HUMAN RELATIONS IN ORGANIZATIONS

APPLICATIONS AND SKILL BUILDING

NINTH EDITION

HUMAN RELATIONS IN ORGANIZATIONS

APPLICATIONS AND SKILL BUILDING

NINTH EDITION

Robert N. Lussier, Ph.D.
Springfield College

McGraw-Hill Irwin

HUMAN RELATIONS IN ORGANIZATIONS: APPLICATIONS AND SKILL BUILDING, NINTH EDITION
Published by McGraw-Hill/Irwin, a business unit of The McGraw-Hill Companies, Inc., 1221 Avenue of the Americas, New York, NY, 10020.

This book is printed on acid-free paper.

1 2 3 4 5 6 7 8 9 0 DOW/DOW 1 0 9 8 7 6 5 4 3 2

ISBN 978-0-07-131528-9
MHID 0-07-131528-4

Chapter opener photo credits: Chapter 1, Polka Dot Images/Jupiterimages; **Chapter 2,** © Glow Images; **Chapter 3,** © LWA/Dann Tardif/Blend Images LLC; **Chapter 4,** © Ronnie Kaufman/Blend Images LLC; **Chapter 5,** © Fancy/Veer; **Chapter 6,** © Getty Images; **Chapter 7,** © Robert Nicholas/Getty Images; **Chapter 8,** © BananaStock/PictureQuest; **Chapter 9,** © Andersen Ross/Blend Images LLC; **Chapter 10,** © Design Pics/Don Hammond; **Chapter 11,** © Tom Grill/Corbis; **Chapter 12,** © PhotoAlto/SuperStock; **Chapter 13,** © Andersen Ross/Blend Images LLC

www.mhhe.com

I would like to dedicate this book to my wife, Marie, and our children, Jesse, Justin, Danielle, Nicole, Brian, and Renee, for their loving support.

CONTENTS IN BRIEF

CONTENTS

PREFACE

In his book *Power Tools,* John Nirenberg asks: "Why are so many well-intended students learning so much and yet able to apply so little in their personal and professional lives?" Is it surprising that students can neither apply what they read nor develop skills when most textbooks continue to focus on reading about concepts and examples, rather than taking the next step and teaching them how to apply what they read and develop the skills required for using the concepts? *I wrote this book to give students the opportunity to apply the concepts and develop skills used in their personal and professional lives.*

I wrote the first edition back in 1988, prior to AACSB calls for skill development and outcomes assessment, to help professors develop their students' ability to apply the concepts and develop organizational behavior/human relations skills. Unlike competitors, I don't just tell you about the concepts. With networking, for instance—the way most people get jobs and promotions today—I tell you step-by-step how to network and provide you with self-assessment exercises, application exercises, skill development exercises, and often, videos. So rather than simply knowing the concepts, you can actually develop skills.

But is the skills approach any good? John Bigelow compared skills texts in his article, "Managerial Skills Texts: How Do They Stack Up?" in the *Journal of Management Education,* and he gave *Human Relations in Organizations* a top rating for a general OB course. *Reviewers continue to say it is the best "how to work with people" textbook on the market.* Although competing texts now include exercises, reviewers continue to say that no competitor offers the quality and quantity of application and skill-building material.

ENGAGING NetGen STUDENTS

Today's traditional students are being called the Digital Millennial or NetGen learners. Being brought up on the Internet, they have different preferred learning styles than students in prior generations. NetGens prefer active, collaborative, and team-based learning.[1] *Human Relations in Organizations,* Ninth Edition, is designed to be flexible enough to be used with the traditional lecture method, while offering a wide range of engaging activities to select from that best meet students' and professors' educational goals and preferred teaching/learning styles. Below

NetGen Learning Preference	How *Human Relations in Organizations* Engages NetGens
Reading: Students prefer active learning to reading.	Students find the text easy to read and understand. Plus, this new edition covers the material more concisely.
Attention and variety through applications and skill-building exercises: Breaking reading and class time into "chunks" helps keep their attention and improve learning.	The text is broken into "chunks," with concepts, followed by interactive applications and skill-building exercises (see below). Each section consists of a major heading with concepts and application material. Unlike many books with exercises that are simply discussion-based, *Human Relations* develops actual skills that can be used immediately.
Directions: Students benefit from checklists, formulas, and recipes for learning and for life.	*Human Relations* is the most "how to" textbook available, including behavioral model steps for handling common human relations issues, such as conflict, and exercises to develop skills.
Internet: NetGens are comfortable with online environments.	An Online Learning Center (www.mhhe.com/lussier9e) provides chapter review material as well as interactive exercises and videos.

Source: Erika Matulich, Raymond Papp, and Diana Haytko, "Continuous Improvement Through Teaching Innovations: A Requirement for Today's Learners," *Marketing Education Review* 18(1) 2008: 1–7.

[1] Erika Matulich, Raymond Papp, & Diana Haytko, "Continuous Improvement Through Teaching Innovations: A Requirement for Today's Learners," *Marketing Education Review* 18(1) 2008: 1–7.

is a list of learning preferences of NetGens and how this text can be used to engage them both in and out of the classroom.

INTEGRATION WITH FLEXIBILITY

This book continues to have a balanced three-pronged approach:

- A clear, concise understanding of human relations/ organizational behavior (HR/OB) concepts (second to none);
- The application of HR/OB concepts for critical thinking in the business world (there are nine types of applications, including videos and the Test Bank and Instructor's Manual);
- The development of HR/OB skills (there are eight types of skills-activities, including videos and the Test Bank and Instructor's Manual).

In addition to this text and its supporting ancillary package to support these distinct but integrated parts, this new edition includes tests to assess student performance in all three areas. I wrote almost every application and skill exercise in this text and the Instructor's Manual to ensure complete integration and a seamless course experience.

The concepts, applications, and skill-building material are clearly identified and delineated in this preface, text, and IM/test bank. Our package offers more quality and quantity of application and skill-building material to allow professors to create their unique courses using only the features that will achieve their objectives. Thus, it is the most flexible package on the market. Next is an explanation of features to choose from for concepts, applications, and skill building.

CONCEPTS

- *Research-based and current.* The book is based on research, not opinion. The ninth edition has been completely updated. There are more than 900 new references (96 percent), for an average of 70 new references per chapter. This is from 30 to 50 percent more references per chapter than major competitors. Earlier references are primarily classics, such as the motivation (Maslow) and leadership (Fiedler) theories.
- *Comprehensive coverage.* The text includes more topics than most competing texts.
- *Systems orientation.* The text is organized in two ways. First, the parts of the book are based on the competency model of managerial education, building from intrapersonal skills, to interpersonal skills, to leadership skills. Second, it also follows the levels of behavior approach, going from individual, to group, to organizational levels of behavior. The systems effect is discussed throughout the book. Cases from Chapters 2 through 13 have questions based on previous chapters to integrate the concepts of multiple chapters.
- *Recurring themes.* Chapters 2 through 13 begin with a discussion of how the chapter concepts affect behavior, human relations, and performance. Most chapters include a discussion of how the concepts differ globally.
- *Pedagogy.* Each chapter contains the following: (1) Learning outcomes at the beginning and in the body of the chapter where the objective can be met. A summary of each learning outcome is given in the Review section at the end of the chapter. (2) Key terms at the beginning of each chapter and again at the end of the Review. The key terms appear in ***boldface*** and *are defined within the chapter in italic* so they are easy to find. (3) Chapter outlines. (4) Exhibits, some of which contain multiple concepts or theories. See Exhibits 7.7, 8.7, and 11.7, for example. (5) Review. The unique feature of the Review is that it is active in two ways. Students first answer true/false questions. Then they must fill in the blanks with the appropriate key terms in one of three ways: from memory, from a list of key terms at the end of the review, or from the key terms at the beginning of the chapter.
- *Test Bank Assessment of Concepts.* The test bank includes true/false and multiple-choice questions for the concepts, including the key terms, presented in each chapter. The test bank also includes the learning outcomes from each chapter, which can be used as short-answer questions to test concept understanding. A summary of the learning outcomes appears in the Review, the Instructor's Manual, and the test bank.

APPLICATIONS

1. *Opening Case.* Each chapter opens with a case. Throughout the chapter, the ways the text concepts apply to the case are presented so that students can understand the application of the concepts to actual people in organizations.

2. *Work Applications.* Throughout each chapter there are approximately 11 questions (more than 140 total) that require the students to apply the concepts to their own work experience. Work experience can be present or past and may include part-time, summer, or full-time employment. Work applications require the students to think critically and bridge the gap between the concepts and their world.
3. *Application Situations.* Each chapter contains two to six boxes, each with 5 to 10 questions (325 total) that require students to apply the concept illustrated in a specific, short example. The questions develop critical thinking skills through the application process.
4. *Cases—with Internet use and cumulative questions; plus role play exercises.* Each chapter has a case study from a real-world organization. At the end of the case, the organization's Web site is given so that students can visit the Web to get updated information on the case. Chapters 2 through 13 include cumulative questions. Cumulative questions include concepts from previous chapters. For example, the case for Chapter 13 has four questions related to Chapter 11, followed by four questions relating to concepts from Chapters 2, 3, 6, 11, and 12. Thus, students continually review and integrate concepts from earlier chapters. Following each case is a role-play exercise to develop skills based on the concepts illustrated in the case.
5. *Objective Cases.* At the end of each chapter there is a short objective case. The unique feature is the "objective" part, with 10 multiple-choice questions, followed by one or more open-ended questions. These cases require students to apply the concepts to people and organizations.
6. *Internet Exercises.* Online at mhhe.com/lussier9e, (which also has self testing and other features).
7. *Communication Skills Questions.* There are more than 125 communication skills questions, an average of approximately 9 per chapter, which can be used for class discussion and/or written assignments.
8. *Test Bank Assessment of Applications and Instructor's Manual.* The test bank includes the work applications from the text as well as multiple-choice questions, similar to the Application Situations and case questions, to evaluate critical thinking skills. The Instructor's Manual includes the recommended answers for all the application features above, except the opening case, which is illustrated throughout the chapter text.

SKILL BUILDING

1. *Self-Assessment Exercises.* Each chapter has between one and five (more than 45 total, an average of 3 per chapter) self-assessment exercises to enable students to gain personal knowledge. Some of the exercises are tied to skill-building exercises to enhance the impact of the self-assessment. All information for completing and scoring, and self-assessment, is contained within each exercise. A unique new feature includes determining a personality profile (in Chapter 3); in all other chapters, students find out how their personality relates to their use of the chapter concepts.
2. *Group Skill-Building Exercises.* Around 30 percent of the skill-building exercises focus primarily on small group (2 to 6 members) activities. Thus, breaking into small groups is required.
3. *Role-Play Skill-Building Exercises.* Around 10 percent of the skill-building exercises focus primarily on developing skills through behavior modeling, as discussed next. Thus, breaking into groups and role-playing is required. Again, all 13 cases include a role-play exercise.
4. *Models, Behavior Model Videos, and Skill-Building Exercises.* Throughout the book are more than 25 models with step-by-step instructions for handling day-to-day human relations situations. How to use several of the models is illustrated in the behavior-modeling videos. For example, students read the model in the book and watch people send messages, give praise, resolve conflicts, handle complaints, and coach an employee, following the steps in the model. After viewing the video, students role-play how they would handle these human relations situations. Students may also give each other feedback on the effectiveness of their role-plays. Videos can also be used as stand-alone activities. The lecture may stop and skill-building begin in class to break up the lecture.
5. *Behavior Model Videos.* There are one or more behavior model videos (20 total) for most chapters. Behavior model videos 2 through 20 show people successfully handling day-to-day human relations

situations. Videos can be followed by class discussion. Also, many videos are used in conjunction with skill-building exercises.

6. *Test Bank Assessment of Skill-Building and Instructor's Manual.* The test bank includes skill-building questions to assess skill building. The Instructor's Manual gives detailed instructions on using all skill-building exercises and answers to skill-building exercises. It also states how students can be tested on the exercises and provides instructions to give to students.
7. *Skill-Building Objectives and AACSB Competencies.* Each skill-building exercise begins by listing its objective. The objective is followed by listing the Association to Advance Collegiate Schools of Business (AACSB) competencies developed through the exercise.
8. *Individual and Group Skill-Building Exercises.* Around 60 percent of the skill-building exercises focus primarily on individual skill building, most of which is done outside class as preparation for the exercise. However, in-class work in groups using the concepts and sharing answers can enhance skill building. Thus, the instructor has the flexibility to (1) simply have students complete the preparations outside class and during class, and then go over the answers, giving concluding remarks and/or leading a class discussion without using any small-group time, or (2) spend group class time as directed in the exercise.

SUMMARY OF INNOVATIONS

- The three-pronged approach to the text: concepts, applications, skills.
- The three-pronged test bank: concepts, applications, skills.
- Eight types of applications, clearly marked in the text, for developing critical thinking skills.
- Eight types of skill-building exercises, clearly marked in the text, that truly develop skills that can be used in one's personal and professional lives.
- Flexibility—use all or only some of the features; select the ones that work for you.

CHANGES TO THE NINTH EDITION

I'm excited about this new ninth edition as I have made major changes to the text content, topic coverage, and features of this edition as follows.

Text Content

- While keeping the same part structure, I have combined the two chapters on communications and the two chapters on teams. This takes the book from 15 chapters down to 13 so that the book is more easily covered in one quarter or semester.
- While revising each chapter, I rewrote some content to make it more personal to students, while making it a bit less focused on management and more on personal human relations both on and off the job.
- As listed by chapter below, several *new topics* have been added. Of particular note is the new coverage of working together in a digital world.
- While adding new current topics and keeping almost all of the same comprehensive coverage, I carefully edited each chapter to cut back on some of the detailed discussion and moved some material into exhibits. This cuts down on the length of most chapters and the entire book.

New and Expanded Topic Coverage by Chapter

Here are just some of the major changes. For a more detailed list, see the Instructor's Manual. *New topics* are identified in *italic* by chapter.

1. Exhibit 1-5 now includes a *model for improving human relations skills.*
2. The section on personality in Chapter 2 has been reorganized to more clearly present four classifications of personality types. A new section, "Using Behavior That Matches the Big Five Personality Types," has been added to illustrate how to deal with different personality types.
3. A new Model 3.1 has been added to identify the *steps to improving one's self-concept.* The section "Does Ethical Behavior Pay?" has been rewritten with all new references.
4. In Chapter 4, the section on multitasking has been expanded and three of the five questions in Self-Assessment Exercise 4-1 have been changed.
5. Chapters 5 and 6 from the eighth edition have been combined in the new Chapter 5, Communications, Emotions, and Criticism, which progresses from organizational structure and communication, to interpersonal communications, and to emotions and criticism. A new section titled "Digital Information Technology" has also been added.

6. In Chapter 6, the subsection "Anger and Violence in the Workplace" is now a new major section.
7. A new section on *repairing trust* is included in Chapter 7.
8. Chapter 8 includes new sections on *motivating with incentive and recognition programs, thank-you videos and notes,* and *self-motivation.*
9. Formerly covered with ethics, etiquette now follows politics in Chapter 9 and is presented in three parts: personal etiquette, *digital etiquette,* and in a new section "Customer Satisfaction and Etiquette," along with a new *model for handling customer complaints.*
10. A new section in Chapter 10 discusses how to conduct *digital networking.*
11. Eighth edition Chapters 12 and 13 have been combined and condensed into a new Chapter 11, Team Dynamics, Creativity, and Problem Solving, and Decision Making. New sections on *virtual teams—working digitally* and how to deal with *social loafing* team members have also been added.
12. In Chapter 13, new subsections discuss *dating coworkers* and *political correctness.* The subsection "How Women Are Progressing in Management and the Glass Ceiling" has been completely rewritten will all new references. Self-Assessment 13-2 now includes *attitudes toward* minorities, as well as women at work.

New and Improved Features

- A new *role-play exercise* has been added to each of the end-of-chapter cases (13 total).
- To make it easier to break the chapter into separate parts (chunking to break up the lecture with applications and skill-building exercises in addition to the current work applications and application situations), an *icon* has been added in the margin where the *communication skills questions* at the back of the chapter can be discussed.
- A new *icon* also indicates when the *skill-building exercises* at the back of the chapter can be completed, based on the text concepts being covered.
- There are more *behavior models* to help develop human relations skills by following a step-by-step approach to handling common human relations issues, such as conflict. The behavior models are now clearly delineated from the exhibits, by being labeled models.
- At the end of each chapter, a new *review* feature helps tie the chapter concepts together to help students understand the relationship among the concepts.
- More than half of the cases are new to this edition, using real-world companies and people whom students can relate to, including Facebook, Jay-Z, Under Armour, Nike, Coca-Cola, Starbucks, and McDonald's, and other cases have been updated.
- Some of the learning outcomes, key terms, exhibits, self-assessments, and skill-building exercises are new or have been revised.

SUPPLEMENTS FOR INSTRUCTORS AND STUDENTS

Online Learning Center—Instructor's Edition, www.mhhe.com/lussier9e

- *Instructor's Manual:* Written by the author, the Instructor's Manual includes the recommended answers for the application features, chapter outlines, learning outcomes, application situations, cases, and objective cases; sample answers to work applications; and support material for video cases and skill-building exercises.
- *Testbank:* Three types of questions are included—concept, application, and skill-building. Questions are also labeled with level of difficulty and text page references.
- *PowerPoint:* Slides include figures, tables, and graphics from the text, as well as additional material not found in the book.
- *Behavior Model Videos.* The Behavior Model Videos focus on the following topics:

Overview	2:50
Learning Styles	4:20
Attitudes	5:08
Success	4:38
Response Styles	8:26
Situational Communications	5:22
Initiating Conflict Resolution	4:00
Mediating Conflict Resolution	8.35
Situational Supervision	4:45
Giving Praise	1:10
Power	3:25
Groups	7:00
Situational Problem Solving and Decision Making	7:00
Coaching Model (increasing performance)	3:10
Evaluative Performance Appraisal	8:17
Developmental Performance Appraisal	5:00
Force Field Analysis	5:20
Handling Complaints	6:10

Online Learning Center—Student Edition, www.mhhe.com/lussier9e

The student site includes self-grading quizzes and chapter review materials. In addition, a premium content access code allows students to access online Self-Assessments, Test Your Knowledge exercises, and Manager's Hot Seat interactive videos.

The Manager's Hot Seat Videos Online, www.mhhe.com/MHS

In today's workplace, managers are confronted daily with issues like ethics, diversity, working in teams, and the virtual workplace. The Manager's Hot Seat videos allow students to watch as real managers apply their years of experience to confront these issues. Students assume the role of the manager as they watch the video and answer multiple choice questions that pop up forcing them to make decisions on the spot. They learn from the manager's mistakes and successes, and then do a report critiquing the manager's approach by defending their reasoning. Reports can be e-mailed or printed out for credit.

Organizational Behavior Video DVD

This collection of videos features interesting and timely issues, companies, and people related to organizational behavior and interpersonal skills.

ACKNOWLEDGMENTS

I want to thank Dr. Herbert Sherman, Professor of Management—Long Island University (Brooklyn Campus), for writing seven new cases and updating three others.

Special thanks to the reviewers of the ninth edition of my manuscript for their excellent recommendations:

Pamela K. Ball, *Clark State Community College*
Daniel Bialas, *Muskegon Community College*
Teresa R. Campbell, *Clark State Community College*
Shannon Durham, *Middle Georgia Technical College*
Wayne Gawlik, *Joliet Junior College*
Samira B. Hussein, *Johnson County Community College*
Jennifer Susan Malarski, *Minneapolis Community and Technical College*
Keith D. Matthews, *Northeast Community College*
Connie Smejkal, *Centralia Community College*

Thanks also to reviewers of past editions:

Mary Hedberg, *Johnson County Community College*
Jane Bowerman, *University of Oklahoma*
Margaret Ryan, *Highline Community College*
Mofidul Islam, *Columbia Southern University*
Lydia E. Anderson, *Fresno City College*
Marilyn J. Carlson, *Clark State Community College*
John Thiele, *Cañada College*
Rachel Erickson, *National College of Business and Technology*
Daniel Bialas, *Muskegon Community College*
Cindy Brown, *South Plains College*
Robert Losik, *Southern New Hampshire University*
Daniel Lybrook, *Purdue University*
Thomas McDermott, *Pittsburgh Technical Institute*
Therese Palacios, *Palo Alto College*
Margaret V. Ryan, *Highline Community College*
Thomas J. Shaughnessy, *Illinois Central College*
Mary Alice Smith, *Tarrant County College*
Joseph Wright, *Portland Community College*
Boyd Dallos, *Lake Superior College*
Sally Martin Egge, *Cardinal Stritch University*
Brian E. Perryman, *University of Phoenix*
Glenna Vanderhoof, *Southwest Missouri State University*
Marion Weldon, *Edmonds Community College*
Lee Higgins, *Southeast Community College—Beatrice Campus*
Janet Weber, *McCook Community College*
William Weisgerber, *Saddleback College*
Andy C. Saucedo, *Dona Ana Community College*
Charleen Jaeb, *Cuyahoga Community College*
John J. Heinsius, *Modesto Junior College*
Roger E. Besst, *Muskingum Area Technical College*
Rebecca S. Ross, *Shenango Valley School of Business*
Thomas E. Schillar, *University of Puget Sound*
Rosemary Birkel Wilson, *Washtenaw Community College*
Thomas J. Shaughnessy, *Illinois Central College*
Edward J. LeMay, *Massasoit Community College*
Julie Campbell, *Adams State College*
John Gubbay, *Moraine Valley Community College*
Ruth Dixon, *Diablo Valley College*
John J. Harrington, *New Hampshire College*
Robert Wall Edge, *Commonwealth College*
Abbas Nadim, *University of New Haven*
Steve Kober, *Pierce College*
Dee Dunn, *Commonwealth College*
Marlene Frederick, *New Mexico State University at Carlsbad*
Linda Saarela, *Pierce College*
David Backstrom, *Allan Hancock College*
Rob Taylor, *Indiana Vocational Technical College*
Warren Sargent, *College of the Sequoias*
Jane Binns, *Washtenaw Community College*
Charles W. Beem, *Bucks County Community College*
Robert Nixon, *Prairie State College*
Leo Kiesewetter, *Illinois Central College*
Stephen C. Branz, *Triton College*
William T. Price, *Jr., Virginia Polytechnic Institute and State University*
Jerry F. Gooddard, *Aims Community College*
Rex L. Bishop, *Charles Community College*
Bill Anton, *DeVard Community College*
Stew Rosencrans, *University of Central Florida*
John Magnuson, *Spokane Community College*
Doug Richardson, *Eastfield College*

Thanks to the following students for suggesting improvements:

Doug Nguyen, *Truckee Meadows Community College of Nevada*
Richard Gardner, *New Hampshire College*
Peter Blunt, *New Hampshire College*

Christianne Erwin, *Truckee Meadows Community College*
Robert Neal Chase, *New Hampshire College*
Cheryl Guiff, *Taylor University Online*

CONTACT ME WITH FEEDBACK

I wrote this book for you. Let me know what you think of it. Write to me and tell me what you did and/or didn't like about it. More specifically, how could it be improved? I will be responsive to your feedback. If I use your suggestion for improvement, your name and college will be listed in the acknowledgment section of the next edition. I sincerely hope that you will develop your human relations skills through this book.

Robert N. Lussier, Professor of Management
Management Department
Springfield College
Springfield, MA 01109
413-748-3202
rlussier@springfieldcollege.edu

PART 1

Intrapersonal Skills: Behavior, Human Relations, and Performance Begin with You

CHAPTER 1

Understanding Behavior, Human Relations, and Performance

LEARNING OUTCOMES

After completing this chapter, you should be able to:

LO 1-1 Explain why human relations skills are important.

LO 1-2 Discuss the goal of human relations.

LO 1-3 Describe the relationship between individual and group behavior and organizational performance.

LO 1-4 Briefly describe the history of the study of human relations.

LO 1-5 State some of the trends and challenges in the field of human relations.

LO 1-6 List 10 guidelines for effective human relations.

LO 1-7 Identify your personal low and high human relations ability and skill levels.

LO 1-8 Identify five personal human relations goals for the course.

LO 1-9 Define the following 17 key terms (in order of appearance in the chapter):

human relations (HR)	**performance**
goal of human relations	**systems effect**
win–win situation	**Elton Mayo**
total person approach	**Hawthorne effect**
behavior	**Theory Z**
levels of behavior	**intrapersonal skills**
group behavior	**interpersonal skill**
organization	**leadership skill**
organizational behavior (OB)	

/// International Business Machines (IBM) is a 100-year-old world-leading information technologies company, headquartered in Armonk, New York. With close to $15 billion in net income, IBM has 426,751 employees who require lots of effective human relations. IBM translates advanced technologies into value for customers through professional solutions, services, and consulting businesses worldwide.[1] For more information on IBM, visit its Web site at www.ibm.com.

When Olin Ready graduated from college, he accepted his first full-time job with IBM. As he drove to work on his first day, he thought: How will I fit in? Will my peers and new boss Nancy Westwood like me? Will I be challenged by my job? Will I be able to get raises and promotions? At about the same time, Nancy was also driving to work thinking about Olin: Will Olin fit in with his peers? Will he be open to my suggestions and leadership? Will Olin work hard and be a high performer?

What would you do to ensure success if you were Olin? What would you do to ensure Olin's success if you were Nancy? Meeting employees' needs while achieving the organization's objectives is the goal of positive human relations in any organization. ///

WHY HUMAN RELATIONS SKILLS ARE SO IMPORTANT

Learning Outcome 1-1

Explain why human relations skills are important.

We begin by discussing what's in this book for you, followed by a look at some of the major myths about human relations and the realities of why human relations skills are so important. We then discuss the goal of human relations and the total person approach to human relations.

What's in It for Me?

It's natural to be thinking, What can I get from this book, or What's in it for me? This is a common question in all human relations, although it is seldom directly asked and answered. Here is the short, bottom-line answer: The better you can work with people—and that is what the course is all about—the more successful you will be in your personal and professional lives.[2] Life is about relationships;[3] it's all people, people, people.[4] This may be one of the few courses you take in which you can actually use what you learn during the course in your personal life. You don't need to wait until you graduate to apply what you learn, and you can develop your human relations skills. Now let's expand on what's in it for you by exploring some of the myths and realities surrounding human relations.

Myths and Reality about Human Relations

Three myths about human relations are: (1) Technical skills are more important than human relations skills; (2) it's just common sense; and (3) leaders are born, not made.

Myth 1: Technical Skills Are More Important Than Human Relations Skills Some people believe that a human relations or organizational behavior (OB) course is less important than more technical courses, such as computer science and accounting. However, the reality is that in a survey of job recruiters, of the 26 attributes identified, organizations are looking for human relations skill identified as (1) communication and interpersonal skills (89 percent) and (2) ability to work well within a team (87 percent).[5] It is commonly said that people are an organization's greatest asset, or key to success,[6] not technology, because people working together develop the technology. By studying human relations, you will learn skills that will help you in situations like Nancy's and Olin's in the opening case.

The technology-oriented IBM gives the average employee 40 hours of training per year, with about 32 of those hours related to human relations.

Myth 2: Human Relations Is Just Common Sense Some people believe that human relations is simple and just common sense. Do all the people in organizations get along and work well together? If human relations is just common sense, then why are people issues some of the most prominent concerns of business owners and managers?[7] It's because high-quality relationships are so important to success.[8] Think about the jobs you've had. Did everyone get along and work well together? How did human relations affect your personal and job satisfaction?

Myth 3: Leaders Are Born, Not Made Some people believe they can't develop their leadership skill, but they can if they work at it. Effective leaders have good human relations skills.[9] The question "Are leaders born or made?" has been researched over the years.[10] Leadership experts generally agree that leadership skills can be developed. Virtually all the large, major corporations spend millions of dollars each year on leadership training. Why would they spend all that money if human relations skills could not be developed? Regardless of your natural ability to get along and work well with people, using the material in this book, you can develop your human relations skills.

Communication Skills
Refer to CS Question 1.

WORK APPLICATION 1-1

In your own words, explain why human relations skills are important to you. How will they help you in your career?

Throughout this book we use many important, or key, terms. To ensure that you have a clear understanding of these terms, when a key term first appears, we present it in **bold letters** with its definition *italicized.*

Goal of Human Relations

Learning Outcome 1-2

Discuss the goal of human relations.

The term **human relations (HR)** *means interactions among people.* When Olin Ready arrives at IBM on his first day of work, he will interact with his new boss, Nancy. Next, a variety of people will help orient and train Olin. Later, as he performs his daily tasks, Olin will interact with Nancy and his coworkers, as well as with people from other departments and with customers. Olin's success at IBM will be based on human relations, and his job satisfaction will affect his personal life.

The **goal of human relations** *is to create a win–win situation by satisfying employee needs while achieving organizational objectives.* A **win–win situation** *occurs when the organization and the employees get what they want.* When an employee wonders, What's in it for me?, that employee is expressing his or her needs. When a manager expects high levels of performance from employees, that manager is identifying organizational objectives. When employees' and organizational goals align, performance tends to follow.[11]

Creating a win–win situation applies to human relations at all levels. When there isn't a win–win situation, performance often suffers, and one person can have a negative effect on relationships of others.[12] For example, members of a department often must share the work. If Olin does not do his share of the work at IBM, he creates problems within the department. (This would be an I-win–coworkers-lose situation.) Coworker Mary may decide it is not fair that she has to do more work than Olin. Consequently, Mary may argue with Olin, slow down her performance, or complain to their boss, Nancy. Nancy's job is to make sure the human relations within her department have a positive effect on her department's performance. Conflicts usually arise because of a lack of a win–win situation.[13] In Chapter 6, you will learn how to create win–win situations when facing conflicts.

WORK APPLICATION 1-2

Give an example, personal if possible, of a situation in which the goal of human relations was met. Explain how the individual's needs were met and how the organizational objectives were achieved.

This book discusses the goal of human relations as it applies to various topics. One goal of this book is to develop your ability to create win–win situations in a variety of settings, including your professional and personal lives.

The Total Person Approach

WORK APPLICATION 1-3

Give a specific example, personal if possible, that supports the total person approach. Explain how an individual's job performance was affected by off-the-job problems.

The **total person approach** *realizes that an organization employs the whole person, not just his or her job skills.* So it is important to understand the whole person.[14] People play many roles throughout their lives, indeed, throughout each day.[15] Olin, therefore, is more than just an employee; he is also a father, a member of the PTA, a scout leader, a jogger, a student, and a fisherman. At work, Olin will not completely discard all his other roles to be a worker only. His off-the-job life will affect his job performance at IBM. Thus, if Olin has a bad day at work, it may not be related to his job, but to another of his life's roles. Also, a bad day at work can affect personal life satisfaction.

BEHAVIOR, HUMAN RELATIONS, AND ORGANIZATIONAL PERFORMANCE

Levels of Behavior

The study of human relations looks closely at the way people behave, why people behave the way they do, or what makes them and the people around them tick?[16] **Behavior** *is what people do and say.* Human relations fuel behavior. The three **levels of behavior** *are individual, group, and organizational.* Human relations take place at the group and organizational levels.

Individual- and Group-Level Behavior As Olin types a letter on the computer or fills out requisition forms, he is engaged in individual behavior. **Group behavior** *consists of the things two or more people do and say as they interact.* Individual behavior influences group behavior. For example, as Olin and Mary work on a project together or attend department meetings, their actions are considered group behavior. Studying the chapters in this book, particularly Chapters 1 through 4, should help you understand and predict your own behavior, and that of others, in an organizational setting. In addition, Chapter 11 will help you gain a better understanding of how your behavior affects others, and how their behavior affects you in teams.

Organizational-Level Behavior An **organization** *is a group of people working to achieve one or more objectives*. This book focuses on human relations in both profit and nonprofit organizations in which people work to make a living. Organizations are created to produce goods and services for the larger society. If you have ever worked, you have been a part of an organization. You also come into contact with organizations on a regular basis, such as when you go into a store, school, church, post office, or health club.

As individuals and groups interact, their collective behavior constitutes the organization's behavior. Thus **organizational behavior (OB)** *is the collective behavior of an organization's individuals and groups*. IBM is an organization, and its collective behavior is based on Olin's behavior, the behavior of Nancy's department, and the behavior of all other departments combined.

This book explores all three levels of behavior. Chapters 2 through 4 focus primarily on individual behavior, Chapters 5 through 10 examine the skills influencing all three levels of behavior, and Chapters 11 through 13 focus on group and organizational behavior.

Exhibit 1.1 illustrates the three levels of behavior. The focus of level three is on the organization as a whole. At this level, the responsibility of the board of directors and the

EXHIBIT 1.1 | Levels of Behavior

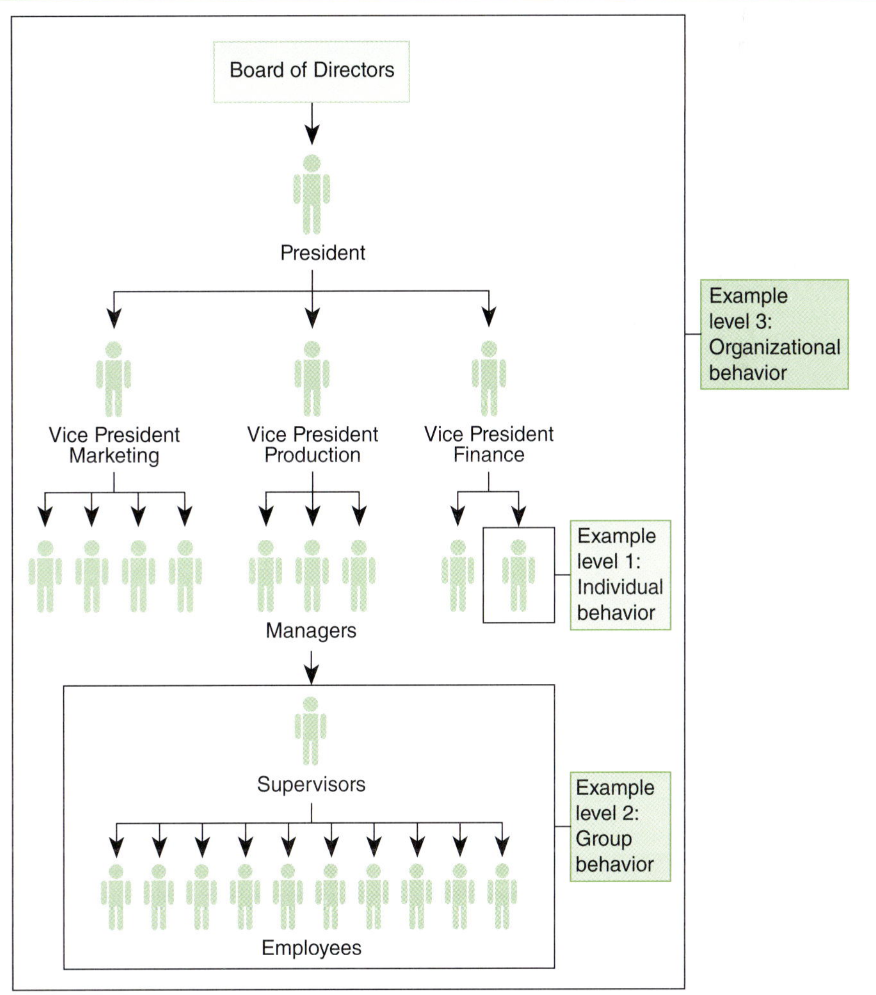

Each manager would have one or more supervisors reporting to him or her, and each supervisor would have several employees reporting to him or her.

WORK APPLICATION 1-4

Give two specific examples of your involvement in human relations—one positive and one negative. Also identify the level of behavior for each example.

president is to focus on the entire organization. The focus of level two is on the behavior and human relations within and between groups such as the marketing, production, and finance departments. The focus of level one is on the behavior of any one person in the organization.[17]

Exhibit 1.1 is a formal organization structure showing authority and reporting relationships. However, it does not show the multiple possible human relations that exist outside the formal structure. For example, the president could interact with any employee, an employee could interact with a manager, and a supervisor could interact with a vice president's administrative assistant.

The Relationship between Individual and Group Behavior and Organizational Performance

Learning Outcome 1-3

Describe the relationship between individual and group behavior and organizational performance.

Throughout this course you will learn how human relations affects individual and group behavior, and the resulting effects on organizational performance. **Performance** *is the extent to which expectations or objectives have been met. Performance* is a relative term. Performance levels are more meaningful when compared to past performance or the performance of others within and/or outside the organization. Since relationships are the lifeblood of organizations, poor relations impede individual, group, and organizational performance.[18]

APPLICATION SITUATIONS / / /

Understanding Important Terms AS 1-1

Identify each statement by its key term.

A. Behavior
B. Goal of human relations
C. Human relations
D. Organization
E. Performance
F. Total person approach

_______ 1. Bill and Sara are discussing how to complete a project they are working on together.

_______ 2. Julio just delivered his report to the outgoing mailbox.

_______ 3. It's 4:50 P.M. and Cindy typed the last bill to be sent out today with the 5:00 P.M. mail.

_______ 4. All the people listed above are members of a(n) _______.

_______ 5. "Because I've been doing a good job, I got a raise; now I can buy that new car I want so badly."

WORK APPLICATION 1-5

Give two specific examples of how human relations affected your performance—one positive and the other negative. Be specific in explaining the effects of human relations in both cases.

The Systems Effect A system is a set of two or more interactive elements. The systems approach, developed by Russell Ackoff, focuses on the whole system with an emphasis on the relationships between its parts. For our purposes, under the **systems effect** *all people in the organization are affected by at least one other person, and each person affects the whole group or organization.* The organization's performance is based on the combined performance of each individual and group. To have high levels of performance, the organization must have high-performing individuals and groups. Groups are the building blocks of the organization. As a result of the systems effect, the destructive behavior of one individual hurts that group and other departments as well.[19] In addition, the destructive behavior of one department affects other departments and the organization's performance.

The challenge to management is to develop high-performing individuals and groups. In a sense, individuals and groups are the foundation of an organization. If either is ineffective, the organization cannot stand. See Exhibit 1.2 for a graphic illustration.

EXHIBIT 1.2 | The Relationship between Individual and Group Behavior and Organizational Performance

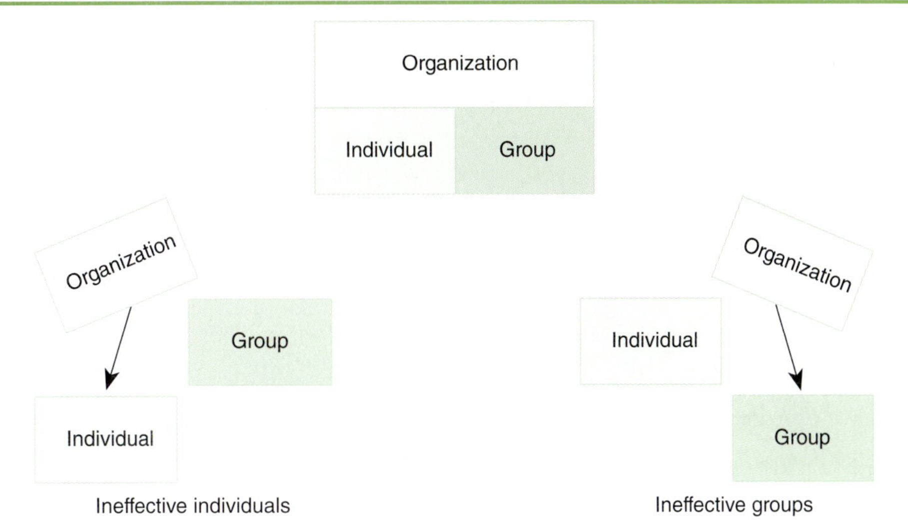

APPLICATION SITUATIONS / / /

Focus of Study AS 1-2

Identify the focus of study in each statement below by selecting two answers. First select the level of behavior:

A. Individual B. Group C. Organizational

Then select the scope of study:

A. Behavior B. Human relations C. Performance

_______ _______ 6. Bill and Sara are discussing how to complete a project they are working on together.

_______ _______ 7. The management hierarchy is from the president down to the employee level.

_______ _______ 8. Carl is writing a letter to a supplier to correct an error in billing.

_______ _______ 9. The marketing department has just exceeded its sales quota for the quarter.

_______ _______10. IBM has just completed its income statement for the quarter.

Just as people are the foundation of the organization, behavior and human relations are the foundation supporting performance. If either is ineffective, performance will fall.[20] Exhibit 1.3 gives a graphic illustration.

HUMAN RELATIONS: PAST, PRESENT, AND FUTURE

Human Relations Is a Multidisciplined Science

Learning Outcome 1-4

Briefly describe the history of the study of human relations.

Popularly called *organizational behavior* and rooted in the behavioral sciences, the science of human relations was developed in the late 1940s. It is based primarily on psychology (which attempts to determine why individuals behave the way they do) and sociology (which attempts to determine how group dynamics affect organizational performance); social psychology, economics, and political science have also contributed to organizational behavior.

During the 1950s, research in human behavior was conducted in large organizations. By the late 1970s, organizational behavior was recognized as a discipline in its own right, with teachers, researchers, and practitioners being trained in organizational behavior itself. Organizational behavior is a social science that has built its knowledge base on a sound

EXHIBIT 1.3 | The Relationship between Behavior, Human Relations, and Performance

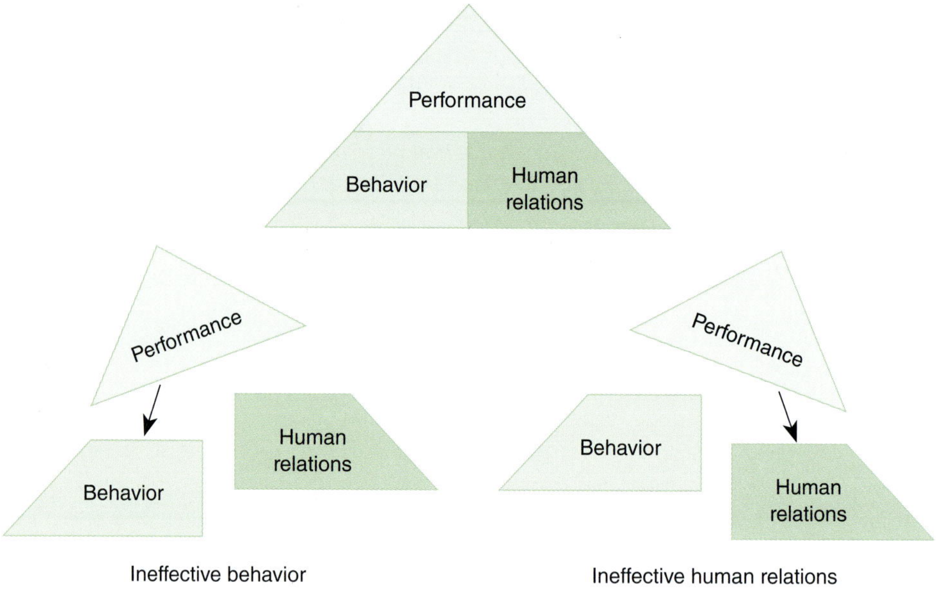

foundation of scientific theory and research.[21] Human relations takes a practical, applied approach. It attempts to anticipate and prevent problems before they occur and to solve existing problems of interpersonal relations in organizations.

The Early Years: Frederick Taylor and Robert Owen

In early America, most people worked on farms or were self-employed tailors, carpenters, shoemakers, or blacksmiths. Then, during the Industrial Revolution people left the farms to work in factories that were all privately owned. These businesses were concerned with profits, not employees, and managers viewed people only as a source of production. Most of the early owner-managers gave little thought to the working conditions, health, or safety of their employees. Working conditions were very poor—people worked from dawn until dusk under intolerable conditions of disease, filth, danger, and scarcity of resources. They had to work this way just to survive; there was no welfare system—you worked or you starved.

Frederick Taylor Frederick Taylor, an engineer known as the "father of scientific management," focused on analyzing and redesigning jobs more efficiently in the late 1800s and early 1900s, which led to the idea of mass production. Scientific managers focused on production, not people.[22] They assumed that workers always acted rationally and were motivated simply by money. Also, Taylor failed to recognize the social needs of employees, and placed them in isolated jobs.

Robert Owen In 1800, Robert Owen was considered the first manager-entrepreneur to understand the need to improve the work environment and the employee's overall situation. In 1920, Owen was called "the real father" of personnel administration.[23] He believed that profit would be increased if employees worked shorter hours, were paid adequately, and were provided with sufficient food and housing. He refused to employ children under the age of 11. (In the early 1800s, children went to work full-time at the age of 9.) Owen taught his employees cleanliness and temperance and improved their working conditions. Other entrepreneurs of that time did not follow his ideas.

Elton Mayo and the Hawthorne Studies

From the mid-1920s to the early 1930s, Elton Mayo and his associates from Harvard University conducted research at the Western Electric Hawthorne Plant near Chicago. The research conducted through the Hawthorne Studies has become a landmark in the human relations field. In fact, **Elton Mayo** *is called the "father of human relations."* As a consequence of these studies, the Hawthorne effect was discovered.[24]

WORK APPLICATION 1-6

Give a specific example, personal if possible, of the Hawthorne effect. It could be when a teacher, coach, or boss gave you special attention that resulted in your increased performance.

The **Hawthorne effect** *refers to an increase in performance caused by the special attention given to employees, rather than tangible changes in the work.* During the research, Mayo changed the lighting and ventilation. To his surprise, performance went up regardless of the working conditions. Through interviews, Mayo realized that the control group during the research felt important because of all the attention it got; therefore performance increased because of the special attention given to employees. With the knowledge of the results of the Hawthorne Studies, some managers used human relations as a means of manipulating employees, while others took the attitude that a happy worker is a productive worker. Studies have shown that happy workers are usually, but not always, more productive than unhappy workers.

The 1930s to the 1990s

During the depression of the 1930s, unions gained strength and in many cases literally forced management to look more closely at the human side of the organization and meet employees' needs for better working conditions, higher pay, and shorter hours.

During the 1940s and 1950s, other major research projects were conducted in a number of organizations. Some of the research was conducted by the *University of Michigan,* which conducted studies in leadership and motivation; *Ohio State University,* which also studied leadership and motivation; the *Tavistock Institute of Human Relations* in London, which studied various subjects; and the *National Training Laboratories* in Bethel, Maine, which studied group dynamics. *Peter Drucker's management by objectives* was popular in the 1950s.

During the 1960s, *Douglas McGregor* published *Theory X and Theory Y.*[25] A discussion of his theories, which contrast the way managers view employees, appears in Chapter 3. In the same time period, *Eric Berne* introduced *transactional analysis (TA).* (See Chapter 7 for a detailed discussion of TA.) Sensitivity training was popular in the 1960s.

During the 1970s, interest in human relations probably peaked. Quality circles were popular. By the late 1970s, the term *human relations* was primarily replaced with the more commonly used term *organizational behavior.*

In the 1980s, the U.S. rate of productivity was much lower than that of Japan. William Ouchi discovered that a few particularly successful firms did not follow the typical U.S. model. After years of research and investigation, Ouchi developed Theory Z.[26] **Theory Z** *integrates common business practices in the United States and Japan into one middle-ground framework appropriate for use in the United States.*

In their book *In Search of Excellence,* Thomas Peters and Robert Waterman conducted research to determine the characteristics of successful organizations.[27] During the 1980s, their work was criticized as companies identified as excellent began to have problems. Total quality management was popular in the 1980s.

Communication Skills
Refer to CS Question 2.

In the 1990s, the trend toward increased participation of employees as a means of improving human relations and organizational performance continued. This trend included greater levels of participation at the lowest level of the organization. As a result, employees have more input into management decisions and how they perform their jobs. The use of groups and teams also became popular in the 1990s and continues to be today.

APPLICATION SITUATIONS / / /

Human Relations History AS 1-3

Identify the following people with their contribution to human relations:

A. Eric Berne	C. William Ouchi	E. Tom Peters
B. Elton Mayo	D. Robert Owen	F. Frederick Taylor

_______ 11. Excellence in American corporations.

_______ 12. Theory Z.

_______ 13. Transactional analysis.

_______ 14. The father of personnel administration.

_______ 15. The Hawthorne Studies.

Current and Future Challenges in the 21st Century

Learning Outcome 1-5

State some of the trends and challenges in the field of human relations.

We've discussed the history of human relations; now let's briefly discuss its current and future trends and challenges. In Chapters 2 through 13, we will discuss these topics in detail.

- **Globalization, change, innovation, and speed.** Chief executive officers (CEOs) rate globalization as a challenge to business leadership in the 21st century. The trend toward globalization has clearly changed the speed and the way we do business today.[28]
- **Technology.** Technology has enabled the innovation and speed we have now in the global economy; the rate of technology change will not slow down. Because technology is created by people, they have to use it effectively to compete.
- **Diversity.** Due to globalization, diversity becomes more important. You need to understand how to work with people around the world.[29]
- **Learning and knowledge.** The key to success today is using knowledge effectively to continually innovate in order to compete in the new global economy.[30]
- **Ethics.** Media coverage of Enron, WorldCom, and other business scandals has heightened awareness of the need for ethical business practices, as well as new corporate governance requirements.[31]
- **Crisis.** In the wake of September 11, 2001, organizations have developed plans to prevent and/or deal with crises that may occur. Safety and security issues have led to new human relations behaviors.[32]

As stated, we will talk more about all of these challenges in later chapters.

Communication Skills
Refer to CS Question 3.

WORK APPLICATION 1-7

Explain how one of the above trends or challenges could personally affect your human relations.

APPLICATION SITUATIONS / / /

Trends and Challenges of Human Relations AS 1-4

Identify the factor in each statement as:

A. External forces B. Changing workforce C. Technology

_______ 16. "First we had to contend with the Japanese; now the Koreans and Chinese are serious competitors as well."

_______ 17. "The number of immigrants employed is increasing because they are the only ones applying for the jobs."

_______ 18. "Every time I look in the business section of the paper, it seems as though someone is coming out with a new or improved computer. How do I know which one to choose?"

_______ 19. "We had better do some training to help prevent getting charged with sexual harassment."

_______ 20. "These kids today don't have the dedication to come to work, and on time, like we did when we were their age."

DEVELOPING HUMAN RELATIONS SKILLS

Scholars are asking for a bridge between theory and practice, between research and teaching, and for practical techniques that are evidence-based to improve success; that is what we do in this book.[33] Through gaining a better understanding of your behavior and that of others in organizations, you will be more skilled at interacting with people and better prepared to anticipate and eliminate human relations problems before they occur. But people are complex and different, and the approach you use to solve a human relations problem with one person may not work with a different person.

WORK APPLICATION 1-8

Do you believe that you can and will develop your human relations abilities and skills through this course? Explain your answer.

This book gives you suggestions, guidelines, and models to follow to improve your people skills. Although these guidelines do not guarantee success, they will increase your probability of successful human relations in organizations.

"Knowing is not enough; we must apply what we learn."[34] Human relations is one of the few courses you can use immediately. Most of the material you will learn can and should be used in your daily personal life with your family, friends, and other people with whom you interact. If you presently work, use this material on the job to develop your human relations skills.

Human Relations Guidelines

Learning Outcome 1-6

List 10 guidelines for effective human relations.

Being likable is important to personal happiness and career success.[35] Are you the kind of person others enjoy being around? Find out by completing Self-Assessment Exercise 1-1. Then read on.

/// Self-Assessment Exercise 1-1 ///

Likability

Select the number from 1 to 5 that best describes your use of the following behavior, and write it on the line before each statement.

(5) Usually (4) Frequently (3) Occasionally (2) Seldom (1) Rarely

_____ 1. I'm an optimist. I look for the good in people and situations, rather than the negative.

_____ 2. I avoid complaining about people, things, and situations.

_____ 3. I show a genuine interest in other people. I compliment them on their success.

_____ 4. I smile.

_____ 5. I have a sense of humor. I can laugh at myself.

_____ 6. I make an effort to learn people's names and address them by name during conversations.

_____ 7. I truly listen to others.

_____ 8. I help other people cheerfully.

_____ 9. I think before I act and avoid hurting others with my behavior.

_____ 10. If I were to ask all the people I work/worked with to answer these nine questions for me, they would select the same responses that I did.

To determine your likability, add the 10 numbers you selected as your answers. The total will range from 10 to 50. Place it here _____ and on the continuum below.

Unlikable 10 -------- 20 -------- 30 -------- 40 -------- 50 Likable

If you want to get ahead in an organization, it is important to do a good job. But it is also important that people like you. If people like you, they will forgive just about anything you do wrong. If they don't like you, you can do everything right and it will not matter. Many hardworking, talented people have been bypassed for promotion and fired simply because their bosses or some other high-level managers didn't like them.

No one can tell you exactly how to be likable. People who try too hard are usually not well liked. However, in this section you will learn guidelines for being likable through successful human relations. The guidelines are based on the behavior of successful, likable people who possess human relations skills. Although general in nature, these guidelines apply to most situations. Throughout the book, you will learn specific skills for dealing with a wide variety of people issues.

The 10 human relations guidelines are (1) be optimistic, (2) be positive, (3) be genuinely interested in other people, (4) smile and develop a sense of humor, (5) call people by name, (6) listen to people, (7) help others, (8) think before you act, (9) apologize; and (10) create win–win situations.

Be Optimistic Football coach Lou Holtz has said that you choose to be optimistic (happy) or pessimistic (sad). Happiness is nothing more than a poor memory for the bad things that happen to you. We usually find what we're looking for. If you look for, and emphasize, the positive, you will find it. Most successful people are optimistic. Do you like being with pesimistic people?

Be Positive Praise and encourage people. People generally don't like to listen to others complain. People often avoid complainers, and you should too. Associating with complainers will only depress you. Don't go around criticizing (putting people down), condemning, or spreading rumors. Do you like negative people who criticize you?

Be Genuinely Interested in Other People Think about your favorite boss and friends. One of the reasons you like them is that they show a genuine interest in you. One of the reasons people fail is the "me only" (or narcissistic, self-focused, preoccupied with receiving attention and expecting special treatment)[36] syndrome. People who feel as though you don't care about them will not come through for you. Do you like self-centered people?

Smile and Develop a Sense of Humor A smile shows interest and caring. It takes fewer muscles to smile than it does to frown. The adage "Smile and the world smiles with you; weep and you weep alone" has a lot of truth to it. You have probably noticed that frowners are usually unhappy and pessimistic.

Develop a sense of humor. Relax, laugh, and enjoy yourself. Be willing to laugh at yourself. Likable people do not take their jobs or themselves too seriously. Do you like people who always frown and never laugh?

Skill-Building Exercise 1-1 develops this skill.

Call People by Name A person's name is the most important sound in any language. Calling people by the name they prefer shows an interest in them and makes them feel important. If you're not good at remembering names, work at it. Like any skill, it takes a conscious effort and some practice to develop. One simple technique you can use to help you remember people's names when you are introduced is to call them by name two or three times while talking to them. Then call them by name the next time you greet them. If you forget a person's name, whenever possible, ask someone else what it is before contacting the person. Remember that in some cultures, however, it is not polite to call a person by his or her first name. In such a culture, use last names, titles, or positions, as expected. Do you like people who don't call you by your name?

Listen to People We learn more by listening than we do by talking. Show respect for the other person's opinions. Don't say "You're wrong" even when the other person is wrong. Such statements only make people defensive and cause arguments, which you should avoid. Saying you disagree has less of an emotional connotation to it. However, when you are wrong, admit it quickly and emphatically.[37] Admitting you're wrong is not a sign of weakness and is often interpreted as a strength. However, not admitting you are wrong is often interpreted as a weakness.

Encourage others to talk about themselves. Ask them questions about themselves, rather than telling them about yourself. This gives you the opportunity to listen and learn while making people feel important. Listening also shows your interest in people.[38] Do you like people who don't listen to you?

Help Others If you want to help yourself, you can do so by helping others.[39] It's a basic law of success. People who use people may be somewhat successful in the short run, but those being used usually catch on. Open and honest relationships in which people help each other meet their needs are usually the best ones. Help others, but don't pry when help is not welcomed. Do you like people who don't help you when you need help?

Think Before You Act Feel your emotions, but control your behavior.[40] Try not to do and say things you will regret later. Watch your language; don't offend people. It is not always what you say but how you say it that can have a negative impact on human relations. Before you say and do things, think about the possible consequences. Being right is not good enough if it hurts human relations. Conduct your human relations in a positive way. Do you like impulsive people who hurt others?

Apologize We all sometimes do or say things (behavior) that offends or hurts others in some way. To truly repair relationships, the best starting point is to admit mistakes and give a "sincere" apology. However, some people, and more so men than women, are reluctant to apologize, and people apologize more often to strangers than to their romantic partners and family members.[41] Even if you don't believe you did anything wrong, you can apologize for offending or hurting the other person. For example, you can say in a sincere voice, "I'm sorry I upset you with my (state the specific behavior, i.e., comment); I will try not to do it again." It takes only a minute to give a sincere apology, and apologizing can help develop, maintain, and repair human relations. Think about it: If someone offends or hurts you, are you more willing to forgive and forget and maintain an effective relationship if the person sincerely apologizes?

Communication Skills
Refer to CS Question 4.

Create Win–Win Situations Human relations is about how we behave and treat others. The goal of human relations is to create win–win situations. The best way to get what you want is to help other people get what they want and vice versa. Throughout the book you will be given specific examples of how to create win–win situations. Do you like people who win at your expense?

If Olin follows these 10 human relations guidelines at IBM, he will increase his chances of success. If you follow these general guidelines, you too will increase your chances of success in all walks of life. These guidelines are just the starting point of what you will learn in this course. For a review of the 10 guidelines to effective human relations, see Exhibit 1.4.

WORK APPLICATION 1-9

Which 2 of the 10 human relations guidelines need the most effort on your part? Which 2 need the least? Explain your answers.

Remember that what you think about affects how you feel, and how you feel affects your behavior, human relations, and performance. So think about and actually use these guidelines to improve your human relations.

Handling Human Relations Problems

Even though you follow the human relations guidelines, in any organization there are bound to be times when you disagree with other employees. And you will more than likely have to interact with people who do not follow the guidelines.

Human relations problems often occur when the psychological contract is not met. The *psychological contract* is the shared expectations between people. At work you have

EXHIBIT 1.4 | Ten Guidelines to Effective Human Relations

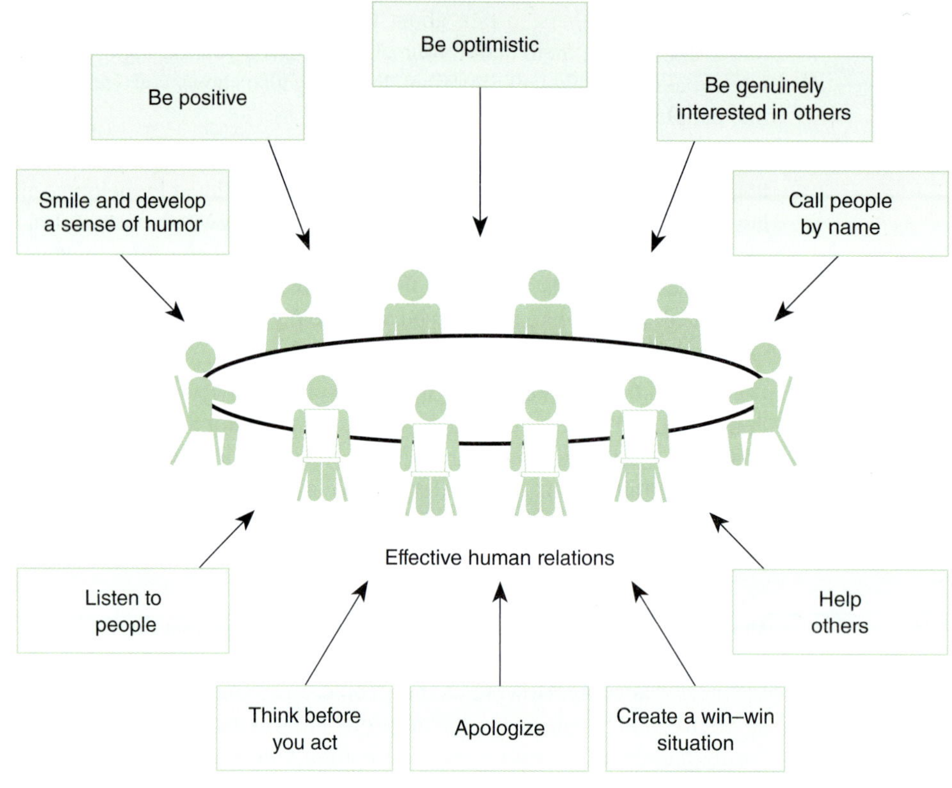

expectations of the things your boss and coworkers should and should not do, and they in turn have expectations of you. As long as expectations are met, things go well. However, if expectations are not met, human relations problems occur.[42] Thus, when people share information and negotiate expectations, have clear roles, and are committed to meeting others' expectations, things go well. We'll focus on sharing information and negotiating expectations throughout this book.

When you encounter a human relations problem, you have to decide whether to avoid the problem or to solve it. In most cases, it is advisable to solve human relations problems rather than ignore them. Problems usually get worse rather than solve themselves. When you decide to resolve a human relations problem, you have at least three alternatives:

1. Change the Other Person Whenever there is a human relations problem, it is easy to blame the other party and expect her or him to make the necessary changes in behavior to meet your expectations. In reality, few human relations problems can be blamed entirely on one party. Both parties usually contribute to the human relations problem. Blaming the other party without taking some responsibility usually results in resentment and defensive behavior. Also, many self-centered people view themselves as nearly perfect and in no need of personal change.[43] The more you force people to change to meet your expectations, the more difficult it is to maintain effective human relations.

2. Change the Situation If you have a problem getting along with the person or people you work with, you can try to change the situation by working with another person or other people. You may tell your boss you cannot work with so-and-so because of a personality conflict, and ask for a change in jobs. There are cases where this is the only solution; however, when you complain to the boss, the boss often figures that you, not the other party, are the problem. Blaming the other party and trying to change the situation enables you to ignore your own behavior, which may be the actual cause of the problem.

3. Change Yourself Throughout this book, particularly in Part 1, you will be examining your own behavior. Knowing yourself is important in good human relations.[44] In many situations, your own behavior is the only thing you can control. In most human relations problems, the best alternative is to examine others' behavior and try to understand why they are doing and saying the things they are; then examine your own behavior to determine why you are behaving the way you are. In most cases, the logical choice is to change your own behavior. That does not mean doing whatever other people request. In fact, you should be assertive. You will learn how to be assertive in Chapter 6. You are not being forced to change; rather, you are changing your behavior because you elect to do so. When you change your behavior, others may also change. In fact, you can also resolve differences through both of you agreeing to change your behavior, and you will learn how to resolve conflicts in Chapter 6.

Communication Skills
Refer to CS Question 5.

WORK APPLICATION 1-10

Give a specific example of a human relations problem in which you elected to change yourself rather than the other person or situation. Be sure to identify your changed behavior.

In each chapter, there are two or more self-assessment instruments to help you better understand your behavior and that of others. It is helpful to examine behavior and to change it, when appropriate, not only throughout this course but throughout life.[45]

OBJECTIVES AND ORGANIZATION OF THE BOOK

Let's discuss what we are trying to do throughout this book (objectives) and how we are going to do it (organization).

Objectives of the Book

Management gurus say that professors should be teaching students how to apply the principles learned.[46] "Through learning and application of what you learn, you can solve any problem."[47] This is the overarching objective of the book. Unlike most other courses that teach you concepts, this course takes you to the next level, as you apply the concepts and develop your human relations skills.

As indicated in the title of the book, it has a three-pronged approach to the objectives:

- To teach you the concepts and theories of human relations.
- To develop your ability to apply the human relations concepts through critical thinking.
- To develop your human relations skills in your personal and professional lives.

This book offers some unique features related to each of the three objectives; these features are listed in Exhibit 1.5. To get the most from this book, turn back to the preface and read the descriptions of these features.

EXHIBIT 1.5 | The Three-Pronged Approach: Features of the Book

Model to Improve:	Learn the Concepts	+	Apply the Concepts	+	Develop Skills	=	Effective Human Relations
	Research-based and current		Opening cases		Self-assessment exercises		
	Comprehensive coverage		Work applications		Skill-building objectives and AACSB		
	Systems-oriented		Application situations		Skill-building exercises (three types)		
					Role-playing exercises		
	Learning outcomes		Cases		Behavior models		
	Key terms		Objective cases		Behavior model videos		
	Exhibits						
	Chapter review and glossary				Manager's hot seat videos		

Flexibility There are so many features that your professor will most likely not use every feature with every chapter. Students have different learning style preferences. There is no one right way of doing things. You have the flexibility to use your own approach. You may also use features that your professor does not include in the course requirements.

AACSB Learning Standards

It is important to develop human relations competencies. So how do you know what specific competencies will be important to your career success? For the answer, we have turned to the Association to Advance Collegiate Schools of Business (AACSB), which gives accreditation to business schools. AACSB accreditation is highly sought after, and even the business schools that don't achieve accreditation tend to strive to meet AACSB standards. Below is a list of competencies that are based on AACSB learning standards related to this course.[48]

- **Reflective thinking and self-management.** Students develop reflective thinking through identifying personal strengths and developmental needs as a first step. Each chapter has self-assessment exercises to help you better understand yourself and how to improve your competencies.
- **Analytic skills.** Students learn to set goals, adjust, and resolve problems and make decisions. You will learn how to write objectives in Chapter 8 and how to use participation in decision making in Chapter 11. Essentially all of the application and skill material in every chapter will help you develop your analytical skills.
- **Communication abilities.** Students learn to effectively listen, share ideas, negotiate, and facilitate the flow of information to improve performance. You will develop communication competency in Chapter 5 and negotiation skills in Chapter 10.
- **Global, multicultural, diversity, and ethical perspectives.** Students are challenged to recognize the impact of global trends on an organization, to value diversity, and to conduct business in an ethical manner. You will develop these competencies in Chapter 3.
- **Teamwork.** Students enhance group and individual dynamics in organizations to create a healthy team environment by combining talents and resources for collaboration and information sharing. You will develop team competencies in Chapter 11, as well as through the exercises in most chapters.
- **Leadership.** Students develop the capacity to lead in organizational situations. Leadership is the focus of last two parts of the book, Chapters 7 through 13.

Each of the skill-building exercises indicates the AACSB learning standard skill(s) to which the exercise relates.

Organization of the Book

The book is organized in two ways. The first is by the *levels of behavior*. The parts, as well as the chapters within each part, progress from the individual, to the group, to the organizational levels of behavior.

Second, the parts of the book are based on the *domain model of managerial education*. In this model the concept of *skills* has evolved into the concept of competencies. *Competencies* are performance capabilities that distinguish effective from ineffective behavior, human relations, and performance: they are the underlying characteristics of a person that lead to or cause effective and outstanding performance. Every current competency model can be organized in terms of four competency domains: intrapersonal skills, interpersonal skills, leadership skills, and business skills.[49] The first three are human relations skills, and the last is a technical skill.

The three human relations domains, which are discussed below, as well as the levels of behavior, are reflected in the table of contents and the profile form on pp. 19–20. This form lists the parts and the chapters within each part.

Part 1. Intrapersonal Skills: Behavior, Human Relations, and Performance Begin with You *Intra* means "within"; thus, **intrapersonal skills** *are within the individual and include characteristics such as personality, attitudes, self-concept, and integrity*. Intrapersonal skills have also been called self-management abilities. Intrapersonal skills are the foundation on which careers are built. You will learn about, apply, and develop intrapersonal skills in Chapters 2 to 4. We end the book by coming back to intrapersonal skills in Appendix A, by developing a plan for applying human relations skills.

Part 2. Interpersonal Skills: The Foundation of Human Relations *Inter* means "between"; thus, interpersonal skills are between people, as are human relations. **Interpersonal skill** *is the ability to work well with a diversity of people*. People with interpersonal, or human relations, skills have the ability to initiate, build, and maintain relationships. They have good communication and conflict resolution skills. Clearly, interpersonal skills are based on, and overlap to some extent, intrapersonal skills. You will learn about, apply, and develop interpersonal skills in Chapters 5 and 6.

Part 3. Leadership Skills: Influencing Others and Part 4. Leadership Skills: Team and Organizational Behavior, Human Relations, and Performance **Leadership skill** *is the ability to influence others and work well in teams*. You can be a leader without being a manager. Leadership courses and programs directed toward training future leaders are increasing.[50] Leadership skill includes persistency and the ability to motivate others. You will learn about, apply, and develop leadership skills in Chapters 7 through 13. Leadership skills are based on intrapersonal and interpersonal skills. Thus, the sequence of parts in the book, as well as the chapters within each part, constitutes a logical set of building blocks for your competency and skill development.

Communication Skills
Refer to CS Question 6.

It's time to assess your intrapersonal skills, interpersonal skills, and leadership skills. Together, these skills are called human relations skills. The following section focuses on self-assessment, an important intrapersonal skill. People with good intrapersonal skills use self-assessment as the basis for improving their human relations skills,[51] which we will be doing throughout the book.

ASSESSING YOUR HUMAN RELATIONS ABILITIES AND SKILLS

For each of the 43 statements below, record in the blank the number from 1 to 7 that best describes your level of ability or skill. You are not expected to have all high numbers. This assessment will give you an overview of what you will learn in this course. Appendix A contains the same assessment to enable you to compare your skills at the beginning and end of the course.

Low ability/skill						High ability/skill
1	2	3	4	5	6	7

_____ 1. I understand how personality and perception affect people's behavior, human relations, and performance.

_____ 2. I can describe several ways to handle stress effectively.

_____ 3. I know my preferred learning style (accommodator, diverger, converger, assimilator) and how it affects my behavior, human relations, and performance.

_____ 4. I understand how people acquire attitudes and how attitudes affect behavior, human relations, and performance.

_____ 5. I can describe self-concept and self-efficacy and how they affect behavior, human relations, and performance.

_____ 6. I can list several areas of personal values and state how values affect behavior, human relations, and performance.

(continued)

Low ability/skill (*Continued*)						High ability/skill
1	2	3	4	5	6	7

_____ 7. I understand how to use a time management system.

_____ 8. I understand how to use time management techniques to get more done in less time with better results.

_____ 9. I know how to develop a career plan and manage my career successfully.

_____ 10. I can describe the communication process.

_____ 11. I can list several transmission media and when to use each.

_____ 12. I can identify and use various message response styles.

_____ 13. I understand organizational communications.

_____ 14. I can list barriers to communications and how to overcome them.

_____ 15. I know my preferred communication style and how to use other communication styles to meet the needs of the situation.

_____ 16. I can describe transactional analysis.

_____ 17. I can identify the differences between aggressive, passive, and assertive behavior. I am assertive.

_____ 18. I can identify different conflict resolution styles. I understand how to resolve conflicts in a way that does not hurt relationships.

_____ 19. I can identify behavioral leadership theories.

_____ 20. I can identify contingency leadership theories.

_____ 21. I know my preferred leadership style and how to change it to meet the needs of the situation.

_____ 22. I understand the process people go through to meet their needs.

_____ 23. I know several content and process motivation theories and can use them to motivate people.

_____ 24. I can list and use motivation techniques.

_____ 25. I can identify bases and sources of power.

_____ 26. I know how to gain power in an organization.

_____ 27. I can list political techniques to increase success.

_____ 28. I have 100 people I can call on for career help.

_____ 29. I know how to open a conversation to get people to give me career assistance.

_____ 30. I know two critical things to do during a negotiation to get what I want.

_____ 31. I understand how to plan and conduct effective meetings.

_____ 32. I can identify components of group dynamics and how they affect behavior, human relations, and performance.

_____ 33. I know the stages groups go through as they develop.

_____ 34. I understand the roles and various types of groups in organizations.

_____ 35. I can help groups make better decisions through consensus.

_____ 36. I know when, and when not, to use employee participation in decision making.

_____ 37. I understand why people resist change and know how to overcome that resistance.

_____ 38. I can identify and use organizational development techniques.

_____ 39. I understand how to develop a positive organizational culture and climate.

_____ 40. I understand equal employment opportunity (EEO) and the rights of legally protected groups such as ethnic and racial minorities, people with disabilities, people who are addicted to drugs or alcohol, and people living with AIDS.

_____ 41. I can define sexism and sexual harassment in organizations.

_____ 42. I can handle a complaint using the complaint model.

_____ 43. I understand how to plan for improved human relations.

To use the profile form below, place an X in the box whose number corresponds to the score you gave each statement above.

Learning Outcome 1-7

Identify your personal low and high human relations ability and skill levels.

Skill-Building Exercise 1-2 develops this skill.

Review your profile form. Your lower score numbers indicate areas where behavior changes are most warranted. Select the top five areas, abilities or skills, you want to develop through this course. Write them out below. In Chapter 8, we will discuss how to set objectives. At that time you may want to return to write what you wish to learn as objectives.

1.

2.

3.

Learning Outcome 1-8

Identify five personal human relations goals for the course.

4.

5.

As the course progresses, be sure to review your course goals and work toward attaining them.

Profile Form

	Your Score							Parts and Chapters in Which the Information Will Be Covered in the Book
	1	2	3	4	5	6	7	
								Part 1. Intrapersonal Skills: Behavior, Human Relations, and Performance Begin with You
1.								2. Personality, Stress, Learning, and Perception
2.								
3.								
4.								3. Attitudes, Self-Concept, Values, and Ethics
5.								
6.								
7.								4. Time and Career Management
8.								
9.								
								Part 2. Interpersonal Skills: The Foundation of Human Relations
10.								5. Communications, Emotions, and Criticism
11.								
12.								
13.								
14.								
15.								
16.								6. Dealing with Conflict
17.								
18.								

Profile Form (*continued*)

	Your Score							Parts and Chapters in Which the Information Will Be Covered in the Book
	1	2	3	4	5	6	7	
								Part 3. Leadership Skills: Influencing Others
19.								7. Leading and Trust
20.								
21.								
22.								8. Motivating Performance
23.								
24.								
25.								9. Ethical Power and Politics, and Etiquette
26.								
27.								
28.								10. Networking and Negotiating
29.								
30.								
								Part 4. Leadership Skills: Team and Organizational Behavior, Human Relations, and Performance
31.								11. Team Dynamics, Creativity and Problem Solving, and Decision Making
32.								
33.								
34.								
35.								
36.								
37.								12. Organizational Change and Culture
38.								
39.								
40.								13. Valuing Diversity Globally
41.								
42.								
43.								Appendix A. Applying Human Relations Skills

Skill-Building Exercise 1-3 develops this skill.

Don't be too concerned if your scores were not as high as you would like them to be. If you work at it, you will develop your human relations skills through this book.

In this chapter we have discussed how your behavior affects your human relations and performance; why human relations skills are so important; that what you learn in this course can be used immediately in your personal and professional lives; a brief history of human relations; the importance of changing your behavior; and 10 guidelines to follow in developing effective human relations. Next is a chapter review with a glossary and more application and skill-building material to develop your human relations skills based on Chapter 1 concepts.

/ / / REVIEW / / /

The chapter review is organized to help you master the nine learning outcomes for Chapter 1. First provide your own response to each learning outcome, and then check the summary provided to see how well you understand the material. Next, identify the final statement in each section as either true or false (T/F). Correct each false statement. Answers are given at the end of the chapter.

LO 1-1 Explain why human relations skills are important.

People are an organization's most valuable resource. It is the people who cause the success or failure of an organization. Faulty human relations skill is the most common cause of management failure.

The myths of human relations (HR) are: (1) Technical skills are more important than HR skills; (2) HR is just common sense; (3) global diversity is overemphasized; and (4) leaders are born, not made. T F

LO 1-2 Discuss the goal of human relations.

Organizations that can create a win–win situation for all have a greater chance of succeeding. If the organization offers everyone what they need, all benefit. Satisfying needs is not easy; rather, it is a goal to strive for, which may never be met.

Organizations expect that employees will not let their personal lives affect their work. T F

LO 1-3 Describe the relationship between individual and group behavior and organizational performance.

Through the systems effect, we learn that individuals affect each other's performance and that of the group and organization. The organization is made up of individuals and groups. Its performance is based on individual and group performance.

Human relations takes place only at the group and organizational levels. T F

LO 1-4 Briefly describe the history of the study of human relations.

In the 1800s Frederick Taylor developed scientific management, which focused on redesigning jobs. Also in the 1800s Robert Owen was the first manager-owner to understand the need to improve the work environment and the employee's overall situation. Elton Mayo is called the "father of human relations." In the mid-1920s to the early 1930s he conducted the Hawthorne Studies and thereby identified the Hawthorne effect, an increase in performance due to the special attention given to employees, rather than tangible changes in the work. Through the 1930s to the 1980s much attention has been paid to the human side of the organization. Teamwork and increased employee participation became popular during the 1990s.

Thomas Peters and Robert Waterman developed Theory Z. T F

LO 1-5 State some of the trends and challenges in the field of human relations.

Trends and challenges in the field of human relations include: (1) globalization, change, innovation, and speed; (2) technology; (3) diversity; (4) learning and knowledge; (5) ethics; and (6) crisis.

The rate of change and technology is slowing down. T F

LO 1-6 List 10 guidelines for effective human relations.

Guidelines for effective human relations include: (1) be optimistic; (2) be positive; (3) be genuinely interested in other people; (4) smile and develop a sense of humor; (5) call people by name; (6) listen to people; (7) help others; (8) think before you act; (9) apologize; and (10) create win–win situations.

The goal of human relations is within guideline 7: help others. T F

LO 1-7 Identify your personal low and high human relations ability and skill levels.

Answers will vary from student to student.

Most people will have the same score on most abilities and skills. T F

LO 1-8 Identify five personal human relations goals for the course.

Answers will vary from student to student.

The goals you select for this course are neither right nor wrong. T F

LO 1-9 Define the following 17 key terms.

Select one or more methods: (1) fill in the missing key terms from memory; (2) match the key terms from the end of the review with their definitions below; and/or (3) copy the key terms in order from the key terms at the beginning of the chapter.

____________________ are interactions among people, while the

____________________ is to create a win–win situation by satisfying employee needs while achieving organizational objectives.

A(n) ____________________ occurs when the organization and employees get what they want.

The ________________ realizes that an organization employs the whole person, not just his or her job skills.

________________ is what people do and say.

The ________________ are individual, group, and organizational.

________________ is the things two or more people do and say as they interact (human relations).

A(n) ________________ is a group of people working to achieve one or more objectives.

________________ is the collective behavior of its individuals and groups.

________________ is the extent to which expectations or objectives have been met.

Under the ________________, all people in the organization are affected by at least one other person, and each person affects the whole group or organization.

________________ is called the "father of human relations" and conducted the Hawthorne Studies in the mid-1920s to the early 1930s, considered the first true human relations research.

The ________________ refers to an increase in performance due to the special attention given to employees, rather than tangible changes in the work.

________________ integrates common business practices in the United States and Japan into one middle-ground framework.

________________ are within the individual and include characteristics such as personality, attitudes, self-concept, and integrity.

________________ is the ability to work well with a diversity of people.

________________ is the ability to influence others and work well in teams.

/ / / KEY TERMS / / /

behavior 4
Elton Mayo 9
goal of human relations 4
group behavior 4
Hawthorne effect 9
human relations 4
interpersonal skill 17
intrapersonal skills 17
leadership skill 17
levels of behavior 4
organization 5
organizational behavior 5
performance 6
systems effect 6
Theory Z 9
total person approach 4
win–win situation 4

/ / / COMMUNICATION SKILLS / / /

The following critical thinking questions can be used for class discussion and/or as written assignments to develop communication skills. Be sure to give complete explanations for all questions.

1. In your opinion, which myth about human relations holds back the development of human relations skills more than any of the others?
2. Which person's contribution to the history of human relations do you find to be the most impressive?
3. Which one of the trends or challenges do you believe is the most relevant to the field of human relations?
4. Which one of the 10 guidelines for effective human relations do you think is the most important?
5. Of the three ways to handle human relations problems, which ones are the easiest and hardest for you?
6. Of the intrapersonal, interpersonal, and leadership skills, which one is your strongest? Your weakest?

CASE / / / W. L. Gore & Associates: How Employees Relate to One Another Sets Gore Apart.

Founded in 1958, W. L. Gore & Associates, Inc. has become a modern-day success story as a uniquely managed, privately owned family business that truly understands the connection between behavior, human relations, and performance. Founders Bill and Vieve Gore set out to create a business where innovation was a way of life and not a by-product. Today, Gore is best known for its GORE-TEX range of high-performance fabrics and Elixir Strings for guitars. Gore is the leading manufacturer of thousands of advanced technology products for the medical, electronics, industrial, and fabrics markets. With annual revenues of $2.5 billion, the company employs approximately 9,000 associates at more than 50 facilities around the world.

Terri Kelly replaced Chuck Carroll as the president and CEO of W. L. Gore & Associates in April 2005. Gore has repeatedly been named among the "100 Best Companies to Work For" in the United States by *Fortune* magazine. In a recent interview, Kelly was asked what would be the most distinctive elements of the Gore management model to an outsider. She listed four factors: "We don't operate in a hierarchy; we try to resist titles; our associates, who are all owners in the company, self-commit to what they want to do; and our leaders have positions of authority because they have followers." According to Kelly, these four attributes enable Gore to maximize individual potential while cultivating an environment that fosters creativity and also to operate with high integrity. She is quick to remind everyone that all of Gore's practices and ways of doing business reflect the innovative and entrepreneurial spirit of its founders.

Kelly attributes Gore's success to its unique culture. As she put it, how work is conducted at Gore and how employees relate to one another set Gore apart. There are no titles, no bosses, and no formal hierarchy. Compensation and promotion decisions are determined by peer rankings of each other's performance. To avoid dampening employee creativity, the company has an organizational structure and culture that goes against conventional wisdom. Bill Gore (the founder) referred to the company's structure as a "lattice organization." Gore's lattice structure includes the following features:[52]

- Direct lines of communication—person to person—with no intermediary
- No fixed or assigned authority
- Sponsors, not bosses
- Natural leadership as evidenced by the willingness of others to follow
- Objectives set by those who must "make them happen"
- Tasks and functions organized through commitments
- Complete avoidance of the hierarchical command and control structure

The lattice structure as described by the people at Gore encourages hands-on innovation and discourages bureaucratic red tape by involving those closest to a project in decision making. Instead of a pyramid of bosses and managers, Gore has a flat organizational structure. There are no chains of command, no predetermined channels of communication. It sounds very much like a self-managed team at a much broader scale.

Why has Gore achieved such remarkable success? W. L. Gore & Associates prefers to think of the various people who play key roles in the organization as being leaders, not managers. While Bill Gore did not believe in smothering the company in thick layers of formal management, he also knew that as the company grew, he had to find ways to assist new people and to follow their progress. Thus, W. L. Gore & Associates came up with its "sponsor" program—a human relations partnership between an incumbent, experienced employee and a newly hired, inexperienced employee. Before a candidate is hired, an associate has to agree to be his or her sponsor or what others refer to as a mentor. The sponsor's role is to take a personal interest in the new associate's contributions, problems, and goals, acting as both a coach and an advocate. The sponsor tracks the new associate's progress, offers help and encouragement, points out weaknesses and suggests ways to correct them, and concentrates on how the associate might better exploit his or her strengths. It's about improving the intrapersonal skills of the new hire.

Sponsoring is not a short-term commitment. All associates have sponsors, and many have more than one. When individuals are hired, at first they are likely to have a sponsor in their immediate work area. As associates' commitments change or grow, it's normal for them to acquire additional sponsors. For instance, if they move to a new job in another area of the company, they typically gain a sponsor there. Sponsors help associates chart a course in the organization that will offer personal fulfillment while maximizing their contribution to the enterprise. Leaders emerge naturally by demonstrating special knowledge, skill, or experience that advances a business objective.

An internal memo describes the three kinds of sponsorship and how they might work:

- **Starting sponsor**—a sponsor who helps a new associate get started on his or her first job at Gore, or helps a present associate get started on a new job.
- **Advocate sponsor**—a sponsor who sees to it that the associate being sponsored gets credit and recognition for contributions and accomplishments.
- **Compensation sponsor**—a sponsor who sees to it that the associate being sponsored is fairly paid for contributions to the success of the enterprise.

An associate can perform any one or all three kinds of sponsorship. Quite frequently, a sponsoring associate is a good friend, and it's not uncommon for two associates to sponsor each other as advocates.

Being an associate is a natural commitment to four basic human relations principles articulated by Bill Gore and still a key belief of the company: fairness to each other and everyone we come in contact with; freedom to encourage, help, and allow other associates to grow in knowledge, skill, and scope of responsibility; the ability to make one's own commitments and keep them; and consultation with other associates before undertaking actions that could affect the reputation of the company. These principles underscore the importance of developing high interpersonal skills for Gore employees.

Over the years, W. L. Gore & Associates has faced a number of unionization drives. The company neither tries to dissuade associates from attending organizational meetings nor retaliates against associates who pass out union flyers. However, Bill Gore believes there is no need for third-party representation under the lattice structure. He asks, "Why would associates join a union when they own the company? It seems rather absurd."

Commitment is seen as a two-way street at W. L. Gore & Associates—while associates are expected to commit to making a contribution to the company's success, the company is committed to providing a challenging, opportunity-rich work environment, and reasonable job security. The company tries to avoid laying off associates. If a workforce reduction becomes necessary, the company uses a system of temporary transfers within a plant or cluster of plants, and requests voluntary layoffs. According to CEO Kelly, Gore's structure, systems, and culture have continued to yield impressive results for the company. In the more than 50 years that Gore has been in business, it has always made a profit.[53]

Go to the Internet: To learn more about W. L. Gore & Associates, visit its Web site (www.gore.com).

Support your answers to the following questions with specific information from the case and text or with other information you get from the Web or other sources.

1. What evidence is there that W. L. Gore & Associates aspires to meet the goal of human relations?
2. How does Gore & Associates depict an organization that fully appreciates the "systems effect"?
3. One can argue that W. L. Gore's lattice structure encompasses some of the unexpected discoveries brought out by Elton Mayo and the Hawthorne Studies. Identify some features of the lattice structure that align with some of the unexpected discoveries of the Hawthorne Studies.
4. How does Gore's "sponsorship" program contribute toward meeting some of the 10 human relations guidelines outlined in the chapter?

Case Exercise and Role-Play

Preparation: You are a manager in an organization that wants to communicate in practical terms the meaning and importance of the the systems effect and the total person approach to new employees during the orientation process. The manager is supposed to use examples to make his or her points. Based on your understanding of these two concepts, create a five-minute oral presentation on the meaning and importance of:

a. The systems effect
b. The total person approach

Role-Play: The instructor forms students into manager–new employee pairs and has each pair dramatize exercise a and b in front of the rest of the class. The student playing the role of new employee should then paraphrase the manager's message. After each presentation, the class is to discuss and critique the effectiveness with which the manager clearly communicated the meaning and importance of these two concepts and the effectiveness of the new employee in replaying the message.

OBJECTIVE CASE / / / Supervisor Susan's Human Relations

Peter has been working for York Bakery for about three months now. He has been doing an acceptable job until this week. Peter's supervisor, Susan, has called him in to discuss the drop in performance. (*Note:* Susan's meeting with Peter and/or a meeting held by Tim with Susan and Peter can be role-played in class.)

SUSAN: Peter, I called you in here to talk to you about the drop in the amount of work you completed this week. What do you have to say?

PETER: Well, I've been having a personal problem at home.

SUSAN: That's no excuse. You have to keep your personal life separate from your job. Get back to work, and shape up or ship out.

PETER: (Says nothing, just leaves.)

Susan goes to her boss, Tim.

SUSAN: Tim, I want you to know that I've warned Peter to increase his performance or he will be fired.

TIM: Have you tried to resolve this without resorting to firing him?

SUSAN: Of course I have.

TIM: This isn't the first problem you have had with employees. You have fired more employees than any other supervisor at York.

SUSAN: It's not my fault if Peter and others do not want to do a good job. I'm a supervisor, not a babysitter.

TIM: I'm not very comfortable with this situation. I'll get back to you later this afternoon.

SUSAN: See you later. I'm going to lunch.

Answer the following questions. Then in the space between questions, state why you selected that answer.

_______ 1. There _______ a human relations problem between Susan and Peter.

a. is *b.* is not

_______ 2. Susan has attempted to create a _______ situation.

a. lose–lose *b.* win–lose *c.* win–win

_______ 3. Susan _______ an advocate of the total person approach.

a. is *b.* is not

_______ 4. Through the systems effect, Peter's decrease in output affects which level of behavior?

a. individual *c.* organizational
b. group *d.* all three levels

_______ 5. The scope of study illustrated in this case covers:

a. behavior *c.* performance
b. human relations *d.* all three

_______ 6. The focus of study by Susan is:

a. individual/behavior *c.* group/human relations
b. individual/performance *d.* organizational/performance

_______ 7. The focus of study by Tim should be:

a. individual/behavior *c.* group/human relations
b. group/behavior *d.* organizational/performance

_______ 8. Later that afternoon Tim should:

a. reprimand Peter
b. talk to Peter and tell him not to worry about it
c. bring Susan and Peter together to resolve the problem
d. do nothing, letting Susan handle the problem herself
e. fire Susan

_______ 9. The major human relations skill lacking in Susan is:

a. being optimistic
b. smiling and developing a sense of humor
c. thinking before you act
d. being genuinely interested in other people

_______ 10. Tim _______ work with Susan to develop her human relations skills.

a. should *b.* should not

11. Will Peter's performance increase? If you were Peter, would you increase your performance?

12. Have you ever had a supervisor with Susan's attitude? Assume you are in Susan's position. How would you handle Peter's decrease in performance?

13. Assume you are in Tim's position. How would you handle this situation?

/ / / SKILL-BUILDING EXERCISE 1-1 / / /

Getting to Know You by Name

In-Class Exercise (Individual)

Objectives:

1. *A.* To get acquainted with the members of your permanent group and to name the group.
   B. To get acquainted with some of your classmates.

AACSB: The primary AACSB learning standard skill developed through this exercise is communication ability.

2. To get to know more about your instructor.

Experience: You will be involved in a small-group discussion, and one person from each group will ask the instructor questions.

Procedure 1 (2–5 minutes)
A. Your instructor will assign you to your permanent group.
B. Break into groups of three to six, preferably with people you do not know or do not know well.

Procedure 2 (8–12 minutes)
Each group member tells the others his or her name and two or three significant things about himself or herself. After all members have finished, ask each other questions to get to know each other better.

Procedure 3 (2–4 minutes) Permanent groups only
Everyone writes down the names of all group members. Addresses and telephone numbers are also recommended.

Procedure 4 (2–3 minutes) All groups
Each person calls all members by name, without looking at written names. Continue until all members call the others by name. Be sure to use the guidelines for remembering people's names on p. 12.

Procedure 5 (5–10 minutes) Permanent groups only
Members decide on a name for the group; a logo is optional.

Procedure 6 (5–12 minutes)
Elect a spokesperson to record and ask your group's questions. The members select specific questions to ask the instructor under the three categories below. The spokesperson should not identify who asked which questions.

1. Questions about course expectations. Questions about doubts or concerns about this course.
2. Questions about the instructor. (What would you like to know about the instructor to get to know him or her?)

Procedure 7 (10–20 minutes)
Each spokesperson asks the group's question under one category at a time. When all questions from category 1 are asked and answered, proceed to category 2. Spokespersons should not repeat questions asked by other groups.

Questions (2–10 minutes): For the groups or class.

1. Is it important to know and call people by name? Why or why not?
2. What can you do to improve your ability to remember people's names when you first meet them, and at later times?

Conclusion: The instructor may make concluding remarks.

Application (2–4 minutes): What have I learned through this exercise? How will I use this knowledge in the future?

Sharing: Volunteers give their answers to the application section.

/ / / SKILL-BUILDING EXERCISE 1-2 / / /

Course Objectives

In-Class Exercise (Individual)

Objective: To share your course objectives.

AACSB: The primary AACSB learning standard skills developed through this exercise are reflective thinking and self-management, analytic skills, and communication abilities.

Experience: You will share your course objectives in small groups or with the entire class.

Preparation: You should have completed the self-assessment section of this chapter, including five written objectives.

Procedure 1 (5–30 minutes)

Option A: Volunteers state one or more of their course objectives to the class. The instructor may make comments.

Option B: Break into groups of three to six members and share your course objectives.

Option C1: Same procedure as Option B with the addition of having the group select a member to share five of the group's objectives.

Option C2: Each group's spokesperson reports its five objectives.

Conclusion: The instructor leads a class discussion and/or makes concluding remarks.

Application (2–4 minutes): Should I change any of my objectives? If yes, rewrite it or them below.

Sharing: Volunteers give their answers to the application section.

/ / / SKILL-BUILDING EXERCISE 1-3 / / /

Human Relations Overview: OBingo Icebreaker

In-Class Exercise (Group)

Objective: To get an overview of some of the many human relations topics through an icebreaker game of bingo.

AACSB: The primary AACSB learning standard skill developed through this exercise is communication ability.

Experience: You will play an interactive game of bingo related to human relations.

Procedure (5–10 minutes)

Go around the room and get signatures of peers who fit the descriptions in the squares on the OBingo card.

Tell the person your name, and sign only if the description really does fit you.

Each person can sign only one square on your card.

Say "bingo" when you get it.

If you get bingo before the time is up, keep getting as many signatures as you can until the time is up.

The number in the square identifies the chapter in which the topic will be covered.

Conclusion: The instructor may make concluding remarks.

Source: This exercise was adapted from Joan Benek-Rivera, Bloomsburg University of Pennsylvania. Dr. Rivera's exercise was presented at the 2002 Organizational Behavior Teaching Conference (OBTC).

HUMAN RELATIONS

OB	I	N	G	O
2. Has an introverted personality	6. Doesn't like structure	9. Is good at motivating others	11. Has a network of at least 50 people for career help	13. Likes to create new things or new ways to do things
2. Has little or no stress	7. Has an ego	9. Is a high achiever	11. Is a tough negotiator	14. Is concerned about doing a quality job
3. Has a satisfying job	7. Avoids conflict	Your name	12. Likes status symbols (name brands that show, trophy)	14. Does not like change
4. Is poor at managing time	8. Likes to be in charge	10. Does as the boss requests	12. Looks out for number one	15. Is a minority
5. Uses paraphrasing regularly	8. Uses an autocratic leader style	10. Enjoys playing organizational politics	13. Likes to solve problems	15. Has lived in a foreign country

/ / ANSWERS TO TRUE/FALSE QUESTIONS / /

1. T.
2. F. Organizations employ the total person and realize that personal lives do affect work, so they try to help employees balance their work and personal lives.
3. T.
4. F. William Ouchi developed Theory Z, Peters and Waterman wrote *In Search of Excellence*.
5. F. The rate of change and technology will continue to increase.
6. F. The goal of human relations is (10): create win–win situations.
7. F. People are different and score differently.
8. T.

CHAPTER 2

Personality, Stress, Learning, and Perception

LEARNING OUTCOMES

After completing this chapter, you should be able to:

LO 2-1 Describe the Big Five personality dimensions.

LO 2-2 Explain the benefits of understanding and identifying personality profiles.

LO 2-3 Describe your stress personality type.

LO 2-4 List causes of stress, and describe how to be more effective at controlling stress.

LO 2-5 Describe the four learning styles and know which is your preferred learning style.

LO 2-6 Describe six biases affecting perception.

LO 2-7 Explain the importance of first impressions and how to project a positive image.

LO 2-8 Define the following 15 key terms (in order of appearance in the chapter):

personality	**perception**
Type A personality	**stereotyping**
locus of control	**perceptual congruence**
Big Five Model of Personality	**primacy effect**
stress	**four-minute barrier**
stressors	**image**
burnout	
controlling stress plan	
intelligence	

/ / / You have most likely consumed a Pepsi drink. But did you know the PepsiCo company also owns Frito-Lay snacks, Tropicana juices, Quaker Oats cereal and granola bars, and Gatorade sport drinks? PepsiCo sells hundreds of products in nearly 200 countries.[1] To learn more about PepsiCo, visit its Web site at www.pepsico.com.

June Peterson was walking alone to the lunchroom. As she walked, she was thinking about her coworker, Rod Wills. June has trouble getting along with Rod because they are complete opposites. As June walked, two general thoughts came to her mind: Why does Rod do the things he does? Why are we so different? More specific questions came to mind: (1) We do the same job—why is he so stressed out and I'm not? (2) Why am I so emotional and interested in people—while Rod isn't? (3) Why am I so eager to get involved and help—while he sits back and watches? (4) Why is Rod so quiet—while I'm so outgoing? (5) Why do I dislike routine and detail so much—while Rod enjoys it so much? (6) Why does he believe that everything that happens is because of fate—while I don't? (7) When we have to agree on a decision, why is he so slow and analytical—while I'm not? (8) Why is it that we see our jobs so differently when they are the same? (9) When I first met Rod, I thought we would hit it off fine. Why was I so wrong?

Although June's questions have no simple answers, this chapter will give you a better understanding of behavioral differences. / / /

HOW PERSONALITY, STRESS, INTELLIGENCE AND LEARNING, PERCEPTION, AND FIRST IMPRESSIONS AFFECT BEHAVIOR, HUMAN RELATIONS, AND PERFORMANCE

Recall that in Part 1 of the book, in Chapters 2 and 3, we discuss intrapersonal skills that affect behavior, human relations, and performance. In this chapter we cover several different yet related topics, so let's start with an overview. Your *personality* affects your behavior and human relations,[2] so your personality is a good predictor of your job performance.[3] Your personality also affects your level of *stress,*[4] and when you are under too much stress it tends to have a negative effect on your behavior, human relations, and job performance.[5] Your personality is also related to your level of *intelligence* and preferred method of learning, so intelligence also influences your behavior and human relations and is a good predictor of job success.[6] Finally, your personality and intelligence influence your *perception,*[7] which, in turn, affects your *first impressions* of others. Since behavior is the product of perception, it also affects human relations and performance.[8]

Throughout this chapter, you will learn how personality, stress, intelligence, perceptions, and first impressions make us similar and different. You will understand how these concepts affect your behavior, human relations, and performance and that of others, so that you can better understand yourself and others and work more effectively. Intrapersonal skills are harder to develop than interpersonal and leadership skills, and since intrapersonal skills are the foundation of effective interpersonal and leadership skills,[9] you will need to give this and the next chapter your best shot.

PERSONALITY

As June Peterson's dilemma illustrates, different people behave differently in their everyday lives. Personality, or personal style, is a very complex subject, yet in our daily lives we use trait adjectives such as *warm, aggressive,* and *easygoing* to describe people's behavior. *Personality* is the word commonly used to describe an individual's collection (total person) of such behavioral traits or characteristics. Personal style or **personality** *is a relatively stable set of traits that aids in explaining and predicting individual behavior.* As noted, individuals are all different, yet similar, in many ways.

Substantial progress in the development of personality theory and traits has been made.[10] Psychoanalyst Carl Jung was a pioneer in developing the theory of psychological types, but others took his work further to develop personality classification methods. In this section you will learn about personality and the personality classifications of Type A and Type B; locus of control; the Big Five Model of Personality; and the MBTI. Throughout this chapter and book, you will gain a better understanding of your personality traits, which will help explain why you and others do the things you do (behavior).

Personality Development and Classification Methods

Why are some people outgoing and others shy, some loud and others quiet, some warm and others cold, some aggressive and others passive? This list of behaviors is made up of individual traits. *Traits* are distinguishing personal characteristics. Personality development is based on genetics and environmental factors. The genes you received before you were born influence your personality traits. Your family, friends, school, and work also influence your personality. In short, personality is the sum of genetics and a lifetime of learning. Personality traits, however, can be changed, with work. For example, people who are shy can become more outgoing.

Type A, Type B, and Locus of Control

Type A and Type B Personalities Let's begin here with the simple two-dimensional method Type A, Type B. A **Type A personality** *is characterized as fast moving, hard driving, time conscious, competitive, impatient, and preoccupied with work.* Because a *Type B personality* is the opposite of Type A, often it is called laid-back or easygoing. The Type A personality is commonly associated with a high level of stress, so we discuss it further in the section on causes of stress.

Locus of Control Another simple two-dimensional personality classification method is locus of control. Before we discuss it, complete Self-Assessment Exercise 2-1 to determine if you are more of an internalizer or externalizer.

/// Self-Assessment Exercise 2-1 ///

Your Locus of Control

Below are five statements. In the blank beside each statement, assign 1 to 5 points based on your agreement with the statement:

Agree		Neutral		Disagree
5	4	3	2	1

_____ 1. Getting ahead in life is a matter of hard work, rather than being in the right place at the right time.

_____ 2. I determine what I do and say, rather than allowing people and situations to upset me and affect how I behave.

_____ 3. Getting a raise and promotion is based on hard work, rather than who you know.

_____ 4. I, rather than other people and situations, determine what happens to my life.

_____ 5. Students earn their grades; teachers don't determine students' grades.

_____ Total. Add the five numbers (1–5). Below, place an X on the continuum that represents your score:

Externalizer 5 – – – – 10 – – – – 15 – – – – 20 – – – – 25 Internalizer

The lower your score, the greater is your belief that you are controlled by external sources such as fate, chance, other people, or environmental situations. The higher your score, the greater is your belief that you are in control of your destiny.

There is no right or wrong score, and a simple five-question instrument may not be totally accurate, but it should be helpful. If you disagree with the score, review the questions and think about why you selected the answers.

Locus of control *is a continuum representing one's belief as to whether external or internal forces control one's destiny.* People with an external locus of control (externalizers) believe that they have little control over their performance and are closed to new experiences. Internalizers believe they are in control and are open to new experiences to improve performance.[11]

Do you believe that you determine your own career success? The message that you need to have an internal locus of control cannot be overstated; it determines your level of satisfaction with self, your stress level, and your career path. Thus, it is absolutely significant that you embrace the message that you control your own destiny.

If you believe that if you try hard, it doesn't matter, that you cannot be successful, you will most likely be unhappy, give up easily, and not have a successful career. Successful people know that they are in control of their lives, and they are happy and successful because they work at it. Successful people have lots of failures, but they keep trying. Internal locus of control can be changed.

Learning Outcome 2-1

Describe the Big Five personality dimensions.

The Big Five Model of Personality

Let's begin by completing Self-Assessment Exercise 2-2 to determine your personality profile. The purpose of the Big Five model is to reliably categorize most, if not all, of the traits that you would use to describe someone. The model is organized into five dimensions, and each dimension includes multiple traits.[12] The **Big Five Model of Personality** *categorizes traits into the dimensions of surgency, agreeableness, adjustment, conscientiousness, and openness to experience.* The dimensions are listed in Exhibit 2.1 and described below. Note, however, that the five dimensions are sometimes published with slightly different descriptor names.

/// Self-Assessment Exercise 2-2 ///

Your Big Five Personality Profile

There are no right or wrong answers, so by being honest you can really increase your self-awareness. We suggest doing this exercise in pencil or making a copy before you write on it. We will explain why later.

Identify each of the 25 statements according to how accurately they describe you. Place a number from 1 to 7 on the line before each statement.

Like me			Somewhat like me			Not like me
7	6	5	4	3	2	1

_____ 1. I step forward and take charge in leaderless situations.

_____ 2. I am concerned about getting along well with others.

_____ 3. I have good self-control; I don't get emotional and get angry and yell.

_____ 4. I'm dependable; when I say I will do something, it's done well and on time.

_____ 5. I try to do things differently to improve my performance.

_____ 6. I enjoy competing and winning; losing bothers me.

_____ 7. I enjoy having lots of friends and going to parties.

_____ 8. I perform well under pressure.

_____ 9. I work hard to be successful.

_____ 10. I go to new places and enjoy traveling.

_____ 11. I am outgoing and willing to confront people when in conflict.

_____ 12. I try to see things from other people's points of view.

_____ 13. I am an optimistic person who sees the positive side of situations (the cup is half full).

_____ 14. I am a well-organized person.

_____ 15. When I go to a new restaurant, I order foods I haven't tried.

_____ 16. I want to climb the corporate ladder to as high a level of management as I can.

_____ 17. I want other people to like me and to be viewed as very friendly.

_____ 18. I give people lots of praise and encouragement; I don't put people down and criticize.

_____ 19. I conform by following the rules of an organization.

_____ 20. I volunteer to be the first to learn or do new tasks at work.

_____ 21. I try to influence other people to get my way.

_____ 22. I enjoy working with others more than working alone.

_____ 23. I view myself as being relaxed and secure, rather than nervous and insecure.

_____ 24. I am considered credible because I do a good job and come through for people.

_____ 25. When people suggest doing things differently, I support them and help bring about change; I don't make statements such as, "It will not work," "We never did it before," "Who else did it?" or "We can't do it."

The columns in the chart below represent specific personality dimensions. To determine *your personality profile,* (1) place the number (1–7) that represents your score for each statement, (2) total each column (5–35), and (3) make a bar chart by marking the total scores on the vertical bars.

Surgency		**Agreeableness**		**Adjustment**		**Conscientiousness**		**Openness to experience**	
	35		**35**		**35**		**35**		**35**
_____ **1.**	**25**	_____ **2.**	**25**	_____ **3.**	**25**	_____ **4.**	**25**	_____ **5.**	**25**
_____ **6.**	**20**	_____ **7.**	**20**	_____ **8.**	**20**	_____ **9.**	**20**	_____ **10.**	**20**
_____ **11.**	**15**	_____ **12.**	**15**	_____ **13.**	**15**	_____ **14.**	**15**	_____ **15.**	**15**
_____ **16.**	**10**	_____ **17.**	**10**	_____ **18.**	**10**	_____ **19.**	**10**	_____ **20.**	**10**
_____ **21.**	**5**	_____ **22.**	**5**	_____ **23.**	**5**	_____ **24.**	**5**	_____ **25.**	**5**
_____ **Total**	**Bar**	_____ **Total**	**Bar**	_____ **Total**	**Bar**	_____ **Total**	**Bar**	_____ **Total**	**Bar**

The higher the total number, the stronger is the personality dimension that describes your personality. What are your strongest and weakest dimensions? Continue reading the chapter to find out the specifics of your personality in each of the five dimensions.

EXHIBIT 2.1 | Big Five Dimensions of Traits

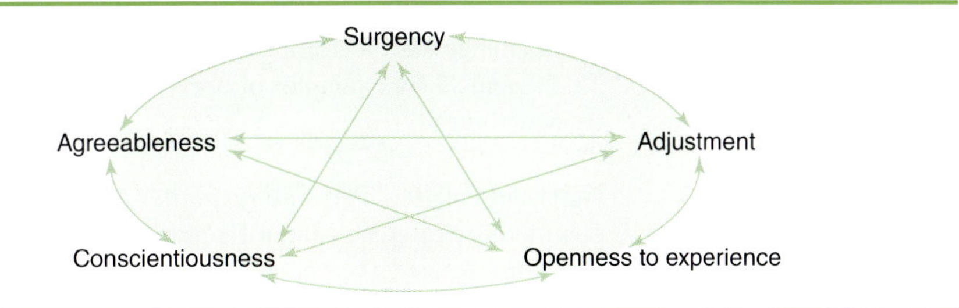

Surgency The *surgency personality dimension* includes leadership and extroversion traits. (1) People strong in leadership, more commonly called dominance, personality traits want to be in charge. They are energetic, assertive, active, and ambitious, with an interest in getting ahead and leading through competing and influencing.[13] The late Steve Jobs had a high surgency personality type.[14] People weak in surgency want to be followers, and they don't like to compete or influence. (2) Extroversion is on a continuum between being an extrovert and being an introvert. Extroverts are outgoing, sociable, and gregarious, like to meet new people, and are willing to confront others, whereas introverts are shy. In Self-Assessment Exercise 2-2, review statements 1, 6, 11, 16, and 21 for examples of surgency traits. How strong is your desire to be a leader?

Agreeableness Unlike the surgency behavior trait of wanting to get ahead of others, the *agreeableness personality dimension* includes traits related to getting along with people. Agreeable personality behavior is strong when someone is called warm, easygoing, courteous, good-natured, cooperative, tolerant, compassionate, friendly, and sociable; it is weak when someone is called cold, difficult, uncompassionate, unfriendly, and unsociable. Strong agreeable personality types are sociable, spend most of their time with other people, and have lots of friends. In Self-Assessment Exercise 2-2, review statements 2, 7, 12, 17, and 22 for examples of agreeableness traits. How important is having good relationships to you?

Adjustment The *adjustment personality dimension* includes traits related to emotional stability. Adjustment is on a continuum between being emotionally stable and being emotionally unstable. Stability refers to self-control, calmness—good under pressure, relaxed, secure, and positive—and a willingness to praise others. Being emotionally unstable means being out of control—poor under pressure, nervous, insecure, moody, depressed, angry, and negative—and quick to criticize others. Bill Gates is said to be more in control of his emotions than Steve Jobs, who was sometimes emotional.[15] People with poor adjustment are often called narcissists and tend to cause problems.[16] In Self-Assessment Exercise 2-2, review statements 3, 8, 13, 18, and 23 for examples of adjustment traits. How emotionally stable are you?

Conscientiousness The *conscientiousness personality dimension* includes traits related to achievement. Conscientiousness is on a continuum between being responsible and dependable and being irresponsible and undependable. Other traits of high conscientiousness include persistence, credibility, conformity, and organization. This trait is characterized as the willingness to work hard and put in extra time and effort to accomplish goals to achieve success. In Self-Assessment Exercise 2-2, review statements 4, 9, 14, 19, and 24 for examples of conscientiousness. Conscientiousness is a good predictor of job success. How strong is your desire to be successful?

Openness to Experience The *openness to experience personality dimension* includes traits related to being willing to change and try new things. People strong in openness to

WORK APPLICATION 2-1

Describe your Big Five personality profile.

experience are imaginative, intellectual, open-minded, autonomous, and creative, they seek change, and they are willing to try new things, while those who are weak in this dimension avoid change and new things. In Self-Assessment Exercise 2-2, review statements 5, 10, 15, 20, and 25 for examples of openness to experience. How willing are you to change and try new things?

Learning Outcome 2-2

Explain the benefits of understanding and identifying personality profiles.

Personality Profiles *Personality profiles* identify individual strong and weak traits. Students completing Self-Assessment Exercise 2–2 tend to have a range of scores for the five dimensions. Review your personality profile. Do you have high scores (strong traits) and low scores (weak traits) on some dimensions? Think about the people you enjoy being with the most at school and work. Are their personalities similar to or different from yours?

APPLICATION SITUATIONS / / /

Personality Dimensions AS 2-1

Identify the personality dimension for each of the five traits or behaviors described below.

A. Surgency C. Adjustment E. Openness to experience
B. Agreeableness D. Conscientiousness

_______ 1. The manager is influencing the follower to do the job the way he, the leader, wants it done.

_______ 2. The sales rep turned in the monthly expense report on time as usual.

_______ 3. The leader is saying a warm, friendly good morning to followers as they arrive at work.

_______ 4. The leader is seeking ideas from followers on how to speed up the flow of work.

_______ 5. As a follower is yelling a complaint, the leader calmly explains what went wrong.

Communication Skills
Refer to CS Question 1.

Recall June's question about why she and Rod are so different. A major reason is that they have different personalities that affect their behavior, human relations, and performance. June has a Type B personality, while Rod has Type A. June is a surgency extrovert, while Rod is an introvert. Not surprisingly, June has a higher agreeableness personality dimension than Rod. They may be similar on the adjustment and conscientiousness personality dimension. June is an internalizer and more open to experience than Rod, who is an externalizer.

WORK APPLICATION 2-2

Select a present or past boss and describe how his or her personality profile affected behavior, human relations, and performance in your department.

The Big Five Model of Personality Has Universal Applications Across Cultures Studies have shown that people from Asian, Western European, Middle Eastern, Eastern European, and North and South American cultures seem to exhibit the same five personality dimensions.[17] However, some cultures do place varying importance on different personality dimensions. Overall, the best predictor of job success on a global basis is the conscientiousness dimension.

Using Behavior That Matches the Big Five Personality Types

People are different, and we should deal with them as individuals. To improve our human relations, it is helpful for us to adjust our behavior based on the other person's personality type, especially our bosses, because they evaluate our performance, which affects our career. That subject is what this section is all about.

1. **Determine Personality Type**—First, we have to understand the personality types and determine an individual's personality profile. As you know, people are complex, and identifying a person's personality type is not always easy, especially when they are between the two ends of the personality type continuum. However, understanding

personality can help you understand and predict behavior, human relations, and performance in a given situation.

2. **Match Personality Type**—Next, we select the behavior we will use to match the other person's personality type. How to deal with each personality type is presented below.

Surgency

Extraverts: They like to talk, so be talkative while showing an interest in them and talking about things they are interested in. If you are not really talkative, ask them questions to get them to do the talking.

Introverts: Take it slow. Be laid-back and don't pressure them, but try to draw them out by asking questions they can easily answer. Ask for ideas and opinions. Don't worry about moments of silence; introverts often like to think before they respond.

Agreeableness

Agreeable: They are easy to get along with, so be friendly and supportive of them. However, remember that they don't tend to disagree with you to your face, so don't assume that just because they don't disagree with you, it means that they actually *do* agree with you. Asking direct questions helps, and be sure to watch for nonverbal behavior that does not match a verbal statement of "I agree with you."

Disagreeable: Try not to do things that will get them upset, but don't put up with mistreatment; be assertive (you will learn how in Chapter 7). Be patient and tolerant, because their behavior is sometimes defensive to keep them from being hurt, but inside, they do want friends. So keep being friendly and trying to win them over.

Adjustment

Emotionally stable: They tend to be easy to get along with.

Emotionally unstable: They tend to be highly emotional and unpredictable, so try to be calm yourself and keep them calm by being supportive while showing concern for them. Also, follow the guidelines of dealing with disagreeable types. You will learn how to deal with emotions and emotional people in Chapter 5.

Conscientiousness

Conscientious: They will come through for you, so don't nag; be supportive and thank them when the task is done.

Unconscientious: They tend to need prompting to complete tasks. Set clear deadlines and follow up regularly; express appreciation for progress and task completion.

Open to Experience

Open: They like change and trying new things. Focus on sharing information, ideas, and creative problem solving.

Closed: They don't want change and tend to focus on the short-term without considering how things will be better in the long-term if they change now. Focus on telling them what they have to lose and how they will benefit from the change, and use facts and figures to support their need for change. You will learn how to overcome resistance to change in Chapter 12.

The Myers-Briggs Type Indicator (MBTI)

Our fourth, and most complex, personality classification method is the Myers-Briggs Type Indicator (MBTI). The MBTI model of personality identifies your personality *preferences.* It is based on your four preferences (or inclinations) for certain ways of thinking and behaving.[18] Complete Self-Assessment Exercise 2-3 to determine your MBTI personality preference.

/// Self-Assessment Exercise 2-3 ///

Your MBTI Personality Preference

Classify yourself on each of the four preferences by selecting the one statement that best describes you:

1. *Where you focus your attention*—**Extrovert or Introvert**

_____ I'm outgoing and prefer to deal with people, things, situations, the outer world. (E)

_____ I'm shy and prefer to deal with ideas, information, explanations, or beliefs, the inner world. (I)

2. *How you take in information*—**Sensing or Intuitive**

_____ I prefer facts to have clarity, to describe what I sense with a focus on the present. (S)

_____ I prefer to deal with ideas, look into unknown possibilities with a focus on the future. (N)

3. *How you make decisions*—**Thinking or Feeling**

_____ I prefer to make decisions based on objective logic, using an analytic and detached approach. (T)

_____ I prefer to make decisions using values and/or personal beliefs, with a concern for others. (F)

4. *How you prefer to organize your life*—**Judging or Perceiving**

_____ I prefer my life to be planned, stable, and organized. (J)

_____ I prefer to go with the flow, to maintain flexibility and to respond to things as they arise. (P)

Place the four letters of preferences here _____ _____ _____ _____

There are 16 combinations, or personality preferences, often presented in the form of a table. Remember, this indicates *preferences* only. You may also use the other traits that you did not select.

ISTJ	ISFJ	INFJ	INTJ
ISTP	ISFP	INFP	INTP
ESTP	ESFP	ENFP	ENTP
ESTJ	ESFJ	ENFJ	ENTJ

Completing Self-Assessment Exercise 2-3 gives you an idea of the types of questions included in the MBTI. There are actually multiple forms of the MBTI for various uses. For more information on the MBTI, and to complete a more detailed assessment, for a fee visit its Web site at www.myersbriggs.org. Think about your friends and family and the people you work with. What MBTI type are they? How can you improve your human relations with them based on the MBTI?

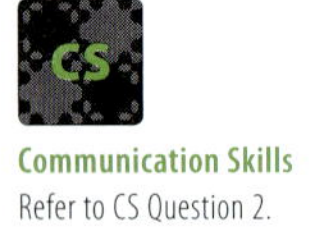

Communication Skills
Refer to CS Question 2.

STRESS

Learning Outcome 2-3

Describe your stress personality type.

In this section, we discuss what stress is, problems associated with stress, causes of stress and stress as it relates to Type A and Type B personalities, signs of stress, and how to control stress.

What Is Stress?

People react to external stimuli internally. **Stress** *is an emotional and/or physical reaction to environmental activities and events.*

Situations in which too much pressure exists are known as stressors. **Stressors** *are situations in which people feel anxiety, tension, and pressure.* Stressors are events and situations to which people must adjust, and the impact of the stressor and how people react depend on the circumstances and on each person's physical and psychological characteristics. Stress is an individual matter. In a given situation one person may be very comfortable while another feels stress. For example, June and Rod have the same job, but Rod is stressed and June isn't.

The Positive Side Some stress helps improve performance by challenging and motivating us.[19] Many people perform best under some pressure. When deadlines are approaching, their adrenaline flows and they rise to the occasion with top-level performance. To meet deadlines, managers often have to apply pressure to themselves and their employees.

Problems Associated with Too Much Stress Stress is a major problem as corporate downsizing requires employees to increase their job responsibilities. Too much stress affects your behavior, human relations, and performance.[20] Stress depletes your energy, weakens your brain and relationships, can cause aging and weight gain, weakens your immune system, can ruin your sleep, make you ill, and can even be a cause of death.[21] Thus, stress is a major cause of absenteeism.[22]

Learning Outcome 2-4

List causes of stress, and describe how to be more effective at controlling stress.

Causes of Stress

There are four common stressors related to work: Complete the questionnaire in Self-Assessment Exercise 2-4 to determine your personality type as it relates to stress.

/// Self-Assessment Exercise 2-4 ///

Your Stress Personality Type

Below are 20 statements. Identify how frequently each item applies to you.

(5) Usually (4) Often (3) Occasionally (2) Seldom (1) Rarely

Place the number 1, 2, 3, 4, or 5 on the line before each statement.

_____ 1. I work at a fast pace.

_____ 2. I work on days off.

_____ 3. I set short deadlines for myself.

_____ 4. I enjoy work/school more than other activities.

_____ 5. I talk and walk fast.

_____ 6. I set high standards for myself and work hard to meet them.

_____ 7. I enjoy competition, I work/play to win; I do not like to lose.

_____ 8. I skip lunch or eat it fast when there is work to do.

_____ 9. I'm in a hurry.

_____ 10. I do more than one thing at a time.

_____ 11. I'm angry and upset.

_____ 12. I get nervous or anxious when I have to wait.

_____ 13. I measure progress in terms of time and performance.

_____ 14. I push myself to the point of getting tired.

_____ 15. I take on more work when I already have plenty to do.

_____ 16. I take criticism as a personal put-down of my ability.

_____ 17. I try to outperform my coworkers/classmates.

_____ 18. I get upset when my routine has to be changed.

(continued)

/// Self-Assessment Exercise 2-4 /// (*continued*)

_____ 19. I consistently try to get more done in less time.

_____ 20. I compare my accomplishments with those of others who are highly productive.

_____ Total. Add up the numbers (1–5) you have for all 20 items. Your score will range from 20 to 100. Below place an X on the continuum that represents your score.

Type A 100 _ _ _ _ _ _ _ _ 80 _ _ _ _ _ _ _ _ 60 _ _ _ _ _ _ _ _ 40 _ _ _ _ _ _ _ _ 20 Type B
A A− B+ B

The higher your score, the more characteristic you are of the Type A stress personality. The lower your score, the more characteristic you are of the Type B stress personality. An explanation of these two stress personality types follows.

WORK APPLICATION 2-3

What was your stress personality type score and letter? Should you work at changing your personality type? Explain why or why not. Will you change?

Personality Type The degree to which stressors affect us is caused, in part, by our personality type. Since stress comes from within, the things we do can cause us stress. As noted earlier, there are Type A and Type B personalities. The 20 statements of Self-Assessment Exercise 2-4 relate to these personality types. People with Type A personalities have more stress than people with Type B personalities. If you scored 60 or above, you have a Type A personality and could end up with some of the problems associated with stress.

- **Organizational Climate.** The amount of cooperation, the level of motivation, and the overall morale in an organization affect stress levels. The more positive the organizational climate and work culture, the less stress there is.
- **Management Behavior.** Calm, participative management styles produce less stress. Tight control through autocratic management tends to create more stress. Some bosses use awful behavior; some are even abusive and have caused stress to the point of driving employees to quit their jobs.
- **Degree of Job Satisfaction.** People who enjoy their jobs and derive satisfaction from them handle stress better than those who do not. In some cases, a change of jobs is a wise move that can lower or get rid of one of your stressors.

APPLICATION SITUATIONS ///

Stressors AS 2-2

Identify the stressor in each statement below.

A. Personality type
B. Organizational climate
C. Management behavior
D. Degree of job satisfaction

_______ 6. "The morale in our department is poor."

_______ 7. "This job is OK, I guess."

_______ 8. "I'm always racing against the clock."

_______ 9. "Our priorities keep changing from week to week. It is very confusing when you're not sure what's expected of you."

_______ 10. "I work at a comfortable pace."

Signs of Stress

Some of the mild signs of stress are an increase in the rate of breathing and increased amounts of perspiration. When you continually look at the clock and/or calendar, feel pressured, and fear that you will not meet a deadline, you are experiencing stress.

People often lose interest in and motivation to do their work because of stress. Stress that is constant, chronic, and severe can lead to burnout over a period of time.[23] **Burnout** *is the constant lack of interest and motivation to perform one's job because of stress.* People sometimes experience temporary burnout during busy periods, as is the case with students studying for exams and retailers trying to cope with a holiday shopping season. The use of stress-controlling techniques can often prevent stress and burnout.

Controlling Stress

Controlling stress is the process of adjusting to circumstances that disrupt or threaten to disrupt a person's equilibrium. Ideally, we should identify what causes stress in our lives and eliminate or decrease it.[24] We can better control stress by following a three-stage plan. The **controlling stress plan** *includes step 1, identify stressors; step 2, determine their causes and consequences; and step 3, plan to eliminate or decrease the stress.* Below are five ways you can help eliminate or decrease stress.

Exercise Physical exercise is an excellent way to release tension and reduce weight.[25]

Aerobic exercise that increases the heart rate and maintains that rate for 30 minutes or more for at least three or more days per week, is generally considered the best type of exercise.[26] Exercises such as fast walking or jogging, biking, swimming, and aerobic dancing fall in this category. Yoga and other exercises that require you to increase your heart rate are also beneficial.

Before starting an exercise program, however, check with a doctor to make sure you are able to do so safely. Start gradually and slowly work your way up to 20 to 30 minutes.

Nutrition Good health is essential to everyone, and nutrition is a major factor in your health. Watch your waistline. Reducing stress, exercising, and getting proper nutrition can help you control your waistline.

Breakfast is considered the most important meal of the day. A good high-protein (eggs/yogurt), high-fiber (whole-grain bread/fruit) breakfast gets you off to a good start. When you eat, take your time because rushing is stressful and leads to overeating.

Try to minimize your intake of junk food containing high levels of salt, sugar, and white flour. Consume less fat, salt, caffeine (in coffee, tea, cola), alcohol, and drugs. Eat and drink more natural foods, such as fruits and vegetables, and drink plenty of water (not soda or sports drinks).

Relaxation Get enough rest and sleep. Most adults require 7–8 hours of sleep, but Americans are not getting enough sleep. Our brains don't work effectively without enough sleep.[27] Here are some signs that you may need more sleep: trouble retaining information, irritability, minor illness, poor judgment, increased mistakes, and weight gain.

Slow down and enjoy yourself. Have some off-the-job interests that are relaxing. Have some fun, and laugh. Some of the things you can do to relax include praying, meditating, listening to music, reading, watching TV or movies, and having hobbies.

When you feel stress, you can perform some simple relaxation exercises. One of the most popular and simplest is *deep breathing.* You simply take a deep breath, hold it for a few seconds (you may count to five), and then let it out slowly. If you feel tension in one muscle, you may do a specific relaxation exercise, or you may relax your entire body, going from head to toe or vice versa. For a list of relaxation exercises that can be done almost anywhere, see Exhibit 2.2.

Positive Thinking Be optimistic and stay positive.[28] Optimism can be learned. Make statements to yourself in the affirmative, such as I will do it. Be patient, honest, and realistic. No one is perfect. Admit your mistakes and learn from them; don't let them get you down. Have self-confidence; develop your time management skills (as discussed in Chapters 3 and 4). Positive thinkers are happier than negative thinkers.

EXHIBIT 2.2 | Relaxation Exercises

Muscles	Tensing Method
Forehead	Wrinkle forehead. Try to make your eyebrows touch your hairline for 5 seconds. Relax.
Eyes and nose	Close your eyes as tightly as you can for 5 seconds. Relax.
Lips, cheeks, jaw	Draw corners of your mouth back and grimace for 5 seconds. Relax.
Neck	Drop your chin to your chest; then slowly rotate your head in a complete circle in one direction and then in the other. Relax.
Hands	Extend arms in front of you; clench fists tightly for 5 seconds. Relax.
Forearms	Extend arms out against an invisible wall and push forward with hands for 5 seconds. Relax.
Upper arms	Bend elbows. Tense biceps for 5 seconds. Relax.
Shoulders	Shrug shoulders up to your ears for 5 seconds. Relax.
Back	Arch your back off the floor or bed for 5 seconds. Relax.
Stomach	Tighten your stomach muscles for 5 seconds. Relax.
Hips, buttocks	Tighten buttocks for 5 seconds. Relax.
Thighs	Tighten thigh muscles by pressing legs together as tightly as you can for 5 seconds. Relax.
Feet	Flex your feet up toward your body as far as you can for 5 seconds. Relax.
Toes	Curl toes under as tightly as you can for 5 seconds. Relax.

Communication Skills
Refer to CS Question 3.

WORK APPLICATION 2-4

Following the controlling stress plan, (1) identify your major stressor, (2) determine its cause and consequences, and (3) develop a plan to eliminate or decrease the stress. Identify each step in your answer.

Support System We all need people we can depend on. Have family and friends you can go to for help with your problems. Having someone to talk to can be very helpful, but don't take advantage of others and use stress to get attention or to get out of doing what you should do.[29] Build relationships at work.

For an illustration of the causes of stress and how to control it, see Exhibit 2.3. If you try all the stress-controlling techniques and none of them work, you should seriously consider getting out of the situation.

EXHIBIT 2.3 | Causes of Stress and How to Control Stress

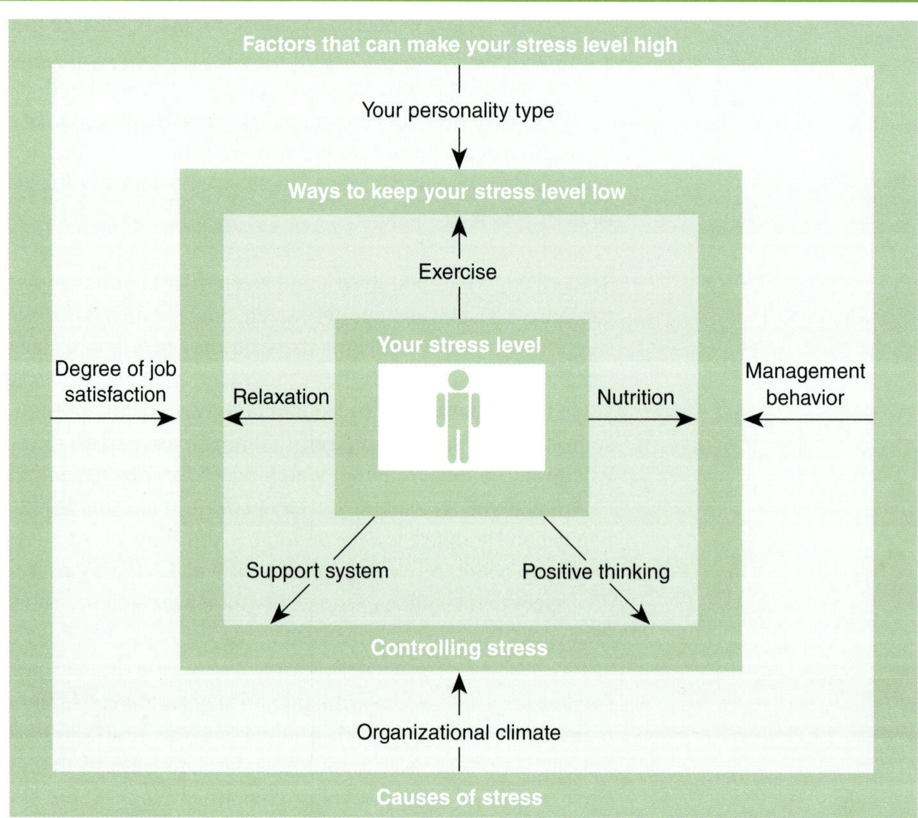

WORK APPLICATION 2-5

Of the five ways to eliminate or decrease stress, which do you do best? Which needs the most improvement and why? What will you do, if anything, to improve in that area?

Let's end this section with a confirmation of your lifestyle or an incentive to change it. According to a research study, if you exercise, don't smoke (or quit), drink only moderately, and eat right (lots of fruits and vegetables and limited junk food), you can live an average of 14 years longer.[30]

Remember that what you think about affects how you feel, and how you feel affects your behavior, human relations, and performance. So think happy, confident thoughts and if you feel stress, use these guidelines to reduce your stress.

INTELLIGENCE, EMOTIONAL INTELLIGENCE, AND LEARNING

This section discusses the development of intelligence, learning styles, and learning organizations.

Intelligence

There are numerous theories of intelligence, many of which view intelligence as the ability to learn and the use of cognitive processes. It is often called general mental ability. For our purposes we will say that **intelligence** *is the level of one's capacity for new learning, problem solving, and decision making.* Today it is generally agreed that intelligence is a product of both genetics and the environment. Most scientists today believe there are at least two and perhaps as many as seven or more different components or kinds of intelligence.

People often perform at different levels for different tasks. As you know, you are good at doing some things (math, tennis, etc.) and not as good at doing others (biology, writing, etc.). Therefore, people have multiple intelligences.

Communication Skills
Refer to CS Question 4.

Intelligence is a strong predictor of many important outcomes in life, such as educational and occupational attainment.[31] Microsoft values intelligence over all other qualifications for all jobs. Although learning new things can cause anxiety, in this fast-changing global environment, if you don't keep up, you will be left behind.

Emotional Intelligence

An offshoot of IQ is EQ (emotional quotient or emotional intelligence [EI]),[32] which is clearly related to the adjustment Big Five personality dimension. EI is all about working well with people, and up to 90 percent of the difference between star performers and average performers is EI.[33] The good news is EI is a learned competence,[34] so you can improve your EI by working at it.[35] That is what this course is all about. So here we list and briefly explain EI components, but you will develop EI skills throughout the course, especially in Chapters 5 and 6. EI is part of multiple intelligences. It has been said, "IQ gets you the job, EQ and I got a clue gets you promoted."

There are five components of EI:

1. Self-awareness (being conscious of your emotions within you; gut feelings).
2. Managing emotions (not letting your emotions get in the way of getting the job done).
3. Motivating yourself (being optimistic despite obstacles, setbacks, and failure).
4. Empathy (putting yourself in someone else's situation and understanding that person's emotions).
5. Social skills (to build relationships, respond to emotions, and influence others).

Remember that what you think about affects how you feel, and how you feel affects your behavior, human relations, and performance. So think happy, confident thoughts to help you stay calm and in control of your emotional behavior. Also, visit the Consortium for Research on Emotional Intelligence in Organizations at www.eiconsortium.org for more information about EI.

You should now have a better understanding of why June and Rod are different, other than personality. June has greater emotional intelligence according to the five components of EI. Based on the opening case information, June is more outgoing, in touch with feelings, interested in people, and eager to get involved and help others, while Rod is not.

Learning Styles

Learning Outcome 2-5

Describe the four learning styles and know which is your preferred learning style.

Our capacity to learn new things is an important aspect of our intelligence. However, we have different preferred learning styles.[36] We will examine four styles people use when learning. Before we describe the four Kolb learning styles, determine your preferred learning style. Complete Self-Assessment Exercise 2-5 before reading on.

/// Self-Assessment Exercise 2-5 ///

Your Learning Style

Below are 10 statements. For each statement distribute 5 points between the A and B alternatives. If the A statement is very characteristic of you and the B statement is not, place a 5 on the ______ A. line and a 0 on the ______ B. line. If the A statement is characteristic of you and the B statement is occasionally or somewhat characteristic of you, place a 4 on the ______ A. line and a 1 on the ______ B. line. If both statements are characteristic of you, place a 3 on the line that is more characteristic of you and a 2 on the line that is less characteristic of you. Be sure to distribute 5 points between each A and B alternative for each of the 10 statements. When distributing the 5 points, try to recall recent situations on the job or in school.

1. When learning:

______ A. I watch and listen.

______ B. I get involved and participate.

2. When learning:

______ A. I rely on my hunches and feelings.

______ B. I rely on logical and rational thinking.

3. When making decisions:

______ A. I take my time.

______ B. I make them quickly.

4. When making decisions:

______ A. I rely on my gut feelings about the best alternative course of action.

______ B. I rely on a logical analysis of the situation.

5. When doing things:

______ A. I am careful.

______ B. I am practical.

6. When doing things:

______ A. I have strong feelings and reactions.

______ B. I reason things out.

7. I would describe myself in the following way:

______ A. I am a reflective person.

______ B. I am an active person.

8. I would describe myself in the following way:

______ A. I am influenced by my emotions.

______ B. I am influenced by my thoughts.

9. When interacting in small groups:

______ A. I listen, watch, and get involved slowly.

______ B. I am quick to get involved.

10. When interacting in small groups:

______ A. I express what I am feeling.

______ B. I say what I am thinking.

/// Self-Assessment Exercise 2-5 /// (*continued*)

Scoring: Place your answer numbers (0–5) on the lines below. Then add the numbers in each column vertically. Each of the four columns should have a total number between 0 and 25. The total of the two A and B columns should equal 25.

	1. _____ A. _____ B.		(5)	2. _____ A. _____ B.		(5)
	3. _____ A. _____ B.		(5)	4. _____ A. _____ B.		(5)
	5. _____ A. _____ B.		(5)	6. _____ A. _____ B.		(5)
	7. _____ A. _____ B.		(5)	8. _____ A. _____ B.		(5)
	9. _____ A. _____ B.		(5)	10. _____ A. _____ B.		(5)
Totals	_____ A. _____ B.		(25)	_____ A. _____ B.		(25)
Style	Observing	Doing		Feeling	Thinking	

There is no best or right learning style; each of the four learning styles has its pros and cons. The more evenly distributed your scores are between the A's and B's, the more flexible you are at changing styles. Understanding your preferred learning style can help you get the most from your learning experiences.

Determining your preferred learning style: The five odd-numbered A statements refer to your self-description as being "observing," and the five odd-numbered B statements refer to your self-description as "doing." The column with the highest number is your preferred style of learning. Write it below:

I described myself as preferring to learn by ____________________.

The five even-numbered A statements refer to your self-description as being a "feeling" person, and the five even-numbered B statements refer to your self-description as being a "thinking" person. The column with the highest number is your preferred style. Write it below:

I described myself as preferring to learn by ____________________.

Putting the two preferences together gives you your preferred dimension of learning. Check it off below:

_____ Accommodator (combines doing and feeling).

_____ Diverger (combines observing and feeling).

_____ Converger (combines doing and thinking).

_____ Assimilator (combines observing and thinking).

Exhibit 2.4 illustrates the four learning styles.

As stated above, people learn based on two personality dimensions or types—feeling versus thinking and doing versus observing. Even though people have a preferred learning style, they cannot always use it. For example, the accommodator and converger prefer to learn by active involvement rather than by observing, while the diverger and assimilator prefer to observe rather than to be actively involved. In this course, you probably don't determine how the instructor will teach it. If the instructor spends more time in class completing and discussing skill-building exercises, the accommodators and convergers will be enjoying their preferred learning style and using their feelings or thoughts when being actively involved. On the other hand, if the instructor spends more class time lecturing on the material and showing films, the diverger and assimilator will be using their preferred learning style, while emphasizing feelings or thinking. Your instructor's preferred learning style will most likely influence the way he or she teaches this course. For example, the author of this book is a converger, which influenced his use of a skill-building approach that includes more emphasis on thinking (than feelings) and doing (than observing); however, all four styles of learning are included.

After reading about the four learning styles, you should realize that there is no best learning style; each has its own pros and cons. You probably realize that you have one preferred learning style, but you also have characteristics of other styles as well.

In addition to having different personalities and levels of emotional intelligence, June and Rod have different learning styles. June combines doing and feeling as an

WORK APPLICATION 2-6

What is your preferred learning style? Are the characteristics of the style a good description of you? Explain. Can you change your learning style?

WORK APPLICATION 2-7

Think about the person you enjoy or have enjoyed working with the most. Identify that person's learning style. Is it the same as yours? What is it that you enjoy about the person?

WORK APPLICATION 2-8

Think about the person you dislike or have disliked working with the most. Identify that person's learning style. Is it the same as yours? What is it that you dislike about the person?

EXHIBIT 2.4 | The Four Learning Styles

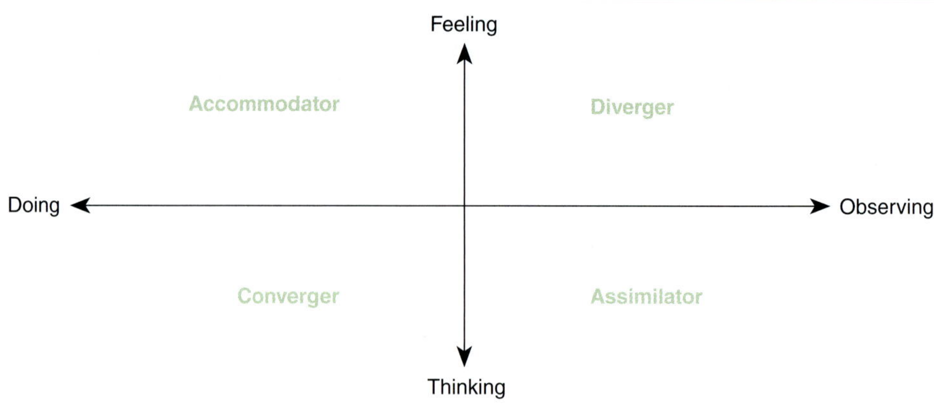

Style	Definition	Characteristics
Accommodators	Prefer learning by doing and feeling.	Tend to learn primarily from hands-on experience. Act on gut feelings, relying more on other people for information than on technical analysis.
Divergers	Prefer learning by observing and feeling.	Have the ability to view concrete situations from many different points of view. Take their time gathering and analyzing many alternatives.
Convergers	Prefer learning by doing and thinking.	Seek practical uses for information focusing on solutions. Prefer dealing with technical tasks and problems rather than with interpersonal issues.
Assimilators	Prefer learning by observing and thinking.	Effective at understanding a wide range of information and putting it into concise, logical form. Tend to be more concerned with abstract ideas and concepts than with people.

Skill-Building Exercise 2-1 develops this skill.

accommodator. Rod combines observing and thinking as an assimilator. They make decisions differently. People with similar personalities and learning styles tend to get along better than those that are different. Thus, because June and Rod are different, it is not surprising that they don't hit it off well. It takes good intrapersonal skills and interpersonal skills to get along with people who are different from you.

APPLICATION SITUATIONS / / /

Learning Styles AS 2-3

Identify the learning style of the people by the statements made about them.

A. Accommodator C. Converger

B. Diverger D. Assimilator

_______ 11. "The reason I don't like to work with Wendy is that she is slow to make decisions; she keeps analyzing the problem to death."

_______ 12. "Auto repair is a good job for Lou Ann because she enjoys fixing things and solving problems."

_______ 13. "I don't want Ted on the committee because he is a daydreamer. We can't use his ideas on the job."

_______ 14. "Ken doesn't use any standard approach like I do when selling. Ken says he feels out the customer and then decides his approach."

_______ 15. "Identify which style would be most likely to have made the comment about Ted in situation 13."

The Learning Organization

Recall from Chapter 1 the organization's need for innovation and speed to be competitive in a global environment. There is a relationship between learning, or intelligence, and innovation. An organization's ability to learn and translate that learning into action is the ultimate competitive advantage.[37] Probably the most important skill that college provides is the ability to continuously learn. Do not view your education as being over when you get your degree, but consider it as only the beginning. Much of what college graduates do on the job is learned at work because much of the work being done did not exist when the person was going to school. Organizations can also learn since they are based on individual learning. *Learning organizations* cultivate the capacity to learn, adapt, and change with the environment in order to be innovative with speed.

The learning organization focuses on improving learning and determining how knowledge is circulated throughout the organization. The learning organization questions old beliefs and ways of doing things, yet it makes the learning process as painless as possible.

PERCEPTION

In this section we discuss the nature of perception and bias in perception.

The Nature of Perception

The term **perception** *refers to a person's interpretation of reality.* In the perception process, you select, organize, and interpret stimuli through your senses. Your perception is influenced by heredity, environment, and more specifically, by your personality, intelligence, needs, self-concept, attitudes, and values. Notice that the definition of perception refers to the "interpretation of reality." In human relations, perception is just as important as reality.[38] People often encounter the same thing and perceive it differently. For example, June and Rod have the same job, but they see their job differently. In such situations, who is right?

What is the reality of any situation? We tend to believe that our perception is reality and the other party's perception is not reality. With an increasing global and diverse work environment, perception differences will continue to increase. Remember, people will behave according to their perception, not yours. Thus, it is important to realize that people often see things differently than you do.[39] So we need to look at things from the other person's perspective.

Bias in Perception

Learning Outcome 2-6

Describe six biases affecting perception.

Some of the biases affecting perception are stereotypes, frame of reference, expectations, selective exposure, interest, and projection.

Stereotypes Consider the bias of **stereotyping,** *which is the process of generalizing the behavior of all members of a group.* Stereotypes are drawn along all kinds of lines, including race, religion, nationality, and sex. Most of us stereotype people as a way of quickly perceiving a person's behavior. Women and minorities are often stereotyped in organizations.[40] Women managers have been stereotyped as being ineffective leaders. Research has shown this stereotype to be incorrect, as there is no real difference in leadership style.[41]

Avoid stereotypes. Consciously attempt to get to know people as individuals, rather than to stereotype.

Frame of Reference Our frame of reference is our tendency to see things from a narrow focus that directly affects us. It is common for employees and management to perceive the same situation from different frames of reference. For example, if managers want to make a change to increase productivity, they perceive the change as positive (ignoring the union's perception), while employees may perceive the change as negative (ignoring management's perception). Parents and their children often have frame-of-reference perception differences.

To be effective in our human relations, we should try to perceive things from the other person's frame of reference and be willing to work together for the benefit of all parties to create a win–win situation.

Expectations What we expect often influences our perceptions of what we see and experience.[42] For example, read the phrase in the triangle below:

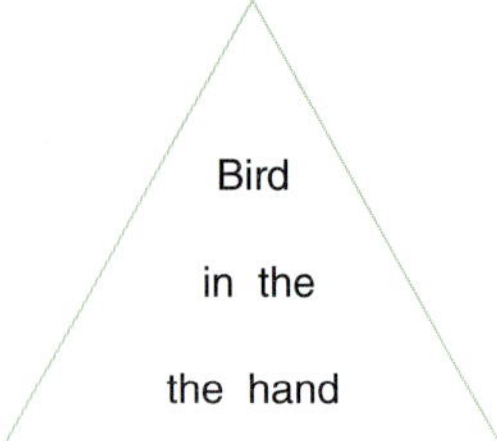

Did you read the word *the* twice? Or, like most people, did you read what you expected, only one *the*? We perceive, select, organize, and interpret information as we expect it to appear.

Often people, especially those who know each other well, do not really listen to each other. They simply hear what they expect to hear. We have expectations of others in relationships; when they do things we don't expect or like, we have human relations problems.

So our preconceived notions and labels can undermine accurate perceptions and effective judgment and decision making.[43] To improve our human relations, we must be careful to understand other people's reality, rather than what we expect reality to be.

Selective Exposure We tend to see and hear what we want to. People sometimes selectively pick information they want to hear and ignore information they don't want to hear. Sometimes when a manager delegates a task with a specific deadline, the employee selectively does not hear, and therefore misses the deadline.

To ensure effective human relations, we should listen to the entire message, rather than use selective exposure.

WORK APPLICATION 2-9

Give an example of when you and another person experienced the same situation but perceived it differently. Which of the six biases affecting perception was responsible for the difference in perception? Explain your answer.

Interest What interests you also affects how you perceive and approach things. Have you ever taken a course and not liked it, while others in the class thought it was great? This difference in perception may be due to different levels of interest in the subject. Interest influences job selection and satisfaction.

Projection To avoid psychological threat, people use a defense mechanism known as *projection.* Projection means attributing one's attitudes or shortcomings to others. People who steal and cheat may make statements like, "Everyone steals from the company" and "All students cheat in college." Projection may be an effective defense mechanism, but it generally does not help human relations.

APPLICATION SITUATIONS / / /

Bias in Perception AS 2-4

Identify the particular perception bias in the statements below.

A. Stereotypes	C. Expectations	E. Interest
B. Frame of reference	D. Selective exposure	F. Projection

_______ 16. "Wayne gets on his employees' nerves because he doesn't really listen to their opinions. He thinks he knows what they want, and he makes decisions without their input all the time."

_______ 17. "Lily is always accusing others of taking long breaks, when in reality she is the violator."

_______ 18. "Ben keeps asking me about basketball. Just because I'm a tall African American doesn't mean I like the game or the L.A. Lakers."

_______ 19. "A major problem between the Arabs and Israelis is their . . ."

_______ 20. "Val has communication problems because she hears only what she wants to hear."

EXHIBIT 2.5 | Biases Affecting Perception

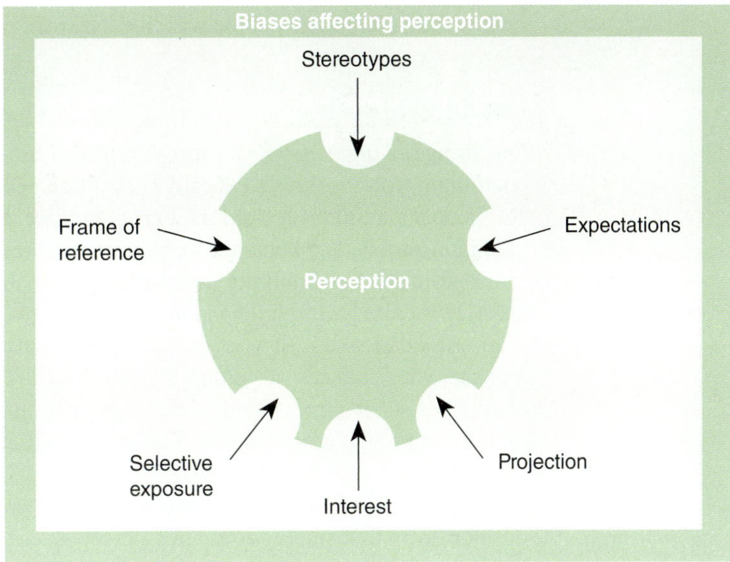

Skill-Building Exercise 2-2 develops this skill.

Communication Skills Refer to CS Question 5.

The term **perceptual congruence** *refers to the degree to which people see things the same way.* When people perceive things the same way, it generally has positive consequences in the organization. However, perception biases also can result in lower performance.[44] The exact relationship between perceptual congruence and performance is not known. Employees who perceive management as supportive are generally happier with their jobs and perceive management's performance more favorably.[45]

For a review of the biases affecting perception, see Exhibit 2.5.

DEVELOPING POSITIVE FIRST IMPRESSIONS

Learning Outcome 2-7

Explain the importance of first impressions and how to project a positive image.

In this section we discuss first impressions: the primacy effect and the four-minute barrier. We also examine image projection.

The Primacy Effect and the Four-Minute Barrier

When we meet people, we form quick impressions of them. Social psychologists call this process the primacy effect. The **primacy effect** *is the way people perceive one another during their first impressions.* It is the "enduring effect" of first impressions. Recall that our perceptions are open to six biases. These first impressions establish the mental framework within which people view one another, so first impressions do matter.[46]

The **four-minute barrier** *is the time we have to make a good impression.* It is also called the *four-minute sell* because it is the average time during which people make up their minds to continue the contact or separate during social situations. However, in business and social situations, the time could be less. Some say first impressions are developed between 30 seconds and two minutes.[47]

During this short period of time, human relations will be established, denied, or reconfirmed. If our first impressions are favorable, we tend to be nice to the person and continue the contact; if not, we end the contact. In ongoing work situations, first impressions of our fellow employees set the tone for our human relations.[48]

First impressions usually linger, but they can be changed. Have you ever disliked someone as a result of first impressions that linger to the present time? On the other hand, can you recall meeting someone you disliked at first, but once you got to know the person, you changed your impression? Recall that June's first impression of Rod was positive, but they did not hit it off for long.

During the four-minute barrier, if you register negative first impressions in other people, you will have to "prove" yourself to change those impressions. It is easier to begin by projecting an image people will like. Next we discuss how to project a positive image.

Image Projection

Our **image** *is other people's attitudes toward us.* Image can be thought of as being on a continuum from positive to negative. To a large extent, we can control the image we project. People's attitudes toward us, our image, are developed by our appearance, nonverbal communications, and behavior. Each of these three areas is discussed separately below.

Before we begin talking about image, you should realize that image from your perspective is called *impression management.* Impression management is associated with job offers. In other words, if you project a positive image during a job interview, you greatly increase your chances of getting the job offer.[49] The image of each of the organization's employees sends a message to customers, who judge the organization by its people. The image you project as an employee has an impact on the organizational image.

Appearance When people first see you, before you can do or say anything, they begin to develop their first impressions. If a person doesn't like the way you look, your clothes, hairstyle, or grooming, he or she may not give you the opportunity to show who you really are. If you want to be successful, you should dress appropriately for the situation. A simple rule to follow is to adopt the dress and grooming standards of the organization and, specifically, of the job you want.

You will learn more tips on apparel and grooming in Chapter 4, on career management.

Nonverbal Communication Our facial expressions, eye contact, and handshake all project our image, as does the tone and the volume of our voice. Our nonverbal communication tends to convey how we are feeling.[50]

After noticing someone's appearance, we tend to look at a person's face. Facial expressions convey feelings more accurately than words. A smile tends to say that things are OK, while a frown tends to say that something is wrong. One of the eight guidelines to human relations is to smile. It is especially important when we first meet someone; we want to project a positive, caring image.

When you first meet someone, eye contact is very important. If you don't look a person directly in the eye, he or she may assume that you do not like him or her, that you are not listening, or that you are not a trusting individual. Maintaining eye contact is important, but don't make others uncomfortable by staring at them. Look in one eye, then the other; then briefly look away. Be aware, however, that in some cultures eye contact is considered differently than in North America.

In many introductions the handshake is used. Your handshake can convey that you are a warm, yet strong person. Your handshake is judged on five factors: (1) firmness—people tend to think that a firm handshake communicates a caring attitude, while a weak grip conveys indifference; (2) dryness—people don't like to hold a clammy hand; it sends a message of being nervous; (3) duration—an extended handshake can convey interest; (4) interlock—a full, deep grip conveys friendship and strength; shallow grips are often interpreted as a weakness; and (5) eye contact—you should maintain eye contact throughout the handshake.

You will learn more about nonverbal communication in Chapter 5.

WORK APPLICATION 2-10

Give examples of situations when others formed a positive and a negative first impression of you. Explain the causes (appearance, nonverbal communication, behavior) of those impressions.

WORK APPLICATION 2-11

Which area of projecting a positive image (appearance, nonverbal communication, behavior) is your strongest? Which is your weakest? Explain your answers. What will you do to project a more positive image in the future?

Behavior After the other person notices our appearance and nonverbal expressions, she or he observes our behavior. As stated earlier in the guidelines to effective human relations, while talking to the person, be upbeat and optimistic, don't complain, show a genuine interest in the person, smile, laugh if appropriate, call the person by name, listen, be helpful, and think before you act. Do not do or say anything that is offensive to the person. Be agreeable and complimentary. Watch your manners and be polite. During the four-minute barrier, avoid discussing controversial topics and expressing personal views about them.

Remember that what you think about affects how you feel, and how you feel affects your behavior, human relations, and performance. So think happy, confident thoughts that you are a winner and you will act and be perceived as a winner and make a good first and lasting image.

Skill-Building Exercise 2-3 develops this skill.

Following the above guidelines on appearance, nonverbal communication, and behavior should help you develop positive first impressions. You will learn more about behavior throughout this book and more about etiquette in Chapter 9.

CS

Communication Skills Refer to CS Question 6.

As we bring this chapter to a close, you should understand how your *personality* affects your behavior, which in turn affects your human relations and performance, and how to match your behavior to other people's personality type. Your personality type (A vs. B) also affects your behavior, and too much *stress* tends to have a negative effect on behavior, human relations, and performance. Your personality is also related to your level of *intelligence,* and you should know your preferred method of learning. You should realize that people don't see things the same way (*perception*), and understand biases that influence people's perceptions. Finally, you should realize the importance of making a good *first impression* and know how to project a positive image.

/ / / REVIEW / / /

The chapter review is organized to help you master the 8 learning outcomes for Chapter 2. First provide your own response to each learning outcome, and then check the summary provided to see how well you understand the material. Next, identify the final statement in each section as either true or false (T/F). Correct each false statement. Answers are given at the end of the chapter.

LO 2-1 Describe the Big Five personality dimensions

The *surgency* personality dimension includes leadership and extroversion traits; people high in surgency strive to get ahead of others. In contrast, the *agreeableness* personality dimension includes traits related to getting along with people. The *adjustment* personality dimension includes traits related to emotional stability. The *conscientiousness* personality dimension includes traits related to achievement. The *openness to experience* personality dimension includes traits related to being willing to change and try new things.

The Myers-Briggs Type Indicator (MBTI) is a more complex personality classification method than the Big Five. T F

LO 2-2 Explain the benefits of understanding and identifying personality profiles.

Understanding and identifying personality profiles can help you to understand and predict behavior, human relations, and performance. One can intentionally change behavior to improve human relations and performance when working with different personality types.

The locus of control is not part of a personality profile. T F

LO 2-3 Describe your stress personality type.

Student answers will vary from Self-Assessment Exercise 2-4: Your Stress Personality Type. People who have a Type A personality are characterized as fast moving, hard driving, time conscious, competitive, impatient, and preoccupied with work; those with a Type B personality are the opposite.

The Type A personality is more prone to stress. T F

LO 2-4 List causes of stress, and describe how to be more effective at controlling stress.

Causes of stress include: personality type, organizational climate, management behavior, and degree of job satisfaction. We can help control stress through exercise, nutrition, relaxation, positive thinking, and support systems. To control stress one should: (1) identify stressors, (2) determine their causes and consequences, and (3) plan to eliminate or decrease the stress.

The five ways recommended to help eliminate or decrease stress are: exercise, nutrition, relaxation, medication, and support systems. T F

LO 2-5 Describe the four learning styles and know which is your preferred learning style.

Accommodators prefer learning by doing and feeling. Divergers prefer learning by observing and feeling. Convergers prefer learning by doing and thinking. Assimilators prefer learning by observing and thinking. Student answers will vary.

The converger learning style is the most effective learning style. T F

LO 2-6 Describe six biases affecting perception.

- *Stereotyping* is the process of generalizing the behavior of all members of a group.
- *Frame of reference* refers to our tendency to see things from a narrow focus that directly affects us.
- *Expectations* refers to how we perceive, select, organize, and interpret information based on how we expect it to appear.
- *Selective exposure* means we tend to see and hear what we want to.

- Our degree of *interest* influences how we perceive things.
- *Projection* refers to our use of defense mechanisms to justify our behavior.

Given a good explanation, people perceive things the same way. T F

LO 2-7 Explain the importance of first impressions and how to project a positive image.

We have up to only four minutes to project a positive image. If we present a negative first impression to people, our future human relations with them can suffer. To project a positive first impression, we need to present an appropriate appearance, send positive nonverbal communications, and behave in a manner befitting the occasion.

Our perceptions are the bases for our first impressions. T F

LO 2-8 Define the following 15 key terms.

Select one or more methods: (1) fill in the missing key terms from memory; (2) match the key terms from the end of the review with their definitions below; and/or (3) copy the key terms in order from the key terms at the beginning of the chapter.

______________ is a relatively stable set of traits that aids in explaining and predicting individual behavior.

The ______________ is characterized as fast moving, hard driving, time conscious, competitive, impatient, and preoccupied with work.

______________ is a continuum representing one's belief as to whether external or internal forces control one's destiny.

______________ categorizes traits into the dimensions of surgency, agreeableness, adjustment, conscientiousness, and openness to experience.

______________ is an emotional and/or physical reaction to environmental activities and events.

______________ are situations in which people feel anxiety, tension, and pressure.

______________ is the constant lack of interest and motivation to perform one's job because of stress.

The ______________ includes step (1) identify stressors; step (2) determine their causes and consequences; and step (3) plan to eliminate or decrease the stress.

______________ is the level of one's capacity for new learning, problem solving, and decision making.

______________ is a person's interpretation of reality.

______________ is the process of generalizing the behavior of all members of a group.

______________ refers to the degree to which people see things the same way.

The ______________ is the way people perceive one another during their first impressions.

The ______________ is the time we have to make a good impression.

Our ______________ is other people's attitudes toward us.

/ / / KEY TERMS / / /

/ / / COMMUNICATION SKILLS / / /

The following critical thinking questions can be used for class discussion and/or as written assignments to develop communication skills. Be sure to give complete explanations for all questions.

1. Which personality traits exhibited by others tend to irritate you? Which of your personality traits tend to irritate others? How can you improve your personality?

2. Do you think that the Big Five Model of Personality or the Myers-Briggs Type Indicator is a more effective measure of personality?
3. Which cause of stress do you think is the major contributor to employee stress in organizations? What can organizations do to help eliminate or reduce employee stress?
4. Do you agree that intelligence (general mental ability) is the most valid predictor of job performance? Should organizations give an IQ test and hire based on the results? Why or why not?
5. How do you know if your perception or that of others is the correct interpretation of reality?
6. Is it ethical to judge and stereotype people based on a few seconds or minutes during first impressions? How do your first impressions help and hinder your human relations?

CASE /// Mark Cuban: Billionaire Entrepreneur with Unique Personality Traits

On January 14, 2000, Mark Cuban purchased the Dallas Mavericks and nothing has been the same since. Almost immediately, Mavericks games took on a festive atmosphere as the American Airlines Center Arena rocked with jubilant fans. Mavericks games became more than just ordinary NBA games—they were a total entertainment experience. This transformation was directly attributed to Cuban's energetic personality, positive attitude, and unique leadership style.

Cuban's personality has been the subject of many news headlines since he became the owner of the Dallas Mavericks. He has been repeatedly fined for violating league policies. Dressed in his jeans and t-shirt, he does not resemble the typical NBA executive. Cuban sits in the front row next to the floor, cheering the team along with thousands of loyal fans. At any other arena, the executives come to the games dressed in suit and tie and are segregated from the crowds in their luxury skybox seats. His personality and unorthodox style of motivating the team is frowned upon by the NBA executives and loved by the fans and players. In many instances in which fines were levied against Cuban for various league violations, he promised to match the fines by donating matching amounts to various charities. He has yelled at players of opposing teams during games, and even called some "thugs."

His whatever-it-takes attitude and commitment to winning has turned a team that was known for its losing streak into a winning team that ultimately won the NBA championship in 2011. In the 20 years before Cuban bought the team, the Mavericks had a winning percentage of 40 percent and playoff record of 21–32. In the 10 years following, the team won 69 percent of their regular season games, and reached the playoffs in each of those seasons. The Mavericks playoff record with Cuban is 49 wins and 57 losses, including their first trip to the NBA finals in 2006, where they lost to the Miami Heat. In a rematch five years later, they won the championship.[51,52]

Running an NBA team is not the only success Cuban has had in his life. He has been called the "billionaire entrepreneur" for a reason. Prior to his purchase of the Mavericks, Cuban co-founded Broadcast.com in 1995, the leading provider of multimedia and streaming on the Internet, and sold it to Yahoo! in July of 1999 for billions of dollars in Yahoo stock. Before Broadcast.com, Cuban co-founded MicroSolutions, a leading National Systems Integrator, in 1983, and later sold it to CompuServe. Cuban's other entrepreneurial ventures include cable channel HDNet, Landmark Theatres, and filmmaker Magnolia Pictures.[53] As of 2010, Cuban is number 459 on Forbes's "World's Richest People" list, with a net worth of $2.4 billion. The *Guinness Book of World Records* credits Cuban with the "largest single e-commerce transaction," after paying $40 million for his Gulfstream jet in October 1999.

Based on the image Cuban projects, especially during Mavericks games, it is possible for some to see him as a self-centered and uncaring individual. However, nothing could be further from the truth. He is a person who cares for others and gives back to help those who are less fortunate. Cuban started the Fallen Patriot Fund to help families of U.S. military persons killed or injured during the Iraq War, personally matching the first $1 million in contributions with funds from the Mark Cuban Foundation, which is run by his brother Brian Cuban. Cuban financed the movie *Redacted* through his film company, Magnolia Pictures, a documentary based on the Mahmudiyah Killings. The story involves the March 2006 rape, murder, and burning of a 14-year-old Iraqi girl, Abeer Hamza al-Janabi, and the murder of her parents and younger sister by U.S. soldiers. Two of the soldiers were convicted and three pleaded guilty, receiving sentences up to 110 years.

Mark Cuban was born on July 31, 1958, in Pittsburgh, Pennsylvania. He graduated from Indiana University in 1981 with a degree in business. His last name was shortened from "Chabenisky" when his Russian grandparents landed on Ellis Island decades ago. Cuban's father Norton was an automobile upholsterer. Cuban's first attempt at entrepreneurship started at age 12, when he sold garbage bags to pay for a pair of expensive basketball shoes. While in school, he worked in a variety of jobs, including bartender, disco dancing instructor, and party promoter. He paid for college by collecting and selling stamps, and once earned about $1,100 from starting a chain letter. He is clearly a person with an internal locus of control. It's impossible to know what Mark Cuban will create, produce, buy, or sell next, but no one doubts that he will certainly do something innovative.

Go to the Internet: To learn more about Mark Cuban and the Dallas Mavericks, visit their Web site at www.nba.com/mavericks/index_main.htm.

Support your answers to the following questions with specific information from the case and text, or with information you get from the web or another source.

1. Personality is a relatively stable set of traits that aids in explaining and predicting individual behavior. What are some of Mark Cuban's traits that can explain his behavior during Mavericks games?

2. Would you describe Mark Cuban as a Type A or Type B personality type?

3. Why is Mark Cuban described as someone with an internal locus of control?

4. The Big Five Model of Personality categorizes traits into the dimensions of surgency, agreeableness, adjustment, conscientiousness, and openness to experience. Which of these dimensions are strongest or clearly evident in Mark Cuban's personality?

5. Is Mark Cuban projecting a positive or negative image with his eccentric behavior during Mavericks games?

Cumulative Case Question

6. Mark Cuban has had several disagreements with the NBA commissioner that have resulted in fines totaling almost a million dollars. Each incident brings a lot of publicity to the team and Cuban himself; most of it negative. Chapter 1 discusses three alternatives for resolving human relations problems—change the other person, change the situation, or change yourself. Which approach or combination of approaches will you recommend for Mark Cuban, and why?

Case Exercise And Role-Play

Preparation: Return to question 5 above, in which we talked about Mark Cuban projecting a negative or positive image by his appearance, nonverbal communication, and behavior. Using a debate format, divide the class into two teams. One team takes the viewpoint that Cuban's appearance, nonverbal communication, and behavior are projecting a negative image for the Dallas Mavericks, while another team takes the opposite viewpoint. Each team prepares a brief narrative to support its position.

In-Class Groups: Form two groups of four to six members to share ideas and develop the statement supporting their positions.

Role-Play: Each group presents its statement to the entire class, with the class acting as judges of the debate. Each group is given one chance to respond to the other group's points. The judges represented by the rest of the class then decide who has won the debate.

OBJECTIVE CASE /// Personality Conflict

Carol is the branch manager of a bank. Two of her employees, Rich and Wonda, came to her and said that they could not work together. Carol asked them why, and they both said, "We have a personality conflict." She asked them to be more specific, and this is what they told her:

RICH: Well, Wonda is very pushy; she tells me what to do all the time, and I let her get away with it because I'm a peace-loving man.

WONDA: That's because Rich is so gullible; he believes anything he is told. I have to look out for him.

RICH: We have different outlooks on life. Wonda believes that if we work hard, we can get ahead in this bank, but I don't agree. I believe you have to be political, and I'm not.

WONDA: That's because I'm motivated and enjoy working.

RICH: Motivated—is that what you call it? She's preoccupied with work. Wonda is rushing all the time, she is impatient, and she always wants to make a contest out of everything.

WONDA: If you were more cooperative, and morale was better, I would not feel stressed the way I do.

RICH: We cannot make decisions together because I am very logical and like to get lots of information, while Wonda wants to make decisions based on what she calls intuition.

WONDA: I thought working here was going to be different. I didn't know I was going to be stuck working with a person who is uncooperative.

RICH: Me? I feel the same way about you.

At this point Carol stopped the discussion.

Answer the following questions. Then in the space between questions, state why you selected that answer.

_______ 1. In Rich's first statement it appears that Wonda has a(n) _______ personality trait, while he has a(n) _______ personality trait.

a. outgoing, reserved *c.* conscientious, expedient
b. aggressive, passive *d.* imaginative, practical

_______ 2. In statement 2, it appears that Wonda is _______ and Rich is _______.

a. shrewd, forthright *c.* stable, emotional
b. high, low intelligence *d.* suspicious, trusting

_______ 3. In statement 3, it appears that Rich has an _______ locus of control while Wonda has an _______ locus of control.

a. internal, external *b.* external, internal

_______ 4. In statement 4, Wonda appears to be an:

a. internalizer *b.* externalizer

_______ 5. In statement 5, Wonda appears to have a Type _______ personality.

a. A *b.* B

_______ 6. In statement 6, Wonda states that _______ is the cause of her stress.

a. personality *c.* management effectiveness
b. organizational climate *d.* job satisfaction

_______ 7. In statement 7, Rich has described himself as having a(n) _______ learning style.

a. accommodator *c.* converger
b. diverger *d.* assimilator

_______ 8. In statement 7, Rich has described Wonda as having a(n) _______ learning style.

a. accommodator *c.* converger
b. diverger *d.* assimilator

_______ 9. In statement 8, the perception problem appears to be due to:

a. stereotyping *d.* selective exposure
b. frame of reference *e.* projection
c. expectations *f.* interest

_______ 10. Who needs to change their behavior?

a. Rich *b.* Wonda *c.* both

11. Overall, are your personality, locus of control, stress type, and learning style more like Rich's or Wonda's? If you were Rich or Wonda, what would you do?

12. If you were Carol, what would you do?

Note: Carol's meeting can be role-played in class.

/ / / SKILL-BUILDING EXERCISE 2-1 / / /

Learning Styles

In-Class Exercise (Group)

Objectives: To better understand your learning style and how to work more effectively with people with different learning styles.

AACSB: The primary AACSB learning standard skills developed through this exercise are reflective thinking and self-management, analytic skills, communication abilities, and teamwork.

Preparation: You should have read the chapter and determined your preferred learning style in Self-Assessment Exercise 2-5.

Procedure 1 (2–3 minutes)
The entire class breaks into four groups: The accommodators, divergers, convergers, and assimilators meet in different groups.

Procedure 2 (5–10 minutes)
Each of the four groups elects a spokesperson-recorder. Assume the class was shipwrecked on a deserted island and had to develop an economic system with a division of labor. During this process, what strengths would your group offer each of the other three groups if you were working one-on-one with them? For example, the accommodators state how they would help the divergers if they were the only two styles on the island. Then they assume the convergers and then the assimilators are the only other learning style on the island. Each group does the same. Feel free to refer to the book at any time.

Procedure 3 (5–15 minutes)
The spokesperson for the accommodators tells the other three groups how they would be helpful to that group if they were the only two styles on the island. The divergers go next, followed by the convergers, and then the assimilators.

Procedure 4 (3–7 minutes)
Break into as many discussion groups as there are members of the smallest of the four learning style groups. Each discussion group must have at least one person from all four learning styles; some will have more. For example, if the smallest group is the assimilators with five members, establish five discussion groups. If there are nine convergers, send two members to four groups and one to the remaining group. If there are six divergers, send one to four of the groups and two to one of the groups. Try to make the number of students in each discussion group as even as possible.

Procedure 5 (3–7 minutes)
Elect a spokesperson-recorder. Each group decides which learning style(s) to include in establishing the economic system. During the discussion, the instructor writes the four styles on the board for voting in procedure 6.

Procedure 6 (2–3 minutes)
The instructor records the votes from each group to be included in establishing the economic system.

Conclusion: The instructor leads a class discussion and/or makes concluding remarks.

Application (2–4 minutes): What have I learned from this exercise? What will I do to be more open to working with people of different learning styles?

Sharing: Volunteers give their answers to the application section.

/ / / SKILL-BUILDING EXERCISE 2-2 / / /

Personality Perceptions

Preparation (Group)

You should read the sections on personality traits and complete Self-Assessment Exercise 2-2. From this exercise, rank yourself below from highest score (1) to lowest score (5) for each of the Big Five. Do not tell anyone your ranking until told to do so.

_______ Surgency _______ Agreeableness _______ Adjustment

_______ Conscientiousness _______ Openness to experience

In-Class Exercise

Objective: To develop your skill at perceiving others' personality traits. With this skill, you can better understand and predict people's behavior, which is helpful to leaders in influencing followers.

AACSB: The primary AACSB learning standard skills developed through this exercise are analytic skills and communication abilities.

Procedure 1 (2–4 minutes)
Break into groups of three with people you know the best in the class. You may need some groups of two. If you don't know people in the class and you did Skill-Building Exercise 1-1: Human Relations, get in a group with those people.

Procedure 2 (4–6 minutes)
Each person in the group writes down his or her perception of each of the other two group members. Simply rank which trait you believe to be the highest and lowest (put the Big Five dimension name on the line) for each person. Write a short reason for your perception, which should include some specific behavior you have observed that led you to your perception.

Name _____________ Highest personality score _____________ Lowest score _____________

Reason for ranking ____

Name _____________ Highest personality score _____________ Lowest score _____________

Reason for ranking ____

Procedure 3 (4–6 minutes)
One of the group members volunteers to go first to hear the other group members' perceptions.

1. One person tells the volunteer which Big Five dimensions he or she selected as the person's highest and lowest scores, and why they were selected. Do not discuss them yet.
2. The other person also tells the volunteer the same information.
3. The volunteer tells the two others what his or her actual highest and lowest scores are. The three group members discuss the accuracy of the perceptions.

Procedure 4 (4–6 minutes)
A second group member volunteers to go next to receive perceptions. Follow the same procedure as above.

Procedure 5 (4–6 minutes)
The third group member goes last. Follow the same procedure as above.

Conclusion: The instructor may lead a class discussion and/or make concluding remarks.

Application (2–4 minutes): What did I learn from this exercise? How will I use this knowledge in the future?

Sharing: Volunteers give their answers to the application section.

/ / / SKILL-BUILDING EXERCISE 2-3 / / /

First Impressions

In-Class Exercise (Group)

Objectives: To practice projecting a positive first impression. To receive feedback on the image you project. To develop your ability to project a positive first impression.

AACSB: The primary AACSB learning standard skills developed through this exercise are reflective thinking and self-management, analytic skills, and communication abilities.

Preparation: You should have read and now understand how to project a positive first impression.

Procedure 1 (2–4 minutes)
Pair off with someone you do not know. If you know everyone, select a partner you don't know well. Make one group of three if necessary. Do not begin your discussion until asked to do so.

Procedure 2 (Exactly 4 minutes)
Assume you are meeting for the first time. A mutual friend brought you together but was called to the telephone before introducing you. The mutual friend has asked you to introduce yourselves and get acquainted until he or she returns. When told to begin, introduce yourselves and get acquainted. Be sure to shake hands.

Procedure 3 (7–12 minutes)
Using the Image Feedback sheet below, give each other feedback on the image you projected. To be useful, the feedback must be an honest assessment of the image your partner received of you. So answer the questions with the input of your partner.

IMAGE FEEDBACK

Human Relations Guidelines

1. I was optimistic ________, neutral ________, pessimistic ________.
2. I did ________, did not ________ complain and criticize.
3. I did ________, did not ________ show genuine interest in the other person.
4. I did ________, did not ________ smile and laugh when appropriate.
5. I did ________, did not ________ call the person by name two or three times.
6. I was a good ________, fair ________, poor ________ listener.
7. I was/tried to be ________, wasn't ________ helpful to the other person.
8. I did ________, did not ________ do or say anything that offended the other person.

Image Projection

Appearance:

9. My appearance projected a positive ________, neutral ________, negative ________ image to the other person.

Nonverbal communication:

10. My facial expressions projected a caring ________, neutral ________, uncaring ________ attitude toward the other person.
11. My eye contact was too little ________, about right ________, too much ________.
12. My handshake was firm ________, weak ________; dry ________, wet ________; long ________, short ________; full grip ________, shallow grip ________; with eye contact ________, without eye contact ________.
13. The behavior the other person liked most was ____.
14. The behavior the other person liked least was ____.

Overall

By receiving this feedback, I realize that I could improve my image projection by:

Perception

It is important to understand both our first impression of others and theirs of us (image). After discussing your images, do you think you made any perception errors? If yes, which one(s)?

Conclusion: The instructor leads a class discussion and/or makes concluding remarks.

Application (2–4 minutes): What did I learn from this exercise? How will I use this knowledge in the future?

Sharing: Volunteers give their answers to the application section.

// ANSWERS TO TRUE/FALSE QUESTIONS //

1. T.
2. F. A personality profile includes all types of traits, depending on the personality measurement.
3. T.
4. F. The fourth recommended method is positive thinking, not medication.
5. F. There is no one most effective learning style. We each have a preferred way of learning that works best for us.
6. F. People don't tend to "listen" to an explanation; they perceive based on their bias.
7. T.

CHAPTER 3

Attitudes, Self-Concept, Values, and Ethics

LEARNING OUTCOMES

After completing this chapter, you should be able to:

LO 3-1 Define attitudes and explain how they affect behavior, human relations, and performance.

LO 3-2 Describe how to change your attitudes.

LO 3-3 List seven job satisfaction determinants.

LO 3-4 Determine whether you have a positive self-concept and how it affects your behavior, human relations, and performance.

LO 3-5 Understand how your manager's and your own expectations affect your performance.

LO 3-6 Demonstrate how to develop a more positive self-concept.

LO 3-7 Identify your personal values.

LO 3-8 Compare the three levels of moral development.

LO 3-9 Define the following 13 key terms (in order of appearance in the chapter):

attitude
Theory X
Theory Y
Pygmalion effect
job satisfaction
job satisfaction survey
self-concept
self-efficacy
self-fulfilling prophecy
attribution
values
value system
ethics

/// The Red Cross is committed to saving lives and easing suffering. This diverse nonprofit organization serves humanity and helps people by providing relief to victims of disaster, both locally and globally. The organization gives health and safety training to the public and provides social services to U.S. military members and their families. In the wake of an earthquake, tornado, flood, fire, hurricane, or other disaster, it provides relief services to communities across the country. The Red Cross is the largest supplier of blood and blood products in the United States.[1]

Rayanne was walking back to work after a meeting with her supervisor, Kent. Rayanne recalled that Kent had said she had a negative attitude and that it was affecting her performance, which was below standard. Kent had asked Rayanne if she was satisfied with her job. She had said, "No, I really don't like working, and I've messed up on all the jobs I've had. I guess I'm a failure." Kent had tried to explain how her poor attitude and negative self-concept were the cause of her poor performance. But Rayanne hadn't really listened, since work is not important to her. Rayanne has an external locus of control; thus, she believes that her poor performance is not her fault. She doesn't believe Kent knows what he's talking about. Rayanne thinks that Kent is not being ethical, that he is trying to manipulate her to get more work out of her. Is Kent's or Rayanne's analysis correct? Can Rayanne change? ///

HOW ATTITUDES, JOB SATISFACTION, SELF-CONCEPT, VALUES, AND ETHICS AFFECT BEHAVIOR, HUMAN RELATIONS, AND PERFORMANCE

In this chapter, we continue to focus on developing intrapersonal skills that affect behavior, human relations, and performance. We cover several different yet related topics, so let's start with an overview. *Attitudes* are critical to success.[2] Our attitudes toward others, and their attitudes toward us, clearly affect our behavior, human relations, and performance.[3] Attitudes are the foundation of our *job satisfaction.*[4] Making employees happier can increase their contributions, effort, and productivity;[5] plus, they stay in their jobs longer.[6] Satisfied workers have a positive impact on customers' satisfaction with the organization and its products.[7] Our *self-concept* is based on our attitude about ourself, and our confidence affects our career success and overall performance in any aspect of life.[8] Our work *values* are our standards of behavior, which affect our human relations and performance.[9] *Unethical* behavior hurts both human relations and performance.[10]

Kent, in the opening case, tries to get Rayanne to understand how her poor attitude and negative self-concept are affecting her job performance, but she does not value work. Do you believe Kent is correct? Do you have a positive attitude and self-concept? Are you happy? Would you like to improve your attitude and self-concept? This chapter can help you improve.

ATTITUDES

Learning Outcome 3-1

Define attitudes and explain how they affect behavior, human relations, and performance.

In this section, we examine what an attitude is and the importance of attitudes, how you acquire attitudes, types of management attitudes and how they affect performance, and how to change attitudes.

What Is an Attitude and Are Attitudes Important?

WORK APPLICATION 3-1

Describe your attitude about college in general and the specific college you are attending.

An **attitude** *is a strong belief or feeling toward people, things, and situations.* We all have favorable, or positive, attitudes and unfavorable, or negative, attitudes about life, human relations, work, school, and everything else. Attitudes are not quick judgments we change easily but we *can* change our attitudes.[11] People interpret our attitudes by our behavior. Rayanne appears to have a negative attitude toward many things.

Attitudes are definitely important.[12] Employers place great emphasis on attitude. A Xerox executive stated that organizations want to affect not only employees' behavior, but also their attitudes. J. S. Marriott, Jr., president of Marriott Corporation, stated, "We have found that our success depends more upon employee attitudes than any other single factor." This is largely due to the fact that customers evaluate service quality by the employees' attitudes; employee attitudes affect customer attitudes.[13]

How We Acquire Attitudes

Communication Skills
Refer to CS Question 1.

Attitudes are developed primarily through experiences. As people develop from childhood to adulthood, they interact with parents, family, teachers, friends, employees, and managers. From all these people, they learn what is right and wrong and how to behave.

When encountering new people or situations, you are the most open and impressionable because you usually haven't had time to form an attitude toward them. Recall the importance of first impressions from the last chapter. Before entering a new situation, people often ask others with experience about it. This begins the development of attitudes before the encounter. For example, before you signed up for this class, you may have asked others questions about it. If they had positive or negative attitudes, you too may have developed a positive attitude you may have started the course with or a negative attitude. Getting information from others is fine, but you should develop your own attitudes.

Management's Attitudes and How They Affect Performance

Before reading on, answer the 10 questions in Self-Assessment Exercise 3-1 to determine if you have Theory X or Theory Y attitudes.

Management Attitudes Douglas McGregor classified attitudes, which he called *assumptions,* as Theory X and Theory Y.[14] Managers with **Theory X** *attitudes hold that employees dislike work and must be closely supervised to get them to do their work.* Theory Y managers tend to look for the natural goodness in people.[15] **Theory Y** *attitudes hold that employees like to work and do not need to be closely supervised to get them to do their work.* Managers with dominant personalities often do not trust employees; thus, they have Theory X attitudes.

Communication Skills
Refer to CS Question 2.

Over the years research has shown that managers with Theory Y attitudes tend to have employees with higher levels of job satisfaction than the employees of Theory X managers. However, managers with Theory Y assumptions do not always have higher levels of productivity in their departments.[16]

/// Self-Assessment Exercise 3-1 ///

Your Management Attitudes

Circle the letter that best describes what you would actually do as a supervisor. There are no right or wrong answers.

Usually (U) Frequently (F) Occasionally (O) Seldom (S)

U F O S 1. I would set the objectives for my department alone (rather than include employee input).

U F O S 2. I would allow employees to develop their own plans (rather than develop them for them).

U F O S 3. I would delegate several tasks I enjoy doing (rather than doing them myself).

U F O S 4. I would allow employees to make decisions (rather than make them for employees).

U F O S 5. I would recruit and select new employees alone (rather than include employees' input).

U F O S 6. I would train new employees myself (rather than have employees do it).

U F O S 7. I would tell employees what they need to know (rather than everything I know).

U F O S 8. I would spend time praising and recognizing my employees' work efforts (rather than not do it).

U F O S 9. I would set several (rather than few) controls to ensure that objectives are met.

U F O S 10. I would closely supervise my employees (rather than leave them on their own) to ensure that they are working.

To better understand your own attitudes toward human nature, score your answers. For items 1, 5, 6, 7, 9, and 10, give yourself 1 point for each usually (U) answer; 2 points for each frequently (F) answer; 3 points for each occasionally (O) answer; and 4 points for each seldom (S) answer. For items 2, 3, 4, and 8, give yourself 1 point for each seldom (S) answer; 2 points for each occasionally (O) answer; 3 points for each frequently (F) answer; and 4 points for each usually (U) answer. Total all points. Your score should be between 10 and 40. Place your score here ______. Theory X and Theory Y are on opposite ends of a continuum. Most people's attitudes fall somewhere between the two extremes. Place an X on the continuum below at the point that represents your score.

Theory X 10 ----- --- ------ -- 20 ----- ----- ----- ----- 30 ---- - -- --------- 40 Theory Y

The lower your score, the stronger the Theory X attitude; the higher your score, the stronger the Theory Y attitude. A score of 10 to 19 could be considered a Theory X attitude. A score of 31 to 40 could be considered a Theory Y attitude. A score of 20 to 30 could be considered balanced between the two theories. Your score may not accurately measure how you would behave in an actual job; however, it should help you understand your own attitudes toward people at work.

APPLICATION SITUATIONS / / /

Theory X, Theory Y AS 3-1

Identify each manager's comments about employees as:

A. Theory X B. Theory Y

_______ 1. "Be careful with it now. I don't want you to mess it up like you did the last time."

_______ 2. "Thanks, I'm confident you will do a good job."

_______ 3. "Select the format you want to use and get it to me when you finish it."

_______ 4. "I'll be checking up on you to make sure the job gets done on time."

_______ 5. "I know you probably think it's a lousy job, but someone has to do it."

Communication Skills
Refer to CS Question 3.

WORK APPLICATION 3-2

Give two examples of when your attitude affected your performance. One should be a positive effect and the other a negative one. Be sure to fully explain how your attitudes affected performance.

WORK APPLICATION 3-3

Give an example of when you lived up to (or down to) someone else's expectations of your performance (the Pygmalion effect). It could be a parent's, teacher's, coach's, or boss's expectations. Be specific.

How Management's Attitudes Affect Employees' Performance Managers' attitudes and the way they treat employees affect employees' job behavior and performance.[17] Research has supported this theory. It is called the *Pygmalion effect.* The **Pygmalion effect** *states that supervisors' attitudes and expectations of employees and how they treat them largely determine their performance.* In a study of welding students, the foreman who was training the group was given the names of students who were quite intelligent and would do well. Actually, the students were selected at random. The only difference was the foreman's expectations. The so-called intelligent students significantly outperformed the other group members. Why this happened is what this theory is all about. The foreman's expectations became the foreman's self-fulfilling prophecy.

In a sense, the Hawthorne effect is related to the Pygmalion effect because both affect performance. In the Hawthorne Studies, the special attention and treatment given the workers by the management resulted in increased performance.

Through the positive expectations of others, people increase their level of performance. Unfortunately, many managers tend to stereotype and see what they expect to see: low performance. And their employees see and do as the managers expect. We all need to expect and treat people as though they are high achievers to get the best from them.

Although others' attitudes can affect your behavior, human relations, and performance, you are responsible for your own actions. Try to ignore negative comments and stay away from people with negative attitudes. Focus on the positives.[18]

Treat workers well and they will work harder. Treat them badly and they will get even. As a manager, create a win–win situation. Expect high performance and treat employees as being capable and special, and you will get the best performance from them.

Learning Outcome 3-2

Describe how to change your attitudes.

Changing Attitudes

Complete Self-Assessment Exercise 3-2. Determine your own job attitude.

/// Self-Assessment Exercise 3-2 ///

Your Job Attitude

For each of the 10 statements below, identify how often each describes your behavior at work. Place a number from 1 to 5 next to each of the 10 statements.

(5) Always (4) Usually (3) Frequently (2) Occasionally (1) Seldom

_____ 1. I smile and am friendly and courteous to everyone at work.

_____ 2. I make positive, rather than negative, comments at work.

(*continued*)

/// Self-Assessment Exercise 3-2 /// (*continued*)

_____ 3. When my boss asks me to do extra work, I accept it cheerfully.

_____ 4. I avoid making excuses, passing the buck, or blaming others when things go wrong.

_____ 5. I am an active self-starter at getting work done.

_____ 6. I avoid spreading rumors and gossip among employees.

_____ 7. I am a team player willing to make personal sacrifices for the good of the work group.

_____ 8. I accept criticism gracefully and make the necessary changes.

_____ 9. I lift coworkers' spirits and bring them up emotionally.

_____ 10. If I were to ask my boss and coworkers to answer the nine questions for me, they would put the same answers that I did.

_____ Total: Add up the 10 numbers.

Interpreting your score. You can think of your job attitude as being on a continuum from positive to negative. Place an X on the continuum below at the point that represents your score.

Negative attitude 10 — — — — — — — — 20 — — — — — — — — — 30 — — — — — — — — — 40 — — — — — — — — — 50 Positive attitude

Generally, the higher your score, the more positive your job attitude is. You may want to have your boss and trusted coworkers answer the first nine questions, as suggested in question 10, to determine if their perception of your job attitude is the same as your perception.

WORK APPLICATION 3-4

Based on your answers in Self-Assessment Exercise 3-2, what will you do to improve your job attitude? Be specific.

Would you rather work with people who have good, moderate, or poor job attitudes? We may not be able to change our coworkers' job attitudes and behavior, but we can change our own. Review your answers to the first nine questions in Self-Assessment Exercise 3-2, and think about ways you can improve your job attitude.

Changing Your Attitudes The environment around us influences our attitudes. Usually we cannot control our environment, but we can control and change our attitudes. You can choose to be and learn to be either optimistic or pessimistic. You can choose to look for the positive and be happier and get more out of life.[19] The following hints can help you change your attitudes:

1. Remember that what you think about affects how you feel, and how you feel affects your behavior, human relations, and performance. Football commentator Lou Holtz said, you choose to be happy or sad (or optimistic and pessimistic); happiness comes from having a poor memory for the bad things that happen to us. So if you think about the good things, you will feel happy and have more effective behavior, human relations, and performance.
2. Be aware of your attitudes. People who are optimistic have higher levels of job satisfaction. Consciously try to have and maintain a positive attitude. Make the best of situations by looking for the positive.[20]

   If you catch yourself complaining or being negative in any way, stop and change to a positive attitude. With time you can become more positive.
3. Realize that there are few, if any, benefits to harboring negative attitudes. Negative attitudes, such as holding a grudge, can only hurt your human relations, and hurt yourself in the end.
4. Keep an open mind. Listen to other people's input. Use it to develop your positive attitudes.

You can gain control of your attitudes and change the direction of your life. Start today. We become what we think about,[21] or "what we think determines what happens to us."[22] So think and act like a winner, and you will become one. Rayanne, in the opening case, does not seem to be interested in changing her attitude. If she doesn't change, Rayanne will never be successful.

EXHIBIT 3.1 | Changing Attitudes

Shaping and Changing Employee Attitudes It is difficult to change your own attitudes; it is even more difficult to change other people's attitudes. But it can be done. The following hints can help you, as a manager, change employee attitudes:

1. Give employees feedback. Employees must be made aware of their negative attitudes if they are to change. The manager must talk to the employee about the negative attitude. The employee must understand that the attitude has negative consequences for her or him and the department. The manager should offer an alternative attitude. In the opening case, Kent has done this.
2. Accentuate positive conditions. Employees tend to have positive attitudes toward the things they do well. Make working conditions as pleasant as possible, and make sure employees have all the necessary resources and training to do a good job.
3. Provide consequences. Employees tend to repeat activities or events followed by positive consequences. On the other hand, they tend to avoid things followed by negative consequences. Try to keep negative attitudes from developing and spreading.
4. Be a positive role model. If the manager has a positive attitude, employees may also.

See Exhibit 3.1 for a review of how to change your attitudes and those of your employees.

APPLICATION SITUATIONS / / /

Job Attitudes AS 3-2

Identify each employee's attitude statement as:

A. Positive B. Negative

_______ 6. "Why do I have to do it?"

_______ 7. "I'd be happy to go pick up the mail for you."

_______ 8. "Get out of the way. Can't you see I'm trying to get through here?"

_______ 9. "It's not my fault. The guy didn't give me enough time."

_______ 10. "I heard you missed your sales quota this month. Don't worry. You'll make it up next month."

JOB SATISFACTION

In this section we discuss the importance and nature of job satisfaction, the determinants of job satisfaction, and facts about job satisfaction.

The Importance and Nature of Job Satisfaction

A person's **job satisfaction** *is a set of attitudes toward work.* Work is an important part of life,[23] and people want to be happy, so naturally people want job satisfaction.[24] Employees who are more satisfied with their jobs are generally better workers.[25]

WORK APPLICATION 3-5

Has job or school satisfaction affected your absenteeism? Explain your answer. For example, do you attend a class or job more if you are satisfied with it or if you are dissatisfied with it?

A **job satisfaction survey** *is a process of determining employee attitudes about the job and work environment.* Organizations such as the Red Cross measure job satisfaction and work to improve it. Today managers see a decline in employees' job dedication, attendance, and punctuality. Improving job satisfaction may lead to better human relations and organizational performance by creating a win–win situation.[26]

When employees are hired, they come to the organization with a set of desires, needs, and past experiences that combine to form job expectations about work. If their expectations are met, they generally have high levels of job satisfaction, and vice versa. Employees who don't have job satisfaction during high unemployment often stay at the current job.[27] But they will leave once they can find a better job.[28].

Job satisfaction is a part of life satisfaction.[29] As Chapter 1 stated, the total person comes to work. Your off-the-job life also affects your job satisfaction, and in turn your job satisfaction affects your life satisfaction. For example, Rayanne has brought a negative attitude to work, which in turn has affected her job satisfaction.

Determinants of Job Satisfaction

Learning Outcome 3-3

List seven job satisfaction determinants.

Job satisfaction is on a continuum from low to high. It can refer to a single employee, a group or department, or an entire organization. Notice that the definition of job satisfaction identifies an overall attitude toward work. It does so because people usually have positive attitudes about some aspects of work, such as the work itself, and negative attitudes about other aspects of work, such as pay. Job satisfaction is our overall attitude toward our jobs.

There are a variety of determinants of job satisfaction. Each of these determinants may be of great importance to some people and of little importance to others.

The Work Itself Whether a person enjoys performing the work itself has a major effect on overall job satisfaction. People who view their jobs as boring, dull, or unchallenging tend to have low levels of job satisfaction.[30]

Pay and Benefits A person's satisfaction with the pay received affects overall job satisfaction.[31] And the rising cost of health care, along with faltering retirement benefits, make benefits more important than ever.[32] Employees who are not satisfied with their pay and benefits may not perform to their full potential.

Growth and Upward Mobility Whether a person is satisfied with personal or company growth and whether the potential for upward mobility exists may affect job satisfaction.[33] Many, but not all, people want to be challenged and to learn new things. Some people want to be promoted to higher-level jobs.

Supervision Whether a person is satisfied with the supervision received affects overall job satisfaction. Employees who feel their boss does not provide appropriate direction or too much control may become frustrated and dissatisfied with work. The personal relationship between the boss and the employee also affects job satisfaction.

Communication Skills
Refer to CS Question 4.

Coworkers Whether a person has positive human relations with his or her coworkers affects overall job satisfaction. People who like their coworkers often have higher levels of job satisfaction than employees who dislike their coworkers.

EXHIBIT 3.2 | Determinants of Job Satisfaction

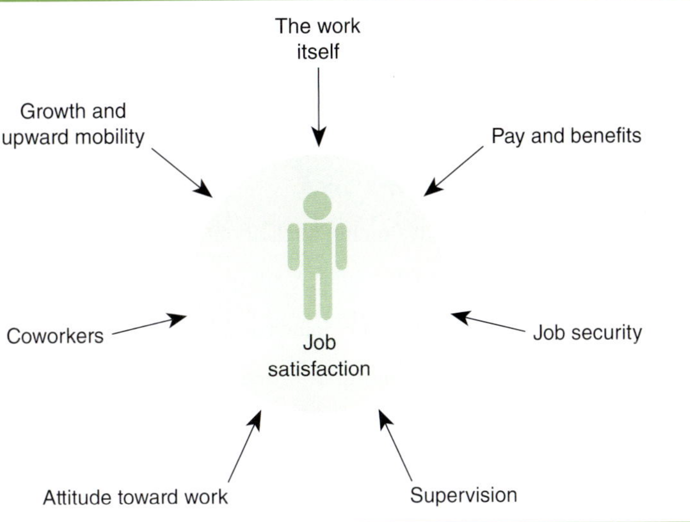

Job Security During times of high unemployment, employees are concerned about avoiding layoffs.[34] Worrying about being laid off can be stressful and affect job satisfaction.

Attitude toward Work Some people view work (attitude) as fun and interesting, while others do not. Some people have been satisfied with many different jobs, while others have remained dissatisfied in numerous work situations. People with a positive attitude toward work tend to have higher levels of job satisfaction. Personality is associated with work attitude and behavior.

People differ in the ways they prioritize the above determinants of job satisfaction. A person can be highly satisfied in some areas and dissatisfied in others yet have overall job satisfaction. Unfortunately, Rayanne doesn't seem happy with any of these determinants of job satisfaction. Remember that what you think about affects how you feel, and how you feel affects your behavior, human relations, and performance. So if you keep thinking about the bad parts about your job, you will feel bad and have less effective behavior, human relations, and performance. So think about the things you like about the job. For a review of the seven determinants of job satisfaction, see Exhibit 3.2.

WORK APPLICATION 3-6

Consider a specific job you hold or have held. Measure your job satisfaction for the job by rating each of the seven determinants of job satisfaction using a scale from 1 (not satisfied) to 5 (satisfied); then add up the total points and divide by seven to get your average, or overall, job satisfaction level. Be sure to write down the seven determinants and your ratings.

WORK APPLICATION 3-7

Has job or school satisfaction affected your performance? Explain your answer. For example, compared to your work in classes or jobs that you are satisfied with, do you work as hard and produce as much for classes or jobs that you are dissatisfied with?

Job Satisfaction in the United States and Other Countries

Most people start a new job with high expectations of job satisfaction, but the initial satisfaction often wears off. Companies that work to improve job satisfaction have above-average customer service, sales, and profits because real satisfaction among employees leads to real money for the company.[35, 36] But internationally, education and income do increase job satisfaction.[37] Job satisfaction differences may be driven by the extent to which people in different countries hold jobs that differ in level of interest, promotion prospects, and job security. People in professional and managerial jobs and those performing non-manual work reported more job satisfaction than those who perform manual work. Also, people working under long-term job contracts reported greater job satisfaction than those under short-term or no contracts.[38]

There are different levels of job satisfaction across cultures. With increased global competition to increase productivity, companies need to be careful not to push employees to the point of decreased job satisfaction; such behavior can have negative consequences on performance.

APPLICATION SITUATIONS / / /

Job Satisfaction AS 3-3

Identify each statement by its determinant of job satisfaction:

A. Work itself
B. Pay
C. Growth and mobility
D. Supervision
E. Coworkers
F. General work attitude
G. Job security

_______ 11. "The boss is always on my back about something."

_______ 12. "I'd like to buy a DVD player, but my bills are piling up. I certainly deserve more than I make."

_______ 13. "I enjoy working with my hands and fixing the machines."

_______ 14. "I'm applying for a promotion, and I think I'll get it."

_______ 15. "Pete and Ann are real jerks. I don't get along well with either of them. They think they know it all."

SELF-CONCEPT

Learning Outcome 3-4

Determine whether you have a positive self-concept and how it affects your behavior, human relations, and performance.

In this section, we explain self-concept and how it is formed, self-efficacy, attribution theory and self-concept, and the steps of how to build a positive self-concept.

Self-Concept and How It Is Formed

Your **self-concept** *is your overall attitude about yourself.* Self-concept is also called *self-esteem* and *self-image.* Self-concept can be thought of as being on a continuum from positive to negative, or high to low. Do you like yourself? Are you a valuable person? Are you satisfied with the way you live your life? When faced with a challenge, are your thoughts positive or negative? Do you believe you can meet the challenge or that you're not very good at doing things? If your beliefs and feelings about yourself are positive, you tend to have a high self-concept. Your personality is based, in part, on your self-concept.[39]

Your self-concept includes perceptions about several aspects of yourself. You can have a positive self-concept and still want to change some things about yourself. Self-concept is your perception of yourself, which may not be the way others perceive you. Your thoughts and feelings about yourself have greater influence in determining your self-concept than does your behavior.[40] Even if individuals don't consider themselves likable, others probably do like them.

You develop your self-concept over the years through the messages you receive about yourself from others. Your present self-concept has been strongly influenced by the way others have treated you—the attitudes and expectations others have had of you (Pygmalion effect). Your parents were the first to contribute to your self-concept. Did your parents build you up with statements like, "You're smart—you can do it," or destroy you with "You're dumb—you cannot do it"? If you have siblings, were they positive or negative? Your early self-concept still affects your self-concept today. As you grew through adolescence, your teachers and peers also had a profound impact on your self-concept. Were you popular? Did you have friends who encouraged you? By the time you reach adulthood in your early 20s, your self-concept is fairly well developed. However, when you take on more responsibilities, such as a full-time job, marriage, and children, your self-concept can change. Your job and boss, for example, do or will affect your success (Pygmalion effect) and self-concept.[41]

Apparently, Rayanne came to work for Kent with a negative self-concept. Rayanne stated that she messed up on all her previous jobs, and she called herself a failure. Her self-concept, like yours, however, is dynamic and capable of changing. Kent is trying to develop a win–win situation by trying to get Rayanne to develop a more positive attitude and self-concept so that she can be happier and more productive. Rayanne can change her attitude and self-concept if she really wants to and is willing to work at it. Are you willing to develop a more positive self-concept so that you can be happier and more productive?

In addition to receiving messages from others, we also make social comparisons. We compare ourselves with others all the time. You might think to yourself, Am I smarter, better looking, more successful than the people I associate with? Such comparisons can have positive or negative influences on your self-concept. Focusing on negative comparisons can cause you to have a negative self-concept and to be unhappy, so don't do it.

WORK APPLICATION 3-8

Describe your self-concept.

Self-Efficacy

Learning Outcome 3-5

Understand how your manager's and your own expectations affect your performance.

Self-efficacy *is your belief in your capability to perform in a specific situation.* Self-efficacy affects your effort, persistence, expressed interest, and the difficulty of goals you select.[42] For example, if your major is business, your self-efficacy may be high for a management course but low for a language or biology course that you may be required to take.

APPLICATION SITUATIONS / / /

Self-Concept AS 3-4

Identify each statement as:

A. Positive B. Negative

_______ 16. "Darn, that's the fifth mistake I've made today."

_______ 17. "Sure, I can do that. No problem."

_______ 18. "It's been three weeks, and I still cannot understand why I did not get the promotion I wanted so badly."

_______ 19. "I enjoy going on sales calls and meeting new people."

_______ 20. "I cannot do math."

Your expectations affect your performance.[43] If you think you will be successful, you will be. If you think you will fail, you will, because you will fulfill your expectations. You will live up to or down to your expectations. This expectation phenomenon is often referred to as the *self-fulfilling prophecy* and the Galatea effect. The **self-fulfilling prophecy** *occurs when your expectations affect your success or failure.* Rayanne stated that she had messed up on all the jobs she had, and she called herself a failure. Is it any surprise to find that Rayanne is having problems in her new job working for Kent?

WORK APPLICATION 3-9

Give an example of when you lived up to or down to your own expectations (self-efficacy leading to self-fulfilling prophecy).

As you can see, self-efficacy and the self-fulfilling prophecy go hand in hand. Your self-efficacy becomes your self-fulfilling prophecy. So you need self-efficacy, or the confidence to put forth the effort needed to succeed at challenging tasks.[44]

Attribution Theory and Self-Concept

Let's discuss attribution theory and how it relates to your self-concept. **Attribution** *is one's perception that the cause of behavior is either internal or external. Internal* behavior is within the control of the person, and *external* behavior is out of the person's control or it is based on the situation. For example, a worker may usually be nice (internal), but when overstressed, he may be rude and yell (external). When we observe others' behavior, we do not know the reason for it. So we make a judgment as to why people do the things they do. If you believe the cause to be external, you may respond with positive human relations. If you believe the cause to be internal, you may yell back, which leads to negative human relations. So attribution theory is how we perceive the causes of behavior, which in turn affects our subsequent choices and behaviors.

You can improve your self-concept only if you are willing to take responsibility for your actions and change to improve. Rayanne is not willing to take responsibility for her poor performance; she says it's not her fault. Nor is she willing to change to improve. Until she takes responsibility and is willing to change, she will not improve. Are you willing to change to improve?

Building a Positive Self-Concept

Learning Outcome 3-6

Demonstrate how to develop a more positive self-concept.

You are the ultimate creator of your self-concept.[45] People with a positive self-concept are happier and more likable, have better relationships, and are more productive. You can always improve your self-concept, even though it is not easy to evaluate yourself and it is even more difficult to change. But as Jack Welch says, you have to take charge of yourself. Once you recognize the importance of a positive self-concept, you will see that it is worth the time and effort to improve your self-concept. You can change; you don't have to be who you were in the past or are in the present. The general guidelines below are followed by an action plan that will help you develop a more positive self-concept.

As a manager (coach, parent, teacher, friend), you can work with employees using these ideas to help them develop a more positive self-concept. One thing to keep in mind is that you need to be positive and give praise and encouragement. However, real self-esteem is based on achievement, not praise for low performance. If you give praise for poor performance, performance usually does not improve and it often gets worse.

Kent can teach Rayanne how to improve her self-concept; he should praise her for improvements, but he should not praise her if she does not improve her performance. If Rayanne's performance does not improve and Kent takes no action, her self-concept will not improve.

General Guidelines The following are general guidelines you can implement in your daily life to improve your self-concept:

1. View mistakes as learning experiences. Realize that we all make mistakes. Talk to any successful businessperson with a positive self-concept and he or she will admit making mistakes. But he or she will tell you that you need to take some risks to be successful.[46] Don't hide in the dugout; go to bat. You get some strikeouts and some hits. That's how life is. Try to be future-oriented. Don't worry about past mistakes. Dwelling on past mistakes will only have a negative effect on your self-concept.
2. Accept failure and bounce back. Inability to rebound from disappointments is one of the main reasons people fail. Dwelling on failure and disappointment will only have a negative effect on your self-concept. Realize that you will have disappointments but will most likely go on to bigger and better things. Recall our definition of success (Chapter 1).
3. Control negative behavior and thoughts. Become aware of your emotions (develop your emotional intelligence), and work to control your behavior.[47]

   Thoughts are also very important because we become what we think about,[48] and what we think determines what happens to us.[49] If you keep thinking you are a loser, you will be a loser, so think about being a winner. If your thoughts are full of failure, you will fail. Silence the voice that says you can't succeed.[50] If you catch yourself thinking negative thoughts, be aware of what is happening and replace the negative thoughts and beliefs with positive ones, such as "I can do this. It's easy." With time you will have fewer and fewer negative thoughts. Always accept a compliment with a thank you. Don't minimize the compliment with a statement such as, "Anyone could have done it" or "It was not a big deal." Never put yourself down in your thoughts, words, or actions. If you catch yourself doing this, stop and replace the thoughts or behavior with positive ones.
4. Tap into your spirituality. Use any religious or spiritual beliefs you have that can help you develop a more positive self-concept: For example, "God will help me succeed."

Action Plan for Building a Positive Self-Concept The three-part action plan for building a positive self-concept is listed in Model 3.1 and discussed below.

MODEL 3.1 | Building a Positive Self-Concept

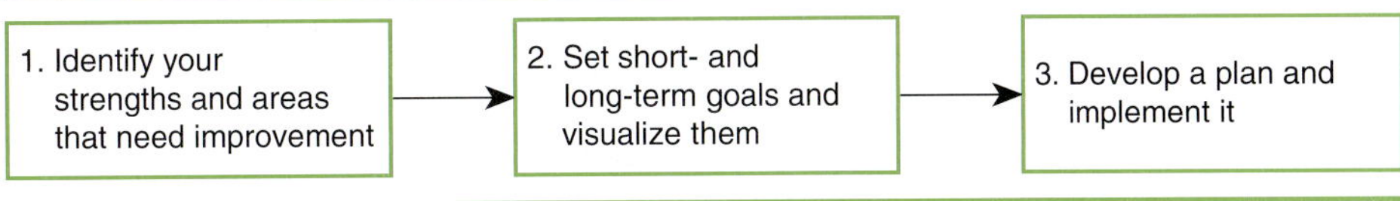

Step 1: Identify Your Strengths and Areas That Need Improvement What are the things about yourself that you like? What can you do well? What do you have to offer other people and organizations?

What are the things about yourself or the behavior that could be improved? Be aware of your limitations.[51] No one is good at everything. Focus on your strengths, not on your weaknesses. In areas where you are weak, get help and help others in their weak areas.

Step 2: Set Short- and Long-Term Goals and Visualize Them Before you can get anywhere or get anything out of life, you must first determine where you want to go or what you want. Based on step 1, set some goals for the things about yourself or your behavior that you want to change for the better. Write them down in positive, affirmative language. For example, write:

- "I am calm when talking to others" (not "I don't yell at people").
- "I am a slim ____________ pounds [select a weight 5 to 10 pounds less than your current weight]" (not "I must lose weight").
- "I am outgoing and enjoy meeting new people" (not "I must stop being shy").
- "I am smart and get good grades," or "I am good at my job."

Place your goals where you can review them several times each day. Put copies on your mirror, refrigerator, car visor, or desk, or record them so you can play them several times each day. Start and end each day thinking positive thoughts about yourself.

People often procrastinate because the whole goal or project seems overwhelming. When you don't know where to start, you don't do anything. Remember, success comes one step at a time. Reaching one goal helps motivate you to continue, and each success helps you develop a more positive self-concept. Therefore, set short-term goals you can reach. For example, if you presently weigh 150 pounds, start with the goal "I am a slim 110 pounds," but break it up into doable parts: "I will weigh 145 pounds by January 1, 2014," and "I will weigh 140 pounds by March 1, 2014." Compliment and reward yourself regularly as you achieve your short-term goals. Rewards do not have to be big. When you hit the new weight, treat yourself to a small ice cream cone or a movie. Rewards will help motivate you to continue until you reach the final 110 pounds. As you continue to set and achieve short-term goals, you will continue to build your self-concept as being successful. You will learn about goal setting and motivation in Chapter 8.

Each day, visualize yourself as you want to be, as set forth in your goals. For example, picture yourself being calm when talking to a person you usually yell at. Mentally see yourself at a slim 110 pounds. Picture yourself meeting new people or being successful on the job, and so forth.

Skill Building Exercises 3-2 and 3-3 develop this skill.

Step 3: Develop a Plan and Implement It What specific action will you take to improve your self-concept through changing your thoughts or behavior? Some goals take much planning, while others do not. For example, if you want to lose weight to get down to 110 pounds, you will have to do more than just imagine yourself being 110 pounds. What will be your plan to lose the weight? Exercise? Diet? What are the specifics? With other goals, such as not yelling at people, making detailed plans is not so easy. However, you can determine what it is that gets you angry and try to eliminate it. What will you do differently?

Communication Skills Refer to CS Question 5.

Stop comparing yourself with others and downgrading yourself, because this hurts your self-concept. We can all find someone who is better than we are. Even the best are eventually topped. Set your goals, develop plans, and achieve them. Compare yourself with *you.* Be the best that *you* can be. Continue to improve yourself by setting goals, developing plans,

EXHIBIT 3.3 | Developing a Positive Self-Concept

Accept failure and bounce back

Control negative behavior and thoughts

View mistakes as learning experiences

Tap into your spirituality

1. Identify your strengths and areas that need improvement.
2. Set short- and long-term goals and visualize them.
3. Develop a plan and implement it.

and achieving them. Through this process, you will develop your self-concept. If you continually improve yourself, there is less chance of a midlife crisis. You are less likely to look back at your life and ask, What have I accomplished? You will know and be proud of yourself. See Exhibit 3.3 for a review of how to develop a positive self-concept. Skill-Building Exercise 3-2 gives you the opportunity to develop a plan to improve your self-concept.

WORK APPLICATION 3-10

Which of the four general guidelines to building a positive self-concept needs the least work? The most work? Explain your answer.

VALUES

Learning Outcome 3-7

Identify your personal values.

In this section, we cover individual values and how they are related to, yet different from, attitudes. A person's **values** *are the things that have worth for or are important to the individual,* and a **value system** *is the set of standards by which the individual lives.* Values concern what "should be"; they influence the choices we make among alternative behaviors.[52] Values direct the form that motivated behavior will take. For example, if you have three job offers, you will select the one that is of the highest value to you.

Values help shape your attitudes. When something is of value to you, you tend to have positive attitudes toward it. Since work is not important to Rayanne, it is not surprising that she has a negative attitude toward work. What is of value to you? Take time and identify what is truly important to you, and be sure you devote time to your values.[53] Complete Self-Assessment Exercise 3-3 to identify your personal values in eight broad areas of life.

/// Self-Assessment Exercise 3-3 ///

Your Personal Values

Below are 16 items. Rate how important each one is to you on a scale of 0 (not important) to 100 (very important). Write a number from 0 to 100 on the line to the left of each item.

Not important					Somewhat important					Very important
0	10	20	30	40	50	60	70	80	90	100

_____ 1. An enjoyable, satisfying job.

_____ 2. A high-paying job.

_____ 3. A good marriage.

_____ 4. Meeting new people, social events.

_____ 5. Involvement in community activities.

_____ 6. My religion.

_____ 7. Exercising, playing sports.

_____ 8. Intellectual development.

_____ 9. A career with challenging opportunities.

/// Self-Assessment Exercise 3-3 /// (*continued*)

_____ 10. Nice cars, clothes, home, etc.

_____ 11. Spending time with family.

_____ 12. Having several close friends.

_____ 13. Volunteer work for not-for-profit organizations such as the cancer society.

_____ 14. Meditation, quiet time to think, pray, etc.

_____ 15. A healthy, balanced diet.

_____ 16. Educational reading, self-improvement programs, etc.

Below, transfer the numbers for each of the 16 items to the appropriate column; then add the two numbers in each column.

	Professional	Financial	Family	Social
	1. _____	2. _____	3. _____	4. _____
	9. _____	10. _____	11. _____	12. _____
Totals	_____	_____	_____	_____
	Community	**Spiritual**	**Physical**	**Intellectual**
	5. _____	6. _____	7. _____	8. _____
	13. _____	14. _____	15. _____	16. _____
Totals	_____	_____	_____	_____

The higher the total in any area, the higher the value you place on that particular area. The closer the numbers are in all eight areas, the more well-rounded you are.

Think about the time and effort you put forth in your top three values. Is it sufficient to allow you to achieve the level of success you want in each area? If not, what can you do to change? Is there any area in which you feel you should have a higher value total? If yes, which one? What can you do to change?

WORK APPLICATION 3-11

What is your attitude toward your personal values in the eight areas of Self-Assessment Exercise 3-3? Do you plan to work at changing any of your values? Why or why not?

Values are developed in much the same way as attitudes. However, values are more stable than attitudes. Attitudes reflect multiple, often changing, opinions. Values about some things do change, but the process is usually slower than a change in attitude. Society influences our value system. What was considered unacceptable in the past may become commonplace in the future, or vice versa. For example, the percentage of smokers and the social acceptance of smoking have decreased over the years. Value changes over the years are often a major part of what is referred to as the *generation gap.*

Getting to know people and understanding their values can improve human relations. For example, if Juan knows that Carla has great respect for the president, he can avoid making negative comments about the president in front of her. Likewise, if Carla knows that Juan is a big baseball fan, she can ask him how his favorite team is doing.

Skill Building Exercise 3-1 develops this skill.

Discussions over value issues, such as abortion and homosexuality, rarely lead to changes in others' values. They usually just end in arguments. Therefore, we should try to be open-minded about others' values and avoid arguments that will only hurt human relations.

Spirituality in the Workplace

People want to be happy.[54] Many people are seeking spirituality as a means of fulfillment in their lives. Dr. Edward Wilson, Harvard University professor and two-time Pulitzer Prize–winning expert on human nature, says, "I believe the search for spirituality is going to be one of the major historical episodes of the 21st century."[55]

Judith Neal, director of the Tyson Center for Faith and Spirituality in the Workplace at the University of Arkansas (http://tfsw.uark.edu), has defined spirituality in the workplace and developed guidelines for leading from a spiritual perspective.[56]

Defining Spirituality in the Workplace The Latin origin of the word spirit is *spirare,* meaning "to breathe." At its most basic, then, spirit is what inhabits us when we are alive and breathing; it is the life force.

Spirituality in the workplace is about people seeing their work as a spiritual path, as an opportunity to grow personally and to contribute to society in a meaningful way. It is about learning to be more caring and compassionate with fellow employees, with bosses, with subordinates, and with customers. It is about having integrity, being true to oneself, and telling the truth to others. Spirituality in the workplace can refer to an individual's attempts to live his or her values more fully in the workplace. Or it can refer to the ways organizations structure themselves to support the spiritual growth of employees. In the final analysis, one's understanding of spirit and of spirituality in the workplace is a very individual and personal matter.

Guidelines for Leading from a Spiritual Perspective Here are five spiritual principles that have been useful to many leaders in their personal and professional development:

1. *Know thyself.* All spiritual growth processes incorporate the principle of self-awareness. Examine why you respond to situations the way you do.
2. *Act with authenticity.* Followers learn a lot more from who we are and how we behave than from what we say. Authenticity means being oneself and not playing a role.
3. *Respect and honor the beliefs of others.* It can be very risky and maybe even inappropriate to talk about your own spirituality in the workplace. Yet if spirituality is a guiding force in your life and your leading, and if you follow the guideline of authenticity, you cannot hide that part of yourself. It is a fine line to walk. It is extremely important that employees do not feel that you are imposing your belief system (spiritual, religious, or otherwise) on them.
4. *Be as trusting as you can be.* This guideline operates on many levels. On the personal level, this guideline applies to trusting oneself, one's inner voice, or one's source of spiritual guidance. This means trusting that there is a Higher Power in your life and that if you ask, you will receive guidance on important issues.
5. *Maintain a spiritual practice.* In a research study on people who integrate their spirituality and their work, the most frequently mentioned spiritual practice is spending time in nature. Examples of other practices are attending religious services, meditating, praying, reading inspirational literature, doing hatha yoga, or writing in a journal.

Secular institutional research has found that during moments of anger and distress, turning to prayer or meditation, encouraged in nearly all religions, diminishes the harmful effects of negative emotions and stress. Also, people who attend religious services at least once a week enjoy better-than-average health and wealth. A survey reported that 90 percent of Americans pray.[57]

By implementing the ideas presented in this chapter, you can develop positive attitudes and a more positive self-concept, as well as clarify your values. Begin today.

ETHICS

Communication Skills
Refer to CS Question 6.

Communication Skills
Refer to CS Question 7.

As related to values, **ethics** *refers to the moral standard of right and wrong behavior.* Business is often viewed as being unethical,[58] and today more businesses are focusing on ensuring ethical business practices.[59] In this section, we discuss whether ethical behavior does pay, how personality and attitudes affect ethical behavior, how people justify unethical behavior, some ethical guidelines, the stakeholders' approach to ethics, and global ethics. Before we begin, complete Self-Assessment Exercise 3-4 to determine how ethical your behavior is.

/// Self-Assessment Exercise 3-4 ///

How Ethical Is Your Behavior?

For this exercise, you will be using the same set of statements twice. The first time you answer them, focus on your own behavior and the frequency with which you use it. On the line before the question number, place the number from 1 (frequently) to 4 (never) that represents how often you have done the behavior in the past, do the behavior now, or would do the behavior if you had the chance. These numbers will allow you to determine your level of ethics. You can be honest without fear of having to tell others your score in class. *Sharing ethics scores is not part of the exercise.*

Frequently			Never
1	2	3	4

The second time you use the statements, focus on other people in an organization with whom you work or have worked. Place an O on the line after the number if you have observed someone doing this behavior. Also place an R on the line if you have reported (blown the whistle on) this behavior either within the organization or externally.

O———Observed R———Reported

1–4 **O, R**

College

_____ 1. _____ Cheating on homework assignments.

_____ 2. _____ Cheating on exams.

_____ 3. _____ Passing in papers that were completed by someone else as your own work.

Job

_____ 4. _____ Lying to others to get what you want or to stay out of trouble.

_____ 5. _____ Coming to work late, leaving work early, or taking long breaks or lunches and getting paid for it.

_____ 6. _____ Socializing, goofing off, or doing personal work rather than doing the work that should be done and getting paid for it.

_____ 7. _____ Calling in sick to get a day off when you are not sick.

_____ 8. _____ Using the organization's phone, computer, Internet, copier, mail, car, etc. for personal use.

_____ 9. _____ Taking home company tools or equipment without permission for personal use and returning the items.

_____ 10. _____ Taking home organizational supplies or merchandise and keeping the items.

_____ 11. _____ Giving company supplies or merchandise to friends or allowing them to take the items without saying anything.

_____ 12. _____ Putting in for reimbursement for meals and travel or other expenses that weren't actually eaten or taken.

_____ 13. _____ Taking your spouse or friends out to eat or on a business trip and charging it to the organizational expense account.

_____ 14. _____ Accepting gifts from customers or suppliers in exchange for giving them business.

_____ 15. _____ Cheating on your taxes.

_____ 16. _____ Misleading customers, such as promising short delivery dates, to make a sale.

_____ 17. _____ Misleading competitors, such as pretending to be a customer or supplier, to get information to use to compete against them.

_____ 18. _____ Planting false information to enhance your chances of getting reelected.

_____ 19. _____ Selling a customer more product than the customer needs just to get the commission.

_____ 20. _____ Spreading false rumors about coworkers or competitors to make yourself look better for advancement or to make more sales.

_____ 21. _____ Lying for your boss when asked or told to do so.

_____ 22. _____ Deleting information that makes you look bad or changing information to look better than the actual results.

(*continued*)

/// Self-Assessment Exercise 3-4 /// (*continued*)

1–4 **O, R**

_____ 23. _____ Being pressured, or pressuring others, to sign off on documents that contain false information.

_____ 24. _____ Being pressured to sign off on documents you haven't read, knowing they may contain information or decisions that may be considered inappropriate, or pressuring others to do so.

_____ 25. If you were to give this assessment to a person with whom you work and with whom you do not get along very well, would she or he agree with your answers? Use 4 (yes) or 1 (no). Place the appropriate number on the line before the number 25. (No O or R responses are necessary for this question.)

Other Unethical Behavior: On the lines below, add other unethical behaviors you have observed. If you reported the behavior, write an R before the behavior.

26. _____ ____

27. _____ ____

28. _____ ____

Note: This self-assessment is not meant to be a precise measure of your ethical behavior. It is designed to get you thinking about your behavior and that of others from an ethical perspective. There is no right or wrong score; however, each of these actions is considered unethical behavior in most organizations. Another ethical issue in this exercise is your honesty when rating the frequencies of your behavior. How honest were you?

Scoring: To determine your ethics score, add the numbers you recorded. Your total will be between 25 and 100. Place the number here _____ and on the continuum below place an X at the point that represents your score. The higher your score, the more ethical your behavior is; the lower your score, the less ethical your behavior is.

Unethical 25 -- — - 30 —- --40 — --50 - ---60 - ---70 - ---80 - ---90 - ---100 Ethical

Does Ethical Behavior Pay?

Generally, the answer is yes. Unethical behavior hurts business and society.[60] Contrary to what some people believe, people who are nice and ethical are more likely to rise to power.[61] Successful people generally have high integrity—they are honest and ethical, and honor their word.[62] Bill Gates and Warren Buffett, two of the world's richest men, say that ethics pays; don't cut corners.[63] Unethical behavior can cause human relations problems.[64]

How Personality Traits and Attitudes, Moral Development, and the Situation Affect Ethical Behavior

Personality Traits and Attitudes The use of ethical behavior is related to our individual needs and personality traits. Leaders with *surgency* dominance personality traits have two choices: to use power for personal benefit or to help others.[65] To gain power and to be *conscientious* with high achievement, some people will use unethical behavior; also, irresponsible people often cut corners. An *agreeableness* personality, sensitive to others, can lead to following the crowd in either ethical or unethical behavior. *Emotionally unstable* people and those with an external locus of control are more likely to use unethical behavior.[66] People *open to new experiences* are often ethical.

People with *positive attitudes* about ethics tend to be more ethical than those with negative or weak attitudes about ethics. The firm's internal ethical context can help or hurt employee attitudes and behavior—being ethical or unethical. When you complete Self-Assessment Exercise 3-5 at the end of this section, you will have a better understanding of how your personality affects your ethical behavior.

Learning Outcome 3-8

Compare the three levels of moral development.

Moral Development A second factor affecting ethical behavior is *moral development,* which refers to understanding right from wrong and choosing to do the right thing. Our ability to make ethical choices is related to our level of moral development.[67] There are three levels of

EXHIBIT 3.4 | Levels of Moral Development

Level 3: Postconventional

Behavior is motivated by universal principles of right and wrong, regardless of the expectations of the leader or group. One seeks to balance the concerns for self with those of others and the common good. At the risk of social rejection, economic loss, and physical punishment, the individual will follow ethical principles even if they violate the law (Martin Luther King, Jr., for example, broke what he considered unjust laws and spent time in jail seeking universal dignity and justice).

"I don't lie to customers because it is wrong."

The common leadership style is visionary and committed to serving others and a higher cause while empowering followers to reach this level.

Level 2: Conventional

Living up to expectations of acceptable behavior defined by others motivates behavior to fulfill duties and obligations. It is common for followers to copy the behavior of the leaders and group. If the group (this could be society, an organization, or a department) accepts lying, cheating, and stealing when dealing with customers, suppliers, the government, or competitors, so will the individual. On the other hand, if these behaviors are not accepted, the individual will not do them either. Peer pressure is used to enforce group norms.

"I lie to customers because the other sales reps do it too."

It is common for lower-level managers to use a leadership style similar to that of the higher-level managers.

Level 1: Preconventional

Self-interest motivates behavior to meet one's own needs and to gain rewards while following rules and being obedient to authority to avoid punishment.

"I lie to customers to sell more products and get higher commission checks."

The common leadership style is autocratic toward others while using one's position for personal advantage.

Source: Based on Lawrence Kohlberg, "Moral Stages and Moralization: The Cognitive-Development Approach," in *Moral Development and Behavior: Theory, Research, and Social Issues,* ed. Thomas Likona (Austin, TX: Holt, Rinehart and Winston, 1976), pp. 31–53.

personal moral development, as discussed in Exhibit 3.4. At the first level, preconventional, you choose right and wrong behavior based on your self-interest and the consequences (reward and punishment). With ethical reasoning at the second level, conventional, you seek to maintain expected standards and live up to the expectations of others. At the third level, postconventional, you make an effort to define moral principles regardless of the leader's or group's ethics. Although most of us have the ability to reach this third level, only about 20 percent of people actually do reach it. Most people behave at the second level, conventional. How do you handle peer pressure? What level of moral development have you attained? What can you do to further develop your ethical behavior?

WORK APPLICATION 3-12

Give an organizational example of behavior at each of the three levels of moral development.

The Situation People respond to "incentives" and can often be manipulated to do the ethical or unethical thing based on the situation's circumstances.[68] Highly competitive and unsupervised situations increase the odds of unethical behavior. Unethical behavior occurs more often when there is no formal ethics policy or code of ethics and when unethical behavior is not punished. Unethical behavior is especially prevalent when it is rewarded. People are also less likely to report unethical behavior (blow the whistle) when they perceive the violation as not being serious and when the potential whistle-blower is friends with the offender.

To tie together the three factors affecting ethical behavior, we need to realize that personality traits and attitudes and our moral development interact with the situation to determine if a person will use ethical or unethical behavior. In this chapter we use the individual level of analysis: Am I ethical? How can I improve my ethical behavior? At the organizational level, many firms offer training programs and develop codes of ethics to help employees behave ethically. We will talk about ethics again, as it relates to power and politics, in Chapter 9.

How People Justify Unethical Behavior

Most people understand right and wrong behavior and have a conscience, or they live by a personal code of conduct. So why do good people do bad things? In most cases, when people use unethical behavior it is not due to some type of character flaw or being born a bad person. Few people see themselves as unethical. We all want to view ourselves in a positive manner. Therefore, when we do use unethical behavior, we often justify the behavior to protect our *self-concept* so that we don't have a guilty conscience or feel remorse.[69] Let's discuss several thinking processes used to justify unethical behavior.

- *Moral justification* is the process of reinterpreting immoral behavior in terms of a higher purpose. The terrorists of 9/11/01 killed innocent people, as do suicide bombers, yet they believe their killing is for the good and that they will go to heaven for their actions. People sometimes state that they have conducted unethical behavior (lying about a competitor to hurt its reputation, fixing prices, stealing confidential information, etc.) for the good of the organization and employees.
- *Displacement of responsibility* is the process of blaming one's unethical behavior on others: "I was only following orders; my boss told me to inflate the figures."
- *Diffusion of responsibility* is the process of a group engaging in unethical behavior, with no one person being held responsible: "We all take bribes or kickbacks; it's the way we do business"; "We all take merchandise home." As related to conventional morality, peer pressure is used to enforce group norms.
- *Advantageous comparison* is the process of comparing oneself to others who are worse: "I call in sick when I'm not sick only a few times a year; Tom and Ellen do it all the time"; "We pollute less than our competitors do."
- *Disregard for or distortion of consequences* is the process of minimizing the harm caused by the unethical behavior: "If I inflate the figures, no one will be hurt and I will not get caught. And if I do, I'll just get a slap on the wrist anyway." Was this the case at Enron and Global Crossing?
- *Attribution of blame* is the process of claiming the victim deserved whatever happened, or the unethical behavior was caused by someone else's behavior: "It's my coworker's fault that I repeatedly hit him. He called me XXX, so I had to hit him."
- *Euphemistic labeling* is the process of using "cosmetic" words to make the behavior sound acceptable. "Terrorist group" sounds bad, but "freedom fighters" sounds justifiable. "Misleading" or "covering up" sounds better than "lying to others."

WORK APPLICATION 3-13

Give at least two organizational examples of unethical behavior and the process of justification.

Human Relations Guide to Ethical Decisions

When making decisions, try to meet the goal of human relations by creating a win–win situation for all stakeholders. Some of the relevant stakeholder parties include peers, your boss, subordinates, other department members, the organization, and people and organizations outside the organization you work for as well.

Communication Skills
Refer to CS Question 8.

Here is a simple stakeholders guide to making ethical decisions: *If, after making a decision, you are proud to tell all the relevant parties your decision, the decision is probably ethical. If you are embarrassed to tell others your decision, or if you keep rationalizing the decision, it may not be ethical.*

A second, simple guide is the golden rule: "Do unto others as you want them to do unto you." Or, "Don't do anything to anyone that you would not want them to do to you." Or, "Do to others what they want you to do."

Skill Building Exercise 3-4
develops this skill.

A third guide is the Rotary International four-way test: (1) Is it the truth? (2) Is it fair to all concerned? (3) Will it build goodwill and better friendship? (4) Will it be beneficial to all concerned?

Some final guidelines are to have integrity (be honest—don't lie, cheat, or steal);[70] when tempted to be unethical refer to the ethical guide you use;[71] when you are not sure if something is ethical, ask an ethical person who will not just tell you what you want to hear. Remember that what you think about affects how you feel, and how you feel affects your

EXHIBIT 3.5 | Levels of Global Corporate Social Responsibility (GCSR) and Action

Level of GCSR	Action
4. Philanthropic	Be a good global citizen by doing what is desired by global stakeholders.
3. Ethical	Be ethical by doing what is expected by global stakeholders.
2. Legal	Be lawful by doing what is required by global stakeholders.
1. Economic	Be profitable by doing what is required by global capitalism.

Source: Adapted from A.B. Carroll, "Managing Ethically with Global Stakeholders: A Present and Future Challenge," *Academy of Management Executive* 18(2) (2004): 114–120.

behavior, human relations, and performance. If you keep thinking about doing something unethical and justifying it, you may give in to the temptation by using unethical behavior. So stop thinking about it and remind yourself it is unethical.

WORK APPLICATION 3-14

Give an example, preferably from an organization for which you work or have worked, of an individual creating a win–win situation for all parties involved. Identify all parties involved and how they were winners. Use Exhibit 9.2, Human Relations Guide to Ethical Decision Making (page 282), to help you answer the question.

Global Ethics

A difficult challenge to multinational corporation (MNC) managers is the fact that different countries have different levels of ethical standards.[72] For example, it is unethical to give bribes in America, but it is the way in which business is conducted in some countries. Managers typically have two choices. According to *universalism,* managers should make the same ethical decisions across countries, whereas *relativism* calls for decisions to be made based on the ethical standards of the particular country. Thus, the MNC manager using universalism would not give any bribes, whereas the manager using relativism would give bribes in some countries. Today, governments and MNCs are working to develop more universal ethical standards.[73] Think of the complexity of conducting business in 100 to 200 countries.

The increasing concern for global managerial ethics calls for a better understanding through cross-national comparisons. To this end, and getting back to justification of unethical behavior, researchers have found that the same justifications presented earlier are used globally.[74]

MNCs can choose their level of global corporate social responsibility (GCSR); see Exhibit 3.5 for a list of the four levels. Corporate executives of MNCs expressed the conviction that GCSR and citizenship were the trend, which will continue with universal ethical standards.[75]

Rayanne accused Kent of being unethical by trying to manipulate her into doing more work. Was Kent unethical? Before we end the discussion of ethics, complete Self-Assessment Exercise 3-5 to better understand how your personality and attitudes affect your ethical behavior, your moral development, and your justifications for using unethical behavior.

/// Self-Assessment Exercise 3-5 ///

Your Personality Profile and Ethics

Return to Self-Assessment Exercise 2-2, Your Big Five Personality Profile, on page 32 and place your personality profile scores below:

Surgency _____ Agreeableness _____ Adjustment _____ Conscientiousness _____ Openness to experience _____

Review the discussion of ethics above as it relates to your personality profile. How does your personality affect your ethical behavior? Which guides for ethical decisions will you use?

____

____

____

Which level of moral development have you attained? How can you improve?

____

____

____

(*continued*)

/// Self-Assessment Exercise 3-5 /// (*continued*)

Which justifications have you used? How can you improve your ethical behavior by not using justifications?

____

____

____

As we bring this chapter to a close, you should understand the importance of *attitude* and that it affects your behavior, human relations, performance, and *job satisfaction* and how to change your attitudes to be more positive. Your attitude about yourself forms your *self-concept,* and you should understand how to build a more positive self-concept. You should know what is important to you (*values*). You should realize that it does pay to be ethical, as using unethical behavior hurts human relations. You should also understand your level of moral development and how you justify unethical behavior, and be able to use guides to help you use ethical behavior.

/ / / REVIEW / / /

The chapter review is organized to help you master the 9 learning outcomes for Chapter 3. First provide your own response to each learning outcome, and then check the summary provided to see how well you understand the material. Next, identify the final statement in each section as either true or false (T/F). Correct each false statement. Answers are given at the end of the chapter.

LO 3-1 Define attitudes and explain how they affect behavior, human relations, and performance.

Attitudes are strong beliefs or feelings toward people, things, and situations. If we have a positive attitude toward a person, our behavior and interactions with them will be different than our behavior with a person toward whom we have a negative attitude. A supervisor's attitude and expectations of an employee largely determine his or her performance. This is referred to as the Pygmalion effect. Positive attitudes tend to lead to higher levels of performance than negative attitudes, but not always.

Theory Y attitudes are outdated. T F

LO 1-2 Describe how to change your attitudes.

The first thing we must do is be aware of our attitudes, and make a conscious effort to change negative attitudes into positive ones. When we catch ourselves being negative, we must stop and change to a more positive attitude. We should think for ourselves, let negative attitudes go, and keep an open mind.

To change employee attitudes: (1) give them feedback, (2) accentuate positive conditions, (3) provide consequences, and (4) be a positive role model. T F

LO 3-3 List seven job satisfaction determinants.

Seven determinants of job satisfaction are: (1) satisfaction with the work itself, (2) pay and benefits, (3) growth and upward mobility, (4) supervision, (5) coworkers, (6) job security, and (7) attitude toward work.

Most American workers are dissatisfied with their jobs. T F

LO 3-4 Determine whether you have a positive self-concept and how it affects your behavior, human relations, and performance.

Answers will vary from positive to negative self-concepts. Generally, people with positive self-concepts are more outgoing and have more friends than people with negative self-concepts. They also tend to have higher levels of performance.

Your self-concept is influenced by how others treat you—their attitudes and expectations. T F

LO 3-5 Understand how your manager's and your own expectations affect your performance.

When supervisors and coworkers believe and act like employees will be successful, those employees usually are high performers. On the other hand, when supervisors and coworkers believe and act like employees will not be successful, they usually are not high performers. The Pygmalion effect, self-efficacy, and the self-fulfilling prophecy all hold true.

The Pygmalion effect tends to be based on the specific situation, whereas self-efficacy and the self-fulfilling prophecy are more constant. T F

LO 3-6 Demonstrate how to develop a more positive self-concept.

General guidelines for developing a more positive self-concept are: (1) view mistakes as a learning experience, (2) accept failure and bounce back, (3) control negative behavior and thoughts, and (4) tap into your spirituality. An action plan for building a positive self-concept includes the following steps: (1) identify your strengths and areas that need improvement, (2) set goals and visualize them, and (3) develop a plan and implement it.

Having a more positive self-concept can help you succeed in your personal and professional lives. T F

LO 3-7 Identify your personal values.

Answers will vary among students. Some personal values include professional, financial, family, social, community, spiritual, physical, and intellectual.

Spirituality in the workplace is a fad that is decreasing in popularity. T F

LO 3-8 Compare the three levels of moral development.

At the lowest level of moral development, preconventional, behavior is motivated by self-interest; one seeks to gain rewards and avoid punishment. At the second level, conventional, behavior is motivated by meeting the group's expectations to fit in by copying others' behavior. At the highest level, postconventional, behavior is motivated by the desire to do the right thing, even at the risk of alienating the group. The higher the level of moral development, the more ethical the behavior.

Most people are on the preconventional level of moral development. T F

LO 3-9 Define the following 13 key terms.

Select one or more methods: (1) Fill in the missing key terms from memory, (2) match the key terms from the end of the review with their definitions below, and/or (3) copy the key terms in order from the key terms at the beginning of the chapter.

A(n) ______________ is a strong belief or feeling toward people, things, and situations.

______________ attitudes hold that employees dislike work and must be closely supervised to get them to do their work.

______________ attitudes hold that employees like to work and do not need to be closely supervised to get them to do their work.

The ______________ states that management's attitudes and expectations of employees, and how they treat them, largely determine their employees' performance.

______________ is a set of attitudes toward work.

A(n) ______________ is a process of determining employee attitudes about the job and work environment.

Our ______________ is our overall attitude about ourselves.

______________ is our belief in our capability to perform in a specific situation.

A(n) ______________ occurs when your expectations affect your successes or failures.

______________ is the perception of the cause of behavior as being internal or external.

______________ are the things that have worth or are important to the individual.

A(n) ______________ is the set of standards by which the individual lives.

______________ is the moral standard of right and wrong behavior.

/ / / KEY TERMS / / /

attitude 59
attribution 67
ethics 72
job satisfaction 64
job satisfaction survey 64
Pygmalion effect 61
self-concept 66
self-efficacy 67
self-fulfilling prophecy 67
Theory X 60
Theory Y 60
values 70
value system 70

/ / / COMMUNICATION SKILLS / / /

The following critical thinking questions can be used for class discussion and/or as written assignments to develop communication skills. Be sure to give complete explanations for all questions.

1. What is your attitude toward life? Do you agree with the statement, "Life sucks, then you die"?
2. Do more managers have Theory X or Theory Y attitudes today? Be sure to give examples to back up your statements.
3. Do you really believe that you can get better results with people using the Pygmalion effect—being positive and encouraging, rather than negative and threatening? Be sure to give examples to back up your statements.
4. Do you believe that most organizations really try to provide employees with job satisfaction? Give examples of what firms do to increase job satisfaction.
5. Is having a positive self-concept really all that important?
6. What is your view of spirituality in the workplace?
7. Do most people behave ethically at work, or do they lie, cheat, and steal?
8. Which method of justifying unethical behavior do you think is most commonly used?

CASE / / / Coca-Cola: More Than Just a Soft Drink

The Coca-Cola Company is the world's largest beverage company, refreshing consumers with more than 500 sparkling and still brands. Led by Coca-Cola, the world's most valuable brand, the company's portfolio features $14 billion brands including Diet Coke, Fanta, Sprite, Coca-Cola Zero, vitaminwater, Powerade, Minute Maid, Simply, and Georgia. Globally, it is the number one provider of beverages. Through the world's largest beverage distribution system, consumers in more than 200 countries enjoy its beverages at a rate of 1.7 billion servings a day. With an enduring commitment to building sustainable communities, the company is focused on initiatives that reduce its environmental footprint; support active, healthy living; create a safe, inclusive work environment for its associates; and enhance the economic development of the communities where it operates.[76]

Coke's strategic vision is the cornerstone of the firm and sets the tone for the business and work environment, as noted by Muhtar Kent, president and CEO of the firm. Coke is "committed to serving and supporting sustainable communities because our business succeeds where communities thrive. Together with our bottling partners, our business partners, and members of the communities where we operate, The Coca-Cola Company works to identify and address existing and emerging social and environmental issues, as well as potential solutions."[77]

According to Kent, this strategic vision is incorporated in the manifest for growth. "The Coca-Cola Company is on a journey. It is a bold journey, inspired by our simple desire for sustainable growth, and fueled by our deep conviction that collectively we can create anything we desire. . . . The goals are simple: We will reinvigorate growth for our Company, and we will inspire our people. Likewise, our strategy is simple: We will accomplish our goals by building a portfolio of branded beverages, anchored in our icon, Coca-Cola,® and by enabling superior market execution globally and locally—aligning and leveraging the power of our global network."[78]

According to the company's Web site,

> Coke is built around two core assets, its brand and its people. That's what makes working here so special. We believe that work is more than a place you go every day. It should be a place of exploration, creativity, professional growth and interpersonal relationships. It's about being inspired and motivated to achieve extraordinary things. We want our people to take pride in their work and in building brands others love. After all, it's the combined talents, skills, knowledge, experience and passion of our people that make us who we are.
>
> Nearly 140,000 associates around the world live and work in the markets we serve—more than 86 percent of them outside the U.S. In this geographically diverse environment, we learn from each market and share those learnings quickly. As a result, our Company culture is ever more collaborative. From beverage concept and development to merchandising, our associates are sharing ideas across departments and markets in new ways. Consequently, our associates are increasingly enthusiastic about their work and inspired to turn plans into action.[79]

According to Kent, "Ultimately, this journey will be propelled by unleashing the collective genius of our organization that will make sustainable growth a reality. We take this journey because it is in our very nature to innovate, create and excel. . . . It is who we are."[80]

Go to the Internet: For more information on Muhtar Kent and an update on the information provided in this case, do a name search on the Internet and visit www.coca-cola.com.

Support your answers to the following questions with specific information from the case and text, or other information you get from the Web or other sources.

1. What seems to be Muhtar Kent's attitude toward Coca-Cola's local communities, its brands, and its people?

2. Using Theory X, Theory Y, describe Kent's management attitude.

3. What determinants of job satisfaction are addressed by Kent in his description of the firm?

4. Does Coca-Cola help develop employees' self-concept?

5. How are values illustrated in this case?

6. Coca-Cola and Kent's vision statement and manifest for growth do not seem to directly address the issue of spirituality in the workplace. What guidelines could he and Coca-Cola employ to rework these statements to address the issue of workplace spirituality?

7. Coca-Cola is a multinational corporation (MNC). What level of moral development and global corporate social responsibility (GCSR) do Coca-Cola and Kent seem to be operating on?

Cumulative Questions

8. How does Coca-Cola's vision statement and manifest for growth deal with the issue of human relations (Chapter 1)?

9. Is Coca-Cola a learning organization (Chapter 2)?

Case Exercise and Role-Play

Preparation: Coca-Cola's success is based on its brand and its people. Assume you are the CEO. As an individual or group, prepare a 2- to 3-minute motivational speech reminding employees of the importance of their attitude and how Coke helps create job satisfaction. Encourage employees to continue to grow Coke brand sales. Be sure to use the text information and answers to the case questions when developing your speech.

Role-Play: Individuals (or one representative of a group) present their motivational talk to the class, followed by a question-and-answer period.

OBJECTIVE CASE /// Job Satisfaction

Kathy Barns was the first woman hired by Kelly Construction Co. to perform a "man's job." When Kathy was interviewed for the job by Jean Rossi, the personnel director, Kathy was excited to get the opportunity to prove a woman could do a man's job. During the first month Kathy never missed a day. However, in the second month she missed four days of work, and by the end of the month she came to tell Rossi she was quitting. Jean was surprised and wanted to find out what happened, so she asked Kathy some questions.

JEAN: How did your orientation for the job go?

KATHY: Well, the boss, Jack, started things off by telling me that he was against my being hired. He told me that a woman couldn't do the job and that I would not last very long.

JEAN: Did Jack teach you the job?

KATHY: He taught me the different parts of the job by beginning with a statement about how difficult it was. Jack made comments like "I'm watching you—don't mess up." He was constantly looking over my shoulder waiting for me to make a mistake, and when I did, he would give me the old "I told you so" speech. A couple of the guys gave me some help, but for the most part they ignored me.

JEAN: Is your job performance satisfactory?

KATHY: It's not as good as it could be, but it cannot be too bad because Jack hasn't fired me. I enjoy the work when Jack leaves me alone, and I do better work, too. But it seems he's always around.

JEAN: Are you really sure you want to quit?

KATHY: *Pauses and thinks.*

Answer the following questions. Then in the space between questions, state why you selected that answer.

_______ 1. Jack had Theory _______ attitudes toward Kathy.

a. X *b.* Y

_______ 2. Kathy started at Kelly with a _______ job attitude.

a. positive *b.* negative

_______ 3. Most likely there _______ a relationship between Kathy's job satisfaction and her absenteeism.

a. is *b.* is not

_______ 4. The major determinant of Kathy's job dissatisfaction is:

a. the work itself *c.* growth and mobility *e.* coworkers

b. pay *d.* supervision *f.* general work attitude

_______ 5. Job satisfaction _______ the major reason for Kathy's performance being below her potential.

a. is *b.* is not

_______ 6. Jack's behavior contributed to the _______ of Kathy's self-efficacy.

a. development *b.* deterioration

_______ 7. The attribution cause for Kathy's lack of success at Kelly is:

a. internal *b.* external

_______ 8. There _______ a relationship between Kathy's job satisfaction and her quitting (turnover).

a. is *b.* is not

_______ 9. Kathy's _______ changed over the two months at Kelly Construction.

a. attitude *b.* job satisfaction *c.* values

_______ 10. This case best illustrates:

a. Theory X *c.* Pygmalion effect *e.* self-fulfilling prophecy

b. value system *d.* self-efficacy

11. How could Jean have prevented this situation?

12. What would you do if you were in Kathy's situation?

Note: Jean's meeting with Kathy can be role-played in class.

/ / / SKILL-BUILDING EXERCISE 3-1 / / /

Self-Learning

In-Class Exercise (Individual and Group)

Objective: To better understand human behavior.

AACSB: The primary AACSB learning standard skills developed through this exercise are reflective thinking and self-management, analytic skills, and communication abilities.

Preparation: You should have completed Self-Assessment Exercises 3-1, 3-2, and 3-3 in this chapter.

Experience: You will share your self-learning in small groups to better understand your behavior and that of others.

Procedure 1 (5–15 minutes)
Break into groups of two or three members, and share the answers you feel comfortable sharing in Self-Assessment Exercises 3-1, 3-2, and/or 3-3. Do not pressure anyone to share anything that makes him or her uncomfortable. Focus on your similarities and differences and the reasons for them. Your instructor will tell you if you will be doing the sharing in the next section of this exercise.

Sharing: Volunteers state the similarities and differences within their group.

Conclusion: The instructor leads a class discussion and/or makes concluding remarks.

Application: What have I learned from this exercise? How will I use this knowledge in the future?

/ / / SKILL-BUILDING EXERCISE 3-2 / / /

Building a More Positive Self-Concept

Preparation (Individual and Group)

This may not be an easy exercise for you, but it could result in improving your self-concept, which has a major impact on your success in life. Below, follow the three-step plan for building a positive self-concept.

You may be asked to share your plan with a person of your choice in class. Your instructor should tell you if you will be asked to share during class. If you will share during class, do not include anything you do not wish to share. Write in the space provided, using additional pages if needed. Write a separate personal plan for yourself if you do not want to share it.

Step 1. Identify your strengths and areas for improvement.
What do I like about myself?

What can I do well? (Reflect on some of your accomplishments.)

What skills and abilities do I have to offer people and organizations?

What are the things about myself or behaviors that could be improved to help me build a more positive self-concept?

Step 2. Set goals and visualize them.

Based on your area(s) for improvement, write down some goals in a positive, affirmative format. Three to five goals are recommended as a start. Once you achieve them, go on to others.

For example:

1. I am positive and successful (not: I need to stop thinking/worrying about failure).
2. I enjoy listening to others (not: I need to stop dominating the conversation).

Visualize yourself achieving your goals. For example, imagine yourself succeeding without worrying, or visualize having a conversation you know you will have, without dominating it.

Optional. If you have a negative attitude toward yourself or others—or you would like to improve your behavior with others (family, coworkers), things, or issues (disliking school or work)—try following the internationally known motivational speaker and trainer Zig Ziglar's system. Thousands of people have used this system successfully. This system can be used for changing personality traits as well.

Here are the steps to follow, with an example plan for a person who has a negative self-concept and also wants to be more sensitive to others. Use this example as a guide for developing your own plan.

1. *Self-concept.* Write down everything you like about yourself. List all your strengths. Then go on and list all your weaknesses. Get a good friend to help you.
2. *Make a clean new list, and using positive affirmations, write down all your strengths.* Example: "I am sensitive to others' needs."
3. *On another sheet of paper, again using positive affirmations, list all your weaknesses.* For example, don't write, "I need to lose weight." Write, "I am a slim (whatever you realistically can weigh in 30 days) pounds." Don't write, "I have to stop criticizing myself." Write, "I positively praise myself often every day." Write, "I have good communications skills," not "I am a weak communicator." The following list gives example affirmations for improving sensitivity to others. Note the repetition; you can use a thesaurus to help.

   I am sensitive to others.

   My behavior with others conveys my warmth for them.

   I convey my concern for others.

   My behavior conveys kindness toward others.

   My behavior helps others build their self-esteem.

   People find me easy to talk to.

   I give others my full attention.

   I patiently listen to others talk.

   I answer others in a polite manner.

   I answer questions and make comments with useful information.

   My comments to others help them feel good about themselves.

   I compliment others regularly.

4. *Practice.* Every morning and night for at least the next 30 days, look at yourself in the mirror and read your list of positive affirmations. Be sure to look at yourself between each affirmation as you read. Or record the list on a tape recorder and listen to it while looking at yourself in the mirror. If you are really motivated, you can repeat this step at other times of the day. Start with your areas for improvement. If it takes five minutes or more, don't bother with the list of your strengths. Or stop at five minutes; this exercise is effective in short sessions. Although miracles won't happen overnight, you may become more aware of your behavior in the first week. In the second or third week, you may become aware of yourself using new behavior successfully. You may still see some negatives, but the number will decrease in time as the positive increases.

   Psychological research has shown that if a person hears something believable repeated for 30 days, they will tend to believe it. Ziglar says that you cannot consistently perform in a manner that is inconsistent with the way you see yourself. So, as you listen to your positive affirmations, you will believe them, and you will behave in a manner that is consistent with your belief. Put simply, your behavior will change with your thoughts without a lot of hard work. For example, if you listen to the affirmation, "I am an honest person" (not, "I have to stop lying"), in time—without having to work at it—you will tell the truth. At first you may feel uncomfortable reading or listening to positive affirmations that you don't really believe you have. But keep looking at yourself in the mirror and reading or listening, and with time you will feel comfortable and believe it and live it.

   Are you thinking you don't need to improve, or that this method will not work? Yes, this system often does work. Zig Ziglar has trained thousands of satisfied people. I tried the system myself, and within two or three weeks, I could see improvement in my behavior. The question isn't, Will the system work for you? but rather, Will you work the system to improve?

5. *When you slip, and we all do, don't get down on yourself.* In the sensitivity-to-others example, if you are rude to someone and catch yourself, apologize and change to a positive tone. Effective leaders admit when they are wrong and apologize. If you have a hard time admitting you are wrong and saying you are sorry, at least be obviously nice so that the other person realizes you are saying you are sorry indirectly. Then forget about it and keep trying. Focus on your successes, not your slips. Don't let 10 good discussions be ruined by one insensitive comment. If you were a baseball player and got 9 out of 10 hits, you'd be the best in the world.

6. *Set another goal.* After 30 days, select a new topic, such as developing a positive attitude toward work or school, or trying a specific leadership style that you want to develop. You can also include more than one area to work on.

Step 3. Develop a plan and implement it.

For each of your goals, state what you will do to achieve it. What specific action will you take to improve your self-concept through changing your thoughts or behavior? Number your plans to correspond with your goals.

In-Class Exercise

Objective: To build a more positive self-concept.

AACSB: The primary AACSB learning standard skills developed through this exercise are reflective thinking and self-management and analytic skills.

Preparation: You should have completed the three-step action plan for building a positive self-concept on the preceding pages.

Experience: In groups of two, you will share your plan to build a more positive self-concept.

Procedure 1 (2–4 minutes)

Break into teams of two. You may make a group of three if you prefer. Try to work with someone with whom you feel comfortable sharing your plan.

Procedure 2 (10–20 minutes)

Using your preparation plan, share your answers one at a time. It is recommended that you both share on each step and question before proceeding to the next. The choice is yours, but be sure you get equal time. For example, one person states, "what I like about myself." The other person follows with his or her response. After both share, go on to cover "what I do well," and so on. During your sharing, you may offer each other helpful suggestions, but do so in a positive way; remember you are helping one another build a more positive self-concept. Avoid saying anything that could be considered a put-down.

Conclusion: The instructor may lead a class discussion and/or make concluding remarks.

Application (2–4 minutes): Will I implement my plan? If so, will I succeed at developing a more positive self-concept? What have I learned through this experience?

/ / / SKILL-BUILDING EXERCISE 3-3 / / /

Giving and Accepting Compliments

In-Class Exercise (Group)

Objective: To give and accept compliments as a means to improving self-concept.

AACSB: The primary AACSB learning standard skills developed through this exercise are analytic skills and communication abilities.

Procedure 1 (2 minutes)
Preparation: Recall that one of the human relations guidelines is to help others. One way to help others is to give them compliments that will help them develop and maintain a positive self-concept. Also, as stated in this chapter, never minimize compliments, but accept them with a thank you. This exercise is based on these two points.

Experience: In groups you will give and accept compliments.

Break into groups of four to six, preferably with people you know.

Procedure 2 (4–8 minutes)
Each person in the group thinks of a sincere, positive compliment to give to each group member (for instance, make a comment on why you like the person). When everyone is ready, one person volunteers to receive first. All the other members give that person a compliment. Proceed until everyone, one at a time, has received a compliment from everyone else.

Procedure 3 (3–6 minutes)
Each group discusses the following questions:

1. How did it feel to receive the compliments? Were you tempted to—or did you—minimize a compliment?

2. How do you feel about people who give you compliments versus those who give you criticism? Is there a difference in your human relations between people in these two groups?

3. How did it feel to give the compliments?

4. What is the value of giving compliments?

5. Will you make an effort to compliment yourself and others?

Conclusion: The instructor may lead a class discussion and/or make concluding remarks. In Chapter 8, Skill-Building Exercise 8-2, Giving Praise (page 251), you can develop the skill of giving compliments.

Application: Write out your answer to question 5 above as the application question.

/ / / SKILL-BUILDING EXERCISE 3-4 / / /

Ethics and Whistle-Blowing

In-Class Exercise (Individual and Group)

Objective: To better understand ethics and whistle-blowing.

AACSB: The primary AACSB learning standard skills developed through this exercise are reflective thinking and self-management, analytic skills, and communication abilities.

Preparation: You should have completed Self-Assessment Exercise 3-4, How Ethical Is Your Behavior?

Experience: You will share your answers to the questions below.

Procedure 1 (5 minutes)

Briefly answer the following questions related to Self-Assessment Exercise 3-4:

1. For "College" items 1 through 3, who is harmed and who benefits from these unethical behaviors?

2. For "Job" items 4 through 24, select the three (circle their numbers) that you consider the most severe unethical behavior. Who is harmed and who benefits by these unethical behaviors?

3. If you observed unethical behavior but didn't report it, why didn't you blow the whistle? If you did, why did you report the unethical behavior? What was the result?

4. As a manager, it is your responsibility to uphold ethical behavior. If you know employees are using unethical behavior, will you take action to enforce compliance with ethical standards?

5. What can you do to prevent unethical behavior?

6. As part of the class discussion, share the "Other Unethical Behavior" you have observed. If you didn't add any, try to do so until the time is up.

Procedure 2 (15–30 minutes)

Option A: Break into groups of five or six, and share your answers to the questions. The instructor will tell the group if they should select a spokesperson to report to the entire class.

Option B: The instructor leads a discussion in which students share their answers to the questions. (The instructor may begin by going over the statements and have students who have observed the behavior raise their hands.) Then the instructor will have them raise their hands if they reported the behavior.

Conclusion: The instructor may lead a class discussion and/or make concluding remarks.

Application (2–4 minutes): What did I learn from this exercise? How will I use this knowledge in the future?

Sharing: Volunteers give their answers to the application section.

/ / ANSWERS TO TRUE/FALSE QUESTIONS / /

1. F. Theory X attitudes are outdated and being replaced with Theory Y attitudes.
2. T.
3. F. Two-thirds of Americans would take the same job again and 90 percent are at least somewhat satisfied with their jobs.
4. T.
5. F. Self-efficacy is your belief in your ability to perform in a specific situation. The Pygmalion effect and self-fulfilling prophecy are more constant.
6. T.
7. F. This was not stated in the book, and it is not true.
8. F. Most people are on the conventional level of moral development.

CHAPTER 4

Time and Career Management

LEARNING OUTCOMES

After completing this chapter, you should be able to:

LO 4-1 Explain how to analyze your use of time with a time log.

LO 4-2 State the three priority determination questions and determine when an activity on the to-do list should be delegated or assigned a high, medium, or low priority.

LO 4-3 List the three steps in the time management system.

LO 4-4 Identify at least three time management techniques you presently do not use but will use in the future.

LO 4-5 Describe the four career stages.

LO 4-6 List the five steps in the career planning model.

LO 4-7 Explain at least three tips to get ahead that you can use to improve your chances of getting a job, raises, and promotions.

LO 4-8 Define the following 11 key terms (in order of appearance in the chapter):

time management	**time management steps**
time log	**career planning**
priority	**career development**
priority determination questions	**career planning model**
to-do list	**career path**
	job shock

/// Whitney and Shane were talking during lunch hour in a Friendly's Restaurant in Tampa, Florida. Whitney was complaining about all the tasks she had to get done. She had all kinds of deadlines to meet. Whitney was a nervous wreck as she listed the many tasks. After a while, Shane interrupted to say that he used to be in the same situation until he took a time management workshop that taught him to get more done in less time with better results. Shane gave Whitney the details so she could take the course. In return, Whitney told Shane about a career development course she took. It not only helped her to get the job she has now, but also to know what she wants to accomplish in the future.

Have you ever felt as though you have more to do than the time you have to do it in? Do you ever wonder about your career? If you answered yes to either of these two questions, this chapter can help you. ///

HOW TIME MANAGEMENT AND CAREER SKILLS AFFECT BEHAVIOR, HUMAN RELATIONS, AND PERFORMANCE

Some people may question whether time management belongs in a human relations textbook. It is here because one of the major reasons people and especially managers do not have better human relations is their lack of time.[1] If you manage your time better, you will have more time to spend developing effective human relations. Developing time management skills is also an effective way to better balance work–family life,[2] reduce stress (Chapter 2),[3] increase personal productivity,[4] and experience inner peace.[5] It is possible for you to gain control of your life by controlling your time. How well you manage your time will affect your career success.

WORK APPLICATION 4-1

Why are time management skills important? How can you benefit by using the time management information discussed in this chapter?

Many people are concerned about their careers,[6] especially in today's environment.[7] Career planning is not just about getting a job; it's also about continually developing yourself[8] so that you can advance throughout your career.[9] Time and career management skills lead to better behavior, more effective human relations, higher levels of performance, and career success.

TIME MANAGEMENT

The term **time management** *refers to techniques designed to enable people to get more done in less time with better results.* In this section, we examine ways to analyze your present use of time, a priority determination system, ways to use a time management system, and time management techniques.

Analyzing Time Use

Learning Outcome 4-1

Explain how to analyze your use of time with a time log.

The first step to successful time management is to determine current time use. People often do not realize how much time they waste until they analyze time use.[10] Anyone at a desk loses 2.1 hours of productivity every day owing to poor time management.[11] An analysis of how you use your time will indicate areas for improvement.

Time Log The **time log** *is a daily diary that tracks activities and enables a person to determine how time is used.* You use one time log for each day. See Exhibit 4.1 for an example. It is recommended that you keep track of your daily time use for one or two typical weeks. Make 5 to 10 copies of Exhibit 4.1; you may need to change the hours to match your working hours. Try to keep the time log with you throughout the day. Fill in each 15-minute time slot, if possible. Try not to go for longer than one hour without filling in the log. Each time shown represents 15 minutes of time. Beside each time write the activity or activities completed. For example, on the 8:15 line, record the activity or activities completed from 8:00 to 8:15.

Analyzing Time Logs After keeping time logs for 5 to 10 working days, you can analyze them by answering the following questions:

1. Review the time logs to determine how much time you are spending on your primary responsibilities. How do you spend most of your time?
2. Identify areas where you are spending too much time.[12]
3. Identify areas where you are not spending enough time.
4. Identify major interruptions that keep you from doing what you want to get done. How can you eliminate them?[13]
5. Identify tasks you are performing that you do not have to be involved with. If you are a manager, look for nonmanagement tasks. To whom can you delegate these tasks?[14]

EXHIBIT 4.1 | Time Log

Date ____________

8:00
8:15
8:30
8:45

9:00
9:15
9:30
9:45

10:00
10:15
10:30
10:45

11:00
11:15
11:30
11:45

12:00
12:15
12:30
12:45

1:00
1:15
1:30
1:45

2:00
2:15
2:30
2:45

3:00
3:15
3:30
3:45

4:00
4:15
4:30
4:45

5:00
5:15
5:30
5:45

6. How much time is controlled by your boss? How much time is controlled by your employees? How much time is controlled by others outside your department? How much time do you actually control? How can you gain more control of your own time?
7. Look for crisis situations. Were they caused by something you did or did not do? Do you have recurring crises? How can you plan to eliminate recurring crises?
8. Look for habits, patterns, and tendencies. Do they help or hurt you in getting the job done? How can you change them to your advantage?
9. List three to five of your biggest time wasters. What can you do to eliminate them?
10. Determine how you can manage your time more efficiently.

WORK APPLICATION 4-2

Identify your three biggest time wasters, preferably with the use of a time log. How can you cut down or eliminate these time wasters?

Multitasking As you analyze your time, are you finding that you try to do too many things at the same time—multitasking? Research has found that people who multitask are actually less efficient than those who focus on one "complex" project at a time.[15] The brain is not actually capable of doing two things at once. Think of it as a single-screen TV. You can't watch two shows at once, but you can flip back and forth, missing some of each show; the more shows you watch, the more you miss of each one. Time is lost when switching between tasks, and the time loss increases with the complexity of the task. Managing two tasks at once reduces the brainpower available for either task, and it increases stress. Multitasking decreases your ability to concentrate.[16] With things binging and bonging and tweeting at you, you don't think. You can save time by shutting off these interruptions and distractions.[17] Complete Self-Assessment Exercise 4-1 to determine if you are multitasking too much.

/// Self-Assessment Exercise 4-1 ///

Multitasking

Identify how frequently you experience each statement.

Not frequently				Frequently
1	2	3	4	5

_____ 1. I have a hard time paying attention; my mind wanders when I'm listening to someone or reading.

_____ 2. I have a hard time concentrating; I can't do just one work/homework task for an hour or longer.

_____ 3. I have short-term memory loss; I forget if I did something recently.

_____ 4. I'm easily bored, distracted, and interrupted while doing work/homework.

_____ 5. I continually check for text, phone, and e-mail messages and go online while doing work/homework.

Add up your score (5 to 25) and place it here _____. On the continuum below, mark the point that represents your total score.

Multitasking not an issue 1 - - - 5 - - - 10 - - - 15 - - - 20 - - - 25 Possible over-multitasking

The five statements are all warning signs of over-multitasking. However, other issues, such as fatigue, could also cause these signs. Can you improve your time management by cutting down on multitasking and focusing more on one task at a time? If you don't like to spend much time doing one thing or get bored easily, at least try to select a good stopping point so that when you return to a task, you don't lose too much time figuring out where you left off. You can also write notes to help you quickly get back to being productive at the task when you return to it.

The remainder of this section presents ideas to help you improve your time management.

Communication Skills
Refer to CS Question 1.

Priority Determination

At any given time, you face having to do many different tasks. One of the things that separates successful from unsuccessful people is their ability to do the important things later. Set only a few priorities.[18] Bill Gates said that Steve Jobs had the ability to focus on a few

Learning Outcome 4-2

State the three priority determination questions and determine when an activity on the to-do list should be delegated or assigned a high, medium, or low priority.

things that were really important, leading to Apple's success.[19] A **priority** *is the preference given to one activity over other activities.*

Tasks that you must get done should be placed on a to-do list and then prioritized, ranking the order of performance.[20] According to Peter Drucker, a few people seem to do an incredible number of things; however, their impressive versatility is based mainly on doing one thing at a time.

Priority Determination Questions Set priorities[21] by answering three priority determination questions. The three questions are:[22]

1. Do I need to be personally involved because of my unique knowledge or skills?
2. Is the task within my major area of responsibility or will it affect the performance or finances of my department? Managers must oversee the performance of their departments and keep the finances in line with the budget.
3. When is the deadline? Is quick action needed? Should I work on this activity right now, or can it wait? Time is a relative term. In one situation, taking months or even a year may be considered quick action, while in another situation a matter of minutes may be considered quick action.

To summarize, **priority determination questions** *ask (1) Do I need to be personally involved? (2) Is the task my responsibility or will it affect the performance or finances of my department? and (3) Is quick action needed?*

Assigning Priorities Based on the answers to the three priority determination questions, a manager can delegate a task or assign it a high, medium, or low priority.

Delegate (D) The task is delegated if the answer to question 1, Do I need to be personally involved?, is no. If the answer to question 1 is no, it is not necessary to answer questions 2 and 3 because a priority has not been assigned to the task. However, planning the delegation and delegating the task are prioritized.

High (H) Priority A high priority is assigned if you answer yes to all three questions. You need to be involved, it is your major responsibility, and quick action is needed.

Medium (M) Priority A medium priority is assigned if you answer yes to question 1 (you need to be involved) but no to either question 2 (it is not your major responsibility) or question 3 (quick action is not needed; it can wait).

Low (L) Priority A low priority is assigned if you answer yes to question 1 (you need to be involved) but no to both questions 2 and 3. It is not your major responsibility, and quick action is not needed.

WORK APPLICATION 4-3

Identify at least three high priorities related to your education.

The To-Do List The three priority determination questions are on the to-do list in Exhibit 4.2 and also appear in Application Situation 4-1 to help you develop your ability to assign priorities. The **to-do list** *is the written list of activities the individual has to complete.* Feel free to make copies of Exhibit 4.2 and use it on the job. In summary, decide what is really important, put it on your list, and find the time to do it.

WORK APPLICATION 4-4

List at least five activities on your to-do list. Based on the three priority determination questions, prioritize each activity as H, M, L, or D.

When using the to-do list, write each activity you have to accomplish on one or more lines and assign a priority to it. Remember that priorities may change several times during the day as a result of unexpected tasks that must be added to your to-do list. Look at the high (H) priority activities and start by performing the most important one. When it's done, cross it off and select the next, until all high-priority activities are done. Then do the same with the medium (M) priorities, then the low (L) priorities. Be sure to update the priorities with your boss.[23] As deadlines come nearer or get changed, priorities will change.[24] With time, low priorities often become high priorities.

EXHIBIT 4.2 | To-Do List

D Delegate—no to 1
H High priority—yes to all three questions (YYY)
M Medium priority—yes to 1 and 2 or 3 (YYN or YNY)
L Low priority—yes to 1, no to 2 and 3 (YNN)

Activity	1 Involvement Needed?	2 Responsibility/ Performance/ Finances?	3 Quick Action/ Deadline?	Time Needed?	Priority

Source: Adapted from Harbridge House Training Materials (Boston).

APPLICATION SITUATIONS / / /

Prioritizing To-Do List Activities AS 4-1

Prioritize the following 10 activities on the to-do list of a supervisor of a production department in a large company.

Priority Determination	Questions 1	2	3		
D Delegate—no to question 1 **H** High priority—yes to all three questions (YYY) **M** Medium priority—yes to 1 and 2 or 3 (YYN or YNY) **L** Low priority—yes to 1, no to 2 and 3 (YNN)	Do I Need to Be Involved?	Is It My Responsibility/ Performance/Finances?	Is Quick Action Needed?	Deadline?	Priority
Activity					
1. Chen, the sales manager, told you that three customers stopped doing business with the company because your products have decreased in quality.					
2. Your secretary, Rita, told you that there is a salesperson waiting to see you. He does not have an appointment. You don't do any purchasing.					
3. Jan, a vice president, wants to see you to discuss a new product to be introduced in one month.					
4. Chen, the sales manager, sent you a memo stating that the sales forecast was incorrect. Sales are expected to increase by 20 percent starting next month. Inventories are as scheduled.					
5. Dan, the personnel director, sent you a memo informing you that one of your employees has resigned. Your turnover rate is one of the highest in the company.					
6. Rita told you that a John Smith called while you were out. He asked you to return his call, but wouldn't state why he was calling. You don't know who he is or what he wants.					
7. Sherise, one of your best workers, wants an appointment to tell you about a situation that happened in the shop.					
8. Chen called and asked you to meet with him and a prospective customer for your product. The customer wants to meet you.					
9. Tom, your boss, called and said he wants to see you about the decrease in the quality of your product.					
10. In the mail you got a note from Frank, the president of your company, and an article from *The Wall Street Journal.* The note said FYI (for your information).					

Source: Adapted from Harbridge House Training Materials (Boston).

Time Management System

Learning Outcome 4-3

List the three steps in the time management system.

The problem you face is not a shortage of time—we all have the same 24 hours a day—but how to use your time to manage important activities.[25] Experts say that many people waste 2 hours a day.[26]

The time management system that is presented in this section has a proven record of success with thousands of managers. It can also be used by nonmanagers and students. You should try it for three weeks. After that time, you may adjust it to meet your own needs.

The four major parts to the time management system are priorities, objectives, plans, and schedules:

- *Priorities.* Setting priorities on a to-do list helps increase performance.[27]
- *Objectives.* Objectives state *what* we want to accomplish within a given period of time. Set objectives following the guidelines stated in Chapter 8.
- *Plans.* Plans state *how* you will achieve your objectives. They list the necessary activities to be performed.[28]
- *Schedules.* Schedules state *when* the activities planned will be carried out. You should schedule each workday. [29]

Time management techniques all boil down to making a plan and sticking to it as much as possible. The **time management steps** *are as follows: step (1) plan each week, step (2) schedule each week, and step (3) schedule each day.*

Step 1: Plan Each Week On the last day of each week, plan the coming week. Do this every week. Using your to-do list and the previous week's plan and departmental objectives, fill in the weekly planning sheet (see Exhibit 4.3). Start by listing the objectives you want to accomplish during the week. The objectives should not be routine tasks you perform weekly or daily. For example, if an employee's annual review is coming due, plan for it. Planning too much becomes frustrating when you cannot get it all done. On the other hand, if you do not plan enough activities, you will end up wasting time.

Step 2: Schedule Each Week Scheduling your week gets you organized to achieve your important objectives. You may schedule the week at the same time you plan it, or after, whichever you prefer. Planning and scheduling the week should take about 30 minutes. See Exhibit 4.4 for a weekly schedule. Make copies of Exhibits 4.3 and 4.4 for use on the job. When scheduling your plans for the week, select times when you do not have other time commitments, such as meetings. Schedule around 65 percent of your available weekly and daily time for unexpected events, but avoid unnecessary interruptions and distractions. If you turn off digitals (text, phone, e-mail, Internet) and check them only every couple of hours, you will be surprised at how much you can get done.[30] With practice, you will perfect weekly planning and scheduling. Steven Covey says, *The key to success is not to prioritize your schedule, but to schedule your priorities weekly and daily.*

Step 3: Schedule Each Day At the end of each day, you should schedule the next day. Or you can begin each day by scheduling it. This should take 15 minutes or less.[31] Using your plan and schedule for the week, and your to-do list, schedule each day on the form in Exhibit 4.5. Make copies of it as needed on the job.

Begin by scheduling the activities over which you have no control, such as meetings you must attend, and be punctual.[32] But don't forget to leave time for unexpected events.However, don't procrastinate; schedule the task and just do it.[33] And again, turn off your digitals.[34]

Schedule your high-priority items during your prime time. Prime time is the period of time when you perform at your best. For most people this time is early in the morning. Determine your prime time and schedule the tasks that need your full attention then. Do routine things, like checking your mail, during non-prime-time hours, after high-priority items are done.

EXHIBIT 4.3 | Weekly Planning Sheet

Plan for the week of ___________________________

Objectives: (What is to be done, by when) (To + action verb + singular behavior result + target date [Chapter 8, Exhibit 8.6, page 256])

Activities	Priority	Time Needed	Day to Schedule
Total time for the week			

EXHIBIT 4.4 | Weekly Schedule

Schedule for the week of ______________

	Monday	**Tuesday**	**Wednesday**	**Thursday**	**Friday**
8:00 8:15 8:30 8:45					
9:00 9:15 9:30 9:45					
10:00 10:15 10:30 10:45					
11:00 11:15 11:30 11:45					
12:00 12:15 12:30 12:45					
1:00 1:15 1:30 1:45					
2:00 2:15 2:30 2:45					
3:00 3:15 3:30 3:45					
4:00 4:15 4:30 4:45					
5:00 5:15 5:30 5:45					

EXHIBIT 4.5 | Daily Schedule

Day ____________________ **Date** ____________________

8:00	
8:15	
8:30	
8:45	
9:00	
9:15	
9:30	
9:45	
10:00	
10:15	
10:30	
10:45	
11:00	
11:15	
11:30	
11:45	
12:00	
12:15	
12:30	
12:45	
1:00	
1:15	
1:30	
1:45	
2:00	
2:15	
2:30	
2:45	
3:00	
3:15	
3:30	
3:45	
4:00	
4:15	
4:30	
4:45	
5:00	
5:15	
5:30	
5:45	

Skill-Building Exercise 4-1 develops this skill.

Communication Skills Refer to CS Question 2.

Do not perform an unscheduled task before a scheduled task without prioritizing it first. If you are working on a high-priority item and a medium-priority item is brought to you, let it wait. Often, the so-called urgent things can wait.

Forms similar to Exhibits 4.1 to 4.5 can be purchased in pad, book, computerized, and Web versions. Cell phones are also popular time management tools. In addition, you may copy the exhibits in the text for your own use.

APPLICATION SITUATIONS / / /

Time Management AS 4-2

Match each statement with its part in the time management system.

A. Priorities
B. Objectives
C. Plans
D. Weekly schedule
E. Daily schedule

_______ 11. "I set up my appointments for May 5."

_______ 12. "I know what I want to accomplish."

_______ 13. "I've decided how to get the work done."

_______ 14. "I know my major responsibilities."

_______ 15. "I've planned my week; now I'm going to . . ."

Learning Outcome 4-4

Identify at least three time management techniques you presently do not use but will use in the future.

Time Management Techniques

Self-Assessment Exercise 4-2 includes 68 time management techniques. They include major time wasters and ways to overcome them. Complete the exercise to determine which techniques you presently use and techniques that can help you get more done in less time with better results. Review and prioritize the items in the "Should" column. Select at least your top priority item now to work on each week. Write it on your to-do list, and schedule it, if appropriate. Once you have completed the "Should" column, do the same with the items in the "Could" and "Do" columns. Then review the "N/A" ("not applicable") column items to be sure they do not apply.

/ / / Self-Assessment Exercise 4-2 / / /

Time Management Techniques

This list of 68 ideas can be used to improve your time management skills. Check off the appropriate box for each item.

(1) I *should* do this.
(2) I *could* do this.
(3) I *do* this now.
(4) *Does not apply* to me.

Planning and Controlling	(1) Should	(2) Could	(3) Do	(4) N/A
1. Set objectives—long- and short-term.				
2. Plan your week, how you will achieve your objectives.				

/// Self-Assessment Exercise 4-2 /// (*continued*)

	(1) Should	(2) Could	(3) Do	(4) N/A
3. Use a to-do list; write all assignments on it.				
4. Prioritize the items on your to-do list. Do the important things rather than urgent things.				
5. Get an early, productive start on your top-priority items.				
6. During your best working hours—prime time—do only high-priority items.				
7. Don't spend time performing unproductive activities to avoid or escape job-related anxiety. It doesn't really work.				
8. Throughout the day ask yourself, "Should I be doing this now?"				
9. Plan before you act.				
10. Plan for recurring crises, and plan to eliminate crises.				
11. Make decisions. It is better to make a wrong decision than none at all.				
12. Have a schedule for the day. Don't let your day be planned by the unexpected.				
13. Schedule the next day before you leave work.				
14 Schedule unpleasant or difficult tasks during prime time.				
15. Schedule enough time to do the job right the first time. Don't be too optimistic on the length of time to do a job.				
16. Schedule a quiet hour(s). Be interrupted only by true emergencies. Have someone take a message, or ask people to call you back during scheduled unexpected event time.				
17. Establish a quiet time for the entire organization, department, or other group. The first hour of the day is usually the best time.				
18. Schedule large blocks of uninterrupted (emergencies only) time for projects, etc. If this doesn't work, hide somewhere.				
19. Break large (long) projects into parts (time periods).				
20. If you don't follow your schedule, ask the priority question (is the unscheduled event more important than the scheduled event?).				
21. Schedule a time for doing similar activities (e.g., make and return calls, write letters and memos).				
22. Keep your schedule flexible—allow _____ % of time for unexpected events.				
23. Schedule unexpected event time and answer mail; do routine things in between events.				
24. Ask people to see or call you during your scheduled unexpected event time only, unless it's an emergency.				
25. If staff members ask to see you—"got a minute?"—tell them you're busy and ask if it can wait until X o'clock (scheduled unexpected time).				
26. Set a schedule time, agenda, and time limit for all visitors, and keep on topic.				
27. Control your time. Cut down on the time controlled by the boss, the organization, and your subordinates.				
Organizing				
28. Keep a clean desk.				
29. Rearrange your desk for increased productivity.				
30. All non-work-related or distracting objects should be removed from your desk.				
31. Do one task at a time.				
32. With paperwork, make a decision at once. Don't read it again later and decide.				
33. Keep files well arranged and labeled.				

/// Self-Assessment Exercise 4-2 /// (*continued*)

	(1) Should	(2) Could	(3) Do	(4) N/A
34. Have an active and inactive file section.				
35. If you file an item, put a destruction date on it.				
36. Call rather than write, when appropriate.				
37. Have someone else (delegate) write letters, memos, etc.				
38. Dictate rather than write letters, memos, etc.				
39. Use form letters and/or form paragraphs.				
40. Answer letters or memos on the document itself.				
41. Have someone read things for you and summarize them for you.				
42. Divide reading requirements with others and share summaries.				
43. Have calls screened to be sure the right person handles them.				
44. Plan before calling. Have an agenda and all necessary information ready—take notes on the agenda.				
45. Ask people to call you back during your scheduled unexpected event time. Ask when is the best time to call them.				
46. Have a specific objective or purpose for every meeting.				
47. For meetings, invite only the necessary participants and keep them only for as long as they are needed.				
48. Always have an agenda for a meeting and stick to it. Start and end as scheduled.				
49. Conclude each meeting with a summary, and get a commitment on who will do what by when.				
50. Call rather than visit, if possible.				
51. Set objectives for travel. List everyone you will meet with. Send them agendas and have a file folder for each person with all necessary data for your meeting.				
52. Combine and/or modify activities to save time.				
Leadership and Staffing				
53. Set clear objectives for subordinates with accountability—give them feedback and evaluate results often.				
54. Use your subordinates' time well. Don't make them wait idly for decisions, instructions, or materials, or in meetings.				
55. Communicate well. Wait for a convenient time, rather than interrupting your subordinates and wasting their time.				
56. Train your subordinates. Don't do their work for them.				
57. Delegate activities in which you personally do not need to be involved.				
58. Delegate nonmanagement functions.				
59. Set deadlines when delegating.				
60. Set deadlines that are earlier than the actual deadline.				
61. Use the input of your staff. Don't reinvent the wheel.				
62. Teach time management skills to your subordinates.				
63. Don't procrastinate; do it.				
64. Don't be a perfectionist; define acceptable and stop there.				
65. Learn to stay calm. Getting emotional only causes more problems.				
66. Reduce socializing without causing antisociality.				
67. Identify your time wasters and work to minimize them.				
68. If there are other ideas you have that are not listed above, add them here.				

Communication Skills
Refer to CS Question 3.

In the opening case, Whitney could benefit from implementing the time management system and techniques presented here.

CAREER MANAGEMENT

WORK APPLICATION 4-5

From the 68 time management techniques presented in Self-Assessment Exercise 4-2, list the three most important ones you should be using. Explain how you will implement each technique.

You must take the responsibility for managing your career.[35] If you expect others to give you jobs, raises, and promotions, they may never come your way. In this section, you will learn how to manage your career successfully. The topics covered are career stages, career planning and development, getting a job, resumes, getting raises and promotions, global careers, and apparel and grooming.

Career Stages

Learning Outcome 4-5

Describe the four career stages.

Before planning your career, you must consider your career stage. As people get older, they have different career stage needs.

The 20s This is the time when you are just getting started. The challenge is to prove that you have what it takes to get the job done well—and on time. There is a lot of pressure to be the best. Women and minorities who seek advancement in a world dominated by men tend to feel personal pressure to try harder. You must develop the job skills needed to do the present job and to prepare for advancement. Initiative is needed. Young people often have unrealistic expectations and don't realize they need to work long, hard hours to get ahead.[36]

Today's young people are impatient and feel pressured to quickly advance up the corporate ladder (which is shaky at best and is better viewed as a pyramid,[37] or you may need to make lateral moves to advance.[38] So don't view your career as a linear progression. It is now common to work for many different organizations during a career.

The 30s This decade is the time when people develop expertise. In their 30s people often question their careers: Where am I going? Should I be here? Am I secure in my position? This time of doubt is especially tough on women, who must decide whether and how to combine children and careers.[39] Men especially feel trapped by financial demands and are frightened of changing careers even when they are not happy, because a change in career often requires a cut in pay to start at a lower position.

The 40s and 50s By age 45, most people have weathered a failure or two and know whether or not they have a shot at advancement. The majority don't make it and must accept that the race is over. In the past, people at this stage would settle into a secure job. However, many organizations have cut back. People in their 40s and 50s are sometimes forced to seek new employers or new careers. This can be difficult when trying to cope with growing older.

WORK APPLICATION 4-6

Which career stage are you in? Does the information stated about your career stage relate to your career? Explain.

The 60s and 70s At this stage, people begin to prepare for retirement, or may transition to part-time work. They can pass along what they have learned and provide continuity. People at this stage make good role models and mentors. Mentors can boost young careers. Although few employees are given such an opportunity, get a mentor if you can, and then return the favor. Mentoring others can help you as well.

Career Planning and Development

Learning Outcome 4-6

List the five steps in the career planning model.

There is a difference between career planning and career development. **Career planning** is *the process of setting career objectives and determining how to accomplish them.* **Career development** *is the process of gaining skill, experience, and education to achieve career objectives.* You must take responsibility for your career and develop a career plan.

Most colleges and large organizations offer career planning and development services. The career planning counselor's role is not to find people jobs but to help them set realistic

Skill-Building Exercise 4-2 develops this skill.

career objectives and plans. Many colleges also offer career placement services designed to help students find jobs. But it is the students' responsibility to obtain the job offer.

The career planning model can help you develop your own career plan. In preparation for Skill-Building Exercise 4-2, you will find working papers to guide you in the development of your own career plan. The **career planning model** *steps are these: step (1) self-assessment, step (2) career preferences and exploration, step (3) set career objectives, step (4) develop a plan, and step (5) control.*

Step 1: Self-Assessment The starting point in career planning is the self-assessment inventory. Who are you? What are your interests, values, needs, skills, and experience? What do you want to do during your career? If you don't have the answers to these questions, most college career services offer free or low-cost tests that can help.

Communication Skills
Refer to CS Question 4.

The key to career success is to determine the following: What do you do well? What do you enjoy doing? How do you get a job that combines your interests and skills? To be successful, you need to view yourself as successful. To be successful, develop some realistic short-term objectives and achieve them.

Step 2: Career Preferences and Exploration Based on your self-assessment, you must decide what you want from your job and career, and prioritize those wants. Career planning is not just a determination of what you want to do. It is also important to determine why you want to do these things. What motivates you? How much do you want it? What is your commitment to your career? Without the appropriate motivation and commitment to career objectives and plans, you will not be successful in attaining them.

Some of the things you should consider are (1) which industry you want to work for; (2) what size organization you want to work for; (3) what type of job(s) you want in your career, including which functional areas interest you (production/operations, marketing, finance, human resources, and so on) and, if you want to be a manager, what department(s) you want to manage; (4) what city, state, or country you want to work in (people who are willing to relocate often find more opportunities); and (5) how much income you expect to earn when you start your career, as well as 5 years and 10 years from then.

Once you have made these determinations, read about your primary career area. Conduct networking interviews. Talk to people in career planning and to people who hold the types of jobs you are interested in. People in these positions can help provide information that you can use in developing your career plan. Get their advice. Determine the requirements and qualifications you need to get a job in the career that interests you.[40] Getting an internship, fieldwork position, cooperative job, part-time job, and/or summer job in your field of interest can help you land the job you want after graduation. In the long run, it is often more profitable to take a job that pays less but gives you experience that will help you in your career progression.

Step 3: Set Career Objectives Set short- and long-range objectives using the guidelines from Chapter 8. Objectives should not simply be a listing for the next job(s). For example (assuming graduation from college in May 2014):

- To attain a sales position with a large insurance company by June 30, 2014.
- To attain a starting first-year income of $48,000.
- To attain my MBA by June 30, 2018.
- To become a sales manager in the insurance industry by June 30, 2020.
- To attain a salary of $65,000 by June 30, 2020.

Step 4: Develop a Plan Develop a plan that will enable you to attain your objectives. A college degree is becoming more important for developing skills and earning pay increases. This is where career development fits in. You must determine what skills, experience, and

EXHIBIT 4.6 | Career Planning Model

Step 1. Self-assessment.
Step 2. Career preferences and exploration.
Step 3. Set career objectives.
Step 4. Develop a plan.
Step 5. Control.

education you need to get where you want to go and plan to develop as needed. Talking to others can help you develop a career plan.

You should have a written career plan, but this does not mean that it cannot be changed. You should be open to unplanned opportunities and take advantage of them when it is in your best interest to do so.

WORK APPLICATION 4-7

What career development efforts are you making?

Step 5: Control It is your responsibility to achieve your objectives. You may have to take corrective action. Review your objectives, check your progress at least once a year, and change and develop new objectives and plans. Update your resume (to be discussed) at the same time.

Exhibit 4.6 lists the steps in the career planning model.

APPLICATION SITUATIONS / / /

Career Planning Steps AS 4-3

Match each statement with its step in the career planning model.

A. 1 B. 2 C. 3 D. 4 E. 5

_______ 16. "First, I have to get my degree; then I'll apply for a management trainee position with the major banks in the Midwest."

_______ 17. "I'm very good in math and computers."

_______ 18. "I want to be a partner in a CPA firm within seven years."

_______ 19. "Once a year I sit down and reassess who I am and where I'm going."

_______ 20. "I want to get into the co op program because I'm not sure what I want to do when I graduate. I figure it will help me decide."

Getting a Job

Communication Skills
Refer to CS Question 5.

It has been said that getting a good job is a job in itself. Unfortunately, jobs are harder to come by these days, and more firms are hiring independent contractors instead of full-time employees.[41] In attaining any good job, you need to develop a career plan; develop a resume and cover letter; conduct research; and prepare for the interview. Networking (Chapter 10) can be helpful at each stage.

Career Plan Interviewers are often turned off by candidates who have no idea of what they want in a job and career. On the other hand, they are usually impressed by candidates with realistic career plans. Having a good career plan gives you a competitive advantage over those who do not.

Resume and Cover Letter A recruiting executive at Xerox once said that the resume is about 40 percent of getting a job. The cover letter and resume are your introduction to the organization you wish to work for. If the resume is not neat, has errors, or contains mistakes, you may not get an interview.

The cover letter should be short—one page or less, as some recruiters don't even read it.[42] Its purpose is to introduce your resume and to request an interview. The standard cover letter states the job you are applying for and summarizes your qualifications. Be sure to talk about the firm and why you want to work for it. State how the company can benefit by hiring you, and end by asking for an interview.

The use of a resume for part-time and summer employment can also give a positive impression that makes you stand out from the competition. Give copies to friends and relatives who can help you get a job.

Communication Skills
Refer to CS Question 6.

Research Research is required to determine where to send your resume. Many colleges offer seminars in job search strategies. There are also a number of articles and books on the subject. Most people today find jobs through networking. Help-wanted ads in newspapers and online are common places to research jobs.

Once you land an interview, but before you go to it, you should research the organization. You want to determine as much about the organization as you can.[43] For example, you should know the products and/or services it offers, know about the industry and its trends, and know about the organization's profits and future plans; www.hoovers.com may have the company information. For organizations that are publicly owned, you can get an annual report that has much of this information; they are also online at most company Web sites. If you know people who work at the organization, talk to them about these issues.

You should also develop a list of questions you want to ask the interviewer during or at the end of the interview. Asking questions is a sign of intelligence and shows interest in the organization.[44] Two good areas to ask questions about are job responsibilities and career opportunities.

Communication Skills
Refer to CS Question 7.

Prepare for Questions You should also prepare to answer possible questions that you could be asked during a job interview (see Exhibit 4.7 for a list of common interview questions). If you are asked to state strengths and weaknesses, don't give direct weaknesses; they should be strengths in disguise. For example, don't say, "Sometimes I have trouble getting along with others." Instead say, "I'm very accomplishment-oriented, and sometimes I push people to work harder and cause some conflict."

EXHIBIT 4.7 | Common Interview Questions

Answering these questions prior to going to a job interview is good preparation that will help you get the job; written answers are better than verbal.

- How would you describe yourself?
- What two or three things are most important to you in your job and career?
- Why did you choose this job and career?
- What do you consider to be your greatest strengths and weaknesses?
- What have you learned from your mistakes?
- What would your last boss say about your work performance?
- What motivates you to go the extra mile on a project or job?
- What have you accomplished that shows your initiative and willingness to work?
- What two or three accomplishments have given you the most satisfaction? Why?
- Why should I hire you?
- What skills do you have?
- What makes you qualified for this position?
- In what ways do you think you can make a contribution to our company?
- Do you consider yourself a leader?
- How do you work under pressure?
- Why did you decide to seek a position in this company?
- What can you tell us about our company?
- What are your expectations regarding promotions and salary increases?
- Are you willing to travel and relocate?
- What are your long-range and short-range goals and objectives?
- What do you see yourself doing five years from now? Ten years from now?
- What do you expect to be earning in five years?

The Interview The interview is given the most weight in job decisions in most cases. It is vital to make a very positive first impression (Chapter 2). This means conveying a relaxed presence and an ability to convey accomplishments and to pique the interviewer's interest quickly. Be sure to follow job interview etiquette (Chapter 9). You also want to dress for success, which we discuss at the end of this chapter.

Many college career placement services offer workshops on how to interview for a job. Some offer mock interviews on camera that allow you to see how you conduct yourself during an interview. If this service is available, take advantage of it. During the interview, smile, be pleasant and agreeable, and offer compliments to interviewers.

After the interview, evaluate how well you did. Make some notes on what you did and did not do well. If you want the job, send a thank-you letter,[45] add anything you forgot to say, and state your interest in the job and the fact that you look forward to hearing from the interviewer. Enclose a copy of your resume.

If you did not get the job, ask the interviewer how you can improve. An honest answer can be helpful in preparation for future interviews.

WORK APPLICATION 4-8

Which specific idea(s) on getting a job do you plan to use?

Resumes Now we will get into the details of how to write a resume that will get you the job you have identified through your career plan and job search. To begin, complete Self-Assessment Exercise 4-3 to evaluate your resume, or resume knowledge.

/// Self-Assessment Exercise 4-3 ///

Your Resume Evaluation

Rate either your current resume or your resume knowledge for each question as:

Describes my resume 5 4 3 2 1 Doesn't describe my resume

_____ 1. My resume is based on a good career plan.

_____ 2. My resume is customized; it's not simply a copy of some format blueprint.

_____ 3. My resume does not include the word "I," and it has incomplete sentences.

_____ 4. My resume is customized for each individual job; one size doesn't fit all.

_____ 5. My resume is neat, attractive, and free of errors.

_____ 6. My resume is one page long, or two pages max for five or more years of experience.

_____ 7. My resume has digital/Internet capabilities.

_____ 8. My most important selling points are listed first and given the most space.

_____ 9. My resume states the specific job I'm applying for; it's not a general statement.

_____ 10. My job objective includes my personal qualities and skills with the job.

_____ 11. My resume has a qualification summary, or in 10–15 seconds, the recruiter can understand the job I want and that I am qualified to do the job.

_____ 12. My resume includes accomplishments that are quantified.

_____ 13. My resume includes concrete examples of skills, not just fluff words like *communication skills, team player, driven, organization,* and *interpersonal skills.*

_____ 14. My experience includes employment by months and years; plus employer, address, telephone, and supervisor, if they want a reference.

_____ 15. My experience that is not directly related to a job applied for focuses on transferable skills related to the job.

_____ Total. Add up the number of points and place it on the continuum below.

Effective resume 75 70 60 50 40 30 20 15 Ineffective resume

The higher your score, the better are the chances of getting the job you apply for.

EXHIBIT 4.8 | Sample Resume

John Smith
10 Oak Street
Springfield, MA 01118
413-748-3000 jsmith@aol.com

Objective

Competitive team player with excellent sales and communication skills seeks sales position.

Qualification Summary

Degree in business with a concentration in marketing. Marketing internship and marketing research experience. Sales and customer relations experience. Increased sales by 5 percent for employer. Developed communications, sales, and leadership skills through a variety of courses and jobs. Captain of the basketball team.

Education

BS Business Administration/ Marketing	Springfield College, Springfield, MA 01109. Business major with a concentration in marketing. 3.0 GPA. Graduation May 2014.
Courses	Sales—developed communication skills through three class presentations.
	Sales skills developed through 10 sales role-playing exercises.
	Marketing research—developed a questionnaire and conducted survey research for a local business, developing a customer profile to be used to target market sales promotions.
Marketing Internship	Big Y Supermarkets, 1050 Roosevelt Ave., Springfield, MA 01117, 413-745-2395. Supervisor: VP of Marketing John Jefferson. Worked directly for the VP on a variety of tasks/projects. Helped with the weekly newspaper ad inserts. Suggested a layout change that is being used. Spring Semester 2014.
Basketball Team	Member of the varsity basketball team for four years, captain senior year.

Experience

Salesperson	Eblens, 100 Cooley St., Chicopee, MA 01020, 413-534-0927. Sold clothing and footwear to a diverse set of customers. Employee of the month in July for the highest sales volume. Supervisor: Susan Miller. May to August 2013.
Landscaper	Eastern Landscaping, 10 Front St., East Longmeadow, MA 01876, 413-980-7527. Helped attract two new customers, a 5% increase. Interacted with customers and resolved complaints. Supervisor: Owner Thomas Shea. May to August 2011 and 2012.

Let's begin by stating some general guidelines to resume writing, followed by the major parts of the resume: contact information, objective, qualification summary, education, experience, and other possible additional parts. Although there is no one right way to write a resume, most resumes do include these parts. Also, note that the advice is from experts, but you can find people who do not agree with everything presented here, or there may be exceptions to these rules. While reading about the resume, refer to Exhibit 4.8, Sample Resume.

General Resume Guidelines It is fine to follow some resume format, but you have to customize your resume, and you should have a unique resume for each job you apply for. Resumes are written with incomplete sentences to keep them short and to the point, without stating "I." For people with less than five years of experience, a one-page resume is recommended, and two pages is the max. Today, many employers are using some form of digital/online resumes. Even if you send a print copy, many companies scan your resume. We will discuss the e-resume later in this section.

Your most important selling points should be the most visible. Thus, place the most job-relevant qualifications first and give them the most coverage. If you have professional full-time work experience related to the job you are applying for, list experience before education. If you are a recent college graduate with the degree as your major qualification, list education first.

Contact Information At the top of your resume, without a heading, list your name, address, telephone, and e-mail address where you can be reached to set up an interview. Note that your telephone message and e-mail address should be appropriate for business.

Also, be aware that many employers do a search on social networks (i.e., Facebook and MySpace) and if they find pictures of you not behaving well, undressed or dressed sexually, or engaging in drugs and drinking, they may not hire you. So you may want to do a search on yourself and delete any material that would be inappropriate for the job you are seeking.

Objective The objective—the job you are applying for—is critical because the rest of your resume needs to focus on your qualifications to do the job. Companies are matching people with specific skills to related jobs, so you need to clearly state the job that you are applying for, such as sales representative.

Be sure to include with your job objective your personal qualities and skills that the employer would want. For example, don't just write: Seeking sales position. Do write: Self-starting team player with excellent time management and communication skills seeks sales position. In the resume you can provide details of your qualities and skills. You can find out desired qualities and skills by reading job descriptions.

Qualification Summary Experts say recruiters spend only 10 to 15 seconds looking at each resume. So you need to state the job you want and that you can do the job—quickly. Start with your objective, followed by a qualification summary stating why you can do the job. The details of your qualifications should appear in the other parts of the resume.

If you have very limited job-related qualifications, you can skip this part of the resume.

Education Throughout your resume, you want to be sure to quantify your accomplishments, such as a good GPA, and include specific examples of personal qualities and skills, such as *driven, communicator,* and *team player.* Only list high school education if your resume does not fill a full page, or if you had some outstanding accomplishments related to the job you're applying for.

- State your degree received with major, minor/concentration, and the name and address of your college/university.
- Avoid a listing of college courses. Select a few that are directly relevant to the job you are applying for, and briefly identify knowledge and skills developed to help you on the job.
- Describe internships under the education section, stating knowledge, qualities, and skills you developed that can help you on the job you are applying for.
- List any activities, such as sports and clubs. Be sure to state any leadership positions, accomplishments, and any honors received. Describe job-related qualities and skills you developed through these activities, such as goal setting and teamwork skills.

Experience List any full-time, part-time, or summer jobs and any volunteer work.

- List job title, employer name, address, telephone number, and supervisor and/or other person, if you want the person contacted for a reference. State length of employment in both months and years.
- Describe knowledge, qualities, and skills you developed that can help you on the job you are applying for.
- State quantifiable accomplishments.[46]

Communication Skills
Refer to CS Question 8.

Other List any specific skills/training (computer programs), foreign language fluency, certifications (e.g., real estate), or talents that are related to the job you are applying for—using an appropriate heading. Again, focus on knowledge, qualities, and skills you developed that can help you on the job you are applying for.

WORK APPLICATION 4-9

Make a resume following the chapter guidelines. Bring your resume to class. Your professor may allow class time for you to see other students' resumes so that you can give and receive feedback.

The e-Resume: As you may know, many organizations are requesting that resumes be sent electronically via e-mail. Be sure to follow their instructions. Here are a few do's and don'ts of e-resumes: (1) Do develop your resume in a word processing file. However, don't send it as an attachment. (2) Save your resume in ASCII file format; use "save as text file" in your word processing document or save your resume as a PDF file. Your resume is now an e-resume. (3) Write your cover letter in the e-mail, and then copy your e-resume in the body of the e-mail. (4) Before sending it to an employer, send it to yourself so that you can see what it looks like. If it's a mess, fix it; then resend it to yourself until it reads and looks good. (5) Send it to the employer.

Learning Outcome 4-7

Explain at least three tips to get ahead that you can use to improve your chances of getting a job, raises, and promotions.

Getting Raises and Promotions

This section discusses tips to help you get ahead, career paths, preparation for getting a raise or promotion, asking for a raise or promotion, changing organizations, and job shock.

Tips to Help You Get Ahead Below are 10 ways to enhance your chances of career advancement:

- Be a top performer at your present job. If you are not successful at your present job, you are not a likely candidate for a raise or promotion.
- Finish assignments early. When your boss delegates a task, finish it before the deadline. This shows initiative.
- Volunteer for extra assignments and responsibility.[47] If you can handle additional work, you should get paid more, and you show your ability to take on a new position.
- Keep up with the latest technology. Request the opportunity for training. Take the time to learn to use the latest technology. Read publications that pertain to your field.
- Develop good human relations with the important people in the organization. (Follow the ideas throughout this book.)
- Know when to approach your boss.[48] Make requests when your boss is in a good mood; stay clear when the boss is in a bad mood unless you can help resolve the reason for the bad mood.
- Be polite. Say "thank you" both orally and in writing. Sending a thank you note keeps your name in front of people. Saying "please" and "thank you," "pardon me," and so on, shows concern for others.
- Never say anything negative about anyone. You never know who will find out what you've said. That "nobody" may be a good friend of an important person.
- Be approachable. Smile, and go out of your way to say hi to people. Take time to talk to people who want your help.

WORK APPLICATION 4-10

Which of the 10 tips for getting ahead need the most and the least conscious effort on your part? Explain your answer.

Career Paths A **career path** *is a sequence of job assignments that lead to more responsibility, with raises and promotions.* In organizations that have career paths, it is easier to develop a career plan, because in a sense that's what career paths are. In the fast-food industry, career paths are common. For example, management trainees start out by going to a formal training program for a few weeks; then they are assigned to a store as a trainee for six months; then they go to a different store as an assistant store manager for a year; then they become a store manager.

Preparation for Getting a Raise or Promotion It is very important to understand your job responsibilities and how you are evaluated by your boss, both formally and informally. Know your boss's expectations and exceed them, or at least meet them. Do what needs to be done to get a high performance appraisal. If you don't get a good performance appraisal, your chances of getting a raise or promotion will be hurt.

If you want a raise or promotion, it's your responsibility to prove that you deserve one; prepare your case.[49] The way to prove it is through self-documentation.

Keep a critical incidents file of every positive thing you do that is not generally required but that helps the organization. Keeping the boss appraised of your success on a regular basis is not bragging. Some of the things to include are:

- Any additional work you now perform.
- Times when you volunteered or cooperated to help other departments.
- Ideas you suggested that helped the organization.
- Any increases in the performance of your department or personal work.[50] Be specific. For example, productivity was up by 5 percent last year, absenteeism was down 10 percent last year, returns were down by 100 units this period, sales increased by $5,000 this quarter.
- If during the last performance appraisal you were told of areas that needed improvement, gather evidence to show how you have improved.

The first four suggestions also apply to getting a job—adding value.

If you plan to ask for a raise, state a specific amount. Check to find out what other people in similar jobs are getting for raises, and what other organizations pay their employees for similar jobs.[51] Check Web sites (www.salaryexpert.com, www.indeed.com/salary, www.salary.com, www.payscale.com) for market rates for salaries, posted by occupation. If your boss is a negotiator, start with a request for a higher raise than you expect to get. This way you can compromise and still get what you feel you deserve.

Asking for a Raise or Promotion Pay and benefits and advancement opportunity are important to career success.[52] When asking for a raise or promotion, don't catch your boss by surprise. The best time to ask is usually during the performance appraisal process. Present your critical incidents to help you get a good review and raise.

WORK APPLICATION 4-11

Which specific idea(s) do you plan to use to help you get raises and promotions?

Aspiration is an advancement-related trait. So requests for promotion should be known before a specific position is open. Your boss and the human resources or personnel department should know your career plan. Ask them where you stand, what the chances of promotion are, and when promotion may come. Have them help you prepare for a promotion.

Changing Organizations If you are satisfied that you are meeting your career plan with one organization, stay with it. If not, search out new opportunities elsewhere. Companies report difficulty finding well-qualified employees, so even with high unemployment, you may get a better job.[53]

If you are open to making a career move, have an updated resume ready and let your network of contacts know you are willing to make a move if the right opportunity comes along. Don't quit your job until you get another one, and around your boss and peers, don't publicize that you are looking for a new job.

In the opening case, Shane could benefit by developing a career plan, with a strong resume supporting his plans.

Job Shock Few jobs, if any, meet all expectations. **Job shock** *occurs when the employee's expectations are not met.* Expectations that the workplace is fair and that good work will always be recognized and rewarded are the leading cause of job shock. It is also common for employers to say, "Don't worry, we'll take care of you," and nothing happens, to your dismay. People also find part or many of their day-to-day tasks boring. Job shock has no quick cure. However, it is helpful to learn to cope with unsettling on-the-job realities by developing a "real-world" mindset. Talk to other people to find out if your situation is unique. If it's not, you probably have unrealistic job expectations. People often change jobs only to find the same frustrations they hoped to leave behind. Learn to realize that your unhappiness often springs from unrealistic job expectations. Developing a real-world mindset can help shield you from future shocks.

Through personal development, you can improve your human relations skills and time management skills and advance in your career. Good luck in doing so.

Global Careers

Globalization will affect your career in one way or another. You could end up like William Lussier by taking a job in Europe working for a Japanese company. To advance to the top of some firms, you must leave the country and work abroad for a year or more. You could take a job working in the United States for a foreign-owned company, for example, Shell (Netherlands), Nestlé (Switzerland), Nokia (Finland), Samsung (South Korea), or Columbia Records or Aiwa (Japan). Even if you work in America for a U.S. company, there is a good chance that you will work with employees from other countries here and with employees in other countries. You will likely deal with customers or suppliers from other countries. At the least, in the corporate world, you will compete with foreign companies for business. What type of global career do you want? Regardless of your career goals, possessing good human relations skills with a diversity of people is critical to your career success.

Apparel and Grooming

Communication Skills
Refer to CS Question 9.

Communication Skills
Refer to CS Question 10.

Apparel and grooming play a major role in making a good first impression because they help you get and keep a job.[54] They are also important in maintaining your image to help you get raises and promotions. Your clothes should be proper business apparel that is well coordinated, well tailored, and well maintained.[55] Your hair should be neat, trimmed, clean, and away from your face. Clean teeth and fingernails and fresh breath are expected. Avoid tattoos, body-piercing jewelry, and flashy jewelry that shows at work.[56]

There are hundreds of image consultants, and etiquette classes are popular.[57] Here are some generally agreed-on suggestions if you want to dress for a successful career in most organizations.

Dress for the Organization and Job Dress and groom like the people in the organization and specific job that you want. If you are not sure of the dress style, call or visit the organization before the job interview and find out, or at least possibly overdress, as suggested for job interviews. Once you are on the job, at least dress like your peers.

Job Interview As a general guide, during a job interview never underdress (such as jeans and T-shirts) and possibly overdress. As a college graduate seeking a professional job, wear a suit if managers do (tie for men), even if you will not need to wear one for the job. However, some companies, like Google, advise casual clothes. Do some research so you know what to wear.

Wear Quality Clothes Quality clothes project a quality image. Start with a quality suit for job interviews and important days at work, such as your first day, to develop a good first impression.[58] Look for sales when buying apparel, but don't buy a suit, or anything else you will wear to work, unless you really like it. If you feel good about the way you look, you will generally project a more positive self-image of confidence, which will help your career. So never buy anything you don't really like, even if it is on sale.

Dress and Groom Conservatively The latest dress fad is often inappropriate in the professional business setting. You may not be taken seriously if you exhibit faddish or flashy apparel and grooming. Don't dress like you are going to a nightclub, and don't show any underwear, such as bra straps; dress like you are going to work.[59]

Casual Dress What is considered casual business dress does vary, and because of poor choices on the part of some employees, many organizations have dress codes.[60] In most cases, casual doesn't include jeans and T-shirts for professional employees. Dress similar to others in the firm when you get the job.

Suggestions for Men Men may want to follow these guidelines:

- **Grooming.** If other men in the organization do not have facial hair, long hair, or wear earrings, you may consider shaving, getting a haircut, and leaving the earrings at home, at least for the job interview.
- **Suit.** The suit is still the most appropriate apparel in many organizations. A typical business suit is blue or gray, commonly dark, and stripes are acceptable. It is conservatively cut, and the width of the lapels and the pants are conservative in style.
- **Shirt.** The business shirt is a solid color and may have thin stripes, though not loud. The shirt has long sleeves, and they show about ½ inch from the suit sleeves when your arms are by your side.
- **Tie.** The wrong tie can hurt the quality image of your suit. The business tie is silk and usually has some conservative design—no animals, sayings, or cartoon characters. A tie tack is not needed, but a small, conservative one is acceptable.
- **Shoes.** Conservative dark leather business shoes, not sneakers, are worn with a suit. If in doubt about whether your shoes, or any other parts of your business attire, are properly conservative for business, ask a qualified sales rep.
- **Matching.** The suit, shirt, and tie all match. Be careful not to mix three sets of stripes. Generally, with a striped suit, wear a solid-color shirt. Match the color of the design in the tie to the suit and shirt. The color of the conservative belt (small, simple buckle) is the same color as your shoes. The color of the thin socks match the color of the pants (no heavy wool or white socks), and the socks are long enough so that your legs never show.[61]

Suggestions for Women Women may want to follow these guidelines:

- **Grooming and jewelry.** Wearing heavy makeup, such as very obvious eye shadow, dark outlined lips, and excessive-smelling perfumes, is not appropriate for business; don't wear it. Makeup should be subtle to the point that people don't think you are wearing any, and if worn, perfume should be light. Jewelry is simple and tasteful, never overdone. Avoid long, dangly earrings.[62]
- **Skirted suit.** The professional skirted suit is most appropriate; however, the conservative business dress with coordinated jacket is also acceptable. The skirt matches the blazer-cut jacket, and it reaches to the middle of the knee.[63] With proper business apparel, you are not trying to make a fashion statement. Women have more color choice, but black, dark blue, and gray are good for the first suit.
- **Blouse.** The business blouse is silk or cotton and free of frills, patterns, or unusual collars; it is not low-cut. Low necklines come across as seductive, and people usually assume the sexual innuendo is intentional. Do not show your cleavage, even at business socials, because the image set forth will be lasting. You want people talking about your accomplishments, not your figure. Solid colors are preferred, with a greater range of collars acceptable so long as they contrast and coordinate with the color of the suit. The top button should be open.

Communication Skills
Refer to CS Question 11.

- **No tie, scarf optional.** Don't dress like the guys.[64] It is generally agreed that a woman wearing a tie may appear as though she is trying to imitate male apparel. However, a conservative scarf is acceptable if you want to wear one.
- **Shoes.** Leather shoes match the suit and are conservative. Avoid open-toe shoes.[65] Shoes are not a fashion statement—they are comfortable, with a moderate heel; plain pumps are a good choice.
- **Matching, and attaché case.** All apparel matches. Neutral or skin-tone pantyhose are worn with your business suit. Businesswomen carry an attaché case, which replaces a purse or handbag, whenever feasible.

If you are thinking that it is unfair to be judged by your appearance rather than for who you really are and what you can do, you are correct. However, if you haven't found out yet, life is not always fair. Fair or not, in most organizations, your appearance will affect your career success. Remember that you are judged on your appearance and how you look affects the business's image and success.[66] However, your appearance is something over which you have control.

Remember that what you think about affects how you feel, and how you feel affects your behavior, human relations, and performance. So think happy, confident thoughts that you are a winner and you will act and be perceived as a winner and career success will follow. Complete Self-Assessment Exercise 4-4 to determine how your personality affects your time and career management.

/// Self-Assessment Exercise 4-4 ///

Personality and Time and Career Management

If you are *open to new experiences,* you probably are time-conscious and seek improvements. Being open and flexible, you may be good at career development.

If you have a high *agreeableness* personality, with a high need for affiliation, you may not be too concerned about time management and may freely give your time to others. However, you may need to work at saying no to requests that you don't have to do, so that you don't spread yourself too thin, you can get your own work done, and you can keep your stress level down. You also may not be too concerned about career advancement, because relationships tend to be more important to you than being a manager and climbing the corporate ladder.

If you scored high on *conscientiousness,* with a high need for achievement, you may tend to be time-conscious to achieve your goals by the dates you set. You are concerned about career success, but without a high surgency need, your concern may not be to advance in management.

If you have *surgency,* with a high need for power, you like to be in control and may need to work at trusting people and delegating to save time. You most likely have aspirations to climb the corporate ladder. But be sure to use ethical power and politics.

Action plan: Based on your personality, what specific things can you do to improve your time management and career skills?

____

____

As we bring this chapter to a close, you should realize that better *time management* leads to more effective behavior and performance, which in turn leaves more time to improve human relations. You should understand the importance of setting and sticking to priorities, how to set priorities using a to-do list, and how to use the time management system of planning your week, scheduling each week and each day. You should also be able to use time management techniques to get more done in less time with better results. How well you manage your time will affect your *career management* success. You should know how to develop a career plan, get a job, write a resume, get raises and promotions, and how to dress for success.

/ / / REVIEW / / /

The chapter review is organized to help you master the 8 learning outcomes for Chapter 4. First provide your own response to each learning outcome, and then check the summary provided to see how well you understand the material. Next, identify the final statement in each section as either true or false (T/F). Correct each false statement. Answers are given at the end of the chapter.

LO 4-1 Explain how to analyze your use of time with a time log.

To analyze your time, keep a time log for one or two typical weeks. Then answer the 10 questions in the text to analyze areas where your time can be spent more effectively.

Multitasking complex tasks is a good time management technique. T F

LO 4-2 State the three priority determination questions and determine when an activity on the to-do list should be delegated or assigned a high, medium, or low priority.

The three priority determination questions are: (1) Do I need to be personally involved? (2) Is the task my responsibility or will it affect the performance or finances of my department? and (3) Is quick action needed? An activity is high priority when you answer yes to all three questions. An activity is medium priority when you say yes to question 1 and no to either question 2 or 3. An activity is low priority when you say yes to question 1 and no to both questions 2 and 3. If the answer to question 1 is no, the activity should be delegated.

After answering the three priority determination questions, you rank order each task on your to-do list. T F

LO 4-3 List the three steps in the time management system.

Following the time management system, step (1) is to plan each week, step (2) is to schedule each week, and step (3) is to schedule each day.

Begin scheduling by listing activities over which you have no control, such as meetings. T F

LO 4-4 Identify at least three time management techniques you presently do not use but will use in the future.

Answers among students will vary.

Procrastination is a time waster that leads to stress. T F

LO 4-5 Describe the four career stages.

The four career stages are characterized as follows. The 20s are a time for proving one's ability as one gets started. The 30s involve the development of expertise and often some questioning of one's career path. By the 40s and 50s, most individuals have reached their highest level of advancement. In the 60s and 70s people begin to prepare for retirement.

Younger people face a greater threat of being laid off; with age comes job security. T F

LO 4-6 List the five steps in the career planning model.

The five steps in the career planning model are (1) self-assessment, (2) career preferences and exploration, (3) set career objectives, (4) develop a plan, and (5) control.

Following graduation from college is a good time to begin determining career preferences and exploration. T F

LO 4-7 Explain at least three tips to get ahead that you can use to improve your chances of getting a job, raises, and promotions.

Answers among students will vary.

When applying for a job, it is best not to specify a job title so that employers can match your talents to the jobs they have open. T F

LO 4-8 Define the following 11 key terms.

Select one or more methods: (1) fill in the missing key terms from memory; (2) match the key terms from the end of the review with their definitions; and/or (3) copy the key terms in order from the key terms list at the beginning of the chapter.

__________________ refers to techniques designed to enable people to get more done in less time with better results.

A(n) __________________ is a daily diary that tracks activities, enabling you to determine how your time is used.

__________________ is the preference given to one activity over other activities.

The __________________ ask (1) Do I need to be personally involved? (2) Is the task my responsibility or will it affect the performance or finances of my department? and (3) Is quick action needed?

A(n) __________________ is the written list of activities the individual has to complete.

The __________________ are as follows: step (1) plan each week, step (2) schedule each week, and step (3) schedule each day.

__________________ is the process of setting career objectives and determining how to accomplish them.

__________________ is the process of gaining skill, experience, and education to achieve career objectives.

The __________________ steps are these: step (1) self-assessment, step (2) career preferences and exploration, step (3) set career objectives, step (4) develop a plan, and step (5) control.

A(n) ________________________ is a sequence of job assignments that lead to more responsibility, with raises and promotions.

________________________ occurs when the employee's expectations are not met.

/ / / KEY TERMS / / /

/ / / COMMUNICATION SKILLS / / /

The following critical thinking questions can be used for class discussion and/or as written assignments to develop communication skills. Be sure to give complete explanations for all questions.

1. Based on your experience or observation, list ways in which people in organizations waste time. How can these time-wasting activities be cut back or eliminated?
2. It takes time to follow a time management system. Is the time taken worth the benefits? Will you use a time management system? Why or why not?
3. Are you a procrastinator? Are you a perfectionist? What are the pros and cons to being a procrastinator and perfectionist?
4. Have you done a career self-assessment? Was it easy or difficult? Why? Do you believe you could benefit from taking a career test? Why or why not?
5. Select a job you are interested in getting. Go online to one or more of the following Web sites to determine the compensation for the job you want: www.salaryexpert.com, www.indeed.com/salary, www.salary.com, www.payscale.com.
6. Do a job search for the job you are interested in getting. Go online to one or more of the following Web sites (or others related to your field) to find job opportunities: www.collegejournal.com (jobs and tips for new college grads); www.collegerecruiter.com (internships, and entry-level jobs); www.careerbuilder.com (jobs and advice); and www.monster.com (a listing of jobs).
7. From question 6, or based on other sources, select an organization you would like to work for. Research the company and develop some questions in preparation for a job interview.
8. Prepare or revise your resume, and then evaluate it using Self-Assessment Exercise 4-3. How did you score? Based on your assessment, revise your resume.
9. How would you feel about working for a domestic company and competing against foreign companies? How would you feel about working for a foreign company at home? How would you feel about working in another country and, if you are interested, what countries would you be willing to work in?
10. Will your apparel and grooming really affect your career success? Why or why not?
11. What are your thoughts on women showing cleavage at work? Should cleavage be covered or shown? Why? In your opinion, is a low neckline meant to be seductive, with intentional sexual innuendo?

CASE / / / Jay-Z the Rap Artist and Business Mogul: His Rise to the Top

Jay-Z is one of the most financially successful hip-hop artists and entrepreneurs in America today, with a net worth of over $450 million as of 2010. He has sold approximately 50 million albums worldwide. He holds the record for most number one albums by a solo artist on the Billboard 200.[67] Jay-Z also has had four number ones on the Billboard Hot 100.[68] He has won at least 13 Grammys so far for his musical work. Not bad for someone who grew up in a housing project in New York City, was abandoned by his father, never graduated from high school, and sold drugs on the streets. Just how did he overcome the odds? Jay-Z has shown a remarkable skill at career planning and development.

From early on, it seems Jay-Z, whose real name is Shawn Corey Carter, had a sense of his career preference. Carter was known as "Jazzy," a nickname that eventually developed into his stage name, "Jay-Z." As his mother, Gloria Carter, recalls, a young Jay-Z was the family entertainer. He was known to wake up his siblings at night banging out drum patterns on the kitchen table. Eventually, Ms. Carter bought him a boom box on his birthday, sparking his interest in music. He began rapping, writing lyrics, and following the music of many popular artists at the time. He found a way to combine his interests and skills into an entertainment career as a rap artist. Jay-Z has also established himself as an entrepreneur like his fellow hip-hop moguls and friends, Russell Simmons, Dr. Dre, and Sean "Diddy" Combs, who also have business holdings such as record companies and clothing lines.

Career success is more likely when one sets career objectives and develops plans for achieving them. In Jay-Z's case, he clearly understood the value of taking control of his career, rather than leaving it up to others. He made this his objective and set about to make it happen. In 2004 he became CEO of Def Jam. The music industry was going through some changes that threatened its sales and profits. The recording industry was rapidly losing revenue owing to two emerging trends—online piracy and illegal downloading of songs. Jay-Z acknowledged this threat in interviews, stating that much of his time was spent trying to discover alternative ways for the industry to make money. Artists who had signed under his label, most notably LL Cool J, complained of his lack of promotion for them. As Jay-Z pointed out, it made little sense to promote artists when their record sales were unlikely to make much money. In 2007, Jay-Z made the critical decision to step down as CEO. Unfortunately, he still was signed to Def Jam as an artist, meaning that he had to release his next album under Def Jam. In order to release himself from his Def Jam contract, Jay-Z had to pay Def Jam $5 million. He opted to release the album as a partnership with Roc Nation, his label, Live Nation (primarily a concert company), and Atlantic Records. Jay-Z explains his reasoning this way: "I wanted to have it back for a number of reasons, the most important being that it wasn't consistent with the type of business I planned for me or where I was positioning myself. Everything in my life I had taken charge of, but yet I was still an artist signed to a label. It seemed a little archaic in my plans."[69] This decision gave Jay-Z substantial control over his career, which is very rare for recording artists. According to some in the industry, his example represents a serious threat to the recording industry establishment.

Jay-Z has elevated multitasking to a new level. In addition to his musical accomplishments, he also co-owns the 40/40 Club, is part-owner of the NBA's New Jersey Nets, and is the creator of the clothing line Rocawear. He is the former CEO of Def Jam Recordings, one of the three founders of Roc-A-Fella Records, and the founder of Roc Nation. And as a leading entrepreneur within the hip-hop fashion industry, Jay-Z is single-handedly responsible for redirecting old-school hip-hop culture from oversized sweatshirts and baggy jeans to more refined dress shirts and tailored pants.[70] His rise from the projects to business success can be attributed to his unorthodox business style and entrepreneurial instincts. He is no doubt a very creative individual.

Underneath his on-stage Type A personality is a soft-spoken, considerate, respectful, and kind individual. On a visit to Africa a few years ago, Jay-Z became aware of the drought problem facing many African countries. Upon his return, the rapper pledged to raise awareness of and combat global water shortage during his world tour. The effort took place in partnership with the United Nations, as well as MTV, which produced a documentary titled *Diary of Jay-Z: Water for Life*, which aired in November 2006. Along with his friend, fellow rap artist Sean "Diddy" Combs, Jay-Z pledged $1 million to the American Red Cross's relief effort after Hurricane Katrina.

The boy from the projects married the girl from the suburbs. On April 4, 2008, Jay-Z married R&B superstar Beyoncé Knowles. According to the *New York Daily News,* the couple just had their first child (a baby girl) over the weekend of January 6–8, 2012. Jay-Z's career success so far is inspiring, especially given the obstacles he has had to overcome.

Go to the Internet: To learn more about Jay-Z and his business ventures, go to www.mtv.com/music/artist/jay_z/artist.jhtml or search his name on any search engine on the web.

Support your answers to the following questions with specific information from the case and text, or with information you get from the web or another source.

1. As mentioned in the case, Jay-Z wears several hats with respect to the business ventures he manages. What does this say about his time management skills?

2. Steps 1 and 2 in the career planning model are self-assessment and career preference and exploration. What in the case will support the possibility that Jay-Z implicitly did a self-assessment before launching into a music career as a rapper?

3. Assume you are Jay-Z. Based on the facts of the case, what are some specific objectives that you would set for yourself as part of your career plan?

4. Step 4 in the career planning model is to develop a plan that will enable you to attain your objectives. Cite an example in the case of how Jay-Z went about achieving his objective of taking control of his music career.

Cumulative Case Questions

5. In terms of locus of control (Chapter 2), do you think Jay-Z has an internal or external locus of control and why?

6. In your opinion, does Jay-Z have a sense of his self-concept (Chapter 3), and what do you think influenced it?

Case Exercise and Role-Play

Preparation: The case mentions that as a leading entrepreneur within the hip-hop fashion industry, Jay-Z is single-handedly responsible for redirecting old-school hip-hop culture from oversized sweatshirts and baggy jeans to more refined dress shirts and tailored pants.

In-Class Groups: Form pairs of students, one representing Jay-Z (the business executive) and the other representing a young hip-hop fan who still believes in wearing baggy jeans and T-shirt or team jersey shirt as a fashion statement.

Role-Play: Have each pair of students role-play a job interview scenario with the Jay-Z character charged with explaining to the interviewee the importance of appropriate apparel and grooming during an interview.

OBJECTIVE CASE /// Overworked?

In the following discussion, Iris is a middle manager and Peggy is a first-line supervisor who reports to her.

IRIS: Peggy, I've called you into my office to speak to you again about the late report.

PEGGY: I know it's late again, but I'm so busy getting the work out that I don't have time to do it. I'm always the first to arrive for work and the last to go home. I push hard to get the job done. Sometimes I end up redoing employees' work because it's not done properly. I often get headaches and stomach cramps from working so intensely.

IRIS: I know you do. Maybe the problem lies in your time management ability. What do you usually do each day?

PEGGY: Most of each day is spent putting out fires. My employees constantly need me to help them with their work. The days just seem to speed by. Other than putting out fires, I don't do much.

IRIS: So you can't get the reports done on time because of the number of fires. What is your approach to getting the reports done on time?

PEGGY: I just wait until there are no fires to put out; then I do them. Sometimes it's after the deadline.

IRIS: You are going to have to make some definite changes if you are going to be a successful supervisor. Do you enjoy being a supervisor?

PEGGY: For the most part I do. I think I might like to move up the ladder some day. But I like the hands-on stuff; I'm not too thrilled about doing paperwork.

IRIS: If you develop your time management skills, I believe you will find that you can get the job done on time with less stress. On Monday the company is offering a time management workshop. I took the course myself; it's excellent. It really helped me a lot when I was in your position, and still does today. It teaches you a three-step approach. Do you want to attend?

PEGGY: Yes, but what about the work in my department?

IRIS: I'll cover for you. On Tuesday, I want you to come see me first thing in the morning so that we can discuss what you learned and how you are going to apply it on the job.

Answer the following questions. Then in the space between questions, state why you selected that answer.

______ 1. Keeping a time log and using a to-do list would be helpful to Peggy.

a. true *b.* false

_______ 2. Peggy seems to be effective at setting priorities.

a. true *b.* false

_______ 3. Peggy seems to delegate _______ activities.

a. many *b.* few

_______ 4. Setting weekly objectives, plans, and schedules would help Peggy get the reports done on time.

a. true *b.* false

_______ 5. Peggy seems to have a Type _______ personality.

a. A *b.* B

_______ 6. Peggy appears to be in the _______ career stage.

a. 20s *c.* 40s and 50s

b. 30s *d.* 60s and 70s

_______ 7. Peggy has a career plan.

a. true *b.* false

_______ 8. The time management workshop is best classified as:

a. career planning *c.* career development

b. career planning model *d.* career path

_______ 9. From the case information, we can assume that this company has career paths.

a. true *b.* false

_______ 10. It appears that Peggy will be a good candidate for raises and promotions.

a. true *b.* false

_______ 11. How would you conduct the Tuesday morning session with Peggy?

/ / / SKILL-BUILDING EXERCISE 4-1 / / /

Time Management System

Preparation (Individual and Group)

Before using the time management system, you will find it helpful to keep a time log for one or two typical weeks. It is strongly recommended that you keep a time log and analyze it.

Note: For this exercise you will need copies of Exhibits 4.1, 4.3, 4.4, and 4.5. You may make photocopies of the exhibits or make your own copies on sheets of paper. While performing the steps below, refer to the text guidelines.

Step 1: Plan Your Week. Use Exhibit 4.3 to develop a plan for the rest of this week. Begin with today.

Step 2: Schedule Your Week. Use Exhibit 4.4 to schedule the rest of this week. Be sure to schedule a 30-minute period to plan and schedule next week, preferably on the last day of the week.

Step 3: Schedule Your Day. Schedule each day using Exhibit 4.5. Do this each day, at least until the class period for which this exercise is assigned.

Be sure to bring your plans and schedules to class.

In-Class Exercise

Objective: To understand how to use the time management system to enable you to get more done in less time with better results.

AACSB: The primary AACSB learning standard skills developed through this exercise are reflective thinking and self-management and analytic skills.

Preparation: You need your completed plans and schedules.

Experience: You will share and discuss your plans and schedules for the week and your daily schedules.

Procedure 1 (5–10 minutes)

Break into groups of five or six, and share and discuss your plans and schedules. Pass them around so that you and others can make comparisons. The comparisons serve as a guide to improving future plans and schedules.

Conclusion: The instructor leads a class discussion and/or makes concluding remarks.

Application (2–4 minutes): What did I learn from this experience? How will I use this knowledge in the future?

Sharing: Volunteers give their answers to the application section.

/ / / SKILL-BUILDING EXERCISE 4-2 / / /

Career Planning

Preparation (Individual and Group)

Answering the following questions will help you develop a career plan. Use additional paper if needed. Do not reveal anything about yourself that you prefer not to share with classmates during the in-class exercise.

Step 1: Self-Assessment

a. List two or three statements that answer the question, "Who am I?"

b. Think about two or three of your major accomplishments. (They can be in school, work, sports, hobbies, etc.) List the skills it took to achieve each accomplishment.

c. Identify skills and abilities you already possess that you can use in your career (for example, planning, organizing, communicating, leading).

Step 2: Career Preferences and Exploration

a. What type of industry would you like to work in? (You may list more than one.)

b. What type and size of organization do you want to work for?

c. List by priority the five factors that will most influence your job or career decisions (opportunity for advancement, challenge, security, salary, hours, location of job, travel involved, educational opportunities, recognition, prestige, environment, coworkers, boss, responsibility, variety of tasks, etc.).

d. Describe the perfect job.

e. What type of job(s) do you want during your career (marketing, finance, operations, personnel, and so forth)? After selecting a field, select a specific job—for example, salesperson, manager, accountant.

Step 3: Set Career Objectives

a. What are your short-range objectives for the first year after graduation?

b. What are your intermediate objectives for the second through fifth years after graduation?

c. What are your long-range objectives?

Step 4: Develop a Plan

Use the following form to develop an action plan to help you achieve your objectives.

Career Plan

Objective ____________________

Starting date ____________________ **Due date** ____________________

Steps (what, where, how, resources, etc.—subobjectives)	When	
	Start	**End**

In-Class Exercise

Objective: To experience career planning; to develop a career plan.

AACSB: The primary AACSB learning standard skills developed through this exercise are reflective thinking and self-management and analytic skills.

Preparation: You will need the completed preparation that serves as your career plan.

Experience: You will share your career plan with one or two classmates to help make improvements.

Procedure 1 (10–20 minutes)
Break into teams of two or three. One at a time, go through your career plans while the others ask questions and/or make recommendations to help you improve your career plan.

Conclusion: The instructor leads a class discussion and/or makes concluding remarks.

Application (2–4 minutes): What did I learn from this experience? How will I use this knowledge in the future?

Sharing: Volunteers give their answers to the application section.

/ / ANSWERS TO TRUE/FALSE QUESTIONS / /

1. F. Multitasking is effective for juggling simple, not complex, tasks.
2. F. You should not rank order tasks because you will waste time renumbering them as new ones are added.
3. T.
4. T.
5. F. In the global economy, people of all ages are being laid off.
6. F. Career preferences and explorations, such as internships, should take place during college.
7. F. Recruiters are filling jobs that have specific titles, not matching talents with jobs. Resumes without specific job titles are usually put in the reject pile.Learning Outcome 4-8

Define the following 11 key terms.

PART 2

Interpersonal Skills: The Foundation of Human Relations

CHAPTER 5

Communications, Emotions, and Criticism

LEARNING OUTCOMES

After completing this chapter, you should be able to:

LO 5-1 Describe how communication flows through organizations.

LO 5-2 List and explain the four steps in the communication process.

LO 5-3 List the five steps in the message-sending process.

LO 5-4 Describe how to get feedback.

LO 5-5 List the three steps in the message-receiving process.

LO 5-6 Define five response styles.

LO 5-7 List the four situational supervisory styles and the four variables to consider in selecting the appropriate communication style.

LO 5-8 Discuss what should and should not be done to calm an emotional person.

LO 5-9 Describe how to get criticism effectively.

LO 5-10 Define the following 14 key terms (in order of appearance in the chapter):

organizational structure	**encoding**
organizational communication	**message**
vertical communication	**decoding**
horizontal communication	**paraphrasing**
grapevine	**feedback**
communication process	**emotional labor**
	empathic listening
	reflecting statements

/ / / Ford Motor Company has 166,000 people working in plants and offices all over the world to make its motor vehicles. Janet Low was driving to her new job at the Ford Twin Cities Assembly Plant in St. Paul, Minnesota, where approximately 900 employees make Ford Ranger pickup trucks. Janet was thinking about Ford's organizational structure and how she would fit in and communicate with her boss and peers. Would people talk to her and be willing to listen to her and get to know her personally, and would she make new friends? Janet is sensitive, and on her last job the boss was very critical. She was dedicated to doing her best in the hopes that her new boss wouldn't have to criticize her too often. Janet was feeling emotionally excited and wondered how she would like the job.[1] / / /

HOW COMMUNICATIONS, EMOTIONS, AND CRITICISM AFFECT BEHAVIOR, HUMAN RELATIONS, AND PERFORMANCE

In this chapter, we take the intrapersonal skills foundation from the first four chapters and start building interpersonal skills in this second section of the book. We present communications from two levels. We start with the organizational level in the next section and proceed to interpersonal communications in sections three to six. In the last section we discuss how emotions and criticism affect communications.

Communication is vital for the success of contemporary organizations.[2] That is why communication and interpersonal skills were ranked as the most important attributes recruiters look for in job candidates,[3] and why AACSB accreditation requires teaching and assessing communication abilities.[4] Communication skills are the foundation of human relations, as we initiate, build, and maintain relationships through communications. Recall that behavior is what we do and say; thus, communication is behavior. When communicating, if people get too emotional, such as when being criticized, it can negatively affect their behavior, human relations, and performance.

Clearly, communication skills are important in your personal life and for career success. Communications with employees and organizational support affect our behavior, human relations, and job satisfaction and performance.[5] Our behavior during communications also affects other people's behavior and our human relations.[6] For example, if you are polite and friendly, chances are the other person will behave in a similar way. However, if you are rude, the other person may retaliate. Saying the right thing to people can motivate them to succeed at a given task.[7]

WORK APPLICATION 5-1

Give a specific example in which communication affected your behavior, human relations, and performance.

The general public's and the customer's perception of the organization is often based on interpersonal communications with employees. Employee communication directly affects customer satisfaction and loyalty, which in turn affect organizational revenue, growth, profitability, and shareholder value.[8]

WORK APPLICATION 5-2

Select an organization for which you work or have worked. Is the division of labor specialized? Identify the chain of command from your job to the top of the organization. How many people are in your boss's span of management? Is authority centralized or decentralized? How is work coordinated?

ORGANIZATIONAL STRUCTURE AND COMMUNICATION

In this section we describe how communications flows through organizations. We begin by identifying how organizations are structured, which influences the flow of communications.

Organizational Structure

Organizational structure *refers to the way managers design their firm to achieve the organization's mission and goals.* Organizational theory is the management of collective effort through organizational design.[9] The organization's structure determines who works together, and organizational communication flows through this structure. Through structure come policies, procedures, and rules.[10] In the development of an organizational structure, there are five important questions to be answered. See Exhibit 5.1 for the questions and the principles used to find the answers. Also see Exhibit 5.2 for an illustration of an organization chart.

WORK APPLICATION 5-3

Draw an organization chart illustrating the departments in the organization for which you work or have worked.

Learning Outcome 5-1

Describe how communication flows through organizations.

Some of the organizational structure trends are as follows. Organizations are redesigning organizing processes.[11] Top managers are streamlining structures by getting rid of layers of management.[12] Organizations are increasingly using a team-based structure;[13] as a result, the second most desirable attribute recruiters seek in job candidates is the ability to work well within a team.[14] Large multinational companies (MNCs) tend to have multibusinesses (companies within one company) and refer to them as business units (BUs), and these BUs create what is called an M-form structure that focuses on particular products, customers, or geographies.[15]

Organizational Communication

In general, **organizational communication** *is the compounded interpersonal communication process across an organization.* Communication within an organization flows in a

EXHIBIT 5.1 | Designing Organizational Structure

Question	Organization Principle Used to Answer Question
1. How should we subdivide the work?	**Division of labor** (the degree to which tasks are subdivided into separate jobs) **Departmentalization** (grouping of related activities into units)
2. To whom should departments and individuals report?	**Chain of command** (the line of authority from the top to the bottom of the organization, which is shown in an organization chart)
3. How many individuals should report to each manager?	**Span of management** (number of subordinates)
4. At what level should decisions be made?	**Centralized or decentralized authority** (With *centralized* authority, top managers make important decisions. With *decentralized* authority, lower-level managers make important decisions.)
5. How do we get everyone to work together as a system?	**Coordination** (implementing the other four principles to achieve organizational mission and goals)

EXHIBIT 5.2 | Organization Chart

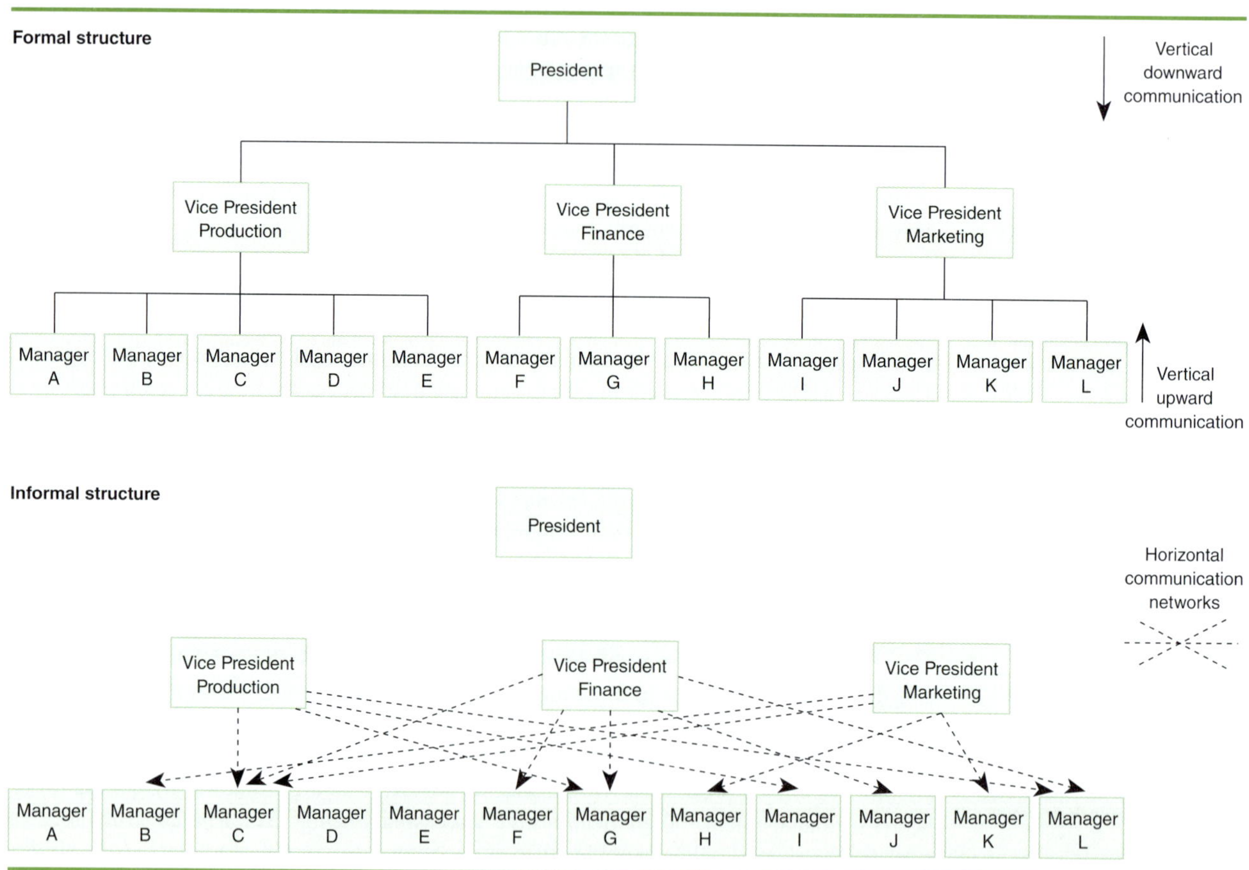

vertical, horizontal, or lateral way throughout the firm. It may also be conveyed through the grapevine, which goes in all directions.

Vertical Communication **Vertical communication** *is the flow of information both up and down the chain of command.* It is often called *formal communication* because it follows the chain of command and is recognized as official. It flows both upward and downward.

Downward Communication When upper-level managers make decisions, they are often communicated down the chain of command. It is the process of higher-level management communicating with those below them (subordinates). So when your boss tells you what to do, the manager is using downward communication.

WORK APPLICATION 5-4

Give a specific example of when you used vertical communication. Identify it as upward or downward.

Upward Communication When employees send a message to managers above them, they are using upward communication, and it is vital to organizational success.[16] So when you communicate with your boss or higher-level managers, you are using upward communication.

For an illustration of downward and upward vertical communication, see Exhibit 5.2.

Horizontal Communication **Horizontal communication** *is the flow of information between colleagues and peers.* It is often called *informal communication* because it does not follow the chain of command and is often not recognized as official. Communication outside the chain of command is horizontal. It is also called *lateral communication.* Most messages processed by an organization are carried via informal channels. As an employee, you may find it necessary to communicate with your peers, employees in other departments, and people outside the organization, such as customers, in order to meet your objectives.

WORK APPLICATION 5-5

Give a specific example of when you used horizontal communication.

Grapevine Communication The **grapevine** *is the informal vehicle through which messages flow throughout the organization.* The grapevine is a useful organizational reality that will always exist. It should be considered as much a communication vehicle as the company newsletter or employee meetings. Unfortunately, employees tend to say they first hear about major changes at work through the grapevine, rather than vertical downward communication. Rumors often start when management disastrously tries to hide things from employees.

Communication Skills
Refer to CS Question 1.

Rather than ignore or try to repress the grapevine, tune in to it. Identify the key people in the organization's grapevine and feed them information. To help prevent incorrect rumors, keep the information flowing through the grapevine as accurate and rumor-free as possible. Share all nonconfidential information with employees; tell them of changes as far in advance as possible. Encourage employees to ask questions about rumors they hear.

WORK APPLICATION 5-6

Give a specific example of a message you heard through the grapevine. How accurate was it? Was it the exact same message management sent?

Gossiping about people can really hurt your human relations with them when they find out about it. In a diverse workplace, it is even more important to be careful about what you say about those who are different from you. The adage "If you can't say anything good about someone, don't say anything at all" is a good human relations rule to follow.

APPLICATION SITUATIONS / / /

Communication Flow AS 5-1

Identify the communication flow as:

A. Vertical—downward
B. Vertical—upward
C. Horizontal
D. Grapevine

_______ 1. "Hey, Jim, have you heard that Mr. Smith and Cindy went out on a date last night? They went to the . . ."

_______ 2. "Pete, will you come here and hold this so I can get the plate on straight—the way I do it for you all the time?"

_______ 3. "Karen, here is the letter you asked me to type. Proofread it and I'll make any necessary changes."

_______ 4. "Ronald, I have a new customer here who wants to set up a charge account. Please do the credit check and make the decision soon. I can sell them lots of our merchandise, and you can bill them for it."

_______ 5. "Ed, take this over to Carl for me."

Digital Information Technology

Some people prefer personal face-to-face communication, whereas other prefer electronic communications.[17] Either way, digital information technology has clearly changed the way we communicate in our personal and professional lives. Information technology is so important that it is listed as one of the important learning and assessment standards for AACSB accreditation.[18] Here we briefly describe the Internet, e-mail, texting, and wireless communications; e-commerce, mobile workers, and m-commerce; social media; and cloud computing. In Chapter 9 we will discuss *digital etiquette* to follow when communicating digitally.

Communication Skills
Refer to CS Question 2.

The Internet, E-Mail, Texting, and Wireless Communications The Internet is a global collection of computer networks linked together to exchange data and information, and the World Wide Web (WWW) is a segment of the Internet in which information is presented in the form of web pages. Three key information technologies used to access the Internet are computers, phones, and handheld devices. E-mail is now the most common way people communicate at work.[19] E-mail and texting is replacing U.S. Postal Service mail, which is losing money.[20] We went from using hardwired computers to wireless laptops, to notebooks and smartphones. Will the **Apple** iPad tablet usher in a new era of computing?[21]

E-Commerce, Mobile Workers, and M-Commerce *E-commerce* or *e-business* (E = electronic) is work done by using electronic linkages (including the Internet) between employees, partners, suppliers, and customers. Much e-business is done within an organization between employees using an *intranet.* E-commerce is more narrowly defined as business exchanges or transactions that occur electronically. Exhibit 5-3 illustrates how information networks

EXHIBIT 5.3 | E-Commerce

Business-to-Business (B2B)

Ford	←	(B2B)	→	Firestone

Ford buys tires from Firestone.

Business-to-Employee (B2E)

Business/Database	←	(B2E)	→	Employees

FedEx and **UPS** drivers get electronic orders to pick up packages along their routes and send electronic information for tracking deliveries.

Business-to-Customer (B2C)

Amazon.com	←	(B2C)	→	John Smith

Amazon.com sells a Kindle and book to John Smith.

Peer-to-Peer (P2P)

Employee	←	(P2P)	→	Employee

An **Apple** employee in the United States electronically contacts an employee in China to find out why an iPad order is behind schedule.

Customer-to-Customer (C2C)

		eBay (online auctions)		
		↑↓		
John Smith	←	(C2C)	→	Jean Jones

John Smith buys a watch from Jean Jones and sells a cell phone to Jones through eBay.

are used in conducting e-commerce. A new trend is machine-to-machine (M2M) to connect all our digital devices.[22]

Today, many employees don't have to come to the office to work. For many mobile workers, smartphones give them much of what they need to work, with a lot less hassle than their old laptops.[23] Both on and off the job, more people continue to access the Internet daily on their mobile phones, and this trend will continue.[24] Mobile technology will be the most powerful way to influence consumers in the next 15 years[25] as more people shop using mobile *(m-commerce)* devices.[26] Are you an m-commerce buyer?

Social Media The social networking sites are not only being used by individuals as a way to communicate with friends. To better connect with younger workers and customers, many companies are increasing their presence on social media.[27] Many businesses are using **Facebook** and others to their advantage. For example, **Dell** and **Ernst & Young** are using the social network as a recruiting tool, while companies such as **Calvin Klein, Pizza Hut,** and **Forever 21** post promotions, contests, and coupons for their fans. Facebook's role in the American political process was demonstrated back in the January 2008 Republican and Democratic debates when Facebook teamed up with **ABC** and **Saint Anselm College** to allow users to post questions to the presidential candidates and give live feedback. CEO Mark Zuckerberg's ultimate goal is to turn Facebook into the planet's standardized communication platform and the main tool that people use to communicate for work and pleasure. With over 500 million users, 35 percent of the entire Internet population, already using Facebook, it seems he is well on his way.[28]

Communication Skills
Refer to CS Question 3.

Cloud Computing *Cloud computing,* broadly speaking, is any service or program sent over an Internet connection. World-class business technology used to require millions of dollars and months of installation; now all it takes is a couple of days and the ability to pay fees.[29] An outside vendor runs the service and software, so the buyer doesn't have to worry about the technical issues in-house.[30] Cloud computing enables a company to tap into raw computing power, storage, software applications, and data from large data centers over the Internet. Customer companies pay only for the computing resources they need, when they need them. So using the cloud lets businesses avoid building their own data centers and buying servers and disks.[31] Using the cloud cuts IT costs and eliminates the need to continually upgrade both software and local servers; cloud computing can also be a bargain for many small businesses.[32] A whole generation of Internet companies wouldn't be in business today without the cloud. For example, the **Netflix** Web site runs on the cloud and **Zynga** uses it to handle spikes in play.[33] But the cloud is not right for all businesses.[34] Here are some of the many providers with their cloud-based services. The *Elastic Compute Cloud* is from **Amazon, IBM** offers *Cloudburst,* **EMC** has *Decho,* and **Microsoft** provides *Azure.*[35]

WORK APPLICATION 5-7

Give specific examples of how you use digital information technology to communicate.

THE COMMUNICATION PROCESS, BARRIERS, AND DIFFERENCES

Now that we have a foundation in organizational structure and communication flow and the digital information technology used to communicate organization wide, for the rest of the chapter, let's focus more on interpersonal communications, which are often between two people. In this section, we begin with an explanation of the communication process, followed by barriers to communications. Next we discuss differences in communications between genders, and end with difference by culture.

Learning Outcome 5-2

List and explain the four steps in the communication process.

The Communication Process

The **communication process** *consists of a sender who encodes a message and transmits it through a channel to a receiver who decodes it and may give feedback.* Exhibit 5.4 illustrates the communication process. Below is a brief explanation of each step in the communication process; you will learn the details of each step in separate sections of this chapter.

EXHIBIT 5.4 | The Communication Process

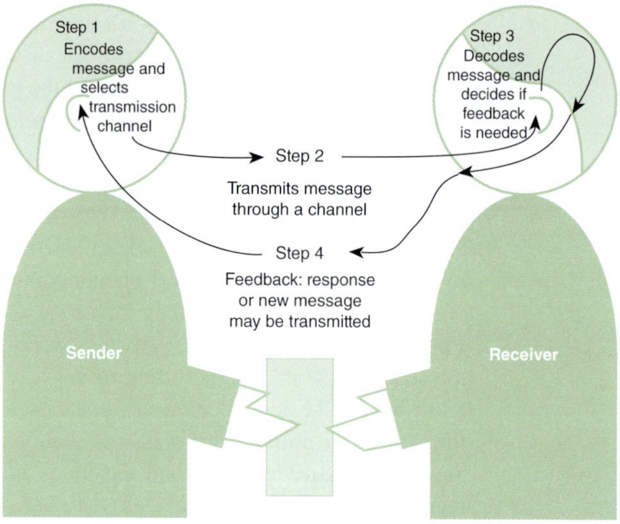

Step 1
Encodes message and selects transmission channel

Step 2
Transmits message through a channel

Step 3
Decodes message and decides if feedback is needed

Step 4
Feedback: response or new message may be transmitted

Sender

Receiver

1. The Sender Encodes the Message and Selects the Transmission Channel

Encoding the Message The *sender* of the message is the person who initiates the communication of *information and meaning that are to be communicated.* **Encoding** *is the sender's process of putting the message into a form that the receiver will understand.* You should consider the receiver of the message to determine the best way to encode the message to ensure clear transmission of the information and meaning. Do the words we select matter? Duke University Coach Mike Krzyzewski said his job is as much about words as it is about basketball—choosing the right words to motivate players is as important to the outcome of a game as choosing the right players and strategies for the court.[36]

Selecting the Transmission Channel The **message** *is the physical form of the encoded information.* The message is transmitted through a channel. The three primary *communication channels* you can use are oral, nonverbal, and written. See Exhibit 5.5 for the various transmission channel options.

EXHIBIT 5.5 | Message Transmission Channels

Oral Communication	Nonverbal Communication	Written Communication

Face-to-face conversations
Presentations
Meetings
Telephone conversations
Voice-mail messages
	Setting
	Body language
	  Facial expressions
	  Vocal quality
	  Gestures
	  Posture
	Posters (pictures)
		Memos
		Letters
		Reports
		E-mails, instant messages, texts
		Faxes
		Bulletin boards
		Posters (words)
		Newsletters

Personal or Digital	**Personal or Digital**	**Personal or Digital**
Face-to-face is personal communications; presentations can use digital PowerPoint; meetings can be in person or via webcam teleconferencing; and telephone calls and messages use digital technology.	Nonverbal communications can be seen in person and digitally via webcam teleconferencing	Most of these channels can be a more personal hard copy or digital copy. Memos are commonly used for internal communications and sent digitally or e-mailed, whereas letters are commonly on company letterhead and mailed.

It's important to select the most appropriate channel of transmission for any message. When selecting a channel, we need to remember that people do have different preferences in terms of which channel they like to receive messages from.[37] For example, many younger people like to text, whereas older people do not. *Media richness* should also be considered. It refers to the amount of information and meaning conveyed through a channel. The more information and meaning, the "richer" the channel is. Face-to-face is the richest channel because it allows the sender and receiver to take full advantage of both oral and nonverbal communication. The telephone is less rich than face-to-face because most nonverbal cues are lost when you cannot see facial expressions and gestures. All forms of oral communication are richer than written communication because oral communication allows transmission of at least some nonverbal cues, which are lost with written messages.[38]

WORK APPLICATION 5-8

Which message transmission channels do you use most often at work?

APPLICATION SITUATIONS / / /

Channel Selection AS 5-2

Select the most appropriate channel for each message.

A. Face-to-face
B. Telephone
C. Meeting
D. Presentation
E. Memo
F. Letter
G. Report
H. Poster

_______ 6. The supervisor has to assign a new customer order to Karen and Ralph.

_______ 7. The supervisor is expecting needed material for production this afternoon. She wants to know if it will arrive on time.

_______ 8. Employees have been leaving the lights on when no one is in the stockroom. The managers want employees to shut off the lights when they leave.

_______ 9. The boss asked for the production figures for the month.

_______ 10. An employee broke a rule and needs to be disciplined.

2. The Sender Transmits the Message through a Channel As the sender, after you encode the message and select the channel, you transmit the message through the channel to one or more receivers. Don't forget the importance of your nonverbal communications when sending oral messages;[39] a smile versus a frown sends a different message.[40]

3. The Receiver Decodes the Message and Decides If Feedback Is Needed The person receiving the message decodes it. **Decoding** *is the receiver's process of translating the message into a meaningful form.* The receiver combines the message with other ideas and interprets the meaning of the message. We all decode words so that the message makes sense to us. The receiver decides if feedback, a response, or a new message is needed.[41] With oral communication, feedback is commonly given immediately. However, with written communication, it may not be necessary to reply.

4. Feedback: A Response or a New Message May Be Transmitted After decoding the message, the receiver may give feedback to the sender, and people are seeking honest communications.[42] You should realize that the role of sender and receiver can change during a communication exchange; communication is often a two-way process of giving information and getting feedback. Giving positive feedback tends to increase performance.[43]

Here is an example of the communication process: (1) A professor (sender) prepares for a class and encodes a message by preparing a lecture; (2) the professor transmits the message orally through a lecture during class; (3) the students (receivers) decode the lecture (message) by listening and/or taking notes in a meaningful way; and (4) students usually have the option of asking questions (feedback) during or after class.

Communication Skills
Refer to CS Question 4.

WORK APPLICATION 5-9

Give at least two different barriers to communication you have experienced at work. Explain the situation and how the barrier could have been overcome.

Communication Barriers

When we communicate, there are barriers that can lead to miscommunications. The top of Exhibit 5.6 lists 11 common barriers that interfere with effective communication. The bottom of Exhibit 5.6 lists the barriers, their descriptions, and ways to overcome the communication barriers to help prevent communication breakdowns. Emotions are important barriers, so we will discuss this topic in more detail in the last section of this chapter.

EXHIBIT 5.6 | Communication Barriers

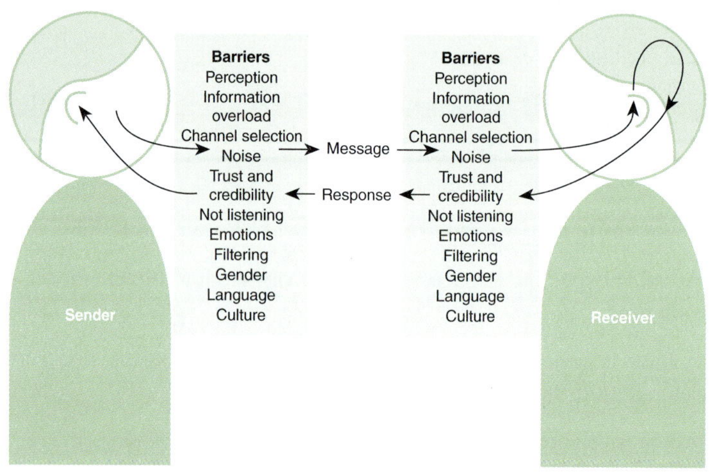

Barrier	Description	Overcoming the Barrier
a. Perception	Receivers use their perceptions to decode messages. *Semantics* and *jargon* can be communication barriers.	Consider how the receiver will perceive the message and select appropriate words and terminology.
b. Information overload	People have a limit on the amount of information they can understand at any given time.	Send messages in a quantity that the receiver can understand.
c. Channel selection	Some channels are more appropriate for certain messages than others.	Give careful thought to selecting the most effective channel for the situation.
d. Noise	Noise is anything that interferes with message transmission.	Stop the noise or distraction, or move to a quiet location.
e. Trust and credibility	People who lack credibility and fail to create a climate of trust and openness aren't believed.	Be open and honest with people, and get the facts straight before you communicate.
f. Not listening	People don't always pay attention and listen to the message or understand it.	Question receivers and have them paraphrase the message back to you.
g. Emotions	When people are emotional, it is difficult to be objective and to listen.	Remain calm and be careful not to make others emotional by your behavior.
h. Filtering	Filtering is altering or distorting information (lying) to project a more favorable image.	Be honest and treat errors as a learning experience rather than as an opportunity to blame and criticize others.
i. Gender	Gender difference can lead to miscommunications.	Be empathetic with the other gender.
j. Language	Speaking different languages makes communication very difficult.	Try to use a translator or nonverbal methods to get the message across.
k. Culture	Having different cultures can lead to miscommunications.	Get to know the other person's culture.

APPLICATION SITUATIONS / / /

Communication Barriers AS 5-3

Using Exhibit 5.6, identify the communication barriers indicated by the statements below using the letters a through k.

_______ 11. "You shouldn't be upset. Listen to me."

_______ 12. "Buddy, why did you send the boss a text message? Don't you know he is behind the times technologically?"

_______ 13. "That's a lot to remember; I'm not sure I got it all."

_______ 14. "Why did you say the job is going well, when you know it's not? You haven't even finished the third or fourth part yet."

_______ 15. "I cannot hear you. Shut that thing off! Now, what did you say?"

_______ 16. "I said I'd do it in a little while. It's only been 10 minutes. Why do you expect it done now?"

_______ 17. "Why should I listen to you? You don't know what you're talking about."

_______ 18. "Can you explain it to him in Spanish?

_______ 19. "I'm sorry, I didn't get it. What did you say?"

_______ 20. "Putting up your thumb like that is an insult in my country."

Gender Conversation Differences

Gender biases influence communications and cause communication barriers.[44] Research has shown that, generally, men and women behave differently,[45] and that they converse for different reasons.[46] When they do converse, gender style becomes a barrier to communication between the sexes. Men tend to talk to emphasize status. Women tend to talk to create connections and develop relationships.[47] Women spend more time talking about their feelings and personal lives, including their families, than do men. Women who have worked together for a few weeks may know much about one another's personal lives, whereas men can work together for years and not know much about one another's personal lives.

Communication Skills
Refer to CS Question 5.

WORK APPLICATION 5-10

Describe a gender communication difference you have observed at work.

As a result of gender diversity in conversation, men tend to complain that women talk on and on about their problems, and women criticize men for not listening. When men hear a problem, they tend to want to assert their independence and control by providing a solution. However, when women mention a problem or their feelings, it tends to be to promote closeness; they generally are not looking for advice. So women may want to vent their feelings and problems with other women, instead of men; and men may want to just listen and give reflecting responses, rather than focusing on solving problems. Men may also talk more about their feelings and personal lives to improve human relations. You'll learn how to listen and reflect later in the chapter.

Cross-Cultural Communication Differences

In the global economy, when conducting international business, you should be aware that cultural differences can cause barriers to communication. Some of the areas of possible barriers include cultural context; social conventions; language, etiquette, and politeness; and nonverbal communication.

Cultural Context The process of encoding and decoding is based on an individual's culture; therefore the message meaning is different for people of diverse cultures. The greater the difference in culture between the sender and receiver, the greater are the chances of

EXHIBIT 5.7 | High-Context to Low-Context Cultures

High-Context

- Chinese
- Korean
- Vietnamese
- Arab
- Greek
- Spanish
- Italian
- English
- North American
- Scandinavian
- Swiss
- German

Low-Context

Source: Based on the work of E.T. Hall, from R.E. Dulck, J.S. Fielden, and J.S. Hill, "International Communication: An Executive Primer," *Business Horizons,* January–February 1991, p. 21.

EXHIBIT 5.8 | High-Context versus Low-Context Cultures: Communication Importance

Context	High-Context Culture	Low-Context Culture
Focus on nonverbal communications and subtle cues	X	
Focus on actual spoken and written word		X
Importance of credibility and trust	X	
The need to develop relationships	X	
Importance of position, age, and seniority	X	
Use of precisely written legal contracts		X
Use of direct, get-down-to-business conversation		X
Managers telling employees (giving orders) what to do		X

encountering communication barriers. People around the globe see, interpret, and evaluate behavior differently. As a result, they act on behavior differently. Thus, the chances of running into perception communication barriers increase.

Understanding high- and low-context culture differences can help us better understand potential barriers to communication and how to overcome them. The importance to which context influences the meaning individuals take from a message—not only the specific words (oral and written) but also the person's behavioral actions—varies by culture.

See Exhibit 5.7 for a list of high- and low-context cultures. See Exhibit 5.8 for a list of some of the differences between high-context and low-context cultures in terms of communication.

Communication Skills
Refer to CS Question 6.

Social Conventions The directness of how business is conducted varies. North Americans tend to favor getting down to business quickly and concisely. If you use this approach with Arab or Japanese people, however, you may lose the business because they prefer a more indirect, informal chat to begin business meetings. What constitutes punctuality varies greatly around the world. North American and Japanese people want you to be on time, while being late for a meeting with an Arab or Latin American person is not viewed as negative.

Language, Etiquette, and Politeness Even when you are speaking English to people outside North America, words mean different things, and the same thing may be called by different names (e.g., *lift* rather than *elevator,* and *petrol* rather than *gasoline*). What is considered rude in one country may not be rude in another. So be careful not to accidentally offend people in other cultures. For example, the Japanese want to maintain interdependence and harmony. They have 16 subtle ways to say no. Rather than saying, "I don't want to buy your product," a Japanese businessperson would be more likely to say, "A sale will be very difficult." The Japanese person would think it is clear to the American that he is saying no. The American, however, would tend to reply with a statement about how the difficulty can be overcome rather than realizing the deal is off and giving up. Continuing to try to sell is an insult to the Japanese.

Nonverbal Communication People do prefer different channels of communication.[48] As Exhibit 5.8 shows, nonverbals are important,[49] and more so in some cultures than others. Gestures do not translate well across cultures because they involve symbolism that is not shared. One gesture can mean very different things in different cultures. A raised thumb in the United States is a signal of approval, but in Greece it is an insult, meaning the same as a raised middle finger in America. Latin Americans and Arabs expect extensive eye contact, while Europeans would be uncomfortable and would interpret this as being stared at. Arabs, Latin Americans, and southern Europeans want to touch, while northern Europeans and North Americans don't want to be touched.

Overcoming Global Barriers This section is not meant to teach you how to overcome all the possible barriers to global communication. The objective is to make you realize the importance of learning the cultures of other countries if you plan to do business with them successfully. Most major multinational companies train their employees to be sensitive to specific cultural differences when doing business with people from other cultures.

To help overcome global barriers to communications, you can follow these guidelines:[50]

- Believe there are differences until similarity is proved. We need to ignore our natural tendency to think that people are like us until we are sure they really are.
- Delay judgment of a person's behavior until you are sure you are being culturally sensitive. You may think a particular behavioral statement or action is inappropriate or insulting to you, but that may not be the intended meaning; the behavior may be appropriate in the other person's culture. For example, if a Japanese businessperson gives you a gift, it is most likely a gift, not a bribe to get your business.
- Put yourself in the receiver's position. As the sender, try to decode your message with a focus on the receiver's cross-cultural differences. For example, if you don't give a Japanese businessperson a gift, you may be considered impolite and hurt your chances of developing a relationship.
- When in doubt, ask. If you are not sure what is appropriate, ask someone who knows. Then, for example, you will know to expect a gift exchange.
- Follow the other person's lead, and watch his or her behavior. For example, if a person bows, bow back. If you do or don't do something and the other person's nonverbal communication indicates discomfort, be quick to apologize and to do it or avoid the behavior.

WORK APPLICATION 5-11

Describe a cross-cultural barrier to communication you have experienced. Explain the situation and how the barrier could have been overcome.

Keep in mind the overview of the steps in the communication process and the potential barriers as we discuss the details of sending, receiving, and responding to messages in the rest of this chapter.

SENDING MESSAGES

Have you ever heard a manager say, "This isn't what I asked for"? When this happens, it is usually the manager's fault for not taking 100 percent of the responsibility for ensuring the message has been transmitted with mutual understanding. In this section, we discuss the first two steps in the message-sending process including planning and sending the message and then checking understanding to ensure the message has been transmitted successfully.

Planning the Message

Recall that before we send a message we should carefully encode it and select the channel—this is planning how to send the message. Before sending a message, we should plan what, who, how, when, and where. *What* is the goal of the message? What do we want as the end result of the communication? Set objectives.[51] *Who* should receive the message? With the receiver(s) in mind, plan *how* you will encode the message so that it will be understood. *When* will the message be transmitted? Timing is important. Finally, decide *where* the message will be transmitted.

Learning Outcome 5-3

List the five steps in the message-sending process.

Sending the Message Face-to-Face

It is helpful to follow the steps in the *message-sending process*. Below is a discussion of the five steps.

Step 1: Develop rapport. Put the receiver at ease. It is usually appropriate to begin communication with small talk related to the message. It helps prepare the person to receive the message, and to form relationships.

Skill-Building Exercise 5-1 develops this skill.

WORK APPLICATION 5-12

Recall a present or past boss. How well did the boss send messages? Which steps in the message-sending process were followed, and which were not commonly followed?

MODEL 5.1 | The Message-Sending Process

Step 2: State the communication objective. If the goal of the business communication is to influence, it is helpful for the receiver to know the end result of the communication before getting to all the details as to why it is important.

Step 3: Transmit the message. To influence, tell the people what you want them to do, give instructions, and so forth. And be sure to set deadlines for completing tasks. If the goal is to inform, tell the people the information. Avoid talking too fast and giving too much detail.

Step 4: Check understanding. After transmitting the message, the sender has two options. The sender can either (1) simply assume that the receiver understands the message and that there is mutual understanding (this is known as one-way communication) or (2) check to see if the message has been understood with mutual understanding. Questioning and paraphrasing are two techniques that can be used to ensure mutual understanding (these are two-way communication methods).

Paraphrasing *is the process of having the receiver restate the message in his or her own words.* About the only time we may not want to check understanding is when the goal is to express feelings. When influencing and giving information, we should ask direct questions and/or use paraphrasing. To simply ask "Do you have any questions?" does not check understanding.

Step 5: Get a commitment and follow up. When the goal is to influence, it is important to get a commitment to the action. We should make sure the other person can do the task and have it done by a certain time or date. In situations in which the person does not intend to get the task done, it is better to know when sending the message rather than wait until the deadline to find out. When communicating to influence, follow up to ensure that the necessary action has been taken. Model 5.1 lists the five steps in the message-sending process.

Checking Understanding: Feedback

Learning Outcome 5-4

Describe how to get feedback.

When we are communicating a message, the best way to ensure mutual understanding is to get feedback from the receiver. **Feedback** *is the process of verifying messages.* Questioning, paraphrasing, and allowing comments and suggestions are all forms of feedback. Feedback facilitates job performance.[52]

The Common Approach to Getting Feedback on Messages and Why It Doesn't Work The most common approach to getting feedback is to send the entire message, followed by asking, "Do you have any questions?" Feedback usually does not follow because people have a tendency not to ask questions. Regardless of the reason, the result is the same: Employees don't ask questions; generally, students don't either.

After sending messages and asking if there are questions, we often proceed to make another common error. We assume that no questions means communication is complete and that there is mutual understanding of the message. In reality, the message is often misunderstood. When a message does not result in communication, the most common cause is the sender's lack of getting feedback to ensure mutual understanding. The proper use of questioning and paraphrasing can help ensure that our messages are communicated successfully.

How to Get Feedback on Messages Below are four guidelines we should use when getting feedback on messages:

Be Open to Feedback First of all, we must be open to feedback and must ask for it. When someone asks a question, we need to be responsive and patiently answer questions and explain things.

Be Aware of Nonverbal Communication We must be sure that our nonverbals encourage feedback.[53] For example, if we say we encourage questions, but when people ask questions, we act impatient or look at them as though they are stupid, people will learn not to ask us questions. We must also be aware of the receivers' nonverbal communications. For example, if we are explaining a task to Larry, and Larry has a puzzled look on his face, he is probably confused but may not be willing to say so. In such a case, we should stop and clarify things before going on.

CS

Communication Skills
Refer to CS Question 7.

Ask Questions Direct questions dealing with the specific information we have given will indicate whether the receivers have been listening and whether or not they understand enough to give a direct reply. If the response is not accurate, repeating, giving more examples, or elaborating the message is needed.

WORK APPLICATION 5-13

Describe how a boss in either your present or your past used feedback. How could his or her feedback skills be improved?

WORK APPLICATION 5-14

Do you use paraphrasing now? Will you use it more, less, or with the same frequency in the future? Why?

Use Paraphrasing The most accurate indicator of understanding is paraphrasing. However, the way we ask others to paraphrase will affect their attitude. For example, if we say, "John, tell me what I just said so that I can be sure you will not make a mistake as usual," the result will probably be defensive behavior. Here are two proper requests for paraphrasing:

- "Now tell me what you are going to do so we will be sure that we are in agreement."
- "Please tell me what you are going to do so that I can be sure that I explained myself clearly."

RECEIVING MESSAGES

To receive messages orally, we must listen effectively. So let's begin this section by completing Self-Assessment Exercise 5-1 to determine how good a listener you are.

/// Self-Assessment Exercise 5-1 ///

Your Listening Skills

Select the response that best describes the frequency of your actual behavior. Place the letter A, U, F, O, or S on the line before each of the 15 statements.

Almost always (A) Usually (U) Frequently (F) Occasionally (O) Seldom (S)

_____ 1. I like to listen to people talk. I encourage them to talk by showing interest, by smiling and nodding, and so forth.

_____ 2. I pay closer attention to speakers who are more interesting or similar to me.

_____ 3. I evaluate speakers' words and nonverbal communication ability as they talk.

_____ 4. I avoid distractions; if it's noisy, I suggest moving to a quieter spot.

_____ 5. When people interrupt me to talk, I put what I was doing out of sight and mind and give them my complete attention.

_____ 6. When people are talking, I allow them time to finish. I do not interrupt, anticipate what they are going to say, or jump to conclusions.

_____ 7. I tune out people whose views do not agree with mine.

(continued)

/// Self-Assessment Exercise 5-1 /// *(continued)*

_____ 8. While the other person is talking or the professor is lecturing, my mind wanders to personal topics.

_____ 9. While the other person is talking, I pay close attention to the nonverbal communication to help me fully understand what the sender is trying to get across.

_____ 10. I tune out and pretend I understand when the topic is difficult.

_____ 11. When the other person is talking, I think about what I am going to say in reply.

_____ 12. When I feel there is something missing or contradictory, I ask direct questions to get the person to explain the idea more fully.

_____ 13. When I don't understand something, I let the sender know.

_____ 14. When listening to other people, I try to put myself in their position and see things from their perspective.

_____ 15. During conversations, I repeat back to the sender what has been said in my own words (paraphrase) to be sure I understand correctly what has been said.

If you were to have people to whom you talk regularly answer these questions about you, would they have the same responses that you selected? Have friends fill out the questions for you and compare answers.

To determine your score, give yourself 5 points for each A, 4 for each U, 3 for each F, 2 for each O, and 1 for each S for statements 1, 4, 5, 6, 9, 12, 13, 14, and 15. Place the scores on the line next to your response letter. For items 2, 3, 7, 8, 10, and 11, the score reverses: Give yourself 5 points for each S, 4 for each O, 3 for each F, 2 for each U, and 1 for each A. Place these scores on the line next to your response letter. Now add your total number of points. Your score should be between 15 and 75. Place your score here and place an X on the continuum below at the point that represents your score. Generally, the higher your score, the better your listening skills.

Poor listener 15 - - - - - - - - 25 - - - - - - - - 35 - - - - - - - - 45 - - - - - - - - 55 - - - - - - - - 65 - - - - - - - - 75 Good listener

If someone asked us are you a good listener, most likely we would say yes. What was your score on the self-assessment? Unfortunately, a recent survey found that the number one thing lacking in new college grads is listening skills.[54] All the digital screens are robbing our ability to focus.[55] Constant multitasking is deteriorating our ability to pay attention for long and listen.[56] For how long can you pay attention and listen effectively at school and work without checking your messages or doing other things? Next time you begin reading a textbook, time how long you can go before you "have" to stop and do something else.

Do you prefer people who talk at you or listen to you? We learn by listening, not talking. Do you talk more than you listen? To be sure your perception is correct, ask your boss, coworkers, and friends who will give you an honest answer. If you spend more time talking than listening, you may want to listen more. Whether you talk or listen more now, by using the message-receiving process and listening tips in this section, you can become a better listener.

Learning Outcome 5-5

List the three steps in the message-receiving process.

The Message-Receiving Process

The message-receiving process has three parts. First we have to listen to the message, next we should analyze what was said as we decode the message, and then we should check understanding through paraphrasing and watching nonverbal behavior to ensure the message was received accurately.

To improve your listening skills, focus your attention on listening for a week by concentrating on both what other people say and their nonverbal communication. Notice if their verbal and nonverbal communication are consistent. Talk only when necessary so that you can listen to what others are saying. If you follow the 13 listening tips below, you will improve your listening skills. The tips will be presented in the sequence of the message-receiving process.

Listening Tips

Listening

1. *Pay attention.* When people interrupt you to talk, stop what you are doing and give them your complete attention. Quickly relax and clear your mind so that you are receptive to the speaker. This will get you started correctly. If you miss the first few words, you may miss the message.
2. *Avoid distractions.* Shut off your digital machines and other distractions. Keep your eye on the speaker.
3. *Stay tuned in.* While the other person is talking or the professor is lecturing, do not let your mind wander to personal topics. If it does, gently bring it back. It is also very helpful to repeat in your mind what the speaker is saying. If the topic is difficult, do not tune out; ask questions. Do not think about what you are going to say in reply; just listen.
4. *Do not assume and interrupt.* Do not assume you know what the speaker is going to say or listen at the beginning and jump to conclusions. Listen to the entire message without interrupting the speaker other than to clarify the message.
5. *Watch for nonverbal cues.* Understand both the feelings and the content of the message. People sometimes say one thing and mean something else. So watch as you listen to be sure that the speaker's eyes, body, and face are sending the same message as the verbal message. If something seems out of place, clarify by asking questions.
6. *Ask questions.* When you feel there is something missing or contradictory, or you just do not understand, ask direct questions to get the person to explain the idea more fully.
7. *Take notes.* Part of listening is writing down important things and documenting them when necessary so you can remember them later. This is especially true when listening to instructions.
8. *Convey meaning.* The way to let the speaker know you are listening to the message is to use verbal clues such as "you feel . . . ," "uh huh," "I see," and "I understand." You should also use nonverbal communication such as eye contact, appropriate facial expressions, nodding of the head, and sitting on the edge of the chair, leaning slightly forward to indicate you are interested and listening.

Communication Skills
Refer to CS Question 8.

Analyzing

9. *Think.* Listen actively by organizing, summarizing, reviewing, interpreting, and critiquing often. Again, repeat in your mind what the speaker is saying.
10. *Evaluate after listening.* When people try to listen and analyze or evaluate what is said at the same time, they tend to miss part or all of the message. You should just listen to the entire message and then come to your conclusions.
11. *Evaluate facts presented.* When you evaluate the message, base your conclusion on the facts presented rather than on opinions, stereotypes, and generalities.

Skill-Building Exercise 5-2 develops this skill.

Checking Understanding

12. *Paraphrase.* Begin speaking by paraphrasing the message back to the sender. When you can paraphrase correctly, you convey that you have listened and understood the other person. Now you are ready to offer your ideas, advice, solution, or decision in response to the sender of the message.
13. *Watch for nonverbal cues.* Pay attention to the other person's nonverbal communication. If the person does not seem to understand what you are talking about, clarify the message before finishing the conversation.

WORK APPLICATION 5-15

Refer to Self-Assessment Exercise 5-1 and the 13 tips to improve your listening skills. What is your weakest listening skill? How will you improve your listening ability?

MODEL 5.2 | The Message-Receiving Process

1. Listening	→	2. Analyzing	→	3. Check understanding
1. Pay attention 2. Avoid distractions 3. Stay tuned in 4. Do not assume and interrupt 5. Watch for nonverbal cues 6. Ask questions 7. Take notes 8. Convey meaning		9. Think 10. Evaluate after listening 11. Evaluate facts presented		12. Paraphrase 13. Watch for nonverbal cues

See Model 5.2 for a review of the message-sending process with the 13 listening tips.

APPLICATION SITUATIONS / / /

Listening AS 5-4

Identify each statement by its number (1 to 13) from the 13 listening tips above.

_______ 21. "I'm sorry; I just got a text. What did you say again?"

_______ 22. "Hold on; let me write this down so I don't forget it."

_______ 23. "Forgive me; I missed the beginning of what you said. Please start again."

_______ 24. "You look overwhelmed. Let me go over it again."

_______ 25. "So you want me to take this letter over to Pete in the service department now."

_______ 26. "How long do you think it will take me to get the task done?"

_______ 27. "OK, I got it. That's all I need to know."

_______ 28. "Are you finished? I can see some problems in implementing this suggestion."

_______ 29. "I get it. That is a great idea."

_______ 30. "Do you have any supporting information to back up your ideas?"

RESPONDING TO MESSAGES

Learning Outcome 5-6

Define five response styles.

The fourth and last step in the communication process is responding to the message. Not all messages require a response, but most face-to-face messages do. In this section, we present five response styles to choose from and explain how to deal with emotional people and how to give and take criticism.

Response Styles

Before learning about response styles, complete Self-Assessment Exercise 5-2 to determine your preferred response style.

/// Self-Assessment Exercise 5-2 ///

Your Preferred Response Style

Select the response you would actually make as the supervisor in the five situations that follow:

_____ 1. I cannot work with Paul. That guy drives me crazy. He is always complaining about me and everyone else, including you, boss. Why does he have to be my job partner? We cannot work together. You have to assign someone else to be my partner.

A. I'm sure there are things that you do that bother Paul. You'll have to work things out with him.

B. What has he said about me?

C. Can you give me some examples of the specific things that he does that bother you?

D. I'll talk to Paul. I'm sure we can improve or change the situation.

E. So Paul is really getting to you.

_____ 2. We cannot make the deadline on the Procter Project without more help. We've been having some problems. A major problem is that Betty and Phil are recent college grads, and you know they don't know anything. I end up doing all the work for them. Without another experienced person, my team will not get the job done on time.

A. Tell me more about these problems you are having.

B. Did you see the game last night?

C. You are really concerned about this project, aren't you?

D. You will have to stop doing the work and train the new people. They will come through for you if you give them a chance.

E. Don't worry. You're a great project leader. I'm sure you will get the job done.

_____ 3. Congratulations on being promoted to supervisor. I was wondering about what to expect. After all, we go back five years as good friends in this department. It will seem strange to have you as my boss.

A. Things will work out fine, you'll see.

B. I take it that you don't like to see things change. Is that what you mean?

C. Just do a good job and there will not be any problems between us.

D. Is Chris feeling any better?

E. Tell me how you think things will change.

_____ 4. I wish you would do something about Gloria. Because of her short, tight clothes, the men are always finding some excuse to come by here. She loves it; you can tell the way she is always flirting with all the guys. Gloria could turn this place into a soap opera if you don't do something.

A. So you think this situation is indecent, is that it?

B. I cannot tell Gloria how to dress. Why don't you turn your desk so you don't have to watch.

C. Don't let it bother you. I'm sure it's innocent and that nothing is really going on. You know how these younger kids are these days.

D. What do you think I should do?

E. Are you feeling well today?

_____ 5. I cannot take it anymore. I've been running around like a fool waiting on all these customers and all they do is yell at me and complain.

A. Are you going to the party tonight?

B. What is the most irritating thing the customers are doing?

C. With Erin being out today, it's been crazy. But tomorrow she should be back and things should be back to normal. Hang in there; you can handle it.

D. The customers are really getting to you today, hey?

E. I told you during the job interview that this is how it is. You have to learn to ignore the comments.

(continued)

/// Self-Assessment Exercise 5–2 /// (*continued*)

To determine your preferred response style, in the following table circle the letter you selected in situations 1 to 5. The column headings indicate the style you selected.

	Advising	Diverting	Probing	Reassuring	Reflecting
1	A	B	C	D	E
2	D	B	A	E	C
3	C	D	E	A	B
4	B	E	D	C	A
5	E	A	B	C	D
	_____	_____	_____	_____	_____
Total	_____	_____	_____	_____	_____

Add up the number of circled responses per column. The total for all columns should equal 5. The column with the highest number represents your preferred response style. The more evenly distributed the numbers are among the styles, the more flexible you are at responding.

Communication Skills
Refer to CS Question 9.

WORK APPLICATION 5-16

Give situations in which any two of the five response styles would be appropriate. Give the sender's message and your response. Identify its style.

As the sender transmits a message, how you respond to the message directly affects communication. Of the five styles, students tend to have the most difficulty with the reflective statement: wondering why they should paraphrase back the message already given. A major reason is to show an interest in the other person and to let him or her know you are open and listening to what he or she has to say. Psychologist Carl Rogers stated that reflecting responses should be used in the beginning stages of most communications because they lead to developing good human relations—as people want to be listened to and know that they are valued. However, there is no one best response style. The response should be appropriate for the situation. See Exhibit 5.9 for a list of the five response styles, their definitions, and when it is appropriate to use each style.

EXHIBIT 5.9 | Response Styles

Style	Definition	Appropriate Use
Advising	Providing evaluation, personal opinion, direction, or instructions.	Give advice when directly asked for it.
Diverting	Switching the message; changing the subject.	Use to avoid needless arguments.
Probing	Asking for more information.	Ensure understanding by getting more information.
Reassuring	Giving supportive statements.	Give to provide confidence.
Reflecting	Paraphrasing the message back to the sender.	Use to convey understanding and acceptance.

APPLICATION SITUATIONS / / /

Identifying Response Styles AS 5-5

Below are two situations with 10 responses. Identify each as:

A. Advising C. Probing E. Reflecting

B. Diverting D. Reassuring

LYNN: Michael, do you have a minute to talk?

MICHAEL: Sure, what's up?

LYNN: Can you do something about all the swearing the men use around the plant? It carries through these thin walls into my work area. It's disgusting. I'm surprised you haven't done anything.

MICHAEL:

_______ 31. I didn't know anyone was swearing. I'll look into it.

_______ 32. You don't have to listen to it. Just ignore it.

_______ 33. Are you feeling well today?

_______ 34. What kind of swear words are they using?

_______ 35. You find this swearing offensive?

JIM: Mary, I have a complaint.

MARY: Sit down and tell me about it.

JIM: Being the AD [athletic director], you know that I use the weight room after the football team. Well, my track team has to return the plates to the racks, put the dumbbells back, and so forth. I don't get paid to pick up after the football team. After all, they have the use of the room longer than we do. I've complained to Ted [the football coach], but all he says is that's the way he finds it, or that he'll try to get the team to do a better job. But nothing happens.

MARY:

_______ 36. Before I forget, congratulations on beating Harvard.

_______ 37. You feel it's unfair to pick up after them?

_______ 38. How long has this been going on?

_______ 39. You work it out with Ted.

_______ 40. Thanks for telling me about it; I'll talk to Ted to see what's going on.

In the above two situations, which response is the most appropriate?

SITUATIONAL COMMUNICATION

Learning Outcome 5-7

List the four situational supervisory styles and the four variables to consider in selecting the appropriate communication style.

The following is the process used with each of the four situational communications styles. Each style is based primarily on four behaviors. Notice that behavior can be characterized as a combination of two dimensions—task and relationship. In task behavior, the sender focuses on getting the job done primarily through directing the receiver in what to do and how to do it. In relationship behavior, the sender elicits others' input and listens and responds with supportive behavior. Both task and relationship can be described as high or low depending on the amount of emphasis placed on each of the two dimensions during communication.

Situational Communication Styles

- *Autocratic communication style (S-A)* demonstrates high task–low relationship (HT–LR) behavior, initiating a closed presentation. The other party has little, if any, information and is generally low in capability. You initiate and control the communication with minimal, if any, response. You make a presentation letting the other parties know they are expected to comply with your message.

- *Consultative communication style (S-C)* demonstrates high task–high relationship (HT–HR) behavior, using a closed presentation for the task with an open elicitation for the relationship. The other party has moderate information and capability. You initiate the communication by letting the other party know that you want him or her to buy into your influence. You are closed to having your message accepted (task), but open to the person's feelings (relationship).
- *Participative communication style (S-P)* demonstrates low task–high relationship (LT–HR) behavior, responding with open elicitation, some initiation, and little presentation. The other party is high in information and capability. You respond by eliciting others' input on how to do thing, or convey personal support in the situation.
- *Laissez-faire communication style (S-L)* demonstrates low task–low relationship (LT–LR) behavior, responding with the necessary open presentation. The other party is outstanding in information and capability. You respond to the other party with the information, structure, and so forth that the sender wants.

Situational Variables

When selecting the appropriate communication style, you should consider four variables: time, information, acceptance, and capability. Answering the questions related to each variable below can help you select the appropriate style for the situation.

- **Time:** Do I have enough time to use two-way communication? When there is no time, the other three variables are not considered; the autocratic style is appropriate. When time is available, any of the other styles may be appropriate, depending on the other variables. Time is a relative term; in one situation a few minutes may be considered a short time period, while in another a month may be a short period of time.
- **Information:** Do I have the necessary information to communicate my message, make a decision, or take action? When you have all the information you need, the autocratic style may be appropriate. When you have some of the information, the consultative style may be appropriate. When you have little information, the participative or laissez-faire style may be appropriate.
- **Acceptance:** Will the other party accept my message without any input? If the receiver will accept the message, the autocratic style may be appropriate. If the receiver will be reluctant to accept it, the consultative style may be appropriate. If the receiver will reject the message, the participative or laissez-faire style may be appropriate to gain acceptance.
- **Capability:** Capability has two parts: (1) Ability—does the other party have the experience or knowledge to participate in two-way communication? Will the receiver put the organization's goals ahead of personal needs or goals? (2) Motivation—does the other party want to participate?

When the other party is low in capability, the autocratic style may be appropriate; moderate in capability, the consultative style may be appropriate; high in capability, the participative style may be appropriate; outstanding in capability, the laissez-faire style may be appropriate. Capability levels can change from one task to another. For example, a professor may have outstanding capability in classroom teaching, but be low in capability for advising students.

Skill-Building Exercise 5-3 develops this skill.

DEALING WITH EMOTIONS AND CRITICISM

Communicating with people brings out emotions, and our feelings affect our behavior, human relations, and performance in our personal and professional lives.[57] Recall from Chapter 2 that adjustment (or emotional stability) is part of our personality and the importance of emotional intelligence. As the economy has become more service-oriented, dealing with the emotions of employees and customers has become increasingly important to business success.[58]

Emotions, Emotional Labor, and Global Differences

Dealing effectively with emotions reduces stress and improves human relations and performance.[59] Here we discuss these three related topics, which are the foundation for our next topic, dealing with emotional people.

Understanding Feelings Emotions are often just called feelings. There are six universal emotions: happiness, surprise, fear, sadness, anger, and disgust.

We can Control Behavior, Not Feelings We should realize that feelings are subjective; they tell us people's attitudes and needs. Feelings are usually disguised as factual statements. Most important, feelings are neither right nor wrong, but behavior is, so we should not make judgments and evaluate feelings, only behavior.

It is important to suppress negative emotionally driven behavior.[60] We cannot choose our feelings or control them. However, we can control how we express our feelings. For example, if someone says something that upsets you, you will feel the emotion and then choose your behavior, such as to say nothing, give the person a dirty look, yell, throw something, or hit the person. People can't see our feelings, only our behavior that expresses those feelings. So we will feel our emotions, but should control our behavior.

Nonverbals Convey Feelings Emotions are often more clearly revealed through nonverbal communications than verbally. For example, if a person is angry, he or she won't usually tell us. But we can tell by the look on the person's face, the tone of his or her voice, the pointing of a finger at us, and so on. A person's smile or frown conveys happy or sad feelings to us. So to truly understand a person's feeling, pay attention to his or her nonverbal behavior as you communicate.

Communication Skills
Refer to CS Question 10.

Emotional Labor At work, we are expected to control our behavior, not our feelings. **Emotional labor** *requires the expression of feeling through desired behavior.* For example, employees are expected to be cheerful with customers, to be pleasant with coworkers, and to avoid expressing feeling through negative behavior—especially aggression and violence at work.[61] Thus, emotional regulation of behavior is important for good human relations and performance.[62]

Managers should encourage employees to express their feelings in a positive way. However, they shouldn't allow employees to go around yelling, swearing, bullying, or hitting others. Unfortunately, a lack of self-control over negative behavior is resulting in an increase in workplace violence.[63] Therefore, dealing with emotions effectively, which you are learning to do, can help prevent negative behavior. Although we may not like some of our coworkers, we should treat them with respectful emotional labor.

WORK APPLICATION 5-17

How well do you hide your feelings from others, such as being disappointed or upset, while using emotional labor?

Also, we shouldn't get caught up in others' emotions. Because people express their feelings with negative behavior doesn't mean we have to match their negative behavior. For example, when someone yells at us, it doesn't mean we have to yell back. Returning negative behavior usually only makes the interaction worse and hurts human relations. You will learn how to deal with emotional people after we discuss global differences.

Global Differences What is acceptable in one culture may not be acceptable in another. Some cultures lack words to express feelings such as anxiety, depression, sadness, and guilt, and they interpret the same emotions differently. Emotional labor expectations vary culturally. For example, in the United States, employees are generally expected to be friendly and to smile at customers. However, in Muslim cultures, smiling is commonly taken as a sign of sexual attraction, so women are discouraged from smiling at men.

Learning Outcome 5-8

Discuss what should and should not be done to calm an emotional person.

Dealing with Emotional People

You will have better communications and human relations if you can deal with emotional employees effectively. The first thing to remember is to follow the guidelines to effective

Communication Skills
Refer to CS Question 11.

human relations and avoid behavior that will get people emotional—that way you don't have to deal with emotional people. Unfortunately, we do sometimes get people emotional with our behavior, and others get people emotional and we have to deal with them, especially managers. Let's begin by discussing what not to do and then what to do when dealing with emotional people.

Don't Argue, Return Negative Behavior, or Belittle the Emotional Person When dealing with an emotional person, don't argue with him or her. And don't return the negative behavior. Unfortunately, negative feelings and behavior tend to occur more frequently at work and have greater consequences for performance than positive feelings do.[64] In the early days of Apple and Microsoft, when Bill Gates worked together with Steve Jobs to create software for Apple, Steve would sometimes express his anger through rude behavior, but Bill responded by becoming very calm. Bill is good when people are emotional.[65] If Bill argued and was rude back, the two might have parted ways and both Apple and Microsoft might not have become as successful as they are today. Think about it: Does arguing or negative behavior really help?

When someone is emotional, *never* make put-down statements like these: "You shouldn't be angry," "Don't be upset," "Don't be a baby," "Just sit down and be quiet," or "I know how you feel." (No one knows how anyone else feels; recall perceptions in Chapter 2). Don't try to make the person feel guilty or bad with statements like, "I'm ashamed of you," "I'm disappointed in you," or "You should be ashamed of yourself." These types of statements only make the feelings stronger. While you may get the person to be quiet, effective communication will not take place. The problem will still exist, and your human relations with the person will suffer because of it, as will your relations with others who see or hear about what you said and did.

Be Empathic and Use Reflecting Statements Recall that strong emotions are a barrier to communications because people can't think and talk logically when they are highly emotional. Being logical with them doesn't work because when we are highly emotional, it doesn't matter what we know or don't know; all that counts is what we feel.[66] Therefore, we have to first deal with the emotion and calm them, and then deal with the content of the issue to resolve any conflicts. To calm emotional people, encourage them to express their feelings in a positive way by being empathic and using reflective responses. However, if emotions are too strong (yours or theirs), it may be wiser to wait until a later time after emotions cool down.[67] Make statements like, "Let's wait until after lunch (do set a time) to discuss this issue."

Be empathic by attempting to see things from the other person's perception and use empathic listening. **Empathic listening** *is the ability to understand and relate to another's situation and feelings.* To listen with empathy doesn't mean you have to agree with the person. Just try to put yourself in his or her place. Do not agree or disagree with the feelings (recall that feelings are not right or wrong—so don't belittle people); simply identify them verbally with reflecting statements.

Reflecting statements *paraphrase feelings back to the person.* Use statements like these: "You were *hurt* when you didn't get the assignment." "You *resent* Bill for not doing his share of the work. Is that what you mean?" "You are *doubtful* that the job will be done on time. Is that what you're saying?" Using empathic listening allows the person to get out the feelings, thus calming him or her. After you deal with emotions, you can go on to work on content (solving problems). Understanding feelings is often the solution, as sometimes all people want is someone to listen to them and understand what they are going though; they are not seeking advice or solutions.

WORK APPLICATION 5-18

Recall a situation in which a manager had to handle an emotional employee (which can be you). Did the manager follow the guidelines for calming an emotional person?

Getting and Giving Criticism

Criticism (finding fault with our behavior) and emotions are related topics because criticism tends to bring out feelings, as people tend to get emotional and defend their behavior

Learning Outcome 5-9

Describe how to get criticism effectively.

even when it's negative and hurts human relations and performance.[68] So when we deal with criticism, we tend to have to deal with emotions. Here are some tips on getting and giving criticism.

Getting Criticism It is great to hear praise for the job we are doing, and we need to hear it, but the only way we can improve is to openly seek criticism.[69] However, if you ask someone for critical feedback, remember that you are asking to hear things that may surprise, upset, or insult you, or hurt your feelings. Let's face it, criticism of our behavior from our boss, peers, or employees is painful. We do not really enjoy being criticized, even when it is constructive, and many people handle criticism poorly.[70] Do you like being told you did something wrong or your performance was not up to par? How well do you listen to criticism and change your behavior to improve? Here are some do's and don'ts for when you get criticism.

First we need to accept the fact that the only way to improve our behavior, human relations, and performance is to accept criticism and change our behavior accordingly. Keep in mind the phrase "no pain, no gain" when it comes to criticism. Recognize that, more often than not, your boss and others want to help you succeed. When you get criticism, whether you ask for it or not, think before you react.[71] We tend to make excuses to preserve our self-image in the face of criticism.[72] But bosses don't want excuses, so view criticism as an opportunity to improve. Stay calm (even when the other person is emotional). Don't blame other people or factors for your behavior and performance.[73] Don't be defensive—listen carefully and change to improve.[74]

If you become emotional, defensive, and blameful (and it is hard not to when you feel attacked), your boss may stop giving feedback and your performance will not improve and your chances for career success with the organization will be limited because you will continue to get mediocre reviews and not understand why.

Communication Skills
Refer to CS Question 12.

WORK APPLICATION 5-19

How would you rate yourself on your ability to accept criticism without getting emotional and defensive? How could you improve your ability to accept criticism?

We can learn great lessons from our mistakes (and we all make them), but we need to avoid repeating mistakes and change our behavior to improve.[75] After you have listened carefully without making excuses, or even if you did, take some time to become more objective and think about the feedback. If you objectively don't agree with the criticism, if you hear it consistently, it doesn't matter what you think. The truth is, you're being perceived that way (Chapter 2), and if you don't change you may not improve and advance.[76]

Create a personal continuous improvement mentality, and keep improving your performance. Although it hurts to get it, in most criticism (no matter how poorly given), regardless of who gives it, there is opportunity for improvement. So don't get bummed out by criticism; instead get fired up and motivated to do better, and change your behavior.[77] Also, when your boss criticizes you, take the initiative to create an action plan and follow-up to check to see how you are doing. Let the boss know that you have changed and improved.[78]

Giving Criticism An important part of the manager's job is to improve employee performance through constructive criticism. If you are (or want to be) a manager, if you are not willing to criticize, maybe you should ask yourself this question: Do I really want to be a manager?[79] In our personal lives, and if we are not managers at work, we don't have the authority to tell people that they need to change their behavior through criticism. However, if we want to help people improve their behavior on or off the job, we need to give criticism.

Criticize carefully using behavior that will not get the person emotional or defensive. A good approach is not to just come out with criticism. Ask the person if he or she wants it. For example, if you see a person do a task that is not effective ask, "Would you like me to show you an easier way to do that?" If the person says yes, he or she is open to your criticism. Give feedback on performance quickly, concisely, privately, and don't humiliate.[80] Keep it short, but clearly and descriptively state the undesired performance and tell the person exactly what needs to be changed to improve.[81] Chapter 6 will provide more details on how to accomplish this task.

Remember that what you think about affects how you feel, and how you feel affects your behavior, human relations, and performance. So think happy, confident thoughts that you will improve to help you stay calm and in control of your emotional behavior and deal effectively with emotional people. Keep in mind that we will continue to deal with emotions in the next chapter, as people are often emotional when they deal with conflict. Complete Self-Assessment Exercise 5-3 to determine how your personality affects your communications, emotions, and acceptance of criticism.

/// Self-Assessment Exercise 5-3 ///

Your Personality Traits and Communications, Emotions, and Criticism

Let's tie personality traits from Chapter 2 together with what we've covered in this chapter. We are going to present some general statements about how your personality may affect your behavior, human relations, and performance. For each area, determine how the information relates to you. This will help you better understand your behavioral strengths and weakness and the areas you may want to improve.

If you have a high *surgency* personality, you most likely are an extrovert and have no difficulty initiating conversations and communicating with others orally. However, you may be dominating communication and prefer vertical communications following the chain of command with centralized authority. Be a team player. Surgency types are often not good at dealing with emotions. You may need to be more attentive to nonverbal communication and emotions. You may be better at giving than getting feedback, so you may need to work at being receptive to feedback. You may also need to work at giving more praise and less criticism.

If you are high in *agreeableness* personality traits, you are most likely a good listener and communicator, preferring oral horizontal communications as a team player. You are probably connected to the grapevine, so be careful not to spread false rumors. You are probably in tune with emotions and nonverbal communication cues. You may be reluctant to give criticism even though it will help others improve.

Your *adjustment* level affects the emotional tone of your communications. If you tend to get emotional, and it is a barrier to communications, you may want to work to keep your emotional response behavior under control. Watch your nonverbal communication because it tells people how you feel about them and it can hurt your human relations. Try not to be sensitive to criticism and not to become defensive, blame others, and give excuses for your negative behavior and performance. At the same time, don't be too critical of others.

If you are high in *conscientiousness,* you tend to have reliable communications. If you are not conscientious, you may want to work at returning messages quickly. You may be so concerned with your own success that you don't pay attention to emotions and nonverbal communication. Criticism may be painful to you, because you try hard to do a good job. But remember that it can lead to more conscientiousness and greater success.

People who are *open to new experience* often initiate communications, because communicating is often part of the new experience. If you are not open to new experience, you may be reluctant to change organizational structure and flows of communication.

Action plan: Based on your personality, what specific things will you do to improve your communications, emotional labor, and acceptance of criticism?

____

____

____

As we bring this chapter to a close, you should understand how organizations are structured and the *flow of communications* throughout the organization. You should know the *communication process* and *barriers* to communications and how to overcome them. You should be able to effectively send, receive, and respond to *messages.* You should understand how *emotions* affect communications and be able to deal effectively with emotional people. You should be able to effectively give and receive *criticism.*

/ / / REVIEW / / /

The chapter review is organized to help you master the 10 learning outcomes for Chapter 5. First provide your own response to each learning outcome, and then check the summary provided to see how well you understand the material. Next, identify the final statement in each section as either true or false (T/F). Correct each false statement. Answers are given at the end of the chapter.

LO 5-1 Describe how communication flows through organizations.

Formal communication flows through communication networks in vertical and horizontal directions. The grapevine is also a major source of informal communication flowing in all directions.

When an employee goes to talk to the boss, the employee is using vertical upward communication. T F

LO 5-2 List and explain the four steps in the communication process.

The four steps in the communication process are: (1) The sender encodes the message and selects the transmission channel; (2) the sender transmits the message; (3) the receiver decodes the message and decides if feedback is needed; and (4) feedback, in the form of a response or a new message, may be transmitted.

Low-context cultures rely heavily on nonverbal communication and subtle situational cues during the communication process. T F

LO 5-3 List the five steps in the message-sending process.

The steps in the message-sending process are: (1) develop rapport, (2) state the communication objective, (3) transmit the message, (4) check understanding, and (5) get a commitment and follow up.

A good way to check understanding is to just ask, "Do you have any questions?" T F

LO 5-4 Describe how to get feedback.

To get feedback, one must be open to feedback, be aware of nonverbal communication, ask questions, and paraphrase.

Effective managers take the time to listen to employee complaints and suggestions for change. T F

LO 5-5 List the three steps in the message-receiving process.

The first step is to listen to the message; the second step is to analyze what has been communicated; the third step is to check understanding by paraphrasing what has been said while watching for nonverbal cues.

Asking questions while listening is part of effective listening. T F

LO 5-6 Define five response styles.

(1) Advising responses provide evaluation, opinion, direction, or instructions. (2) Diverting responses switch the message; change the subject. (3) Probing responses ask for more information. (4) Reassuring responses give supportive statements. (5) Reflecting responses paraphrase the message back to the sender.

Reflecting responses should be used in the beginning stages of most communications. T F

LO 5-7 List the four situational supervisory styles and the four variables to consider in selecting the appropriate communication style.

The autocratic communication style (S-A) demonstrates high task–low relationship (HT–LR) behavior, initiating a closed presentation. The consultative communication style (S-C) demonstrates high task–high relationship (HT–HR) behavior, using a closed presentation for the task with an open elicitation for the relationship. The participative communication style (S-P) demonstrates low task–high relationship (LT–HR) behavior, responding with open elicitation, some initiation, and little presentation. The laissez-faire communication style (S-L) demonstrates low task–low relationship (LT–LR) behavior, responding with the necessary open presentation. The other party is outstanding in information and capability. You respond to the other party with the information, structure, and so forth that the sender wants.

When selecting the appropriate communication style, you should consider four variables: Time—Do I have enough time to use two-way communication? Information—Do I have the necessary information to communicate my message, make a decision, or take action? Acceptance—Will the other party accept my message without any input? Capability (two parts): Ability—Does the other party have the experience or knowledge to participate in two-way communication? Motivation—Does the other party want to participate?

If you don't have time, you use the laissez-fair communication style. T F

LO 5-8 Discuss what should and should not be done to calm an emotional person.

First, don't use behavior that gets people emotional so you don't have to calm them. Don't argue, return negative behavior, or belittle the emotional person because these behaviors tend to make the feelings stronger. Do use empathic listening and reflecting statements because this behavior calms emotions.

When dealing with an emotional person, it is a good idea to determine what the feeling is and if it is right or wrong. T F

LO 5-9 Describe how to get criticism effectively.

First we need to accept the fact that the only way to improve our behavior, human relations, and performance is to accept criticism and change our behavior accordingly. To this end, realizing that criticism is painful, but that without pain there is no gain, openly seek criticism without becoming emotional, defensive, and blameful with excuses for our faulty behavior and performance.

If we don't believe we need to change our behavior, but others do, there is a perception problem and in most cases we should change our behavior. T F

LO 5-10 Define the following 14 key terms.

Select one or more methods: (1) fill in the missing key terms from memory; (2) match the key terms from the end of the review with their definitions below; and/or (3) copy the key terms in order from the key terms at the beginning of the chapter.

__________ refers to the way managers design their firms to achieve the organization's mission and goals.

__________ is the compounded interpersonal communications process across an organization.

__________ is the flow of information both up and down the chain of command.

__________ is the flow of information between colleagues and peers.

The __________ is the informal vehicle through which messages flow throughout the organization.

The __________ consists of a sender who encodes a message and transmits it through a channel to a receiver who decodes it and may give feedback.

__________ is the sender's process of putting the message into a form that the receiver will understand.

The __________ is the physical form of the encoded information.

__________ is the receiver's process of translating the message into a meaningful form.

__________ is the process of having the receiver restate the message in his or her own words.

__________ is the process of verifying messages.

__________ requires the expression of feelings through desired behavior.

__________ is the ability to understand and relate to another's situation and feelings.

__________ paraphrase feelings back to the person.

/ / / KEY TERMS / / /

communication process 131
decoding 133
emotional labor 147
empathic listening 148
encoding 132
feedback 138
grapevine 129
horizontal communication 129
message 132
organizational communication 127
organizational structure 127
paraphrasing 138
reflecting statements 148
vertical communication 128

/ / / COMMUNICATION SKILLS / / /

The following critical thinking questions can be used for class discussion and/or as written assignments to develop communication skills. Be sure to give complete explanations for all questions.

1. Many employees, including managers, complain about organizational communications. What are some of the complaints and how can communications be improved?
2. E-mail is preferred over oral communication at work, and texting is increasingly used. What are the pros and cons of oral versus e-mail or text communication? Which form of communication do you use more often? Which one do you prefer?
3. Many employees waste time using social media at work. Should organizations ban the use of social media for personal reasons during work hours? If so, how?
4. Which two barriers to communication do you believe are the most common in organizations today? What can firms do to help eliminate these two barriers?

5. Do men and women really converse differently? Do you speak about different things with your male and female friends and coworkers? If so, what do you talk about with men versus women?
6. Which is preferable to you, a high-context culture or a low-context culture?
7. How often do you use paraphrasing and ask others to paraphrase to ensure mutual understanding? How effective are you at paraphrasing and asking others to paraphrase, and how can you improve your paraphrasing skills?
8. Select a few friends and/or coworkers. Do you spend more time talking or listening, or do you spend an equal amount of time talking and listening when you are with them? Write down each person's name and the percentage of time you spend talking and listening; for example, 25 percent talking and 75 percent listening, 50–50, 35–65, and so on. After recording the percentages, ask each person what percentage he or she believes you talk and listen. How accurate was your perception? Should you change the amount of time you spend talking versus listening, and if so, how will you go about changing?
9. Which response style do you believe is most commonly used at work? Should the most commonly used response style be reflecting? Why or why not?
10. How do you rate your ability to read nonverbal communications (e.g., facial expressions, vocal quality, gestures, and posture)? What can you do to improve your ability to understand nonverbal communications?
11. Do you agree that women are more emotional than men? Do they show greater emotional expression, experience emotions more intensely, express both positive and negative feelings (except anger) more often, feel more comfortable expressing feelings, and read nonverbal clues better than men?
12. Do you actively seek criticism? How do you rate your ability to accept criticism? Do you get emotional and defensive? How can you improve your ability to accept criticism? After getting criticized, do you change to improve? What advice would you give others to help them accept criticism and change to improve performance?

CASE /// Peter and Korby Clark: The Ranch Golf Club

The Ranch Golf Club, where every player is a special guest for the day, opened in 2001 in Southwick, Massachusetts. The Ranch's competitive advantage is the upscale public course, with links, woods, and a variety of elevations, and unsurpassed service. In less than a year, the Ranch earned a four-star course rating, one of only four in New England. In the January 2003 issue of *Golf Digest,* the Ranch was rated number three in the country in the "new upscale public golf course" category, and it was ranked as the best public golf course in Massachusetts in 2007. The Ranch was voted in the top 50 of all public golf courses in the Golf World's 2010 Readers' Choice Awards. The Ranch was one of only two courses in all of New England that made the list.

Peter and Korby Clark are one-third owners of the Ranch, and Peter is the managing partner with the assistance of his wife, Korby. The Halls, who provided the land for the Ranch, are one-third owners, and Bernard Chiu and Ronald Izen are one-third investment owners.

The key to success at the Ranch is clear, open communication. Peter has to continually communicate with his partners and managers, and nothing takes the place of sitting down face-to-face during regular weekly meetings and listening to each other to continually improve operations. Meetings of department managers with employees focus on the importance of communicating the philosophy of unsurpassed professional service. To communicate professionalism, all employees wear Ranch uniforms and are trained on how to perform high-quality service. Even the words used are chosen to communicate professionalism. For example, the Ranch has player assistants, not rangers; golf cars, not golf carts; and a golf shop, not a pro shop.

Feedback is critical to success at the Ranch; it is how the Clarks and the other Ranch managers know if the players are getting quality service and how to improve service. The Clarks, Ranch managers, and employees are open to player criticism because they realize that the only way to improve is to listen and make changes to improve performance. In fact, Peter and Korby Clark spend much of their time at the Ranch talking to players about their experiences, with the focus on listening for ways to make improvements.

The Clarks and the Ranch managers set clear objectives and have regular meetings with employees to get and give feedback on how the Ranch is progressing toward meeting its objectives. The Ranch managers who evaluate employee performance interact regularly with each employee, employee peers, the players, and other managers at the Ranch, and they use the feedback from others in their performance appraisals.

Peter and Korby Clark are former part owners of nearly 50 Jiffy Lubes, and Peter professionally coached college and high school football and high school baseball. Peter says there are more similarities than differences in running a Jiffy Lube business, managing a golf club, and coaching sports. The focus is the same—high-quality service. You have to treat the customer or player right. Peter uses the same three I's coaching philosophy in all three situations. You need *intensity* to be prepared to do the job right, *integrity* to do the right thing when no one is watching, and *intimacy* to be a team player. If one person does not do the job right, everyone is negatively affected. In business and sports, you need to strive to be the best. You need to set and meet challenging goals. Peter strongly believes in being positive and in the need to develop a supportive working relationship, which includes sitting down to talk and really listening to the other person.

Go to the Internet: For current information about the Ranch Golf Club, use the Internet address www.theranchgolfclub.com. You can take a virtual tour of the golf course online.

Support your answers to the following questions with specific information from the case and text, or other information you get from the web or other sources.

1. Briefly describe the organizational communications flow at the Ranch.

2. How do the interpersonal communication skills of Peter Clark affect behavior, human relations, and performance at the Ranch?

3. Do you think Peter Clark spends more time sending or receiving messages, or an equal amount of time doing both?

4. Which of the 13 listening tips do you think are most relevant for Peter Clark?

5. Assess Peter and Korby Clark's use of feedback.

6. Which response style do you think Peter Clark uses most often?

Cumulative Questions

7. How do Peter and Korby Clark strive to meet the goal of human relations (Chapter 1)?

8. Assess Peter Clark's personality in relation to each of the Big Five dimensions (Chapter 2).

9. Assess Peter Clark's attitude, self-concept, values, and ethics (Chapter 3).

Case Exercise and Role-play

Preparation: Here is your situation. Peter Clark was at lunch and overheard the employee server Chris Smith being a bit rude to a diner. The customer said, "I ordered the steak rare, and you screwed up and brought me a well-done steak." The server, in an emotionally loud voice, said "I didn't screw up, you did. But I will get you another one anyway," and walked away to get it.

Your instructor will assign you to be Peter Clark or the employee server Chris Smith. Peter prepares to talk to the server about being rude to customers. Be sure to follow the steps in Model 5.1, the message-sending process. The server role-players should put themselves in the situation knowing that Chris had a big fight with his significant other the night before and they broke up, so he has been upset all day. But prepare for the meeting following the steps in Model 5.2, the message-receiving process.

Role-Play: Matched pairs of Peter Clark and the server Chris Smith role-play the meeting. The meeting may be done in small groups, or two people may role-play before the entire class.

After the meeting, the group or class discusses and critiques the effectiveness of the meeting. Identify any statements that hurt the conflict resolution, and offer alternatives. Also, identify things not said and done that could have helped resolve the conflict. Was empathy used with reflecting statements? How well were emotional behaviors handled?

OBJECTIVE CASE /// Communication?

In the following dialogue, Chris is the manager and Sandy is the employee.

CHRIS: I need you to get a metal plate ready for the Stern job.

SANDY: OK.

CHRIS: I need a ¾-inch plate. I want a ½-inch hole a little off center. No, you'd better make it ⅝. In the left corner I need about a ⅜-inch hole. And on the right top portion, about ⅞ of an inch from the left side, drill a ¼-inch hole. You got it?

SANDY: I think so.

CHRIS: Good, I'll be back later.

Later.

CHRIS: Do you have the plate ready?

SANDY: It's right here.

CHRIS: This isn't what I asked for. I said a ½-inch hole a little off center; this is too much off center. Do it again so it will fit.

SANDY: You're the boss. I'll do it again.

Answer the following questions. Then in the space between questions, state why you selected that answer.

_______ 1. Chris and Sandy communicated.
a. true
b. false

_______ 2. Chris's primary goal of communication was to:
a. influence
b. inform
c. express feelings

_______ 3. Chris was the:
a. sender/decoder
b. receiver/decoder
c. sender/encoder
d. receiver/encoder

_______ 4. Sandy was the:
a. sender/decoder
b. receiver/decoder
c. sender/encoder
d. receiver/encoder

_______ 5. The message transmission medium was:
a. oral
b. written
c. nonverbal
d. combined

_______ 6. Chris followed guidelines to getting feedback on messages by
a. being open to feedback
b. being aware of nonverbal communication
c. asking questions
d. paraphrasing communication
e. none of these

_______ 7. Which step(s) did Chris follow in the message-sending process? (You may select more than one answer.)
a. step 1
b. step 2
c. step 3
d. step 4
e. step 5

_______ 8. Sandy was an active listener.
a. true
b. false

_______ 9. Sandy's response style was primarily:
a. advising
b. diverting
c. probing
d. reassuring
e. reflecting

_______ 10. Chris used the _______________ supervisory style.
a. autocratic
b. consultative
c. participative
d. laissez-faire

_______ 11. In Chris's situation, how would you have given the instructions to Sandy?

Note: Students may role-play giving instructions.

/ / / SKILL-BUILDING EXERCISE 5-1 / / /

Giving Instructions

In-Class Exercise (Group)

Objective: To develop your ability to give and receive messages (communication skills).

AACSB: The primary AACSB learning standard skill developed through this exercise is communication abilities.

Experience: You will plan, give, and receive instructions for the completion of a drawing of three objects.

Preparation: No preparation is necessary except reading the chapter. The instructor will provide the original drawings.

Procedure 1 (3–7 minutes)

Read all of procedure 1 twice. The task is for the manager to give an employee instructions for completing a drawing of three objects. The objects must be drawn to scale and look like photocopies of the originals. You will have 15 minutes to complete the task.

The exercise has four separate parts, or steps.

1. The manager plans.
2. The manager gives the instructions.
3. The employee does the drawing.
4. The results are evaluated.

Rules: The rules are numbered to correlate with the four parts above.

1. *Planning.* While planning, the manager may write out instructions for the employee but may not do any drawing of any kind.
2. *Instructions.* While giving instructions, the manager may not show the original drawing to the employee. (The instructor will give it to you.) The instructions may be given orally, and/or in writing, but no nonverbal hand gestures are allowed. The employee may take notes while the instructions are being given but cannot do any drawing with or without a pen. The manager must give the instructions for all three objects before drawing begins.
3. *Drawing.* Once the employee begins the drawing, the manager should watch but no longer communicate in any way.
4. *Evaluation.* When the employee is finished or the time is up, the manager shows the employee the original drawing. Discuss how you did. Turn to the integration section and answer the questions. The manager writes down the answers.

Procedure 2 (2–5 minutes)

Half of the class members act as the manager first and give instructions. Managers move their seats to one of the four walls (spread out). They should be facing the center of the room with their backs close to the wall.

Employees sit in the middle of the room until called on by a manager. When called on, they bring a seat to the manager. They sit facing the manager so that they will not be able to see any manager's drawing.

Procedure 3 (15–20 minutes)

The instructor gives each manager a copy of the drawing. Be careful not to let any employees see it. The manager plans the instructions. When managers are ready, they call an employee and give the instructions. It may be helpful to use the message-sending process. Be sure to follow the rules. The employee should do the drawing on the page titled "Employee

Drawing." If using written instructions, use nonbook paper. You have 15 minutes to complete the drawing, and possibly 5 minutes for integration (evaluation). When you finish the drawing, turn to the evaluation questions in the integration section below.

Procedure 4 (15–20 minutes)

The employees are now the managers and sit in the seats facing the center of the room. New employees go to the center of the room until called on.

Follow procedure 3, with the instructor giving a different drawing. Do not work with the same person; change partners.

Evaluating Questions: You may select more than one answer.

_______ 1. The goal of communication was to:

a. influence *b.* inform *c.* express feelings

_______ 2. Feedback was:

a. immediate *c.* performance-oriented

b. specific and accurate *d.* positive

_______ 3. The manager transmitted the message:

a. orally *c.* nonverbally

b. in writing *d.* using a combined method

_______ 4. The manager spent _______ time planning

a. too much *b.* too little *c.* the right amount of

The next six questions relate to the message-sending process:

_______ 5. The manager developed rapport (step 1).

a. true *b.* false

_______ 6. The manager stated the communication objective (step 2).

a. true *b.* false

_______ 7. The manager transmitted the message _______ (step 3).

a. effectively *b.* ineffectively

_______ 8. The manager checked understanding by using _______ (step 4).

a. direct questions *c.* both direct questions and paraphrasing

b. paraphrasing *d.* neither direct questions nor paraphrasing

Integration

_______ 9. The amount of checking was:

a. too frequent *b.* too infrequent *c.* about right

_______ 10. The manager got a commitment and followed up (step 5).

a. true *b.* false

_______ 11. The manager and/or employee got emotional.

a. true *b.* false

_______ 12. The primary response style used by the manager was:

a. advising *c.* probing *e.* reflecting

b. diverting *d.* reassuring

_______ 13. The primary response style used by the employee was:

a. advising *c.* probing *e.* reflecting

b. diverting *d.* reassuring

_____ **14.** The manager used the _____ supervisory style.

a. autocratic *c.* participative

b. consultative *d.* laissez-faire

_____ **15.** The appropriate style was:

a. autocratic *c.* participative

b. consultative *d.* laissez-faire

_____ **16.** Were the objects drawn to approximate scale? If not, why not?

_____ **17.** Did you follow the rules? If not, why not?

_____ **18.** If you could do this exercise over again, what would you do differently?

Conclusion: The instructor leads a class discussion and/or makes concluding remarks.

Application (2–4 minutes): What did I learn from this experience? How will I use this knowledge in the future?

Sharing: Volunteers give their answers to the application section.

/ / / EMPLOYEE DRAWING / / /

/// SKILL-BUILDING EXERCISE 5-2 ///

Listening Skills

Preparation: In-Class Exercise

Recall a time when you did something really good that you shared with a friend. It should take around 5 minutes to describe. Write a brief description. ______________________________

____

Objective: To experience and/or observe and assess listening skills.

AACSB: The primary AACSB learning standard skill developed through this exercise is communication abilities. Select an option and set up for the role-play.

Procedure 1 (2–3 minutes)

Option A: One person tells his or her good news to one other person as the class observes.

Option B: Break into groups of 6 to 8. One person tells his or her good news to one other person as the other group members observe.

Procedure 2 (5–7 minutes)

Tell the other person your good news as though it just happened.

Procedure 3 (8–12 minutes)

Assess the listening skills below by giving specific examples of how the person did or did not do a good job of listening. Was the person an empathic listener? Explain.

Assess the listener on the 13 listening tips: Turn to the tips on page 142 and assess the person on each of the 13 tips, with examples of what was done well and what could be improved. Which response styles did the listener use (advising, diverting, probing, reassuring, or reflecting)?

Conclusion: The instructor leads a class discussion and/or makes concluding remarks.

Application (2– 4 minutes): What did I learn from this experience? How will I use this knowledge in the future?

Sharing: Volunteers give their answers to the application section.

/// SKILL-BUILDING EXERCISE 5-3 ///

Situational Communication

Preparation (Individual and Group)

Begin this exercise by determining your preferred communication style in Self-Assessment Exercise 5-4.

/// BMV–6 Self-Assessment Exercise 5-4 ///

Determining Your Preferred Communication Style

To determine your preferred communication style, select the *one* alternative that most closely describes what you would do in each of the 12 situations below. Do not be concerned with trying to pick the correct answer; select the alternative that best describes what *you* would actually do. Circle the letter *a, b, c,* or *d*. Ignore the _____ time _____ information _____ acceptance _____ capability/ _____ style and S _____ lines. They will be explained later.

_____ 1. Wendy, a knowledgeable person from another department, comes to you, the engineering supervisor, and requests that you design a special product to her specifications. You would: _____ time _____ information _____ acceptance _____ capability/ _____ style

/// BMV–6 Self-Assessment Exercise 5-4 /// (*continued*)

a. Control the conversation and tell Wendy what you will do for her. S _____
b. Ask Wendy to describe the product. Once you understand it, you would present your ideas. Let her realize that you are concerned and want to help with your ideas. S _____
c. Respond to Wendy's request by conveying understanding and support. Help clarify what is to be done by you. Offer ideas, but do it her way. S _____
d. Find out what you need to know. Let Wendy know you will do it her way. S _____

_____ 2. Your department has designed a product that is to be fabricated by Saul's department. Saul has been with the company longer than you have; he knows his department. Saul comes to you to change the product design. You decide to: _____ time _____ information _____ acceptance _____ capability/_____ style

a. Listen to the change and why it would be beneficial. If you believe Saul's way is better, change it; if not, explain why the original design is superior. If necessary, insist that it be done your way. S _____
b. Tell Saul to fabricate it any way he wants to. S _____
c. You are busy; tell Saul to do it your way. You don't have time to listen and argue with him. S _____
d. Be supportive; make changes together as a team. S _____

_____ 3. Upper management has a decision to make. The managers call you to a meeting and tell you they need some information to solve a problem they describe to you. You: _____ time _____ information _____ acceptance _____ capability/_____ style

a. Respond in a manner that conveys personal support and offer alternative ways to solve the problem. S _____
b. Respond to their questions. S _____
c. Explain how to solve the problem. S _____
d. Show your concern by explaining how to solve the problem and why your solution is an effective one. S _____

_____ 4. You have a routine work order. The work order is to be placed verbally and completed in three days. Sue, the receiver, is very experienced and willing to be of service to you. You decide to: _____ time _____ information _____ acceptance _____ capability/_____ style

a. Explain your needs, but let Sue make the order decision. S _____
b. Tell Sue what you want and why you need it. S _____
c. Decide together what to order. S _____
d. Simply give Sue the order. S _____

_____ 5. Work orders from the staff department normally take three days; however, you have an emergency and need the order today. Your colleague, Jim, the department supervisor, is knowledgeable and somewhat cooperative. You decide to: _____ time _____ information _____ acceptance _____ capability/_____ style

a. Tell Jim that you need the work order by three o'clock and will return at that time to pick it up. S _____
b. Explain the situation and how the organization will benefit by expediting the order. Volunteer to help in any way you can. S _____
c. Explain the situation and ask Jim when the order will be ready. S _____
d. Explain the situation and together come to a solution to your problem. S _____

_____ 6. Danielle, a peer with a record of high performance, has recently had a drop in productivity. Her problem is affecting your performance. You know Danielle has a family problem. You: _____ time _____ information _____ acceptance _____ capability/_____ style

a. Discuss the problem; help Danielle realize the problem is affecting her work and yours. Supportively discuss ways to improve the situation. S _____
b. Tell the boss about it and let him decide what to do about it. S _____
c. Tell Danielle to get back on the job. S _____
d. Discuss the problem and tell Danielle how to solve the work situation; be supportive. S _____

_____ 7. You are a knowledgeable supervisor. You buy supplies from Peter regularly.
He is an excellent salesperson and very knowledgeable about your situation. You are placing your weekly order. You decide to: _____ time _____ information _____ acceptance _____ capability/_____ style

a. Explain what you want and why. Develop a supportive relationship. S _____
b. Explain what you want and ask Peter to recommend products. S _____
c. Give Peter the order. S _____
d. Explain your situation and allow Peter to make the order. S _____

(*continued*)

/// BMV–6 Self-Assessment Exercise 5-4 /// (*continued*)

_____ 8. Jean, a knowledgeable person from another department, has asked you to perform a routine staff function to her specifications. You decide to: _____ time _____ information _____ acceptance _____ capability/ _____ style

a. Perform the task to her specifications without questioning her. S _____
b. Tell her that you will do it the usual way. S _____
c. Explain what you will do and why. S _____
d. Show your willingness to help; offer alternative ways to do it. S _____

_____ 9. Tom, a salesperson, has requested an order for your department's services with a short delivery date. As usual, Tom claims it is a take-it-or-leave-it offer. He wants your decision now, or within a few minutes, because he is in the customer's office. Your action is to: _____ time _____ information _____ acceptance _____ capability/ _____ style

a. Convince Tom to work together to come up with a later date. S _____
b. Give Tom a yes or no answer. S _____
c. Explain your situation and let Tom decide if you should take the order. S _____
d. Offer an alternative delivery date. Work on your relationship; show your support. S _____

_____ 10. As a time-and-motion expert, you have been called in regard to a complaint about the standard time it takes to perform a job. As you analyze the entire job, you realize one element of the complaint should take longer, but other elements should take less time. The end result is a shorter total standard time for the job. You decide to: _____ time _____ information _____ acceptance _____ capability/ _____ style

a. Tell the operator and supervisor that the total time must be decreased and why. S _____
b. Agree with the operator and increase the standard time. S _____
c. Explain your findings. Deal with the operator's or supervisor's concerns, but ensure compliance with your new standard. S _____
d. Together with the operator, develop a standard time. S _____

_____ 11. You approve budget allocations for projects. Marie, who is very competent in developing budgets, has come to you. You: _____ time _____ information _____ acceptance _____ capability/ _____ style

a. Review the budget, make revisions, and explain them in a supportive way. Deal with concerns, but insist on your changes. S _____
b. Review the proposal and suggest areas where changes may be needed. Make changes together, if needed. S _____
c. Review the proposed budget, make revisions, and explain them. S _____
d. Answer any questions or concerns Marie has and approve the budget as is. S _____

_____ 12. You are a sales manager. A customer has offered you a contract for your product with a short delivery date. The offer is open for two days. The contract would be profitable for you and the organization. The cooperation of the production department is essential to meet the deadline. Tim, the production manager, and you do not get along very well because of your repeated requests for quick delivery. Your action is to: _____ time _____ information _____ acceptance _____ capability/ _____ style

a. Contact Tim and try to work together to complete the contract. S _____
b. Accept the contract and convince Tim in a supportive way to meet the obligation. S _____
c. Contact Tim and explain the situation. Ask him if you and he should accept the contract, but let him decide. S _____
d. Accept the contract. Contact Tim and tell him to meet the obligation. If he resists, tell him you will go to his boss. S _____

To determine your preferred communication style, in the table below, circle the letter corresponding to the alternative you chose in situations 1 to 12. The column headings indicate the style you selected.

/// BMV–6 Self-Assessment Exercise 5-4 /// (*continued*)

	Autocratic	Consultative	Participative	Laissez-faire
1.	a	b	c	d
2.	c	a	d	b
3.	c	d	a	b
4.	d	b	c	a
5.	a	b	d	c
6.	c	d	a	b
7.	c	a	b	d
8.	b	c	d	a
9.	b	d	a	c
10.	a	c	d	b
11.	c	a	b	d
12.	d	b	a	c
Total	______	______	______	______

Add the number of circled items per column. Adding the numbers in the Total row should equal 12. The column with the highest number represents your preferred communication style. There is no one best style in all situations. The more evenly distributed the numbers are between the four styles, the more flexible your communication style is. A total of 0 or 1 in any column may indicate a reluctance to use that style. You could have problems in situations calling for the use of that style.

Selecting the Appropriate Communication Style

Successful people understand different styles of communication and select communication styles based on the situation. There are three steps to follow when selecting the appropriate communication style in a given situation.

- *Step 1: Diagnose the situation.* Answer the questions for each of the four situation variables. In Self-Assessment Exercise 5-4 you were asked to select one alternative situation. You were told to ignore the _____ time _____ information _____ acceptance _____ capability/ _____ style and S _____ lines. Now you will complete this part in the In-Class Skill-Building Exercise 5-3 by placing the style letters (S-A, S-C, S-P, S-L) on the lines provided for each of the 12 situations.
- *Step 2: Select the appropriate style for the situation.* After analyzing the four variables, select the appropriate style for the situation. In some situations, where variables support conflicting styles, select the style of the most important variable for the situation. For example, capability may be outstanding (C-4), but you have all the information needed (S-A). If the information is more important, use the autocratic style even though the capability is outstanding. When doing In-Class Skill-Building Exercise 5-3, place the letters (S-A, S-C, S-P, S-L) for the appropriate styles on the style lines.
- *Step 3: Implement the appropriate communication style.* During In-Class Skill-Building Exercise 5-3, you will identify one of the four communication styles for each alternative action; place the S-A, S-C, S-P, or S-L on the S lines. Select the alternative *a, b, c,* or *d* that represents the appropriate communication for each of the 12 situations.

The table below summarizes the material from the chapter on pages 145–146 and in this section. Use it to determine the appropriate communication style in situation 1 below and during In-Class Skill-Building Exercise 5-3.

MODEL 5.3 | Situational Communications

Step 1: Diagnose the Situation.

Variable	Use of Communication Style
Time	No S-A (do not consider the other three variables) Yes S-A, S-C, S-P, or S-L (consider other three variables)
Information	All S-A, some S-C, little S-P or S-L
Acceptance	Accept S-A, reluctance S-C, reject S-P or S-L
Capability	Low S-A, moderate S-C, high S-P, outstanding S-L

Step 2: Select the Appropriate Style for the Situation.

Autocratic (S-A)	Consultative (S-C)	Participative (S-P)	Laissez-Faire (S-L)
High task–low relationship behavior	High task–high relationship behavior	Low task–high relationship behavior	Low task–low relationship behavior
You take charge. You want things done your way.	You want things done your way, but you are willing to discuss thing.	You are seeking others' input on how to do things, or supporting them.	You are willing to do things the other person's way; help as needed.

Step 3: Implement the Appropriate Communication Style.

During In-Class Skill-Building Exercise 5-3, you will identify each communication style and select the alternative (*a*, *b*, *c*, or *d*) that represents the appropriate style.

Determining the Appropriate Communication Style for Situation 1

Step 1: Diagnose the situation. Answer the four variable questions from the model, and place the letters on the four variable lines below.

1. Wendy, a knowledgeable person from another department, comes to you, the engineering supervisor, and requests that you design a special product to her specifications. You would: time _____ information _____ acceptance _____ capability/ _____ style
   a. Control the conversation and tell Wendy what you will do for her. S_____
   b. Ask Wendy to describe the product. Once you understand it, you would present your ideas. Let her realize that you are concerned and want to help with your ideas. S _____
   c. Respond to Wendy's request by conveying understanding and support. Help clarify what is to be done by you. Offer ideas, but do it her way. S _____
   d. Find out what you need to know. Let Wendy know you will do it her way. S _____

Step 2: Select the appropriate style for the situation. Review the four variables. If they are all consistent, select one style. If they are conflicting, select the most important variable as the style to use. Place its letters (S-A, S-C, S-P, or S-L) on the style line.

Step 3: Select the appropriate action. Review the four alternative actions. Identify the communication style for each, placing its letters on the S _____ line, then check the appropriate match alternative.

Let's see how you did.

1. *Time* is available; it can be either S-C, S-P, or S-L. *Information:* You have little information, so you need to use a participative or laissez-faire style to find out what Wendy wants done: S-P or S-L. *Acceptance:* If you try to do it your way rather than Wendy's way, she will most likely reject it. You need to use a participative or laissez-faire style: S-P or S-L. *Capability:* Wendy is knowledgeable and is highly capable: S-P.
2. Reviewing the four variables, you see that there is a mixture of S-P and S-L. Since you are an engineer, it is appropriate to participate with Wendy to give her what she needs. Therefore, the choice is S-P.
3. *Alternative a* is S-A; this is the autocratic style, high task–low relationship. *Alternative b* is S-C; this is the consultative style, high task–high relationship. *Alternative c* is S-P; this is the participative style, low task–high relationship. *Alternative d* is S-L; this is laissez-faire, low task–low relationship behavior.

If you selected *c* as your action, you chose the most appropriate action for the situation. This was a 3-point answer. If you selected *d* as your answer, this is also a good alternative; it scores 2 points. If you selected *b,* you get 1 point for overdirecting. If you selected *a,* you get zero points; this is too much directing and will most likely hurt communication.

The better you match your communication style to the situation, the more effective you will be at communicating.

In-Class Exercise

Objective: To develop your ability to communicate using the appropriate style for the situation.

AACSB: The primary AACSB learning standard skills developed through this exercise are analytic skills and communication abilities.

Preparation: You should have completed the 12 situations in Self-Assessment Exercise 5-4. In the self-assessment, you were selecting the alternative that *you* would choose in the situation. In this part of the skill-building exercise, you are trying to select the *most appropriate* alternative that will result in the most effective communication. Thus, you may be selecting different answers.

Experience: You will work at selecting the appropriate style for the 12 situations in Self-Assessment Exercise 5-4. On the time, information, acceptance, and capability lines, place the letters S-A, S-C, S-P, or S-L, whichever is appropriate for the situation. Based on your diagnoses, select the one style you would use. Place the letters S-A, S-C, S-P, or S-L on the style line. On the four S lines write the letters S-A, S-C, S-P, or S-L to identify each style being used.

Procedure 1 (3–8 minutes)
The instructor reviews the Situational Communications Model and explains how to apply it to determine the appropriate style for situation 1.

Procedure 2 (6–8 minutes)
Turn to situation 2. Using the model, select the appropriate style. If you have time, identify each alternative style (3–4 minutes). The instructor goes over the recommended answers (3–4 minutes).

Procedure 3 (20–50 minutes)

A. Break into groups of two or three. As a team, apply the model to situations 3 through 7 (15–20 minutes). The instructor will go over the appropriate answers when all teams are done or the time is up (4–6 minutes).

B. (Optional) Break into new groups of two or three and do situations 8 through 12 (15–20 minutes). The instructor will go over the appropriate answers (4–6 minutes).

Conclusion: The instructor leads a class discussion and/or makes concluding remarks.

Application (2–4 minutes): What did I learn from this experience? How will I use this knowledge in the future?

Sharing: Volunteers give their answers to the application section.

/ / ANSWERS TO TRUE/FALSE QUESTIONS / /

1. T.
2. F. High-context cultures rely heavily on nonverbal communication and subtle situational cues during the communication process.
3. F. Asking direct questions and paraphrasing are two techniques used to check understanding.
4. T.
5. T.
6. T.
7. F. With no time, you use the autocratic communication style.
8. F. Feelings are neither right or wrong, and identifying a feeling as wrong is a form of belittling a person, which should be avoided. Again, we can't control our feelings, just how we express our feelings as behavior.
9. T.

CHAPTER 6

Dealing with Conflict

LEARNING OUTCOMES

After completing this chapter, you should be able to:

LO 6-1 Describe the three ego states of transactional analysis.

LO 6-2 Explain the three types of transactions.

LO 6-3 Identify the differences between passive, aggressive, and assertive behavior.

LO 6-4 List the four steps of assertive behavior.

LO 6-5 State when and how to use five conflict management styles.

LO 6-6 List the steps of initiating, responding to, and mediating conflict resolutions.

LO 6-7 Define the following 14 key terms (in order of appearance in the chapter):

transactional analysis (TA)
ego states
types of transactions
assertiveness
conflict
forcing conflict style
avoiding conflict style
accommodating conflict style
compromising conflict style
collaborating conflict style
initiating conflict resolution steps
XYZ model
responding to conflict resolution steps
mediating conflict resolution steps

/ / / Larry and Helen work together doing the same job at Harvey's, a department store in Springfield. They share a special calculator because it is expensive and it is used for only part of their job. The calculator is generally kept in one person's possession until the other person requests it. Recently, the amount of time each needs to use the calculator has increased.

When Larry wants the calculator, he says, "I need the calculator now" (in a bold, intimidating voice), and Helen gives it to him, even when she is using it. When Helen needs the calculator, she says, "I don't like to bother you, but I need the calculator." If Larry is using it, he tells Helen that he will give it to her when he is finished with it, and Helen says, "OK." Helen doesn't think this arrangement is fair and is getting upset with Larry. But she hasn't said anything to Larry yet. Larry comes over to Helen's desk, and this conversation takes place:

LARRY: I need the calculator right now.

HELEN: I'm sick and tired of your pushing me around. Go back to your desk, and I'll bring it to you when I'm good and ready.

LARRY: What's wrong with you? You've never acted like this before.

HELEN: Just take the calculator and go back to your desk and leave me alone.

LARRY: *(Says nothing; just takes the calculator and leaves.)*

HELEN: *(Watches Larry walk back to his desk with the calculator, feels a bit guilty, and thinks to herself)* Why do I let little annoyances build up until I explode and end up yelling at people? It's rather childish behavior to let people walk all over me, then to reverse and be tough and rude. I wish I could stand up for my rights in a positive way without hurting my relations. ///

HOW INTERPERSONAL DYNAMICS AFFECT BEHAVIOR, HUMAN RELATIONS, AND PERFORMANCE

The three topics of this chapter—transactional analysis, assertiveness, and conflict management—all involve interpersonal dynamics through communication. All three deal with your *emotions* and those of others in an effective way to enhance behavior, human relations, and performance.[1] Dealing with emotions, your own and others', is part of emotional intelligence.[2]

Transactional analysis is a method for determining how people interact. When we interact, behavior can be passive, aggressive, or assertive. During human relations, transactions can go poorly, people can be aggressive, and it is common for people to disagree and be in *conflict*.[3] Behavior used when people agree and when they are in conflict differs, and those differences affect human relations.[4] How teams manage conflict is a crucial factor in their success.[5] Putting these topics together, you should realize that during human relations (transactional analysis), the behavior used (passive, aggressive, or assertive) affects whether or not there is a conflict and performance.

When you interact with people, you can try to push people around, you can let people push you around, or you can stand up for your rights (assertiveness).[6] When you are in disagreement with others (conflict), you can decide to ignore or to resolve your differences.[7] Dealing with your emotions and transacting with people on the appropriate level, assertively standing up for your rights, and resolving your conflicts without hurting human relations will improve your effectiveness in organizations and in your personal life.[8] That's what this chapter is about.

TRANSACTIONAL ANALYSIS

Before we begin, complete Self-Assessment Exercise 6-1 to determine your preferred transactional analysis (TA) style.

/// Self-Assessment Exercise 6-1 ///

Your Preferred Transactional Analysis Style

Turn to Skill-Building Exercise 6-1, Transactional Analysis, on page 194. Ignore the directions, steps 1 to 4. Go directly to the 10 situations. Put yourself in the responder's position (1—Sue, 2—Saul, . . . 10—Mike), and place a check mark after the letter (*not* on the line) of the one response that best describes what you would say in each situation. Be honest; don't try to pick the response you think is correct. After selecting your 10 responses, circle the letter of your response for each situation in the table on the next page.

(continued)

/// Self-Assessment Exercise 6-1 /// (*continued*)

Situation	Critical Parent	Sympathetic Parent	Natural Child	Adapted Child	Adult
1.	*a*	*b*	*d*	*c*	*e*
2.	*d*	*c*	*e*	*a*	*b*
3.	*b*	*d*	*a*	*c*	*e*
4.	*c*	*e*	*b*	*d*	*a*
5.	*e*	*b*	*d*	*a*	*c*
6.	*a*	*b*	*e*	*d*	*c*
7.	*e*	*a*	*b*	*c*	*d*
8.	*b*	*c*	*e*	*d*	*a*
9.	*a*	*c*	*d*	*b*	*e*
10.	*a*	*e*	*d*	*c*	*b*
Total					

Scoring: Add the number of letters circled in each column. The number in each column should be between 0 and 10, and the total of all columns should equal 10. The column with your highest total is your preferred TA style. If it's not adult, or even if it is, you may want to improve your TA behavior.

Communication Skills
Refer to CS Question 1.

Transactional analysis (TA) *is a method of understanding behavior in interpersonal dynamics.* In fact, there is an International Transactional Analysis Association (itaaworld.org) that publishes the *Transactional Analysis Journal.* Eric Berne developed TA in 1960 in the field of psychology. A few years after its development, Berne applied TA to business in his bestselling book, *Games People Play.*[9]

In this section you will learn about your preferred TA style (called ego state in TA jargon), the types of human relations transactions you have, and your attitude toward yourself and others (called life positions). You will also learn about giving positive and negative feedback (called stroking) during human relations.

Learning Outcome 6-1

Describe the three ego states of transactional analysis.

Ego States and Types of Transactions

Ego States According to Berne, we all have three major ego states that affect our behavior or the way we transact through communication. The three **ego states** are the *parent, child,* and *adult.* We change ego states throughout the day; even during a single discussion, a series of transactions can take place between different ego states. Your parent, child, and adult ego states interact with other people's parent, child, and adult ego states. Understanding the ego state of the person you are interacting with can help you understand his or her behavior and how to transact in an effective way.[10] The three ego states of TA are (1) *parent:* the critical parent is evaluative while the sympathetic parent is supportive; (2) *child:* the natural child is curious while the adapted child is rebellious; and (3) *adult:* the adult is a thinking, unemotional state of ego. See Exhibit 6.1 for a more detailed description of the ego states.

Generally, the most effective behavior, human relations, and performance come from the adult ego state.[11] When interacting with others, you should be aware of their ego state. Are they acting like a parent, a child, or an adult? Identifying their ego state will help you understand why they are behaving the way they are and help you determine which ego state you should use during the interaction. For example, if the person is acting like an adult, you most likely should too. If the person is acting like a child, it may be appropriate for you to

EXHIBIT 6.1 | Transactional Analysis Ego States

TA Ego State	Description
Parent	
1. Critical parent	Controls the conversation using advising responses (Chapter 5) that are judgmental, opinionated, demanding, disapproving, or disciplining, telling others what to do.
2. Sympathetic parent	Uses reassuring responses (Chapter 5) that are protecting, permitting, consoling, caring, or nurturing, to be supportive.
Child	
1. Natural child	Uses probing responses (Chapter 5) that show curiosity, fun, fantasy, or impulsiveness.
2. Adapted child	Responds with confrontational advising responses (Chapter 5) that express rebelliousness, pouting, anger, fear, anxiety, inadequacy, or procrastination.
Adult	Behaves in a thinking, rational, calculating, factual, unemotional manner with cool and calm behavior. Avoids getting caught up in others' emotions.

act like a parent rather than an adult. And there are times when it is appropriate to act out of the child ego state and have a good time.

Learning Outcome 6-2

Explain the three types of transactions

Communication Skills
Refer to CS Question 2.

Types of Transactions Within ego states there are three different **types of transactions:** *complementary, crossed, and ulterior.* The three types of transactions are (1) *complementary:* the sender of the message gets the intended response from the receiver; (2) *crossed:* the sender does not get the expected response; and (3) *ulterior:* the person appears to be in one ego state, but his or her behavior comes from a different ego state. See Exhibit 6.2 for examples and common results of each transaction.

APPLICATION SITUATIONS / / /

Transactional Analysis AS 6-1

Identify each transaction as being:

A. Complementary B. Crossed C. Ulterior

_______ 1. "Would you help me move this package over there?" "Sure thing."

_______ 2. "Will you serve on my committee?" "Yes, I think the experience will be helpful to me" (thinking—I want to get to know you, you're cute).

_______ 3. "Will you help me fill out this report?" "You have done several of them. Do it on your own; then I will check it for you."

_______ 4. "How much will you pay me to do the job?" "$10." "What! You're either joking or trying to take advantage of me."

_______ 5. "You're lying." "No, I'm not! You're the one who is lying."

WORK APPLICATION 6-1

Give an example of a complementary transaction you experienced. Be sure to identify the ego states involved.

WORK APPLICATION 6-2

Give an example of a crossed transaction you experienced. Be sure to identify the ego states involved.

WORK APPLICATION 6-3

Give an example of an ulterior transaction you experienced. Be sure to identify the ego states involved.

EXHIBIT 6.2 | Types of Transactions

Transaction	Example	Common Result
Complementary	An employee makes a mistake and, wanting some sympathy, apologizes to the boss. *Employee:* "I just dropped the thing when I was almost done. Now I have to do it all over again." *Supervisor*: "It happens to all of us; don't worry about it."	Generally, complementary transactions result in more effective communication with fewer hurt feelings and arguments. Exceptions are if an employee uses an adapted child or critical parent ego state and the supervisor does too. These complementary transactions can lead to problem transactions.
Crossed	Let's return to our first example. *Employee:* "I just dropped the thing when I was almost done. Now I have to do it all over again." *Supervisor*: "You are so clumsy.	Generally, crossed transactions result in surprise, disappointment, and hurt feelings for the sender of the message. The unexpected response often gets the person emotional, which often results in his or her changing to the adapted child ego state, which causes the communication to deteriorate further, often into an argument. Crossed transactions can be helpful when the negative parent or child ego response is crossed with an adult response. This crossover may result in the preferred adult-to-adult conversation.
Ulterior	A person came up to a consultant and complained about his boss in the adult ego state. When the consultant gave advice, the participant twice had quick responses as to why the advice would not work (child rather than adult behavior). The consultant realized that what the participant actually wanted was sympathetic understanding for his situation, not advice. The consultant stopped making suggestions and used reflecting responses (Chapter 5) from the sympathetic parent ego state.	Sometimes people don't know what they want or how to ask for it in a direct way, so they use ulterior transactions. When possible, it is best to avoid ulterior transactions because they tend to waste time. Avoid making people search for your hidden meaning. Plan your message (Chapter 5) before you send it. When receiving messages, look for ulterior transactions and turn them into complementary transactions as illustrated in the ulterior example.

Life Positions and Stroking

Life Positions As stated in Chapter 3, attitudes affect your behavior and human relations. Within the transactional analysis framework, you have attitudes toward yourself and toward others. Positive attitudes are described as "OK," and negative attitudes are described as "not OK." The four life positions are illustrated in Exhibit 6.3.

The most desirable life position is shown in the upper right-hand box: "I'm OK—You're OK." With a positive attitude toward yourself and others, you have a greater chance for having adult-to-adult ego state communication. You can change your attitudes (Chapter 3), and you should if they are not positive, to create win–win situations. People with positive self-concepts (Chapter 3) tend to have positive attitudes.

EXHIBIT 6.3 | Life Positions

Attitude toward Oneself		Negative	Positive
	Positive	I'm OK—You're not OK	I'm OK—You're OK
	Negative	I'm not OK—You're not OK	I'm not OK—You're OK

Attitude toward Others

Communication Skills
Refer to CS Question 3.

Stroking Stroking is any behavior that implies recognition of another's presence. Strokes can be positive and make people feel good about themselves, or they can be negative and hurt people in some way.

We all want praise and recognition. Giving praise (positive strokes) is a powerful motivation technique that is easy to use and costs nothing. We should all give positive strokes and avoid giving negative strokes.

Skill-Building Exercise 6-1 develops this skill.

Through work and effort, you can learn to control your emotional behavior and transact on an adult-to-adult level in most situations. Skill-Building Exercise 6-1 presents 10 situations in which you are required to identify the ego states being used to help you communicate on an adult-to-adult level. Remember that what you think about affects how you feel, and how you feel affects your behavior, human relations, and performance. So think "I'm OK—You're OK" thoughts to help you communicate from the adult ego state, and give lots of stroke.

In the opening case, Larry was behaving out of the critical parent ego state. He showed disapproval of Helen by asking, "What's wrong with you? You never acted like this before." Helen responded to Larry's request for the calculator from the adapted child ego state. Helen was rebellious and showed her anger by saying, "I'm sick and tired of your pushing me around. Go back to your desk and I'll bring it to you when I'm good and ready." They had a crossed transaction because Larry opened in his usual manner but was surprised when Helen did not respond in her typical manner. Larry was in the "I'm OK—You're not OK" life position, while Helen was in the "I'm not OK—You're not OK" life position. Both used negative strokes. In this case, chances are that what they are fighting about (the calculator) isn't really what they are fighting about. It can be a deeper issue, such as respect, that has surfaced. This is known as the iceberg rule.

WORK APPLICATION 6-4

Identify your present or past boss's life position and use of stroking.

Learning Outcome 6-3

Identify the differences between passive, aggressive, and assertive behavior.

ASSERTIVENESS

Begin this section by completing Self-Assessment Exercise 6-2 to determine your use of the assertiveness style, which is sometimes included with the situational communication styles discussed in Chapter 5.

/// Self-Assessment Exercise 6-2 ///

Your Use of the Assertiveness Style

Turn to Skill-Building Exercise 6-2, Assertiveness, on page 197. Ignore the directions. Go directly to the 10 situations. Put yourself in the situation, and place a check mark after the letter (*not* on the line) of the one response that best describes what

(continued)

/// Self-Assessment Exercise 6-2 /// (*continued*)

you would say or do in each situation. Be honest; don't try to pick the response you think is correct. After selecting your 10 responses, circle the letter of your response for each situation in the table below.

Situation	Passive	Assertive	Aggressive
1.	*b* *d*	*c*	*a* *e*
2.	*d* *e*	*c*	*a* *b*
3.	*c* *e*	*a*	*b* *d*
4.	*b* *d*	*c*	*a* *e*
5.	*a* *e*	*b*	*c* *d*
6.	*a* *d*	*b*	*c* *e*
7.	*b* *d*	*a*	*c* *e*
8.	*b* *c*	*d*	*a* *e*
9.	*a* *c*	*d*	*b* *e*
10.	*b* *c*	*a*	*d* *e*
Total			

Scoring: Add the number of letters circled in each column. The number in each column should be between 0 and 10, and the total of all three columns should equal 10. The column with your highest total is your preferred style. If it's not assertive, or even if it is, you may want to improve your assertiveness behavior.

In this section, you will learn to express feelings, ask for favors, give and receive compliments, request behavior changes, and refuse unreasonable requests. You can ask for what you want in a direct, straightforward, deliberate, and honest way that conveys self-confidence without being obnoxious or abusive. When people stand up for their rights without violating the rights of others, they are using assertive behavior.[12]

Assertiveness *is the process of expressing thoughts and feelings while asking for what one wants in an appropriate way.* You need to present your message without falling into stereotypical "too pushy" (aggressive) or "not tough enough" (nonassertive–passive) traps.

Assertiveness Is Becoming More Global For example, the employees in Thailand are becoming more assertive, and the Japanese now include more strategies of assertiveness.

In China, workers are assertively asking for raises and better working conditions, and getting them.

Passive Behavior

Passive or nonassertive behavior comes primarily through the obedient child or supportive parent ego state. Passive people are in an "I'm not OK" life position. Passive behavior is an avoidance of behavior or an accommodation of the other party's wishes without standing up for one's own rights.[13] It involves self-denial and sacrifice. Passive people tend to deny the importance of things. They rationalize things—"It doesn't matter to me."

When people know someone is passive, they tend to take advantage of the person. They make unreasonable requests, knowing the person cannot say no, and refuse to meet the passive person's rare mild request. When the passive person does speak, others tend not to listen and tend to interrupt. In fact, some men freely interrupt women and dismiss women's ideas—and many women tolerate this! But women can and do assert themselves.[14]

Communication Skills
Refer to CS Question 4.

Passivity is often based on fear: fear of rejection, fear of retaliation, fear of hurting others, fear of being hurt, fear of getting into trouble, and so on. Continued passive behavior is usually unproductive for both the individual and the organization. If you tend to be passive, determine what really is important, and stand up for your rights in an assertive way.

Aggressive Behavior

As you read, you will realize that aggressive behavior is not the same as assertive; aggression is "abusive mistreatment of others," and not appropriate behavior.[15]

Aggressive behavior comes primarily through the adapted child and the critical parent ego states. Aggressive people are demanding, tough, rude, and pushy.[16] They insist on getting their own way and use force to gain control.[17] They are very competitive, hate to lose to the point of cheating, and tend to violate the rights of others to get what they want.

When faced with aggressive behavior, the other party often retaliates with aggressive behavior (fights back) or withdraws and gives in (takes flight). People often avoid contact with the aggressive person or prepare themselves for a fight when transacting. Abusive supervisors' behavior results in an annual loss of an estimated $23.8 billion in increased health care costs, workplace withdrawal, and lost productivity.[18]

Some women become aggressive because they feel it is necessary to compete in the business world. No one should feel as though he or she has to be aggressive to be taken seriously; assertiveness is more effective.[19] Violence is clearly aggressive behavior at the extreme level. Because anger and workplace violence are so important, we will discuss these issues separately in the next major section.

If you are continually aggressive, work at becoming more sensitive to the needs of others. Learn to replace aggressive behavior with assertive behavior.

Passive–Aggressive Behavior

Passive–aggressive behavior is displayed in three major ways:

1. The person uses both types of behavior sporadically. For example, a manager may be very aggressive with subordinates, yet passive with superiors. Or the person may be passive one day or moment and aggressive the next. This type of person is difficult to work with because no one knows what to expect.
2. The person uses passive behavior during the situation, then shortly after uses aggressive behavior. For example, an employee may agree to do something, then leave and slam the door, yell at the next person he or she sees, or sabotage the task.
3. The person uses passive behavior but inside is building up hostility. After the repeated behavior happens often enough, the passive person becomes aggressive. Too often the person who was attacked really doesn't understand the full situation and blames everything on the exploder, rather than examining his or her self-behavior, and changing it.

   The person who becomes aggressive often feels guilty. The end result is usually hurt human relations and no change in the situation. For example, during a meeting, Carl interrupted June three times when she was speaking. June said nothing each time, but was building up hostility. The fourth time Carl interrupted June, she attacked him by yelling at him for being so inconsiderate of her. He simply said, "What's wrong with you?" It would have been better for June to assertively tell Carl not to interrupt her the first time he did it.

   If you use passive–aggressive behavior, try to learn to be assertive on a consistent basis and you will be easier to work with. You will also get the results you want more often.

Communication Skills
Refer to CS Question 5.

WORK APPLICATION 6-5

Recall an example of when you used or observed passive–aggressive behavior. How did it affect human relations?

Assertive Behavior

Assertive behavior comes through the adult ego state, with an "I'm OK—You're OK" life position. As stated earlier, the assertive person expresses feelings and thoughts and asks for things without aggressive behavior.[20] The person stands up for his or her rights without violating the rights of others.

People who use assertive behavior tend to have a positive self-concept. They are not threatened by others, and they do not let others control their behavior. When others are out of the adult ego state, people using assertive behavior continue to transact in an adult ego state. Assertive people project a positive image (Chapter 3) of being confident, friendly, and honest. Using assertive behavior wins the respect of others.[21] Use it on a consistent basis.

Being Assertive Assertive behavior is generally the most effective method of getting what you want while not taking advantage of others. Being assertive can create a win–win situation. Assertive behavior is different from aggressive behavior and the terms are not interchangeable. To better understand the differences between passive, aggressive, and assertive behavior, see Exhibit 6.4. The phrases can be thought of as do's and don'ts. Do make assertive phrases and don't make passive and aggressive phrases. But remember, there are times when passive and aggressive behavior are appropriate. You will learn when later in this chapter.

Below is an example that puts it all together. When a person who is talking is interrupted, he or she can behave in one of three ways:

1. Passively. The person can say and do nothing.
2. Aggressively. The person can say, "I'm talking; mind your manners and wait your turn," in a loud voice, while pointing to the interrupter.
3. Assertively. The person can say, "Excuse me; I haven't finished making my point," with a smile and in a friendly but firm voice.

EXHIBIT 6.4 | Passive, Assertive, and Aggressive Phrases

Passive Phrases

Passive speakers use self-limiting, qualifying expressions without stating their position or needs.

- I don't know/care (when I do).
- It doesn't matter (when it does).
- Either one/way is fine with me (when I have a preference).
- I'm sorry (when I don't mean it).
- It's just my opinion . . .
- I don't want to bother you, but . . .
- It's not really important, but . . .

Assertive Phrases

Assertive speakers state their position or needs without violating the rights of others.

- I don't understand . . .
- I need/want/prefer . . .
- I would like . . .
- No, I won't be able to . . .
- I'd prefer that you don't tell me these jokes anymore.
- My opinion is . . .
- I need some of your time to . . .
- I thought that you would like to know . . .

Aggressive Phrases

Aggressive speakers state their position or needs while violating the rights of others using "you-messages" and absolutes.

- You don't need/want . . .
- Your opinion is wrong.
- You don't know what you're talking about.
- You're doing it wrong.
- That won't work!
- You have to . . .
- You need to know . . .

MODEL 6.1 | Assertiveness Steps

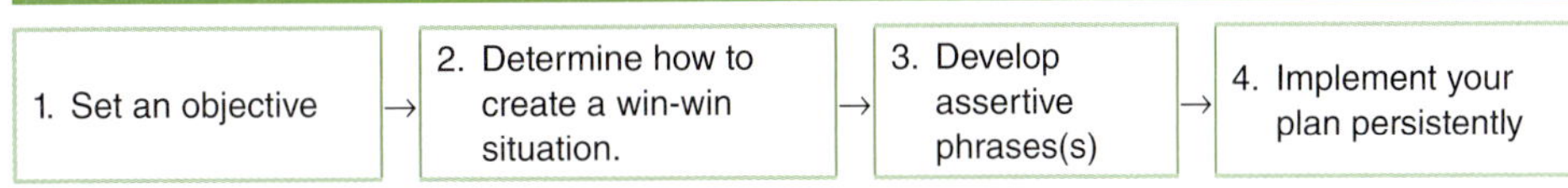

Communication Skills
Refer to CS Question 6.

The passive behavior will most likely lead to the person's being cut off and not listened to on a regular basis. The aggressive behavior will most likely lead to hurt human relations and may lead to an argument, while the assertive response will most likely lead to the interrupted person's getting to finish now and in the future, without hurting human relations.

We will further explain how to be assertive in the next section, which deals with conflict management.

In the opening case introduction, before the conversation took place, Helen used passive behavior, while Larry used aggressive behavior. During the confrontation Helen used aggressive behavior, but when Larry responded with aggressive behavior, she returned to passive behavior, giving him the calculator. In other words, Helen used passive–aggressive–passive behavior with Larry.

WORK APPLICATION 6-6

Recall an actual conflict you faced. Identify passive, aggressive, and assertive responses to the situation.

Learning Outcome 6-4

List the four steps of assertive behavior.

Assertiveness Steps Below are the four assertive steps that Helen, in the opening case, could have used. These steps are summarized in Model 6.1

Step 1: Set an objective. Specify what you want to accomplish. Helen's objective could have been "to tell Larry that I will give him the calculator after I'm finished with it."

Step 2: Determine how to create a win–win situation. Assess the situation in terms of meeting your needs and the other person's needs. Larry's needs are already being met by Helen's giving him the calculator any time he wants it. Presently, there is a win–lose situation. Helen needs to be assertive to meet her own needs to get her work done. Equitably sharing the use of the calculator will create a win–win situation. The present system of giving it to each other when done may work fine if Helen finishes using it before giving it to Larry.

Step 3: Develop assertive phrase(s): Before confronting Larry, Helen could have developed a statement such as, "I'm using it now, and I'll give it to you as soon as I'm finished with it."

Step 4: Implement your plan persistently. Helen could have used the above statement. If Larry continued to use aggressive behavior to get the calculator, Helen could persistently repeat the phrase until it sinks in, until Larry leaves without the calculator. It is not necessary, but Helen could explain why she feels the situation is not fair and repeat that she will give the calculator to Larry when she is done with it.

Skill-Building Exercise 6-2
develops this skill.

APPLICATION SITUATIONS / / /

Assertiveness AS 6-2

Identify each response to a supervisor's request for an employee to make a personal purchase for him on company time:

A. Passive B. Aggressive C. Assertive

________ 6. "I'm not doing that, and I'll report you to the union if you ask again."

________ 7. "Is that part of my job description?"

________ 8. "I'll get on it just as soon as I finish this."

________ 9. "You know I'm not going to do a stupid thing like that. Do your own shopping."

________ 10. "Your request is unreasonable because it is not part of my job. I will not do it because we could both get in trouble."

Remember that what you think about affects how you feel, and how you feel affects your behavior, human relations, and performance. So think about being assertive, not passive, be aware of your feelings of anger, and keep your aggressive behavior under control to help you have effective human relations.

ANGER AND VIOLENCE IN THE WORKPLACE

Now that we know the difference between passive, aggressive, and assertive behavior, let's focus on aggressive behavior with anger that can lead to violence, and how to prevent it. Human resource managers have reported increased incivility and violence, stating it can happen anywhere. The key to preventing workplace violence is to recognize and handle suspicious behavior before it becomes violent.[22]

Causes of Anger and Violence

Anger can lead to violence. You have most likely heard of road rage. In business we have *desk rage* and *customer rage,* which can take the form of yelling, verbal abuse, and physical violence. Today, 70 percent of customers who have a product or service problem are in rage by the time they talk with a customer-service worker.[23] People low on the personality adjustment dimension, using aggressive behavior, are more apt to become angry and violent.[24] Frustration, stress, and fear bring out anger. In fact violence is almost always prompted by unresolved conflict, and the violence is often a form of sabotage on other employees (back stabbing, spreading false rumors) or on the organization (property damage) to get even.

The physical work environment, such as work space, noise, odors, temperature (hot), ventilation, and color, can contribute to making people angry. A hostile work environment, called toxicity, leads to violence. People tend to copy, or model, others' behavior. For example, If employees see others being aggressive, especially managers, and nothing is done about it, they are more apt to also use aggressive behavior at work.[25] Violence in the community, which includes family violence, surrounding an organization is brought into the workplace. Some, but not all, experts report that drugs contribute to violence.

Dealing with Anger

Anger can be tough to deal with, especially in an organizational setting.

Your Anger and Emotional Behavior Control A secondary feeling of anger follows many of our feelings. Your boss may surprise you with extra work, which makes you angry. Disappointment often leads to anger. Your coworker doesn't do his share of the work, so you get mad at him. Buddha said, "You will not be punished *for* your anger; you will be punished *by* your anger." Anger can lead to perception problems, poor decisions, and hostility, which is stressful and can harm your health.[26] On the positive side, anger can lead to assertive behavior to resolve problems.

Recall our discussion of emotions in Chapter 5. It is natural to get angry sometimes. Although we cannot control the feeling of anger, we can control our behavior; we can learn to deal with anger in more positive ways to get rid of it.[27] Letting anger build up often leads to passive–aggressive behavior. Here are some tips for effectively getting rid of your anger:

- Remember that what you think about affects how you feel, and how you feel affects your behavior, human relations, and performance. So don't think about and dwell on your angry feelings. Let it go because you only get more upset. Be assertive, not passive, to help keep from using passive aggressive behavior.
- Develop a positive attitude about how you deal with anger. Use the techniques from Chapter 3 for changing your attitudes and building a positive self-concept. Review Skill-Building Exercise 3-2. Develop positive affirmations, such as "I stay calm when in traffic" (not "I must stop getting mad in traffic"); "I get along well with Joe" (not "I must stop letting Joe make me angry").

- Use rational thinking. For example, when dealing with customers, tell yourself their anger is to be expected; it's part of your job to stay calm.
- Look for positives. In many bad situations, there is some good.
- Look for the humor in the situation to help defuse the anger. Finding appropriate humor can help keep you from moping and getting angry.
- A key factor in controlling your anger is using assertive behavior. If you tend to be passive or aggressive, work at being assertive.
- Use an anger journal. A first step to emotional control of anger is self-awareness. Answer these questions: How often do you get irritated or angry each day? What makes you irritated or angry? How upset do you get? What feelings do you have when you are angry? What behavior (yell, say specific words, pound desk, or do and say nothing, accommodate) do you use when you are angry? Are you good at dealing with your irritations or anger? One good way to improve your ability to control your anger is to write the answers to these questions in an anger journal. It is a method of letting out the anger in an effective way. People who use a journal change their behavior without even trying.

Anger of Others and Emotional Behavior Control Below are some tips from the Crisis Prevention Institute and the National Institute for Occupational Safety and Health (NIOSH) to help you deal with the anger of others through your emotional control and to prevent violence. We start this discussion with a review.

- Think and be like Bill Gates. When people get angry, Bill responds by becoming very calm. "I'm good at when people get emotional."[28]
- Remember to be empathic and use reflecting statements (Chapter 5) to calm the person. Apologize even if you didn't do anything wrong. For example say, "I'm sorry this happened. How can we make it right?"[29]
- Our tips in Chapter 5 for dealing with emotional employees apply here. Again, never make any type of put-down statement; that type of response can make the person angrier. As stated above, you may use appropriate humor to cut the tension, but be careful that the humor is not viewed as being sarcastic. Such behavior can lead to violence.
- Don't respond to anger and threats with the same behavior. Angry people are rarely in the adult ego state, and they are often aggressive (although they may be passive). The key to success in maintaining your emotional control is to stay in the adult ego state.
- Don't give orders or ultimatums. This approach can increase anger and push the person to violence.
- Watch your nonverbal communication; show concern and avoid appearing aggressive. Use eye contact to show concern, but be aware that staring or glaring can make you appear aggressive. Maintain a calm, soothing tone to defuse anger and frustration. Talking loud and with frustration, anger, or annoyance in your tone of voice will convey aggression. Don't move rapidly, point at the person, get too close (stay 2 to 5 feet apart), or touch the person.
- Realize that anger is natural, and encourage people to vent in appropriate ways. With the aggressor, the problem is usually to keep the behavior acceptable. With the passive person, you may need to ask probing questions to get her or him to vent, such as "What is making you angry? What did I do to make you mad?"
- Acknowledge the person's feelings. Using reflecting responses by paraphrasing the way the person is feeling shows that you care and helps calm the person so that he or she can get back in the adult ego state.
- Get away from the person if necessary. If possible, call in a third party (security) to deal with the person; then leave.

Preventing Violence

Signs of Potential Violence Workplace violence is rarely spontaneous; it's more commonly passive–aggressive behavior in rising steps, related to an unresolved conflict. Employees do give warning signs that violence is possible, so it can be prevented if you look for these signs and take action to defuse the anger before it becomes violent.[30]

- Take verbal threats seriously. Most violent people do make a threat of some kind before they act. If you hear a threat, or hear about a threat from someone, talk to the person who made the threat and try to resolve the issue.
- Watch nonverbal communication. Gestures or other body language that convey anger can indicate a threat of violence just as much as behavior such as yelling can. Talk to the person to find out what's going on.
- Watch for stalking and harassment. It usually starts small but can lead to violence. Put a stop to it.
- Watch for damage to property. If an employee kicks a desk, punches a wall, or the like, talk to the person to get to the reason for the behavior. People who damage property can become violent to coworkers.
- Watch for indications of alcohol and drug use. People can become violent under the influence of these substances. Get them out of the workplace and get them professional help if it's a recurring problem.
- Include the isolated employee. It is common for violent people to be employees who don't fit in, especially if they are picked on or harassed by coworkers. Reach out to such employees and help them fit in, or get them to a place where they do.
- Look for the presence of weapons or objects that might be used as weapons. You may trying talking to the person if you feel safe, but get security personnel involved.

Communication Skills
Refer to CS Question 7.

WORK APPLICATION 6-7

Recall a situation in which someone was angry with you, preferably your boss. What was the cause of the anger? Did the person display any signs of potential violence? If so, what were they? How well did the person deal with his or her anger? Give the specific tips the person did and did not follow.

WORK APPLICATION 6-8

Recall a situation in which you were angry with someone. What was the cause of your anger? Did you display any signs of potential violence? If so, what were they? How well did you deal with your anger? Give the specific tips you did and did not follow.

Organizational Prevention of Violence The number one preventive method is to train all employees to deal with anger and prevent violence, which is what you are learning now. However, the starting place is with a written policy addressing workplace violence, and a zero-tolerance policy is the best preventive policy. From the manager's perspective, it is very important to take quick disciplinary action against employees who are violent at work. Otherwise, aggression will spread in the organization and it will become more difficult to stop. Managers especially need to avoid using aggression at work, because employees more readily copy managers' behavior than that of other employees.[31] The organization should have a system for dealing with grievances and should track incidents of violence as part of its policy.

Organizations can also screen job applicants for past or potential violence so that they are not hired. Organizations should also develop a good work environment that addresses the issues listed above as causes of violence. Demotions, firings, and layoffs should be handled in a humane way, following the guidelines for dealing with anger. Outplacement services to help employees find new jobs can help cut down on violence.

Individual Prevention of Violence One thing you should realize is that the police department will not help you prevent personal or workplace violence. Police get involved only after violence takes place. Here are a few more tips for preventing violence. Keep in mind that there is always the potential for violence; look for escalating frustration and anger so that you can defuse the situation before it becomes violent by being empathic using reflecting statements.[32] Never be alone with a potentially violent person or stand between the person and the exit. Know when to get away from the person. Be aware of the organization's policy for calling in security help. Report any troubling incidents to security staff.

CONFLICT MANAGEMENT STYLES

Some people think that a conflict exists only in serious issues with anger. However, in human relations, a **conflict** *exists whenever two or more parties are in disagreement.* Do you agree with everything people do and say in your human relations? If not, you are in conflict, most likely every day. Your ability to manage conflict is critical to your success.[33] In this section, we discuss reasons for conflict and avoiding conflicts as well as the five conflict management styles you can use when you are in conflict.

Reasons for Conflict and Avoiding Conflicts

All human relations rely on unwritten, implicit expectations by each party, called the psychological contract.[34] Often we are not aware of our expectations until they have not been met. Communication problems or conflicts arise for three primary reasons: (1) we fail to make our expectations known to other parties, (2) we fail to find out the expectations of other parties, and (3) we assume that the other parties have the same expectations that we have.

In any relationship, to avoid conflict, share information and assertively discuss expectations early, before the conflict escalates. Unfortunately, avoiding conflict is easier said than done.

WORK APPLICATION 6-9

Describe a conflict you observed in an organization, preferably an organization with which you are or were associated. Explain the conflict by the people involved and the reasons for the conflict.

In the opening case, Larry expected Helen to give him the calculator when he wanted it, which he made explicit to Helen. Larry failed to find out Helen's expectations (probably did not care), and may have assumed that she did not mind giving him the calculator whenever he wanted it. Helen's expectation was that Larry would share the calculator, and she found out his expectations were not the same as hers. However, she did not assertively tell Larry this early. Thus, they are in conflict and need to talk about their expectations. Also, there are times when the other party (Larry) is emotional and/or not being reasonable, making conflict more common and more difficult to resolve.[35] Helen is going to need to be assertive with Larry.

Conflict Has Benefits People often think of conflict as fighting and view it as disruptive. Conflict, however, can be beneficial. The question today is not whether conflict is good or bad but rather how to manage conflict to benefit the organization. A balance of conflict is essential to all organizations. Too little or too much conflict is usually a sign of management's unwillingness or inability to adapt to a changing environment. Challenging present methods and presenting innovative change causes conflict, but can lead to improved performance as conflict affects individual and team creativity, satisfaction, and performance.[36]

Communication Skills
Refer to CS Question 8.

Before learning the five conflict management styles, complete Self-Assessment Exercise 6-3 to determine your preferred style.

/// Self-Assessment Exercise 6-3 ///

Determining Your Preferred Conflict Management Style

Below are four situations. Rank all five alternative actions from 1, the first approach you would use (most desirable), to 5, the last approach you would use (least desirable). Don't try to pick a best answer. Select the alternative that best describes what you would actually do in the situation based on your past experiences.

1. You are the general manager of a manufacturing plant. The purchasing department has found a source of material at a lower cost than the one being used. However, the production manager says the current material is superior, and he doesn't want to change. The quality control manager says that both will pass inspection with similar results. You would:

   _____ *a.* Do nothing; let the purchasing and production managers work it out between themselves.

   _____ *b.* Suggest having the purchasing manager find an alternative material that is cheaper but acceptable to the production manager.

   _____ *c.* Have the purchasing and production managers compromise.

   _____ *d.* Decide who is right and make the other comply.

   _____ *e.* Get the purchasing and production managers together and work out an agreement acceptable to both parties.

(continued)

/// Self-Assessment Exercise 6-3 /// *(continued)*

2. You are a professor at a college. You have started a consulting organization and have the title of director of consulting services, which the dean has approved. You run the organization through the business department, using other faculty and yourself to consult. It has been going well. Randy, the director of continuing education, says that your consulting services should come under his department and not be a separate department. You would:

   _____ *a.* Suggest that some services be under continuing education, but that others, like your consulting service, remain with you in the business department.

   _____ *b.* Do what you can to stop the move. Go to the dean and request that the consulting services stay under your direction in the business department, as originally approved by the dean.

   _____ *c.* Do nothing. The dean will surely see through this "power grab" and turn Randy down.

   _____ *d.* Go and talk to Randy. Try to come up with an agreement you are both satisfied with.

   _____ *e.* Go along with Randy's request. It's not worth fighting about; you can still consult.

3. You are a branch manager for a bank. One of your colleagues cut you off twice during a managers' meeting that just ended. You would:

   _____ *a.* Do nothing; it's no big deal.

   _____ *b.* Discuss it in a friendly manner, but try to get the colleague to stop this behavior.

   _____ *c.* Don't do or say anything because it might hurt your relations, even if you're a little upset about it.

   _____ *d.* Forcefully tell the colleague that you put up with being cut off, but will not tolerate it in the future.

   _____ *e.* Tell the colleague that you will listen without interrupting if he or she does the same for you.

4. You are the human resources/personnel manager. You have decided to have visitors sign in and wear guest passes. However, only about half of the employees sign their guests in before taking them to their offices to do business. You would:

   _____ *a.* Go talk to the general manager about why employees are not signing in visitors.

   _____ *b.* Try to find a method that will please most employees.

   _____ *c.* Go to the general manager and request that she require employees to follow your procedures. If the general manager says to do it, employees will comply.

   _____ *d.* Do not require visitors to sign in; require them only to wear guest passes.

   _____ *e.* Let employees do things the way they want to.

To determine your preferred conflict management style, place your numbers 1 to 5 on the lines below.

Situation 1

_____ *a.* Avoiding
_____ *b.* Accommodating
_____ *c.* Compromising
_____ *d.* Forcing
_____ *e.* Collaborating

Situation 2

_____ *a.* Compromising
_____ *b.* Forcing
_____ *c.* Avoiding
_____ *d.* Collaborating
_____ *e.* Accommodating

Situation 3

_____ *a.* Avoiding
_____ *b.* Collaborating
_____ *c.* Accommodating
_____ *d.* Forcing
_____ *e.* Compromising

Situation 4

_____ *a.* Collaborating
_____ *b.* Accommodating
_____ *c.* Forcing
_____ *d.* Compromising
_____ *e.* Avoiding

/// Self-Assessment Exercise 6-3 /// *(continued)*

Now place your ranking numbers 1 to 5 that correspond to the styles from the four situations in order; then add the four numbers.

Situation 1	Situation 2	Situation 3	Situation 4		
_____ *a.*	_____ *b.*	_____ *d.*	_____ *c.*	= _____	total, Forcing style
_____ *b.*	_____ *c.*	_____ *a.*	_____ *e.*	= _____	total, Avoiding style
_____ *c.*	_____ *e.*	_____ *c.*	_____ *b.*	= _____	total, Accommodating style
_____ *d.*	_____ *a.*	_____ *e.*	_____ *d.*	= _____	total, Compromising style
_____ *e.*	_____ *d.*	_____ *b.*	_____ *a.*	= _____	total, Collaborating style

The total with the lowest score is your preferred conflict management style. There is no one best conflict style in all situations. The more even the totals are, the more flexible you are at changing conflict management styles. Very high and very low totals indicate less flexibility.

It is also helpful to identify others' preferred styles so that you can plan how to resolve conflicts with them.

Learning Outcome 6-5

State when and how to use five conflict management styles.

The five conflict management styles—forcing, avoiding, accommodating, compromising, and collaborating—are presented next. See Exhibit 6.5 for an overview of the five styles integrated with TA and assertiveness.

Forcing Conflict Style

The **forcing conflict style** *user attempts to resolve the conflict by using aggressive behavior.* The forcing approach uses an uncooperative, autocratic attempt to satisfy one's own needs at the expense of others, if necessary. A win–lose situation is created. Forcers use authority, threaten, intimidate, and call for majority rule when they know they will win. For example, a manager tells an employee, "If you don't do it now, you're fired!"

Advantages and Disadvantages of the Forcing Conflict Style The advantage of the forcing style is that better organizational decisions will be made (assuming the forcer is correct), rather than less effective, compromised decisions. The disadvantage is that overuse of this style leads to hostility and resentment toward its user.

EXHIBIT 6.5 | Conflict Management Styles

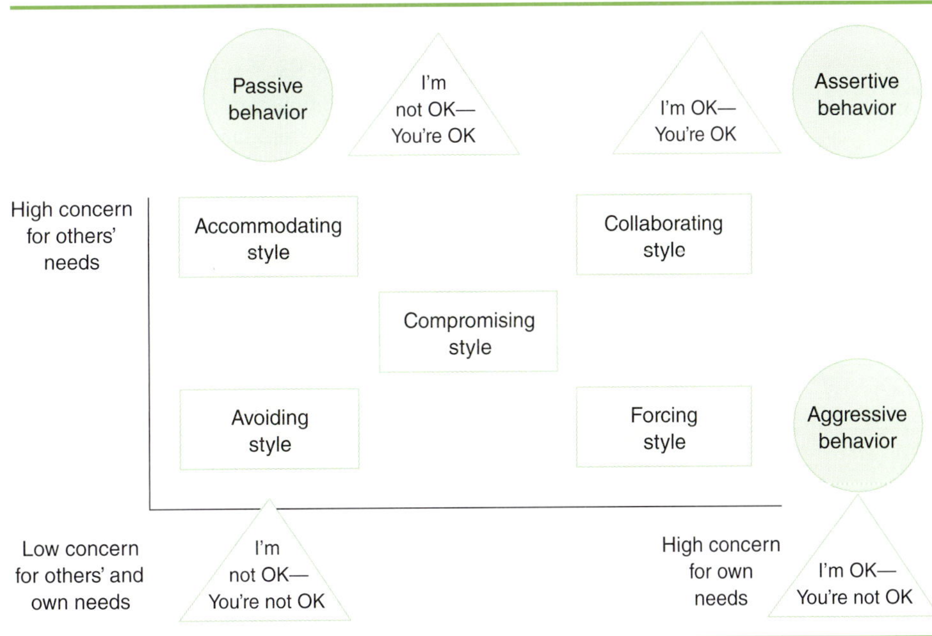

Appropriate Use of the Forcing Conflict Style The forcing style is appropriate to use when (1) the conflict is about personal differences (particularly values that are hard to change); (2) maintaining close, supportive relationships is not critical; and (3) conflict resolution is urgent.

Communication Skills
Refer to CS Question 9.

Avoiding Conflict Style

The **avoiding conflict style** *user attempts to passively ignore the conflict rather than resolve it.* Its user is unassertive and uncooperative, and wants to avoid or postpone confrontation. A lose–lose situation is created because the conflict is not resolved.[37] People avoid the conflict by refusing to take a stance, physically leaving it, or escaping the conflict by mentally leaving the conflict.

Advantages and Disadvantages of the Avoiding Conflict Style The advantage of the avoiding style is that it may maintain relationships that would be hurt through conflict resolution. The disadvantage of this style is the fact that conflicts do not get resolved. An overuse of this style leads to conflict within the individual. People tend to walk all over the avoider. Supervisors use this style when they allow employees to break rules without confronting them. Avoiding problems usually does not make them go away; the problems usually get worse. Being afraid to be assertive is not a problem; it's not being assertive when you are afraid that's the problem.

Appropriate Use of the Avoiding Conflict Style The avoiding style is appropriate to use when (1) one's stake in the issue is not high, (2) confrontation will damage a critical working relationship, and (3) a time constraint necessitates avoidance. Some people use the avoiding style out of fear that they will handle the confrontation poorly, making the situation worse rather than better. After studying this chapter and following its guidelines, you should be able to handle confrontations effectively.

Accommodating Conflict Style

The **accommodating conflict style** *user attempts to resolve the conflict by passively giving in to the other party.* The accommodating approach is unassertive and cooperative. It attempts to satisfy the other party while neglecting one's own needs. A win–lose situation is created, with the other party being the winner.

Advantages and Disadvantages of the Accommodating Conflict Style The advantage of the accommodating style is that relationships are maintained. The disadvantage is that giving in to the other party may be counterproductive. The accommodating person may have a better solution. An overuse of this style leads to people's taking advantage of the accommodator, and the relationship the accommodator tries to maintain is often lost.

Appropriate Use of the Accommodating Conflict Style The accommodating style is appropriate when (1) maintaining the relationship outweighs all other considerations; (2) the changes agreed to are not important to the accommodator, but are to the other party; and (3) the time to resolve the conflict is limited. This is often the only style one can use with an autocratic boss.

The Difference between Avoiding and Accommodating With the avoiding style, you can simply say or do nothing. However, with the accommodating style, you have to do or say something you don't want to. For example, if your boss says something you disagree with, you can avoid by saying nothing. However, if your boss asks you to take a letter to the mailroom, and you don't want to but do it anyway, you have accommodated the boss.

Compromising Conflict Style

The **compromising conflict style** *user attempts to resolve the conflict through assertive give-and-take concessions.* This approach attempts to meet one's need for harmonious relationships. An I-win-part–I-lose-part situation is created through compromise, making the compromising style intermediate in assertiveness and cooperation. It is used in negotiations.[38]

Advantages and Disadvantages of the Compromising Conflict Style The advantage of the compromising style is that the conflict is resolved quickly and relationships are maintained. The disadvantage is that the compromise often leads to counterproductive results (suboptimum decisions). An overuse of this style leads to people's playing games, such as asking for twice as much as they need in order to get what they want. It is commonly used during management and labor collective bargaining.

Appropriate Use of the Compromising Conflict Style The compromising style is appropriate to use when (1) the issues are complex and critical, and there is no simple and clear solution; (2) all parties have a strong interest in different solutions; and (3) time is short.

Collaborating Conflict Style

The **collaborating conflict style** *user assertively attempts to resolve the conflict with the best solution agreeable to all parties.* It is also called the *problem-solving style.* The collaborating approach is assertive and cooperative. The collaborator attempts to fully address the concerns of all. The focus is on finding the best solution to the problem that is satisfactory to all parties. Unlike the forcer, the collaborator is willing to change if a better solution is presented. This is the only style that creates a true win–win situation. Collaborating is based on creative problem solving and decision making, and we will discuss it in Chapter 11.

Advantages and Disadvantages of the Collaborating Conflict Style The advantage of the collaborating style is that it tends to lead to the best solution to the conflict using assertive behavior. One great disadvantage is that the time and effort it takes to resolve the conflict is usually greater and longer than with the other styles.

Appropriate Use of the Collaborating Conflict Style The collaborating style is appropriate when (1) maintaining relationships is important, (2) time is available, and (3) it is a peer conflict. To be successful, one must confront conflict. The collaborating conflict style is generally considered the best style because it confronts the conflict assertively,[39] rather than passively ignoring it or aggressively fighting one's way through it.

The Difference between Compromising and Collaborating Let's explain with an example. With the compromising style, when you and a coworker are delivering furniture, you take turns listening to the radio station you like; thus, each of you wins and loses some. With collaborating, you would agree on a station you both like to listen to—you both win. Unfortunately, collaboration is not always possible.

The situational perspective states that there is no one best style for resolving all conflicts. A person's preferred style tends to meet his or her needs. Some people enjoy forcing, others prefer to avoid conflict, and so forth. Success lies in one's ability to use the appropriate style to meet the situation. Of the five styles, the most difficult to implement successfully (and probably the most underutilized when appropriate) is the collaborative style. Therefore, the collaborative style is the only one that will be given detailed coverage in the next section of this chapter. In Chapter 10 you will learn how to use the compromising style when negotiating.

WORK APPLICATION 6-10

Give an example of a conflict situation you face or have faced. Identify and explain the appropriate conflict management style to use.

In the opening case, Larry consistently used the forcing conflict resolution style, while Helen began by using the accommodating style, changed to the forcing style, and returned to the accommodating style. To create a true win–win situation for all parties, Helen could have used the collaborating conflict management style.

APPLICATION SITUATIONS / / /

Selecting Conflict Management Styles AS 6-3

Identify the most appropriate conflict management style as:

A. Forcing
B. Avoiding
C. Compromising
D. Accommodating
E. Collaborating

_______ 11. You are in a class that uses small groups for the entire semester. Under normal class conditions the most appropriate style is _______.

_______ 12. You have joined a committee so that you can meet people. Your interest in its function itself is low. While serving on the committee, you make a recommendation that is opposed by another member. You realize that you have the better idea. The other party is using a forcing style.

_______ 13. You are the supervisor of a production department. An important order is behind schedule. Two of your employees are in conflict, as usual, over how to meet the deadline.

_______ 14. You are on a committee that has to select a new computer. The four alternatives will all do the job. It's the brand, price, and service that people disagree on.

_______ 15. You are a sales manager. One of your competent salespersons is trying to close a big sale. The two of you are discussing the next sales call she will make. You disagree on strategy.

_______ 16. You are on your way to an important meeting. You're late. As you turn a corner, at the end of the shop you see one of your employees goofing off instead of working.

_______ 17. You have a department crisis. Your boss calls you and tells you, in a stern voice, "Get up here right away."

_______ 18. You are in a special one-hour budget meeting with your boss and fellow supervisors. You have to finalize the total budget for each department.

_______ 19. You and a fellow supervisor are working on a report. You disagree on the format to use.

_______ 20. You're over budget for labor this month. It's slow today so you asked a part-time employee to go home early. He tells you he doesn't want to go because he needs the money.

RESOLVING CONFLICTS WITH THE COLLABORATING CONFLICT STYLE

Learning Outcome 6-6

List the steps of initiating, responding to, and mediating conflict resolutions.

When a conflict exists, determine the appropriate style to use. Collaboration is not always appropriate in supervisor–employee conflicts. However, it is generally the appropriate style for conflict between colleagues and peers. It is important to bring conflict out into the open and agree to resolve it,[40] because conflicts can produce severe negative consequences for individuals and organizations.[41] Thus, conflict management skills are important.[42]

The objective of this section is to develop your ability to assertively confront (or be confronted by) people you are in conflict with, in a manner that resolves the conflict without damaging interpersonal relationships. We examine the roles of initiator, responder, and mediator in conflict resolution.

Initiating Conflict Resolution

An initiator is a person who confronts another person (or other people) about a conflict. The initiator's attitude will have a major effect on the outcome of the confrontation.[43] We tend to get what we are looking for. If you go into a confrontation expecting to argue and fight, you probably will. If you expect a successful resolution, you will probably get it. (See our discussion of the self-fulfilling prophecy in Chapter 3.)

To resolve conflicts, you should develop a plan of action. When you initiate a conflict resolution using the collaborating style, follow the **initiating conflict resolution steps:** *step (1) plan to maintain ownership of the problem using the XYZ model; step (2) implement your plan persistently; and step (3) make an agreement for change.* (See Model 6.2.)

Step 1: Plan to Maintain Ownership of the Problem Using the XYZ Model Part of the reason confronters are not successful at resolving conflict is that they wait too long before confronting the other party, and they do it in an emotional state without planning (passive–aggressive behavior). People end up saying things they don't mean because they haven't given thought to what it is they want to say and accomplish through confrontation.

You should realize that when you are upset and frustrated, the problem is yours, not the other party's. For example, you don't smoke and someone visits you who does smoke. The smoke bothers you, not the smoker. It's your problem. Open the confrontation with a request for the respondent to help you solve your problem. This approach reduces defensiveness and establishes an atmosphere of problem solving.

There are four things we should not do during the opening XYZ statement: (1) Don't *judge* the person's behavior. For example, don't say "You shouldn't smoke; it's bad for you." (2) Don't give *advice* (this is done in steps 2 and 3). (3) Don't make *threats.* For example, if you do smoke again I will report you to the boss. (4) Don't try to determine who is to *blame*. Both parties are usually partly to blame. Fixing blame only gets people defensive, which is counterproductive to conflict resolution.

Skill-Building Exercise 6-3 develops this skill.

WORK APPLICATION 6-11

Use the XYZ model to describe a conflict problem you face or have faced.

Keep the opening statement short. The longer the statement, the longer it will take to resolve the conflict. People get defensive when kept waiting for their turn to talk. Use the XYZ model. The **XYZ model** *describes a problem in terms of behavior, consequences, and feelings.* For example: When you do X (behavior), Y (consequences) happens, and I feel Z (feelings). For example, when you smoke in my room (behavior), I have trouble breathing and become nauseated (consequence), and I feel uncomfortable and irritated (feeling). You can vary the sequence and start with a feeling or consequence to fit the situation.

Timing is also important. If the other party is busy, set an appointment to discuss the conflict. In addition, don't confront a person on several unrelated issues at once, or when they are highly emotional.

Step 2: Implement Your Plan Persistently After making your short, planned XYZ statement, let the other party respond. If the confronted party acknowledges the problem and says he or she will change, you may have succeeded. Often people do not realize there is a conflict and when approached properly, they are willing to change. However, if the other party does not understand or avoids acknowledgment of the problem, persist. You cannot resolve a conflict if the other party will not even acknowledge its existence. Repeat your planned statement several times, and/or explain it in different terms, until you get an acknowledgment or realize that the situation is hopeless. But don't give up too easily, and be sure to listen to the other party and watch for nonverbal clues.

When the other party acknowledges the problem, but is not responsive to resolving it, appeal to common goals. Make the other party realize the benefits to him or her and the organization as well.

Step 3: Make an Agreement for Change Try to agree on a specific action you both will take to resolve the conflict. Remember that you are collaborating, not forcing. If possible, get a commitment statement describing the change.

Below is an example of conflict resolution:

PAM: Hi, Bill! Got a few minutes to talk?

BILL: Sure, what's up?

PAM: Something's been bothering me lately, and I wanted you to know about it. When you come to class without doing your homework [*behavior*], I get irritated [*feeling*], and our group has to wait for you to read the material, or make a decision without your input [*consequences*].

BILL: Hey, I'm busy!

PAM: Do you think the rest of the group isn't?

BILL: No.

PAM: Are grades important to you?

BILL: Yeah. If I don't get good grades, I can't play on the football team.

PAM: You get a grade for doing your homework, and we all get the same group grade. Your input helps us all get a better grade.

BILL: You're right; sometimes I forget about that. Well, sometimes I don't do it because I don't understand the assignment.

PAM: I'll tell you what; when you don't understand it, call me, or come over, and I'll explain it. You know my number and address.

BILL: I'd appreciate that.

Skill-Building Exercise 6-4 develops this skill.

PAM: So you agree to do your homework before class, and I agree to help you when you need it.

BILL: OK, I'll do it from now on.

Responding to Conflict Resolution

A responder is a person confronted by an initiator. Most initiators do not follow the model above. Therefore, the responder must take responsibility for successful conflict resolution by following the conflict resolution model. The **responding to conflict resolution steps** *are as follows: step (1) listen to and paraphrase the problem using the XYZ model; step (2) agree with some aspect of the complaint; step (3) ask for, and/or give, alternative solutions; and step (4) make an agreement for change.* (See Model 6.2.)

Apologize When confronted, it is important to restore relationships that may have been hurt by the conflict, and apologizing really helps.[44] You will be surprised at how your human relations can improve simply by telling people you are sorry for your behavior that bothers them. So during step 2 it is very helpful to apologize. Even if you don't believe you did anything wrong, it is helpful to at least say something like, "I'm sorry I offended you," or "I'm sorry you are upset."

Mediating Conflict Resolution

Frequently, conflicting employees cannot resolve their dispute. In these cases, the manager or an outside mediator should mediate to help them resolve their differences.

Before bringing the conflicting parties together, the manager should decide whether to start with a joint meeting or individual meetings. If one employee comes to complain, but has not confronted the other party, or if there is a serious discrepancy in employee perceptions, the manager should meet one-on-one with each party before bringing them together.

On the other hand, when both parties have a similar awareness of the problem and are motivated to solve it, the manager can begin with a joint meeting when all parties are calm. The manager should be a mediator, not a judge. Make employees realize it's their problem,

MODEL 6.2 | Conflict Resolution

Initiating Conflict Resolution Steps	Responding to Conflict Resolution	Mediating Conflict Resolution
1. Plan to maintain ownership of the problem using the XYZ model. 2. Implement your plan persistently. 3. Make an agreement for change.	1. Listen to and paraphrase the problem using the XYZ model. 2. Agree with some aspect of the complaint. 3. Ask for, and/or give, alternative solutions. 4. Make an agreement for change.	1. Have each party state his or her complaint using the XYZ model. 2. Agree on the problem(s). 3. Develop alternative solutions. 4. Make an agreement for change, and follow up.

not yours, and that they are responsible for solving it. Get the employees to resolve the conflict, if possible. Remain impartial, unless one party is violating company policies. Don't belittle the parties in conflict. Don't make comments like, "I'm disappointed in you two; you're acting like babies."

When bringing conflicting parties together, follow the mediating conflict model. The **mediating conflict resolution steps** *are as follows: step (1) have each party state his or her complaint using the XYZ model; step (2) agree on the problem(s); step (3) develop alternative solutions; and step (4) make an agreement for change, and follow up.* The steps for initiating, responding to, and mediating conflict resolution are summarized in Model 6.2.

Remember that what you think about affects how you feel, and how you feel affects your behavior, human relations, and performance. So think about the specific behavior that is causing the conflict and how to resolve the issue, not your anger or revenge. Don't confront others when you are emotional, and if they are emotional, try to calm them first or postpone the conflict resolution discussion until you are both calm. If you are mediating a conflict, calm the parties or postpone the discussion until all parties (including you) are calm so you can focus on the behavior changes needed to resolve the human relations and performance problem.

In the discussion of assertiveness, there was an example of how Helen could have been assertive with Larry in the opening case. In addition to being assertive with Larry, Helen could have used the collaborating conflict style to resolve the calculator problem. Helen could have suggested to Larry that the two of them go to the boss and ask for another calculator so that they could each have their own. A second calculator could create a win–win situation for all parties. Helen and Larry would both win because they would not have to wait for the calculator. The department would win because productivity would increase; there would be less time wasted getting and waiting for the calculator. The organization would win because the department would perform more efficiently. Obtaining a second calculator is a good conflict resolution. However, the department or organization may not have the money in the budget to buy a new calculator, or the idle time may actually be cheaper. If this is the case, Helen can be assertive and keep the calculator until she is finished—this is a win–win situation; or she and Larry could work out some other collaborative agreement, such as each having the calculator during specific hours. If Larry is not willing to collaborate, their boss will have to mediate the conflict resolution.

WORK APPLICATION 6-12

Describe an actual situation in which the initiating, responding, and/or mediating conflict resolution model would be appropriate.

PUTTING IT ALL TOGETHER

To see the relationship between TA, assertiveness, and conflict management, see Exhibit 6.6. Notice that the first two columns come from conflict management, the third from assertiveness, and the fourth and fifth from TA. The last column relates to the goal of human

EXHIBIT 6.6 | Interpersonal Dynamics Styles

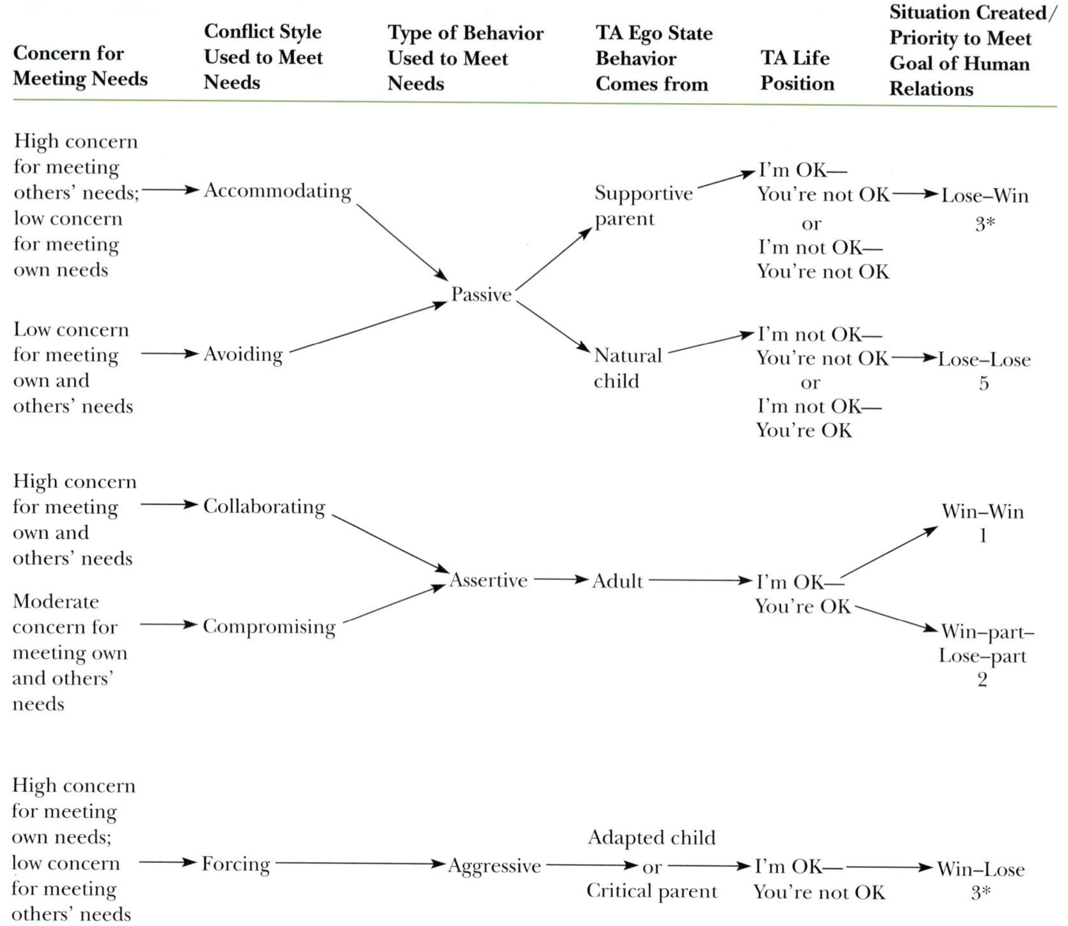

*The win–lose and lose–win situations are equal in priority to the group or organization because both an individual and the group or organization lose. The individual's loss is more important to the loser than to the group.

relations. The last column shows the order of priority of which interpersonal behavior to use to meet the goal of human relations. However, remember that this is general advice. As stated in the chapter, at times other behavior is appropriate. In the majority of your human relations, you should strive to have a high concern for meeting your needs while meeting the needs of others. You should use an assertive, adult, collaborating style to create a win–win situation for all parties.

In reviewing Exhibit 6.6, you should see that the behavior of people using the passive, accommodating, avoiding conflict styles is the opposite of the behavior of people who use the aggressive, forcing conflict styles. Assertive people use the collaborating, compromising conflict styles, and their behavior is between the other two extremes.

You should also understand that people using the passive, accommodating, avoiding conflict styles tend to have human relations that are the opposite of people using the aggressive, forcing conflict styles. The passive person tends to shy away from making friends and being actively involved, while the aggressive person tries to take over and is offensive to the group. Assertive people use the collaborating style and tend to be friendly and outgoing as they work to create win–win situations for all parties. Generally, people who are passive don't get their needs met; they get walked over by the aggressive people. Aggressive people are disliked because they violate the rights of others. Assertive people tend to have the best human relations.

No clear relationship exists between individual performance and the interpersonal dynamic style used. Many passive people work well alone, and so do aggressive people. Aggressive people are sometimes more productive than passive people because they can take advantage of passive people. This happened in the opening case. When it comes to group and organizational performance, the assertive person is generally the most responsible for the group effort. Passive people may have great ideas on doing a good group job, but they don't say how. Aggressive people look out only for themselves. If someone offers an idea different from theirs, they are not willing to collaborate for the good of all. The assertive group member collaboratively shares ideas but is willing to change to a better alternative to create a win–win situation for all. By following the guidelines in this chapter, you can develop assertive collaborating skills.

Let's discuss how your personality affects your ego state, assertiveness, and preferred conflict style in Self-Assessment Exercise 6-4.

/// Self-Assessment Exercise 6-4 ///

Your Personality and Interpersonal Dynamics

People with the same personality type (Chapter 2) tend to get along better and have less conflict than those with different personality types. So be careful during human relations with people different from you.

If you have a high *surgency* personality, watch your use of the critical parent ego state and be sure to give lots of positive strokes to help human relations. You may be in the "I'm OK" life position, but make sure that you treat others as "You're OK." As a surgency, you also need to be careful not to use aggressive behavior to get what you want. You most likely have no problem confronting others when in conflict. However, be careful not to use the forcing style with others.

If you have a high *agreeableness* personality, you tend to get along well with others. But be careful not to use the sympathetic parent ego state, and watch the appropriate use of the child ego state. Don't let others take advantage of you so that you put them in the "You're not OK" life position, and so that you can stay in the "I'm OK" position. Be careful not to be passive and not to use the avoiding and accommodating conflict styles to get out of confronting others; you need to satisfy your needs too.

How well you deal with your emotions, especially anger, is what *adjustment* is about. If you are not high on adjustment personality traits, you will tend to use the parent or child ego states. You may be in the "I'm not OK" position, and others will be in the "You're not OK" position. Based on your adjustment personality, you can be passive (let people take advantage of you) or aggressive (try to take advantage of others), and poor adjustment can lead to violence. Low adjustment people are usually poor at dealing with conflict, because they tend to avoid and accommodate or to force in conflict situations. Try not to be low in adjustment and get too emotional. Use the tips on dealing with emotions, especially anger.

There is a relationship between adjustment and *openness to experience*. If you are not well adjusted, you are probably not open to experience. If you are low on openness, you may not handle conflicts well since their resolution often requires change. So try to be open to new experiences.

If you are a high *conscientious* personality, you can still transact from the parent or child ego state. You may be in the "I'm OK" life position, but be sure not to put others in the "You're not OK" position. Watch your use of aggressive behavior to achieve your objectives. You may be good at conflict resolution, but be careful to meet others' needs too.

Action plan: Based on your personality, what specific things will you do to improve your TA, assertiveness, and conflict management skills?

____

____

____

____

As we bring this chapter to a close, you should understand *transactional analysis* ego states, types of transactions, life positions, and stroking, and use behavior from the adult ego state during human relations. You should know the difference between passive, aggressive, and *assertive* behavior and be able to avoid being passive and aggressive and use assertive behavior. You should be able to deal with your anger, the anger of others, and help prevent workplace violence. You should know the reasons for *conflict and* how to use five conflict management styles, and you should be able to successfully initiate a conflict resolution. Putting these topics together briefly, you should realize that during your human relations (transactional analysis), the behavior you use (passive, aggressive, or assertive) affects whether or not you are in conflict and affects your performance.

/ / / REVIEW / / /

The chapter review is organized to help you master the seven learning outcomes for Chapter 6. First provide your own response to each learning outcome, and then check the summary provided to see how well you understand the material. Next, identify the final statement in each section as either true or false (T/F). Correct each false statement. Answers are given at the end of the chapter.

LO 6-1 Describe the three ego states of transactional analysis.

The three ego states of transactional analysis are: (1) *parent*: the critical parent is evaluative, while the sympathetic parent is supportive; (2) *child:* the natural child is curious, while the adapted child is rebellious; and (3) *adult:* the adult is a thinking, unemotional state of ego.

Transactional analysis was first developed for the field of psychology and later applied to business. T F

LO 6-2 Explain the three types of transactions.

The three types of transactions are: (1) *complementary:* the sender of the message gets the intended response from the receiver; (2) *crossed:* the sender does not get the expected response; and (3) *ulterior:* the person appears to be in one ego state, but his or her behavior comes from a different ego state.

Complementary transactions always come from the same ego state. T F

LO 6-3 Identify the differences between passive, aggressive, and assertive behavior.

Passive behavior is nonassertive. The passive person gives in to the other party without standing up for his or her rights.

Aggressive behavior includes the use of force to get one's own way, often at the expense of violating others' rights.

Assertive behavior involves standing up for one's rights without violating the rights of others.

Passive–aggressive behavior occurs when a person says nothing when irritated, lets anger build up, and then blows up. T F

LO 6-4 List the four steps of assertive behavior.

The four steps of assertive behavior are: (1) set an objective; (2) determine how to create a win–win situation; (3) develop an assertive phrase; and (4) implement your plan persistently.

Assertive behavior should be used to get what you want, while the other party loses. T F

LO 6-5 State when and how to use five conflict management styles.

The five conflict management styles are: (1) *forcing,* when the user attempts to resolve the conflict by using aggressive behavior; it should be used when the conflict is one involving personal differences; (2) *avoiding,* when the user attempts to passively ignore the conflict rather than resolve it; it should be used when one's stake in the issue is not high; (3) *accommodating,* when the user attempts to resolve the conflict by passively giving in to the other party; it should be used when maintaining relations outweighs all other considerations; (4) *compromising,* when the user attempts to resolve the conflict through assertive give-and-take concessions; it should be used when the issues are complex and critical, and when there is no simple and clear solution; and (5) *collaborating,* when the user assertively attempts to jointly resolve the conflict with the best solution agreeable to all parties; it should be used for peer conflicts.

When an employee doesn't do what the supervisor requests, the forcing conflict style is appropriate. T F

LO 6-6 List the steps of initiating, responding to, and mediating conflict resolutions.

The initiating conflict resolution steps are: (1) plan to maintain ownership of the problem using the XYZ model; (2) implement your plan persistently; and (3) make an agreement for change. The responding to conflict resolution steps are: (1) listen to and paraphrase the problem using the XYZ model; (2) agree with some aspect of the complaint; (3) ask for, and/or give, alternative solutions; and (4) make an agreement for change. The mediating conflict resolution steps are: (1) have each party state his or her complaint using the XYZ model; (2) agree on the problem(s); (3) develop alternative solutions; and (4) make an agreement for change, and follow up.

Initiating, responding to, and mediating a conflict all take the same level of skill. T F

LO 6-7 Define the following 14 key terms.

Select one or more methods: (1) fill in the missing key terms from memory; (2) match the key terms from the end of the review with their definitions below; and/or (3) copy the key terms in order from the key terms at the beginning of the chapter.

________________ is a method of understanding behavior in interpersonal dynamics.

________________ are the parent, child, and adult.

________________ are complementary, crossed, and ulterior.

____________________ is the process of expressing thoughts and feelings while asking for what one wants in an appropriate way.

____________________ exists whenever two or more parties are in disagreement.

The ____________________ user attempts to resolve the conflict by using aggressive behavior.

The ____________________ user attempts to passively ignore the conflict rather than resolve it.

The ____________________ user attempts to resolve the conflict by passively giving in to the other party.

The ____________________ user attempts to resolve the conflict through assertive give-and-take concessions.

The ____________________ user assertively attempts to resolve the conflict with the best solution agreeable to all parties.

The ____________________ are these: step (1) plan to maintain ownership of the problem using the XYZ model; step (2) implement your plan persistently; and step (3) make an agreement for change.

The ____________________ describes a problem in terms of behavior, consequences, and feelings.

The ____________________ are as follows: step (1) listen to and paraphrase the problem using the XYZ model; step (2) agree with some aspect of the complaint; step (3) ask for, and/or give, alternative solutions; and step (4) make an agreement for change.

The ____________________ are these: step (1) have each party state his or her complaint using the XYZ model; step (2) agree on the problem(s); step (3) develop alternative solutions; and step (4) make an agreement for change, and follow up.

/ / / KEY TERMS / / /

accommodating conflict style 182
assertiveness 172
avoiding conflict style 182
collaborating conflict style 183
compromising conflict style 183
conflict 178
ego states 168
forcing conflict style 181
initiating conflict resolution steps 185
mediating conflict resolution steps 187
responding to conflict resolution steps 186
transactional analysis 168
types of transactions 169
XYZ model 185

/ / / COMMUNICATION SKILLS / / /

The following critical thinking questions can be used for class discussion and/or as written assignments to develop communication skills. Be sure to give complete explanations for all questions.

1. Some people say that because transactional analysis was developed in the 1960s, it is outdated. Do you agree, or do you believe that TA can help us understand behavior and improve human relations?
2. Some people intentionally use ulterior transactions to get what they want without others knowing it. Are ulterior transactions ethical?
3. Some people have negative attitudes and use negative strokes that hurt others. Is giving negative strokes unethical behavior?
4. Select a person you know who is consistently passive. Do people take advantage of this person, such as getting them to do more work? Do you? Is it ethical to take advantage of passive people?
5. Select a person you know who is consistently aggressive. Do people let this person get his or her way? Do you? What is the best way to deal with an aggressive person? What is the best way to deal with a passive–aggressive person?
6. Select a person you know who is consistently assertive. Do people tend to respect this person, and does this person have effective human relations? Do you have effective human relations? What will you do to improve your assertiveness?
7. Recall an occasion of violence at school or work. Describe the situation. Were there signs that violence was coming? What can you do to help prevent violence?
8. Which conflict management style do you use most often? Why do you tend to use this conflict style? How can you become more collaborative?
9. How do you feel about the use of the forcing conflict style? Do you use it often? Is using the forcing style ethical?

CASE /// Phillip Knight and William Perez's Conflict at Nike

Nike started with a handshake between two co-founding visionary Oregonians—Bill Bowerman and his University of Oregon runner Phil Knight. They and the people they hired evolved and grew the company from a U.S.-based footwear distributor to a global marketer of athletic footwear, apparel, and equipment that is unrivaled in the world. Along the way, Nike established a strong brand portfolio with several wholly owned subsidiaries including Cole Haan, Converse Inc., Hurley International LLC, NIKE Golf, and Umbro Ltd. Today Nike operates in more than 160 countries around the globe. Through its suppliers, shippers, retailers, and other service providers, Nike directly or indirectly employs nearly one million people.[45]

Bowerman was primarily the innovative designer of Nike shoes and Knight was the CEO and board chair. Knight decided to step down as CEO while remaining as chair. Knight hired William D. Perez to replace him. However, the newly appointed CEO Perez and chair Knight didn't see eye-to-eye on how to run the business. Perez soon realized that Knight was battling him on everything from where Nike could sell its sneakers to how much time executives should be spending attending meetings. Knight claimed that the conflict was due to Perez's inability to acclimate to the Nike culture, while Perez felt that Knight was overbearing and overcontrolling as board chair.

Perez said that Knight didn't back off from running day-to-day operations, as board chairs usually do. He said: "He hired me to replace him and he never left. His level of interaction with employees was the same as the day before I got there." As Knight admits, he is not the greatest communicator. Knight would hear that Perez had a different position from him—not from Perez, but from another person Knight talked to at Nike. The incident led to confused employees and a very frustrated CEO. Knight, on the other hand, said that Nike was operating at 80 percent efficiency under Perez—an awkward position to be in when its biggest rivals, Adidas and Reebok, were ganging up on it. Knight did not see the situation getting any better. Perez, however, saw the problem more as a disagreement over the firm's basic strategy and management philosophy.

These dissimilarities filtered down to operational and style issues. Knight was more into the meeting culture whereas. Perez would leave to get things done and move on to the next subject. People were spending a lot of time in frustrating meetings where decisions were not being made. Perez was a data person who wanted to know what the "facts" were. Knight's Nike culture was very different, because "feelings" were considered important. Feelings can't be replaced with facts, but data can be used as a guide. Perez wanted Knight to be involved, but by being inspiring and energizing, not by running the business.[46]

Because of the conflict, Perez left Nike and became CEO of Wm. Wrigley Jr. Company, the world's largest chewing-gum manufacturer.[47] Co-founder Knight remained as board chair and promoted Nike veteran Mark Parker to succeed Perez as president and CEO. Parker has been employed by Nike since 1979, with primary career advancement responsibilities in product research, design and development, marketing, and brand management. Both Knight and Parker retain their positions today.[48]

Go to the Internet: For more information on Nike and to update the information provided in this case, do a name search on the Internet and visit www.nike.com.

Support your answers to the following questions with specific information from the case and text, or other information you get from the web or other sources.

1. Using transactional analysis, describe the implied nature of the interaction between Perez and Knight. What do you believe led to these crossed transactions?

2. Using the terms *assertive, passive,* and *aggressive,* describe the implied behaviors of Knight and Perez in their interactions.

3. What conflict management style is being exhibited in this case?

4. How was the conflict resolved between Knight and Perez? How would you have resolved the conflict between them?

Cumulative Questions

5. What roles do perception (Chapter 2), attitudes, and values (Chapter 3) play in this case?

6. How might active listening (Chapter 5) have assisted Knight and Perez in understanding each other's positions?

7. How is Knight, as Nike board chair, bypassing the traditional chain of command (Chapter 5) at the company?

Case Exercise and Role-Play

Preparation: The instructor assigns students to be either Knight or Perez. Assume the two of you are going to try to work things out. Prepare for a meeting in which you will try to resolve your conflict. Both parties prepare to initiate the conflict resolution and develop an XYZ statement. Write down a list of the specific behaviors that the other party does that bothers you that you would like to have changed.

Role-Play: Matched pairs of Knight and Perez role-play the conflict resolution meeting. The meeting may be done in small groups, or two people may role-play before the entire class.

After the conflict meeting, the group or class discusses and critiques the effectiveness of the conflict resolution. Identify any statements that hurt the conflict resolution, and offer alternatives. Also, identify things not said and done that could have helped resolve the conflict.

OBJECTIVE CASE /// Bill and Saul's Conflict

The following conversation takes place over the telephone between Bill, the salesperson, and Saul, the production manager.

BILL: Listen, Saul, I just got an order for 1,000 units and promised delivery in two days. You'll get them out on time, won't you?

SAUL: Bill, you know the normal delivery time is five days.

BILL: I know, but I had to say two days to get the order, so fill it.

SAUL: We don't have the capability to do it. You should have checked with me before taking the order. The best I can do is four days.

BILL: What are you—my mother, or the production manager?

SAUL: I cannot have 1,000 units ready in two days. We have other orders that need to be filled before yours. Four days is the best I can do on short notice.

BILL: Come on, Saul, you cannot do this to me, I want to keep this account. It can mean a lot of business.

SAUL: I know, Bill; you've told me this on three other orders you had.

BILL: But this is a big one. Don't you care about sales?

SAUL: Yes, I do, but I cannot produce the product as fast as you sales reps are selling it lately.

BILL: If I don't meet my sales quota, are you going to take the blame?

SAUL: Bill, we are going in circles here. I'm sorry, but I cannot fill your request. The order will be ready in four days.

BILL: I was hoping you would be reasonable. But you've forced me to go to Mr. Carlson. You know he'll be telling you to fill my order. Why don't you just do it and save time and aggravation?

SAUL: I'll wait to hear from Mr. Carlson. In the meantime, have a good day, Bill.

Answer the following questions. Then in the space between the questions, state why you selected that answer.

_______ 1. Bill was transacting from the _______ ego state.

a. critical parent *b.* sympathetic parent *c.* adult *d.* natural child *e.* adapted child

_______ 2. Saul was transacting from the _______ ego state.

a. critical parent *b.* sympathetic parent *c.* adult *d.* natural child *e.* adapted child

_______ 3. The telephone discussion was a(n) _______ transaction.

a. complementary *b.* crossed *c.* ulterior

_______ 4. Bill's life position seems to be:

a. I'm OK—You're not OK *b.* I'm OK—You're OK *c.* I'm not OK—You're not OK *d.* I'm not OK—You're OK

_______ 5. Bill's behavior was:

a. passive *b.* aggressive *c.* assertive

_______ 6. Saul's behavior was:

a. passive *b.* aggressive *c.* assertive

_______ 7. Bill and Saul have an _______ conflict.

a. individual *c.* individual/group

b. interpersonal *d.* intragroup

_______ 8. Their source of conflict is:

a. personal differences *c.* objectives

b. information *d.* environment

_______ 9. Bill used the _______ conflict style.

a. forcing *c.* accommodating *e.* collaborating

b. avoiding *d.* compromising

_______ 10. Saul used the _______ conflict style.

a. forcing *c.* accommodating *e.* collaborating

b. avoiding *d.* compromising

11. What would you have done if you were Bill?

12. Assume you are Mr. Carlson, the boss. How will you respond when Bill calls?

Note: The conversation between Bill and Saul and/or their meeting with Mr. Carlson can be role-played in class.

/ / / SKILL-BUILDING EXERCISE 6-1 / / /

Transactional Analysis

Preparation (Individual and Group)

Below are 10 situations. For each situation:

1. Identify the sender's communication ego state as:
   CP—Critical Parent
   SP—Sympathetic Parent
   NC—Natural Child
   AC—Adapted Child
   A—Adult
2. Place the letters CP, SP, NC, AC, or A on the S _______ to the left of each numbered situation.
3. Identify each of the five alternative receiver's ego states as in instruction 1 above. Place the letters CP, SP, NC, AC, or A on the R _______.
4. Select the best alternative to achieve effective communication and human relations. Circle the letter *a, b, c, d,* or *e*.

S _______ 1. Ted delegates a task, saying, "It's not much fun, but someone has to do it. Will you please do it for me?" Sue, the delegatee, says:

a. "A good boss wouldn't make me do it." R _______

b. "I'm always willing to help you out, Ted." R _______

c. "I'm not cleaning that up." R _______

d. "You're not being serious, are you?" R _______

e. "I'll get right on it." R _______

S ______ 2. Helen, a customer, brought a dress to the cleaners, and later she picked it up, paid, and went home. At home she opened the package and found that the dress was not clean. Helen returned to the cleaners and said, "What's wrong with this place? Don't you know how to clean a dress?" The cleaning person, Saul, responds:

a. "It's not my fault. I didn't clean it personally." R ______

b. "I'm sorry this happened. We'll do it again right now." R ______

c. "I can understand your disappointment. Were you planning on wearing it today? What can I do to make this up to you?" R ______

d. "These are stains caused by your carelessness, not ours." R ______

e. "Gee whiz, this is the first time this has happened." R ______

S ______ 3. In an office, Bill drops a tray of papers on the floor. Mary, the manager, comes over and says, "This happens once in a while to all of us. Let me help you pick them up." Bill responds:

a. "Guess I slipped, ha ha ha." R ______

b. "This wouldn't have happened if people didn't stack the papers so high." R ______

c. "It's not my fault; I'm not picking up the papers." R ______

d. "Thanks for helping me pick them up, Mary." R ______

e. "It will not take long to pick them up." R ______

S ______ 4. Karl and Kelly were talking about the merit raise given in their branch of the bank. Karl says: "I heard you did not get a merit raise." Kelly responds:

a. "It's true; how much did you get?" R ______

b. "I really don't need a raise anyway." R ______

c. "The branch manager is unfair." R ______

d. "The branch manager didn't give me a raise because he is prejudiced. The men got bigger raises than the women." R ______

e. "It's nice of you to show your concern. Is there anything I can do to help you out?" R ______

S ______ 5. Beckie, the store manager, says to an employee: "Ed, there is no gum on the counter; please restock it." Ed responds:

a. "Why do I always get stuck doing it?" R ______

b. "I'd be glad to do it. I know how important it is to keep the shelves stocked for our customers." R ______

c. "I'll do it just as soon as I finish this row." R ______

d. "I'll do it if I can have a free pack." R ______

e. "Why don't we buy bigger boxes so I don't have to do it so often?" R ______

S ______ 6. Carol, the manager, asked Tim, an employee, to file some forms. A while later Carol returned and asked Tim why he hadn't filed the forms. Tim said: "Oh, oh! I forgot about it." Carol responds:

a. "I've told you before; write things down so you don't forget to do them." R ______

b. "It's OK. I know you're busy and will do it when you can." R ______

c. "Please do it now." R ______

d. "What's wrong with you?" R ______

e. "You daydreaming or what?" R ______

S ______ 7. Joan just finished making a budget presentation to the controller, Wayne. He says: "This budget is padded." Joan responds:

a. "I'm sorry you feel that way. What is a fair budget amount?" R ______

b. (*laughing*) "I don't pad any more than the others." R ______

c. "You don't know what you're talking about. It's not padded." R ______ *d.* "What items do you believe are padded?" R _______

e. "You can't expect me to run my department without some padding for emergencies, can you?" R _______

S _______ **8.** Jill, a computer repair technician, says to the customer: "What did you do to this computer to make it malfunction like this?" The customer responds:

a. "Can you fix it?" R _______

b. "I take good care of this machine. You'd better fix it fast." R _______

c. "I'm sorry to upset you. Are you having a rough day?" R _______

d. "I'm going to tell your boss what you just said." R _______

e. "I threw it down the stairs, ha ha." R _______

S _______ **9.** Pete is waiting for his friend, Will, whom he hasn't seen for some time. When Will arrives, Pete says, "It's good to see you," and gives Will a hug, spinning him around. Will responds:

a. "Don't hug me on the street; people can see us." R

b. "I'm not late; you got here early." R _______

c. "Sorry I'm late. Is there anything I can do to make it up to you? Just name it." R _______

d. "Let's go party, party, party." R _______

e. "Sorry I'm late; I got held up in traffic." R _______

S _______ **10.** Sally gives her secretary, Mike, a note saying: "Please type this when you get a chance." About an hour later, Sally returns from a meeting and asks: "Mike, is the letter I gave you done yet?" Mike responds:

a. "If you wanted it done by 11, why didn't you say so?" R _______

b. "I'm working on it now. It will be done in about 10 minutes." R _______

c. "You said to do it when I got a chance. I've been too busy doing more important things." R _______

d. "Sure thing, boss lady, I'll get right on it." R _______

e. "I'm sorry, I didn't realize how important it was. Can I type it right now and get it to you in about 15 minutes?" R _______

In-Class Exercise

Objective: To improve your ability to use transactional analysis.

AACSB: The primary AACSB learning standard skills developed through this exercise are analytic skills and communication abilities.

Preparation: You should have completed the preparation (10 situations) for this exercise.

Procedure (5–50 minutes)
Select one option:

1. The instructor goes over the recommended answers to the 10 situations.
2. The instructor asks students for their answers to the situations, followed by giving the recommended answers.
3. Break into groups of two or three and together follow the three-step approach for two to three situations at a time, followed by the instructor's going over the recommended answers. Discuss the possible consequences of each alternative response in the situation. Would it help or hurt human relations and performance? How?

Conclusion: The instructor leads a class discussion and/or makes concluding remarks.

Application: What have I learned from this experience? How will I use this knowledge in the future?

Sharing: Volunteers give their answers to the application section.

/ / / SKILL-BUILDING EXERCISE 6-2 / / /

Assertiveness

Preparation (Individual and Group)

In this exercise there are 10 situations with 5 alternative statements or actions. Identify each as assertive (A), aggressive (G), or passive (P). Place the letter A, G, or P on the line before each of the five alternatives. Circle the letter (*a* to *e*) of the response that is the most appropriate in the situation.

1. In class, you are in small groups discussing this exercise; however, two of the members are talking about personal matters instead. You are interested in this exercise.

   ________ *a.* "Don't you want to learn anything in this class?"

   ________ *b.* Forget the exercise, join the conversation.

   ________ *c.* "This is a valuable exercise. I'd really appreciate your input."

   ________ *d.* "This exercise is boring, isn't it?"

   ________ *e.* "Stop discussing personal matters, or leave the class!"

2. You and your roommate do not smoke. Smoke really bothers you. However, your roommate has friends over who smoke in your room regularly.

   ________ *a.* Throw them out of your room.

   ________ *b.* Purposely cough, repeatedly saying, "I cannot breathe."

   ________ *c.* Ask your roommate to have his guests refrain from smoking, or meet at a different place.

   ________ *d.* Complain to your favorite professor.

   ________ *e.* Do and say nothing.

3. Your boss has repeatedly asked you to go get coffee for the members of the department. It is not part of your job responsibility.

   ________ *a.* "It is not part of my job. Why don't we set up a rotating schedule so that everyone has a turn?"

   ________ *b.* "Go get it yourself."

   ________ *c.* Continue to get the coffee.

   ________ *d.* File a complaint with the personnel department or the union.

   ________ *e.* "Why don't we skip coffee today?"

4. You are riding in a car with a friend. You are nervous because your friend is speeding, changing lanes frequently, and passing in no-passing zones.

   ________ *a.* "Are you trying to kill me?"

   ________ *b.* "What did you think of Professor Lussier's class today?"

   ________ *c.* "Please slow down and stay in one lane."

   ________ *d.* Try not to look where you are going.

   ________ *e.* "Stop driving like this or let me out right here."

5. You are in a department meeting to decide on the new budget. However, some of the members are going off on tangents and wasting time. Your boss hasn't said anything about it.

   ________ *a.* Don't say anything. After all, it's your boss's meeting.

   ________ *b.* "So far we agree on XYZ, and we still need to decide on ABC. Does anyone have any ideas on these line items?"

   ________ *c.* "Let's stop wasting time and stay on the subject."

   ________ *d.* "Let's just vote so we can get out of here."

   ________ *e.* "Excuse me, I have to go to the bathroom."

6. One of your coworkers repeatedly tries to get you to do her work with all kinds of excuses.
   ________ *a.* Do the work.
   ________ *b.* "I have no intention of doing your work, so please stop asking me to do it."
   ________ *c.* "Buzz off. Do it yourself, freeloader."
   ________ *d.* "I'd like to do it for you, but I'm tied up right now."
   ________ *e.* "Get away from me and don't bother me again."
7. You bought a watch. It doesn't work, so you return to the store with the receipt. The salesclerk says you cannot exchange it.
   ________ *a.* Insist on the exchange. Talk to the person's boss and his or her boss if necessary.
   ________ *b.* Leave with the watch.
   ________ *c.* Drop the watch on the counter and pick up a new watch and walk out.
   ________ *d.* Come back when a different salesclerk is there.
   ________ *e.* Create a scene, yell, and get other customers on your side. Disrupt business until you get the new watch.
8. You are about to leave work and go to see your child perform in a play. Your boss comes to you and asks you to stay late to do a report she needs in the morning.
   ________ *a.* "Sorry, I'm on my way to see a play."
   ________ *b.* "I'd be happy to stay and do it."
   ________ *c.* "Are you sure I cannot do it tomorrow?"
   ________ *d.* "I'm on my way to see a play. Can I take it home and do it later tonight?"
   ________ *e.* "Why should I get stuck here? Why don't you do it yourself?"
9. You believe that cheating is wrong. Your roommate just asked you if he could copy the homework you spent hours preparing.
   ________ *a.* "Here you go."
   ________ *b.* "I don't help cheaters."
   ________ *c.* "OK, if you don't copy it word for word."
   ________ *d.* "I'd like to help you. You're my friend, but in good conscience I cannot let you copy my homework."
   ________ *e.* "You go out and have a good time, then you expect me to be a fool and get you off the hook? No way."
10. Some people you know stop by your dorm room. One of them pulls out some drugs, takes some, and passes them along. You don't take drugs.
    ________ *a.* "You can get me into trouble. Please put them away or leave."
    ________ *b.* Grab them and get rid of them.
    ________ *c.* Take some drugs because you don't want to look bad.
    ________ *d.* Pass them along without taking any.
    ________ *e.* "Get out of here with that stuff."

In-Class Exercise

Objective: *To improve your ability to be assertive.*

AACSB: The primary AACSB learning standard skills developed through this exercise are analytic skills and communication abilities.

Preparation: You should have completed the preparation (the 10 situations) for this exercise.

Procedure (5–50 minutes)

Select one option:

1. The instructor goes over the recommended answers to the 10 situations.
2. The instructor asks students for their answers to the situations, followed by giving the recommended answers.

3. Break into groups of two or three and together follow the three-step approach for two or three situations at a time, followed by the instructor's going over the recommended answers. Discuss the possible consequences of each alternative response in the situation. Would it help or hurt human relations and performance? How?

Conclusion: The instructor leads a class discussion and/or makes concluding remarks.

Application: What have I learned from this experience? How will I use this knowledge in the future?

Sharing: Volunteers give their answers to the application section.

/ / / SKILL-BUILDING EXERCISE 6-3 / / /

Using the XYZ Conflict Model

Preparation (Individual and Group)

Below are five conflict situations. Write the XYZ statement you would use to resolve the conflict. Remember the goal of resolving the conflict while maintaining human relations.

1. A coworker has asked you to go out after work for the second time. The first time you gave an excuse for not being able to go, but you really don't want to go out with this person. What would you say?
   X ______
   Y ______
   Z ______
2. A coworker keeps coming to your work area to socialize. You have been talking as long as the person wants to. But it is affecting getting your work done, and you have had to stay late. What would you say?
   X ______
   Y ______
   Z ______
3. A coworker has been taking it easy and not doing his share of the work on your two-person assignment. You have had to do more than your share, and you don't want it to continue. What would you say?
   X ______
   Y ______
   Z ______
4. A coworker has continued to interrupt another coworker friend of yours as she speaks. It is upsetting you, and you have decided to talk to the interrupter privately about it. What would you say?
   X ______
   Y ______
   Z ______
5. A coworker is playing music loud for the third time. You don't like the music, and it affects your ability to concentrate. You haven't said anything, but you plan to now. What would you say?
   X ______
   Y ______
   Z ______

In-Class Exercise

Objective: To improve your ability to initiate conflict resolution with positive statements.

AACSB: The primary AACSB learning standard skills developed through this exercise are analytic skills and communication abilities.

Preparation: You should have completed the preparation (the five situations) for this exercise.

Procedure (5–30 minutes)
Select one option:

1. The instructor goes over possible answers to the five situations.
2. The instructor asks students for their XYZ statements to the situations, followed by giving possible answers.
3. Break into groups of two or three, and together come up with an XYZ statement, followed by the instructor's going over the recommended answers. Discuss the possible consequences of each alternative response in the situation. Would it help or hurt human relations and performance? How?

Conclusion: The instructor leads a class discussion and/or makes concluding remarks.

Application: What have I learned from this experience? How will I use this knowledge in the future?

Sharing: Volunteers give their answers to the application section.

/ / / SKILL-BUILDING EXERCISE 6-4 / / /

Initiating Conflict Resolution

Preparation (Group)

During class you will be given the opportunity to role-play a conflict you face, or have faced, in order to develop your conflict skills. Fill in the information below, and also record your answers on a separate sheet of paper.

Other party (or parties) (You may use fictitious names) ______________________________

Define the situation:

1. List pertinent information about the other party (e.g., relationship with you, knowledge of the situation, age, background).
2. State what you wish to accomplish (objective) as a result of the conflict confrontation or discussion.
3. Identify the other party's possible reaction to your confrontation (resistance to change: intensity, source, focus).

How will you overcome this resistance to change?

Using the three steps in initiating conflict resolution, on a separate sheet of paper write out your plan to initiate the conflict resolution. Bring your written plan to class.

In-Class Exercise

Objective: To experience and develop skills in resolving a conflict.

AACSB: The primary AACSB learning standard skills developed through this exercise are analytic skills and communication abilities.

Preparation: You should have completed the information and written plan in preparation for this exercise.

Experience: You will initiate, respond to, and observe a conflict role-play, and then evaluate the effectiveness of its resolution.

BMV 6-1

Procedure 1 (2–3 minutes)
Break into as many groups of three as possible. If there are any people not in a triad, make one or two groups of two. Each member selects the number 1, 2, or 3. Number 1 will be the first to initiate a conflict role-play, then 2, followed by 3.

Procedure 2 (8–15 minutes)

1. Initiator number 1 gives his or her information from the preparation to number 2 (the responder) to read. Once number 2 understands, role-play (see number 2 below). Number 3 is the observer.

2. Role-play the conflict resolution. Number 3, the observer, writes his or her observations on the feedback sheet (see below).
3. Integration: When the role-play is over, the observer leads a discussion on the effectiveness of the conflict resolution. All three should discuss the effectiveness. Number 3 is not a lecturer. Do not go on until told to do so.

Procedure 3 (8–15 minutes)

Follow procedure 2; this time number 2 is the initiator, number 3 is the responder, and number 1 is the observer.

Procedure 4 (8–15 minutes)

Follow procedure 2; this time number 3 is the initiator, number 1 is the responder, and number 2 is the observer.

Conclusion: The instructor leads a class discussion and/or makes concluding remarks.

Application (2–4 minutes): What did I learn from this experience? How will I use this knowledge in the future?

BMV 6-2

Mediating Conflict Resolution *may be shown.*

Sharing: Volunteers give their answers to the application section.

Feedback for ______________________________

Try to have positive improvement comments for each step in initiating conflict resolution. Remember to be descriptive and specific, and for all improvements have an alternative positive behavior (APB) (i.e., if you would have said /? done . . . , it would have improved the conflict resolution by . . .).

Step 1: Did the initiator *maintain ownership* of the problem?

Did he or she have and implement a well-thought-out *XYZ plan*?

Step 2: Did he or she *persist* until the confrontee acknowledged the problem?

Step 3: Did the initiator get the confrontee to *agree to a change* or solution?

// ANSWERS TO TRUE/FALSE QUESTIONS //

1. T.
2. F. Complementary transactions can come from *any* ego state, such as parent to child.
3. T.
4. F. Assertive behavior is used to create a win–win situation, not a win–lose situation as stated.
5. T.
6. F. It is more difficult to mediate a conflict.

PART 3

Leadership Skills: Influencing Others

CHAPTER 7

Leading and Trust

LEARNING OUTCOMES

After completing this chapter, you should be able to:

LO 7-1 Explain what leadership is and how it affects behavior, human relations, and performance.

LO 7-2 Describe leadership trait theory.

LO 7-3 List and describe three behavioral leadership theories.

LO 7-4 List and describe three contingency leadership theories.

LO 7-5 Explain four situational supervisory styles.

LO 7-6 Identify three characteristics that substitute for leadership.

LO 7-7 Briefly describe the five dimensions of trust.

LO 7-8 Define the following 14 key terms (in order of appearance in the chapter):

leadership
leadership trait theory
behavioral leadership theories
Leadership Grid
contingency leadership theories
contingency leadership theory
leadership continuum
normative leadership theory
situational leadership
autocratic style (S-A)
consultative style (S-C)
participative style (S-P)
laissez-faire style (S-L)
trust

/ / / Mike Templeton is a branch manager at the Northwest Bank in Davenport, Iowa. Mike has authority over subordinates to make decisions regarding hiring and firing, raises, and promotions. Mike gets along well with his subordinates. The branch atmosphere is friendly. His boss has asked for a special report about the loans the branch has made so far this year. Mike could have done the report himself, but he thought it would be better to delegate the task to one of the three loan officers. After thinking about the qualifications of the three loan officers, Mike selected Jean. He called her into his office to talk about the assignment.

MIKE: Hi, Jean, I've called you in here to tell you that I've selected you to do a year-to-date loan report for the branch. It's not mandatory; I can assign the report to someone else. Are you interested?

JEAN: I don't know; I've never done a report before.

MIKE: I realize that, but I'm sure you can handle it. I selected you because of my faith in your ability.

JEAN: Will you help me?

MIKE: Sure. There is more than one way to do the report. I can give you the details on what must be included in the report, but you can use any format you want, as long as I approve it. We can discuss the report now; then as you work on it, you can come to me for input. I'm confident you'll do a great job. Do you want the assignment?

JEAN: OK, I'll do it.

Together, Mike and Jean discuss how she will do the report.

What leadership style would you use to get the report done? This chapter explains 10 leadership theories. Each will be applied to the loan report. / / /

In Part 1 (Chapters 1 to 4) we focused on developing intrapersonal skills, and in Part 2 (Chapters 5 to 6) we built on those skills to develop interpersonal skills. We are now in Part 3, so we turn to developing leadership skills, which are clearly based on intrapersonal and interpersonal skills. These three skills form a natural, overlapping developmental sequence.[1] Leadership is both a skill and a behavior that exhibits that skill.[2]

HOW LEADERSHIP AFFECTS BEHAVIOR, HUMAN RELATIONS, AND PERFORMANCE

Learning Outcome 7-1

Explain what leadership is and how it affects behavior, human relations, and performance.

Leadership *is the process of influencing employees to work toward the achievement of objectives*. Leadership is one of the most talked-about, researched, and written-about management topics.[3] However, even though leadership skills can be taught,[4] recruiters say they often see a lack of interpersonal and leadership skills in job applicants.[5] Strong leadership is needed.[6] With today's focus on teamwork, leadership ability is important to everyone in the organization, not just managers.[7]

There are various styles of leadership.[8] The leader's style affects the leader's behavior.[9] In other words, the leader's behavior actually makes the leader's style. An autocratic leader displays behavior different from that of a democratic leader. The human relations between leader and follower will differ according to the leadership style.[10] This will be explained in more detail throughout the chapter.

Leadership can make a difference in performance.[11] The success of individual careers and the fate of organizations are determined by how effectively leaders behave.[12] In most cases, effective leadership leads to better performance.[13] Transformational leadership has been shown to have a positive relationship with performance.[14] Truly outstanding leaders tend to elicit commitment and high performance from others through trust relationships.[15]

On the other side, abusive leaders mistreat employees,[16] and hurt human relations and performance.[17]

Leadership and Management Are Not the Same People tend to use the terms *manager* and *leader* interchangeably. However, that usage is not correct. Management and leadership are related but different concepts.[18] Leadership is one of the five management functions (planning, organizing, staffing, leading, and controlling). Someone can be a manager without being a true leader.[19] There are managers—you may know of some—who are not leaders because they do not have the ability to influence others. There are also good leaders who are not managers. The informal leader, an employee group member, is a case in point. You may have worked in a situation where one of your peers had more influence in the department than the manager.

Our definition of leadership does not suggest that influencing employees is the task of the manager alone; employees do influence other employees.[20] Anyone can be a leader within any group or department, and everyone in a team is expected to be a leader.[21] Thus, regardless of your position, you are expected to share leadership, because leadership is a shared activity.[22]

Theory and Application Based on learning styles (Chapter 2), some people like leadership theories and want to know about them and the history of leadership, while others just want the practical, "how to lead" material. In this chapter, we provide both. In the first three major sections we provide the history of leadership theory based on the three schools of leadership: trait, behavioral, and contingency. Then in the fourth section, based on the theories, we provide situational supervision that explains how to select the most appropriate leadership style for a given situation. So you can put your focus on one or the other, or both.

WORK APPLICATION 7-1

Give detailed reasons why leadership skills are important to a specific organization.

For years researchers have been trying to answer these questions: "What does it take to be an effective leader?" and "What is the most effective leadership style?" There is no universal agreement about the answers to these questions.[23] We will now turn to a chronological review of how researchers have tried to answer these questions. After studying the major leadership theories, you can select the one you like best, combine some, or develop your own.

LEADERSHIP TRAIT THEORY

Learning Outcome 7-2

Describe leadership trait theory.

In the early 1900s, an organized approach to studying leadership began. The early studies were based on the assumption that leaders are born, not made. This concept was later called the "great man" theory of leadership. Researchers wanted to identify a set of characteristics, or traits, that distinguished leaders from followers or effective from ineffective leaders. **Leadership trait theory** *assumes that there are distinctive physical and psychological characteristics accounting for leadership effectiveness.* In fact, personality traits do affect leadership style and creative outcomes.[24] Researchers analyzed traits, or qualities, such as appearance, aggressiveness, self-reliance, persuasiveness, and dominance in an effort to identify a set of traits that all successful leaders possess. The list of traits was to be used as a prerequisite for the promotion of candidates to leadership positions. Only candidates possessing all the identified traits were to be given leadership positions.

Inconclusive Findings: In 70 years, more than 300 trait studies were conducted. However, no one has come up with a universal list of traits that all successful leaders possess. In all cases, there were exceptions.

People also questioned whether traits such as assertiveness and self-confidence were developed before or after one became a leader. It is practically impossible to uncover a universal set of traits. Indeed, if leaders were simply born and not made (in other words, if leadership skills could not be developed), there would be no need for courses in management and human relations.[25]

The Ghiselli Study

Probably the most widely publicized trait theory study was conducted by Edwin Ghiselli.[26] His study concluded that there are traits important to effective leadership, though not all are necessary for success. Ghiselli identified the following six traits, in order of importance, as being significant traits for effective leadership: (1) *supervisory ability,* (you will develop these skills in this course); (2) *need for occupational achievement*; (3) *intelligence;* (4) *decisiveness;* (5) *self-assurance;* and (6) *initiative.*

In the opening case, Mike appears to have supervisory ability. He is getting the job done through Jean, using the supervisory process. Based on the case, one cannot determine if Mike has the other five traits.

Current Studies

WORK APPLICATION 7-2

What are your views on leadership trait theory? Recall a manager you have now or have had in the past. Which of Ghiselli's six traits does or did the person have? Which traits does or did the person lack?

Even though it is generally agreed that there is no universal set of leadership traits or qualities, people continue to study and write about leadership traits.[27] Current research supports the hypothesis that traits do play a role in predicting leadership qualities. One study found that the Big Five personality does have a preferred leadership profile, with high surgency and conscientiousness being positively related to successful leadership and high agreeableness and low adjustment being negatively related to leadership success.[28] Also, neuroscientists are finding that leaders actually may think differently.[29] In a survey conducted by *The Wall Street Journal*/Gallup, 782 top executives in 282 large corporations were asked, "What are the most important traits for success as a supervisor?"[30] Before the results are revealed, complete Self-Assessment Exercise 7-1 to determine if you have the qualities necessary to be a successful leader.

/// Self-Assessment Exercise 7-1 ///

Your Leadership Traits

Select the response that best describes the frequency of your actual behavior. Place the number 1 to 5 on the line before each statement.

Almost always	Usually	Frequently	Occasionally	Seldom
5	4	3	2	1

_____ 1. I am trustworthy. If I say I will do something by a set time, I do it.

_____ 2. I am loyal. I do not do or say things that hurt my friends, relatives, coworkers, boss, or others.

_____ 3. I can take criticism. If people tell me negative things about myself, I give them serious thought and change when appropriate.

_____ 4. I am honest. I do not lie, steal, cheat, or the like.

_____ 5. I am fair. I treat people equally. I don't take advantage of others.

_____ 6. I want to be successful. I do things to the best of my ability.

_____ 7. I am a self-starter. I get things done without having to be told to do them.

_____ 8. I am a problem solver. If things aren't going the way I want them to, I take corrective action to meet my objectives. I don't give up easily.

_____ 9. I am self-reliant. I don't need the help of others.

_____ 10. I am hardworking. I enjoy working and getting the job done.

_____ 11. I enjoy working with people. I prefer to work with others rather than work alone.

_____ 12. I can motivate others. I can get people to do things they may not really want to do.

_____ 13. I am respected. People enjoy working with me.

_____ 14. I am cooperative. I strive to help the team do well, rather than to be the star.

_____ 15. I am a leader. I enjoy teaching, coaching, and instructing people.

To determine your score, transfer the numbers 1 to 5 that represent your responses below. The column headings represent the trait or quality listed in each statement. Total each column; then add those numbers to determine the grand total.

Integrity	Industriousness	Ability to Get Along with People	
_____ 1.	_____ 6.	_____ 11.	
_____ 2.	_____ 7.	_____ 12.	
_____ 3.	_____ 8.	_____ 13.	
_____ 4.	_____ 9.	_____ 14.	
_____ 5.	_____10.	_____ 15.	
_____ Total	_____ Total	_____ Total	_____ Grand Total

Your total for each column will range from 5 to 25, and your grand total will range from 15 to 75. In general, the higher your score, the better your chances of being a successful manager. If you are interested in being (or are) a manager, you can work on improving your integrity, industriousness, and ability to get along with others. As a start, review the list of traits. In which were you strongest? Weakest? Set objectives and develop plans to improve.

Communication Skills
Refer to CS Question 1.

Answers to *The Wall Street Journal*/Gallup survey revealed integrity, industriousness, and the ability to get along with people as the three most important traits for success.

Learning Outcome 7-3

List and describe four behavioral leadership theories.

BEHAVIORAL LEADERSHIP THEORIES

By the late 1940s, most of the leadership research had switched from trait theory to a focus on the leader's behavior. In the continuing quest to find the one best leadership style in all situations, studies attempted to identify the differences in the behavior of effective leaders versus ineffective leaders. **Behavioral leadership theories** *assume that there are distinctive styles that effective leaders use consistently, that is, that good leadership is rooted in behavior.*

In this section you will learn about two-dimensional leadership styles, the Leadership Grid, and transformational, charismatic, transaction, and servant leadership and stewardship.

Two-Dimensional Leadership Styles

Structuring and Consideration Styles In 1945, Ohio State University began a study to determine effective leadership styles. In their attempt to measure leadership styles, the researchers developed an instrument known as the Leader Behavior Description Questionnaire (LBDQ). Respondents to the questionnaire perceived their leaders' behavior toward them on two distinct dimensions:[31]

- *Initiating structure.* The extent to which the leader takes charge to plan, organize, direct, and control as the employee performs the task.
- *Consideration.* The extent to which the leader communicates to develop trust, friendship, support, and respect.

Job-Centered and Employee-Centered Styles At approximately the same time the Ohio State studies began, the University of Michigan's Survey Research Center began leadership studies. Researchers at Michigan identified the same two dimensions, or styles, of leadership behavior. However, they called the two styles by different names:[32]

- *Job-centered.* This is the same as initiating structure. The Managerial Grid (to be discussed next) refers to this dimension as concern for production.
- *Employee-centered.* This is the same as consideration. The Managerial Grid refers to this dimension as concern for people.

Leadership Styles Different combinations of the two dimensions of leadership result in four leadership styles, illustrated in Exhibit 7.1.

Communication Skills
Refer to CS Question 2.

In the opening case, Mike is using the high-consideration (employee-centered) and low-structure (job-centered) style, box 3, because he is telling Jean what needs to be in the report, but how she does the report is up to her. Mike also offers supportive statements.

EXHIBIT 7.1 | Two-Dimensional Leadership Models

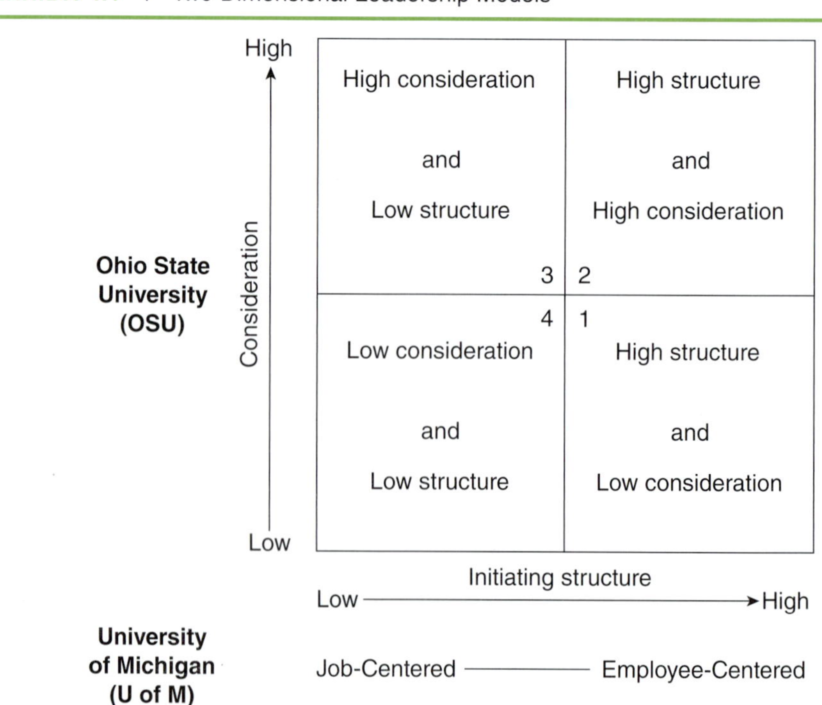

EXHIBIT 7.2 | The Leadership Grid

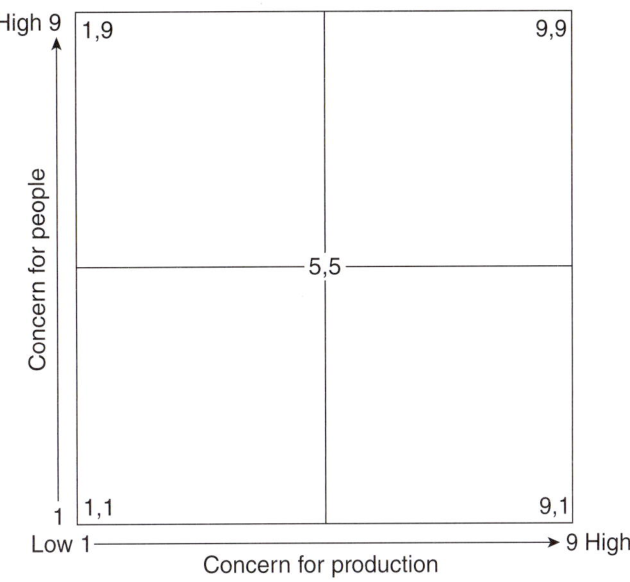

Source: The Leadership Grid Figure (adapted from *Leadership Dilemmas—Grid Solutions* by Robert R. Blake and Anne Adams McCanse. Houston: Gulf Publishing Company, p. 29. Copyright © 1991, by Scientific Methods, Inc.)

The Leadership Grid

Robert Blake and Jane Mouton developed the Managerial Grid. They published it in 1964 and updated it in 1978 and 1985. In 1991 it became the Leadership Grid, with Anne Adams McCanse replacing Mouton. (see Exhibit 7.2)[33]

APPLICATION SITUATIONS / / /

Two-Dimensional Leadership Styles AS 7-1

Using Exhibit 7.1, identify the behavior by its quadrant:

A. 1 B. 2 C. 3 D. 4

_______ 1. "Bill, I want you to take out the mail. It's your turn; you haven't done it for quite awhile."

_______ 2. "I don't care; do whatever you want to do."

_______ 3. "Put out that butt; there is no smoking allowed."

_______ 4. "You're not doing a very good job because you're new. I'll work with you until you get it right. Do it like this."

_______ 5. "I know you can do the task. You're just not too sure of yourself because you never did it before. Try it; if you have a problem, come and get me."

The Leadership Grid is based on the two leadership dimensions called *concern for production* and *concern for people.* The **Leadership Grid** *is Blake and Mouton's model identifying the ideal leadership style as having a high concern for both production and people.* The model identifies five major styles:

The impoverished manager (1,1). This leader has low concern for both production and people. The leader does the minimum required to remain employed in the position.

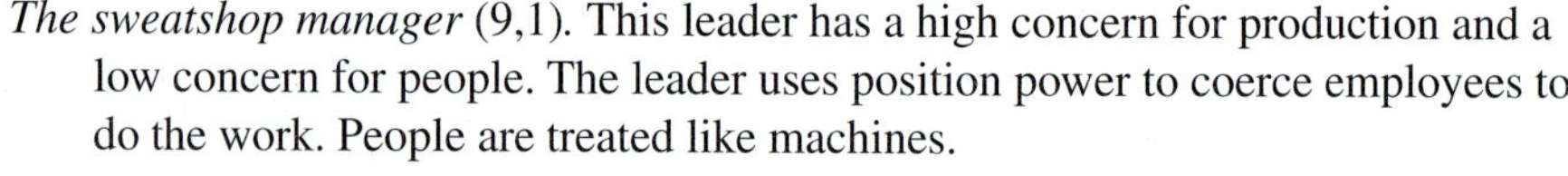

The sweatshop manager (9,1). This leader has a high concern for production and a low concern for people. The leader uses position power to coerce employees to do the work. People are treated like machines.

The country club manager (1,9). This leader has a high concern for people and a low concern for production. The leader strives to maintain good relations and a friendly atmosphere.

The organized-person manager (5,5). This leader has balanced, medium concern for both production and people. The leader strives to maintain satisfactory middle-of-the-road performance and morale.

Communication Skills
Refer to CS Question 3.

The team manager (9,9). This leader has a high concern for both production and people. This leader strives for maximum performance and employee satisfaction. Participation, commitment, and conflict resolution are emphasized.

WORK APPLICATION 7-3

What are your views on the Leadership Grid? Recall a manager you have now or have had. Which of the five styles does or did the manager use?

Leadership Grid training identifies a person's preferred leadership style as 1 of 81 combinations of concern for production and people. Then trainees are taught to always use the one ideal leadership style—the team manager (9,9)—according to Blake and Mouton.

In the opening case, Mike has a high concern for getting the report done and a high concern for Jean. If you had to select one of the five major styles, you would probably choose the 9,9 team manager. However, Mike is giving more support to Jean than direction for doing the report. Mike is actually using closer to a 9,7 leadership style.

APPLICATION SITUATIONS / / /

The Leadership Grid AS 7-2

Match the five situations with the leader's probable style. (Refer to Exhibit 7.2.)

A. 1,1 (impoverished)
B. 1,9 (country club)
C. 9,1 (sweatshop)
D. 5,5 (organized person)
E. 9,9 (team manager)

_______ 6. The group has very high morale; the members enjoy their work. Productivity in the department is one of the lowest in the company.

_______ 7. The group has adequate morale. Members have an average productivity level.

_______ 8. The group is one of the top performers. Members have high morale.

_______ 9. The group has one of the lowest levels of morale. It is one of the top performers.

_______ 10. The group is one of the lowest producers. It has a low level of morale.

Transformational, Charismatic, Transactional, and Servant Leadership and Stewardship

Transformational Leadership Transformational leadership, a contemporary view of leadership, is a behavioral theory because it focuses on the behavior of successful leaders.[34] Studies examine successful leaders to determine the behavior they use to make their organizations successful.[35]

Transformational leadership is about change, innovation, and entrepreneurship. Clearly Steve Jobs was a transformational leader as he transformed Apple, the way we use computers and phones, and the way we listen to music.[36]

Charismatic Leadership Transformational leaders also can be charismatic leaders. Although charisma is not needed to lead, it can help. Charismatic leadership characterizes extraordinary forms of influence, and is frequently associated with leaders who are perceived as exceptional, gifted, and even heroic.[37] Martin Luther King Jr. and Mother Teresa are considered to have been charismatic. Steve Jobs was charismatic because he changed our lives,[38] and he was even called a Pied Piper.[39]

Transactional Leadership Transformational leadership has been contrasted with transactional leadership.[40] The transaction is based on the principle of "you do this work for me and I'll give this reward to you."

Servants and Stewardship Stewardship theory states that leaders should be servants of the organization.[41] Leaders' primary motivations are to serve the organization's best interests and mission, as opposed to more self-serving, opportunistic ends.[42]

CONTINGENCY LEADERSHIP THEORIES

Learning Outcome 7-4

List and describe four contingency leadership theories.

Both the trait and behavioral leadership theories were attempts to find the one best leadership style in all situations. In the late 1960s, it became apparent that there is no one best leadership style in all situations. **Contingency leadership theories** *assume that the appropriate leadership style varies from situation to situation.* Contingency theory is still being researched today.[43]

In this section, we discuss some of the most popular contingency leadership theories, including contingency leadership theory, leadership continuum, normative leadership theory, and situational leadership.

Contingency Leadership Theory

In 1951, Fred E. Fiedler began to develop the first situational leadership theory. He called the theory "Contingency Theory of Leader Effectiveness."[44] Fiedler believed that one's leadership style is a reflection of one's personality (trait theory–oriented) and is basically constant. Leaders do not change styles. **Contingency leadership theory** *developed by Fiedler, is used to determine if a person's leadership style is task- or relationship-oriented and if the situation matches the leader's style.* If there is no match, Fiedler recommends that the leader change the situation, rather than the leadership style.

Leadership Style The first major factor is to determine whether one's leadership style is task- or relationship-oriented. To do so, the leader fills in the Least Preferred Coworker (LPC) scales. This is followed by determining the favorableness of the leader's situation.

Situational Favorableness Situational favorableness refers to the degree to which a situation enables the leader to exert influence over the followers. The more favorable the situation, the more power the leader has. The three variables, in order of importance, are:

1. *Leader–member relations.* Is the relationship good or poor? The better the relations, the more favorable the situation.
2. *Task structure.* Is the task structured or unstructured? Do employees perform routine, unambiguous, standard tasks? The more structured the jobs are, the more favorable the situation.
3. *Position power.* Is position power strong or weak? The more power, the more favorable the situation.

Determining the Appropriate Leadership Style To determine whether task or relationship leadership is appropriate, the user answers the three questions pertaining to situational favorableness, using the Fiedler contingency theory model. See Exhibit 7.3 for an adapted model. The user starts with question 1 and follows the decision tree to determine the situation (1 to 8) and appropriate leadership style (task or relationship).

One of the criticisms of Fiedler's model comes from those who believe that the leader should change his or her style rather than the situation. The other contingency writers in this chapter take this position. Fiedler has thus helped contribute to the other contingency theories.

EXHIBIT 7.3 | Fiedler's Contingency Leadership Theory Model

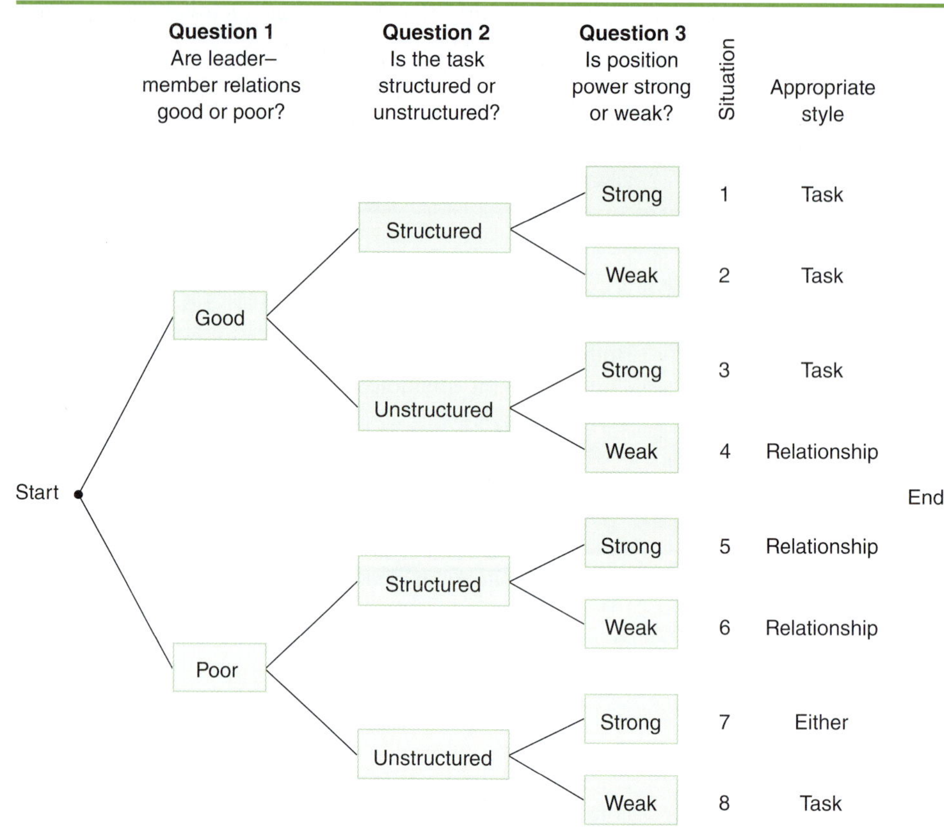

Source: A Theory of Leadership Effectiveness by F. Fiedler, Copyright (copyright symbol) 1967, by McGraw-Hill.

CS
Communication Skills
Refer to CS Question 4.

WORK APPLICATION 7-4

What are your views on contingency leadership theory? Do you agree with Fiedler's recommendation to change the situation rather than the leader's style?

In the opening case, Mike has good relations with Jean, the task is unstructured, and Mike's position power is strong. This is situation 3, in which the appropriate leadership style is task (Exhibit 7.3). However, Mike is using a relationship style. Fiedler would suggest that Mike change the situation to meet his preferred relationship style.

APPLICATION SITUATIONS / / /

Contingency Leadership Theory AS 7-3

Using Exhibit 7.3, match the situation with its corresponding appropriate leadership style. Select two answers for each situation.

A. 1 C. 3 E. 5 G. 7

B. 2 D. 4 F. 6 H. 8

a. Task-oriented b. Relationship-oriented

______ 11. Ben, the supervisor, oversees the assembly of mass-produced containers. He has the power to reward and punish. Ben is viewed as a hard-nosed supervisor.

______ 12. Jean, the manager, is from the corporate planning staff. She helps the other departments plan. Jean is viewed as being a dreamer; she doesn't understand the departments. People tend to be rude in their dealings with Jean.

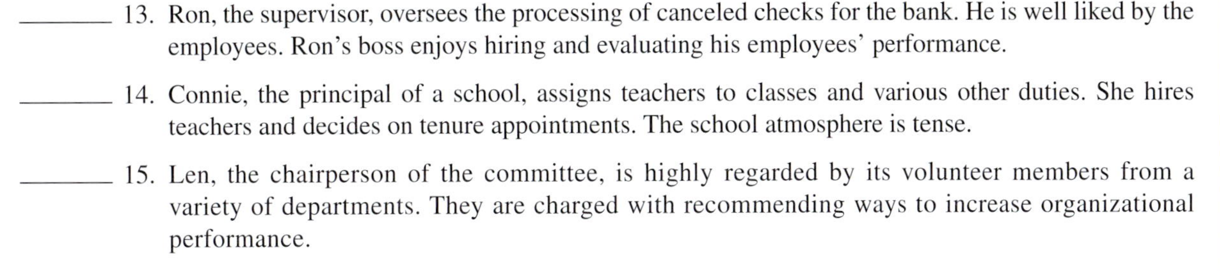

_______ 13. Ron, the supervisor, oversees the processing of canceled checks for the bank. He is well liked by the employees. Ron's boss enjoys hiring and evaluating his employees' performance.

_______ 14. Connie, the principal of a school, assigns teachers to classes and various other duties. She hires teachers and decides on tenure appointments. The school atmosphere is tense.

_______ 15. Len, the chairperson of the committee, is highly regarded by its volunteer members from a variety of departments. They are charged with recommending ways to increase organizational performance.

Leadership Continuum

Robert Tannenbaum and Warren Schmidt state that leadership behavior is on a continuum from boss-centered to employee-centered leadership. Their model focuses on who makes the decisions. They identify seven major styles the leader can choose from. Exhibit 7.4 is an adaptation of their model, which lists the seven styles.[45] The **Leadership continuum,** *developed by Tannenbaum and Schmidt, identifies seven leadership styles based on the use of boss-centered versus employee-centered leadership.*

Before selecting one of the seven leadership styles, the user must consider the following three factors, or variables:

The manager. What is the leader's preferred style, based on experience and confidence in the subordinates?

The subordinates. What is the subordinates' preferred style for the leader? Generally, the more willing and able the subordinates are to participate, the more freedom to participate should be given.

The situation. What are the environmental considerations, such as the organization's size, structure, goals, and technology? Upper-level managers also influence leadership styles.

As you read about the situational variables, you will realize that they are descriptive; the model does not state which style to use in a situation. The leadership styles discussed in the "Situational Supervision" tell the leader which style to use in a given situation.

Skill-Building Exercise 7-2 develops this skill.

In the opening case, Mike began the discussion using style 4, in which the leader presents a tentative decision subject to change. Jean did not have to do the report. Mike would have given it to another employee if she did not want to do it. Mike also used style 5, leader presents problem—the need for the report and what must be included in the report—and told Jean he would allow her to select the form, subject to his final approval.

WORK APPLICATION 7-5

What are your views on the leadership continuum? Recall a manager you have now or have had. Which of the seven styles does or did the manager use?

EXHIBIT 7.4 | The Leadership Continuum

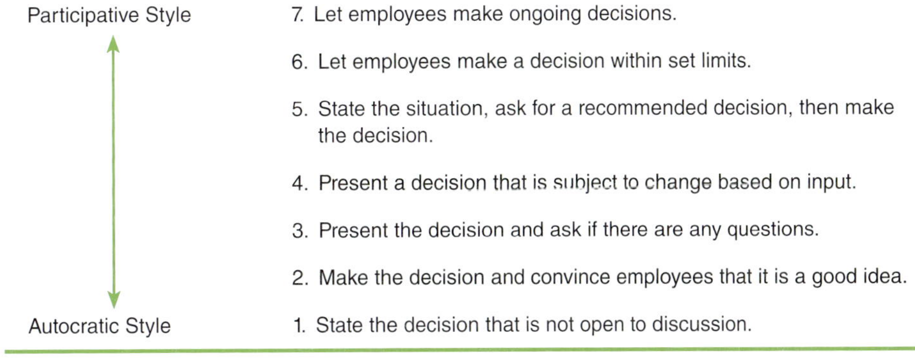

Participative Style	7. Let employees make ongoing decisions.
↑	6. Let employees make a decision within set limits.
	5. State the situation, ask for a recommended decision, then make the decision.
	4. Present a decision that is subject to change based on input.
	3. Present the decision and ask if there are any questions.
↓	2. Make the decision and convince employees that it is a good idea.
Autocratic Style	1. State the decision that is not open to discussion.

APPLICATION SITUATIONS / / /

Leadership Continuum **AS 7-4**

Using Exhibit 7.4, identify the statements by their leadership style:

A. 1 C. 3 E. 5 G. 7

B. 2 D. 4 F. 6

_______ 16. "Samantha, I selected you to be transferred to the new department, but you don't have to go if you don't want to."

_______ 17. "Sally, go clean off the tables right away."

_______ 18. "From now on, this is the way it will be done. Does anyone have any questions about the procedure?"

_______ 19. "These are the two weeks we can go on vacation. You select one."

_______ 20. "I'd like your ideas on how to stop the bottleneck on the line. But I have the final say on the solution we implement."

Normative Leadership Theory

Based on empirical research into managerial decision making, Victor Vroom and Philip Yetton attempted to bridge the gap between leadership theory and managerial practice. To do so, they developed a model that tells the manager which leadership style to use in a given situation. **Normative leadership theory,** *developed by Vroom and Yetton, is a decision-tree model that enables the user to select from five leadership styles the one that is appropriate for the situation.*

Leadership Styles In 2000 Victor Vroom published a revised version of this normative leadership model with the title *Leadership and the Decision Making Process.*[46] In it, he changed the names of the leadership styles. Vroom identified five leadership styles based on the level of participation in the decision by the followers. Vroom adapted the model from Tannenbaum and Schmidt's leadership continuum model (Exhibit 7.4), which ranges from autocratic to participative styles. Here is Vroom's latest version of the five leadership styles:

1. *Decide.* Leader makes decision alone.
2. *Consult individually.* Talk to employees individually to get information and suggestions; then leader makes decision.
3. *Consult group.* Talk to group of employees to get information and suggestions; then leader makes decision.
4. *Facilitate.* Have group meeting for employee participation with leader in making decision.
5. *Delegate.* Group makes the decision.

WORK APPLICATION 7-6

What are your views on normative leadership theory? Recall a manager you have now or have had. Which of the five styles does or did the manager use?

Although the normative leadership model is primarily a leadership model, it is also used to determine the level of participation in decision making. There are actually two different models and a series of seven questions to answer, making it quite complex. Therefore, we will not present the model. Refer to endnote 46 for a copy of the model and details on how to use the model.

In the opening case, Mike used the consult individually style. Mike told Jean that she could select the style subject to his approval. Mike makes the final decision based on Jean's input.

Situational Leadership

Situational leadership, *developed by Paul Hersey and Kenneth Blanchard, is a model for selecting from four leadership styles the one that matches the employees' maturity level in a given situation.* For the most part, situational leadership[47] takes the two-dimensional leadership styles and the four quadrants (see Exhibit 7.1), and develops four leadership styles, which Hersey and Blanchard call *telling* (lower-right quadrant—high task, low relationship); *selling* (upper-right quadrant—high task, high relationship); *participating* (upper-left quadrant—high relationship, low task); and *delegating* (lower-left quadrant—low relationship, low task).

Hersey and Blanchard went beyond the behavioral theory by developing a model that tells the leader which style to use in a given situation. To determine the leadership style, one determines the followers' maturity level. If it is low, the leader uses a telling style; if it is moderate to low, the leader uses a selling style; if it is moderate to high, the leader uses the participating style; and if it is high, the leader uses a delegating style.

In the opening case, Mike used the participating style with Jean. Since Mike had a higher concern for Jean than for the task, he gave Jean more support than directions. Mike gave her the specifics of what had to be included, but he let her decide on the format, subject to his approval.

In general, contingency leadership theories attempt to create a win–win situation by giving the followers the support and direction they need.[48]

See Exhibit 7.5 for a review of the major theories of leadership.

EXHIBIT 7.5 | Leadership Theories

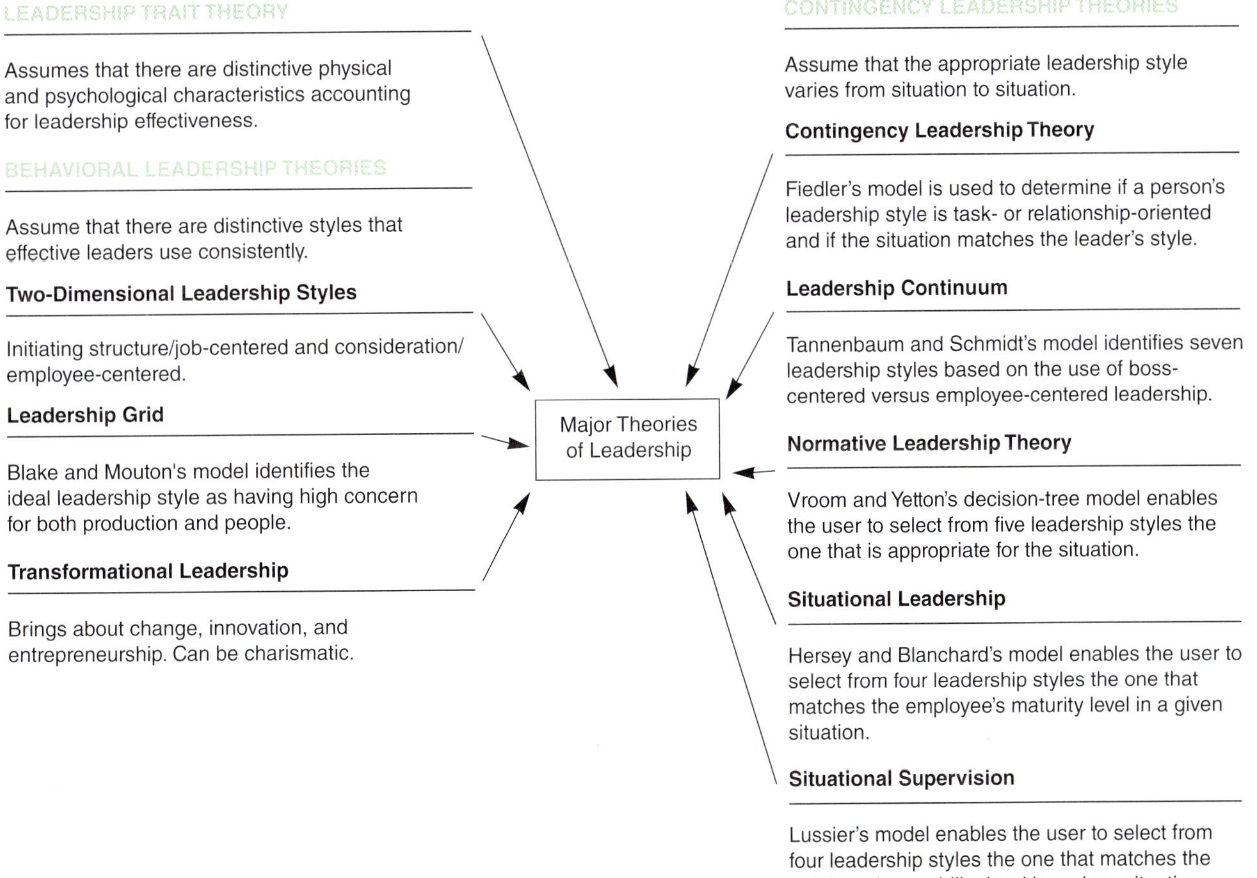

SITUATIONAL SUPERVISION

Now that we have explained the various leadership theories, based on those theories, we now present the practical "how to lead" with the appropriate style for the situation model. Recall that we can all be leaders (supervisors) of others (employees) even if we are not managers. So although the terms *supervisor* and *employee* are used, anyone can use the model in their personal and professional lives. Let's begin with Self-Assessment Exercise 7-2, which identifies your preferred supervisory style.

/// Self-Assessment Exercise 7-2 ///

Determining Your Preferred Supervisory Style

This exercise is designed to determine your preferred supervisory style. Below are 12 situations. Select the one alternative that most closely describes what you would do in each situation. Don't be concerned with trying to pick the right answer; select the alternative you would really use. Circle the letter *a, b, c,* or *d.* Ignore the C _____ and S _____ lines, which will be explained later in this chapter and used in class in Skill-Building Exercise 7–1.

C _____ 1. Your rookie crew members seem to be developing well. Their need for direction and close supervision is diminishing. You would:

a. Stop directing and overseeing performance unless there is a problem. S _____
b. Spend time getting to know them personally, but make sure they maintain performance levels. S _____
c. Make sure things keep going well; continue to direct and oversee closely. S _____
d. Begin to discuss new tasks of interest to them. S _____

C _____ 2. You assigned Joe a task, specifying exactly how you wanted it done. Joe deliberately ignored your directions and did it his way. The job will not meet the customer's standards. This is not the first problem you've had with Joe. You decide to:

a. Listen to Joe's side, but be sure the job gets done right away. S _____
b. Tell Joe to do it again the right way and closely supervise the job. S _____
c. Tell him the customer will not accept the job and let Joe handle it his way. S _____
d. Discuss the problem and what can be done about it. S _____

C _____ 3. Your employees work well together. The department is a real team. It's the top performer in the organization. Because of traffic problems, the president OK'd staggered hours for departments. As a result, you can change your department's hours. Several of your workers have suggested changing. The action you take is to:

a. Allow the group to decide the hours. S _____
b. Decide on new hours, explain why you chose them, and invite questions. S _____
c. Conduct a meeting to get the group members' ideas. Select new hours together, with your approval. S _____
d. Send around a memo stating the hours you want. S _____

C _____ 4. You hired Bill, a new employee. He is not performing at the level expected after one month's training. Bill is trying, but he seems to be a slow learner. You decide to:

a. Clearly explain what needs to be done and oversee his work. Discuss why the procedures are important; support and encourage him. S _____
b. Tell Bill that his training is over and it's time to pull his own weight. S _____
c. Review task procedures and supervise his work closely. S _____
d. Inform Bill that although his training is over, he can feel free to come to you if he has any problems. S _____

C _____ 5. Helen has had an excellent performance record for the past five years. Recently you have noticed a drop in the quality and quantity of her work. She has a family problem. You would:

a. Tell her to get back on track and closely supervise her. S _____
b. Discuss the problem with Helen. Help her realize her personal problem is affecting her work. Discuss ways to improve the situation. Be supportive and encourage her. S _____
c. Tell Helen you're aware of her productivity slip and that you're sure she'll work it out soon. S _____
d. Discuss the problem and solution with Helen and supervise her closely. S _____

/// Self-Assessment Exercise 7-2 /// (*continued*)

C ______ 6. Your organization does not allow smoking in certain areas. You just walked by a restricted area and saw Joan smoking. She has been with the organization for 10 years and is a very productive worker. Joan has never been caught smoking before. The action you take is to:

a. Ask her to put it out, then leave. S ______

b. Discuss why she is smoking and what she intends to do about it. S ______

c. Encourage Joan not to smoke in this area again, and check up on her in the future. S ______

d. Tell her to put it out, watch her do it, and tell her you will check on her in the future. S ______

C ______ 7. Your department usually works well together with little direction. Recently a conflict between Sue and Tom has caused problems. As a result, you:

a. Call Sue and Tom together and make them realize how this conflict is affecting the department. Discuss how to resolve it and how you will check to make sure the problem is solved. S ______

b. Let the group resolve the conflict. S ______

c. Have Sue and Tom sit down and discuss their conflict and how to resolve it. Support their efforts to implement a solution. S ______

d. Tell Sue and Tom how to resolve their conflict and closely supervise them. S ______

C ______ 8. Jim usually does his share of the work with some encouragement and direction. However, he has migraine headaches occasionally and doesn't pull his weight when they occur. The others resent doing Jim's work. You decide to:

a. Discuss his problem and help him come up with ideas for maintaining his work; be supportive. S ______

b. Tell Jim to do his share of the work and closely watch his output. S ______

c. Inform Jim that he is creating a hardship for the others and should resolve the problem by himself. S ______

d. Be supportive, but set minimum performance levels and ensure compliance. S ______

C ______ 9. Bob, your most experienced and productive worker, came to you with a detailed idea that could increase your department's productivity at a very low cost. He can do his present job plus this new assignment. You think it's an excellent idea and you:

a. Set some goals together. Encourage and support his efforts. S ______

b. Set up goals for Bob. Be sure he agrees with them and sees you as being supportive of his efforts. S ______

c. Tell Bob to keep you informed and to come to you if he needs any help. S ______

d. Have Bob check in with you frequently so that you can direct and supervise his activities. S ______

C ______ 10. Your boss asked you for a special report. Fran, a very capable worker who usually needs no direction or support, has all the necessary skills to do the job. However, Fran is reluctant because she has never done a report. You:

a. Tell Fran she has to do it. Give her direction and supervise her closely. S ______

b. Describe the project to Fran and let her do it her own way. S ______

c. Describe the benefits to Fran. Get her ideas on how to do it and check her progress. S ______

d. Discuss possible ways of doing the job. Be supportive; encourage Fran. S ______

C ______ 11. Jean is the top producer in your department. However, her monthly reports are constantly late and contain errors. You are puzzled because she does everything else with no direction or support. You decide to:

a. Go over past reports, explaining exactly what is expected of her. Schedule a meeting so that you can review the next report with her. S ______

b. Discuss the problem with Jean and ask her what can be done about it; be supportive. S ______

c. Explain the importance of the report. Ask her what the problem is. Tell her that you expect the next report to be on time and free of errors. S ______

d. Remind Jean to get the next report in on time and without errors. S ______

C ______ 12. Your workers are very effective and like to participate in decision making. A consultant was hired to develop a new method for your department using the latest technology in the field. You:

a. Explain the consultant's method and let the group decide how to implement it. S ______

b. Teach them the new method and closely supervise them. S ______

c. Explain the new method and why it is important. Teach them the method and make sure the procedure is followed. Answer questions. S ______

d. Explain the new method and get the group's input on ways to improve and implement it. S ______

(*continued*)

/// Self-Assessment Exercise 7-2 /// (*continued*)

To determine your supervisory style:

1. In the table below, circle the letter you selected for each situation. The column headings represent the supervisory style you selected.

Situation	S-A	S-C	S-P	S-L
1.	*c*	*b*	*d*	*a*
2.	*b*	*a*	*d*	*c*
3.	*d*	*b*	*c*	*a*
4.	*c*	*a*	*d*	*b*
5.	*a*	*d*	*b*	*c*
6.	*d*	*c*	*b*	*a*
7.	*d*	*a*	*c*	*b*
8.	*b*	*d*	*a*	*c*
9.	*d*	*b*	*a*	*c*
10.	*a*	*c*	*d*	*b*
11.	*a*	*c*	*b*	*d*
12.	*b*	*c*	*d*	*a*
Total				

S-A Autocratic
S-C Consultative
S-P Participative
S-L Laissez-faire

2. Add the number of circled items per column. The highest number is your preferred supervisory style. Is this the style you tend to use most often?

The more evenly distributed the numbers are, the more flexible your style is. A score of 1 or 0 in any column may indicate a reluctance to use the style.

Note that there is no "right" leadership style. This part of the exercise is designed to enable you to better understand the style you tend to use or prefer to use.

Defining the Situation

Having determined a preferred supervisory style, it is time to learn about the four supervisory styles and when to use each. As mentioned, no one best supervisory style exists for all situations.[49] Instead, the effective supervisor adapts his or her style to meet the capabilities of the individual or group.[50] Based on Ohio State two-dimensional leadership styles, supervisor–employee interactions fall into two distinct categories: directive and supportive. When we use the term *supervisor,* we are referring to *you,* and employees can be others if you are not in an official supervisory role.

- *Directive behavior.* The supervisor focuses on directing and controlling behavior to ensure that the task gets done. The supervisor tells employees what the task is and when, where, and how to do it, and oversees performance.
- *Supportive behavior.* The supervisor focuses on encouraging and motivating behavior. He or she explains things and listens to employee views, helping employees make their own decisions.

In other words, when a supervisor interacts with employees, the focus can be on directing (getting the task done), supporting (developing relationships), or both.

These definitions lead us to the question, What style should I use and why? The answer is, It depends on the situation. And the situation is determined by the capability of the employee(s). There are two distinct aspects of capability:

- *Ability.* Do the employees have the experience, education, skills, and so on to do the task without direction from the supervisor?
- *Motivation.* Do the employees want to do the task? Will they perform the task without a supervisor's encouragement and support?

Employee capability can be located on a continuum from low to outstanding, which the supervisor will determine by selecting the one capability level that best describes the employee's ability and motivation for the specific task. These levels are as follows:

- *Low (C-1).* The employees can't do the task without detailed directions and close supervision. Employees in this category may have the ability to do the task, but they lack the motivation to perform without close supervision.
- *Moderate (C-2).* The employees have moderate ability and need specific direction and support to get the job done properly. The employees may be highly motivated but still need direction, support, and encouragement.
- *High (C-3).* The employees are high in ability but may lack the confidence to do the job. What they need most is support and encouragement to motivate them to get the task done.
- *Outstanding (C-4).* The employees are capable of doing the task without direction or support.

Most people perform a variety of tasks on the job. It is important to realize that their capability may vary depending on the specific task. For example, a bank teller may be a C-4 for routine transactions, but a C-1 for opening new or special accounts. Employees tend to start working with a C-1 capability, needing close direction. As their ability to do the job increases, supervisors can begin to be supportive and stop supervising closely. A supervisor must gradually develop employees from C-1 to C-3 or C-4 levels over time.

Using the Appropriate Supervisory Style

Learning Outcome 7-5

Explain four situational supervisory styles.

As mentioned, the "correct" supervisory style depends on the situation. And the situation, in turn, is a function of employee capability. Each of the supervisory styles, discussed in greater detail below, also involves varying degrees of supportive and directive behavior.

The four supervisory styles—autocratic, consultative, participative, and laissez-faire—are summarized in Model 7.1 in relation to the different levels of employee capability.

The **autocratic style (S-A)** *involves high-directive–low-supportive behavior (HD–LS) and is appropriate when interacting with low-capability employees (C-1).* When interacting with employees, the supervisor gives very detailed instructions, describing exactly what the task is and when, where, and how to perform it. He or she also closely oversees performance. The supportive style is largely absent. The supervisor makes decisions without input from the employees.

The **consultative style (S-C)** *involves high-directive–high-supportive behavior (HD–HS) and is appropriate when interacting with moderate-capability employees (C-2).* Here, the supervisor would give specific instructions, telling employees what the task is and when, where, and how to perform it, as well as overseeing performance at all major stages through completion. At the same time, the supervisor would support the employees by explaining why the task should be performed as requested and answering their questions. Supervisors should work on relationships as they sell the benefits of completing the task their way. When making decisions, they may consult employees, but they have the final say. Once a supervisor makes the decision, which can incorporate employees' ideas, he or she directs and oversees the employees' performance.

MODEL 7.1 | Situational Supervision Model

Capability Level (C)	Supervisory Style (S)
(C-1) Low → The employees are unable and/or unwilling to do the task without direction.	**(S-A) Autocratic** *High-directive–low-supportive.* Tell employees what to do and closely oversee performance. Give little or no support. Make decisions by yourself.
(C-2) Moderate → The employees have moderate ability and are motivated.	**(S-C) Consultative** *High-directive–high-supportive.* Sell employees on doing the job your way and oversee performance at major stages. You may include their input in your decision. Develop a supportive relationship.
(C-3) High → The employees are high in ability but may lack self-confidence or motivation.	**(S-P) Participative** *Low-directive–high-supportive.* Provide little or general direction. Let employees do the task their way. Spend limited time overseeing performance. Focus on end results. Make decisions together, but you have the final say.
(C-4) Outstanding → The employees are very capable and highly motivated.	**(S-L) Laissez-Faire** *Low-directive–low-supportive.* Provide little or no direction and support. Let employees make their own decisions.

The **participative style (S-P)** *is characterized by low-directive–high-supportive behavior (LD–HS) and is appropriate when interacting with employees with high capability (C-3).* When interacting with employees, the supervisor gives general directions and spends limited time overseeing performance, letting employees do the task their way and focusing on the end result. The supervisor should support the employees by encouraging them and building up their self-confidence. If a task needs to be done, the supervisor should not tell them how to do it, but ask them how they will accomplish it. The supervisor should make decisions together with employees or allow employees to make the decision subject to the supervisor's limitations and approval.

The **laissez-faire style (S-L)** *entails low-directive–low-supportive behavior (LD–LS) and is appropriate when interacting with outstanding employees (C-4)***.** When interacting with these employees, supervisors should merely inform employees about what needs to be done. The supervisor answers their questions, but provides little, if any, direction. It is not necessary to oversee performance. These employees are highly motivated and need little, if any, support. The supervisor allows these employees to make their own decisions subject to the supervisor's limitations, although approval by the supervisor will not be necessary.

Applying the Situational Supervision Model

The situation below comes from Self-Assessment Exercise 7-2. Now the information in Model 7.1 will be applied to this situation.

To begin, identify the employee capability level described. The levels are listed in the left-hand column of the exhibit. Indicate the capability level (1 through 4) on the line marked "C" to the left of the situation. Next, determine the management style that each response (*a, b, c,* or *d*) represents. Indicate that style (A, C, P, or L) on the line marked "S" at the end of each response. Finally, identify the most appropriate response by placing a check mark (✓) next to it.

C _____ 1. Your rookie crew members seem to be developing well. Their need for direction and close supervision is diminishing. You would:

a. Stop directing and overseeing performance, unless there is a problem. S _____

b. Spend time getting to know them personally, but make sure they maintain performance levels. S _____

c. Make sure things keep going well; continue to direct and oversee closely. S _____

d. Begin to discuss new tasks of interest to them. S _____

Let's see how well you did.

1. The capability was C-1, but they have now developed to the C-2 level. If you put the number 2 on the C line, you were correct.
2. Alternative *a* is S-L, the laissez-faire style. There is no direction or support. Alternative *b* is S-C, the consultative style. There is both direction and support. Alternative *c* is S-A, the autocratic style. There is direction but no support. Alternative *d* is S-P, the participative style. There is low direction and high support (in discussing employee interests).
3. If you selected *b* as the appropriate response, you were correct. However, in the business world, there is seldom only one way to handle a problem successfully. Therefore, in this exercise, you receive points based on how successful your behavior would be in each situation. In this situation, *b* is the most successful alternative because it involves developing the employees gradually; it's a three-point answer. Alternative *c* is the next best alternative, followed by *d*. It is better to keep things the way they are now than try to rush employee development, which would probably cause problems. So *c* is a two-point answer, and *d* is a one-point answer. Alternative *a* is the least effective because you are going from one extreme of supervision to the other. This is a zero-point answer because the odds are great that this style will cause problems that will affect supervisory success.

SB

Skill-Building Exercise 7-1 develops this skill.

WORK APPLICATION 7-7

What are your views on situational supervision? Recall a manager you have now or have had. Which of the four styles does or did the manager use? Would you use the model on the job?

WORK APPLICATION 7-8

Which of the four supervisory styles would you like your boss to use with you? Why would you prefer this particular style?

WORK APPLICATION 7-9

Which leadership theory or model do you prefer? Why?

WORK APPLICATION 7-10

Describe the type of leader you want to be.

Communication Skills Refer to CS Question 5.

The better a supervisor is at matching his or her supervisory style to employees' capabilities, the greater the chances of being a successful supervisor. Don't forget that you don't have to be a supervisor to use the model when you influence others as a leader.

In completing Skill-Building Exercise 7-1, Situational Supervision, you will apply the model to the remaining situations and be given feedback on your success at applying the model as you develop your situational supervision skills. Remember that what you think about is how you feel, and what you feel is how you behave. So now that you know how to be a situational supervisor, think and act like a leader and others will follow you whether or not you are a manager.

PUTTING THE LEADERSHIP THEORIES TOGETHER

This chapter has presented nine different leadership theories. Exhibit 7.6 puts the nine leadership theories together, converting them into four leadership style categories. A review of this exhibit should lead to a better understanding of the similarities and differences between these leadership theories.

EXHIBIT 7.6 | Leadership Styles

Behavioral Leadership Theories

	Leadership Style Categories			
	Autocratic	**Democratic**		**Laissez-Faire**
Two-dimensional leadership styles	High structure/job-centered Low consideration/employee-centered	High structure/job-centered High consideration/employee-centered	High consideration/employee-centered Low structure/job-centered	Low consideration/employee-centered Low structure/job-centered
Leadership Grid	High concern for production; low concern for people (9,1 sweatshop manager)	High concern for both production and people (9,9 team manager)	High concern for people; low concern for production (1,9 country club manager)	Low to moderate concern for both people and production (1,1 impoverished and 5,5 organized managers)
Transformational leadership	No actual style			

Contingency Leadership Theories

Contingency Leadership Theory	**Task Orientation**		**Relationship Orientation**	
Leadership continuum	1. Make decision and announce it	2. Sell decision 3. Present ideas and invite questions	4. Present tentative decision subject to change 5. Present problem, get suggestions, and make decision	6. Define limits and ask group to make decision 7. Permit subordinates to function within limits defined by leader
Normative leadership theory	Make decision alone using available information (Decide)	Meet individually or as a group with subordinates, explain the situation, get information and ideas on how to solve the problem, make final decision alone (Consult individual and group)	Have group meeting for employee participation with leader in decision making (Facilitate)	Meet with subordinates as a group, explain the situation, and allow the group to make decision (Delegate)
Situational leadership	High task, low relationship (Telling)	High task, high relationship (Selling)	High relationship, low task (Participating)	Low relationship, low task (Delegating)
Situational supervision	High directive, low support (Autocratic)	High directive, high support (Consultative)	High support, low directive (Participative)	Low support, low directive (Laissez-faire)

Leadership Trait Theory

Based on traits of leader; no actual style

Learning Outcome 7-6

Identify three characteristics that substitute for leadership.

SUBSTITUTES FOR LEADERSHIP?

The leadership theories presented assume that some leadership style will be effective in each situation. Steven Kerr and John Jermier argue that certain individual, task, and organizational variables prevent managers from affecting subordinates' attitudes and behaviors.[51] Substitutes for managers, or characteristics that negate or replace managers' influence, are those that structure tasks (directive) for followers or give them positive strokes (support) for their action. Rather than having the managers provide the necessary direction and support, the subordinates, task, or organization may provide them.[52]

Thus, because leadership is a shared process between the group members, there is no substitute for leadership. However, there are substitutes for managers.[53]

The following characteristics may substitute for management by providing direction and/or support:

Communication Skills
Refer to CS Question 6.

WORK APPLICATION 7-11

Do you agree that characteristics of subordinates, task, and the organization can substitute for management direction and support? Explain your answer.

1. *Characteristics of subordinates.* Ability, knowledge, experience, training; need for independence; professional orientation; indifference toward organizational rewards.
2. *Characteristics of task.* Clarity and routine; invariant methodology; provision of own feedback concerning accomplishment; intrinsic satisfaction.
3. *Characteristics of the organization.* Formalization (explicit plans, goals, and areas of responsibility); inflexibility (rigid, unbending rules and procedures); highly specified and active advisory and staff functions; closely knit, cohesive work groups; organizational rewards not within the leader's control; spatial distance between superior and subordinates.

DIVERSITY AND GLOBAL LEADERSHIP

Thinking globally and having global leadership skills are essential to effective organizations.[54] Europeans travel between countries the way Americans travel between states. Most large companies conduct business in many parts of the world. This makes cultural awareness and diversity in leadership necessary for business success in the increasingly global business environment.[55]

Most leadership theories were developed in the United States, so they do have an American bias. Theories assume employee responsibility, rather than employee rights; self-gratification, rather than employee commitment to duty or altruistic motivation; democratic values, rather than autocratic values; rationality, rather than spirituality, religion, or superstition. Thus, the theories may not be as effective in cultures based on different assumptions.[56]

In the 1970s, Japan's productivity rate was increasing faster than that of the United States. Research was conducted to determine why the Japanese were more productive, and it became apparent that Japanese firms were managed and led differently than U.S. organizations. Over the years, many U.S. companies have adopted more collective decision making and responsibilities, and have taken a more holistic view of employees (recall the total person approach from Chapter 1). Furthermore, the number of firms using self-directed virtual work teams has increased.[57]

Within Europe there are diverse management models, which raise a range of management education issues. European managers deal more with cultural than technical issues in the context of diverse value systems and religious backgrounds. Management is organized more as a language than as a set of techniques. Thus, leaders in different MNCs need autonomy to lead differently.[58]

American, European, and Japanese executives realize that they must manage and lead their business units in other countries differently than they do at home. Toyota and Honda run their plants in the United States somewhat differently from those in Japan. Similarly, IBM's management style in Japan differs from its style in the United States.

Here are a few examples of differences in leadership styles based on national culture. Korean leaders are expected to be paternalistic toward employees. Arab leaders are viewed as weak if they show kindness or generosity without being asked to do so. Japanese leaders are expected to be humble and speak infrequently. Scandinavian and Dutch leaders embarrass, rather than motivate, employees with public, individual praise. Autocratic leadership styles tend to be appropriate in high-context cultures (Chapter 5), such as those in Arab, Far Eastern, and Latin American countries, whereas participative leadership styles tend to be appropriate in low-context cultures, such as those in the United States, Norway, Finland, Denmark, and Sweden. Thus, different cultures make cross-business-unit collaboration in MNCs difficult.[59]

Leadership is also different in e-organizations, which are often global companies. According to executives who have worked in e-org and traditional organizations, e-org leaders focus more on speed in decision making, flexibility, and a vision of the future. Online leadership, managing people from all over the world in virtual and boundaryless organizations, calls for much less face-to-face communication and more written communication to get the job done. You may lead or be part of a virtual team, working interdependently with shared purpose across space, time, and organization boundaries, using technology to communicate and collaborate.[60]

Communication Skills
Refer to CS Question 7.

Although cultural differences will continue to affect leadership, the instant communication, individualism, and material acquisition of global products in our society today threaten traditional family, religious, and social structures, as the trend toward the development of a more global blended culture continues.[61] But don't look for a one-size-fits-all solution or leadership style.[62]

TRUST

Let's begin by tying leadership and trust together. You can't be a truly effective leader without trust.[63] High-quality relationships needed to lead are based on trust,[64] as leaders and subordinates have a unique bonding, respect, and trust.[65] Trust affects behavior, human relations, and performance.[66] Unfortunately, worldwide trust in business and government is near a low point, and in America over half of employees do not trust their leaders.[67] As you probably already realize, being trustworthy is important in your personal and professional life.[68] So before reading about trust, complete Self-Assessment Exercise 7-3, Your Trustworthiness.

/// Self-Assessment Exercise 7-3 ///

Your Trustworthiness

For each statement, select the frequency with which you use, or would use, the behavior at work. Be honest; that's part of trustworthiness.

Almost always				Almost never
1	2	3	4	5

_____ 1. I tell the truth; I tell it like it is.

_____ 2. When I make a commitment to do something, I do it.

_____ 3. I strive to be fair by creating a win–win situation for all parties.

_____ 4. I do the task to the best of my ability.

_____ 5. I volunteer to help others when I can, and I seek help when I need it.

_____ 6. I am humble; I don't brag about my accomplishments.

_____ 7. When I make a mistake, I admit it rather than try to cover it up or downplay it.

_____ 8. I don't overcommit to the point of breaking commitments.

_____ 9. I practice what I preach and walk the talk; I don't say one thing and do another.

_____ 10. I treat coworkers—both friends and others—fairly.

/// Self-Assessment Exercise 7-3 /// *(continued)*

_____ 11. I stand by, protect, and save face for coworkers.

_____ 12. When someone tells me something in confidence, I don't tell anyone else.

_____ 13. I say only positive things, or nothing, about coworkers; I don't gossip.

_____ 14. I am viewed by coworkers as being collaborative rather than competitive.

_____ 15. I let coworkers know the real me—what I stand for and what I value. I share my feelings.

_____ 16. When coworkers tell me something private about themselves, I offer acceptance and support and share something about myself.

_____ 17. I deal effectively with diverse opinions, people, and types of conflict.

Place the numbers (1 to 5) you recorded for the situations on the lines below. Total each by column; then add the totals of the five columns and place the grand total on the continuum (17–85) below the totals.

Integrity	Competence	Consistency	Loyalty	Openness
_____ 1.	_____ 4.	_____ 8.	_____ 11.	_____ 15.
_____ 2.	_____ 5.	_____ 9.	_____ 12.	_____ 16.
_____ 3.	_____ 6.	_____ 10.	_____ 13.	_____ 17.
	_____ 7.		_____ 14.	
_____	_____	_____	_____	_____ Totals

Trustworthy 17 - - - 20 - - - 30 - - - 40 - - - 50 - - - 60 - - - 70 - - - 80 - - - 85 Untrustworthy

The lower your score, the more trustworthy you are. Note your strongest (lowest-score column) and weakest (highest-score column) dimensions of developing trust. You will learn how to develop trust in all five dimensions in the following section.

Are you trustworthy? In this section, we discuss types of trust and how to develop trust.

Types of Trust

Trust *is the positive expectation that another will not take advantage of you.*

The three types of trust in human relations are deterrence-, knowledge-, and identification-based trust (see Exhibit 7.7). They can also be called levels of trust, because they form a building block of trust.[69] See Exhibit 7.7 for a list of trust levels and dimensions.

- **Deterrence-based trust.** Most new human relations begin with deterrence-based trust because we lack experience dealing with the other person. Deterrence-based trust is the most fragile since one violation or inconsistency can destroy the human relations.[70] The relationship is based on fear of reprisal if the trust is violated. So we try to avoid being untrustworthy; we are on our best behavior when we first meet people.
- **Knowledge-based trust.** Knowledge-based trust is the most common organizational trust. Trust is based on experience dealing with the other person. Based on our knowledge, we can predict the other person's behavior. The better we know people, the better we can predict their behavior—and trust them.
- **Identification-based trust.** Identification-based trust occurs when there is an emotional connection—friend rather than just coworker. It is the highest level of trust. People look out for each other's best interests and act for the other.

EXHIBIT 7.7 | Three Levels and Five Dimensions of Trust

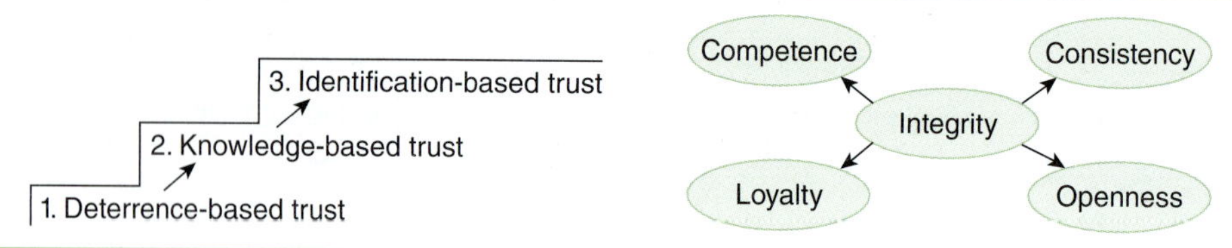

WORK APPLICATION 7-12

Give an example of each of the three levels of trust you have experienced on the job.

- **Deterrence- versus knowledge- and identification-based trust.** Unlike fragile deterrence-based trust, knowledge- and identification-based trust are not broken by inconsistent behavior. If we incorrectly predict behavior and are disappointed or taken advantage of in some way, often we can understand the violation, accept it, forgive the person, and move on with the relationship.

Developing Trust

Learning Outcome 7-7

Briefly describe the five dimensions of trust.

Now let's discuss how to develop trust so that you can achieve the identification-based level of trust. As shown in Exhibit 7.7, there are five dimensions of trust. Note that integrity is in the center, holding the other four dimensions together, because without integrity, trust breaks apart.

The five columns in Self-Assessment Exercise 7-3, Your Trustworthiness, are the five dimensions of trust. Although they are all important, you may want to pay particular attention to your weaker areas.

Integrity People who have *integrity* are honest and sincere.[71] Integrity and dependability are the most important dimension when people assess another's trustworthiness.[72]

Tips to develop your integrity include:

- *Be honest.* Don't lie, steal, or cheat; be sincere, and tell it like it is and people will trust you.
- *Be fair.* According to Joe Lee (CEO of Darden Restaurants, integrity and fairness are the important core values to business. Perceived unfairness causes distrust and a desire for revenge, restitution, and retaliation.[73]

Communication Skills
Refer to CS Questions 8 and 9.

Competence To trust, respect, and have confidence in you, people need to believe that you have the skills and abilities to carry out your commitments.

Tips to develop your competence include:

- *Be conscientious.* Do the job to the best of your ability.
- *Know your strengths and limitations.* Volunteer to help others when you can, and seek assistance when you need it. Don't commit to doing something that you cannot deliver on.
- *Admit your mistakes and apologize.* Others will think, "I can trust you."

Consistency *Consistent* people use the same behavior in similar situations; they are predictable.

Tips to develop your consistency include:

- *Keep your commitments.* To trust you, people must believe that you are dependable.[74] Promises made must be promises kept. You're only as good as your word and commitments, so if you say you will do something, follow through.[75]
- *Practice what you preach.* Walk the talk, because actions speak louder than words. People who say one thing and do another lack credibility.

EXHIBIT 7.8 | The Johari Window

	Known to Self	Unknown to Self
Known to Others	Open	Blind
Unknown to Others	Hidden	Unknown

Source: Of Human Interaction by J. Luft, Copyright © 1969, by National Press.

Loyalty People who are *loyal* look out for others' interests (they don't take advantage of others). Staying loyal to someone preserves trust, allowing people to be able to function without suspecting their motives.[76] Loyalty requires identification-based trust.

Tips to develop your loyalty include:

- *Maintain confidences.* When someone tells you something in confidence, that person is being vulnerable in trusting you, so don't tell others. One time could be your last.
- *Don't gossip negatively about individuals.* If people hear you gossip about others, they may assume you do the same behind their backs. Follow this rule: If you don't have anything nice to say, don't say anything.

Openness People who are *open* accept new ideas and change. They give the full truth.

Tips to develop your openness include:

- *Self-disclosure and the Johari Window.* Self-disclosure enhances human relations and is what takes the level of trust to the identification level.[77] The Johari Window was developed by Joseph Luft and Harry Ingram, who called it by a combination of their first names.[78] As shown in Exhibit 7.8, the window has four regions representing the intersection of two axes: (1) the degree to which information about you (values, attitudes, beliefs) is known to or understood by you, and (2) the degree to which information about you is known by others.

  Based on our understanding of self, we select those aspects of self that are appropriate to share with others; we *open* the *hidden* self areas of the window. As we self-disclose, we also find out things about ourselves that others know, such as irritating things we do; we open the *blind* area. The *unknown* area cannot be open until we experience a new situation, such as getting laid off, because we don't know how we will behave until it happens. Thus, to develop trust and improve human relations, we gradually share self-disclosure to *open* the *hidden* and *blind* areas of the Johari Window.
- *Risk self-disclosure.* Developing trust through self-disclosure does include the risk of being hurt, disappointed, and taken advantage of. Although people often fear the risk of self-disclosure, the rewards of improved human relations and personal friendship are worth the risk. If you follow the guidelines above, you can minimize your risk.

Skill-Building Exercise 7-3 develops this skill.

WORK APPLICATION 7-13

What are your strongest and weakest dimensions of trust at work? How will you improve your trustworthiness? What tips will you implement?

Repairing Trust

Trust is earned and builds over time. It is much easier to destroy trust than to build it.[79] Years of trust can be hurt or destroyed with one bad act of distrust.[80] For example, if you get caught in a lie, miss a deadline or do a poor job, or are disloyal, you may hurt your relationship and you might not be trusted again. With knowledge- and identification-based trust levels you may be forgiven, but you may not. Your relationship may never be the same again, or it could end. So be sure to always be trustworthy to avoid having to repair trust.[81]

Because trust is easily broken, knowing how to repair trust has become a critical competency.[82] After trust is broken, we obviously need to follow all of the tips to building trust. However, to truly repair trust the starting point is to admit mistakes and give a sincere

WORK APPLICATION 7-14

How often do you apologize? Should you apologize more often, and especially to the people closest to you, when you break their trust?

apology. Some people, and more so men than women, are reluctant to apologize, and people apologize more often to strangers than to their romantic partners and family members.[83] When we do something that breaks trust, the other person is likely to be emotional, so we do need to stay calm and calm the other person, and apologizing helps.[84] Even if you don't believe you did anything wrong, you can apologize for breaking trust with the other person. For example, you can say in a sincere voice, "I'm sorry I upset you with my (state the specific behavior, i.e., comment), I will try not to do it again." It takes only a minute to give a sincere apology, and apologizing can help develop, maintain, and repair trust that is critical to effective human relations.

Complete Self-Assessment Exercise 7-4 to determine how your personality affects your leadership style and ability to develop trust.

/// Self-Assessment Exercise 7-4 ///

Your Personality and Leadership and Trust

Recall that your personality is based on traits. So your personality does affect your leadership behavior and your use of contingency leadership styles. What was your preferred situational leadership style? Are you flexible? Can you change styles to meet the situation?

If you have a high *surgency* personality, you most likely have a higher task-oriented leadership style than people-oriented, so you may want to work on the people side. Watch your use of autocratic leadership behavior. Use participation (participative and laissez-faire styles) when appropriate. You may be competent and consistent, but because getting the job done is more important to you than developing human relations, you may need to work on integrity, loyalty, and openness to develop greater *trust.*

If you have a high *agreeableness* personality, you most likely have a high people-oriented leadership style, but you need to make sure the job gets done. You may be reluctant to use the autocratic leadership style when it is appropriate. You are most likely high on openness and are loyal on *trust* dimensions and you may have integrity, but you may need to work on competence and consistency, because getting the job done is less important to you than developing human relations.

How well you deal with your emotions is what *adjustment* is about. If you are not high on adjustment personality traits, you may tend to be reluctant to be a leader. Low adjustment personalities are usually not open to disclosure, so you may have trouble being *trusted* for competence, consistency, and integrity.

If you are a high *conscientious* personality, you may push others to be conscientious too. Are you more task- or people-oriented? That orientation will affect your leadership style more than your conscientiousness. Conscientiousness tends to lead to competence and consistency *trust* dimensions. However, you may need to work on integrity, loyalty, and openness, based on your task or people orientation.

If you have a high *openness to experience,* you may use participative leadership styles to bring about change. You will use openness to develop *trust,* but you may need to work on other dimensions of trust.

Action plan: Based on your personality, what specific things will you do to improve your leadership style and develop trust?

____

____

____

____

As we bring this chapter to a close, you should realize that you can be a leader even if you are not a manager. You should know leadership traits are important, but that there is no universal list of traits that determine leadership success. You should understand the two-dimensional leadership styles of task and relationship behavior, and that they have different terms based on the behavioral theory; and be able to define contemporary behavioral theories. You should also be able to describe four contingency leadership theories. Importantly, you should be able to select the most appropriate leadership style for the situation using the situational supervision model. In addition, there are substitutes for management and there is diversity in global leadership. Leadership is based on trust, so you should understand the types of trust, and be able to develop and repair trust. Remember that what you think is how you feel, and how you feel is how you behave. So think, feel, and act like a leader whom people can trust.

/ / / REVIEW / / /

The chapter review is organized to help you master the 8 learning outcomes for Chapter 7. First provide your own response to each learning outcome, and then check the summary provided to see how well you understand the material. Next, identify the final statement in each section as either true or false (T/F). Correct each false statement. Answers are given at the end of the chapter.

LO 7-1 Explain what leadership is and how it affects behavior, human relations, and performance.

Leadership is the process of influencing employees to work toward the achievement of objectives. A leader using one style will behave differently than another leader using a different style. The leader's style also affects the type of human relations between the leader and followers. Leaders can affect followers' performance, but not always.

The terms *leadership* and *management* mean the same thing. T F

LO 7-2 Describe leadership trait theory.

Leadership trait theory assumes that distinct physical and psychological characteristics account for effective leadership. According to Ghiselli, the major leadership trait needed for success is supervisory ability. However, there is no universally accepted set of effective leadership traits.

Leadership trait theory is outdated and no longer studied. T F

LO 7-3 List and describe three behavioral leadership theories.

Behavioral leadership theories assume that there are distinctive styles that effective leaders use consistently. The three theories are: (1) two-dimensional leadership styles—initiating structure and consideration styles (Ohio State) and job-centered and employee-centered styles (University of Michigan); (2) the Leadership Grid—Blake and Mouton's model identifying the ideal leadership style as having a high concern for both production and people; and (3) transformational leadership—leaders bring about change, innovation, and entrepreneurship.

Charismatic leadership is a behavioral leadership theory. T F

LO 7-4 List and describe four contingency leadership theories.

Contingency leadership theories assume that the appropriate leadership style varies from situation to situation. The four theories are: (1) contingency leadership theory—Fiedler's model used to determine whether leadership style is task- or relationship-oriented, and whether the situation matches the style; (2) leadership continuum—Tannenbaum and Schmidt's identified boss-centered and employee-centered leadership at the extremes; (3) normative leadership theory—Vroom and Yetton's decision-tree model that enables the user to select from five leadership styles the one that is appropriate for the situation; and (4) situational leadership—Hersey and Blanchard's model for selecting from four leadership styles the one that fits the employees' maturity level in a given situation.

Contingency leadership theory is the only one that recommends changing the situation, rather than your leadership style. T F

LO 7-5 Explain four situational supervisory styles.

The four situational supervisory styles are: (1) autocratic—high-directive–low-support; (2) consultative—high-directive–high-support; (3) participative—low-directive–high-support; and (4) laissez-faire—low-directive–low-support.

When the employee's capability level is high (C-3), the consultative leadership style is appropriate. T F

LO 7-6 Identify three characteristics that substitute for leadership.

Characteristics of subordinates, task, and the organization can substitute for management by providing direction and/or support.

Subordinates, task, and the organization are substitutes for management, but they can't substitute for leadership. T F

LO 7-7 Briefly describe the five dimensions of trust.

The five dimensions of trust are: (1) integrity—being honest, truthful, and sincere; (2) competence—having technical and interpersonal knowledge, ability, and skill; (3) consistency—using the same behavior in similar situations; (4) loyalty—looking out for the interests of others; and (5) openness—accepting new ideas and change.

The Johari Window is a measure of openness. T F

LO 7-8 Define the following 14 key terms.

Select one or more methods: (1) Fill in the missing key terms from memory; (2) match the key terms from the end of the review with their definitions below; and/or (3) copy the key terms in order from the key terms at the beginning of the chapter.

________________ is the process of influencing employees to work toward the achievement of objectives.

________________ assumes that there are distinctive physical and psychological characteristics accounting for leadership effectiveness.

________________ assume that there are distinctive styles that effective leaders use consistently.

The ________________ is Blake and Mouton's model identifying the ideal leadership style as having a high concern for both production and people.

________________ assume that the appropriate leadership style varies from situation to situation.

________________ is Fiedler's model, which is used to determine if a person's leadership style is task- or relationship-oriented, and if the situation matches the leader's style.

The ________________ is Tannenbaum and Schmidt's model, which identifies seven leadership styles based on the use of boss-centered versus employee-centered leadership.

________________ is Vroom and Yetton's decision-tree model, which enables the user to select from five leadership styles the one that is appropriate for the situation.

________________ is Hersey and Blanchard's model for selecting from four leadership styles the one that matches the employees' maturity level in a given situation.

The four situational supervision styles are ________________, which involves high-directive–low supportive behavior and is appropriate when interacting with low-capability employees; ________________, which involves high-directive–high-supportive behavior and is appropriate when interacting with moderate-capability employees; ________________, which is characterized by low-directive–high-supportive behavior and is appropriate when interacting with employees with high capability; and ________________, which entails low-directive–low-supportive behavior and is appropriate when interacting with outstanding employees.

________________ is the positive expectation that another will not take advantage of you.

/ / / KEY TERMS / / /

autocratic style 219
behavioral leadership theories 208
consultative style 219
contingency leadership theories 211
contingency leadership theory 211
laissez-faire style 220
leadership 205
leadership continuum 213
Leadership Grid 209
leadership trait theory 206
normative leadership theory 214
participative style 220
situational leadership 215
trust 225

/ / / COMMUNICATION SKILLS / / /

The following critical thinking questions can be used for class discussion and/or as written assignments to develop communication skills. Be sure to give complete explanations for all questions.

1. There are many traits that are said to be important to leadership success. Which three traits do you believe are the most important? List in order of priority.
2. The two-dimensional leadership styles developed at Ohio State University and the University of Michigan back in the 1940s still serve as the bases for the current contingency leadership theories. Are the task and relationship dimensions outdated?
3. The Leadership Grid states that the one best style to use in all situations is the 9,9 team manager style, with a high concern for both people and production. Do you agree with this statement?
4. Fiedler's contingency leadership theory states that managers can't change their leadership style; they are either task- or relationship-oriented. Do you agree with this statement?

5. Which of the five contingency leadership theories (Exhibit 7.5) do you prefer?
6. Do you agree with the statement that you can substitute for management but you can't substitute for leadership, or is this just semantics?
7. Give some examples of global cultural diversity that you have experienced.
8. Do you agree that integrity is at the center of trust, holding the other four dimensions together? Can competence, consistency, loyalty, and/or openness lead to trusting relationships if there is no integrity?
9. Based on your life and work experience, what percentage of people would you say really have integrity (that is, are honest—don't lie, steal, or cheat—and sincere)? Give some examples of how certain people damaged your trust in them.

CASE / / / Howard Schultz: Starbucks

Named after the character from Herman Melville's *Moby Dick*, Starbucks has grown into a large multinational chain of coffee shops with more than 17,000 stores worldwide. Its mission is to inspire and nurture the human spirit—one person, one cup, and one neighborhood at a time. The business has always been, and will always be, about quality coffee and other products and customer service. Sure, it starts with the promise of a perfectly made beverage, but it goes far beyond that. It's really about human connection. Starbucks' customers feel a sense of belonging; stores become a haven, a break from the worries outside, a place where people can meet with friends. Every store is part of a community and takes its responsibility to be a good neighbor seriously. Management knows that if it delivers in each of these areas, it will enjoy the kind of success that rewards shareholders. Starbucks is fully accountable to get each of these elements right so that everyone it touches can endure and thrive.[85]

Sitting in his office, Dr. Sherman, professor of management at Long Island University, stared at a man wearing blue jeans, a T-shirt, and a black leather jacket. It was hard for Dr. Sherman to fathom that the driving force behind Starbucks was a Brooklyn-born man, who went to Northern Michigan University on a football scholarship, and who traveled to Seattle to fall in love not only with a city but also with a way of doing business—the Starbucks way. Howard Schultz's method included the shop owners' dedication to coffee connoisseurship and caring for employees.

His entrepreneurial drive was inspired by what he saw in Italy. That country's plethora of coffeehouses were part of the national social structure, a place for discourse and, of course, for fashionable display. The original Starbucks founders were reluctant to expand into the restaurant business, but Schultz eventually bought the company for $3.8 million.

Sherman found Schultz surprisingly humble for a gentleman who expanded a small firm selling drip coffeemakers into a worldwide, multibillion-dollar business. Schultz's main goal was to serve a great cup of coffee but attached to this goal was a principle: Schultz wanted to build a company with soul. This led to a series of practices that were unprecedented in retail. Schultz insisted that all employees working at least 20 hours a week get comprehensive health coverage. Then he introduced an employee stock-option plan. These moves boosted loyalty and led to extremely low worker turnover, even though employee salaries were fairly low.

"You have to understand," Schultz said, "that employees are the cornerstone of my firm. Without happy employees we cannot have happy customers, and without happy customers we cannot have happy stockholders. So, if you take care of your employees, everything else falls into place." Starbuck's guiding principles include providing a great work environment and treating each other with respect and dignity; embracing diversity as an essential component in the way it does business; applying the highest standards of excellence to the purchasing, roasting, and fresh delivery of its coffee; developing enthusiastic, satisfied customers all of the time; contributing positively to its communities and the environment, and recognizing that profitability is essential to its future success. With Starbucks, Schultz wanted to create "the kind of company that my father never got a chance to work for, in which people were respected."

Asked the secret of his success, Schultz recounts four principles: Don't be threatened by people smarter than you. Compromise anything but your core values. Seek to renew yourself even when you are hitting home runs. And everything matters.

Howard Schultz created Starbucks and served as CEO and board chair for several years. Schultz eventually stepped down from his CEO position, letting Jim Donald take over the day-to-day operations as CEO. However, Starbucks ran into problems and its stock price plunged, so Schultz took back the CEO position. Schultz's turnaround strategy included improving the current state of its U.S. stores by giving store partners better training and tools, launching new products (some of which will have an impact as significant as its Frappuccino products and the Starbucks Card), and introducing new concepts in store design, among other enhancements to the *Starbucks Experience*. At the same time, Starbucks slowed the pace of its U.S. store openings and closed a number of underperforming locations. Starbucks also is focusing on growth outside the United States. However, with the downturn of the economy in 2008, and slow economic growth into 2012 with relatively high unemployment, penny-pinching customers, and competition from Dunkin' Donuts and McDonald's, some question whether Howard Schultz can keep his company from getting creamed (pun intended).[86]

Go to the Internet: For more information on Howard Schultz and Starbucks and to update the information provided in this case, do a name search on the Internet and visit www.starbucks.com.

Support your answers to the following questions with specific information from the case and text, or with other information you get from the Web or other sources.

1. Which traits has Howard Schultz exhibited that would indicate he is an effective leader?

2. Describe Schultz's basic leadership style. How would you rate his leadership using the Leadership Grid?

3. Which factors might lead Dr. Sherman to conclude that Howard Schultz is a transformational and charismatic leader?

4. What actions does Schultz take to build employee trust in his firm? Would you trust him?

5. Which leadership challenges might going international pose to Schultz? In which countries might his style of leadership work or not work?

Cumulative Questions

6. Personality (Chapter 2) is best associated with which leadership theory?

7. What is the role of communication (Chapter 5) in leadership?

8. In implementing the turnaround strategy, which assertiveness (passive, aggressive, assertive) and conflict management styles (Chapter 6) would be most appropriate for Schultz?

OBJECTIVE CASE /// The Cleanup Job

Brenda is the head meat cutter in the Big K Supermarket. Brenda hires and has fired meat cutters; she also determines raises. Although it has never been said, she speculates that the all-male meat-cutting crew isn't friendly toward her because they resent having a female boss. They are all highly skilled.

Once a month the meat and frozen foods cases are supposed to be cleaned by a meat cutter; they are all equally capable of doing it. It is not any one person's job, and no one likes to do it. It's that time of month again, and Brenda has to select someone to clean up. She just happens to see Rif first, so she approaches him.

BRENDA: Rif, I want you to clean the cases this month.

RIF: Why me? I just did it two months ago. Give someone else a turn.

BRENDA: I didn't ask you to tell me when you did it last. I asked you to do it.

RIF: I know, but I'm a meat cutter, not a janitor. Why can't the janitor do it? Or something more fair?

BRENDA: Do I have to take action against you for not following an order?

RIF: OK, I'll do it.

Answer the following questions. Then in the space between questions, state why you selected that answer.

______ 1. The basic leadership style Brenda used with Rif was:

a. autocratic *b.* democratic *c.* laissez-faire

______ 2. With Rif, Brenda used the ______ quadrant leadership style in Exhibit 7.1.

a. 1 *c.* 3

b. 2 *d.* 4

_______ **3.** With Rif, Brenda should have used the _______ quadrant leadership style in Exhibit 7.1.

a. 1 *c.* 3
b. 2 *d.* 4

_______ **4.** The Leadership Grid style Brenda used with Rif was _______ (see Exhibit 7.2).

a. 1,1 *c.* 1,9 *e.* 9,9
b. 9,1 *d.* 5,5

_______ **5.** According to Leadership Grid theory, Brenda used the appropriate leadership style.

a. true *b.* false

_______ **6.** According to Fiedler's contingency theory model (see Exhibit 7.3), Brenda is in a _______ situation, and _______ -oriented behavior is appropriate.

a. task *b.* relationship

_______ **7.** Brenda used the _______ leadership continuum style (see Exhibit 7.4).

a. 1 *c.* 3 *e.* 5 *g.* 7
b. 2 *d.* 4 *f.* 6

_______ **8.** The appropriate normative leadership style to resolve the monthly cleanup job is:

a. decide *c.* consult group *e.* delegate
b. consult individually *d.* facilitate

_______ **9.** The situational supervision style Brenda used with Rif was _______ (see Model 7.1).

a. autocratic *c.* participative
b. consultative *d.* laissez-faire

_______ **10.** The situational supervision style Brenda should use to resolve the monthly cleanup job is _______ (see Model 7.1).

a. autocratic *c.* participative
b. consultative *d.* laissez-faire

_______ **11.** In Brenda's situation, how would you get the cases cleaned each month?

Note: Different leadership styles can be role-played in class.

/ / / SKILL-BUILDING EXERCISE 7-1 / / /

Situational Supervision

In-Class Exercise (Individual and Group)

Objectives: To learn to use the situational supervision model. To develop your ability to supervise employees using the appropriate situational supervisory style for their capability level.

AACSB: The primary AACSB learning standard skills developed through this exercise are reflective thinking, analytic, and leadership skills.

BMV 7-1

Experience: In groups of two, you will apply the Situational Supervision Model in Model 7.1 to situations 2 through 12 in Self-Assessment Exercise 7-2. After you have finished, your instructor will give you the recommended answers, enabling you to determine your level of success at selecting the appropriate style.

For each situation, use the left-hand column in Model 7.1 to identify the employee capability level the situation describes. Write the level (1 through 4) on the line marked "C" to the left of each situation in Self-Assessment Exercise 7-2. Now identify the supervisory style that each response (*a* through *d*) represents. (These are listed in the right-hand column of the exhibit.) Indicate the style (A, C, P, or L) on the line marked "S" at the end of each response. Finally, choose the management style you think is best for each situation by placing a check mark (✓) next to the appropriate response (*a, b, c,* or *d*).

Procedure 1 (3–8 minutes)

The instructor reviews the Situational Supervision Model, Model 7.1, and explains how to use the model for situation 1.

Procedure 2 (29–43 minutes)

1. Turn to situation 2 in Self-Assessment Exercise 7-2, page 218, and to Model 7.1, page 220, Situational Supervision Model. (You may tear the exhibit out of your book.) Apply the model to the situation in an attempt to select the best course of action (3–4 minutes). The instructor will go over the answers and scoring (3–4 minutes).
2. Divide into teams of two; you may have one group of three if there is an odd number in the class. Apply the model as a team to situations 3 through 6. Team members may select different answers if they don't agree (8–12 minutes). Do not do situations 7 through 12 until you are told to do so. Your instructor will go over the answers and scoring for situations 3 through 6 (2–4 minutes).
3. As a team, select your answers to situations 7 through 12 (11–15 minutes). Your instructor will go over the answers and scoring to situations 7 through 12 (2–4 minutes).

Caution: There is no proven relationship between how a person performs on a pencil-and-paper test and how he or she actually performs on the job. People have a tendency to choose the answer they think is correct, rather than what they would actually do. The objective of this exercise is to help you better understand your supervisory style and how to improve it.

Conclusion: The instructor leads a class discussion and/or makes concluding remarks.

Application (2–4 minutes): What have I learned from this experience? How will I use this knowledge in the future?

Sharing: Volunteers give their answers to the application section.

/ / / SKILL-BUILDING EXERCISE 7-2 / / /

A Leadership Style Role-Play

In-Class Exercise (Group)

Objectives: To experience leadership in action. To identify the leadership style, and how using the appropriate versus inappropriate leadership style affects the organization.

AACSB: The primary AACSB learning standard skills developed through this exercise are analytic and leadership skills.

Preparation: All necessary material is below; no preparation is necessary.

Procedure 1 (5–10 minutes)

Break into groups and select the style (autocratic, consultative, participative, or laissez-faire) your group would use to make the following decision:

You are an office manager with four subordinates who all do typing on outdated computers. You will be receiving a new computer to replace one of the outdated ones. (Everyone knows about it because several salespeople have been in the office.) You must decide who gets the new computer. Below is some information about each subordinate.

- Pat—He or she has been with the organization for 20 years, is 50 years old, and presently has a two-year-old computer.
- Chris—He or she has been with the organization for 10 years, is 31 years old, and presently has a one-year-old computer.
- Fran—He or she has been with the organization for five years, is 40 years old, and presently has a three-year-old computer.
- Sandy—He or she has been with the organization for two years, is 23 years old, and presently has a five-year-old computer.

Possible Leadership Styles

Instructor selects one option:

Option A: Continuum of Leadership Behavior Styles 1 through 7. See Exhibit 7.4 for definitions of these seven styles.

Option B: Situational Supervisory Styles

S-A Autocratic

a. Make the decision alone; then tell each subordinate individually your decision and how and why you made it.

b. Make the decision alone; then have a group meeting to announce the decision and how and why you made it. No discussion is allowed.

S-C Consultative

a. Before deciding, talk to the subordinates individually to find out if they want the word processor, and why they think they should get it. Then make the decision and announce it to the group or to each person individually.

b. Before deciding, have a group meeting to listen to why all the subordinates want it, and why they think they should get it. Have no discussion among subordinates. Then make the decision and announce it to the group or to each person individually.

S-P Participative

a. Tentatively decide to whom you want to give it. Then hold a meeting to tell the group your plans, followed with a discussion that can lead to your changing your mind. After the open discussion, you make the decision and announce it, explaining the rationale for selection.

b. Call a group meeting and explain the problem. Lead an open discussion about who should get the word processor. After the discussion, make your decision and explain the rationale for it.

S-L Laissez-faire

a. Call a meeting and explain the situation. Tell the group that they have *X* amount of time (5–7 minutes for the exercise) to make the decision. You do not become a group member; you may or may not stay for the decision. However, if you do stay, you cannot participate.

Procedure 2 (5–10 minutes)

1. Four volunteers from different groups go to the front of the class. Take out a sheet of 8½-by-11-inch paper and write the name of the person you are role-playing (in big, dark letters), fold it in half, and place it in view of the manager and class. While the managers are planning, turn to the end of this exercise and read your role and the roles of your colleagues. Try to put yourself in the person's position, and do and say what he or she actually would during the role-play. No one but the typist should read this additional subordinate role information.
2. The instructor will tell each group which leadership style their manager will role-play; it may or may not be the one selected.
3. The group selects a manager to do the actual role-play of making the decision; and the group plans "who, what, when, where, how." The manager will perform the role-play. No one should read the additional subordinate role information.

Procedure 3 (1–10 minutes)
One manager goes to the front of the class and conducts the leadership role-play.

Procedure 4 (1–5 minutes)
The class members (other than the group being represented) vote for the style (1 to 7 or Tell *a. b.*; Sell *a. b.*; Participate *a. b.*; Delegate *a.*) they think the manager portrayed. Then the manager reveals the style. If several class members didn't vote for the style portrayed, a discussion can take place.

Procedures 3 and 4 continued(25–40 minutes)
Repeat procedures 3 and 4 until all managers have their turn or the time runs out.

Procedure 5 (2–3 minutes)
The class members individually determine the style they would use when making the decision. The class votes for the style the class would use in this situation. The instructor gives his or her recommendation and/or the author's.

Conclusion: The instructor leads a class discussion and/or makes concluding remarks.

Application (2–4 minutes): What did I learn from this experience? How will I apply this knowledge in the future?

Sharing: Volunteers give their answers to the application section.

Subordinate Roles

Additional information (for subordinates' role-playing only):

Pat — You are happy with the way things are now. You do not want the new computer. Be firm and assertive in your stance.

Chris — You are bored with your present job. You really want the new computer. Being second in seniority, you plan to be aggressive in trying to get it. You are afraid that the others will complain because you got the last new computer. So you have a good idea: You will take the new one, and Sandy can have your old one.

Fran — You are interested in having the new computer. You spend more time each day typing than any of the other employees. Therefore, you believe you should get the new computer.

Sandy — You want the new computer. You believe you should get it because you are by far the fastest typist, and you have the oldest computer. You do not want a hand-me-down computer.

/ / / SKILL-BUILDING EXERCISE 7-3 / / /

Self-Disclosure and Trust (Johari Window)

In-Class Exercise (Group)

Objective: To develop trust by self-disclosing to open your Johari Window.

AACSB: The primary AACSB learning standard skill developed through this exercise is communication abilities.

Experience: You will self-disclose by asking and answering questions to develop trust.

Rules:

1. Take turns asking questions.
2. You may refuse to answer a question as long as you did not ask it (or plan to).
3. You don't have to ask the questions in order.
4. You can add your own questions to ask anytime during the exercise.

Procedure 1 (7–15 minutes)
Break into groups of two or three. Take a minute to read the questions. Check questions you want to ask, and add your own questions. Follow the rules above.

1. What is your name and major?
2. Why did you select your major?
3. What career plans do you have?
4. How do you feel about doing this exercise?
5. What do you do in your spare time?
6. What is your Big Five Personality profile, or what do you think my profile is?
7. In Self-Assessment Exercise 7-3 what was your trustworthiness score and what were your strongest and weakest dimensions, or what do you think my score was, and which are my strongest and weakest dimensions?
8. What was your first impression of me?
9. How do you and/or others view me?
10. ______________________________
11. ______________________________
12. ______________________________

Procedure 2 (5–15 minutes)
Review the tips for developing trust. How well did I follow the tips, or did I not follow any of the tips?

Answer the following questions in the same group. Then you may ask the questions from the list above and/or your own questions to further self-disclose.

1. Have I/you taken any risk during this self-disclosure?
2. What level of trust have we developed (deterrence-, knowledge-, identification-based)?
3. Did I/you not follow any of the tips for developing trust?
4. With regard to the Johari Window, have I/you simply focused on opening the unknown to others (hidden), or have I/you opened the unknown to self (blind)?
5. Have I/you learned anything unknown to self?

Conclusion: The instructor may lead a class discussion and/or make concluding remarks.

Application (2–4 minutes): What did I learn from this experience? How will I apply this knowledge in the future?

Sharing: Volunteers give their answers to the application section.

/ / ANSWERS TO TRUE/FALSE QUESTIONS / /

1. F. Leadership and management are not the same thing.
2. F. As stated in the text, although there is no universal list of leadership traits, leadership trait theory is still being studied today.
3. T.
4. T.
5. F. In Model 7.1, with C-3 employees the participative leadership style is appropriate.
6. T.
7. T.

CHAPTER 8

Motivating Performance

LEARNING OUTCOMES

After completing this chapter, you should be able to:

LO 8-1 Explain the motivation process and the three factors affecting performance.

LO 8-2 Describe four content motivation theories.

LO 8-3 Describe two process motivation theories.

LO 8-4 State how reinforcement is used to increase performance.

LO 8-5 List the four steps in the model for giving praise.

LO 8-6 List the criteria for setting objectives.

LO 8-7 Identify the four parts of the model for writing objectives.

LO 8-8 State ways to enrich, design, and simplify jobs.

LO 8-9 Explain possible limitations of using motivation theories outside North America.

LO 8-10 Define the following 16 key terms (in order of appearance in the chapter):

motivation	**equity theory**
performance formula	**reinforcement theory**
content motivation theories	**giving praise**
needs hierarchy	**objectives**
two-factor theory	**management by objectives (MBO)**
manifest needs theory	**job enrichment**
process motivation theories	**job design**
expectancy theory	**job simplification**

/ / / Latoia Henderson was recently promoted to a management position at Ford Motor Company. She is enthusiastic about her work. Generally, things are going well, but Latoia is having a problem with Hank. Hank is often late for work, and even though he can do a good job, he does not regularly perform to expectations. Latoia had a talk with Hank to find out what the problem was. Hank said the money and benefits were great, and the people in the department were nice, but the job was boring. He complained that he didn't have any say about how to do his job and that Latoia was always checking up on him. Hank believes he is treated fairly because of the union, which gives him job protection. But because everyone is paid the same, working hard is a waste of time. If you were in Latoia's position, how would you motivate Hank? This chapter examines specific motivation theories and techniques that can be used to motivate not only Hank but employees in all organizations. / / /

Learning Outcome 8-1

Explain the motivation process and the three factors affecting performance.

THE IMPORTANCE OF MOTIVATION

In this section, we discuss what motivation is and why it is important and how motivation affects behavior, human relations, and performance.

What Is Motivation and Why Is It Important?

Motivation *is the internal process leading to behavior to satisfy needs.* Have you ever wondered why people do the things they do? The primary reason people do what they do is to meet their needs or wants. So motivating is about answering people's often unasked question, "What's in it for me?" by helping them meet their needs and wants. The process people go through to meet their needs is

Need → Motive → Behavior → Satisfaction or Dissatisfaction

WORK APPLICATION 8-1

Give an example of how you have gone through the motivation process. Identify the need, motive, behavior, and satisfaction or dissatisfaction.

For example, you are thirsty (need) and have a drive (motive) to get a drink. You get a drink (behavior) that quenches (satisfaction) your thirst. However, if you could not get a drink, or a drink of what you really wanted, you would be dissatisfied. Satisfaction is usually short-lived. Getting that drink satisfied you, but soon you will need another drink.

Managers often view motivation as an employee's willingness to put forth effort and commitment to achieve organizational objectives.[1] Latoia is concerned because Hank is not motivated to work hard.

Why Knowing How to Motivate Employees Is Important Motivated, engaged employees give companies a competitive advantage through increased performance.[2] Let's face it, motivation leading to behavioral effort has long been recognized as an important determinant of achievement.[3] Circuit City failed while Best Buy continues to be successful. When Best Buy's CEO was asked why he said, "the differential for us has been how we inspire our employees. Without that capability, you won't last."[4] Steve Jobs said he could see how much motivation matters.[5] When he left Apple, its performance went down, but after he returned, his ability to motivate employees brought Apple's performance to record highs.

Thus, your ability to motivate yourself and others is critical to your career success, and the goal of this chapter is to increase your ability to do both.

How Motivation Affects Behavior, Human Relations, and Performance

Clearly, if we are motivated to do something or not motivated to do it, our behavior tends to be different. How we feel about doing something affects our emotions, our feelings tend to affect our behavior, and in turn our behavior affects our human relations and performance—recall the Pygmalion effect (Chapter 2). If you are in a bad mood because you have to do something you don't want to do, are you more apt to display negative behavior that can hurt human relations related to the task, and vice versa? As already discussed, motivation is the key to success or failure because it affects performance.[6]

The Performance Formula However, performance is not based simply on motivation. The level of performance attained is determined by three interdependent factors: ability, motivation, and resources. This relationship can be stated as a **performance formula:** *Performance = Ability × Motivation × Resources.*

For performance levels to be high, all three factors must be high. If any one factor is low or missing, the performance level will be adversely affected. For example, Mary Lou, a very intelligent student, has the books, but because she does not care about grades, she does not study (low motivation) and does not get an A.

As an employee and manager, if you want to attain high levels of performance, you must be sure that you and your employees have the ability, motivation, and resources to meet objectives. When performance is not at the standard level or above, you must determine which performance factor needs to be improved, and improve it. In the opening case, Hank has the ability and resources, but he lacks motivation.

Communication Skills
Refer to CS Question 1.

APPLICATION SITUATIONS / / /

The Performance Formula AS 8-1

Identify the factor contributing to low performance in the five situations below.

A. Ability B. Motivation C. Resources

______ 1. In recent years, the U.S. steel industry has not been as productive as the foreign competition.

______ 2. I don't think you produce as much as the other department members because you're lazy.

______ 3. I practice longer and harder than my track teammates Heather and Linda. I don't understand why they beat me in the races.

______ 4. I could get all A's if I wanted to. But I'd rather relax and have a good time in college.

______ 5. The government would be more efficient if it cut down on waste.

When employee needs are not met through the organization, employees are dissatisfied and are generally lower performers.[7] This is the case with Hank; he finds the job boring and is not performing to expectations. To increase Hank's performance, Latoia must meet the goal of human relations. She must create a win–win situation so that Hank's needs are met to motivate him to perform to her expectations. As each motivation theory and technique is presented, you will learn how Latoia can apply it to motivate Hank or others.

Theory and Application Based on learning styles (Chapter 2), some people like motivation theories and want to know them, while others just want the practical "how to motivate" material. In this chapter, we provide both. In the first three major sections we provide the theories based on the three schools of motivation: content, process, and reinforcement, but we do include advice on how to motivate with each theory. The section on reinforcement theory is also practical because it tells you how to get people to do what you want them to do. Then, based on the theories, we provide motivation techniques that can be used to motivate others and yourself. So you can put your focus on one or the other, or both.

CONTENT MOTIVATION THEORIES

Learning Outcome 8-2

Describe four content motivation theories.

To increase performance, managers must know their own needs and their employees' needs, and they must satisfy them.[8] This is the goal of human relations.

The **content motivation theories** *focus on identifying people's needs in order to understand what motivates them.* In this section, you will learn four content motivation theories: (1) needs hierarchy, (2) ERG theory, (3) two-factor theory, and (4) manifest needs theory. You will also learn how organizations use these theories to motivate employees.

Needs Hierarchy

The **needs hierarchy** *is Maslow's theory of motivation, which is based on five needs.* In the 1940s, Abraham Maslow developed one of the most popular and widely known motivation theories which is still being researched today.[9] His theory is based on three major assumptions:[10]

1. People's needs are arranged in order of importance (hierarchy), going from basic needs (physiological) to more complex needs (self-actualization).
2. People will not be motivated to satisfy a higher-level need unless the lower-level need has been at least minimally satisfied.

EXHIBIT 8.1 | Needs Hierarchy and ERG Theory

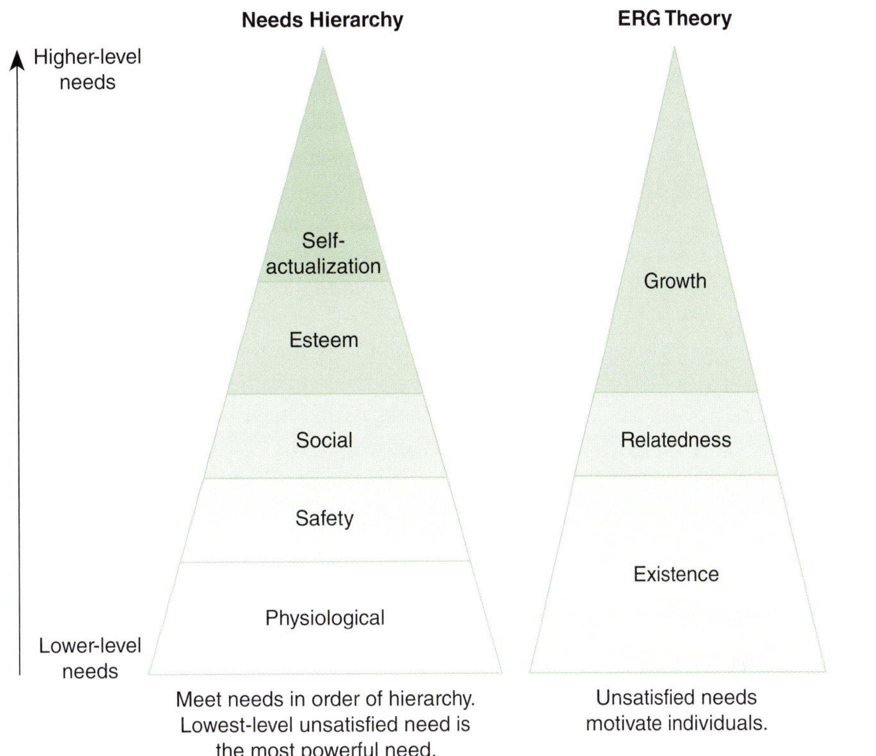

3. There are five classifications of needs. Listed below are these five classes of needs in order of importance to the individual.
   - *Physiological needs.* These are people's primary or basic needs. They include air, food, shelter, sex, and relief or avoidance of pain. In an organizational setting, these needs include adequate salary, breaks, and working conditions.
   - *Safety needs.* The individual is concerned with safety and security. These needs include safe working conditions, salary increases to meet inflation, job security, and fringe benefits that protect the physiological needs.
   - *Social needs.* People look for love, friendship, acceptance, and affection. These needs include the opportunity to interact with others, be accepted, and have friends.
   - *Esteem needs.* The individual focuses on ego, status, self-respect, recognition for accomplishments, and a feeling of self-confidence and prestige. These needs include titles, the satisfaction of completing the job itself, merit pay raises, recognition, challenging tasks, participation in decision making, and the chance for advancement.
   - *Self-actualization.* The highest level of need is to develop one's full potential. To do so, one seeks growth, achievement, and advancement. These needs include the development of one's skills; the chance to be creative; achievement and promotions; and the ability to have complete control over one's job.

   See Exhibit 8.1 for an illustration of Maslow's five needs.

Communication Skills
Refer to CS Question 2.

ERG Theory

As Exhibit 8.1 illustrates, Clayton Alderfer reorganizes Maslow's needs hierarchy into three levels of needs: existence (physiological and safety needs), relatedness (social), and growth (esteem and self-actualization). In the opening case, Hank's performance was poor, but he can be motivated to meet Latoia's expectations if his performance results in satisfying his needs.

Motivating with Needs Hierarchy and ERG Theory The major recommendation is to meet employees' lower-level needs so that they will not dominate the employees' motivational process. Get to know and understand people's needs and strive to meet them as a means of increasing performance. How organizations meet needs is discussed in a later section.

To use ERG theory, answer six questions: (1) What need does the individual have? (2) What needs have been satisfied? (3) Which unsatisfied need is the lowest in the hierarchy? (4) Have some higher-order needs been frustrated? If so, how? (5) Has the person refocused on a lower-level need? (6) How can the unsatisfied needs be satisfied? Latoia observed Hank and took the time to talk to him to determine his needs. Hank's need for existence and relatedness have been met. However, his need for growth has been frustrated. To motivate Hank, Latoia must meet his need for growth. In this chapter, you will learn ways to satisfy growth needs.

Two-Factor Theory

The **two-factor theory** *is Herzberg's classification of needs as hygienes and motivators.* Before learning Herzberg's theory, complete Self-Assessment Exercise 8-1 to learn what motivates you.

In the 1950s, Frederick Herzberg and associates research findings disagreed with the traditional view that satisfaction and dissatisfaction were at opposite ends of a continuum.[11]

/// Self-Assessment Exercise 8-1 ///

Your Motivators and Hygienes

Below are 12 job factors that contribute to job satisfaction. Rate each according to how important it is to you. Place the number 1 to 5 on the line before each factor.

Very important		Somewhat important		Not important
5	4	3	2	1

_____ 1. An interesting job I enjoy doing.

_____ 2. A good boss who treats everyone the same, regardless of circumstances.

_____ 3. Recognition and appreciation for the work I do.

_____ 4. The opportunity for advancement.

_____ 5. A job that is routine, without much change from day to day.

_____ 6. A prestigious job title regardless of pay.

_____ 7. Job responsibility that gives me the freedom to do the job my way.

_____ 8. Good working conditions (nice office).

_____ 9. A focus on following company rules, regulations, procedures, and policies.

_____ 10. The opportunity to grow through learning new things.

_____ 11. A job I can do well and succeed at.

_____ 12. Job security.

To determine if hygienes or motivators are important to you, on the lines below place the numbers (1 to 5) that represent your answers for the statements.

/// Self-Assessment Exercise 8-1 /// (continued)

Hygienes Score	Motivators Score
2. _____	1. _____
5. _____	3. _____
6. _____	4. _____
8. _____	7. _____
9. _____	10. _____
12. _____	11. _____
Total _____	Total _____

Add each column. Did you select hygienes or motivators as being more important to you? Now we'll find out their significance.

Herzberg classifies two needs that he calls *factors.* Herzberg combines lower-level needs (physiological, safety, social/existence, and relatedness) into one classification he calls *hygienes;* and he combines higher-level needs (esteem, self-actualization, growth) into one classification he calls *motivators.* Hygienes are also called *extrinsic factors* because attempts to motivate come from outside the job itself.[12] Motivators are called *intrinsic factors* because motivation comes from the job itself.[13] See Exhibit 8.2 for an illustration of Herzberg's theory.

Herzberg contends that providing hygiene factors keeps people from being dissatisfied, but it does not motivate people. For example, if people are dissatisfied with their pay and they get a raise, they will no longer be dissatisfied. They may even be satisfied for a short period of time. However, before long they get accustomed to the new standard of living and will no longer be satisfied. The vicious cycle goes on. If you got a pay raise, would you be motivated and be more productive?

WORK APPLICATION 8-2

In Self-Assessment Exercise 8-1, did you select motivators or hygienes as being important to you? Explain.

To motivate, Herzberg says that you must first ensure that hygiene factors are adequate. Once employees are satisfied with their environment, they can be motivated through their jobs.

Review Self-Assessment Exercise 8-1. Do not expect external rewards for everything you are asked to do. To be satisfied, you must seek and attain internal rewards.[14]

Using Two-Factor Theory to Motivate Employees In the opening case, Hank said he was not dissatisfied with hygiene factors. He lacked job satisfaction. If Latoia is going to motivate him, she will have to focus on intrinsic motivation, not hygiene. Hank says the job is boring. Will a pay raise or better working conditions make the job more interesting and challenging? Motivation and happiness come from doing what you like and enjoy doing.[15] The best way to motivate employees is to build challenge and opportunity for achievement into the job itself. Herzberg has developed a method for increasing motivation, which he calls *job enrichment.* In a later section of this chapter, you will learn about job enrichment and how Latoia could use it to motivate Hank.

EXHIBIT 8.2 | Two-Factor Theory

Hygiene Factors (Needs) (physiological, safety, social/existence, and relatedness needs)	**Motivator Factors (Needs)** (esteem, self-actualization, and growth needs)
Extrinsic Factors Dissatisfaction ◄——► No Dissatisfaction • Pay • Status • Job security • Fringe benefits • Policies and administrative practices	**Intrinsic Factors** No Job Satisfaction ◄——► Job Satisfaction • Meaningful and challenging work • Recognition for accomplishments • Feeling of achievement • Increased responsibility • Opportunity for growth • Opportunity for advancement

EXHIBIT 8.3 | Classification of Needs by Four Theories of Motivation

Maslow's Needs Hierarchy Theory	Alderfer's ERG Theory	Herzberg's Two-Factor Theory	McClelland's Manifest Needs Theory
Self-actualization	Growth	Motivators	Achievement
Esteem			Power
Social	Relatedness	Hygienes	Affiliation
Safety	Existence		
Physiological			

Communication Skills
Refer to CS Question 3.

Skill-Building Exercise 8-1
develops this skill.

Manifest Needs Theory

The **manifest needs theory** *of motivation is primarily McClelland's classification of needs as achievement, power, and affiliation.* It is a personality-based approach to motivation. McClelland does not have a classification for lower-level needs. His affiliation needs are the same as social and relatedness needs, and power and achievement are related to esteem and self-actualization and growth.[16] See Exhibit 8.3 for a comparison of the need classifications of the four theories of motivation.

Unlike Maslow, he believes that needs are based on personality and are developed as people interact with the environment. All people possess the need for achievement, power, and affiliation, but to varying degrees. One of these three needs tends to be dominant in each one of us and motivate our behavior. Before getting into the details of each need, complete Self-Assessment Exercise 8-2 to determine your dominant or primary need. After you have a better understanding of your needs, you will learn more about all three needs.

/// Self-Assessment Exercise 8-2 ///

Your Manifest Needs

Identify each of the following 15 statements according to how accurately it describes you. Place the number 1 to 5 on the line before each statement.

Like me		Somewhat like me		Not like me
5	4	3	2	1

_____ 1. I enjoy working hard.

_____ 2. I enjoy competition and winning.

_____ 3. I want/have lots of friends.

_____ 4. I enjoy a difficult challenge.

_____ 5. I enjoy leading and being in charge.

_____ 6. I want to be liked by others.

_____ 7. I want to know how I am progressing as I complete tasks.

_____ 8. I confront people who do things I disagree with.

_____ 9. I enjoy frequent parties.

_____ 10. I enjoy setting and achieving realistic goals.

_____ 11. I enjoy influencing other people to get my way.

_____ 12. I enjoy belonging to lots of groups or organizations.

_____ 13. I enjoy the satisfaction of completing a difficult task.

/// Self-Assessment Exercise 8-2 /// (*continued*)

_____ 14. In a leaderless situation I tend to take charge.

_____ 15. I enjoy working with others more than working alone.

To determine your primary need, on the lines below, place the numbers (1 to 5) that represent your scores for the statements.

Achievement	Power	Affiliation
1. _____	2. _____	3. _____
4. _____	5. _____	6. _____
7. _____	8. _____	9. _____
10. _____	11. _____	12. _____
13. _____	14. _____	15. _____
Total _____	Total _____	Total _____

Add the numbers in each column. Each column total should be between 5 and 25. The column with the highest score is your dominant or primary need.

The Need for Achievement (*n*-Ach) People with a high *n*-Ach tend to be characterized as: wanting to take personal responsibility for solving problems; goal-oriented (they set moderate, realistic, attainable goals); seeking challenge, excellence, and individuality; taking calculated, moderate risks; desiring concrete feedback on their performance; willing to work hard. Need for achievement is correlated with performance.[17] Managers tend to have a high, but not a dominant, *n*-Ach.

Motivating Employees with a High* n*-Ach Give them nonroutine, challenging tasks in which there are clear, attainable objectives. Give them fast and frequent feedback on their performance. Continually give them increased responsibility for doing new things.

The Need for Power (*n*-Pow) People with a high need for power tend to be characterized as: wanting to control the situation; wanting influence or control over others; enjoying competition in which they can win (they do not like to lose); willing to confront others. People with high *n*-Pow tend to have a low need for affiliation. Managers tend to have a dominant need for power.

Motivating Employees with a High* n*-Pow Let them plan and control their jobs as much as possible. Try to include them in decision making, especially when they are affected by the decision. They tend to perform best alone rather than as team members. Try to assign them to a whole task rather than just part of a task.

People are motivated to gain power because having it meets their needs. In the opening case, Hank's primary need seems to be power. Hank wants more say in how to do his job, and he wants Latoia to do less checking up on him. If Latoia empowers Hank by giving him more job-related responsibility, it may satisfy Hank's needs and create a win–win situation, resulting in higher performance.

WORK APPLICATION 8-3

Explain how your personal *n*-Ach, *n*-Pow, and *n*-Aff affect your motivation, behavior, and performance. How can you use manifest needs theory to motivate employees?

The Need for Affiliation (*n*-Aff) People with a high *n*-Aff tend to be characterized as: seeking close relationships with others; wanting to be liked by others; enjoying lots of social activities; seeking to belong (they join groups and organizations). They tend to have a low *n*-Pow. They also tend to avoid supervision because they like to be one of the group rather than its leader.

Motivating High* n*-Aff Employees Be sure to let them work as part of a team. They derive satisfaction from the people they work with rather than the task itself. Give them lots of

EXHIBIT 8.4 | How Organizations Meet Employee Needs

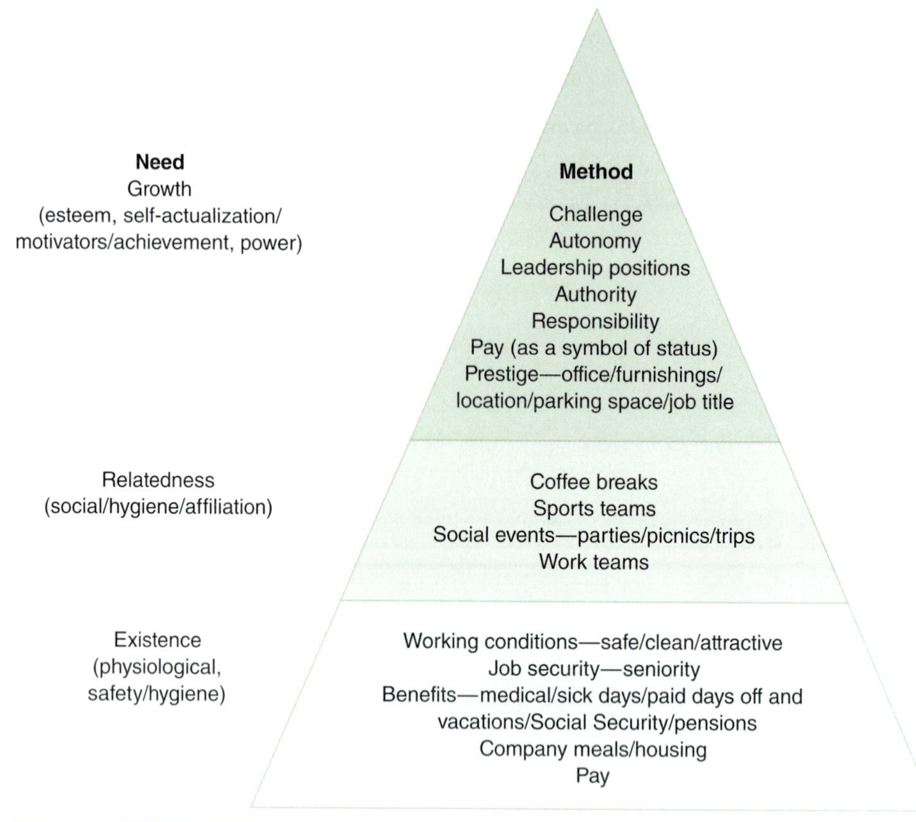

praise and recognition. Delegate responsibility for orienting and training new employees to them. They make great buddies and mentors.

How Organizations Meet Employee Needs

See Exhibit 8.4 for a list of methods used by organizations to meet employee needs. Note that pay is important and can meet both higher- and lower-level needs.[18]

Learning Outcome 8-3

Describe two process motivation theories.

PROCESS MOTIVATION THEORIES

Content motivation theories attempt to understand what motivates people, whereas **process motivation theories** *attempt to understand how and why people are motivated.* Their focus is more on behavior than needs. Why do people select certain goals to work toward?[19] Why do people select particular behavior to meet their needs?[20] How do people evaluate need satisfaction?[21] Expectancy and equity theories attempt to answer these questions.

Expectancy Theory

The **expectancy theory,** *which is Vroom's formula, states that Motivation = Expectancy × Valence.* Under Victor Vroom's theory, motivation depends on how much people want something and how likely they are to get it.[22] Expectancy and valence are two important variables in Vroom's formula that must be met for motivation to take place.

Expectancy Expectancy refers to the person's perception of his or her ability (probability) to accomplish an objective. Generally, the higher one's expectancy, the better the chance for motivation.[23] When employees do not believe that they can accomplish objectives, they will not be motivated to try.

Also important is the perception of the relationship between performance and the outcome or reward. Generally, the higher one's expectancy of the outcome or reward, the better the chance for motivation. This is called *instrumentality*. If employees are certain to get a reward or to be successful, they probably will be motivated. When not sure, employees may not be motivated.

Valence Valence refers to the value a person places on the outcome or reward. Generally, the higher the value (importance) of the outcome or reward, the better the chance of motivation.

Motivating with Expectancy Theory The following conditions should be implemented to motivate employees:

1. Clearly define objectives and the necessary performance needed to achieve them.
2. Tie performance to rewards. High performance should be rewarded. When one employee works harder to produce more than other employees and is not rewarded, he or she may slow down productivity.
3. Be sure rewards are of value to the employee. We need to realize that what motivates us may not motivate someone else. The supervisor should get to know his or her employees as individuals.
4. Make sure your employees believe you will do as what you say you will do. You need people's trust (Chapter 7) to motivate them.

WORK APPLICATION 8-4

Give an example of how expectancy theory has affected your motivation. How can you use expectancy theory to motivate employees?

In the opening case, Hank says that because of the union, everyone is paid the same, so working hard is a waste of time. In the expectancy formula, since expectancy is low, there is no motivation. Latoia may find some other need to help him meet. If Latoia can find a need with expectancy and valence, Hank will be motivated to perform to expectations, creating a win–win situation for all parties.

Equity Theory

The **equity theory** *is primarily Adams's motivation theory, which is based on the comparison of perceived inputs and outputs.* J. Stacy Adams popularized equity theory with his contention that people seek social equity in the rewards they receive (output) for their performance (input).[24]

According to equity theory, people compare their inputs (effort, experience, seniority, status, intelligence, and so forth) and outputs (praise, recognition, pay promotions, increased status, supervisor's approval, and the like) with those of relevant others. A relevant other could be a coworker or a group of employees from the same or from different organizations or even from a hypothetical situation. Notice that our definition mentions *perceived,* not *actual* inputs and outputs. Equity may actually exist. However, if employees believe there is inequity, they will change their behavior to create equity, such as doing less work, changing the situation (like getting a raise), or getting another job.[25]

Most employees tend to inflate their own efforts or performance when comparing themselves with others. They also overestimate what others earn.

Motivating with Equity Theory Using equity theory in practice can be difficult because you don't know (1) who the employee's reference group is, and (2) what his or her view of inputs and outcomes is. However, it does offer some useful general recommendations:

- Be aware that equity is based on perception, which may not be correct. It is possible for the supervisor to create equity or inequity. Some managers have favorite subordinates who get special treatment; others don't.
- Rewards should be equitable. When employees perceive that they are not treated fairly, morale and performance problems occur; resentment and retaliation are common.
- High performance should be rewarded, but employees must understand the inputs needed to attain certain outputs.

WORK APPLICATION 8-5

Give an example of how equity theory has affected your motivation. How can you use equity theory to motivate employees?

- Realize that what people know or don't know isn't important. All that really counts is what they feel.[26] The perception of large inequity gets people emotional. So you have to deal with emotions (follow the guidelines from Chapter 6).

In the opening case, Hank said that he was equitably treated because of the union. Therefore, Latoia does not need to be concerned about equity theory with Hank. However, it could be an issue with another employee.

Communication Skills
Refer to CS Question 4.

Learning Outcome 8-4

State how reinforcement is used to increase performance.

REINFORCEMENT THEORY

Research supports the effect of reinforcement theory on task performance.

As you have seen, content motivation theories focus on what motivates people and process motivation theories focus on how and why people are motivated; reinforcement theory focuses on getting people to do what you want them to do through incentives,[27] because incentives do motivate behavior and performance.[28] **Reinforcement theory** *is primarily Skinner's motivation theory: Behavior can be controlled through the use of positive or negative consequences.* It is also called *behavior modification* and *operant conditioning*.

B. F. Skinner contends that people's behavior is learned through experiences of positive and negative consequences. He believes that rewarded behavior tends to be repeated, while unrewarded behavior tends not to be repeated. The three components of Skinner's framework are[29]

Stimulus ——► Response (Behavior/ Performance) ——► Consequences (Reinforcement/ Positive or Negative)

An employee learns what is, and is not, desired behavior as a result of the consequences for specific behavior.

Reinforcement is not about meeting needs, it's about getting people to do what we want them to do by answering their often unasked question, "What's in it for me?" In essence you are saying, "If you do this behavior [stimulus calling for response behavior] I will give you this reward or this punishment if you don't [consequence—types of reinforcement] and this is how often I will give you the reward or punishment [schedules of reinforcement]."[30] Steve Jobs was very good at getting Apple employees to do what he wanted done in record time. He was known to be a charismatic charmer, but at times to have manipulated other people and coldly pressured them to high levels of performance. But people who could take the pressure were well rewarded.[31]

Skinner states that supervisors can control and shape employees' behavior while at the same time making them feel free. The two important concepts used to control behavior are the types of reinforcement and the schedule of reinforcement.

Types of Reinforcement

The four types of reinforcement are as follows:

Positive Reinforcement A method of encouraging continued behavior is to offer attractive consequences (rewards) for desirable performance. For example, an employee is on time for a meeting and is rewarded by the supervisor's thanking him or her. The praise is used to reinforce punctuality. Other reinforcers are pay, promotions, time off, and increased status. Positive reinforcement is the best motivator for increasing productivity.

Avoidance Reinforcement Avoidance is also called *negative reinforcement*. The employee avoids the negative consequence. For example, an employee is punctual for a meeting to avoid negative reinforcement, such as a reprimand. Rules are designed to get employees to avoid certain behavior. Notice that with avoidance there is no actual punishment; it's the threat of the punishment that controls behavior.

Extinction Extinction attempts to reduce or eliminate undesirable behavior by withholding reinforcement when the behavior occurs. For example, an employee who is late for the meeting is not rewarded with praise. Or a pay raise is withheld until the employee performs to set standards.

Punishment Punishment is used to provide an undesirable consequence for undesirable behavior. For example, an employee who is late for a meeting is reprimanded. Other methods of punishment include harassing, taking away privileges, probation, fining, and demoting. Using punishment may reduce the undesirable behavior, but it may cause other undesirable behavior, such as poor morale, lower productivity, and acts of theft or sabotage. Punishment is the most controversial method and the least effective at motivating employees.

Schedules of Reinforcement

The second reinforcement consideration in controlling behavior is when to reinforce performance. Recall the importance of timely feedback (Chapter 5).[32] The frequency and magnitude of the reinforcement may be as important as the reinforcement itself. The two major classifications are continuous and intermittent:

Continuous Reinforcement With a continuous method, each desired and undesired behavior is reinforced. Examples of this method would be a machine with an automatic counter that lets the employee know, at any given moment, exactly how many units have been produced, or a supervisor who punishes employees for breaking rules every time.

Intermittent Reinforcement With intermittent reinforcement, the reward is given based on the passage of time or output. When the reward is based on the passage of time, it is called an *interval schedule*. When it is based on output, it is called a *ratio schedule*. When electing to use intermittent reinforcement, there are four alternatives:

1. *Fixed interval schedule* (giving a salary paycheck every week, breaks and meals at the same time every day).
2. *Variable interval schedule* (giving praise only now and then, a surprise inspection, a pop quiz).
3. *Fixed ratio schedule* (giving a piece rate or bonus after producing a standard rate).
4. *Variable ratio schedule* (giving praise for excellent work, a lottery for employees who have not been absent for a set time).

Ratios are generally better motivators than intervals. The variable ratio tends to be the most powerful schedule for sustaining behavior.

Motivating with Reinforcement Generally, positive reinforcement is the best motivator. Continuous reinforcement is better at sustaining desired behavior; however, it is not always possible or practical. Following are some general guidelines:

- Make sure employees know exactly what is expected of them. Set clear objectives.
- Select appropriate rewards. A reward to one person could be considered a punishment by another.
- Select the appropriate reinforcement schedule.
- Do not reward mediocre or poor performance.
- Look for the positive and give praise, rather than focusing on the negative and criticizing. Make people feel good about themselves (Pygmalion effect).
- Never go a day without giving praise.
- Do things *for* people, instead of *to* them, and you will see human relations and productivity increases.

In the opening case, Hank has been coming to work late and performing below expectations. Latoia can try giving Hank positive encouraging statements to do a good job. But if it does not change Hank's behavior, Latoia should try some other positive reinforcement such as job enrichment. If positive reinforcement doesn't change Hank's behavior, Latoia can use avoidance reinforcement. Based on her authority, she could tell Hank that the next time he is late or performs below a specific level, he will receive a specific punishment, such as having part of his pay withheld. If Hank does not avoid this behavior, Latoia must follow up and give the punishment. As a manager, try the positive first. Positive reinforcement is a true motivator because it creates a win–win situation by meeting both the employee's and the manager's or organization's needs. From the employees' perspective, avoidance and punishment create a lose–win situation. The organization or manager wins by forcing them to do something they really don't want to do.

Communication Skills
Refer to CS Question 5.

APPLICATION SITUATIONS / / /

Motivation Theories AS 8-2

Identify each supervisor's statement of how to motivate employees by the theory underlying the statement.

A. Expectancy
B. Equity
C. Needs hierarchy
D. Manifest needs
E. Two-factor
F. Reinforcement

_______ 6. "I motivate employees by making their jobs interesting."

_______ 7. "I make sure I treat everyone fairly."

_______ 8. "I know Wendy likes people, so I give her jobs in which she works with other employees."

_______ 9. "Paul would yell in the shop because he knew it got to me. So I decided to ignore his yelling, and he stopped."

_______ 10. "I got to know all of my employees' values fairly well. Now I can offer rewards that will motivate them."

_______ 11. "We offer good working conditions, salaries, and benefits, so I'm working at developing more teamwork."

_______ 12. "When my employees do something outstanding, I write them a thank-you note."

_______ 13. "I used to try to improve working conditions to motivate employees. But I stopped and now focus on giving employees more responsibility so they can grow and develop new skills."

_______ 14. "I set clear objectives that are attainable. And I offer rewards that employees like when they achieve their objectives."

_______ 15. "I now realize that I tend to be an autocratic supervisor because it helps fill my needs. I will work at giving some of my employees more autonomy."

WORK APPLICATION 8-6

What reinforcement type(s) and schedule(s) does/did your present/past supervisor use to motivate you? Explain each. How can you use reinforcement to motivate employees?

MOTIVATION TECHNIQUES

The previous sections discussed the major motivation theories. Now we examine specific on-the-job techniques to motivate employees: incentives and recognition—giving praise, MBO, job enrichment, and job design.

Learning Outcome 8-5

List the four steps in the model for giving praise.

Incentives and Recognition

Incentive and Recognition Programs As discussed with reinforcement theory, people do respond to incentives and we can nearly always get them to do what we want them to do as long as we find the right levers (combination of types and schedules of reinforcement) to motivate the desired behavior. People respond to incentives, even though not necessarily in the expected way. If people don't do what we expect or want, you can certainly find some hidden incentives that explain why.[33]

Because managers know financial incentives (often called *reward programs*) do motivate employees to higher levels of performance, many organizations have formal incentive programs,[34] such as pay-for-performance, bonuses, profit sharing, and stock options.

Many organizations also have recognition programs, which tend to offer nonfinancial (not cash) rewards, such as banquets and employee of the year/month/week awards. Recognition programs can also include things like luncheons, plaques, gift certificates, mugs, t-shirts, and so on. Incentive and recognition programs are generally two separate programs. One great method of recognition that we all can use and that is not part of a formal program is giving praise—our next topic.

Giving Praise Employees want full appreciation for work done. When was the last time your boss gave you a thank-you or some praise for a job well done? When was the last time your boss complained about your work? When was the last time you praised someone? What is the ratio of praise to criticism?

Giving praise develops a positive self-concept and leads to better performance through the Pygmalion effect. Praise is a motivator (not a hygiene) because it meets employees' needs for esteem/self-actualization, growth, and achievement. It is probably the most powerful, least expensive, simplest, and yet most underused motivational technique.[35]

Ken Blanchard and Spencer Johnson popularized giving praise through their best-selling book, *The One-Minute Manager*.[36] They developed a technique that involves giving one minute of praise. Model 8.1 is an adaptation. The steps in **giving praise** are as follows: *step (1) tell the person exactly what was done correctly; step (2) tell the person why the behavior is important; step (3) stop for a moment of silence; and step (4) encourage repeat performance.* Blanchard calls it one-minute praise because it should not take more than one minute to give the praise. It is not necessary for the employee to say anything. The four steps are illustrated below.

Step 1: Tell the person exactly what was done correctly. When giving praise, look the person in the eye to show sincerity. It is important to be very specific and descriptive. General statements like "You're a good worker" are not as effective.

SUPERVISOR: Julio, I just overheard you deal with that customer's complaint. You did an excellent job of keeping your cool; you were polite. That person came in angry and left happy.

Step 2: Tell the person why the behavior is important. Briefly state how the organization and/or person benefits from the action. It is also helpful to tell the employee how you feel about the behavior. Be specific and descriptive.

SUPERVISOR: Without customers we don't have a business. One customer bad-mouthing us can cause hundreds of dollars in lost sales. It really made me proud to see you handle that tough situation the way you did.

Step 3: Stop for a moment of silence. This is a tough one. The rationale for the silence is to give the person the chance to feel the impact of the praise. It's like "the pause that refreshes."

SUPERVISOR: (*Silently counts to five.*)

MODEL 8.1 | Model for Giving Praise

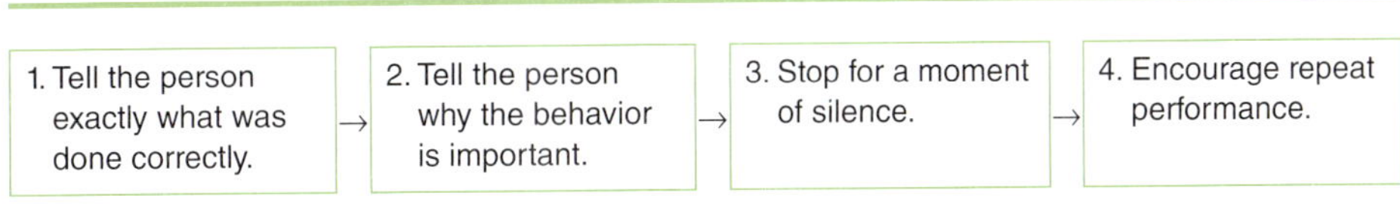

Step 4: Encourage repeat performance. This is the reinforcement that motivates the person to keep up performance. Blanchard recommends touching the person because it has a powerful impact. However, he recommends it only if both parties feel comfortable. Others say not to touch because it could lead to a sexual harassment charge.

SUPERVISOR: Thanks, Julio; keep up the good work (*while touching him on the shoulder or shaking hands*).

As you can see, giving praise is easy, and it doesn't cost a penny. Several managers trained to give praise say it works wonders. It's a much better motivator than giving a raise or other monetary reward. One manager stated that an employee was taking his time stacking cans on a display. He gave the employee praise for stacking the cans so straight. The employee was so pleased with the praise that the display went up with about a 100 percent increase in productivity. Notice that the manager looked for the positive and used positive reinforcement, rather than punishment. The manager could have made a comment such as, "Quit goofing off and get the display up faster." That statement would not have motivated the employee to increase productivity. All it would have done was hurt human relations, and it could have ended in an argument. Notice that in the above example the cans were straight. The employee was not praised for the slow work pace. However, if the praise had not worked, the manager should have used another reinforcement method.

CS

Communication Skills
Refer to CS Question 6.

SB

Skill-Building Exercise 8-2
develops this skill.

In the opening case, Latoia should give him praise for coming in on time and increasing his performance to encourage him to continue this behavior. Praise is a reinforcement that is very effective when used with a variable interval schedule.

Thank-You Videos and Notes In today's global business world, you may never see people you work with face-to-face, but you can video conference or Skype them. Praise can also be given as a written thank-you note (50 to 70 words is all it takes), especially when you can't give praise in person. You can follow the giving praise model steps 1 to 2 and 4, skipping the obvious silence. It can be an e-mail, but even today some people consider the handwritten thank-you note more personal and powerful. Doug Conant, CEO of Campbell Soup, sent out over 30,000 handwritten notes to the company's 20,000 employees because he finds it to be a powerful way to motivate them through recognition.[37]

Learning Outcome 8-6

List the criteria for setting objectives.

Objectives and MBO

For many years, writers have been saying that setting difficult objectives leads to higher levels of motivation and performance, and research supports this statement.[38] In fact, goal setting theory was rated number 1 in importance among 73 management theories.[39]

The **objectives** *state what is to be accomplished within a given period of time.* Objectives are end results; they do not state how the objective will be accomplished. How to achieve the objective is the plan. In this section, you will learn the five criteria objectives should meet, how to write objectives, and how to use management by objectives (MBO).

Criteria for Setting Objectives To motivate people to high levels of performance, objectives should be:

- *Difficult but achievable.* To have high levels of performance, you need to set high standards.[40] Sam Walton (founder of Walmart) said, "High expectations are the key to everything." Individuals perform better when assigned difficult objectives, as opposed to being assigned easy ones, or having no goals, or simply being told to "do your best." However, if people do not believe that the objectives are achievable (expectancy theory), they will not be motivated to work for their accomplishment.[41] Worse, when objectives are too difficult and incentives are high enough, many people will use unethical and illegal means to achieve the objectives, for example, Enron and WorldCom.[42]
- *Observable and measurable.* If people are to achieve objectives, they must be able to observe and measure their progress regularly.[43] Individuals perform better when their performance is measured and evaluated.[44]

- *Specific, with a target date.* To be motivated, employees must know exactly what is expected of them and when they are expected to have the task completed. Employees should have specific objectives with deadlines.[45] However, some objectives do not require or lend themselves to target dates. For example, the objectives in the skill-building exercises do not list a target date.
- *Participatively set when possible.* Groups that participate in setting their objectives generally outperform groups with assigned objectives. Managers should use the appropriate level of participation for the employees' capabilities. The higher the capabilities, the higher the level of participation. (see the section titled "Situational Supervision" in Chapter 7).

Communication Skills
Refer to CS Question 7

- *Accepted.* For objectives to be met, employees must accept them. Without acceptance, even meeting the above four criteria can lead to failure. Using participation helps get employees to accept objectives.

APPLICATION SITUATIONS / / /

Objectives AS 8-3

For each objective, state which criterion is *not* met.

A. Difficult but achievable B. Observable and measurable C. Specific, with a target date

_______ 16. To increase production of widgets during the fiscal year 20 _______.

_______ 17. To increase total sales by 40 percent during 20 _______.

_______ 18. To increase the company's image by June 20 _______.

_______ 19. To write objectives within two weeks.

_______ 20. To pass this human relations course this semester.

Learning Outcome 8-7

Identify the four parts of the model for writing objectives.

Writing Objectives Objectives should be written. To help write objectives that meet the five criteria above, use Max E. Douglas's model, shown in Model 8.2.

Skill-Building Exercise 8-3 develops this skill.

MODEL 8.2 | Model for Writing Objectives

Objectives Model	
To + Action verb + Specific, measurable, and singular behavior + Target date	
Example Objectives for a Student:	
To + receive + a B as my final grade in human relations + in December/May 20____.	
To increase my cumulative grade point average to 3.0 by May 20____.	
Example Objectives for a Manager:	
To produce 1,000 units per day.	
To keep absences to three or fewer per month.	
To decrease accidents by 5 percent during 20____.	
Example Objectives for an Organization:	
Ford:	To increase worldwide sales by 50 percent to 8 million vehicles per year by 2015.[46]
JPMorgan:	To open 2,000 new bank branches by 2016.[47]
Nissan:	To increase world market share from 5.8 to 8 percent by 2017.[48]

Management by Objectives (MBO) **Management by objectives (MBO)** *is the process in which managers and their employees jointly set objectives for the employees, periodically evaluate the performance, and reward according to the results.*

The three steps of an MBO program are as follows:

Step 1. Set Individual Objectives and Plans. Each subordinate jointly sets objectives with the manager. The objectives are the heart of the MBO program and should meet the five criteria discussed earlier.

Step 2. Give Feedback and Evaluate Performance. Employees must know how they are progressing toward their objectives.[49] Thus, the manager and employee must meet frequently to review the latter's progress.

Step 3. Reward According to Performance. Employees' performance should be measured against their objectives. Employees who meet their objectives should be rewarded through recognition, praise, pay raises, promotions, and so on.[50]

Communication Skills
Refer to CS Question 8

An MBO program is a motivator (not a hygiene) because it meets employees' needs for esteem/self-actualization, growth, and power/achievement. An MBO program empowers employees to increase responsibility with an opportunity for creating meaningful, challenging work to help them grow and accomplish what *they* and the manager want to accomplish. An MBO program creates a win–win situation.

In a union situation, such as the opening case, using an MBO program may not be possible without union consent and input.

Job Enrichment

Learning Outcome 8-8

State ways to enrich, design, and simplify jobs.

Job enrichment *is the process of building motivators into the job itself by making it more interesting and challenging.* It is a means of getting job engagement.[51] It differs from job rotation, in which employees learn to perform other employees' jobs, and job enlargement, in which the employee is assigned more tasks of a similar nature.

Before implementing job enrichment, the manager should be sure that the job is of low motivation potential and that the employees want their jobs enriched. Some people are happy with the jobs the way they are. Hygiene factors must also be adequate before using job enrichment.

Here are some simple ways managers can enrich jobs:

- *Delegate more variety and responsibility.* Give employees challenging assignments that help them grow and develop new skills.
- *Form natural work groups.* The work group can also perform its own identifiable work with increased responsibility.
- *Make employees responsible for their own identifiable work.* Let employees make the entire product rather than one part of it.
- *Give employees more autonomy.* Allow employees to plan, schedule, organize, and control their own jobs. Making employees responsible for checking their own work eliminates the need for checkers.

WORK APPLICATION 8-7

Describe how to enrich a present or past job of yours.

Job Design

Job design *is the employee's system for transforming inputs into outputs.* The more effective and efficient the method, the more productive the employee. But we need to create jobs that match employee talent.[52]

A common approach to job design is work simplification. The idea behind work simplification is to work smarter, not harder. **Job simplification** *is the process of eliminating,* *combining, and/or changing the work sequence to increase performance.* To motivate employees, have them break the job down into steps and see if they can:

- *Eliminate.* Does the task have to be done at all? If not, don't waste time doing it.
- *Combine.* Doing more than one thing at a time often saves time.
- *Change sequence.* Often a change in the order of doing things results in a lower total time.

WORK APPLICATION 8-8

Describe how to simplify a present or past job of yours. Does an elimination, combination, or change in sequence help simplify the job?

WORK APPLICATION 8-9

Which motivation theory is the best? Explain why.

WORK APPLICATION 8-10

What is your motivation theory? What are the major methods, techniques, and so on you plan to use on the job as a manager to increase motivation and performance?

When used appropriately, work simplification can be effective at motivating employees. However, the danger lies in making a job too simple and boring rather than making it more interesting and challenging, as with job enrichment.

According to Herzberg, job enrichment and job design are motivators (not hygienes) because they meet employees' needs for esteem, self-actualization, growth, power, and achievement. Thus, job design and job enrichment are processes used to motivate employees.

In a union situation like that in the opening case, job enrichment and/or job design may not be possible without union consent and input. Assuming Latoia can use these techniques, she and Hank could work together to transform Hank's present boring job into a challenging and interesting one. This is the most appropriate motivation technique to use with Hank because it directly addresses the boring job. If Hank finds his job interesting, he will most likely come to work on time and perform to expectation, creating a win–win situation.

Communication Skills

Refer to CS Question 9.

Putting the Motivation Theories Together

Researchers suggest an integration of motivation theories. To this end, review the major motivation theories in Exhibit 8.5. For a review of the four steps in the motivation process, see Exhibit 8.6.

EXHIBIT 8.5 | Motivation Theories

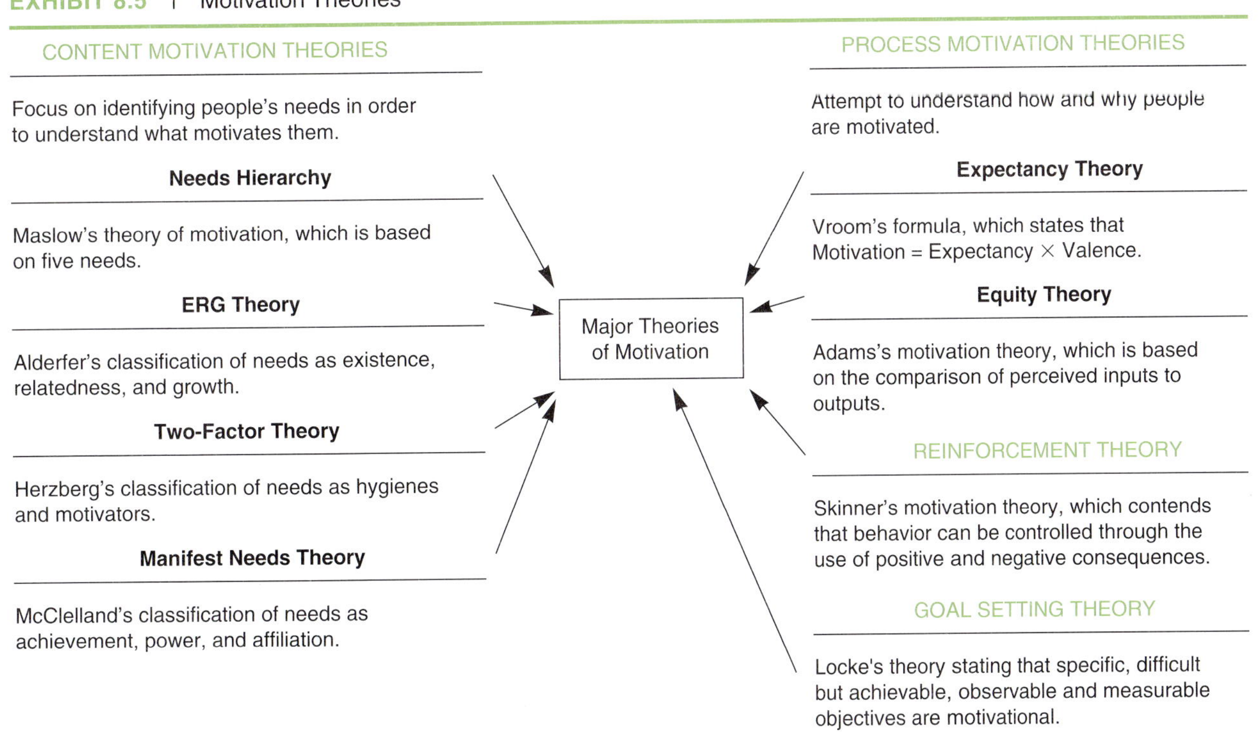

EXHIBIT 8.6 | The Motivation Process

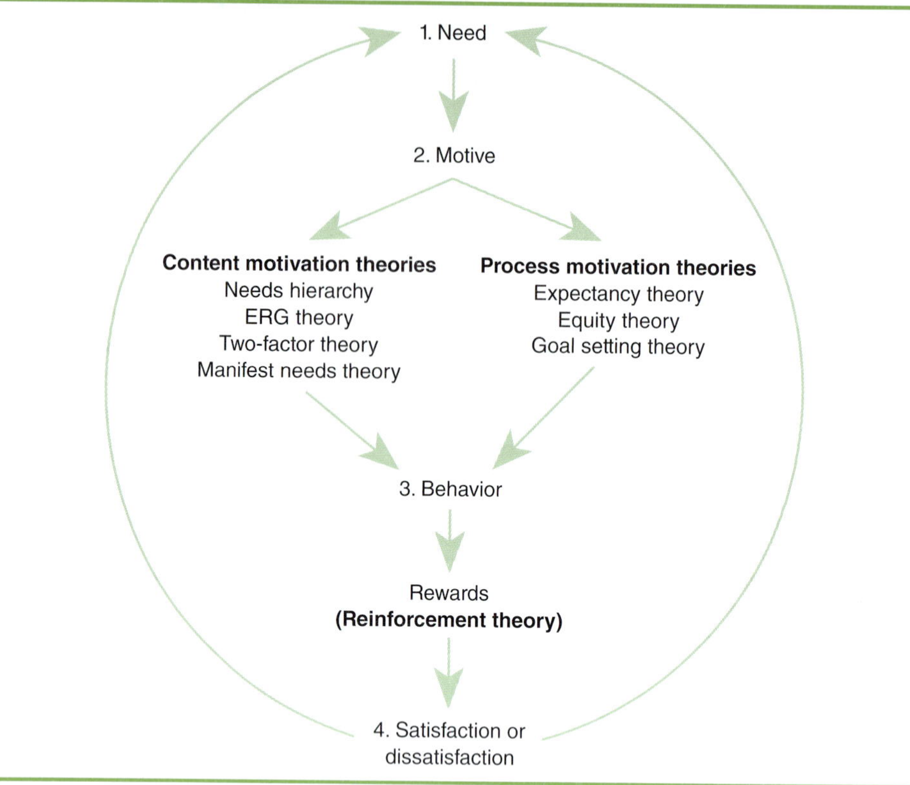

Notice that the motivation process is circular, or ongoing, because meeting needs is a never-ending process.

Self-Motivation

Below is a four-step model to follow to motivate yourself, followed by some other advice if you are not motivated and feel bored or trapped on the job. In either case, you have to take responsibility for motivating yourself and being happy.

Set Objectives First, you've got to know what you want—objective—and be willing to work hard to get whatever it is you want. What do you want? To be motivated, develop objectives using Model 8.2 to be sure to meet the criteria with high expectations for yourself.

Drive and Persistence to Succeed Intelligence is overrated; the drive to win[53] and persistence are better predictors of success.[54] Are you willing to work hard and keep at it until you accomplish your objective?

Develop Plans—Willpower Alone Fails Why do so many people make New Year's resolutions and fail to keep them? It's because willpower, or self-discipline, alone without a plan doesn't work.[55] What exactly are you going to do step-by-step to accomplish your objective? Do you need to improve your skills and qualifications, such as getting a college degree and passing a certification exam, to meet your objective?

Measure Results Get feedback to know how you are progressing toward your objective. Compare your actual performance to your objective.[56] For longer-term objectives, check regularly, not only at the end. How are you progressing—are you there yet?

Reinforce Results Be sure to use reinforcement theory on yourself. If you are missing the objective, consider punishing yourself; for example, if your weight is up, eat less next time. If you are on track to meet the objective, reward yourself in some way (have a special dessert).

MODEL 8.3 | Self-Motivation Model

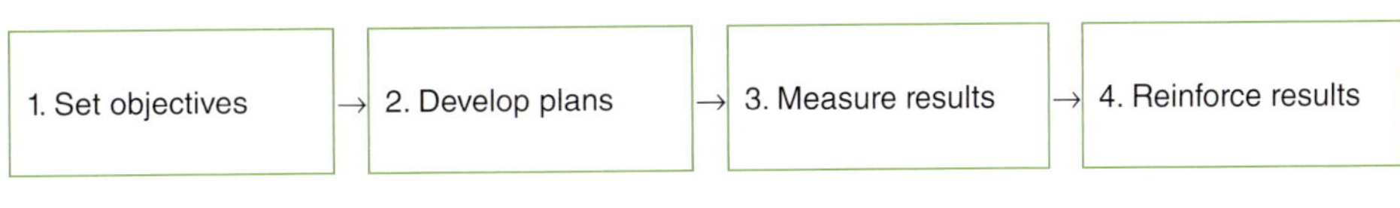

Remember, what you think about is how you feel and what you feel is how you behave. So develop a self-motivation objective and then plan, measure, and reinforce and think about it, and visualize yourself accomplishing the objective. Model 8.3 reviews the steps of self-motivation.

Communication Skills
Refer to CS Question 10.

WORK APPLICATION 8-11

Using Model 8.3, set an objective and develop a plan to achieve it to motivate yourself.

Bored or Feeling Trapped on the Job? If you are in these situations, you can keep things the same, or you can take responsibility and change it with two major alternatives. One, you can look for another job (within or leaving the firm) following the four steps of the self-motivation model, which may require developing new skills, more education, or getting some type of certification. Two, you can think about how your job can be enriched or change the design. With ideas in mind, talk to your boss about implementing ways to improve your job satisfaction.

DO MOTIVATION THEORIES APPLY GLOBALLY?

Learning Outcome 8-9

Explain possible limitations of using motivation theories outside North America.

The motivation theories you have learned were developed in North America. As firms become increasingly global, they must be aware of the cultural limitations of theories. There is support for the idea that motivational concerns vary across nations.[57]

Cross-Cultural Differences in Motivation

Let's discuss how the specific motivation theories differ across cultures.

Hierarchy of Needs, ERG, and Two-Factor Theory Cultural differences suggest that the order of hierarchy may vary across cultures. In risk-averse countries such as Japan, Greece, and Mexico, security needs would be at the top of the needs hierarchy. In countries such as Denmark, Sweden, Norway, the Netherlands, and Finland, which prefer quality of life (relationships) over quantity of life (possessions), social needs would be at the top. As related to two-factor theory, the intrinsic motivation of higher-level needs can be more relevant to wealthy societies than to poor societies.[58]

Manifest Needs Theory Cultures also differ in the extent to which they value need for achievement. The concern for high performance is common in high quantity-of-life countries, including the United States, Canada, and Great Britain; it is almost absent in high quality-of-life countries, including Chile and Portugal.

One major cultural difference is in the focus on individualistic versus group approaches to business. Individualistic societies (the United States, Canada, Great Britain, Australia) tend to value self-accomplishment. Collective societies (Japan, Mexico, Singapore, Pakistan) tend to value group accomplishment and loyalty. So individual versus group incentives tend to vary by country,

Equity Theory Equity theory as it relates to fairness tends to be a value upheld in most cultures. However, equity can call for higher producers to be paid more. This tends to be more of a motivator in individualistic countries than it is in collective countries, where people tend to prefer equality and all are paid the same regardless of output. On the other hand, U.S. unions, including teachers, also tend to prefer equal pay to merit pay.

Expectancy Theory Expectancy theory holds up fairly well cross-culturally because it is flexible. It allows for the possibility that there may be differences in expectations and valences across cultures. For example, societal acceptance may be of higher value than individual recognition in collective societies. So managers in different countries can offer rewards that are of value to their employees.

Reinforcement Theory Reinforcement theory also holds up well cross-culturally. People everywhere tend to use behavior that is reinforced. We all can be told or can figure out what behavior is rewarded and use the behavior to our benefit. Management everywhere tends to set up rules and penalties for breaking them. However, how well the punishment fits the offense can vary. In the United States it is much easier to fire employees than it is in Europe.

Goal Setting An eight-country study found that goal setting is effective for any task in which people have control over their performance.[59] Motivational goal setting relies on a need for achievement and high levels of performance, and it is based on quantity-of-life issues. Thus, the United States sets challenging objectives and achieves them. However, goal setting is less motivational to cultures in which achievement is not important and quality of life is important, such as Portugal and Chile.

Complete Self-Assessment Exercise 8-3 to determine how your personality affects your motivation.

/// Self-Assessment Exercise 8-3 ///

Your Personality and Motivation

If you have a high *surgency* personality, you most likely have a high need for power. You are probably realistic in your expectations, tend to know what you want and set reasonable objectives, and work to achieve your objectives. You may be concerned about being treated equitably but not too concerned if others are. You may like positive reinforcement for yourself, but you have no problem using punishment to get what you want. You like praise, but may not give much praise to others. You tend to like jobs in which you are in control of what you do and how you do it.

If you have a high *agreeableness* personality, you most likely have a high need for affiliation. Your expectations are most likely related more to relationships than to setting task objectives and working to achieve them. You may be concerned about your being treated equitably, and you tend to help others get equal treatment. You may like positive reinforcement for yourself, but you may need to be careful not to use extinction (do nothing and the problem will solve itself) if you are not being treated fairly—be assertive. You need acceptance and like praise, and you tend to give both to others. You tend to like jobs in which you work with others.

If you have a high *conscientious* personality, you most likely have a high need for achievement. You are most likely realistic in your expectations, tend to know what you want and set reasonable objectives, and work to achieve your objectives. You may be concerned about being treated equitably but not too concerned if others are. You like positive reinforcement of your accomplishments and tend to avoid punishment. You like praise, but may not give much praise to others. You tend to like jobs in which you can measure your accomplishments and succeed.

The *adjustment* personality dimension is not a need in the manifest needs motivation theory. However, it clearly affects behavior in a positive or negative way. If you are low in adjustment, you most likely have unrealistic expectations, don't really know what you want, and don't set goals and work to achieve them. You are probably being treated fairly, but you perceive that you are not being treated equitably. You probably get more punishment than rewards. You may not like your job, but changing jobs may not make you happy or more adjusted. A new job will not change your personality; you need to change.

The *openness to experience* personality dimension is not a need in the manifest needs motivation theory. However, it clearly affects behavior in a positive or negative way. If you are open to experience, you are more of a risk taker and tend to set more challenging, realistic objectives than people who are closed to new experiences.

Action plan: Based on your personality, what specific things will you do to improve how you motivate yourself and others?

____

____

____

____

As we bring this chapter to a close, you should understand the motivation process and the importance of motivation and how it affects behavior, human relations, and performance. You should know four content motivation theories (needs hierarchy, ERG, two-factor, and manifest needs) and how organizations meet employee needs, and two process motivation theories (expectancy and equity) and how to motivate others and yourself through these six theories. You should also understand reinforcement theory and how to motivate using types (positive, avoidance, extinction, and punishment) and schedules (continuous and intermittent) of reinforcement. You should be aware of incentive and recognition programs, job enrichment and job design, how the motivation theories fit together, and cross-cultural differences in motivation. More important, you should have the skill to give recognition or praise, to write objectives meeting four criteria, and how to motivate yourself using these three 4-step models.

/ / / REVIEW / / /

The chapter review is organized to help you master the 10 learning outcomes for Chapter 8. First provide your own response to each learning outcome, and then check the summary provided to see how well you understand the material. Next, identify the final statement in each section as either true or false (T/F). Correct each false statement. Answers are given at the end of the chapter.

LO 8-1 Explain the motivation process and the three factors affecting performance.

The motivation process steps are: need → motive → behavior → satisfaction or dissatisfaction. The three factors affecting performance are Ability × Motivation × Resources.

Motivation is the most important factor in the performance formula. T F

LO 8-2 Describe four content motivation theories.

Content motivation theories focus on identifying people's needs in order to understand what motivates them. *Needs hierarchy* is Maslow's theory of motivation based on five categories of needs. Alderfer's *ERG theory* classifies existence, relatedness, and growth needs. The *two-factor theory* is Herzberg's classification of needs as hygienes and motivators. The *manifest needs theory* of motivation is primarily McClelland's classification of needs as achievement, power, and affiliation.

Motivating factors are primarily extrinsic factors. T F

LO 8-3 Describe two process motivation theories.

Process motivation theories attempt to explain how and why people are motivated. *Expectancy theory* is Vroom's formula, which states that Motivation = Expectancy × Valence. *Equity theory* is primarily Adams's motivation theory, which is based on the comparison of perceived inputs to outputs.

Valence refers to one's need for perceived inputs to match outputs. T F

LO 8-4 State how reinforcement is used to increase performance.

Reinforcement theory is primarily Skinner's motivation theory, which contends that behavior can be controlled through the use of positive or negative consequences. Through the use of four types of reinforcement—positive, avoidance, extinction, and punishment—and two schedules of reinforcement—continuous and intermittent—employees can learn which behavior is and is not appropriate. Appropriate behavior that is productive is encouraged, while nonproductive behavior is discouraged.

The two variables of intermittent reinforcement are passage of time (fixed or variable interval) and output (fixed or variable ratio), resulting in four alternative schedules. T F

LO 8-5 List the four steps in the model for giving praise.

The four steps for giving praise are: (1) tell the person exactly what was done correctly; (2) tell the person why the behavior is important; (3) stop for a moment of silence; and (4) encourage repeat performance.

Praise works best when it is not used very often. T F

LO 8-6 List the criteria for setting objectives.

In setting objectives, they should be: difficult but achievable; observable and measurable; specific, with a target date; participatively set when possible; and accepted.

Letting employees set their own objectives generally leads to their acceptance and achievement. T F

LO 8-7 Identify the four parts of the model for writing objectives.

The formula for writing objectives is as follows: To + Action verb + Specific, measurable, and singular behavior + Target date.

"To make a profit this year" is a well-written objective. T F

LO 8-8 State ways to enrich, design, and simplify jobs.
Job enrichment is the process of building motivators into the job itself by making it more interesting and challenging. *Job design* is the employee's system for transforming inputs into outputs. *Job simplification* is the process of eliminating, combining, and/or changing the work sequence to increase performance.
The objective of all three methods is the same—to make the job more interesting and challenging and to motivate employees to higher levels of performance. T F

LO 8-9 Explain possible limitations of using motivation theories outside North America.
People of different cultures have different needs and values. What works well in one country may not be effective in a different one.

Hierarchy of needs, ERG, two-factor, and manifest needs theories don't tend to work well across cultures, but equity, expectancy, reinforcement, and goal setting theories do. T F

LO 8-10 Define the following 16 key terms.
Select one or more methods: (1) fill in the missing key terms from memory; (2) match the key terms from the end of the review with their definitions below; and/or (3) copy the key terms in order from the key terms at the beginning of the chapter.

__________________ is the internal process leading to behavior to satisfy needs.

The __________________ is: Performance = Ability × Motivation × Resources.

__________________ focus on identifying people's needs in order to understand what motivates them.

__________________ is Maslow's theory of motivation, which is based on five needs.

__________________ is Herzberg's classification of needs as hygienes and motivators.

The __________________ of motivation is primarily McClelland's classification of needs as achievement, power, and affiliation.

__________________ attempt to understand how and why people are motivated.

__________________ is Vroom's formula, which states that Motivation = Expectancy × Valence.

__________________ is primarily Adams's motivation theory, which is based on the comparison of perceived inputs and outputs.

__________________ is primarily Skinner's motivation theory: Behavior can be controlled through the use of positive or negative consequences.

The steps in __________________ are as follows: step (1) tell the person exactly what was done correctly; step (2) tell the person why the behavior is important; step (3) stop for a moment of silence; and step (4) encourage repeat performance.

__________________ state what is to be accomplished within a given period of time.

__________________ is the process by which managers and their employees jointly set objectives for the employees, periodically evaluate the performance, and reward according to results.

__________________ is the process of building motivators into the job itself by making it more interesting and challenging.

__________________ is the employee's system for transforming inputs into outputs.

__________________ is the process of eliminating, combining, and/or changing the work sequence to increase performance.

/ / / KEY TERMS / / /

content motivation theories 240
equity theory 247
expectancy theory 246
giving praise 251
job design 254
job enrichment 254
job simplification 254
management by objectives (MBO) 254
manifest needs theory 244
motivation 239
needs hierarchy 240
objectives 252
performance formula 239
process motivation theories 246
reinforcement theory 248
two-factor theory 242

/ / / COMMUNICATION SKILLS / / /

The following critical thinking questions can be used for class discussion and/or as written assignments to develop communication skills. Be sure to give complete explanations for all questions.

1. Some people have stated that the performance formula is oversimplified. Do you agree? Can it really be used to increase performance?
2. Give examples of how all five of your needs in Maslow's hierarchy of needs have been or are being met.
3. Herzberg says that pay is a hygiene factor, whereas others say it is a motivator. What do you say?
4. Which do you believe are more useful in motivating employees: content or process motivation theories?
5. Some people say that reinforcement theory is a means of manipulating employees to do what the company wants them to do. Do you agree? Is the use of reinforcement theory ethical?
6. Does giving praise really motivate employees, or do they view it as a means of getting them to do more work?
7. Some managers say that what gets measured gets done. Do you agree? What does this have to do with setting objectives?
8. What are the advantages and disadvantages of an MBO program?
9. Which of the motivational theories do you prefer? Why?
10. Will you actually use Model 8.3 to motivate yourself?

CASE / / / Kevin Plank: Founder, CEO, and Board Chair of Under Armour

It is often said that necessity is the mother of invention. In 1995 Kevin Plank, then special teams captain of the University of Maryland football team, had an idea born out of a problem every athlete could relate to but could do nothing about; that is, until Plank decided to do something about it. Tired of repeatedly changing the cotton T-shirt under his jersey as it became wet and heavy during the course of a game, Plank set out to develop a different type of shirt that would remain drier and lighter; a shirt that worked with your body to regulate temperature and enhance performance. Working from his grandmother's townhouse in Washington, DC, Plank created a new category of sporting apparel called "performance apparel." He named his company Under Armour and built it into a leading developer, marketer, and distributor of performance apparel, footwear, and accessories. Under Armour's mission is to make all athletes better through passion, design, and the relentless pursuit of innovation. Since 1996, Plank has served as Under Armour's chief executive officer and board chair. Not bad for someone who came in as a walk-on in the University of Maryland's football team and went on to become a special teams captain.[60]

A little more than a decade later, Under Armour is more than a billion-dollar company. Under Armour still sells those shirts it started with, but it has expanded into many corners of the athletic/casual wear market, from compression shorts to sports bras, innovative mouth guards, and basketball shoes. An initial investment of $10,000 in Under Armour when it was founded is worth $140 million today. It seems self-motivation has been a big part of Plank's success. He has always been motivated to achieve whatever he sets his mind to achieve. In a 2003 *Inc* article titled "How I Did It," Plank provides a glimpse into his early motivations to achieve.

Unlike a lot of college football players, Plank never considered football his only option. He always wanted to be a businessman. Even though Nike was a giant in the sports apparel industry, Plank never thought he couldn't make it. He relays a childhood story that led him to believe in his entrepreneurial instincts. As he puts it, "I've always been a hustler. I don't mean that in the literal sense." When he was 14 or 15, he and his brother, Scott, returned from Guatemala with a bunch of knitted bracelets like those you might see at Grateful Dead concert. Scott presented a business proposition to Kevin and his other brother, Colin. "Listen, there's a Dead show coming to town. We'll go down and sell these bracelets and make a lot of money." They took him up on his offer. After just three hours of running around selling the bracelets, the brothers got back together to discuss their progress. As Kevin puts it, his brother Colin said, "I sold the first two. Then I started feeling guilty about how much money I was charging, so I gave the rest away." His brother Scott said, "I made about 70 bucks." Kevin then said, "I have about 580 bucks in my pocket. And I need more bracelets." Right there Kevin knew he was pretty good at this.

Relating another childhood adventure in entrepreneurship, Plank says his first real business was bootlegging T-shirts. "I was just a dumb kid," he says. "You go to a concert and pay $25 for a cotton T-shirt that says 'Rolling Stones,' 'Lollapalooza,' or whatever. On the outside they're 10 or 15 bucks. We were the guys selling them for 10 or 15 bucks."[61]

Plank was determined to succeed with his vision of starting his own business focused on meeting athletes' needs for better performing apparel. Not everyone believed in his vision. As he puts it, "one of my clearest memories of college is my strength coach at Maryland saying, 'Plank, stop worrying about all this other [business] crap and just commit yourself to playing football. You have the rest of your life to do these other things.' But I could never stop. I remember thinking how much fun it would be just to sit at a desk and think, 'All right, how are we going to make a buck?' " His persistence has paid off. Today as CEO and chair of the board at Under Armour, Plank tries to model his work ethic and motivation to his employees. He understands the importance of motivation as a factor in influencing follower behaviors. Plank abides by what he calls the "four pillars of greatness": build a great product, tell a great story, service the business, and build a great team. He employs a lot of the concepts discussed in this chapter, such as positive reinforcement, management by objectives, and job enrichment to realize his pillars of greatness.

In every public presentation that Plank makes, he emphasizes three things—passion, vision, and people—as his set of principles for success in business. On people, Plank says he wants to have the best type of people: "team, team, team. I can't underscore that need [enough]." The relationship between Plank and his employees is based on friendship and respect for one another. It is a very informal culture. According to Hanna, the director of women's sports marketing at Under Armour, it's a "get-it-done attitude." As she explains it, "Essentially, if you need to get something done, any obstacles that are in the way, you find a way to get it done. It's just expected you're going to figure it out somehow. And you get supported." That's why Plank's employees—the majority of whom are around 30 years old—are called "teammates."

Go to the Internet: To learn more about Kevin Plank and Under Armour, visit its Web site at www.underarmour.com.

Support your answers to the following questions with specific information from the case and text or with information you get from the Web or another source.

1. According to Herzberg's two-factor theory of motivation, was Plank's motivation tocreate a new category of performance apparel driven by extrinsic (hygiene) factors or intrinsic (motivator) factors?

2. According to McClelland's manifest theory of motivation, people are motivated by the needs for achievement, power, and affiliation. Which of these needs would you attribute to Plank? If you were to rank them in order of significance to Plank, which will be first, second, and third?

3. What's the evidence in the case that job enrichment is a key part of the way work is done at Under Armour?

Cumulative Questions

4. Chapter 7 distinguished between transformational, charismatic, and transactional leadership theories; which one of these best describes Kevin Plank?

5. Based on the discussion in Chapter 6 on passive, aggressive, and assertive behavior, what type of behavior do you think Kevin Plank has shown in the case narrative on him?

6. The Big Five Model of Personality (Chapter 2) categorizes traits into the dimensions of surgency, agreeableness, adjustment, conscientiousness, and open to experience. Which of these dimensions can you attribute to Kevin Plank?

Case Exercise and Role-Play

Preparation: Under Armour went from $17,000 in revenue in 1996 to more than a billion dollars in sales today. It's one of those only-in-America stories that went from 1 employee to more than 2,700 today. According to the case, one of Kevin Plank's "four pillars of greatness" is to tell a great story.

In-Class Groups: According to the discussion on giving praise in the text, giving recognition to employees motivates them. Divide the class into groups of four or five students. Each group should select a leader to play the role of Kevin Plank and the rest of the group members are employees. Given how far the company has come, Plank wants to give a rousing motivational speech to his employees. He has a vision for the company to become number one in its industry in five years—its 20th anniversary.

Role-Play: Using the different motivational theories presented in the chapter, each group should craft a three-minute speech that will be presented to the class by the group's leader. As Plank puts it, "tell a great story." The instructor or the class as a whole will decide who made the most compelling speech.

OBJECTIVE CASE /// Friedman's Motivation Technique

The following conversation took place between Art Friedman and Bob Lussier. In 1970, Art Friedman implemented a new business technique. At that time the business was called Friedman's Appliances. It employed 15 workers in Oakland, California. Friedman's is an actual business that uses the technique you will read about.

BOB: What is the reason for your success in business?

ART: My business technique.

BOB: What is it? How did you implement it?

ART: I called my 15 employees together and told them, "From now on I want you to feel as though the company is ours, not mine. We are all bosses. From now on you decide what you're worth and tell the accountant to put it in your pay envelope. You decide which days and hours you work and when to take time off. We will have an open petty cash system that will allow anyone to go into the box and borrow money when they need it."

BOB: You're kidding, right?

ART: No, it's true. I really do these things.

BOB: Did anyone ask for a raise?

ART: Yes, several people did. Charlie asked for and received a $100-a-week raise.

BOB: Did he and the others increase their productivity to earn their raises?

ART: Yes, they all did.

BOB: How could you run an appliance store with employees coming and going as they pleased?

ART: The employees made up schedules that were satisfactory to everyone. We had no problems of under- or overstaffing.

BOB: Did anyone steal from the petty cash box?

ART: No.

BOB: Would this technique work in any business?

ART: It did work, it still works, and it will always work for me!

In 1976, Art Friedman changed his business to Friedman's Microwave Ovens. He developed a franchise operation to use his motivation technique of making everyone a boss.

Today, the business is called Friedman's Appliances, and for more information visit its Web site (www.friedmansapplicance.com).

Answer the following questions. Then in the space between questions, state why you selected that answer.

_______ 1. Art's business technique increased performance.

a. true *b.* false

_______ 2. Art focused on the _______ factor in the performance formula.

a. ability *b.* motivation *c.* resources

_______ 3. Art's employees seem to be on the _______ needs level.

a. physiological *c.* social *e.* self-actualization

b. safety *d.* esteem

_______ 4. Art's technique has less emphasis on meeting _______ needs.

a. achievement *b.* power *c.* affiliation

_______ 5. Frederick Herzberg would say Art is using:

a. hygienes *b.* motivators

_______ 6. Victor Vroom would say that Art uses expectancy motivation theory.

a. true *b.* false

_______ 7. J. Stacy Adams would say Art:

a. has equitable rewards *b.* underrewards *c.* overrewards

_______ 8. Art uses _______ reinforcement.

a. positive *c.* extinction

b. avoidance *d.* punishment

_______ 9. Art's technique is most closely associated with:

a. giving praise *c.* job enrichment

b. MBO *d.* job design

_______ 10. Art's technique focuses most on:

a. delegating variety *c.* making work identifiable

b. forming natural work groups *d.* giving autonomy

11. Do you know of any organizations that use any of Art's or other unusual techniques? If yes, what is the organization's name? What does it do?

12. Could Art's technique work in all organizations? Explain your answer.

13. In a position of authority, would you use Art's technique? Explain your answer.

/ / / SKILL-BUILDING EXERCISE 8-1 / / /

What Do You Want from a Job?

In-Class Exercise (Individual and Group)

Objectives: To help you better understand how job factors affect motivation. To help you realize that people are motivated by different factors. What motivates you may turn off someone else.

AACSB: The primary AACSB learning standard skills developed through this exercise are reflective thinking and self-management.

Preparation: You should have completed Self-Assessment Exercise 8–1.

Experience: You will discuss the importance of job factors.

Procedure 1 (8–20 minutes)
Break into groups of five or six, and discuss job factors selected by group members in Self-Assessment Exercise 8–1. Come to a consensus on the three factors that are most important to the group. They can be either motivators or hygienes. If the group mentions other job factors not listed, such as pay, you may add them.

Procedure 2 (3–6 minutes)
A representative from each group goes to the board and writes his or her group's three most important job factors.

Conclusion: The instructor leads a class discussion and/or makes concluding remarks.

Application (2–4 minutes): What did I learn from this experience? How will I use this knowledge in the future?

Sharing: Volunteers give their answers to the application section.

/ / / SKILL-BUILDING EXERCISE 8-2 / / /

Giving Praise

Preparation (Group)

BMV 8-1

Think of a job situation in which you did something well, deserving of praise and recognition. You may have saved the company some money, you may have turned a dissatisfied customer into a happy one, and so on. If you have never worked or done something well, interview someone who has. Put yourself in a supervisory position and write out the praise you would give to an employee for doing what you did.

Briefly describe the situation:

Step 1. Tell the employee exactly what was done correctly.

Step 2. Tell the employee why the behavior is important.

Step 3. Stop for a moment of silence. (Count to five silently.)

Step 4. Encourage repeat performance.

In-Class Exercise

Objective: To develop your skill at giving praise.

AACSB: The primary AACSB learning standard skills developed through this exercise are communication abilities and leadership.

Preparation: You will need your prepared praise.

Experience: You will give and receive praise.

Procedure (12–17 minutes)

Break into groups of five or six. One at a time, give the praise.

1. Explain the situation.
2. Select a group member to receive the praise.
3. Give the praise. (Talk; don't read it off the paper.) Try to select the position you would use if you were actually giving the praise on the job (for example, both standing, both sitting).
4. Integration. The group gives the giver of praise feedback on how he or she did:
   - Step 1. Was the praise very specific and descriptive? Did the giver look the employee in the eye?
   - Step 2. Was the importance of the behavior clearly stated?
   - Step 3. Did the giver stop for a moment of silence?
   - Step 4. Did the giver encourage repeat performance? Did the giver of praise touch the receiver [optional]?
   - Did the praise take less than one minute? Was the praise sincere?

Conclusion: The instructor leads a class discussion and/or makes concluding remarks.

Application (2– 4 minutes): What did I learn from this experience? How will I use this knowledge in the future?

Sharing: Volunteers give their answers to the application section.

/ / / SKILL-BUILDING EXERCISE 8-3 / / /

Setting Objectives

Preparation (Individual)

In Chapter 1, you were asked to write five course objectives. Rewrite the five objectives, or new ones, using the Douglas model below:

To + Action verb + Specific, measurable, and singular behavior + Target date

1.
2.

3.
4.
5.

Also write two personal objectives and two career objectives using Douglas's model:

Personal

1.
2.

Career

1.
2.

In-Class Exercise

Objective: To gain skill at setting objectives.

AACSB: The primary AACSB learning standard skills developed through this exercise are analytic skills and strategic management.

Preparation: You should have written nine objectives in preparation for this exercise.

Procedure (2–12 minutes)

Break into groups of five or six people and share your objectives. One person states one objective and the others give input to be sure it meets the criteria of effective objectives. A second person states one objective, followed by feedback. Continue until all group members have stated all their objectives or the time runs out.

Conclusion: The instructor may lead a discussion and/or make concluding remarks.

Application (2–4 minutes): What did I learn from this experience? How will I use this knowledge in the future?

Sharing: Volunteers give their answers to the application section.

/ / ANSWERS TO TRUE/FALSE QUESTIONS / /

1. F. They are all important because if any of the factors are missing, performance will be lower.
2. F. Motivating factors are primarily "intrinsic" factors.
3. F. Valence refers to the value a person places on the outcome or reward in expectancy theory, not equity theory.
4. T.
5. F. We should praise good behavior often.
6. T.
7. F. Because it is not specific, it is not a well-written objective. How much profit? Also, stating the month and year, rather than simply "this year," would provide a better target date.
8. T.
9. T.

CHAPTER 9

Ethical Power, Politics, and Etiquette

LEARNING OUTCOMES

After completing this chapter, you should be able to:

LO 9-1 State how power, politics, and ethics affect behavior, human relations, and performance.

LO 9-2 Describe seven bases of power.

LO 9-3 List techniques to increase your power bases.

LO 9-4 Describe five influencing tactics.

LO 9-5 Discuss the necessity of organizational politics and three political behaviors.

LO 9-6 Identify techniques to develop effective human relations with superiors, subordinates, peers, and members of other departments.

LO 9-7 State two classifications of business etiquette and how etiquette overlaps between the two classifications.

LO 9-8 List the steps in the handling customer complaints model.

LO 9-9 Define the following 12 key terms (in order of appearance in the chapter):

power
coercive power
connection power
reward power
legitimate power
referent power
information power
expert power
politics
reciprocity
open-door policy
business etiquette

/ / / Bob and Sally are at the water fountain, talking. They both are employed at Scitor Corporation, which is headquartered in Sunnyvale, California.

BOB: I'm sorry the Peterson account was not assigned to you. You deserved it. Roger's claim of being more qualified to handle the job is not true. I'm really surprised that our boss, Ted, believed Roger's claim.

SALLY: I agree. Nobody likes Roger because he always has to get his own way. I can't stand the way Roger puts down coworkers and members of other departments to force them to give him his own way. Roger has pulled the old emergency routine so many times now that purchasing and maintenance ignore his requests. This hurts our department.

BOB: You're right. Roger only thinks of himself; he never considers other people or what's best for the company. I've overheard Ted telling him he has to be a team player if he wants to get ahead.

SALLY: The way he tries to beat everyone out all the time is sickening. He'll do anything to get ahead. But the way he behaves, he will never climb the corporate ladder.

Besides good work, what does it take to get ahead in an organization? In most cases, getting ahead involves gaining power and using ethical political skills with superiors, subordinates, peers, and members of other departments. That's what this chapter is all about. / / /

HOW POWER, POLITICS, ETIQUETTE, AND ETHICS AFFECT BEHAVIOR, HUMAN RELATIONS, AND PERFORMANCE

Learning Outcome 9-1

State how power, politics, and ethics affect behavior, human relations, and performance.

Power is needed to reach objectives in all organizations, and power affects performance.[1] Your boss has a direct influence over your behavior, and the way managers use power also affects human relations and performance.[2] For example, in the opening case, Ted gave the Peterson account to Roger, which will affect both Roger's and Sally's behavior and human relations. Roger may not perform as well as Sally and may hurt department performance. Managers who abuse power using unethical behavior can markedly impair an organization's morale and performance.[3] When organizations use excessive power, workers may give in, but they also may get even by lowering performance.

Like power, *politics* is important to organizational performance.[4] People who use organizational politics tend to use different behavior than those who do not.[5] People using unethical politics tend to lie, cheat, and break the rules. In time, people recognize unethical people and distrust them.[6] Bob and Sally don't have effective human relations with Roger because of his unethical political behavior. The purchasing and maintenance department members ignore Roger's requests because of his behavior, while Bob and Sally have good relations with these departments. As a result of Roger's behavior, the performance of the organization as a whole is affected negatively.

People using proper *etiquette* behave differently than those who don't, and unethical etiquette behavior hurts human relations, and performance. So using proper *etiquette* is also important to behavior, human relations and performance.[7] Along with misusing power and politics, Roger also lacks etiquette skills.

One thing we want to make clear is that power and politics can be helpful or harmful to an organization, depending on the behavior. Most large organizations have codes of conduct to help employees know the difference between ethical and unethical behavior.[8] We classify power and political behavior into two categories: ethical and unethical. *Ethical power and politics* includes behavior that benefits both the individual and the organization. Behavior that helps the individual but does not hurt the organization is also considered ethical. Ethical politics creates a win–win situation, meeting the goal of human relations. On the other hand, *unethical power and politics* includes behavior that benefits the individual and hurts the organization. Unethical politics creates a win–lose situation. Unethical power and politics also includes behavior that helps the organization, but hurts the individual and other stakeholders. The term *organization* includes people inside the firm, because if employees are hurt, so is the organization. When dealing with people outside the firm, use the *stakeholders'* approach to ethics (Chapter 3). By creating a win–win situation for all relevant parties, it increases the firm's performance. So to be successful, be ethical.

WORK APPLICATION 9-1

Give an example of ethical and unethical politics, preferably from an organization for which you work or have worked. Describe the behavior and the consequences for all parties involved.

At first, one may appear to be richly rewarded for knifing people in the back, but retaliation follows, trust is lost, and productivity declines. This is illustrated in the opening case. Roger uses unethical power and politics in hopes of getting ahead. But according to his peers, he will not climb the corporate ladder. It is difficult to get ahead when people don't like you and you make a lot of enemies. Exercising good human relations skills is exercising good ethics. Don't let incentives for personal gain tempt you into using unethical behavior.[9]

APPLICATION SITUATIONS / / /

Ethical and Unethical Politics AS 9-1

Identify the type of politics represented in each statement.

A. Ethical politics B. Unethical politics

_______ 1. Pete goes around telling everyone about any little mistake his peer Sue makes.

_______ 2. Antonio is taking tennis lessons so he can challenge his boss.

_______ 3. Aisha delivers her daily figures at 10:00 each day because she knows she will run into Ms. Big Power on the way.

_______ 4. Carlos goes around asking about what is happening in other departments during his work time.

_______ 5. Frank sent a copy of his department's performance record to three high-level managers to whom he does not report.

Communication Skills
Refer to CS Question 1.

POWER

Some people want and seek power, while others wouldn't take it if you offered it to them. You discovered the reason for this difference in Chapter 8, where you learned about the need for power in McClelland's manifest needs theory. Do you have a need for power? In this section, we discuss the importance of power in organizations, bases of power and how to increase your power, and influencing tactics. Begin by completing Self-Assessment Exercise 9-1, Your Power Base, to determine your preferred use of power.

/// Self-Assessment Exercise 9-1 ///

Your Power Base

When you want to get something and need others' consent or help, which approach do you use most often? Think of a recent specific situation in which you tried to get something. If you cannot develop your own example, assume you and a coworker both want the same job assignment for the day. How would you get it? Rank all seven approaches below from 1, the first approach you would most commonly use, to 7, the last approach you would most commonly use. Be honest.

_______ I did/would somehow use a form of *coercive power*—pressure, blackmail, force, threat, retaliation, and so forth—to get what I want.

_______ I did/would use the influential *connection power* I have. I'd refer to my friend, or actually have my friend tell the person with authority (such as my boss) to let me get (or do) what I want.

_______ I did/would use *reward power* by offering the coworker something of value to him or her as part of the process or in return for compliance.

_______ I did/would convince the coworker to give me what I want by making a *legitimate* request (such as referring to my seniority over the coworker).

_______ I did/would convince the coworker by using *referent power*—relying on our relationship. Others would comply because they like me or are my friends.

_______ I did/would convince my coworker to give me what I want with *information power.* The facts support the reason why he or she should do what I want. I have information my coworker needs.

_______ I did/would convince my coworker to give me what I want by making him or her realize that I have the skill and knowledge. Since I'm the *expert,* it should be done my way.

Your selection rank (1 to 7) prioritizes your preferred use of power. Each power base is a key term and will be explained in this chapter.

Organizational Power

Some people view power as the ability to make people do what they want them to do, or the ability to do something to people or for people. These definitions may be true, but they tend to give power a manipulative, negative connotation, as does the adage "Power corrupts and absolute power corrupts absolutely." Within an organization, power should be viewed in a positive sense.[10] Martin Luther King Jr. said, "Power properly understood is nothing but the ability to achieve purpose. It is the strength to bring about change." Without power, managers could not achieve organizational objectives.[11] Leadership and power go hand in hand. For our purposes, **power** *is a person's ability to influence others to do something they would not otherwise do.* The good news is that power skills can be developed.[12]

Learning Outcome 9-2

Describe seven bases of power.

Learning Outcome 9-3

List techniques to increase your power bases.

Bases of Power and How to Increase Your Power

There are two sources of power—position power and personal power. Position power is derived from top-level management and is delegated down the chain of command. Personal power is derived from the person. Everyone has personal power to varying degrees.

John French and Bertram Raven proposed five bases of power—coercive, reward, legitimate, referent, and expert—which are commonly used today.[13] Below, we will examine seven bases of power and how to increase each. You do not have to take power away from others to increase your power base.[14] Contrary to the Machiavellian cliche, nice people are more likely to rise to power because people give it to others that they genuinely like.[15]

Coercive Power The use of **coercive power** *involves threats and/or punishment to influence compliance.* Out of fear that noncompliance will lead to negative consequences, people do as requested. Other examples of coercive power include verbal abuse, humiliation, and ostracism. In the opening case, when Roger puts down coworkers and members of other departments to force them to give him his own way, he is using coercive power.

Coercive power is appropriate to use in maintaining discipline when enforcing rules. When an employee is not willing to do as the manager requests, the manager may use coercive power to gain compliance. However, it is advisable to keep the use of coercive power to a minimum because it hurts human relations and often productivity as well.[16]

Increasing Coercive Power To have strong coercive position power, you need to have a management job that enables you to gain and maintain the ability to hire, discipline, and fire your employees. However, some people can pressure others to do what they want without management authority.

Communication Skills
Refer to CS Question 2.

Connection Power **Connection power** *is based on the user's relationship with influential people.* It relies on the use of contacts or friends who can influence the person you are dealing with.[17] The right connections can give you the perception of having power, and they can give you actual power. If people know you are friendly with people in power, they are more apt to do as you request. The Objective Case, Politicking, at the end of the chapter illustrates how people use networking connection power to get ahead.

Increasing Connection Power To increase your connection power, expand your network of contacts with important managers who have power. Join the "in crowd" and the "right" clubs. Sports like golf or working out at a gym[18] may help you meet influential people. When you want something, identify the people who can help you attain it, make alliances, and win them over to your side. Get people to know your name. Get all the publicity you can. Have your accomplishments known by the people in power.[19]

Reward Power **Reward power** *is based on the user's ability to influence others with something of value to them.* In a management position, use positive reinforcement with incentives such as praise, recognition, pay raises, and promotions to ensure compliance. With peers, you can exchange favors, known as reciprocity,[20] as a reward or give something of value to the other party.

Let people know what's in it for them. If you have something attractive to others, use it. For example, when Professor Smith is recruiting student aides, he tells candidates that if they are selected and do a good job, he will recommend them for an MBA fellowship at Suffolk University, where he has connection power. As a result, he gets good, qualified help for minimum wages, while helping both his student aide and his alma mater. Professor Smith meets the goal of human relations by creating a win–win situation for himself, the student, and the university.

Increasing Reward Power Get a management position, and gain and maintain control over resources.[21] Have the power to evaluate your employees' performance and determine their raises and promotions. Find out what others value, and try to reward them in that way. Using praise can help increase your power using the giving praise model in Chapter 8. People who feel they are appreciated rather than being used will give you more power.

Legitimate Power **Legitimate power** *is based on the user's position power,* which is given by the organization.[22] Employees tend to feel that they ought to do what the supervisor says within the scope of the job.

The use of legitimate power is appropriate when asking people to do something that is within the scope of their jobs. Most day-to-day interactions are based on legitimate power.

Increasing Legitimate Power Let people know the power you possess, and work at gaining people's perception that you do have power. Remember—people's perception that you have power gives you power.

Referent Power **Referent power** *is based on the user's personal power.* A person using referent power relies on personality and the relationship to gain compliance. For example, say, "Will you please do it for me?" not "This is an order." Identification stems primarily from the attractiveness of the person using power and is manifested in personal feelings of liking someone.[23] Since Roger is not well liked in the organization, he has weak referent power.

The use of referent power is particularly appropriate for people with weak, or no, position power. Today managers are sharing power, or empowering employees.[24] Roger has no position power, so he should increase his referent power.

Increasing Referent Power To gain referent power, develop your relationship with others; stand up for them. Using the guidelines in this book can help you win referent power. Remember that your boss's success depends on you. Gain his or her confidence in order to get more power; work at your relationship with the boss. We will discuss this in more detail later in the chapter.

Information Power **Information power** *is based on the user's information being desired by others.* Managers rely on the other person's need for the information they possess. However, with central computer networks, individual managers today have less of this type of power. Some administrative assistants have more information than the managers they work for. The information is usually, but not always, related to the job.

WORK APPLICATION 9-2

Of the many suggestions for increasing your power bases, which two are your highest priority for using on the job? Explain.

Increasing Information Power Have information flow through you. Know what is going on in the organization. Provide service and information to other departments. Serve on committees; it gives you both information and a chance to increase connection power. Attend seminars and other meetings.

Expert Power **Expert power** *is based on the user's skill and knowledge.* Being an expert makes other people dependent on you. The fewer the people who possess the skill or knowledge, the more power the individual who does possess it has. People often respect an expert. For example, because there are so few people possessing the ability to become top athletes and executives, they command multimillion-dollar contracts.

WORK APPLICATION 9-3

Give two examples, preferably from an organization for which you work or worked, of people using power. Identify the power base and describe the behavior and how it affected human relations and performance.

Expert power is essential to people who have to work with people from other departments and organizations. They have no direct position power to use, so being seen as an expert gives credibility and power. Roger, rather than Sally, got the Peterson account because he convinced Ted of his expertise.

Increasing Expert Power To become an expert, take all the training and educational programs your organization provides. Stay away from routine tasks, in favor of more complex, hard-to-evaluate tasks. Project a positive image.

Skill-Building Exercise 9-1 develops this skill.

Remember to use the appropriate type of power in a given situation. Exhibit 9.1 matches the two sources of power and the seven bases of power with the four situational supervision and communication styles (from Model 8.1). As shown, coercive, connection, and reward power come from position power, while referent, information, and expert power come from personal power.

EXHIBIT 9.1 | Sources and Bases of Power with Situational Supervision and Communication Styles

Personal power →		←	Position power
Expert	Referent	Reward	Coercive
Information	Legitimate	Connection	
Laissez-faire	*Participative*	*Consultative*	*Autocratic*

APPLICATION SITUATIONS / / /

Using Power AS 9-2

Identify the appropriate power base to use in each situation.

A. Coercive
B. Connection
C. Reward or legitimate
D. Referent
E. Information or expert

_______ 6. Carl is one of the best workers you supervise. He needs little direction, but he has slowed down his production level. You know he has a personal problem, but the work needs to get done.

_______ 7. You want a new personal computer to help you do a better job.

_______ 8. José, one of your best workers, wants a promotion. He has asked you to help prepare him for when the opportunity comes.

_______ 9. Your worst employee has ignored one of your directives again.

_______ 10. Wanda, who needs some direction and encouragement to maintain production, is not working to standard today. Wanda claims to be ill, as she does occasionally.

Learning Outcome 9-4

Describe five influencing tactics.

Influencing Tactics

Your power is your ability to influence others to do something they would not otherwise do to help you meet your objectives. So along with power sources and bases, you need to have persuasion skills.[25] Persuasion takes careful preparation and proper presentation of arguments and supporting evidence in an appropriate and compelling way; it is not coercive power or manipulation.

To help persuade people you don't supervise, you can use influencing tactics that focus primarily on personal power. Five influencing tactics are ingratiation (praise), rational persuasion, inspirational appeal, personal appeal, and legitimization. Before we discuss each tactic, let's discuss reading people and creating and presenting a win–win situation so you know which influencing tactic may work best in a given situation.

Reading People Reasons for or an argument presenting your view may sound good to you, but they may seem irrelevant to the other person. If you are going to influence someone, you have to understand the person's values, attitudes, beliefs, and use incentives that will motivate the individual[26] (Chapter 8). Reading people is a key interpersonal skill; it has four parts:

1. Put yourself in the place of the person you want to persuade (your boss, coworker, a person in another department). Anticipate how the person sees the world (perception [Chapter 2]) and what his or her expectations are during your persuasion interaction.
2. Get the other person's expectations right. If you don't, you most likely will not influence the person.
3. Incorporate the information about the other person's expectations into your persuasive presentation. In other words, use the influencing tactic that will work best with the person. For example, if you know the person likes to be praised, use ingratiation.

If the person likes or expects a rational persuasion with facts and figures, use that tactic. If the person doesn't care much about facts and figures and is more emotional, use an inspirational appeal.

4. Keep the focus on the other person's expectations when trying to persuade. This ties in with achieving win–win situations. What's in it for them?

Creating and Presenting a Win–Win Situation When you want someone to do something to help you, it is easy to focus just on yourself. But recall that the key to human relations success is to develop a win–win situation for all relevant parties. So spend time reading the other person, as suggested above, and answer the other person's often unasked question, What's in it for me? Remember that most people are concerned about themselves, not about you. So spending time telling them how you will benefit will be boring to many. What they want to hear is how they will benefit, so, as it says in step 4 above, keep the focus on the other person's expectations.

Ingratiation (Praise) With the *ingratiation tactic,* you are friendly and give praise to get the person in a good mood before making your request. You learned the importance of, and how to give, praise in Chapter 8. Never go a day without giving praise.

Appropriate Use of Ingratiation Ingratiation works best as a long-term influencing strategy to improve relationships. The ingratiation must also be sincere to be effective. If you usually don't compliment a person and all of a sudden you compliment him or her and then ask for a favor, the person will think you are manipulating. Thus, this technique can backfire on you.

Using Ingratiation When using ingratiation, follow these guidelines:

1. Be sensitive to the individual's moods. Ingratiation works well with people who are moody, so asking them at the wrong time can lead to resistance to the change. With moody people, start out with some compliments to determine their mood. If it's good, make the request; if not, wait for a more opportune time, if possible.
2. Compliment the person's past related achievements. Begin by talking about how well the person handled some prior task. Be specific about what she or he did well; use the model for giving praise in Chapter 8. Then move into the request. If you start with the request first, but find resistance, and then proceed to give compliments, the compliments may be seen as insincere manipulation to get what you want.[27]
3. State why the person was selected for the task. Compliment people by saying how uniquely qualified they are to do the task. When people believe the task is important and they are well qualified, they will find it tough to refuse doing you a favor. And yes, ask: would you please do this favor for me?
4. Acknowledge inconvenience posed by your request. Apologize for adding to a busy workload and any inconvenience that will result from doing the task. Praise the individual as you show your appreciation for his or her willingness to be inconvenienced with your request.

Rational Persuasion The *rational persuasion tactic* includes logical arguments with factual evidence to persuade the person that the behavior will result in meeting the objective. Use facts and figures to build a persuasive case; visuals are also helpful. Remember that how information is presented affects persuasiveness.[28]

Appropriate Use of Rational Persuasion Logical arguments generally work well with people whose behavior is more influenced by thinking than by emotions. It works well when you share the same objective and create a true win–win situation.

Using Rational Persuasion When you develop rational persuasion, follow these guidelines:

1. Explain the reason your objective needs to be met. To get a commitment to meet your objective, you want people to know why it needs to be met and why it is important.
2. Explain how the other person will benefit by meeting your objective, again create a win–win situation.
3. Provide evidence that your objective can be met. Remember the importance of expectancy motivation theory (Chapter 8). Offer a detailed, step-by-step plan.
4. Explain how potential problems and concerns will be handled. Know the potential problems and concerns, and deal with them in the rational persuasion. If others bring up problems that you have not anticipated when reading the person, which is likely, be sure to address them. Do not ignore people's concerns or make simple statements like "That will not happen" or "We don't have to worry about that." Get the person's input on how to resolve any possible problems as they come up. This will help gain commitment.
5. If there are competing plans to meet the objective, explain why your proposal is better than the competing ones. Again, do your homework. You need to be well versed about the competition. To simply say "My idea is better than theirs" won't cut it. Be sure to state how your plan is superior to the others and to identify the weaknesses and problems within the other plans.

Inspirational Appeal The *inspirational appeal tactic* attempts to arouse people's enthusiasm through internalization to meet the objective. You appeal to the other person's values, ideals, and aspirations or increase his or her self-confidence by displaying feelings that appeal to the person's emotions and enthusiasm.[29]

Appropriate Use of Inspirational Appeals Inspirational appeals generally work well with people whose behavior is more influenced by emotions than by logical thinking. To be inspirational, you need to understand the values, hopes, fears, and goals of others; having charisma helps.[30] Great sports coaches, such as Vince Lombardi, are well respected for their inspirational appeals to get the team to win the game. Have you heard the saying from Notre Dame, "Win one for the Gipper"?

Using Inspirational Appeals When you develop an inspirational appeal, follow these guidelines:

1. When you use inspirational appeals, you need to develop emotions and enthusiasm.[31] When dealing with multiple individuals, different inspirational appeals may be made to meet individual values.
2. Link the appeal to the person's self-concept. Appeal to his or her self-image as a professional or a member of a team, department, or organization. Accomplishing objectives should help people feel good about themselves, which enhances self-concept.
3. Link the request to a clear, appealing vision. Create a vision of how things will be when your objective is achieved.
4. Be positive and optimistic. Make your confidence and optimism that the objective can be met contagious. For example, talk about when, not if, the objective will be accomplished.
5. Use nonverbal communication to bring emotions to the verbal message. Raise and lower your voice tone, and pause to intensify key points. Maintain eye contact. Using facial expressions, body movement, and gestures such as pounding a table can effectively reinforce verbal messages with emotions.[32]

Personal Appeal With the *personal appeal tactic,* you request the person to meet your objective based on loyalty and friendship. Present your request as a favor to you: "Please do it for me," not "This is an order."

Appropriate Use of Personal Appeals Personal appeals are especially important when you have weak power. Thus, personal appeals are more commonly used with peers and outsiders than with subordinates or bosses. It is also important to have a good relationship with the person. If you ask a personal favor of a person who doesn't like you, the request may end in resistance.

Using Personal Appeals When using personal appeals, follow these guidelines:

1. Begin by stating that you need a favor and why it is important. Then ask for the favor. In effect, you are hoping for a positive commitment before giving the details. When a person understands why it is important to you and agrees to do you the favor, it is tough to say no after finding out what is required. But be sure not to be viewed as manipulative and hurt the relationship.
2. Appeal to your friendship. When you have a relationship, a friendship appeal is usually not needed, and it will generally not work with people you don't know.
3. Tell the person that you are counting on him or her. This helps the person realize the importance to you and your friendship. This statement lets the person know that you don't want the request ignored and that failure to help you could hurt your relationship. Again, friendship is needed for full effect.

Legitimization With the *legitimization tactic,* you rely on organizational authority that a reasonable request is being made and that the person should meet your objective. Yes, legitimization is closely tied to legitimate power, but the tactic is used when you don't have position power, such as with people at higher levels in the organization, so be useful to them.[33]

Communication Skills
Refer to CS Question 3.

Skill-Building Exercises 9-2 and 9-3 develop these skills.

WORK APPLICATION 9-4

Give an example of when you or someone else in an organization for which you work or have worked used one of the five influencing tactics to achieve an objective. Be sure to state the tactic used.

Appropriate Use of Legitimization Legitimization is an appropriate tactic to use when you have legitimate authority or the right to make a particular type of request.

Using Legitimization When using legitimization, follow these guidelines:

1. Refer to organizational policies, procedures, rules, and other documentation. Explain how the request is verified within the organization structure.
2. Refer to written documents. If the person doesn't believe your reference to documents, show the policy manual, contract, letter of agreement, blueprint, work order, or the like that makes your request legitimate.
3. Refer to precedent. If some other person has made the same request, refer to it for equity in support of your request.

You should realize that the five influencing tactics can be used together to help you influence others. For example, praise usually needs to be backed up with another tactic. When one tactic does not work, you may need to change to another. Remember that many people have a hard time saying no when asked directly for a favor.

APPLICATION SITUATIONS / / /

Influencing Tactics AS 9-3

Select the most appropriate individual tactic for each situation.

A. Rational persuasion
B. Inspirational appeal
C. Legitimization
D. Ingratiation
E. Personal appeal

_______ 11. You are in sales and want some information about a new product that has not been produced yet, nor publicly stated internally or externally. You know a person in the production department who has been working on the new product, so you decide to contact this person.

_______ 12. Two of your five crew workers did not come in to work today. You have a large order that should be shipped out at the end of the day. It will be tough for the small crew to meet the deadline.

_______ 13. This situation relates to number 12. Although the crew members have agreed to push to meet the deadline, you would like to give them some help. You have an employee whose job is to perform routine maintenance and cleaning. He is not one of your five crew workers. However, you realize that he could be of help filling in for the two missing workers. You decide to talk to this nonunion employee about working with the crew for two hours today.

_______ 14. The nonunion employee in situation 13 is resisting helping the other workers. He is basically asking, "What's in it for me?"

_______ 15. You believe you deserve a pay raise, so you decide to talk to your boss about it.

ORGANIZATIONAL POLITICS

In this section, you will learn the nature of politics and how to develop political skills. Begin by determining your use of political behavior by completing Self-Assessment Exercise 9-2.

/// Self-Assessment Exercise 9-2 ///

Your Political Behavior

Select the response that best describes your actual or planned use of the following behavior on the job. Place the number 1 to 5 on the line before each statement.

(5) Usually (4) Frequently (3) Occasionally (2) Seldom (1) Rarely

_____ 1. I get along with everyone, even those recognized as difficult. I avoid or delay giving my opinion on controversial issues.

_____ 2. I try to make people feel important and compliment them.

_____ 3. I compromise when working with others and avoid telling people they are wrong; instead, I suggest alternatives that may be more effective.

_____ 4. I try to get to know the managers and what is going on in as many of the other departments as possible.

_____ 5. I take on the same interests as those in power (watch or play sports, join the same clubs, and the like).

_____ 6. I purposely seek contacts and network with higher-level managers so they will know who I am by name and face.

_____ 7. I seek recognition and visibility for my accomplishments.

_____ 8. I form alliances with others to increase my ability to get what I want.

_____ 9. I do favors for others and use their favors in return.

_____ 10. I say I will do things when I am not sure I can deliver; if I cannot meet the obligation, I explain why it was out of my control.

To determine your political behavior, add the 10 numbers you selected as your answers. The number will range from 10 to 50. The higher your score, the more political behavior you use. Place your score here _____ and mark the point that represents your score on the continuum below.

Nonpolitical 10 - - - - 20 - - - - 30 - - - - 40 - - - - 50 Political

These 10 statements are generally considered ethical behavior.

Learning Outcome 9-5

Discuss the necessity of organizational politics and three political behaviors.

The Nature of Organizational Politics

Like power, politics often has a negative connotation due to people who abuse political power. However, politics is critical to your career success.[34] In our economy, money is the medium of exchange; in an organization, politics is the medium of exchange. Managers cannot meet their objectives without the help of other people and departments over which they have no authority or position power. So you need to work with the system to climb the corporate ladder.[35] For example, an executive from IBM came to Apple to work on the iPhone and was unsuccessful at politics, and as a result he is no longer at Apple.[36] **Politics** *is the process of gaining and using power.* As you can see from the definition, power and politics go hand in hand.

The amount and importance of politics varies from organization to organization. However, larger organizations tend to be more political; and the higher the level of management, the more important politics becomes.[37]

Political Behavior

Political behavior is used to develop relationships that are necessary to get the job done. Three primary political behaviors commonly used in organizations are: networking, reciprocity, and coalition building. As you will learn below, these three behaviors are interrelated.

Networking Networking is the process of developing relationship alliances with key people for the purpose of politicking. Your network of people helps you get your job done.[38] Navigating networks of people in organizations has been shown to help win promotions.[39] Networking is such an important topic that we discuss it in detail in the next chapter.

WORK APPLICATION 9-5

Give an example of reciprocity, preferably from an organization for which you work or have worked. Explain the trade-off.

Reciprocity Politics is about reciprocal exchanges.[40] **Reciprocity** *involves creating obligations and debts, developing alliances, and using them to accomplish objectives.* Have you ever heard the expression "You owe me one"? When others do something for you, you incur an obligation that they may expect to be repaid. When you do something for others, you create a debt that you may be able to collect at a later date when you need a favor.

Coalition Building A coalition is a network of alliances that helps you achieve a specific objective. Reciprocity is primarily used to achieve ongoing objectives, whereas coalitions are developed for achieving a specific objective. Many organizational decisions that are supposed to be made during a meeting or vote are actually decided through coalition building. For example, let's say that the selection of the department chair at your college is by election at a department meeting.

Professor Smith would like to replace the current chair. Rather than just put her name on the ballot for the department election at the next meeting, she goes around to several people in the department telling them she wants to be chair. Smith may agree to do things in exchange for votes. Members of her coalition may also get votes for Smith, and someone may have asked her to run. She gets a majority of the department members saying they will vote for her, so Smith puts her name on the ballot. If she did not get the coalition, she would not run. So going into the meeting, the coalition has really already made the decision to elect Smith.

Putting the Political Behaviors Together So to put the three political behaviors together, political success is about developing networks of alliances and coalitions in reciprocal exchanges. When the exchanges create a win–win situation for all members of the alliance and the organization, the goal of human relations is met.

Developing Political Skills

Yes, you can be good at politics without being a jerk. Human relations skills are also political skills in organizations. Following the human relations guidelines throughout this book

Communication Skills
Refer to CS Question 4.

WORK APPLICATION 9-6

Of the 10 political behaviors in Self-Assessment Exercise 9-2, which two need the most effort on your part? Which two need the least? Explain your answers.

can help you develop political skills. More specifically, review the 10 statements in Self-Assessment Exercise 9-2 and consciously increase your use of these behaviors. Successfully implementing these behaviors results in increased political skills. However, if you don't agree with a political behavior, don't use it. You may not need to use all the political behaviors to be successful. Learn what it takes in the organization where you work. Use number 10, saying you will do something when you are not sure you can, sparingly and don't use the word *promise*. You don't want to be viewed as a person who doesn't keep his or her word. Developing trust is very important.[41] And being honest builds trust (Chapter 7).

VERTICAL POLITICS

Vertical politics are relations with superiors and subordinates. Your boss and the employees you supervise and who report to you are the most important persons with whom to develop effective relations.

Relations with Your Boss

Your relationship with your boss will affect your job satisfaction and can mean the difference between success or failure on the job.[42] Needless to say, you should develop a good working relationship with your boss. Doing so is also called *managing* your boss, and *leader–member exchange (LMX) theory*.[43]

Don't try to change your boss. Analyze your boss's style and preferences, and if necessary, change your style to match his or hers. For example, if your boss is very businesslike and you are very informal and talkative, be businesslike when you are with your boss. If your boss likes you and your work to be early, not just on time, be early. Remember, people generally like people who behave like themselves, and being liked can lead to career advancement.

Knowing your boss can lead to better human relations between the two of you. It is helpful to know your boss's primary responsibility, what your boss regards as good performance, how your performance will be evaluated, and what your boss expects of you. So get feedback from your boss to make sure you are on the same page. As discussed in Chapter 7, your boss must trust you.[44] It's your job to help your boss be successful and to offset his or her weaknesses.

Common Expectations of Bosses Your boss will expect loyalty, cooperation, initiative, information, and openness to criticism.

Loyalty Recall that loyalty is an important part of trust. You need to be loyal and have a proper attitude. You should not talk negatively about your boss behind his or her back, even if others are doing so. Regardless of how careful you are, or how trustworthy the other person is, gossip seems to get back to the boss. When it does, it can seriously hurt your relationship. Your boss may never forget it or forgive you for doing it. The benefits, if any, don't outweigh the cost of not being loyal.

Going over Your Boss's Head Also, be careful about going over his or her head (to your boss's boss) because you may be viewed as a betrayer of loyalty and as unethical. Going to complain about your boss can create more problems for you than solutions. Before you do, think, "What are the chances that my boss's boss will take my side against my boss?" It is especially doubtful if you don't have a good relationship with the higher-level manager and your boss does. Going over the boss's head is an issue in the first case at the end of this chapter.

Cooperation Your boss expects you to be cooperative with him or her and with everyone else you must work with. If you cannot get along with others, you can be an embarrassment to your boss. And bosses don't like to be embarrassed. Roger is not cooperative; his boss Ted has told him that if he wants to get ahead, he will have to be a team player.

Initiative Your boss will expect you to know your responsibility and authority and to act without having to be told to do so. Jack Welch says that if you only do what your boss tells you to do, you haven't done enough—overdeliver. Volunteer for assignments.

Information Your boss expects you to keep him or her informed about what your objectives are and how you are progressing. If there are problems, your boss expects you to tell him or her about them. You should not cover up your mistakes, your employees' mistakes, or your boss's mistakes. You can cause your boss embarrassment if he has to learn from others what's going on in his department. Bosses don't like to be surprised.

Openness to Criticism We all make mistakes; part of your boss's job is to help you avoid repeating them. When your boss criticizes you, try not to become defensive and argumentative. Remember that criticism is a means of improving your skills; be open to it even though it hurts. Go back to Chapter 6 and review the guidelines for accepting criticism.

Communication Skills
Refer to CS Question 5.

Regaining Your Boss's Trust If you have done something that makes your boss look bad or in some way hurt your relationship, such as breaking any of the above expectations, you need to earn back his or her trust to reestablish your good working relationship. Your boss can give you poor evaluations and make your life miserable. So *admit shortcomings, apologize,* and state how you will improve. To regain trust, follow the guidelines in Chapter 7.

WORK APPLICATION 9-7

Of the five common expectations of bosses, which is your strongest area? Your weakest area? Explain your answers.

Relations with Subordinates

If the goal of human relations is easy, why are poor human relations common? One reason is the fact that the manager must consider the work to be accomplished as ultimately more important than the needs and desires of those doing the work, including the manager's own needs. Managers get so busy getting the job done that they forget about the needs of the employees doing the work. Employees tend to start a job enthusiastically, but the manager often does not take the time to develop the human relations necessary to maintain that enthusiasm. Think about the best and worst boss you ever had. Chances are the difference was in the relationship you had. As a manager, you must take the time to develop effective human relations.

Developing Manager–Employee Relations In developing manager–employee relations, you should follow the guidelines to human relations throughout this book. The manager should strive for harmonious relations where differences of opinion are encouraged and settled in a peaceful manner. Morale should be kept at high levels, but the manager shouldn't try to please all the people all the time. As a manager, you may face resentment from an employee who resents you for *what* you are (the manager) rather than for *who* you are. Others may not like you for any number of reasons. A manager can have good human relations without being well liked personally or popular. Manager–employee relations should be reciprocal exchanges, so both parties win.[45]

Friendship The relationship between manager and employee cannot be one of real friendship. The nature of supervision excludes true friendship because the manager must evaluate the employee's performance; true friends don't evaluate or judge each other in any formal way. The manager must also give employees directions; friends don't order each other around. The manager must also get the employee to change; friends usually don't try to change each other.

Trying to be friends may cause problems for you, the employee, and the department. Some experts also don't advise being Facebook (or other social media) friends with subordinates. Will your friend try to take advantage of your friendship to get special favors? Will you be able to treat your friend like the other members of the department? The other employees may say you play favorites. They may resent your friend and ostracize him or her. Your friendship could adversely affect department morale.

WORK APPLICATION 9-8

Assume you are hired for or promoted to a management position. Will you develop a relationship with your employees based on friendship? Describe the relationship you plan to develop.

Not being true friends to employees does not mean that managers should not be friendly. If the manager takes an "I'm the boss" attitude, employees may resent him or her and morale problems could result. As in most cases, there are exceptions to the rule. Some managers are friends with employees and are still very effective managers.

WORK APPLICATION 9-9

Does/did your present/past boss use the open-door policy? Explain.

The Open-Door Policy The **open-door policy** *is the practice of being available to employees.* Your management ability is directly proportional to the amount of time your door is open, both literally and figuratively. For effective human relations, you must be available to employees to give them the help they need, when they need it. If employees view the manager as too busy or not willing to help them, poor human relations and low morale can result. An open-door policy does not mean that you must stop everything whenever an employee wants to see you. For nonemergencies the employee should make an appointment. You should prioritize spending time with an employee along with other responsibilities. Managers are also using an *open e-mail policy.*

Communication Skills
Refer to CS Question 6.

Use your power wisely. Remember, your success as a manager depends on your subordinates. If you want employees to meet your expectations, create a win–win situation. Help your subordinates meet their needs while attaining the high performance that will make you a success. When you ask subordinates to do something, answer their unasked question, "What's in it for me?" The Professor Smith–student aide example in the section on reward power is a superior–subordinate win–win situation example.

HORIZONTAL POLITICS

Horizontal politics are your relations with your peers and with members of other departments and organizations. Your peers are the people who are on the same level in the organizational hierarchy as you. Your direct peers also report to your boss. Let's discuss how to develop effective horizontal politics.

Relations with Peers

To be successful, you must cooperate, compete with, and sometimes even criticize your peers.

Cooperating with Peers Your success as an employee is linked to other employees in the organization. If you are cooperative and help them, they should have a positive attitude toward you and be willing to help you meet your objectives. Innovations are created by employees sharing ideas and collaborating.[46] If you don't cooperate with your peers, your boss will know it.

Competing with Peers Even though you are cooperative with your peers, you are still in competition with them. Your boss will compare you with them when evaluating your performance, giving raises, and granting promotions. Like a great athlete, you must learn to be a team player and help your peers be successful, but at the same time, you have to look good as well.

Criticizing Peers Do not go looking for faults in your peers. But if your peers do something they shouldn't, you owe it to them to try to correct the situation or prevent it from recurring. Tactfully and sincerely telling a peer of a shortcoming is often appreciated. Sometimes peers are not aware of the situation. But there are people who don't appreciate criticism or unsolicited advice. Chapter 6 provides details on how to approach peers, and others, to resolve conflicts, and Chapter 5 offers suggestions for giving criticism, including asking if they want feedback that can help them.

Do not go to the boss unless the offense is serious, such as disregarding safety rules, which will endanger the welfare of employees. Unless your own safety is in danger, tell the boss only after discussing the offense with the peer and warning him or her of the

WORK APPLICATION 9-10

Give an example, preferably from an organization for which you work or have worked, of a situation in which you had good human relations with your peers. Describe how you cooperated with, competed with, and/or criticized your peers.

consequences of continuing the behavior. Do not cover for a peer in trouble—you will only make things worse for everyone involved. And don't expect or ask others to cover for you.

Roger violates peer relations. He always has to get his own way. Roger is uncooperative and too competitive; he criticizes coworkers and members of other departments to force them to give him his own way.

Relations with Members of Other Departments

Learning Outcome 9-6

Identify techniques to develop effective human relations with superiors, subordinates, peers, and members of other departments.

As an employee, you will most likely need the help of other departments and organizations to succeed. You will need the human resources department to hire new employees, accounting to approve budgets, purchasing to get materials and supplies, maintenance to keep the department's equipment running efficiently, payroll to approve overtime pay, and so forth.

Some of these departments have procedures you should follow. Develop good human relations through being cooperative and following the guidelines set by the organization. It is also advisable to develop good relations with people in other organizations.

Roger's pulling "the old emergency routine" so many times has resulted in purchasing and maintenance ignoring him. This is an embarrassment for Ted and the department, and it is hurting performance.

WORK APPLICATION 9-11

Give an example, preferably from an organization you work(ed) for, of a situation in which you had good human relations with members of other departments. Describe how your relations affected your performance, the other departments, and the organization as a whole.

Putting It All Together See Exhibit 9.2 for an illustration that puts the concepts of power, politics, and ethics together. Starting in the center, with the goal of human relations, you

EXHIBIT 9.2 | Human Relations Guide to Ethical Decision Making

If you are proud to tell all relevant parties your decision, it is probably ethical.

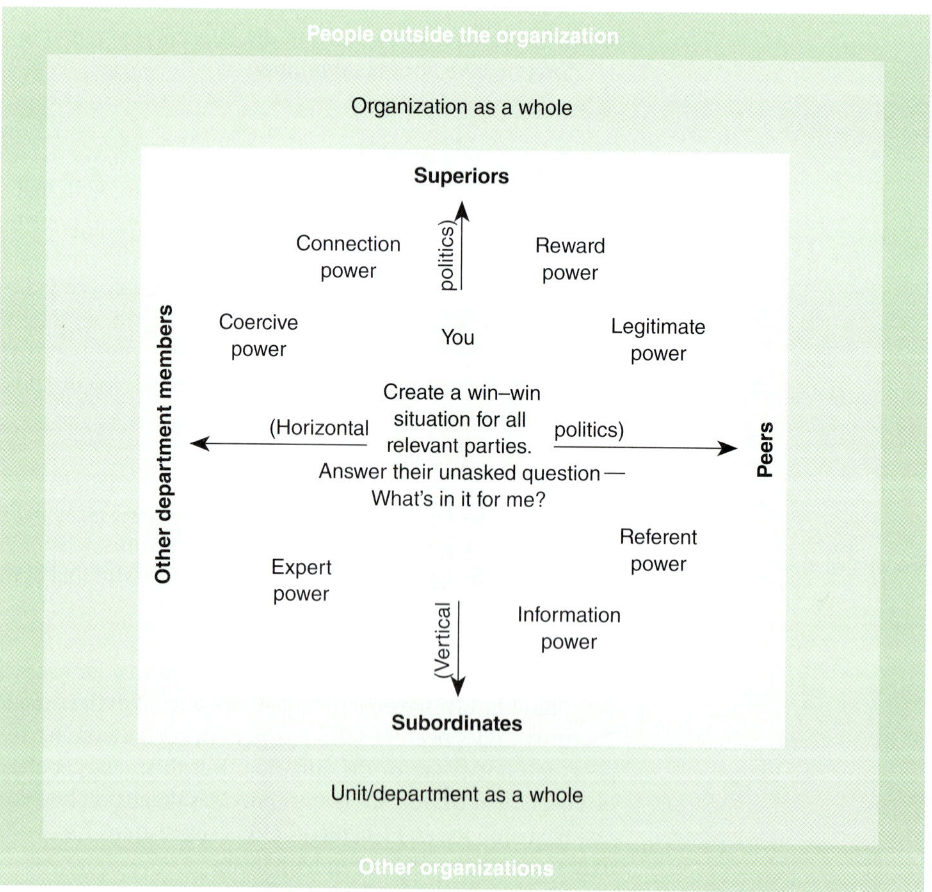

If you are embarrassed to tell all relevant parties your decision or if you keep rationalizing, the decision is probably unethical.

create a win–win situation through horizontal politics with your peers and people in other departments and through vertical politics with your superiors and subordinates. You also use appropriate power with your politics.

APPLICATION SITUATIONS / / /

Relations with Others AS 9-4

Identify the other party being mentioned in each statement.

A. Subordinate B. Superior C. Peers D. Other departments

_______ 16. "As a supervisor, I report to a middle manager named Kim."

_______ 17. "The guys in sales are always trying to rush us to ship the product."

_______ 18. "Abdul is reluctant to accept the task I delegated to him."

_______ 19. "That's the owner of the company."

_______ 20. "The supervisors are getting together for lunch. Will you join us?"

BUSINESS ETIQUETTE

When using power and politics, our behavior should be ethical using proper business etiquette. **Business etiquette,** *often referred to as manners, is the code of behavior expected in work situations.* Many organizations weigh etiquette during the job interview as part of the selection criteria and then for advancement. You may be thinking that it is unfair to judge job candidates by their manners, and you may be right. However, the reality of the business world is that firms do not want employees representing their organization who do not project a favorable image for the organization. Recall that customers, suppliers, and everyone else the organization comes into contact with will judge the organization based on individual behavior. Organizations do not want employees who will embarrass them through rude behavior.

Learning Outcome 9-7

State two classifications of business etiquette and how etiquette overlaps between the two classifications.

Organizations assume that people are taught etiquette at home or that it is learned through experience or observation. However, this is not always the case, and etiquette does change over time, and can be different in various situations. Etiquette skills can be improved and young people today are taking etiquette classes. If you haven't been concerned with business etiquette, start now because it is important.[47] We'll give you some tips in this section regarding in-person, digital, a possible mixture of the two, and customer service etiquette. Follow the human relations guidelines presented throughout this book, especially being ethical and having consideration and respect for "all" others—not engaging in behavior you wouldn't want done to you.

In-Person Etiquette

In this section we discuss in-person etiquette to be used during conversations, while dining, and hoteling.

Conversation Etiquette When you first meet people, especially those at a higher level in the organization, don't assume they want to be called by their first name. Address them with *titles,* such as *Mr.* or *Ms., Dr.,* and so on followed by *last name* unless they tell you to call them by their first name. Use proper business vocabulary, and avoid using obscene language (this goes for digital communication as well). *Profanity* tends to offend some people, but not using such words never seems to offend anyone.

Introducing people using proper etiquette includes presenting the lower-ranking person to the higher-ranking person, stating the higher-ranking person's name first: "Mr. Jones (VP), this is our new sales rep, Carl Jones." When people are of equal rank, mention the older one first. When introducing one employee to a group, present the group to the person: "Carl Jones, these are the other sales reps in our department, Tom Smith, Julio Gonzalis, and Mary Washington." It is also good manners to say a few things about the person being introduced: "Carl is a recent graduate of UNH with a degree in marketing." Recall from Chapter 1 that remembering people's names is important to effective human relations, and the best technique is to say the person's name multiple times during the conversation.

Shaking hands is common business etiquette during introductions. Give a firm, not too strong, handshake with the right hand, and establish eye contact as you greet the person. If the other person extends a fist to your hand, you can change to a fist. Other forms of *touching,* such as hugs, are not common business etiquette but can be very powerful in human relations. The general etiquette is don't touch unless both people feel comfortable with it. When you are not sure but believe he or she is open to touching, wait for the other person to make the first move or make a gesture he or she can take or leave, such as putting out your arms but letting the person come to you to embrace or not.

Dining Etiquette Table manners are important for some jobs because business is sometimes transacted during a meal. In fact, some managers will take the job candidate out to eat and observe etiquette, including table manners. Candidates with poor etiquette are not offered the job, or the business deal. Some of the dining considerations include planning for the meeting, determining seating and who pays the bill (meal, drinks, and the tip), and—of course—using proper table manners. Common etiquette is for the person inviting the other party out to eat to pay the bill. Nina Zagat, co-founder of the Zagat Survey restaurant guide, says: "When ordering food, you are not trying to draw attention to yourself or what you are eating."[48] So avoid food that is messy, such as ribs and lobster. As a general guide, follow the lead of the other person's etiquette. For more details on table manners, see Exhibit 9.3.

EXHIBIT 9.3 | Table Manners

The following are a few simple tips in case you are taken out to eat during the job interview or business meeting. If you get the job and take others out to eat, you are in the interviewer role, even if it's not a job interview. Many of the tips also apply to eating with others during your lunch breaks.

- Don't be starving when you go out to eat. Pigging out is not appropriate behavior and will not make a good impression on the interviewer.
- Do follow the lead of the interviewer; don't take charge.
- Do let the interviewer sit first.
- Do place your napkin on your lap after the interviewer does.
- If the server asks if you want a drink, do wait for the interviewer to respond. Don't ask for alcohol if you are underage.
- Don't order alcohol unless asked if you want a drink by the interviewer. If asked, ask the interviewer if he or she will be having a drink. If the interviewer say yes, have one; if the answer is no, don't have a drink. However, don't have a drink if you will feel its effects. You want to be in top form for the interview questions and discussion, and you want to maintain your proper etiquette.
- Do expect to order an appetizer, main course, and dessert. However, you don't have to order them all, especially if the interviewer does not. For example, if the interviewer asks if you would like an appetizer or a dessert, ask the interviewer if he or she is having one. If the server asks, wait for the interviewer to answer.
- Don't begin to eat any serving until everyone at the table has been served and the interviewer has begun to eat, and pass things around the table to the right.
- Do try to eat at the same pace as the interviewer so that you are not eating each serving much faster or slower than the interviewer.
- Don't talk with food in your mouth. Take small bites to help avoid this problem.
- Don't take the last of anything that you are sharing. It is also polite to leave a little food on your plate, even if you are still hungry.
- Do start using the silverware from the outside in. Follow the interviewer's lead when in doubt.
- Do not offer to pay for part or all of the bill. The general rule is that whoever invites the other out to eat pays the bill, unless otherwise agreed before going to eat.
- Do thank the interviewer for the meal. Also, be polite (say "please" and "thank you") to the server.

Hoteling, Telecommuting, and Cubicle Etiquette *Hoteling* is the sharing of workspace and equipment, such as desks, computers, phones, fax machines, copiers, eating areas, refrigerators, coffee machines, water coolers, and so on. Do follow the general rule to do unto others as you would have them do unto you, such as cleaning up after yourself and making sure the equipment is ready for the next person, paying your fair share of any expenses (coffee, bill for lunch, employee presents), not taking other people's food and drinks without permission (return the favor), respecting others' privacy (don't read or look at things on their desk, computer screen, mail, messages, fax).

Telecommuting is working from off the business premises, usually at home and on the road. Telecommuters usually do at least occasionally go to the work site, so hoteling etiquette applies. Do take advantage of the face-to-face time at work and over the phone, showing enthusiasm for the people and work.

Cubicle etiquette refers to working in an open area close to others who can observe your behavior (see and hear you working and your nonwork activities). Try not to bother others by doing things like talking too loud, displaying things (on walls, desks, computer screens) that can offend others, and doing personal things (letting your cell phone ring, applying makeup, clipping nails). Do dress appropriately (review Chapter 4 for details), and unless it is part of the organizational culture, don't wear hats (like sports baseball caps) indoors.

WORK APPLICATION 9-12

Give a job example of when a coworker behaved with improper in-person etiquette.

Digital Etiquette

As you know, people are communicating more electronically, but don't let screens distract you from your important priorities.[49] Knowing how to use information technology (digital) is important to your career,[50] but you also need to be able to do so with proper business etiquette.[51] So here we discuss using cell phones and texting, e-mail and instant messaging, and telecommuting.

Cell Phone Etiquette The cell (or smart) phone makes it tempting to do personal things while on the job. Business etiquette says not to do personal things in your work area. Because it is a problem, some firms have cell phone rules. So make your personal calls, check Facebook, and surf the Web on your break time and move out of your work area. If you do have a business cell phone, use it only for business, and don't use it (or your personal cell) when you are driving (it is illegal in some states and you greatly increase the chances of getting into an accident). See Exhibit 9.4 for cell phone etiquette, which generally applies to personal or business use.

EXHIBIT 9.4 | Cell Phone Etiquette

- Do speak loudly and clearly enough and speak slowly.
- Do call the person back if you get disconnected; it's the caller's responsibility to call back.
- When you are with others, show sincere interest in them by not constantly looking at your cell phone; place it out of sight and shut it off, or at least put it on vibrate, and don't have a loud, unusual ringtone.
- Don't take a call interrupting a personal conversation, meeting, or other activity unless the message is a true emergency. If you are driving, shut off your cell, or at least pull over to use your cell if it is urgent and you can't wait until getting to your destination (don't check your cell during red lights; they are often too quick and you end up driving while on your cell).
- Don't disrupt others with your cell conversations, such as by talking in meetings and public places (while walking down the street, in a store, restaurant, elevator, or classroom). Do go to a private place, or at least 15 feet away from others.
- Don't eat or drink, talk to others, or talk in the bathroom on your cell phone.
- Don't take multiple calls at one time, keeping people on hold. Do let voice mail take a message and call the person back.
- Do leave a brief message if the person does not answer. But don't use voice mail for bad news, sensitive or confidential information, and complicated information and instructions.
- Do call people back within 24 hours.

EXHIBIT 9.5 | E-Mail Etiquette

- Do use complete sentences that are not filled with acronyms people may not understand.[52] Remember that an e-mail is different from a less formal text/IM, and don't use all CAPS.[53]
- Do keep it short and to the point; the best e-mail replies involve one word—Yes.[54] Remember to let the person know what type of response you want.
- Do proofread your e-mail and spell and grammar check it before sending. Remember that your mistakes are in writing for the world to see, so don't embarrass yourself with poor writing.
- Do use a good but brief description of what the e-mail is about in the subject line.
- Do use the recipient's name in the greeting and sign your name, and be polite (please and thank you).
- Don't send needless e-mails, including CCing others who don't need to know your message.
- Don't send e-mails when you are highly emotional, especially angry, as it is easy to write things you will regret later; 20% of employees have been reprimanded or fired over inappropriate e-mails.[55] So criticize and resolve conflicts in person, when possible; if not, at least be calm.
- Do assume your e-mail will be forwarded, and that it could be read in court. It is generally better not to send confidential information in an e-mail to ensure that it is not forwarded to an unintended person. Hopefully, you will not be doing anything unethical or illegal, or at least not in writing.[56] Also, remember that deleted e-mails can be retrieved.

E-Mail and Texting/Instant Messaging Etiquette Select the most appropriate media to send your messages (Chapter 5), so do use the phone if there will be multiple rounds of responses to save time, and remember that not everyone (especially older people) wants to text. Don't forget the need for human contact through conversation. E-mail should be business formal, with texting and instant messaging (IM) less so. Don't send a text/IM unless it is has immediate job relevance to the person—e-mail instead. See Exhibit 9.5 for e-mail etiquette.

Don't get addicted to constantly checking your phone, e-mail, and text/IM, unless it is required by your job. The typical office employee checks e-mail 50 times and uses instant messaging 77 times. Check at set times throughout the day. And when you have something important to get done, shut off all your digital distractions.[57]

In-Person or Digital Etiquette

WORK APPLICATION 9-13

Give a job example of when a coworker behaved with improper digital etiquette.

In this section we discuss etiquette that can be either in-person or digital: job interviews (by webcam), meetings (via videoconferences), networking (online), presentations (on video and PowerPoint), and dealing with customers (in person or digitally).

Job Interview Etiquette As discussed, the job interview is the major criterion for job selection. Proper dress for in-person and webcam interviews is important (see Chapter 4) to make a good first impression (Chapter 2). The career service department at your college may offer job interview training, and you may be able to use its webcam (commonly Skype) during the actual interview. Take advantage of its services. See Exhibit 9.6 for etiquette do's and don'ts of job interviewing.

Meeting and Presentation Etiquette Do be on time and be properly prepared by having done any assignments. The big issue today is whether or not to use digital technology such as cell phones, laptops, and iPads during *meetings* (including during videoconferences). As a general guide, follow the organizational culture and do as the people running the meeting, above you in rank. However, it is considered poor manners to be talking, texting, or surfing the web while others are talking (this includes presentations); if it's an emergency, take it outside. Even while *videoconferencing*, it's best to dress for business, and don't smoke, eat, or chew gum.[58]

Presentations today commonly use PowerPoint (or Mac Keynote) slides, but don't bore your audience by simply reading the slides to them—talk to them and connect on a

EXHIBIT 9.6 | Job Interviewing Etiquette

In Person and Webcam Interviews

- Do research the organization before the interview so that you can talk intelligently about it.
- Do be sure to get there a little early. Allow plenty of time for traffic and parking. If you are more than 10 minutes early, you can relax and wait before going to the receptionist. For webcams, sign on early enough to start on time.
- Do get the last name and proper pronunciation of the person who will be interviewing you, and greet the interviewer by using her or his last name.
- Don't sit down until the interviewer invites you to sit, and wait for the interviewer to sit first. Not an issue for webcam, just be seated.
- Do be careful of your nonverbal communication (Chapter 5). Sit up straight, leaning a bit forward in the seat, and maintain adequate eye contact to show your interest.
- Do take a little time to think about your answers. Talk clearly and loud enough, while watching your vocabulary to include proper English; avoid street talk or jargon.
- Don't be the first one to bring up salary and benefits.
- Do thank the interviewer for his or her time at the close of the interview.
- Do send a short follow-up, thank-you letter including information discussed during the interview on how you are qualified for the job, or that you thought about after the interview, and send another copy of your resume.
- Do call back if you do not hear whether you got the job by the decision date given by the interviewer, but not before the given date.

Webcam Interviews

In addition to the previous guidelines, here are a few specifically for webcam interviews:

- Do make sure the lighting is even. Don't have a bright light behind you or on the computer to avoid glare and shadows.
- Do try to have the appearance of a professional area. Don't have personal things in view (pets, phone, TV).
- Do turn off all possible distractions (phone, IM, TV, radio) and tell everyone at the interview site to keep the noise down and not to interrupt you during the interview.
- Don't even think about looking at your turned-off phone during the interview.
- Do rehearse to make sure you get the previously mentioned tips right (your college career center may help).

personal level. Lots of companies are making inexpensive videos of presentations, such as product demonstrations, and putting them on YouTube and showing them even during in-person sales calls to ensure professionalism. There are some good iPad applications to help you with presentations: Idea Flight, join.me (allows sharing a presentation with a group of users following along on their iPads), Evernote (allows easily storing and retrieving documents during presentations), and Keynote apps.[59]

Networking Etiquette We've already discussed the importance of political networking; now we cover etiquette during the process. Networking is commonly done both in person and digitally, including Internet Twitter, LinkedIn, and Facebook. In the next chapter, you will learn how to network with manners, but for now remember to be polite and when asking for help, say please; and after getting help, say thank you. Don't ask your boss or people of higher rank to be your Facebook friend, but do so if they ask you. Again, don't do personal social networking on the job.

WORK APPLICATION 9-14

Give a job example of when a coworker behaved with improper meeting, presentation, or networking etiquette.

WORK APPLICATION 9-15

Do an online search on yourself. What were the results?

Online Reputation You need to be concerned about your *online reputation*. You may not think it is fair to be judged at work for your personal life, but remember that companies don't want employees who will embarrass them. Today employers are doing searches before hiring job candidates, and if they find negative information and pictures of you, you may not get the job. If you are employed, be careful about what you post about your employer because people have been fired for providing confidential information and negative comments about their boss and company. So do an online search on yourself, and if you find anything that is not professional, take it down or ask whoever put it there to take it off.

CUSTOMER SATISFACTION AND ETIQUETTE

All organizations provide a good or service or a combination of the two to customers (also called clients, patients, and guests). Therefore, customer service is critical to business success because without customers, you don't have a business. So everyone in the organization should be focusing on customer satisfaction. Although the same human relations skills apply to both employees and customers, dealing with customers is different than dealing with employees. So although customer service etiquette can be in person or digital, we are including it as a separate section of business etiquette. In addition to customer service etiquette, we also provide basic information on customer service. Next we discuss customer satisfaction and etiquette and how to deal with dissatisfied customers.

Customer Satisfaction

The goal of sales is to provide customer satisfaction so that customers will buy your product now and become repeat customers. Customer satisfaction is based on perception (Chapter 2) of the sales and service of the transaction, and perceptions are often more heavily based on emotions than logic—or on how people feel about the experience. So we want to make the experience as pleasant as possible. Satisfied and dissatisfied customers will tell others about their experience, which will result in more or fewer future sales.

Customer Needs and Solving Problems—Listening To provide customer satisfaction, you have to understand what the customers want from your product, or how your product will solve a problem they have. The only way to do this is to listen carefully and ask probing questions to find out. So follow the listening tips from Chapter 5 (listening also refers to written communications in hard copy or digital form).

Attitudes Lead to Behavior The underlying behavior that makes or breaks the customer experience is attitude (Chapter 3). What we think about customers is how we feel, and what we feel is how we behave toward customers. People who enjoy working with customers provide better customer satisfaction. If you don't have a positive attitude toward working directly with customers, jobs dealing directly with customers may not be a good career choice.

Proper Customer Etiquette All of the etiquette tips we discussed so far do in fact refer to customers. So here we add some directly related to customers. You want to develop a welcoming attitude, or service with a smile, not a frown; convey that you care about the customer and want to meet their needs and solve their problems; make the buyer feel good about the sales and service experience as you build effective human relations; and invite the customer back for repeat business.

Improper Customer Etiquette Here we list three major things not to do, followed by what to do to avoid these problems.

Don't Ignore Customers Do you like walking into a business without being acknowledged when you want service? When customers arrive, great them immediately by at least looking at them (eye contact is best) and saying, "I will be with you shortly," and do help them as soon as you can.

Don't Conduct Personal Business While Waiting on Customers Do you like to be kept waiting for service while you can hear the employee talking to a coworker or on a cell phone about personal things, or seeing the employee reading something or working on his or her personal checkbook? Proper etiquette is to give the customer your full undivided attention without nonbusiness distractions.

MODEL 9.1 | Handling Customer Complaints

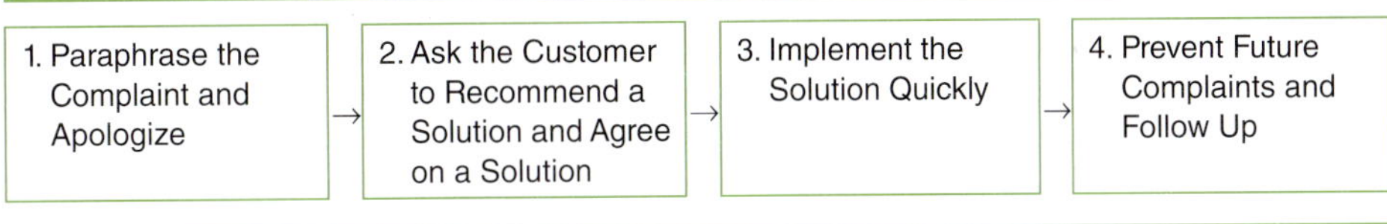

Learning Outcome 9-8

List the steps in the handling customer complaints model.

Don't Use Rude Behavior and Get the Customer Defensive—Do Apologize Even if the customer is being rude to you, don't return the behavior. If you apologize, again even if you didn't do anything wrong, such as by saying "I'm sorry you are not satisfied with the product," it goes a long way to calming an emotional customer. Stay calm and control your behavior; don't raise your voice and verbally abuse customers. Watch your nonverbal communication; don't let your anger show through actions such as giving dirty looks, pointing your finger, or other behavior that will hurt the customer experience.

Dealing with Dissatisfied Customers

Although organizations try hard to satisfy customers, there will be some customers who are dissatisfied for a variety of reasons; mistakes do happen, products don't always meet expectations, some customers make unreasonable requests, and some people have highly disagreeable personalities and like to have something to complain about. If you have to deal with a dissatisfied customer, follow the guidelines. Model 9.1 shows ways to handle customer complaints that will help turn a dissatisfied customer into a satisfied customer.

Step 1: Paraphrase the Complaint and Apologize Realize that you will have to deal with dissatisfied customers and there is a good chance that they will be emotional. So stay calm and deal with emotions (Chapter 5) to calm the customers. Focus on the goal of satisfying them by solving the problem without arguing, because arguing makes them dissatisfied and you lose. Don't get them defensive by blaming them or telling them that they are wrong, and remember the importance of apologizing to calm emotions and retain good human relations.

You can't resolve a complaint unless you clearly understand what the complaint is, so you have to listen carefully (Chapter 5). Repeating the complaint in your own words helps calm the emotional person because he or she realizes that you are listening, and it ensures that you do know what the person is complaining about. When you paraphrase the complaint and apologize, use statements like, "I understand that the problem is . . . , and I'm sorry it happened" or I agree that . . . shouldn't have happened, and I apologize for the inconvenience it has caused you."

Step 2: Ask the Customer to Recommend a Solution and Agree on a Solution If it is routine, like a simple return, ask if the customer would like cash or a store credit, for example. When it is not routine, make statements like, "How would you like us to handle this situation?" or "What can I do to fix this problem?" Often customers have simple solutions that are easy and inexpensive. Letting customers come up with the solution to their problem really turns them around to be satisfied customers.

But asking for a solution doesn't mean you have to do what the customer recommends when it is unreasonable. Realize the customer may be asking for more than he or she expects, hoping to get a good deal (this is negotiation, and you will learn to negotiate in the next chapter). Again, avoid arguing but be firm and calmly repeat the facts that don't justify the customer's solution. Be willing to say no to unreasonable solutions, and state what you are willing to do to resolve the problem. Some customers are not worth keeping anyway.

Step 3: Implement the Solution Quickly The faster the complaint is solved, the happier the customer and the greater the chance of not losing him or her. Let's face it, if your cable is not working and you can't watch TV or go online, do you want a discount coupon, or to have it fixed quickly?

Communication Skills
Refer to CS Question 7.

Step 4: Prevent Future Complaints and Follow Up Take action to make sure the problem doesn't happened again; for example, stop making the same error or stop selling a faulty product. To follow up, you can call or send an e-mail simply asking whether the solution is working. Both prevention and follow-up help satisfy customers and lead to customer retention.

WORK APPLICATION 9-16

Give a job example of when a coworker behaved with improper customer etiquette.

WORK APPLICATION 9-17

Which etiquette tips will you actually use to improve your human relations in your personal and professional lives?

DO POWER, POLITICS, AND ETIQUETTE APPLY GLOBALLY?

If you said no, you are correct. Based on cultural values and history, *power* is perceived and exercised differently around the globe. A method of understanding global differences is called *power distance.* Power distance centers on the extent to which employees feel comfortable interacting across hierarchical levels; In high power distance, employees believe management should have the power and make the decisions, whereas in low power distance, employees want power and want to be involved with management in decision making.

In high power-distance cultures (for example, in Mexico, Venezuela, the Philippines, Yugoslavia, and France), using strong power and politics is acceptable because leaders are expected to behave differently from people in low ranks, and differences in rank are more apparent. In low power-distance cultures (for example, in the United States, Ireland, Australia, New Zealand, Denmark, Israel, and the Netherlands), using strong power and politics is not acceptable because power is expected to be shared with employees through empowerment. In low power-distance cultures, people are less comfortable with differences in power and there is less emphasis on social class distinction and hierarchical rank. Thus, when U.S. companies try to empower their business units in high power-distance cultures, they need to integrate and change the culture within the business unit slowly to be effective.

There still exists a tremendous gap in accepted ethical behavior between the East and West.[60] Like business ethics, proper business *etiquette* in one culture may not be appropriate in another.[61] For example, pointing with the index finger is considered rude in most Asian and Middle Eastern countries. Be aware of possible differences in etiquette, such as gift giving, dining, and drinking alcoholic beverages, as well as when and where to discuss business. When in doubt about whether something is proper etiquette, ask, and if you do offend someone, apologize, stating your ignorance. Also, follow the behavior of the culture, such as bowing back. Other differences in business etiquette have been presented in discussions on global differences in other chapters.

Complete Self-Assessment Exercise 9-3 to determine how your personality affects your use of power and politics.

/// Self-Assessment Exercise 9-3 ///

Your Personality and Power and Politics

If you have a high *surgency* personality, you most likely have a high need for power. Watch your use of coercive power and the use of the autocratic leadership style with subordinates. The way to get power is through politics, so you may be inclined to use political behavior; just make sure you use ethical politics to get what you want. Although you may not be too concerned with what others think of you, watch your use of proper etiquette so that you don't offend others. Being liked does help you gain power. You also need the help of peers and members of other departments, so create win–win situations for all parties. Don't expect your boss to agree with all your ideas. Remember that your relationship with your boss is critical to your advancement. So if you want to advance, do what your boss wants, the way the boss wants it done, no matter how much you disagree.

If you have a high *agreeableness* personality, you most likely have a high need for affiliation. You most likely have a low need for power. However, you may be political to gain relationships. Being concerned about what others think of you, you may be good at etiquette and have good relations with your boss, peers, and others. Watch out for others using power to take advantage of you; be assertive.

If you have a high *conscientious* personality, you most likely have a high need for achievement. You may not care for politics, but you most likely try to gain power to achieve your specific objectives. You most likely use good, rational persuasion; however, you may not be good at reading people and may need to develop this skill to help you get what you want. To maintain a good relationship with your boss, you may need

/// Self-Assessment Exercise 9-3 /// *(continued)*

to make sure what you want to accomplish is what your boss wants you to accomplish. Watch the tendency to seek individual objectives unrelated to those of your peers and others if you want to advance.

How high your *adjustment* is affects how you use power and politics. People low on adjustment (and some can fake it) generally don't use power and politics ethically; they seek to get what they want and to take advantage of others. If you are not high on adjustment personality traits, you may want to stop being self-centered and work on creating win–win situations. You will be surprised at how much more you can get when you give. There is a lot of truth in the adage, "The more you give, the more you receive." Have you ever noticed that the givers are usually happier than the takers? Have you ever done something for someone figuring there is nothing in it for you, only to find out that you got more than you expected?

Your *openness to experience* will have a direct affect on how much power you have. To maintain expert power, you have to keep up with the latest developments in your field. Be the first to get the latest training; volunteer for assignments. Read the appropriate journals to keep up in your field. Go to trade or professional meetings, and network with others outside your organization to stay current. Be a part of the learning organization's quest for continual improvement; try to bring new developments into your department or organization.

Action plan: Based on your personality, what specific things will you do to improve your power, ethical political skills (vertical and horizontal), and etiquette?

____

____

____

____

As we bring this chapter to a close, be aware that what you think is how you feel, and what you feel is how you behave. So if your attitude toward power, politics, and etiquette is positive, you should be better at these skills, which will help you be more successful than if you dislike power and politics and don't want to use proper etiquette. You should understand two sources of power and seven power bases (Exhibit 9.1) and how to increase your power, and be able to better read people and influence them to help you through five influencing tactics. You should realize that power and politics are related, as politics is the process of gaining and using power.

You should be able to use three political behaviors (networking, reciprocity, and coalition building) to get others to help you meet your objectives. You should also be effective in vertical politics (with your boss and subordinates) and horizontal politics (with peers and other departments).

When using power and politics, your behavior should be ethical, using proper business etiquette. Also important is your ability to use proper etiquette in person and digitally, and to satisfy customers and handle dissatisfied customers using Model 9.1. Last, you should realize that how power and politics are used effectively does vary by culture, and that business etiquette varies as well.

/// REVIEW ///

The chapter review is organized to help you master the nine learning outcomes for Chapter 9. First provide your own response to each learning outcome, and then check the summary provided to see how well you understand the material. Next, identify the final statement in each section as either true or false (T/F). Correct each false statement. Answers are given at the end of the chapter.

LO 9-1 State how power, politics, and ethics affect behavior, human relations, and performance.

The use of power and politics is needed in organizations to perform successfully to meet goals. People who use abusive power and politics tend to use unethical behavior and hurt human relations and performance. In the long run, people using ethical power and political behavior with integrity have more positive human relations and outperform people who use unethical behavior.

Power is the ability to influence others to do something they would not otherwise do, and politics is the process of gaining and using power. T F

LO 9-2 Describe seven bases of power.

The seven bases of power are: (1) *coercive power,* which is based on threats and/or punishment to influence compliance; (2) *connection power,* which is based on relationships with influential people; (3) *reward power,* which is based on the ability to influence others with something of value to them; (4) *legitimate power,* which is based on position power; (5) *referent power,* which is based on personal power; (6) *information power,* which is based on information desired by others; and (7) *expert power,* which is based on skill and knowledge.

The bases of position power include coercive, connection, reward, and legitimate; whereas referent, information, and expert power are bases of human relations power. T F

LO 9-3 List techniques to increase your power bases.

Techniques to increase your power bases include: (1) To have *coercive power,* you need to gain and maintain the ability to hire, discipline, and fire employees. (2) To increase your *connection power,* you need to expand your network of contacts with important managers who have power and to get in with the "in crowd." (3) *Reward power* can be gained by evaluating employees' performance and determining their raises and promotions. Using praise can help increase your power. (4) *Legitimate power* can be increased by letting people know the power you do possess, and by working at gaining people's perception that you do have power. (5) To gain *referent power,* you need to develop your relationships with others. Show a sincere interest in others. (6) To increase *information power,* have information flow through you. Know what is going on in the organization. Provide services and information to other departments. Serve on committees; it gives you both information and a chance to increase connection power. (7) To increase your *expert power,* take all the training and educational programs your organization provides. Stay away from routine tasks, in favor of more complex, hard-to-evaluate tasks.

People don't actually have to use power to influence others. T F

LO 9-4 Describe five influencing tactics.

Five influencing tactics include: (1) ingratiation, giving praise; (2) rational persuasion, giving logical arguments with factual evidence; (3) inspirational appeal, arousing people's enthusiasm; (4) personal appeal, focusing on loyalty and friendship; and (5) legitimization, using organizational authority.

Rational persuasion is the most effective influencing tactic. T F

LO 9-5 Discuss the necessity of organizational politics and three political behaviors.

In our economy, money is the medium of exchange; in an organization, politics is the medium of exchange. Political behavior is used to develop relationships that are necessary to get your job done. Three political behaviors that people use include: (1) networking, the process of developing relationship alliances with key people for the purpose of politicking; (2) reciprocity, which involves creating obligations and debts, developing alliances, and using them to accomplish objectives; and (3) coalition building, which involves creating a network of alliances to help you achieve a specific objective.

Power and politics are interrelated, as they are often used together. T F

LO 9-6 Identify techniques to develop effective human relations with superiors, subordinates, peers, and members of other departments.

To develop effective human relations with superiors, meet the common expectations of your boss: be loyal, be cooperative, use initiative, keep your boss informed, and be open to criticism. With subordinates, be friendly, but remember that you cannot be real friends with employees. Use an open-door policy. With peers, be cooperative while competing with them and help them to do an effective job. In your relations with other departments, be cooperative, and follow the requirements they set.

Your relations with your boss and peers are called vertical politics, and your relations with subordinates and other departments are called horizontal politics. T F

LO 9-7 State two classifications of business etiquette and how etiquette overlaps between the two classifications.

Two classifications are in-person (conversation, dining, hoteling, telecommuting, and cubicle etiquette) and digital (cell phone, e-mail, texting, and instant messaging). The two classifications overlap because some business etiquette (job interviewing, attending meetings and giving presentations, and networking) can be done in person and/or digitally.

It is proper etiquette to take personal calls while talking business with coworkers so long as you say excuse me. T F

LO 9-8 List the steps in the handling customer complaints model.

The steps include (1) paraphrase the complaint and apologize; (2) ask the customer to recommend a solution and agree on a solution; (3) implement the solution quickly; and (4) prevent future complaints and follow up.

It is important to know who to blame for the customer complaint. T F

LO 9-9 Define the following 12 key terms.

Select one or more methods: (1) fill in the missing key terms from memory; (2) match the key terms from the end of the review with their definitions below; and/or (3) copy the key terms in order from the key terms at the beginning of the chapter.

____________________ is a person's ability to influence others to do something they would not otherwise do.

The seven bases of power are:

____________________, based on threats and/or punishment to influence compliance.

______________________, based on the user's relationship with influential people.

______________________, based on the user's ability to influence others with something of value to them.

______________________, based on the user's position power.

______________________, based on the user's personal power.

______________________, based on the user's information being desired by others.

______________________, based on the user's skill and knowledge.

______________________, the process of gaining and using power, is an important part of meeting organizational objectives.

______________________ involves creating obligations and debts, developing alliances, and using them to accomplish objectives.

A(n) ______________________ is the practice of being available to employees.

______________________, often referred to as manners, is the code of behavior expected in work situations.

/ / / KEY TERMS / / /

business etiquette 283
coercive power 271
connection power 271
expert power 272
information power 272
legitimate power 272
open-door policy 281
politics 278
power 270
reciprocity 278
referent power 272
reward power 271

/ / / COMMUNICATION SKILLS / / /

The following critical thinking questions can be used for class discussion and/or as written assignments to develop communication skills. Be sure to give complete explanations for all questions.

1. Some people say that power and politics can't be used ethically. Do you agree?
2. Do you agree with the saying, "It's not what you know, it's who you know that is important"? Is it ethical to use connection power to get jobs and other things?
3. When someone tries to influence you, which influencing tactic works best and why? Why doesn't this same tactic work best for everyone?
4. How would you assess your political skill at using networking, reciprocity, and coalition building to help you get what you want? What can you do to improve?
5. Describe your relationship with your current or past boss. Did you meet the five common expectations of bosses? How can you improve your relationship with your current and/or future boss?
6. Describe your relationship with your current peers and members from other departments. How do you cooperate with them, compete with them, and criticize them? How can you improve your relationship with your current peers and members of other departments?
7. Review the list of etiquette tips. Which three tips that you don't use often now might help you in the future? How will you change your etiquette?

CASE / / / Chris Walker: Department of Business

Chris Walker is a tenured professor of business at a small teaching college in the Midwest. The Department of Business (DB) has nine faculty members; it is one of 10 departments in the School of Arts and Sciences (SAS). The business department chair is Judi Jackson, who is in her first year as chair. Six faculty members, including Chris, have been in the department for longer than Judi. She likes to have policies so that faculty members have guides for their behavior. On the collegewide level, there is no policy about the job of graduate assistants. Judi asked the dean of the SAS what the policy was. The dean stated that there is no policy, and he had spoken to the vice president for academic affairs. The vice president and the dean suggested letting the individual departments develop their own policy regarding what graduate assistants can and cannot do. So Judi put "use of graduate assistants" on the department meeting agenda.

During the DB meeting, Judi asked for members' views on what graduate assistants should and should not be allowed to do. Judi was hoping that the department would come to a consensus on a policy. Chris Walker was the only faculty member who was using graduate assistants to grade exams. All but one of the other faculty members spoke out against the use of having graduate assistants grade exams. Other faculty members believed it was the job of the professor to grade the exams. Chris made a few statements in hopes of not having to correct his own exams. He stated that his exams were objective; thus, because there was a correct answer for each item on the exams, it was not necessary for him to personally correct the exams. He also pointed out that across the campus, and across the country, other faculty members were using graduate assistants to teach entire courses and to correct subjective papers and exams. Chris stated that he did not think it would be fair to tell him that he could not use graduate assistants to grade objective exams when others could do so. He also stated that the department did not need to have a policy, and requested that the department not set a policy. However, Judi stated that she wanted a policy. He held a single minority view during the meeting. However, after the meeting, one other member of the department, Ted Brown, who had said nothing during the meeting, told Chris that he agreed that it was not fair to deny him the use of a graduate assistant.

There was no department consensus, as Judi hoped there would be. Judi said that she would draft a department policy, which would be discussed at a future DB meeting. The next day, Chris sent a memo to department members asking if it was ethical and legal to deny him the use of the same resources as others across the campus. He also stated that if the department set a policy stating that he could no longer use graduate assistants to correct objective exams, he would appeal the policy decision to the dean, the vice president, and the president.

Go to the Internet: This case actually did happen. However, the names have been changed for confidentiality. Thus, you cannot go to the college Web site where the case really happened. Therefore, go to your own college Web site and get information that you did not know about your college.

Support your answer to the following questions with specific information from the case and text, or with other information you get from the Web or other sources.

1. What source of power does Judi have, and what type of power is she using during the meeting?

2. (*a*) What source of power does Chris have, and what type of power is he using during the meeting? (*b*) Is the memo a wise political move for Chris? What may be gained/lost by sending it?

3. What would you do if you were Judi? (*a*) Would you talk to the dean, letting him know that Chris said he would appeal the policy decision? (*b*) Which political behavior would that discussion represent? (*c*) Would you draft a policy directly stating that graduate assistants cannot be used to grade objective exams? (*d*) Would your answer to (*c*) be influenced by your answer to (*a*)?

4. If you were Chris, (*a*) knowing you had no verbal supporters during the meeting, would you have continued to defend your position or agreed to stop using a graduate assistant? (*b*) What do you think of Chris's sending the memo? (*c*) As a tenured full professor, Chris is secure in his job. Would your answer change if you had not received tenure or promotion to the top rank?

5. If you were Chris, and Judi drafted a policy and department members agreed with it, what would you do? (*a*) Would you appeal the decision to the dean? (*b*) Again, would your answer change if you had not received tenure or promotion to the top rank?

6. If you were the dean of the SAS, knowing that the vice president does not want to set a collegewide policy, and Chris appealed to you, what would you do? Would you develop a schoolwide policy for the SAS?

7. At what level (collegewide, by schools, or by departments within each school) should a graduate assistant policy be set?

8. (*a*) Should Ted Brown have spoken up in defense of Chris during the meeting? (*b*) If you were Ted, would you have taken Chris's side against the seven other members? (*c*) Would your answer change if you were or were not friends with Chris, and if you were or were not a tenured full professor?

Cumulative Questions

9. What is the role of perception (Chapter 2) and attitudes and values (Chapter 3) in this case?

10. What type of communications (Chapter 5) were used in this case? What was the major barrier to communications?

11. Which conflict management style (Chapter 6) did Judi and Chris use in setting the policy? Which conflict management style would you have used if you were in Chris's situation?

12. Which situational supervisory business style (Chapter 7) was Judi using to set the policy?

13. Which motivation theory (Chapter 8) was Chris using to defend his position to use graduate assistants?

CASE /// Exercise and Role-Play

Preparation: Read the case and think about whether you agree or disagree with using graduate assistants to correct objective exams. If you do this exercise, we recommend that you complete it before discussing the questions and answers to the case.

In-Class Meeting: A person who strongly agrees with Chris Walker's position volunteers to play this role (can be male or female) during a DB meeting. A second person who also agrees with the use of graduate assistants correcting exams plays the role of Ted Brown (can be female). However, recall that Ted cannot say anything during the meeting to support Walker. One person who strongly disagrees with Judi (or Jack) Jackson—who doesn't want graduate assistants to correct exams, and who also feels strongly that there should be a policy stating what graduate assistants can and cannot do—volunteers to play the role of the department chair who runs the DB meeting. Six others who are neutral or disagree with graduate assistants grading exams play the roles of other department members.

The 10 role-players sit in a circle in the center of the room, with the other class members sitting around the outside of the circle. Observers just quietly watch and listen to the meeting discussion.

Role-Play: *(about 15 minutes)* Judi opens the meeting by simply stating that the agenda item is to set a graduate assistants policy stating what they can and cannot do, and that he or she hopes the department can come to a consensus on a policy. Judi states her (or his) position on why graduate students should not be allowed to correct exams, and then asks for other views. Walker and the others, except Ted, jump in anytime with their opinions.

Discussion: After the role-play is over, or when time runs out, the person playing the role of Walker expresses to the class how it felt to have everyone against him (or her). Other department members state how they felt about the discussion, followed by observers' statements as time permits. A discussion of the case questions and answers may follow.

OBJECTIVE CASE /// Politicking

Karen Whitmore is going to be promoted in two months. She will be replaced by one of her subordinates, Jim Green or Lisa Fesco. Both Jim and Lisa know they are competing for the promotion. Their years of experience and quality and quantity of work are about the same. Below is some of the political behavior each used to help get the promotion.

Lisa has been going to night classes and company training programs in management to prepare herself for the promotion. Lisa is very upbeat; she goes out of her way to be nice to people and compliment them. She gets along well with everyone. Knowing that Karen was an officer in a local businesswomen's networking organization, Lisa joined the club six months ago and now serves on a committee. At work Lisa talks regularly to Karen about the women's organization. Lisa makes an effort to know what is going on in the organization. One thing Karen doesn't like about Lisa is the fact that when she points out Lisa's errors, Lisa always has an answer for everything.

Jim is good at sports and has been playing golf and tennis with upper-level managers for over a year now. In the department, especially with Karen, Jim refers to conversations with managers all the time. When Jim does something for someone, he expects that person to do a favor in return. Jim really wants this promotion, but he fears that with more women being promoted to management positions, Lisa will get the job just because she is a woman. To increase his chances of getting the job, Jim stayed late and made a few changes—errors—in the report Lisa was working on. Jim sees nothing wrong with making the changes to get ahead. When Lisa passed in the report, without checking prior work, Karen found the errors. The one thing Karen doesn't like about Jim is the fact that, on occasion, she has to tell him what to do before he acts.

Answer the following questions. Then in the space between the questions, state why you selected that answer.

_______ 1. We know that Karen has _______ power.

a. position *b.* personal

_______ 2. To be promoted, Lisa is stressing _______ power. Refer to the opening statement about Lisa.

a. coercive *c.* reward *e.* referent *g.* expert
b. connection *d.* legitimate *f.* information

_______ 3. To be promoted, Jim is stressing _______ power. Refer to the opening statement about Jim.

a. coercive *c.* reward *e.* referent *g.* expert
b. connection *d.* legitimate *f.* information

_______ 4. _______ appears to use reciprocity the most.

a. Lisa *b.* Jim

_______ 5. Lisa _______ conducted unethical political behavior.

a. has *b.* has not

_______ 6. Jim _______ conducted unethical political behavior.

a. has *b.* has not

_______ 7. Jim has committed _______ behavior in changing the report.

a. Type I *b.* Type II

_______ **8.** Jim's changing the report did *not* affect:

a. supervisors *c.* peers *e.* other departments
b. subordinates *d.* Karen's department *f.* the organization

_______ **9.** Lisa does not meet Karen's expectation of:

a. loyalty *c.* initiative *e.* openness to criticism
b. cooperation *d.* information

_______ **10.** Jim does not meet Karen's expectation of:

a. loyalty *c.* initiative *e.* openness to criticism
b. cooperation *d.* information

11. In Lisa's situation, she suspects Jim made the changes in the report, but she has no proof. What would you do?

12. In Karen's situation, she suspects Jim made the changes in the report, but she has no proof. What would you do?

Note: Meetings between Lisa and Jim, Karen and Jim, or all three may be role-played in class.

/ / / SKILL-BUILDING EXERCISE 9-1 / / /

Who Has the Power?

In-Class Exercise (Group)

Note: This exercise is designed for permanent groups that have worked together at least twice.

Objective: To better understand power and how people gain power.

AACSB: The primary AACSB learning standard skills developed through this exercise are reflective thinking and leadership.

Preparation: You should have read and understood the text chapter.

Experience: Your group will discuss power within the group.

Procedure 1 (5–10 minutes)

Permanent teams get together and decide which member has the most power at this time (greatest ability to influence group members' behavior). Power can change with time. Before discussion, all members select the member they believe has the most power. You may select yourself. Write the most powerful person's name here: ________________.
After everyone has made their selection, each member should state who was selected and explain why. Record the names of those selected below.

Procedure 2 (7–12 minutes)

Come to an agreement on the one person with the most power. Write the group's choice here: ________________.

Was there a struggle for power?

Why is this person the most powerful in the group? To help you answer this question, as a group, answer the following questions about your most powerful person:

1. Which of the 10 human relations guidelines (discussed in Chapter 1) does he or she follow: (1) be optimistic, (2) be positive, (3) be genuinely interested in other people, (4) smile and develop a sense of humor, (5) call people by name, (6) listen to people, (7) help others, (8) think before you act, (9) apologize, and (10) create win–win situations?
2. How does this person project a positive image? What type of image does his or her appearance project? What nonverbal communication does this person project that sends a positive image? What behavior does this person use that gains him or her power?
3. What is the primary source of this person's power (position, personal)?
4. What is the primary base for this person's power in the group (coercive, connection, reward, legitimate, referent, information, expert)?
5. Which political behaviors does this person use (gets along with everyone, makes people feel important and compliments them, compromises and avoids telling people they are wrong)?
6. Does this person use ethical or unethical politics?
7. Does this person cooperate with, compete with, or criticize group members?

Overall, why is this person the most powerful? (Agree and write the reason below.) Share the feeling you experienced doing this exercise. How did you feel about not being, or being, selected as the most powerful group member? Who wanted power and who didn't? Is it wrong or bad to want and seek power?

Optional:

1. A spokesperson from each group tells the class which member was selected as the most powerful, and the overall reason why the person is considered to be the most powerful.
2. A spokesperson from each group does not tell the class which member was selected as the most powerful, but does state the overall reason why the person is considered to be the most powerful.

Conclusion: The instructor leads a class discussion and/or makes concluding remarks.

Application (2–4 minutes): What did I learn from this exercise? How will I use this knowledge in the future?

Sharing: Volunteers give their answers to the application section.

/ / / SKILL-BUILDING EXERCISES 9-2 AND 9-3 / / /

Influencing Tactics

Preparation (individual and Group)

Below are three situations. For each situation, select the most appropriate influencing tactic(s) to use. Write the tactics on the lines following the situations. At this time, don't write out how you would behave (what you would say and do).

1. You are doing a college internship, which is going well. You would like to become a full-time employee a few weeks after you graduate.

Which influencing tactic(s) would you use?

____

Who would you try to influence? How would you do so (behavior)?

____

____

2. You have been working for six months. As you are approaching the elevator, you see a powerful person, one who could potentially help you advance in your career, waiting for the elevator. You have never met her, but you do know that her committee has recently completed a new five-year strategic plan for the company and that she plays

tennis and is active in the same religious organization as you. Although you have only a couple of minutes, you decide to try to develop a connection.

Which influencing tactic(s) would you use?

____

How would you strike up a conversation? What topic(s) would you raise?

____

____

3. You are the manager of the production department. Some of the sales staff has been scheduling delivery dates for your product that your department can't meet. Customers are blaming you for late delivery. This situation is not good for the company, so you decide to talk to the sales staff manager about it over lunch.

Which influencing tactic(s) would you use?

____

How would you handle the situation (behavior)?

____

____

Select one situation that seems real to you, that is, one you can imagine yourself in. Or write in a real-life situation that you can quickly explain to a small group. Now, briefly write out the behavior (what you would do and say) that you would use in the situation to influence the person to do what you want.

Situation # ______ or my situation:

____

____

Influencing tactic(s) to use:

____

Behavior:

____

____

____

____

____

In-Class Exercise

Objective: To develop your persuasion skills by using influencing tactics.

AACSB: The primary AACSB learning standard skills developed through this exercise are analytic skills, leadership, and strategic management.

Preparation: You should understand the five influencing tactics and have completed the preparation.

Experience: You will discuss which influencing tactics are most appropriate for the preparation situations. You may also be given the opportunity to role-play how you would handle the one situation you selected; you will also play the role of the person to be influenced and the observer.

SB 9-2

Procedure 1 (10–20 minutes)

Break up into groups of three, with one or two groups of two if needed. Try not to have in the group two members that selected the same situation; use people who selected their own situation. First, try to agree quickly on which influencing tactics are most appropriate in each situation. Select a spokesperson to give group answers to the class. In preparation for role playing, have each person state the behavior to handle the situation selected. The others give feedback to improve how to handle the situation—by avoiding, changing, and/or adding to the behavior (for example, "I would not say ________; I'd say ________; I'd add ________ to what you have now).

Procedure 2 (5–10 minutes)

SB 9-3

One situation at a time, each group spokesperson tells the class which influencing styles it would use, followed by brief remarks from the instructor. The instructor may also ask people who selected their own situation to tell the class the situation.

Preparation (1–2 minutes)

During the three role-plays, you will be the influencer, influencee, and observer. In preparation, determine who will be the first to role-play the selected situation, who will play the role of the person being influenced, and who will be the observer. Do the same for each of the other two role-plays, giving each person a chance to play all three roles.

Role-play 1 (7–15 minutes)

The influencer role-plays influencing the influencee while the observer takes notes on what was done well and how the influencing could be improved. After the role-play, both the influencee and observer give the influencer feedback for future improvement. Do not start the next role-play until told to do so.

Role-play 2 (7–15 minutes)

The second influencer role-plays influencing the influencee while the observer takes notes on what was done well and how the influencing could be improved. After the role-play, both the influencee and observer give the influencer feedback for future improvement. Do not start the next role-play until told to do so.

Role-play 3 (7–15 minutes)

The third influencer role-plays influencing the influencee while the observer takes notes on what was done well and how the influencing could be improved. After the role-play, both the influencee and observer give the influencer feedback for future improvement.

Conclusion: The instructor may lead a class discussion and/or make concluding remarks.

Application (2–4 minutes): What did I learn from this exercise? How will I use this knowledge in the future?

Sharing: Volunteers give their answers to the application section.

/ / ANSWERS TO TRUE/FALSE QUESTIONS / /

1. T.
2. F. "Human relations" is not a source of power—personal power is the power source.
3. T.
4. F. There is no most effective influencing tactic; it depends on the situation.
5. T.
6. F. Relations with bosses and subordinates are called vertical politics; relations with peers and others are called horizontal politics.
7. F. It is not proper business etiquette to take personal calls during business.
8. F. Placing blame only makes people defensive, so it should be avoided.

CHAPTER 10

Networking and Negotiating

LEARNING OUTCOMES

After completing this chapter, you should be able to:

LO 10-1 List and explain the steps in the networking process.

LO 10-2 Describe what a one-minute self-sell is and what it contains.

LO 10-3 Briefly describe how to conduct a networking interview.

LO 10-4 List and explain the steps in the negotiating process.

LO 10-5 Briefly describe how to plan for negotiations.

LO 10-6 Briefly describe how to bargain.

LO 10-7 Explain the influencing process.

LO 10-8 Define the following 13 key terms (in order of appearance in the chapter):

networking	negotiating
networks	distributive bargaining
networking process	integrative bargaining
one-minute self-sell	negotiating process
networking interview process	negotiating planning
coalition	bargaining
	influencing process

/ / / Toyota started as a family business, and the Toyoda family still has power over the company. Hiroshi Okuda was the first nonfamily member in over 30 years to head Toyota as president. Toyota had become lethargic and overly bureaucratic and had lost market share in Japan to both Mitsubishi and Honda. Hiroshi was not the typical Japanese president, that is, one who would make changes slowly and with consensus.

President Hiroshi Okuda moved quickly and powerfully to change Toyota, going against Japanese cultural traditions to embrace a more global (primarily American) perspective of managing. Even though lifetime employment is common in Japan, Hiroshi replaced almost one-third of the highest-ranking executives. He changed the long-standing Japanese promotion system based on seniority by adding performance as a factor. Some outstanding performers moved up several management levels at one time—a practice unheard of in the history of Toyota.

Hiroshi Okuda turned Toyota around; in a few short years, the company better understood the Japanese customer, and market share and sales were growing. However, it has been speculated that although Hiroshi did a great job, at the same time he offended Toyoda family members. Thus, he was promoted to board chair to keep him out of day-to-day management and then replaced. Today the company is run by family member Akio Toyoda.[1] It was under his leadership that Toyota ran into quality problems. For more information about Toyota and to update the information provided, visit Toyota's Web site at www.toyota.com. / / /

HOW NETWORKING AND NEGOTIATING AFFECT BEHAVIOR, HUMAN RELATIONS, AND PERFORMANCE

Recall that *networking* is a form of political behavior. You can't perform at high levels alone; you need some help and you need to help others through networking reciprocity (Chapter 9).[2] Interpersonal skills are part of initiating, building, and maintaining relationships through networking.[3] Recall that learning organization performance is based on knowledge sharing; it is through networking effort that you gain access to new knowledge.[4] Therefore, networking skills are important to your organization,[5] and to your career success.[6]

WORK APPLICATION 10-1

Explain how networking and/or negotiating have affected behavior, human relations, and performance where you work or have worked.

Negotiation is about coming to an agreement to do something.[7] Negotiation affects the process of work behavior, human relations in resolving conflict and increasing performance, and the advancement of careers.[8] Have you ever noticed that some people consistently get what they want and others don't? A big part of day-to-day success is negotiation skills.[9] Successful organizations, such as Walmart, use their strong bargaining power to keep costs and prices down and profits high.

NETWORKING

Before we get into the details of networking, complete Self-Assessment Exercise 10-1 to determine your networking skill.

/// Self-Assessment Exercise 10-1 ///

Your Networking Skill

Identify each of the 16 statements according to how accurately they describe your behavior. Place the number (1 to 5) on the line before each statement.

Describes me				Does not describe me
5	4	3	2	1

_____ 1. When I take on a task (a new project, a career move, a major purchase), I seek help from people I know and from new contacts.

_____ 2. I view networking as a way to create win–win situations.

_____ 3. I like to meet new people; I can easily strike up a conversation with people I don't know.

_____ 4. I can quickly state two or three of my most important accomplishments.

_____ 5. When I contact businesspeople who can help me (such as with career information), I have goals for the communication.

_____ 6. When I contact businesspeople who can help me, I have a planned, short opening statement.

_____ 7. When I contact businesspeople who can help me, I praise their accomplishments.

_____ 8. When I contact people who can help me, I have a set of questions to ask.

_____ 9. I know contact information for at least 100 people who can potentially help me.

_____ 10. I have a file or database with contact information of people who can help me in my career, and I keep it updated and continue to add new names.

_____ 11. During communications with people who can help me, I ask them for names of others I can contact for more information.

_____ 12. When seeking help from others, I ask how I might help them.

_____ 13. When people help me, I thank them at the time, and for big favors, I write a follow-up thank-you note.

/// Self-Assessment Exercise 10-1 /// *(continued)*

_____ 14. I keep in touch with people who have helped or can potentially help me in my career at least once a year, and I update them on my career progress.

_____ 15. I have regular communications with people in my industry who work for different organizations, such as members of trade or professional organizations.

_____ 16. I attend trade, professional, and career meetings to maintain relationships and to make new contacts.

Add up your score and place it here _____. Then on the continuum below, mark the point that represents your score.

Effective networking 80 - - - - 70 - - - - 60 - - - - 50 - - - - 40 - - - - 30 - - - - 20 - - - - 10 Ineffective networking

If you are a full-time student, you may not score high on networking effectiveness, but that's OK. You can develop networking skills by following the steps and guidelines in this chapter.

Networking is not about asking everyone you know for help.[10] **Networking** *is the ongoing process of building interconnected relationships for the purpose of politicking and socializing.* Networking is about building professional relationships and friendships through effective communications using ethical behavior.[11] **Networks** *are clusters of people joined by a variety of links,*[12] as illustrated in Exhibit 10.1. Your primary connections give you access to their networks, which are secondary connections for you.

Networking is about marketing yourself and thinking of yourself as the CEO of You, Inc.; in other words, *you* are responsible for your career and the exposure of your talents and skills.[13] You will find that a secondary connection (the friend of a friend) is often where you will get the help you need. Whenever you start something—working on a new project, planning a career move, buying a car or a house—use networking.

The Why and Reality of Networking

Why should you network? Because it has benefits,[14] as discussed here. Let's begin to find answers to the questions by stating some of the objectives of networking.

EXHIBIT 10.1 | Networks

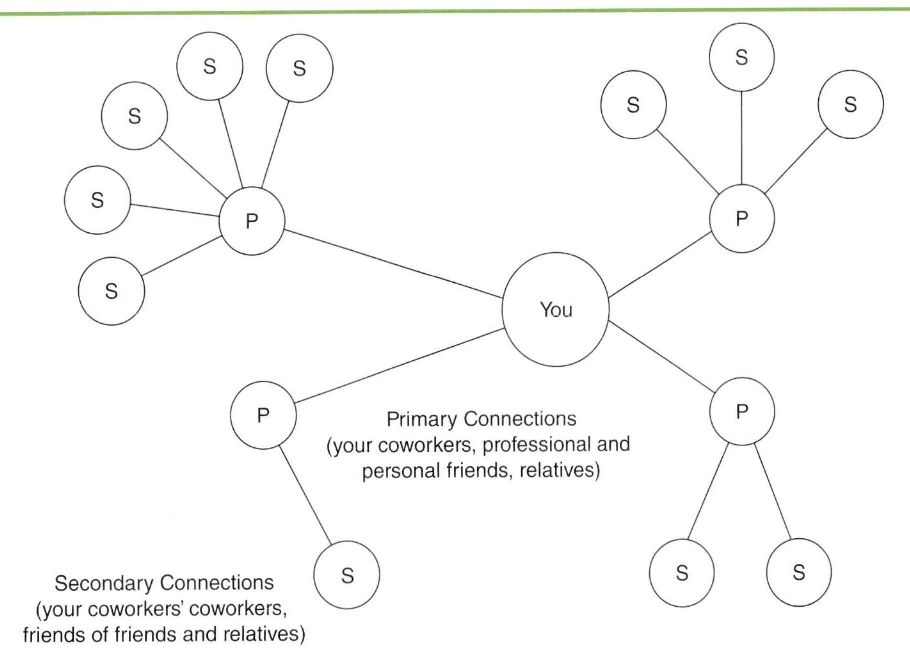

Networking Objectives Here are some of the many reasons to develop your networking skills:

- *To get a job or a better position.* Many jobs being filled today are not posted, and many that are posted are unofficially filled before they are posted. Without networking, you will never know about these job opportunities.[15]
- *To perform better at your current job.* Don't reinvent the wheel; find someone who has "been there and done that" for help. Some jobs, such as sales, require networking to acquire new business.[16]
- *To advance within an organization.* Network to get to know the power players, to gain support and recognition from higher-level managers, and to find a mentor to help you advance.[17]
- *To stay current in your field.* Network through trade and professional organization meetings with people outside your organization to understand the latest developments in your field. You may be able to bring innovations to your organization through expert power.[18]
- *To maintain mobility.* If you think that once you have a job, you don't have to network or stay current in your field, you may be in for a big surprise. If you got laid off today, what would you do? People without a network take much longer to get another job. Think of networking as career insurance—you need it.[19]
- *To develop relationships.* We all want to have both professional and personal friends. Networking is especially important if you take a job in a new location.

Communication Skills
Refer to CS Question 1.

WORK APPLICATION 10-2

Explain how you have used or will use networking to help your career.

It's Not What You Know, It's Who You Know, That's Important To a large extent, this statement is true, but there are exceptions. Here is a general job-related illustration. Sending out resumes and posting them on the Web (Monster.com, Headhunter.net, CareerBuilder.com, and HotJobs.com) are not how most people are getting jobs today. Of the many ways to secure a job, networking is by far the most successful way to discover employment opportunities. According to the U.S. Department of Labor, two-thirds of all jobs are located through word of mouth, informal referrals, relatives, friends, and acquaintances. Networking results in more job opportunities than all the other job search methods combined.[20]

Communication Skills
Refer to CS Question 2.

Learning Outcome 10-1

List and explain the steps in the networking process.

If you get a job through networking, is that fair? Being fair is really not the issue—reality is. You have two choices: complain about how unfair networking is, or develop your networking skills.

Networking sounds easy and we tend to think it should come naturally. However, the reality is that networking is a learned skill that just about everyone struggles with at some time or another. The next five subsections provide a how-to network process that will enhance your career development.[21] The networking process is summarized in Model 10.1. The **networking process** *includes these tasks: (1) perform a self-assessment and set objectives, (2) create a one-minute self-sell, (3) develop a network, (4) conduct networking interviews, and (5) maintain the network.*

Although the same networking process applies to broad career development, as discussed under networking objectives, we'll focus more on the job search.

MODEL 10.1 | The Networking Process

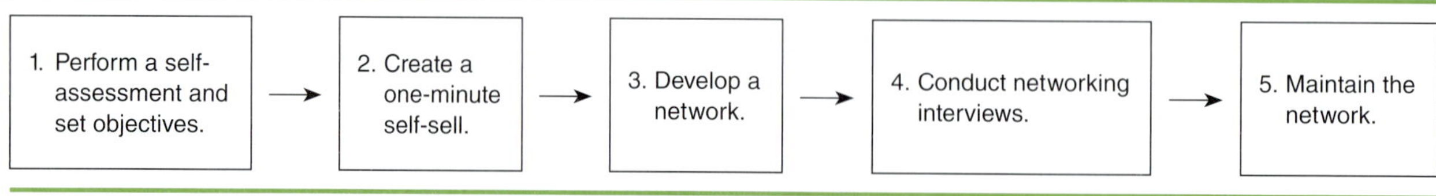

Perform a Self-Assessment and Set Objectives

The task of self-assessment can help clarify your skills, competencies, and knowledge. Self-assessment can also give you insight into your transferable skills and the criteria that are important to you in a new job. If you completed Career Planning Skill-Building Exercise 4-2, you have done a self-assessment. If not, go back to Chapter 4 and do so now.

Accomplishments After completing a self-assessment, you are ready to translate your talents into accomplishments. The results you achieved in your jobs and/or college are the best evidence of your skills. Your future employer knows that your past behavior predicts your future behavior and that if you achieved results in the past, you will likely produce similar results again. Accomplishments are what set you apart and provide evidence of your skills and abilities. You must articulate what you have accomplished in your past in a way that is clear, concise, and compelling. Write down your accomplishments (at least two or three), and include them in your resume. Whether you are looking for a job or not, you should always have an updated resume handy.

Communication Skills
Refer to CS Question 3.

Tying Your Accomplishments to the Job Interview You want to be sure to state those accomplishments that are based on your skills during the job interview. Thus, if you are asked a broad general question, such as, "Tell me about yourself," you can use the accomplishment statements in your resume as your answer.

WORK APPLICATION 10-3

Write a networking objective.

Set Networking Objectives After your self-assessment that focuses on your accomplishments, you need to clearly state your goal,[22] for example, to get a mentor; to determine the expertise, skills, and requirements needed for . . .; to get feedback on my resume and job and/or career preparation for a career move into . . .; to attain a job as . . .; and so on.

Create Your One-Minute Self-Sell

Learning Outcome 10-2

Describe what a one-minute self-sell is and what it contains.

Based on your goal, your next step is to create a one-minute self-sell to help you accomplish your goal. The **one-minute self-sell** *is an opening statement used in networking that quickly summarizes your history and career plan and asks a question.* To take 60 seconds or less, your message must be concise, but it also needs to be clear and compelling. It stimulates conversation by asking your network for help in the area of support, coaching, contacts, knowledge of the industry, and the like.[23]

History Start with a summary of the highlights of your career to date. Include your most recent career and/or school history and a description of the type of work or internship performed and/or the courses you have taken. Be sure to include the industry and type of organization.

Plans Next, state the target career you are seeking, the industry you prefer, and a specific function or role. You can also mention names of organizations you are targeting as well as letting the acquaintance know why you are looking for work.

Question Last, ask a question to encourage two-way communication. The question will vary depending on the contact person and your goal or the reason you are using the one-minute self-sell. Following are some sample questions:

- In what areas might there be opportunities for a person with my experience?
- In what other fields can I use these skills or this degree?
- In what other positions in your organization could my skills be used?
- How does my targeted future career sound to you? Is it a match with my education and skills?
- Do you know of any job openings in my field?

Communication Skills
Refer to CS Question 4.

Write and Practice Your One-Minute Self-Sell Here's a sample self-sell: "Hello, my name is Will Smith. I am a senior at Springfield College, graduating in May with a major in marketing, and I have completed an internship in the marketing department at the Big Y supermarket. I'm seeking a job in sales in the food industry. Can you give me some ideas on the types of sales positions available in the food industry?" Practice delivering your self-sell with family and friends, and get feedback to improve it. Skill-Building Exercise 10-1, Networking Skills, will give you the opportunity to develop and practice a one-minute self-sell.

WORK APPLICATION 10-4

Write a one-minute self-sell to achieve your networking objective from Work Application 10.3.

Develop Your Network

Begin with people you know—your primary contacts. Everyone can create a network list of about 200 people consisting of professional and personal contacts. Address books (paper, Facebook, and e-mail) and phone lists are written network listings. A simple way to start is to set up a separate e-mail or LinkedIn account, the dominant professional networking site.[24] Professional contacts include colleagues (past and present), trade and professional organizations, alumni associations, vendors, suppliers, managers, and mentors. On a personal level, your network includes family, neighbors, friends, religious groups, and personal service providers (doctor, insurance agent, hairstylist, politician).

Ask your primary contacts for secondary contacts with whom you can network. Continually update and add to your list with referrals from others.[25] Your network can get you closer to the decision makers in a hiring position.

Next, expand your list to include people you don't know. Where should you go? Anywhere people gather. Get more involved with professional associations; many have special student memberships and some even have college chapters. If you really want to develop your career reputation, become a leader in your associations, not just a member. Volunteer to be on committees and boards, give presentations, and so on. Other places to go to network with people you don't know include the Chamber of Commerce; college alumni clubs and reunions; civic organizations (Rotary, Lions, Knights of Columbus, Kiwanis, Elks, Moose); trade shows and career fairs; charity, community, and religious groups (Goodwill, American Cancer Society, your local church); and social clubs (exercise, boating, golf, tennis). E-groups and chat rooms are available for all types of interests.

Introduce yourself with your one-minute sell. When you are introduced to people, call them by name two or three times during the conversation. If you think they can help you, don't stop with casual conversation; make an appointment at a later time for a phone conversation, personal meeting, coffee, or lunch. Get their business cards to add to your network list, and give them your card and/or resume when appropriate.[26]

Computer software is available to help you. See Exhibit 10.2 for an example. Of course, you can customize your system to suit your needs.

Conduct Networking Interviews

Set up a networking interview to meet your objective. It may take many interviews to meet a goal, such as the goal of getting a job. An informational interview is a phone call or, preferably, a face-to-face meeting that you initiate to meet objectives, such as to gain information from a contact with hands-on experience in your field of interest. You are the interviewer, so you need to be prepared with specific questions to ask the contact regarding your targeted career or industry.[27]

Ask for a 15- to 20-Minute Meeting Ask for a 15- to 20-minute meeting and many people will talk to you. Such a meeting can be most helpful when you have accessed someone within an organization you'd like to join or have a contact in an industry you are targeting. Be sure not to linger beyond the time you have been offered, unless you are invited to stay. Leave a business card and resume so the person can contact you in case something comes up. If you

EXHIBIT 10.2 | Job Search Network Form

Primary Contact: Bill Smith, fraternity brother
Secondary Contact: John Smith
Smith Brothers Corporation
225 Westwood Street
Anytown, WI 59025
643-986-1182
john_smith@smith.com
Contacts with Person:
6/2/09 Bill called his dad from our fraternity house and I spoke with John and set up an appointment to meet him at his office on 6/5.
6/5/09 Talked for 20 minutes about Smith Brothers and career opportunities. No openings.
6/6/09 Mailed thank-you note for meeting and career info and advice, with copy of business card and resume.
6/18/09 Sent e-mail telling Smith I met with Peter Clark.
Secondary Contacts Received [Make separate page for each.]
Peter Clark, The Ranch Golf Club
Tom Broadhurst, Lobow Mercedes Dealer
Carol Shine, Consultant

are a full-time student or between jobs, you can have professional business cards made up for a relatively low cost. Some college career centers will help you develop business cards and have them printed.

Learning Outcome 10-3

Briefly describe how to conduct a networking interview.

The **networking interview process** *includes these steps: (1) establish rapport—praise and read the person, (2) deliver the one-minute self-sell, (3) ask prepared questions, (4) get additional contacts for your network, (5) ask your contacts how you might help them, and (6) follow up with a thank-you note and status report.* Let's discuss each step.

Establish Rapport—Praise and Read the Person Provide a brief introduction (your name and title—which can be "student at . . . college"), and thank the contact for his or her time. Give the person a copy of your business card and resume. Clearly state the purpose of the meeting. Do some research,[28] and impress the person by stating an accomplishment, such as "I enjoyed your presentation at the CLMA meeting on . . ." As we discussed in Chapter 9, you should read the person and try to match his or her style.

Deliver Your One-Minute Self-Sell Even if the person has already heard it, say it again. This enables you to quickly summarize your background and career direction and start your questions.

Ask Prepared Questions Ask questions.[29] Your questions should vary depending on your objective, the contact, and how the person may be able to help you with your job search. Sample questions include:

- What do you think of my qualifications for this field?
- With your knowledge of the industry, what career opportunities do you see in the future?
- What advice do you have for me as I begin/advance in my career?
- If you were exploring this field, with whom would you talk?

During the interview, if the interviewee mentions anything that could hinder your search, ask how such obstacles could be overcome.

MODEL 10.2 | Networking Interview Process

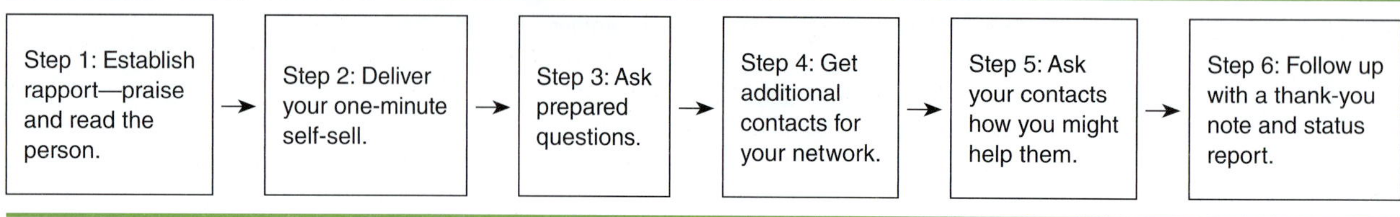

Get Additional Contacts for Your Network The last question above is an example of how to ask for additional contacts. Always ask for names of others you should speak with. Most people can give you three names, so if you are offered only one, ask for others. Add the new contact to your network list. Note that this is done in the job search network form in Exhibit 10.2. When contacting new people, be sure to refer to your primary network person's name as an introduction.

Ask Your Contacts How You Might Help Them Offer a copy of a recent journal article, or any additional information that came up in your conversation. Remember, it's all about building relationships and reciprocity. So do favors for others.[30]

Follow up with a Thank-You Note and Status Report Keeping them posted on your job search progress as well as sending a thank-you note (or e-mail) after the meeting also solidifies the relationship. By sending a thank-you note (or e-mail) with another business card and/or resume and following up with your progress, you are continuing the networking relationship and maintaining a contact for the future. Notice that this is noted in the job search network form in Exhibit 10.2.

It is always helpful to create a log of calls, meetings, and contacts in order to maintain your network as it expands. See Model 10.2 for a review of the networking interview steps.

Maintain Your Network

Keep your network informed of your career progress. If an individual was helpful in finding your new job, be sure to let that person know the outcome. It is also a good idea to notify everyone in your network that you are in a new position and to provide contact information. Networking doesn't stop once you've made a career change. Make a personal commitment to continue networking in order to be in charge of your career development. Continue to update, correct, and add to your network list. Always thank others for their time.

As you have been helped, you should help others. Besides, you will be amazed at how helping others comes back to you. Try to contact everyone on your network list at least once a year.

Coalitions

Like networking, building coalitions is an influencing tactic of political behavior. Recall our discussion of coalitions in Chapter 9, and how to influence others. A **coalition** *is a short-term network used to meet an objective.* Try to get powerful people on your side, and they can help you get other people in your coalition either directly (they can ask others) or indirectly (you can use their name as connection power to get others to join you).

Hiroshi Okuda was good at networking within Toyota and with its family owners. If he hadn't been a good networker, he never would have been the first nonfamily member in over 30 years to head the company. It was through networking that Hiroshi climbed the corporate ladder. A coalition of family members got him promoted to board chair to remove him from day-to-day management.

Digital Networking

Although digital networking is becoming more popular, you should follow the same rules of business etiquette (as discussed in Chapter 9) as you do with in-person networking.[31] Young people are known as the greatest generation of social networkers.[32] You may already be one of the more than 800 million people globally (as of January 2012) with an online Facebook account;[33] that's more than twice the population of the United States. However, if you don't have a professional career–oriented LinkedIn account,[34] you may want to open one to keep your personal and professional friends somewhat separate, although some will be in both groups. Or your LinkedIn account should not just be friends your age; it should include experienced professionals who can help you in your career.

WORK APPLICATION 10-5

Give a job example of how a coalition was used to achieve an objective.

Today, businesses are using social networking Web sites to increase business,[35] and they are using software to monitor what is being said about their company and its products by its customers and employees.[36] Clearly, digital social networks have advantages and perils.[37] Some companies encourage their employees to use social networking on the job while others don't.[38] Some firms claim that personal sharing of information skills can be used to improve workplace collaboration and productivity,[39] whereas others point to studies stating that social networking at work hampers business productivity.[40] The big question that is hard to answer is, "Is it business? Or is it personal?"[41] Many firms have developed digital social networking corporate policies.[42]

Skill-Building Exercise 10-1 develops this skill.

WORK APPLICATION 10-6

What are your strongest and weakest areas of networking? How will you improve your networking skills? Include two or three of the most important tips you learned that you will use.

So how does this relate to you as a student and worker? A study found that the more time young people spend on Facebook, the more likely they are to have weaker study habits and lower grades, as about 25 percent of students check Facebook more than 10 times a day.[43] As a worker, you need to follow the company policy on using digital networking while on the job, and focus on doing business, not on personal socializing with friends at work.

APPLICATION SITUATIONS / / /

Networking Do's and Don'ts AS 10-1

State if you should or should not do each item.

A. Do B. Don't

_______ 1. Start networking with secondary contacts.

_______ 2. Network to know the latest developments in your field.

_______ 3. Network to get help with your current job.

_______ 4. View networking as being unfair.

_______ 5. To keep networking flexible, stay away from having specific goals.

_______ 6. Focus on your weakness during the networking self-assessment.

_______ 7. Develop a self-sell with your history, plans, and question.

_______ 8. During the networking interview, be sure to ask directly for what you want, especially if you are asking for a job.

_______ 9. Ask for a 30-minute networking interview.

_______ 10. Begin the networking interview with your one-minute self-sell.

_______ 11. Be sure to ask for additional contacts during the networking interview; try for three.

_______ 12. When a networking interview is helpful, send a thank-you note and status report.

_______ 13. Contact the people in your network at least once a month.

NEGOTIATING

Like it or not, negotiating is an important skill.[44] In this section, we focus on getting what you want through negotiating. **Negotiating** *is a process in which two or more parties have something the other wants and attempt to come to an exchange agreement.* Negotiation is also called *bargaining.* Networking can lead to negotiating.[45] For example, when you search for a job, you can negotiate the compensation.[46] Sales reps network to negotiate sales.[47]

As with networking, when negotiating, you should be building relationships.[48] Power, influence tactics, and politics can all be used during the negotiation process.[49] In this section, we discuss negotiating and the negotiating process. Before we begin, complete Self-Assessment Exercise 10-2 to determine the behavior you use during negotiating.

Communication Skills
Refer to CS Question 5.

/// Self-Assessment Exercise 10-2 ///

Your Negotiating Skills

Identify each of the 16 statements according to how accurately they describe your behavior. Place the number (1 to 5) on the line before each statement.

Describes me				Does not describe me
5	4	3	2	1

_____ 1. Before I negotiate, if possible, I find out about the person I will negotiate with to determine what she or he wants and would be willing to give up.

_____ 2. Before I negotiate, I set objectives.

_____ 3. When planning my negotiating presentation, I focus on how the other party will benefit.

_____ 4. Before I negotiate, I have a target price I want to pay, a lowest price I will pay, and an opening offer.

_____ 5. Before I negotiate, I think through options and trade-offs in case I don't get my target price.

_____ 6. Before I negotiate, I think of the questions and objections the other party might have, and I prepare answers.

_____ 7. At the beginning of negotiations, I develop rapport and read the person.

_____ 8. I let the other party make the first offer.

_____ 9. I listen to what the other parties are saying and focus on helping them get what they want, rather than focusing on what I want.

_____ 10. I don't give in too quickly to others' offers.

_____ 11. When I compromise and give up something, I ask for something in return.

_____ 12. If the other party tries to postpone the negotiation, I try to create urgency and tell the other party what he or she might lose.

_____ 13. If I want to postpone the negotiation, I don't let the other party pressure me into making a decision.

_____ 14. When I make a deal, I don't second-guess my decision.

_____ 15. If I can't make an agreement, I ask for advice to help me with future negotiations.

_____ 16. During the entire business negotiating process, I'm trying to develop a relationship, not just a one-time deal.

Add up your score and place it here _____. Then on the continuum below, mark the point that represents your score.

Effective negotiating 80 - - - - 70 - - - - 60 - - - - 50 - - - - 40 - - - - 30 - - - - 20 - - - - 10 Ineffective negotiating

If you did not score high on negotiating effectiveness, that's OK. You can develop negotiating skills by following the steps and guidelines in this chapter.

Negotiating Strategies

There are times when negotiations are appropriate, such as management–union collective bargaining, buying and selling goods and services, accepting a new job, getting a raise—all without a fixed price or deal. If there is a set take-it-or-leave-it deal, there is no negotiation. For example, in almost all U.S. retail stores, you either buy the product for the price listed or you don't buy it; you don't negotiate price. However, some individuals and businesses don't simply view routine expenses as nonnegotiable and have negotiated better credit card, cable, and utility rates by asking and negotiating.[50] This works especially well when you have competitors to choose from and threaten to take your business elsewhere. Let's discuss two bargaining strategies.

Distributive Bargaining Strategy **Distributive bargaining** *is negotiating over shares of a fixed pie; it creates a win–lose situation.* It's also called a *zero–sum game* or condition, because any gain you make is at the other party's expense. Every dollar you save on the price is your gain and the seller's loss, or vice versa. So it is more of a win–lose situation than a win–win situation. Parties work out a compromise through give and take.

Communication Skills
Refer to CS Question 6.

Integrative Bargaining Strategy **Integrative bargaining** *is negotiating to give everyone a good deal; it creates a win–win situation.* Let's say you and a friend want to go see a movie. A distributive solution would be to state what movie you want to see and state that you will not go to see any others. Under integrative bargaining, you both list movies you are interested in seeing and find one that you both like. The key is being open to options rather than taking a take-it-or-leave-it approach.

Today the view of distributive bargaining has changed; the fixed pie is considered a mythical fixed pie. Successful firms use integrative strategies to work together to increase the size of the pie for all to share. Steve Jobs was considered to be an excellent negotiator; Microsoft executives were stunned that Jobs was able to negotiate a deal with the music industry to sell songs for a simple 99 cents at the Apple iTunes store.[51]

WORK APPLICATION 10-7

Give a job example of distributive and integrative bargaining.

Learning Outcome 10-4

List and explain the steps in the negotiating process.

The Negotiating Process

The **negotiating process** *has three, and possibly four, steps: (1) planning, (2) bargaining, (3) possibly a postponement, and (4) an agreement or no agreement.* These steps, which are summarized in Model 10.3, are discussed in separate subsections. Like other models in this book, Model 10.3 is meant to give you step-by-step guidelines to follow. However, in applying it to multiple types of negotiations, you may have to make slight adjustments.

MODEL 10.3 | The Negotiating Process

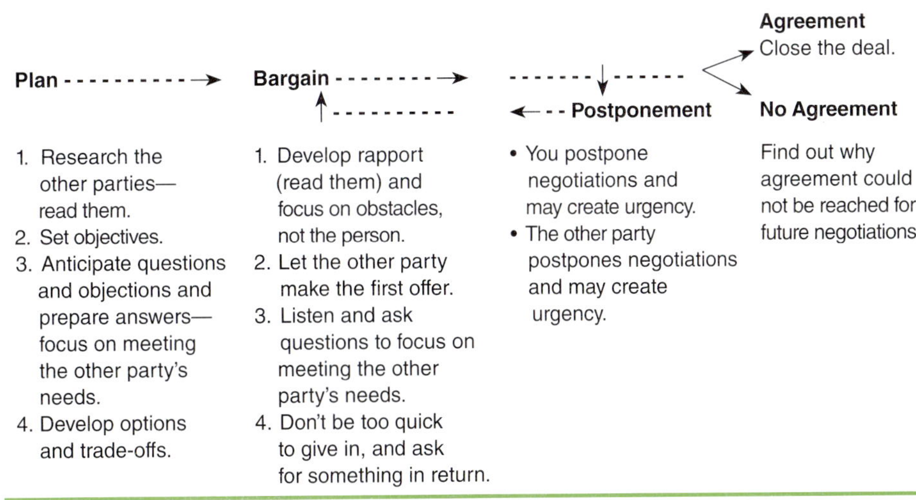

EXHIBIT 10.3 | Sample Negotiating Plan

Negotiating Situation

Job offer from the X Company

1. Research the other parties—read them.

What is the cost of living in the job area? What is the going pay for this job in other organizations? What does this company pay others in this job? What is the job market like? Are there lots of others with my qualifications seeking this job (expert power)? What is the negotiation style of the person who will make me the offer? What can I expect to be offered for compensation?

2. Set objectives.

Based on my research, what is the lowest compensation I will accept? What is my target compensation? What is my opening "asking" compensation, if I make the first offer? What is my best alternative to a negotiated agreement [BATNA]? If I don't get my minimum limit, I'll continue to work part-time/keep my current job/get a job with a temporary agency.

3. Anticipate questions and objections and prepare answers.

I may be asked why I should be paid my target compensation or told that it is too high. If so, I'll say that the competitors pay . . . and your company pays . . . and I have this to offer to earn my compensation. I'll say that I have other possible jobs or that I really need . . . to make it worth moving.

4. Develop options and trade-offs.

If I can't get the pay I want, I'll ask for more days off, more in my retirement account, a nice office, an assistant, or the like.

Learning Outcome 10-5

Briefly describe how to plan for negotiations.

Negotiating Planning

Success or failure in negotiating is often based on preparation.[52] Be clear about what it is you are negotiating over. Is it price, options, delivery time, sales quantity, or all four? **Negotiating planning** *includes researching the other parties, setting objectives, anticipating questions and objections and preparing answers, and developing options and trade-offs.* It is helpful to write out your plan; Exhibit 10.3 is a sample negotiating plan sheet, with a professional job offer compensation. You can use the headings and write in your own plan by answering the types of questions that relate to the situation as shown in Exhibit 10.3 and discussed below.

Step 1: Research the Other Parties—Read Them Researching the other party doesn't mean only the person; it includes the person's situation.[53] For example, if you are buying or selling something, find out about competing brands, quality, prices, and so on. Try to read the other party; follow the guidelines from Chapter 9 before you even meet to negotiate.

Know the key power players. When negotiating with one person, find out to whom that person reports and who really makes the decision. Try to meet with the decision maker to negotiate. Try to find out what the other parties want and what they will and will not be willing to give up *before* you meet to negotiate. Find out their personality traits and negotiation style through networking with people who have negotiated with the person you will negotiate with. The more you know about the other party, the better your chances of reaching an agreement. If possible, establish a personal relationship before the negotiation. If you have worked with the other party, such as your boss or a potential customer, recall what worked and did not work in the past. Figure out how you can use the past experience in your negotiation, such as to get a raise or make a sale.

Step 2: Set Objectives Based on your research, what can you expect? You have to identify the one thing you must come away with. Set limit, target, and opening objectives, and a best alternative to a negotiated agreement (BATNA).

- Set a specific *limit* objective, and be willing to walk away (not come to an agreement) unless you get it. The limit can be considered an upper (most you will pay) or lower (least you will sell for) limit. You need to be willing to walk away from a bad deal.[54]
- Set a *target* objective of what you really want.

- Set an *opening* objective offer that is higher than you expect; you might get it.
- Plan your best alternative to a negotiated agreement (BATNA). Know in advance what you will do if you don't get your limit objective. A BATNA helps you walk away from a bad deal. For example, "If I can't sell my house for my limit by June 10, I'll rent it for six months and then try again." See Exhibit 10.3 for job BATNAs.

Communication Skills
Refer to CS Question 7.

Remember that the other party is probably also setting three objectives with a BATNA. So don't view the opening offer as final. Most successful negotiations result in all parties' reaching an agreement that is between their limit and target objectives. This creates a good deal for all, a win–win situation.

As you know, most people don't come right out and identify their objective range and BATNA. These objectives and alternatives come out through negotiations. We'll discuss objectives again later in this section (see "Agreement or No Agreement").

WORK APPLICATION 10-8

Write negotiating objectives that include limit, target, and opening objectives and a BATNA.

Step 3: Anticipate Questions and Objections and Prepare Answers You need to be prepared to answer the unasked question—"What's in it for me?" Don't focus on what you want, but on how your deal will benefit the other party.[55] Talk in "you" and "we," not "I," terms, unless you are telling others what you will do for them.

There is a good chance that you will be given objections—reasons why the negotiations will not result in an agreement or a sale. Unfortunately, not everyone will come out and directly tell you their real objections. Thus, you need to listen and ask questions to find out what is preventing an agreement.[56] Make things sound positive so that the person believes he or she is getting a good deal.

You need to fully understand your product or deal and project positive self-esteem that shows enthusiasm and confidence. If the other party does not trust you and believes the deal is not a good one, you will not reach an agreement.[57] Thus, during the job selection process, for example, you must convince the manager that you can do the job.

Step 4: Develop Options and Trade-Offs If you have multiple sellers or job offers, you are in a stronger power position to get your target price. It is common practice to quote other offers and to ask if the other party can beat them. Let other parties know what they have to lose. Options should focus on "giving" the other parties what they want while getting what you want so that you all get a good deal.

If you have to give up something, or cannot get exactly what you want, be prepared to ask for something in *return*.[58] When an airline was having financial difficulty, it asked employees to take a pay cut. Rather than simply accept a cut, the union asked for a trade-off and got company stock. If the other party asks for a lower price, ask for a concession, such as a larger-volume sale, or a longer delivery time.

Bargaining

Learning Outcome 10-6

Briefly describe how to bargain.

After you have planned, you are ready to bargain. Face-to-face negotiations are generally preferred because you can see (read) the other person's nonverbal behavior (Chapter 5) and better understand objections. However, telephone and digital written negotiations work too. **Bargaining** *includes (1) developing rapport and focusing on obstacles, not on the person, (2) letting the other party make the first offer, (3) listening and asking questions to focus on meeting the other party's needs, (4) not being too quick to give in, and (5) asking for something in return.* As we go through the bargaining steps, you will realize that you have already planned for each step of bargaining.

Step 1: Develop Rapport (Read the Person) and Focus on Obstacles, Not on the Person Smile and call other parties by name as you greet them. Open with some small talk.[59] Start developing trust and a cooperative relationship.[60] How much time you should wait until you get down to business depends on the other party's style. Some people like to get right down to business, while others want to get to know you before discussing business. So read their style and try to match it.

Focusing on the obstacle, not on the person, means never attacking the other's personality or putting someone down with negative statements, such as, "You are being unfair to ask for such a price cut." If you do so, the other party will become defensive, you may end up arguing, and it will be harder to reach an agreement. Don't make negative comments.[61] Make statements such as, "You think my price is too high?"

People look for four things: inclusion, control, safety, and respect. If people perceive that you are trying to push them into something, threaten them in some way, or belittle them, they will not trust you and may not make the agreement.

Step 2: Let the Other Party Make the First Offer Without setting objectives in preparation for bargaining, how do you know if an offer is any good? With objectives in mind, you have the advantage because if the other party offers you more than your opening and target objective, you can close the agreement. Let's assume you are expecting to be paid $30,000 a year (your target objective), your minimum limit is $27,000, and your opening offer to the employer is $33,000. If the employer offers you $35,000, are you going to say "That's too high; give me $30,000"?

Use the opening offer as a starting point. Remember that the other party probably is starting with an opening offer that can be negotiated up. So start the negotiations from this offer to get to your target objective when you need to. If you are offered $26,000, which is below your limit, you can work the compensation up toward your target. Often, the key to a large raise or beginning salary is bargaining; you must be willing to ask for it and not back down too easily (bargaining step 4), so be persistent.[62]

If the other party seems to be waiting for you to make the first offer, get the other party to make the first offer with questions like these: "What is the salary range?" "What do you expect to pay for such a fine product?"

Try to avoid negotiating simply on price. When others pressure you to make the first offer with a comment like, "Give us your best price, and we'll tell you whether we'll take it," try asking them a question such as, "What do you expect to pay?" or "What is a reasonable price?" When this does not work, say something like, "Our usual [or list] price is . . . However, if you make me a proposal, I'll see what I can do for you."

Communication Skills
Refer to CS Question 8.

If things go well during steps 1 and 2 and you get or exceed your opening offer or target objective, you may skip steps 3 and 4 and go to closing the agreement. If you are not ready to agree, proceed to the next step.

Step 3: Listen and Ask Questions to Focus on Meeting the Other Party's Needs Recall that people want inclusion, control, safety, and respect. When you listen, you give the person all four. So listen with empathy during bargaining, especially when you are in conflict.[63] This is your opportunity to give your prepared answers to the objections while focusing on the other party's needs.

Create opportunities for the other party to disclose reservations and objections. When you speak, you give out information, but when you ask questions and listen, you receive information that will help you overcome the other party's objections.[64] Ask questions like these: "Is the price out of the ballpark?" "Is it fast enough for you?" "Is any feature you wanted missing?" If the objection is something you cannot meet, at least you find out and don't waste time chasing a deal that will not happen.[65]

Steps 4 and 5: Don't Be Too Quick to Give in, and Ask for Something in Return Those who ask for more get more.[66] If you've planned, you have developed options (at least a BATNA) and you have trade-offs ready. After bargaining, you won't have to say, "I should have asked for . . ." Don't simply give up whatever it takes to get the agreement. If your competitive advantage is service and you quickly give in during negotiation for a lower price, you blow all the value in a minute. You want to satisfy the other party without giving up too much during the negotiation. Remember not to go below your limit objective; if that limit is realistic, be prepared to walk away.[67] Having other planned options can help give you bargaining power. If you do walk away, you may be called back, and if not, you may be able to come back for the same deal.

Avoid Desperation and Being Intimidated If others know you are desperate, or just weak, and will accept a low agreement, they will likely take advantage of you. Have you ever seen someone's sign on a product saying, "Must sell, need cash bad"? What type of price do you think such a person gets? You also need to avoid being intimidated by comments such as, in a loud voice, "Are you kidding me? That's too much." Many people will quickly drop the price, but don't be intimidated by such tactics.

Communication Skills
Refer to CS Question 9.

Make the First Concession When you are involved with a complex deal, with trade-offs, be willing to be the first to make a concession. Concessions tend to be reciprocated and to lead to agreements. The other party tends to feel obligated, and then you can come back with a counter trade-off that is larger than the one you gave up.

Postponement

When there doesn't seem to be any progress, it may be wise to postpone the negotiations.

When the Other Party Is Postponing, You May Create Urgency The other party says, "I'll get back to you." Let other parties know what they have to lose. When you are not getting what you want, you may try to create urgency, for example, by saying, "This is on sale and it ends today," "It's our last one," or "They are going fast and it may not be here when you come back." But to create long-term relations, you need to be sure you are giving the other party a good deal.[68] Honesty is the best policy. Establishing a relationship of trust is the necessary first step in closing a deal. If you do have other options, you can use them to create urgency. For example, you might say, "I have another job offer pending; when will you let me know if you want to offer me the job?"

If urgency does not apply or does not work, and the other party says, "I'll think about it," say, "That's a good idea." Then at least review the major features the other party liked about your proposed deal and ask if your offer meets their needs. The other party may decide to come to an agreement. If not, and they don't tell you when they will get back to you, ask, "When can I expect to hear if I got the job?" Try to pin the other party down for a specific time, and tell the person that if you don't hear anything by then, you will call. If you are really interested, follow up with a letter (mail, e-mail, or fax) of thanks for their time and again highlight your features they liked. If you forgot to include any features during the negotiation, add them in the letter.

One thing to remember when the other party resists making the agreement is that the hard sell usually will not work. Take off the pressure. For example, you might say to a boss, "Why don't we think about it and discuss it some more later?"

You also need to learn to read between the lines, watching for nonverbal communications, especially when working with people from different cultures. Some people will not come right out and tell you "no deal."

When You Want to Postpone, the Other Party May Create Urgency If you are not satisfied with the deal, or want to shop around, tell the other party you want to think about it. You may also need to check with your boss, or someone else, which simply may be for advice, before you can finalize the deal. If the other party is creating urgency, be sure it really is urgent. In any case, you may get the same deal at a later date; don't be pressured into making a deal you are not satisfied with or may regret later. If you do want to postpone, give the other party a specific time that you will get back to them, and then do so—whether it is with more prepared negotiations or to simply say you cannot make an agreement.

Agreement or No Agreement

Agreement You may sometimes get your opening offer, or better, if the other party offers more before you open with an offer. If your target and the other party's target are the same, you could both get that target and have a great deal. So when you get your opening offer and both parties get their target objective, there is no real bargaining compromise.

EXHIBIT 10.4 | The Bargaining Range

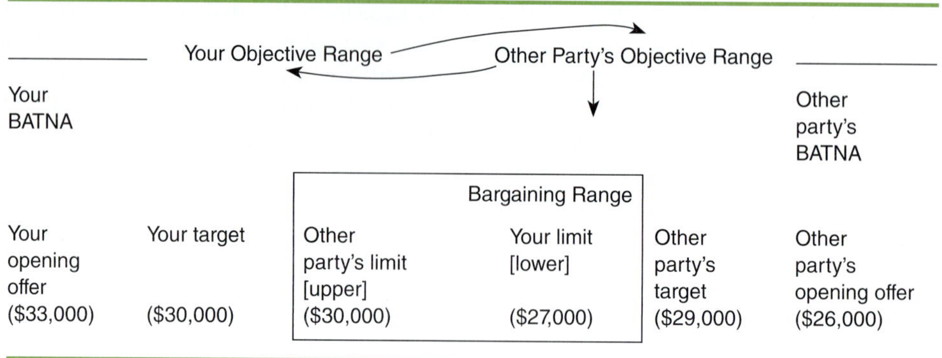

However, it is common for targets to be in opposition. The *bargaining range* is the range between your limit and the other party's limit, which falls between each party's target and limit. Within that range, there is a good deal for both parties. See Exhibit 10.4 for an illustration of the bargaining range; we continue the job example from page 314, using its objectives. Note that the negotiated pay will most likely be between $27,000 and $30,000. In reality, most people don't tell the other parties their objectives and settle between those objectives; it just happens through bargaining.

Once the agreement has been made, restate it and/or put it in writing when appropriate. It is common to follow up an agreement with a letter of thanks and a restatement of the agreement to ensure the other parties have not changed their minds as to what they agreed to.

After the deal is made, stop selling it. Change the subject to a personal one and/or leave, depending on the other person's preferred negotiation style. If the other person wants to work on the relationship, stick around; if not, leave.

Avoid the so-called *winner's curse.* Be happy that you got a good deal. Don't start second-guessing your decision. Don't ask yourself, "Could I have bought (or sold) it for less (or more) than I did?" After you make the deal, it's usually too late to change anything, so why worry about it? By planning (researching the negotiation and setting effective objectives), you can reduce your chances of experiencing the winner's curse and be more confident that you did get a good deal.

No Agreement Rejection, refusal, and failure happen to us all, even the superstars. The difference between the also-rans and the superstars lies in how they respond to the failure. The successful people keep trying and learn from their mistakes and continue to work hard; failures usually don't persevere. Remember that success is the ability to go from failure to failure without losing your enthusiasm, and happiness is nothing more than a poor memory for the bad things (failures) that happen to us.

If you cannot come to an agreement, analyze the situation and try to determine where you went wrong so you can improve in the future. You may also ask the other party for advice. For instance, you could say, "I realize I did not get the job, but thanks for your time. Can you offer me any ideas for improving my resume or my interview skills? Do you have any other ideas to help me get a job in this field?"

Skill-Building Exercises 10-2 develops this skill.

WORK APPLICATION 10-9

What are your strongest and weakest areas of negotiating? How will you improve your negotiating skills? Include two or three of the most important tips you learned that you will use.

Former Toyota chair Hiroshi Okuda was viewed as a tough negotiator who used his power to get what he wanted. He had to negotiate to become president and to take the position of chair. Toyota is also known to be a tough company to negotiate with. It negotiates with hundreds of suppliers to provide top quality at low prices. At the same time, Toyota uses its network and develops long-term relationships with its suppliers. It is agreed that Hiroshi Okuda was a successful businessperson. However, you don't have to try to be like he or anyone else. You need to be you,[69] and to be the best that you can be. Skill Building Exercise 10-2 gives you the opportunity to develop your negotiating skills.

APPLICATION SITUATIONS / / /

Negotiating Do's and Don'ts AS 10-2

State if you should or should not do each item.

A. Do B. Don't

_______ 14. Strive to develop distributive bargaining.

_______ 15. Make sure you get the best deal.

_______ 16. Research the other parties before you meet with them.

_______ 17. Set one objective.

_______ 18. Keep your focus on helping the other person meet his or her objective.

_______ 19. Get down to business quickly.

_______ 20. Make the first offer.

_______ 21. Present a take-it-or-leave-it offer.

_______ 22. Spend most of your negotiating time telling the other parties how great a deal they are getting.

_______ 23. Don't be too quick to give in, and ask for something in return.

_______ 24. Try to postpone bargaining.

_______ 25. If you can't come to an agreement, ask for suggestions that can help you in future negotiations.

DO NETWORKING AND NEGOTIATING APPLY GLOBALLY?

The Internet makes networking even easier. You can communicate with people from all over the world through LinkedIn, Facebook, Twitter, and e-mail and by joining online lists, chat rooms, blogs, and Web boards. As an alternative to traveling around the world, you can negotiate online too. So get online and do some cyber-schmoozing.

Yes there are cultural differences in networking, and you need to appreciate and embrace the host culture.[70] Networking is part of politicking and socializing, which we discussed in the last chapter, so we'll keep it brief here. The need to *network* to develop relationships to get business does vary culturally. We'll discuss networking within the context of negotiating.

With increased globalization, there is an increase in cross-cultural *negotiating*. There is strong support for the existence of negotiating style differences among national cultures.[71] For example, the Israelis like to argue, so a heated emotional negotiation (even yelling) is common behavior, but that is not the case for the Japanese. The amount of time you need to spend researching the other party and the type of information you will need will vary based on the culture, but in general, you need to spend more time when you don't know the customs, practices, and expectations of a particular culture.

There are many implications for negotiating globally. Throughout this section, we refer to classic studies comparing cultural differences regarding the following issues:[72]

- *Time to reach an agreement and deadlines.* The French like conflict and tend to take a long time in negotiating agreements, and they are not too concerned about being liked by the other parties. The Chinese like to drag out negotiations. Americans are different in that they are known globally to be impatient and eager for quick agreement, and they want to be liked. So good negotiators often drag out the negotiations with Americans and make relationships conditional on the final settlement.

- *The focus on task versus relationship.* In Japan and many South American countries, without a relationship there will be no task accomplishment of an agreement, or the task will be to develop the relationship. Like the Japanese, the Chinese tie close networking relationships and negotiating together in conducting business, and gift giving is expected.
- *The use of power and influencing tactics* (plus concessions with reciprocity). The power base to use also varies, based on the power distance of the culture. Influencing tactics (Chapter 9) used during negotiating also vary across cultures. To counter arguments or obstacles to closing the deal, Americans tend to use the rational persuasion tactic, using logical arguments with facts and figures. Arabs tend to use the inspirational tactic, using emotional appeal with feelings. Russians tend to assert their ideas with power, more than with influencing tactics. Concessions are made and reciprocated by both Americans and Arabs, but not often by Russians, because they view concessions as a sign of weakness.
- *Communications—both verbal and nonverbal.* In some cultures (the United States, Germany, England, Switzerland) negotiators use direct verbal messages, whereas in other cultures (Japan, China, Egypt, France, and Saudi Arabia) they rely more on nonverbal communications, so you have to read between the lines.
- *Where the negotiations should take place and the use of alcohol.* These are important considerations. You should know the proper place and when (time of day can vary) to talk business. For example, the CEO of Saber Enterprises says that when Japanese executives come to the United States and when American executives go to Japan, it is almost expected that you will go out to dinner and have several drinks and some sake while talking business. But you certainly don't want to offer and order a drink with a Mormon client.
- *Name, rank or title, dress, greetings, and rituals.* Note that these issues also apply to same-culture negotiations. During your research or, when with the other party, find out how the person prefers to be addressed (is it Christine/Chris, Ms. Smith, President Smith?). Also find out what he or she will wear (a suit, a casual outfit). Note that special or sacred articles may be worn. Know if there are certain greetings (such as bowing) or rituals (such as praying before eating) that you may be expected to participate in.

THE INFLUENCING PROCESS

Learning Outcome 10-7

Explain the influencing process.

Recall that Part 3 of this book is titled Leadership Skills: Influencing Others. In Chapters 7 through 9 and in this chapter, we have covered many factors that can help you influence others to get what you want by developing trust and motivating others with power, influencing tactics, politics, networking, and negotiating. We have focused on getting what we want by being ethical and giving others what they want; thus, we meet the goal of human relations by creating a win–win situation for all parties. Here, we put all the influencing concepts together and create the influencing process.

Review of Influencing Key Terms Let's begin by reviewing definitions. *Leadership* is the process of influencing employees to work toward the achievement of objectives. So leadership is about getting people to do what the organization wants. *Motivation* is the internal process leading to behavior to satisfy needs. *Power* is a person's ability to influence others to do something they would not otherwise do. *Politics* is the process of getting and using power. *Networking* is the ongoing process of building interconnected relationships for the purpose of politicking and socializing. *Negotiating* is a process in which two or more parties have something the other wants and attempt to come to an exchange agreement. *Trust* is the positive expectation that another will not take advantage of you.

EXHIBIT 10.5 | The Influencing Process

Motivation	Behavior	Human Relations	Performance
You begin with a need or something you want, so you set an objective. You need to motivate others to get them to help you meet the objective.	You use power, politics, and networking to motivate others to help you meet the objective. When others have something you want and you have something they want, you negotiate so you both can meet your objectives.	Effective human relations are based on good intrapersonal and interpersonal skills (Chapters 1 to 6) and on using ethical behavior to develop trust.	Using good human relations based on trust leads to a win–win situation for all parties, which results in meeting the objective.

The Influencing Process The **influencing process** *begins with an objective; ethical leadership, power, politics, etiquette, networking, and negotiating are used to motivate others to help reach the objective; and through trust and creating a win–win situation for all parties, the objective is met.* See Exhibit 10.5 for an illustration of this influencing process, which shows the interrelationships among our influencing key terms.

We can view leadership skills from the personal level within and outside organizations as they relate to your behavior, human relations, and performance. You begin with a need or something you want, so you set an objective. (Referring to "setting an objective" rather than to "getting what you want" is using politically correct language; after all, we don't want to appear selfish or to offend anyone.) Often, you need other people to help you get what you want, so you have to motivate them to help you. You use power, politics, and networking behavior to get others to help you meet your objective, and you, in turn, do favors for others in your network. When others have something you want and you have something they want, you negotiate so you both meet your objectives—creating a win–win situation. But to get people to help you, you need to develop trust by using ethical behavior to get what you want.

Communication Skills
Refer to CS Question 10.

Let's discussing how your personality affects your networking and negotiating style, in Self-Assessment Exercise 10-3.

/// Self-Assessment Exercise 10-3 ///

Your Personality and Networking and Negotiating

You should realize that personality can be used more accurately to predict networking behavior than negotiating style. This is why in bargaining, you should focus on obstacles, not on the person. When you research the other party, you do so to find out negotiating style, not personality. Thus, in this exercise, when we discuss negotiating and how it may affect your behavior, the generalities noted may not be accurate in all cases. But keep in mind that there are always exceptions to the generalities presented regarding personality and behavior.

If you have a high *surgency* personality, you most likely have a high need for power and try to network with people who can help you. Remember, however, that even people who you don't think can help you might be the key to something you want down the road. So network with people of all levels. Often the secretary to an important person can get the key person to help you. Watch your use of coercive power during negotiations. Remember that being the first to make a concession usually results in the other person's reciprocating. At that point you can come back with a counter trade-off that is larger than the one you gave up.

If you have a high *agreeableness* personality, you most likely have a high need for affiliation and you enjoy networking at all levels to gain relationships. Watch out for others who might use power during negotiating to take advantage of you. Be assertive, don't give in too easily, and ask for something in return.

If you have a high *conscientious* personality, you most likely have a high need for achievement and don't care too much about having a large network. But you enjoy reciprocity with friends. You may need to work on developing your networking skills, such as making small talk and meeting new people. You probably develop good rational reasons to get what you want in negotiations, but remember to read the other

(continued)

// Self-Assessment Exercise 10-3 /// (*continued*)

parties and focus on giving them what they want so that you get what you want.

How high your *adjustment* is affects how you network and negotiate. People low on adjustment, generally don't use networking and negotiating ethically; they seek to get what they want and to take advantage of others through distributive bargaining. If you are not high on adjustment personality traits, you may want to stop being self-centered and work on creating win–win situations. You will be surprised at how much more you can receive in your network when you learn to give in return. There is truth in the adage, "The more you give, the more you receive." Have you ever done something for someone figuring there was nothing in it for you, only to find out that you got more than you expected?

Your *openness to experience* will have a direct effect on your networking skills. People who are open to new experiences are generally outgoing and enjoy meeting new people. Introverts tend not to enjoy meeting new people and thus are not good at networking, so they may need to work harder at it than others. Openness often leads to compromise and integrative bargaining, which is needed in negotiating successfully.

Action plan: Based on your personality, what specific things will you do to improve your networking and negotiating skills?

____

____

____

____

As we bring this chapter to a close, you should understand the importance of networking and negotiating and be able to network using Model 10.1, the networking process, including interviewing with Model 10.2. You should also be able to negotiate using Model 10.3, the negotiating process.

Where We've Been and Where We are Going To sum up Parts 2 and 3, Chapters 5 through 10, interpersonal and leadership skills are all about how you interact with people and your relationships in your personal and professional lives. It's *not* about what you know or technical skills; it's about how you behave (what you say and do) in teams and organizations, which is the topic of Part 4, Leadership Skills: Team and Organizational Behavior, Human Relations, and Performance.

/// REVIEW ///

The chapter review is organized to help you master the 8 learning outcomes for Chapter 10. First provide your own response to each learning outcome, and then check the summary provided to see how well you understand the material. Next, identify the final statement in each section as either true or false (T/F). Correct each false statement. Answers are given at the end of the chapter.

LO 10-1 List and explain the steps in the networking process.

The first step in the networking process is to perform a self-assessment to determine your accomplishments and to set objectives. Second, create a one-minute self-sell that quickly summarizes your history and career plan and asks a question. Next, develop a written network list. Fourth, conduct networking interviews to meet your objective. Finally, maintain your network for meeting future objectives.

People in the workforce use networking primarily to get a job. T F

LO 10-2 Describe what a one-minute self-sell is and what it contains.

The one-minute self-sell is an opening statement used in networking to begin developing a relationship with another person. It briefly summarizes one's career/educational history, states one's career plans, and asks a question.

A good one-minute self-sell question to ask is, "Can you give me a job?" T F

LO 10-3 Briefly describe how to conduct a networking interview.

The steps for conducting a networking interview are as follows: (1) establish rapport—praise and read the person; (2) deliver the one-minute self-sell; (3) ask prepared questions; (4) get additional contacts for your network; (5) ask your contacts how you might help them; and (6) follow up with a thank-you note and status report.

When establishing rapport, it is a good idea to praise the person and to "read" the person. T F

LO 10-4 List and explain the steps in the negotiating process.
The negotiating process has three, and possibly four, steps: (1) planning, (2) bargaining, (3) possibly a postponement, and (4) an agreement or no agreement.

The best negotiating strategy to use is distributive bargaining. T F

LO 10-5 Briefly describe how to plan for negotiations.
Negotiating planning includes: (1) researching the other parties, (2) setting objectives, (3) anticipating questions and objections and preparing answers, and (4) developing options and trade-offs.

Planning for the negotiation should include three objectives: a limit, a target, and an opening objective. T F

LO 10-6 Briefly describe how to bargain.
Steps for bargaining include: (1) develop rapport and focus on obstacles, not the person; (2) let the other party make the first offer; (3) listen and ask questions to focus on meeting the other party's needs; (4) don't be too quick to give in; and (5) ask for something in return.

If you don't get your limit objective, you should not come to an agreement. T F

LO 10-7 Explain the influencing process.
The influencing process begins with an objective. To achieve it, ethical leadership, power, politics, networking, and negotiating are used to motivate others to help reach the objective. Through trust and creating a win–win situation for all parties, the objective is met.

If people actually followed the influencing process—were ethical and tried to meet the goal of human relations—performance in organizations would increase. T F

LO 10-8 Define the following 13 key terms.
Select one or more methods: (1) Fill in the missing key terms from memory; (2) match the key terms from the end of the review with their definitions below; and/or (3) copy the key terms in order from the key terms at the beginning of the chapter.

________________________ is the ongoing process of building interconnected relationships for the purpose of politicking and socializing.

________________________ are clusters of people joined by a variety of links.

The ________________________ includes these tasks: perform a self-assessment and set objectives, create a one-minute self-sell, develop a network, conduct networking interviews, and maintain the network.

The ________________________ is an opening statement used in networking that quickly summarizes your history and career plan and asks a question.

The ________________________ includes these steps: establish rapport—praise and read the person; deliver your one-minute self-sell; ask prepared questions; get additional contacts for your network; ask your contacts how you might help them; and follow up with a thank-you note and status report.

A(n) ________________________ is a short-term network used to meet an objective.

________________________ is a process in which two or more parties have something the other wants and attempt to come to an exchange agreement.

________________________ is negotiating over shares of a fixed pie; it creates a win–lose situation.

________________________ is negotiating to give everyone a good deal; it creates a win–win situation.

The ________________________ has three, and possibly four, steps: (1) planning, (2) bargaining, (3) possibly a postponement, and (4) an agreement or no agreement.

________________________ includes researching the other parties, setting objectives, anticipating questions and objections and preparing answers, and developing options and trade-offs.

________________________ includes developing rapport and focusing on obstacles, not on the person; letting the other party make the first offer; listening and asking questions to focus on meeting the other party's needs; and not being too quick to give in, and asking for something in return.

The ________________________ begins with an objective. Ethical leadership, power, politics, networking, and negotiating are used to motivate others to help reach the objective. Through trust and creating a win–win situation for all parties, the objective is met.

/ / / KEY TERMS / / /

/ / / COMMUNICATION SKILLS / / /

The following critical thinking questions can be used for class discussion and/or as written assignments to develop communication skills. Be sure to give complete explanations for all questions.

1. This chapter lists six networking objectives (see page 304). For which of these reasons (or for what other reasons) do you have to network?
2. You have heard the expression, "It's not what you know, it's who you know, that's important." Do you agree? If it is true, is it fair?
3. The first step of the networking process is to perform a self-assessment. What are your three most important accomplishments?
4. If you didn't write out a one-minute self-sell for Work Application (10-4), do so now.
5. College students are poor at negotiating. Do you agree with this statement?
6. The text states that the distributive bargaining strategy of fighting over a fixed pie is being replaced by the integrative bargaining strategy, in which the size of the pie is increased, for all to share. Give examples of negotiation situations in which a seemingly fixed pie can be increased and shared.
7. The next time you negotiate, will you actually set three—limit, target, and opening—objectives? Why or why not?
8. In bargaining, does it really matter who makes the first offer?
9. Think of a past, present, or future negotiation situation. Describe the situation and state what you can ask for in return if you don't get your target.
10. Can the influencing process really be conducted ethically and in a way that meets the goal of human relations, or is it just manipulation?

CASE / / / Deborah Kolb and Carol Frohlinger: Cofounders of Negotiating Women, Inc.

Most people fail to recognize the importance of networking and negotiating to their career success. People who are good at networking tend to form better human relations with key individuals who can help them in advancing their professional careers. People who are good at negotiating have a better chance of getting what they truly desire. One's ability to negotiate affects his or her compensation in the workplace.

Negotiating Women, Inc. is a consulting company that focuses on women exclusively by providing negotiation and leadership training for them. The company specializes in live negotiation training, online e-learning courses, and consulting services designed to help women at every stage of their careers claim their value and create conditions for success. Frohlinger and Kolb are cofounders of Negotiating Women, Inc. Both women are successful leaders and scholars in their own right. Frohlinger is a lawyer, negotiation expert, cofounder of Negotiating Women, Inc., and coauthor of *Her Place at the Table: A Woman's Guide to Negotiating Five Key Challenges to Leadership Success.* She recently coauthored *Nice Girls Just Don't Get It: 99 Ways to Win the Respect You Deserve, the Success You've Earned, and the Life You Want*. Kolb is the Deloitte Ellen Gabriel Professor for Women and Leadership at the Simmons School of Management. From 1991 through 1994, she was executive director of the Program on Negotiation at Harvard Law School. She is currently a senior fellow at the program, where she codirects the Negotiations in the Workplace Project. She is also coauthor of *Her Place at the Table: A Woman's Guide to Negotiating Five Key Challenges to Leadership Success* and *The Shadow Negotiation: How Women Can Master the Hidden Agendas That Determine Bargaining Success.* It was named by Harvard Business Review as one of the top 10 business books of 2000. It also received the Best Book award from the International Association of Conflict Management and has been published in paperback under the title, *Everyday Negotiation: Navigating the Hidden Agendas of Bargaining.* The mission statement for Negotiating Women, Inc. is twofold:

- To provide women with the resources—conceptual frameworks as well as practical skill sets—to succeed in the workplace.
- To help organizations create cultures that value and can profit from the diverse talents women bring.

The organization's areas of expertise include negotiating, leadership, conflict resolution, gender analysis, alliances/coalitions, and sales management. Their clients include corporations, nonprofit associations, women's networks in organizations, professional women's associations, individuals, and the government. According to Dr. Kolb, women often are less adroit at winning better salaries, assignments, and jobs, either because they don't ask or because they cave in when they do. Her bottom line is if a woman develops good negotiating skills, she can enhance her career in many ways.

At Networking Women, Inc., workshops are conducted in which participants learn to make their value visible and to avoid sabotaging themselves. Setting goals too low "is likely to become a self-fulfilling prophecy," Dr. Kolb warns. "Backbone really is about preparation." She warns against making unilateral concessions during negotiations. Instead, she advises that you figure out the other side's hidden agenda, devise an alternative if you can't reach agreement, and plan to deflect moves that put you on the defensive. In a recent interview, Frohlinger echoed the view of many when she said that the playing field in the workforce is still not equal, so women are impacted unintentionally in a disproportionately negative way. She said women are left out of the informal networks where information is shared about new positions and openings on the next managerial level. "You may not have access to the hiring manager who could put out a feeler for you. In some industries, women are left out of these networks. It's not intentional, but it is just the way things are. Companies may say they promote solely on performance, but you're naïve if you think that your promotability is based only on your work. It's just as important to have strong relationships with the right people."[71]

On its Web site, Negotiating Women, Inc. has posted 15 questions about women, leadership, and negotiation that Negotiating Women, Inc. can address through their workshops. Among them are the following:[72]

- I have a really exciting plan to change the ways our group does its work. How do I negotiate to make the changes?
- I was just offered a great opportunity to lead a highly visible project at work. I am so excited that I am ready to take it. But I am worried that I won't be able to take on this extra work and do my current job. What should I do?
- My boss just offered me a new job that doesn't interest me very much, but I know that if I say no, that will be the last promotion to come my way. What should I do?
- My boss always supports me and consistently gives me great opportunities. I feel I am underpaid relative to my colleagues, but I hesitate to bring it up because I am afraid he will see me as ungrateful. What should I do?
- I have a hard time negotiating for myself when it comes to salary. I know I bring value to my company; I have the reviews and promotions to show it. But every time I start to negotiate about money, I lose my conviction and accept what is offered. What should I do?
- I have just been appointed to a new leadership role over others in the group. I am concerned that people will not accept me in the role. How can I change their perceptions?
- I am having trouble pulling the team together. There are some people who are trying to make it difficult for me to succeed. What can I do?
- At my annual performance review in a year when my bottom line has been outstanding, my boss surprised me. He didn't discuss my outstanding year but instead focused on my style, telling me that I am too aggressive and that I need to change my style. What should I do?

Many people fail to recognize opportunities to network and negotiate. Organizations such as Negotiating Women, Inc. are emerging to empower individuals with the skills and tools to succeed at these two requirements.

Go to the Internet: To learn more about Deborah Kolb and Carol Frohlinger, visit Negotiating Women, Inc.'s Web site at www.negotiatingwomen.com.

Support your answers to the following questions with specific information from the case and text or with information you get from the Web or another source.

1. Why has Negotiating Women, Inc. focused its attention on women?

2. The text discusses some of the many reasons to develop your networking skills (such as to get a job or a better position, to perform better at your current job, or to advance within your organization). In what ways does Negotiating Women, Inc. address some of these needs?

3. The case listed examples of questions that can be addressed by Negotiating Women Inc. Select any two questions on the list and indicate whether they can be addressed using networking, negotiating, or both.

4. According to Dr. Kolb, setting goals too low "is likely to become a self-fulfilling prophecy." She wants women to develop a backbone, something that takes preparation to accomplish. How can networking help someone in this situation?

5. In the case, Dr. Kolb warns against making unilateral concessions during negotiations. Instead she advises that you figure out the other side's hidden agenda, devise an alternative if you can't reach an agreement, and plan to deflect moves that put you on the defensive. The textbook describes the negotiating process as consisting of four steps: *planning, bargaining, possibly a postponement and an agreement, or no agreement*. In which step does this statement by Dr. Kolb belong?

Cumulative Questions

6. In Chapter 3 we discussed job satisfaction and its determinants—*the work itself, pay, growth and upward mobility, supervision, coworkers, and attitudes toward work*. Which of these determinants can be greatly enhanced through negotiating?

7. In Chapter 4, career planning is defined as the process of setting career objectives and determining how to accomplish them. How can networking help with one's career planning?

Case Exercise and Role-Play

Preparation: Have students read the section on creating your one-minute self-sell in the text. Assume you are attending a Negotiating Women, Inc. workshop and your task is to develop and present your one-minute self-sell.

In-Class Groups: Divide the class into groups of four or five students. Each group member should develop his or her one-minute self-sell and present it to group members for feedback. The group should then select the member with the best one-minute self-sell. This individual will represent the group in front of the rest of the class.

Role-Play: Each person selected from a group will then present his or her one-minute self-sell to the rest of the class. The class will vote on who had the best presentation.

OBJECTIVE CASE /// John Stanton: Amway

Charley Roys wanted to get more consulting jobs, so he went to a Rotary International meeting to make more contacts that could lead to consulting jobs. During the meeting he was talking to different people and giving out his business card.

This one guy, John Stanton, said to Charley, "Hi, my name is John Stanton, and I have an interesting part-time business. I'm looking for people to share this business opportunity with. Would you be interested in making an additional $50,000 a year part-time?" Charley said yes, and he tried to get some ideas of what the business was all about, but all John would say was, "Let's meet for a half hour or so and I will tell you about it." So they agreed to meet the next day at Charley's house.

Charley asked John what the business name was, and John said, "Let me explain the opportunity first." John started drawing layers of people, stating how much Charley would earn from each layer of people selling products for him. All Charley would have to do is sign people up like John was doing and the money would come in. The figures were showing that Charley could make $50,000 a year from a part-time business.

Before John finished, Charley asked, "Is this Amway?" John said, "Yes, it is." Charley said, "I've seen this type of presentation before, and I'm not interested in being an Amway distributor." Charley told him that he did not want to sell products. John replied, "That's not where the money is. You don't have to actually sell the Amway products yourself. You just sign people up and get them to sell the products."

Charley said, "How can I expect others to sell the products if I don't sell any? The whole pyramid is based on selling products." Charley asked John why he did not tell him it was Amway when he asked him at the Rotary Club meeting. John said, "Many people have the wrong impression of Amway, and you really have to have time to see the presentation."

Charley said that he knew that there were some Amway distributors who were really making a lot of money, but that it was not the type of business he would be successful in. Amway was not for him. Before John left, he asked Charley if he knew of anyone who would be interested in making a lot of money part-time. But Charley said no, so John left.

Answer the following questions. Then in the space between questions, state why you selected that answer.

_____ 1. This case is mainly about:

a. networking *b.* negotiating

_____ 2. Was John successful at networking at the Rotary Club meeting?

a. yes *b.* no

_____ 3. To sell Amway products, salespeople need to start with _____ connections.

a. primary *b.* secondary

_____ 4. John's networking objective was to:

a. get a job or a better one
b. perform better at his current job
c. advance within Amway
d. stay current in his field
e. maintain mobility
f. develop relationships

_____ 5. Did John have a good one-minute self-sell?

a. yes *b.* no

_____ 6. Which part of the networking interview did John clearly try to do?

a. develop rapport
b. deliver one-minute self-sell
c. ask questions
d. get additional contacts
e. offer help
f. follow up

_____ 7. Are coalitions needed for John to be successful at Amway?

a. yes *b.* no

_____ 8. Did John and Charley bargain?

a. yes *b.* no

_____ 9. Amway's business is based mainly on _____ bargaining.

a. distributive *b.* integrative

_____ 10. Does Amway, and other similar businesses, try to give all parties a good deal?

a. yes *b.* no

11. Why wasn't John successful in using the influencing process with Charley?

12. Was it unethical for John not to tell Charley the business was Amway at the Rotary Club meeting?

/ / / SKILL-BUILDING EXERCISE 10-1 / / /

Networking Skills

Preparation (Group)

Complete the following steps:

1. Perform a self-assessment and set objectives. List two or three of your accomplishments. Clearly state your goal, which can be to learn more about career opportunities in your major; to get an internship; to get a part-time, summer, or full-time job; and so on.

2. Create your one-minute self-sell. Write it out. See page 306 for an example.

History:

Plan:

Question:

3. Develop your network. List at least five people to be included in your network, preferably people who can help you achieve your objective.

4. Conduct networking interviews. To help meet your objective, select one person to interview by phone if it is difficult to meet in person for a 20-minute interview. List the person and write questions to ask during the interview. This person can be someone in your college career center or a professor in your major.

In-Class Exercise

Objective: To develop networking skills by implementing the steps in the networking process.

AACSB: The primary AACSB learning standard skills developed through this exercise are reflective thinking and communication abilities.

Experience: You will deliver your one-minute self-sell from the preparation and get feedback for improvement. You will also share your network list and interview questions and get feedback for improvement.

Procedure 1 (7–10 minutes)
A. Break into groups of two. Show each other your written one-minute self-sell. Are the history, plan, and question clear (do you understand it?), concise (does it take 60 seconds or less to say?), and compelling (does it generate interest in helping?)? Offer suggestions for improvement.

B. After the self-sell is perfected, each person states (no reading) the one-minute self-sell. Was it stated clearly, concisely, and with confidence? Offer improvements. State it a second and third time, or until told to go on to the next procedure.

Procedure 2 (7–10 minutes)
Break into groups of three with people you did not work with during procedure 1. Follow steps A and B above in your triad. Repeating your self-sell should improve your delivery and confidence.

Procedure 3 (10–20 minutes)
Break into groups of four with people you did not work with during procedures 1 and 2, if possible. Share your answers to preparation steps 3 (your network list) and 4 (your interview questions). Offer each other improvements to the list and the questions.

Application (outside class): Expand your written network list to at least 25 names. Conduct the networking interview using the questions developed through this exercise.

Conclusion: The instructor leads a class discussion and/or makes concluding remarks. Written network lists and/or interview questions and answers may be passed in.

Sharing: Volunteers may share what they have learned about networking.

Source: This exercise was developed by Andra Gumbus, assistant professor, College of Business, Sacred Heart University. © Andra Gumbus, 2002. It is used with Dr. Gumbus's permission.

/ / / SKILL-BUILDING EXERCISE 10-2 / / /

Car Dealer Negotiation

In-Class Exercise (Group)

Objective: To develop negotiation skills.

AACSB: The primary AACSB learning standard skills developed through this exercise are reflective thinking and communication abilities.

Experience: You will be the buyer or seller of a used car.

Preparation: You should have read and should understand the negotiation process.

Procedure 1 (1–2 minutes)
Break into groups of two and sit facing each other so that you cannot read each other's confidential sheet. Each group should be as far away from other groups as possible so that they cannot overhear each other's conversations. If there is an odd number of students in the class, one student will be an observer or work with the instructor. Select who will be the buyer and who will be the seller of the used car.

Procedure 2 (1–2 minutes)
The instructor goes to each group and gives the buyer and seller their confidential sheets.

Procedure 3 (5–6 minutes)

Buyers and sellers read their confidential sheets and in the space below write some plans (what your basic approach will be, what you will say) for the lunch meeting.

Procedure 4 (3–7 minutes)

Negotiate the sale of the car. Try not to overhear your classmates' conversations. You do not have to buy or sell the car. After you make the sale or agree not to sell, read the confidential sheet of your partner in this exercise and discuss the experience.

Integration (3–7 minutes)

Answer the following questions:

1. Which of the seven bases of power (Chapter 9) did you use during the negotiations? Did both parties believe that they got a good deal?

2. Which of the influencing tactics (Chapter 9) did you use during the negotiations?

3. During your planning, did you (1) research the other party, (2) set an objective—(limit, target, open—price to pay or accept), (3) anticipate questions and objections and prepare answers, and (4) develop options and trade-offs?

4. During the negotiations, did you (1) develop a rapport and focus on obstacles, not on the person, (2) let the other party make the first offer, (3) listen and ask questions to focus on meeting the other party's needs, (4) avoid being too quick to give in, and (5) ask for something in return?

5. Did you reach an agreement on the price of the car? If you were the seller, did you get your target price? Or did you get more or less than your target?

6. When you are negotiating, is it a good practice to open high, that is, to ask for more than you expect to receive?

7. When you are negotiating, is it better to be the one to give or to receive the initial offer?

8. When you are negotiating, is it better to appear to be dealing with strong or weak power? In other words, should you try to portray that you have other options and don't really need to make a deal with this person? Or should you appear to be in need of a deal?

9. Can having the power to intimidate others be helpful in negotiations?

Conclusion: The instructor leads a class discussion or simply gives the answers to the integration questions and makes concluding remarks.

Application: What did I learn from this experience? How will I use this knowledge in the future?

Sharing: Volunteers give their answers to the application section.

Source: The car dealer negotiation confidential information is from Arch G. Woodside, Tulane University. The car dealer game is part of a paper, "Bargaining Behavior in Personal Selling and Buying Exchanges," that was presented at the 1980 Eighth Annual Conference of the Association for Business Simulation and Experiential Learning (ABSEL). It is used with Dr. Woodside's permission.

/ / ANSWERS TO TRUE/FALSE QUESTIONS / /

1. F. Most people in the workforce have jobs, so they network primarily for other reasons. Networking is not all about getting a job: it's about developing relationships to help you meet your personal and professional goals.
2. F. In a one-minute self-sell, you should not directly ask for a job.
3. T.
4. F. Distributive bargaining creates a win–lose situation, whereas integrative bargaining creates a win–win situation.
5. T.
6. T.
7. T.

PART 4

Leadership Skills: Team and Organizational Behavior, Human Relations, and Performance

CHAPTER 11

Team Dynamics, Creativity and Problem Solving, and Decision Making

LEARNING OUTCOMES

After completing this chapter, you should be able to:

LO 11-1 Explain the six components of team dynamics and how they affect team performance.

LO 11-2 Describe the five stages of a team's development.

LO 11-3 Explain the four situational supervisory styles to use with a group, based on its stage of development.

LO 11-4 Explain how to plan for and conduct effective meetings.

LO 11-5 Identify six problem members and explain how to handle them so they do not have a negative effect on your meetings.

LO 11-6 List the five steps in the decision-making model.

LO 11-7 Describe five techniques for generating creative alternatives.

LO 11-8 Define the following 16 key terms (in order of appearance in the chapter):

teamwork	**maintenance roles**
team performance model	**self-interest roles**
team dynamics	**problem**
norms	**problem solving**
group cohesiveness	**decision making**
status	**creativity**
roles	**stages in the creative process**
task roles	**brainstorming**

/ / / Bonnie Sue Swinaski is a machine operator for the Western Pacific Manufacturing Company in Jackson, Mississippi. In the past, she has recommended ways to increase performance, which management used. As a result, management appointed Bonnie Sue to lead an ad hoc committee charged with recommending ways to increase performance in her work area. Her group has six members, all from her department, who volunteered to serve on the committee. The committee has been meeting biweekly now for three weeks for one- to two-hour sessions. The members have grown quite close over the weeks, and participation has been fairly equal.

Bonnie Sue, however, has not been very pleased with the group's performance. Only three weeks remain before the group's report is to be presented to management. She has been thinking about some of the problems and wondering how to handle them. At first, the members came to the meetings enthusiastic and came up with crazy ideas. But over time, they lost some of the enthusiasm, even though they were developing better ideas for improving the performance of the department. During meetings, members have been suggesting the need for work to be done outside the meeting, but no one seems to do it. Three of the members cause different kinds of problems in the group. Kirt is destructive—he is constantly putting down other people's ideas, and others have followed his lead. Kirt always thinks his way is better, and he never gives an inch, even when he knows he is wrong. Kirt ends up fighting with members over whose idea is better. Shelby is very

pleasant—she tries to keep peace in the group. The problem with Shelby is that she is consistently getting the group off the topic at hand. Carlos is the opposite of Shelby—he puts the group back on the topic. He doesn't believe in wasting any time, but he's a motor mouth. Carlos dominates the airtime at meetings.

What are the issues? If you were in Bonnie Sue's situation, how would you turn the group into a top performer? / / /

HOW TEAMS, CREATIVITY AND PROBLEM SOLVING, AND DECISION MAKING AFFECT BEHAVIOR, HUMAN RELATIONS, AND PERFORMANCE

We use the term *team* to refer to groups and teams.**Teamwork** *involves working together to achieve something beyond the capabilities of individuals working alone* . The common organizational structure (Chapter 5) today is based on teams.[1] People have different personality types that affect their behavior and human relations, which in turn affect team performance.[2] Recall that our *emotional intelligence* (EQ—Chapter 2) affects our behavior and human relations; people with high EQs tend to make effective performing team players.[3] So EQ is needed for team success. These are a few of the reasons why job recruiters ranked ability to work well within a team as the second most sought after skill in new employees, just below communication and interpersonal skills,[4] which are a foundation for team skills.

Employee *creativity* is crucial for organizational innovation and survival.[5] Personality behavior also affects creative performance.[6] With the increased use of team work units, organizations are counting on creativity from their teams.[7]

Teams are often asked to *solve problems* and make *decisions*.[8] Personality behavior also affects the decisions people make.[9] People behave differently in teams, which affects human relations and the effectiveness of solving problems through decision making. Decisions in turn affect team and firm performance.[10] These are some of the reasons job recruiters ranked analytical and problem-solving skills as the third most sought after skill in new employees.[11] Team skills can be developed,[12] and that is what this chapter is all about.

TEAMS

Now that we know how important teams are, in this section, you will learn about the different types of groups, the team performance model, and team structure.

Types of Teams

There are *formal groups,* which are sanctioned by the organization (i.e., departments), and *informal groups,* which develop spontaneously when members get together voluntarily because of similar interests. Groups can also be *ongoing,*[13] without ending, or *temporary,*[14] discontinuing after the objective is met. Employees are commonly members of multiple teams.[15] Two of the major types of formal groups are functional and task.

Functional Teams **Functional teams** are formal, ongoing teams that consist of managers and their employees. Each work unit or department makes up a functional group. There are also *cross-functional* groups with members from different groups, which can be ongoing or temporary. Some functional groups are called *self-directed* groups or *self-managed* teams because team leadership is shared.[16]

Task Teams **Task teams** work together on a specific activity. Being a member of a task group is in addition to your job in a functional group, so you can have two bosses.[17] Task groups are often called committees. There are two common types of task groups or committees.

The *ad hoc committee,* or *task force,* is a formal, temporary team that discontinues when its purpose is accomplished. For example, a task force can be created to select a new computer. The task force is no longer needed once it has selected the computer, so it disbands. The *standing committee* is a formal, ongoing team that often has rotating members. For example, labor and management commonly have standing committees that work together to negotiate the ongoing collective bargaining agreements that result in a new contract.

Virtual Teams—Working Digitally In the global economy, people from around the world work in teams digitally. *Virtual teams* conduct almost their entire group work by electronic digital communications, rather than face-to-face. Recall that you learned about digital communications, etiquette, and networking in Chapters 5, 9, and 10. This information also applies to virtual teams, as well as developing trust (Chapter 7). An additional digital tool commonly used is groupware. *Groupware* allows team members of any size to edit a document at the same time, or in sequence.

One of the challenges of virtual teams is developing trust with people you don't know and see face-to-face. Can you trust them to do their share of the work, do it right, and meet team objectives on time? Some people tend to be reluctant to trust people with information, even though it is important to teamwork, especially in virtual teams. Effective teamwork is more complex and challenging when working with people in other countries, and we will discuss this in the last section of this chapter.

Communication Skills
Refer to CS Question 1.

Before we get into the details of the components of the team performance model, complete Self-Assessment Exercise 11-1 to determine your use of team behavior.

/// Self-Assessment Exercise 11-1 ///

Your Team Behavior

For each statement, identify how accurately it describes your behavior. Place the number (1 to 5) on the line before each statement.

Describes me				Does not describe me
5	4	3	2	1

_____ 1. I influence the team members to do a good job of meeting organizational objectives.

_____ 2. I try to include the ideas and perspectives of all team members.

_____ 3. I offer creative ways to solve problems that help my team get the job done well.

_____ 4. I offer input in the decisions my team makes.

_____ 5. When there are team conflicts, I help members resolve the differences.

_____ 6. I make sure the team develops clear objectives.

_____ 7. When completing a task, I consider how many members are needed to accomplish the task and include the best team members for the task.

_____ 8. I use behavior that will help meet the organization's or team's objectives, and I encourage others to develop and enforce positive norms.

_____ 9. I try to include every member of the team so that they all feel like full, active members of the team. I don't exclude others in any way.

_____ 10. I'm comfortable with my place on the team; I can be a star or just one of the team's members. I try to help others be comfortable with their status.

_____ 11. I do and say things that directly help the team get the job done.

_____ 12. I do and say things that directly help the team develop and maintain good human relations.

_____ 13. I don't do and say things that benefit me at the expense of the team.

_____ 14. When I join a team that is just starting, such as a new committee, I help the team clarify and set objectives.

/// Self-Assessment Exercise 11-1 /// *(continued)*

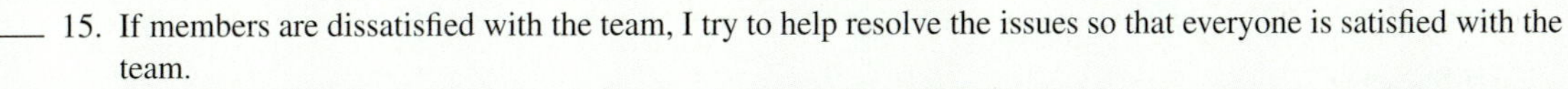

_____ 15. If members are dissatisfied with the team, I try to help resolve the issues so that everyone is satisfied with the team.

_____ 16. If a team member has a drop in commitment to the team, such as having personal problems or a bad day, I try to help that person get through the situation and keep his or her commitment to the team.

_____ 17. When the team is doing a good job, I don't interfere with the team members' getting along or the team's performance.

Add your score and place the total here: Then on the continuum below, mark the point that represents your score.

Effective team behavior	85 - - - 75 - - - 65 - - - 55 - - - 45 - - - 35 - - - 25 - - - 17	Ineffective team behavior

You don't need to do all these things for the team to be effective as long as someone else on the team does them. An important part of team skills is knowing the behavior that is needed to have a successful team and providing the needed behavior to help the team continue to develop.

Questions 1 to 5 refer to team structure, 6 to 13 to team dynamics, and 14 to 17 to team development. As you read about each of the three components, you may want to turn back and review your answers.

The Team Performance Model

The **team performance model** *states that a team's performance is based on its structure, dynamics, and stage of development.* The performance model can be stated as a formula. *Team performance* is a function of team structure + team dynamics + team development stage. The three components of the model are shown in Exhibit 11.1. You should realize that, to have high levels of performance, the team must have an effective structure for working together as a team, have good dynamic human relations, and develop its ability to work as a team.[18] Teams face the systems effect: if any one of the components is weak, performance suffers. In this chapter, we discuss each component in sequence in separate sections, starting with team structure.

CS
Communication Skills
Refer to CS Question 2.

Team Structure

As shown in Exhibit 11.2, there are four team structure components that, along with team dynamics and development, affect team performance. We spend the least amount of time with team structure here because we already discussed some of the components of structure in other chapters, and we will discuss others in detail later in this chapter. *Conflict,* which we discussed in Chapter 6, and effectively resolving conflicts without hurting human relations, is important to performance.[19]

Leadership, covered in Chapter 7, is important to team performance.[20] Leaders need to unlock employee creativity.[21] Therefore, in this chapter we expand the coverage to leading teams as a situational supervisor, based on team development stages. We also cover how to run a meeting using leadership skills.

Composition refers to the diversity of team members. Team mix, or diversity, involves more than gender and race,[22] which we will discuss in Chapter 13. Important to team performance are the knowledge, abilities, and skills of the team members that should complement each other so that the team can achieve better results than its individuals.

EXHIBIT 11.1 | The Team Performance Model

Team Performance	(*f*)*	Team Structure	+	Team Dynamics	+	Team Development Stage

*(*f*) = is a function of.

EXHIBIT 11.2 | Team Structure Components

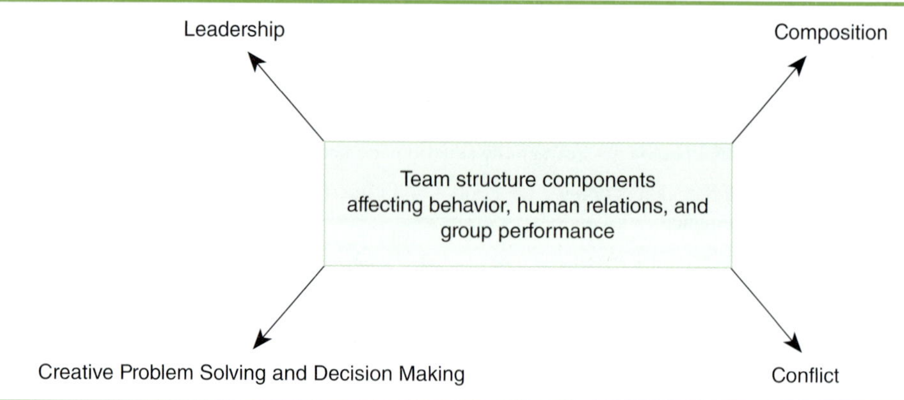

Learning Outcome 11-1

Explain the six components of team dynamics and how they affect team performance.

Creative problem solving and decision making also affect team performance. Teams encounter problems in getting the job done. How the members work together to come up with creative solutions to the problems affects team performance.[23] How decisions are made, autocratic or participative (Chapter 7), and the decisions themselves also affect performance.[24] Problem solving and decision making and creativity are discussed in separate sections later in this chapter.

TEAM DYNAMICS

Team dynamics *refers to the patterns of interactions that emerge as groups develop.* These interactions are also called *group process*. In this section, we discuss the six components of group dynamics: objectives, team size, team norms, group cohesiveness, status within the team, and group roles. As you read the implications for leaders, recall that you don't have to be a manager to be a leader—rise to the occasion to help the group dynamics.

Objectives

To be effective, teams must agree on clear objectives and be committed to achieving them.[25] The leader should allow the group to have input in setting objectives, based on its capability to participate, which you will learn to do later in this chapter.

WORK APPLICATION 11-1

For Work Applications 11-1 through 11-8, recall a specific group to which you belong or have belonged. If you will be doing Skill-Building Exercise 11-1, do not use your class group for this specific group now.

Does the group agree on, and are members committed to, clear objectives? Explain your answer.

Implications for Leaders Get the group to set specific, measurable objectives with a target date following the guidelines in the setting objectives model (Chapter 8).

Team Size

What is the ideal team size? The number varies, depending on the team's purpose. If the group is too small, it tends to be too cautious; if it is too large, it tends to be too slow. Generally, participation is more equal in groups of around 5 members. Groups of 20 or more tend to be too large to reach consensus on decisions, and they tend to form subgroups. But larger groups tend to generate more alternatives and higher-quality ideas because they benefit from diverse participation.

WORK APPLICATION 11-2

How large is the group? Is the size appropriate? Explain.

Implications for Leaders Usually leaders have no say in the size of their functional groups. However, the appropriate leadership style may vary with team size. Leaders who chair a committee may be able to select the team size. In doing so, be sure to get the right people on the committee, while trying to keep the group size appropriate for the task.

Team Norms

Functional groups generally have standing plans (policies and rules) to help provide the necessary guidelines for behavior. However, groups tend to form their own unwritten rules about how things are done.[26] **Norms** *are the group's shared expectations of its members' behavior.* Norms determine what should, ought to, or must be done for the group to maintain consistent and desirable behavior.[27]

How Norms Develop and Teams Enforce Them Norms are developed spontaneously as the group members interact through the routine of the team. Members, influenced by leaders, determine what is acceptable and unacceptable behavior[28] and the way they dress.[29] If a team member does not follow the norm, the other members may try to enforce compliance—*peer pressure*. The common ways teams enforce norms include ridicule, ostracism, sabotage, and physical abuse. You most likely have experienced peer pressure at school, socially, and at work.

Communication Skills
Refer to CS Question 3.

Implications for Leaders Team norms can be positive, helping the team meet its objective(s), or they can be negative, hindering the group from meeting its objective(s). Be aware of the group's norms, and work toward maintaining and developing positive norms, while trying to eliminate negative norms.[30] Confront groups with negative norms and try to work out agreeable solutions to have positive norms.

Group Cohesiveness

WORK APPLICATION 11-3

List at least three of the team's norms. Identify them as positive or negative. How does the team enforce these norms?

The extent to which a group will abide by and enforce its norms depends on its degree of cohesiveness. **Group cohesiveness** *is the attractiveness and closeness group members have for one another and for the group.* The more cohesive the group, the more its members stick together as a team. The more desirable group membership is, the more willing the members are to behave according to the team's norms. For example, if some team members take drugs, the team may develop a norm of taking drugs. This peer pressure to take drugs often wins out. To be accepted by the team, members will behave in ways they really don't agree with.

Factors Influencing Cohesiveness *Six factors* affect group cohesiveness. Realize that these are general statements; there are always exceptions in some groups. The stronger the agreement and commitment made to the achievement of the group's *objectives,* the greater the cohesiveness of the group. The smaller the *group size,* the greater the cohesiveness. The more similar the group members are (*homogeneity*), the greater the cohesiveness. The more equal the level of *participation* among group members, the greater the group's cohesiveness. The greater the external competition, rather than competition within team members, the greater the cohesiveness. The more *success* a group has achieving its objectives, the more cohesive it tends to become. People want to be on a winning team. Have you ever noticed that losing teams tend to argue more than winning teams and complain that other members are messing up and are the cause of lack of success?

How Cohesiveness Affects Team Performance Many research studies have compared cohesive and noncohesive teams and concluded that cohesive teams tend to have a higher level of success at achieving their objectives, with greater job satisfaction. Cohesive team members are closer, more trusting and cooperative.[31] S. E. Seashore and others have conducted research on cohesiveness and found that:

- Groups with the highest levels of productivity were highly cohesive and accepted management's level of productivity.
- Groups with the lowest levels of productivity were also highly cohesive, but rejected management's level of productivity; they set and enforced their own level below that of management.

- Groups with intermediate levels of productivity were low cohesive groups, irrespective of their acceptance of management's level of productivity. The widest variance of individual group members' performance was among the groups with the lower levels of cohesiveness. They tended to be more tolerant of nonconformity with group norms.

Communication Skills
Refer to CS Question 4.

Implications for Leaders Strive to develop cohesive groups that accept positive norms. The use of participation helps the group develop cohesiveness while it builds agreement and commitment toward its objective(s). While some intragroup competition may be helpful, focus primarily on intergroup competition—think like sports. This helps develop a cohesive winning team, which in turn motivates the group to higher levels of success.

Status within the Team

WORK APPLICATION 11-4

Is the group cohesive? How do the six factors listed previously influence the group's cohesiveness? How does the level of cohesiveness affect the group's performance? Explain your answers.

As team members interact, they develop respect for one another on numerous dimensions. The more respect, prestige, influence, and power a group member has, the higher his or her status within the team.[32] **Status** *is the perceived ranking of one member relative to other members of the group.*

The Development of Status and How It Affects Team Performance Status is based on several factors: a member's job title, wage or salary, seniority, knowledge or expertise, interpersonal skills, appearance, education, race, age, sex, and so on.[33] High-status members have more influence on the development of the group's norms, and can more easily get away with breaking norms. Lower-level members tend to copy high-status members' behavior.[34]

Status congruence is the acceptance and satisfaction members receive from their group status. Members who are not satisfied with their status may feel excluded from the team, and they may not be active team participants. They may physically or mentally escape from the team and not perform to their full potential. Or they may cause team conflict as they fight for a higher status level.[35]

Communication Skills
Refer to CS Question 5.

Implications for Leaders To be an effective leader, you need to have high status within the group. Maintain good human relations with the group, particularly with the high-status informal leaders, to be sure they endorse positive norms and objectives. In addition, be aware of conflicts that may be the result of lack of status congruence.[36] Use the conflict management model (Chapter 6) to be sure conflicts are resolved.

Group Roles

WORK APPLICATION 11-5

List each team member in order by status in the team, including yourself. What are some of the characteristics that lead to high or low status on the team?

Team members have their own roles and responsibilities, generating shared representations of actions and tasks, and choose their own behavior in terms of joint objectives.[37] **Roles** *are shared expectations of how group members will fulfill the requirements of their position.* When people join the organization, they learn about the organization's expectations through orientations, job descriptions, and managerial supervision. When interacting with the team, they learn the team's expectations of them—its norms. People often have multiple roles within the same position. For example, a professor may have the roles of teacher, researcher, consultant, adviser, and committee member.

Classifying Group Roles and How They Affect Team Performance Chapter 7 stated that when leaders interact with employees, they can use directive behavior (structuring, job-centered, production- and task-oriented), supportive behavior (consideration, employee-centered, people's- and relationship-oriented), or both. These same two dimensions can also be performed by group members as they interact. When used to relate to group interactions, they are commonly called *task roles* and *maintenance roles.* A third category, called *self-interest roles,* is often added. Below we will discuss each type of role in more detail.

The group's **task roles** *are the things group members do and say that directly aid in the accomplishment of its objective(s).* Task roles focus on getting the job done (and influencing others to help).[38] Task roles can be subclassified as: objective clarifiers, planners, organizers, leaders, and controllers. Clearly, task roles need to be fulfilled for the team to perform its functions.

The group's **maintenance roles** *are the things group members do and say to develop and sustain group dynamics.* Maintenance roles focus on people working effectively together (and influencing others to work as team members). Maintenance roles can be subclassified as: involvers and encouragers of others, consensus seekers, gatekeepers of norms, compromisers, and harmonizers who keep the peace through conflict resolution. As discussed, a group will perform only to the level of how well team members work together effectively to achieve its objectives.

In contrast to these two types of roles that help team performance, **self-interest roles** *are the things group members do and say to meet their own needs or objectives at the expense of the team.* Self-interest seekers often give the impression that they are concerned about others and the organization, when in reality such behavior is a cover to get what they want. They may use unethical politics (Chapter 10) and the forcing conflict style (Chapter 6) to push others to get what they want. People using self-interest roles are problem team members hurting team performance. Self-interest roles can be subclassified as: aggressors, blockers, recognition seekers, and withdrawers.

Communication Skills
Refer to CS Question 6.

Implications for Leaders To be effective, a team must have members who play task roles and maintenance roles, while minimizing self-interest roles. When in a group, you should be aware of the roles its members play. If the members are not playing the task and/or maintenance role required at a given time, you should play the role. The next section discusses group development and the manager's use of task and maintenance roles as the group develops.

In the opening case, the objective is fairly clear, group size is adequate, and cohesiveness, status, and roles are not major problems. Kirt has been discrediting others' ideas, and others have followed his lead. A negative norm has developed that needs to be addressed by Bonnie Sue as the leader to ensure success of the group. Bonnie Sue can begin the next meeting by stating that the norm has developed and explain how it is destructive to the group. She can interrupt when Kirt and others put down ideas by reminding the group to be positive. The group can also discuss whether there are other negative norms that should be stopped. In addition, they can discuss the development of positive norms that can help the group do a better job. In terms of group roles, Carlos is playing a task role for the group. Shelby is playing a maintenance role for the group. Kirt is playing a self-interest role. How to handle Kirt, Shelby, and Carlos as problem individuals will be discussed later in this chapter.

In summary, effective groups should have clear objectives with agreement and commitment to those objectives by its members, appropriate group size to achieve its objectives, positive norms, cohesiveness, status congruence, and members who play task and maintenance roles while minimizing self-interest roles. Developing effective group dynamics that meet the needs of the individuals and the group or organization creates a win–win situation for all parties. See Exhibit 11.3 for a review of the six components of team dynamics.

WORK APPLICATION 11-6

Using your list from Work Application 11-5, identify the major roles played by each group member, including yourself.

EXHIBIT 11.3 | Team Dynamics Components

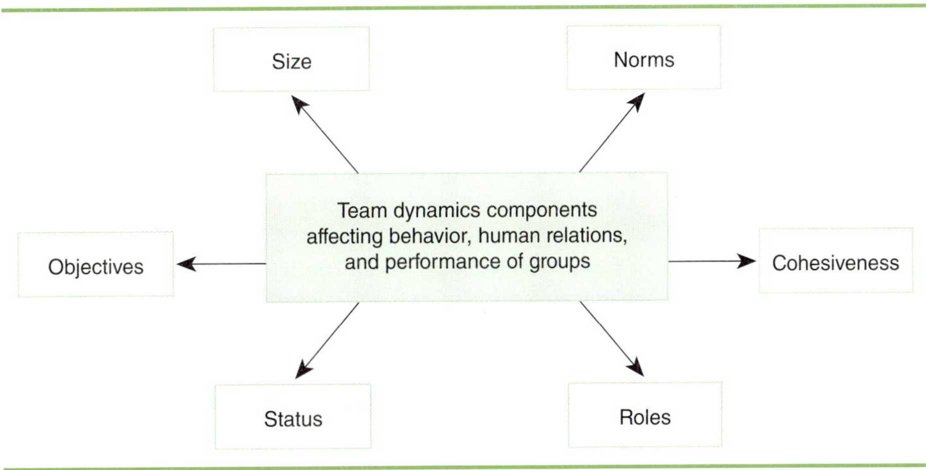

APPLICATION SITUATIONS / / /

Group Dynamics **AS 11-1**

Match each statement with the group dynamics issue it represents.

A. Objectives C. Norms E. Status

B. Size D. Cohesiveness F. Roles

_______ 1. "I'm a union man. If it wasn't for the union, we would not be getting the pay we do. Collective bargaining really works."

_______ 2. "I could use another employee, but there is no workplace available."

_______ 3. "I wish the administration would make up its mind. One month we produce one product, and the next month we change to another."

_______ 4. "When you need advice, go see Sharon; she knows the ropes around here better than anyone."

_______ 5. "Conrad, you're late for the meeting. Everyone else was on time, so we started without you."

APPLICATION SITUATIONS / / /

Roles **AS 11-2**

Match each statement with the role it fulfills.

A. Task B. Maintenance C. Self-interest

_______ 6. "Wait, we have not heard Abdul's idea yet."

_______ 7. "Could you explain why we are doing this again?"

_______ 8. "We tried that before you came here; it does not work. My idea is much better."

_______ 9. "What does this have to do with the problem? We are getting sidetracked."

_______ 10. "I like that idea better than mine. Let's go with it."

TEAM DEVELOPMENT STAGES AND LEADERSHIP

Learning Outcome 11-2

Describe the five stages of a team's development.

In this section, we discuss the stages that teams go through from inception to termination, followed with a model for understanding which situational supervision style (Chapter 7) to use based on the stage of development.

Stages of Team Development

Below we will describe each of the group development stages (GDSs) that task groups may go through. However, not all groups progress through all the stages, or they get stuck in one stage and never reach the group's full potential.

Stage 1: Orientation This *forming* stage is characterized by low development level (D1), high commitment, and low competence. When people first form a group, they tend to come to the group with a moderate to high commitment to the group.[39] However, because they have not worked together, they do not have the competence to achieve the task. Members tend to have anxiety over how they will fit in, what will be required of them, and what the group will be like.

EXHIBIT 11.4 | Team Development Stages 1 through 4

Orientation	Dissatisfaction	Resolution	Production
GDS1	GDS2	GDS3	GDS4

Morale: High / Low

Competence

Commitment (morale)

Note: If a team is at stage 5, it terminates and has no competence and commitment. There is no development.

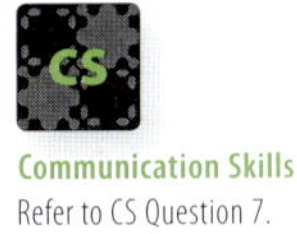

Communication Skills
Refer to CS Question 7.

Stage 2: Dissatisfaction This *storming* stage is characterized by moderate development level (D2), lower commitment, and some competence. As members work together for some time, they tend to become dissatisfied with the group. Members start to question: Why am I a member? Is the group going to accomplish anything? Why don't other group members do what is expected? and so forth. However, the group does develop some competence to perform the task.

Stage 3: Resolution This *norming* stage is characterized by high development level (D3), variable commitment, and high competence. As members develop competence, they often become more satisfied with the group and committed to it.[40] Relationships develop that satisfy group members' affiliation needs. They learn to work together as they develop a group structure with acceptable norms and cohesiveness.

Stage 4: Production This *performing* stage is characterized by outstanding development level (D4), high commitment, and high competence. This high commitment enhances productivity and performance, as does the high competence skill level. The group works as a team and there is a high level of satisfaction of members' affiliation needs. The group maintains a positive group structure and dynamics.

Stage 5: Termination In functional groups, the *adjourning* stage is not reached unless there is some drastic reorganization; however, it does occur in task groups. During this stage, members experience feelings about leaving the group.

WORK APPLICATION 11-7

Identify the group's stage of development and the leader's situational supervisory style. Does the leader use the appropriate style?

WORK APPLICATION 11-8

What can be done to improve the group's dynamics? Explain.

The two key variables identified through each stage of group development are work on the task (*competence*) and the socioemotional tone or morale (*commitment*). The two variables do not progress in the same manner. Competence tends to continue to increase through each of the first four stages, while commitment tends to start high in stage 1, drop in stage 2, and then rise through stages 3 and 4. This pattern is illustrated in Exhibit 11.4.

In the opening case, Bonnie Sue's committee is in stage 2—dissatisfaction. The group has had a decrease in commitment and an increase in competence. The group needs to resolve the dissatisfaction to progress to stages 3 and 4 of development. Being an ad hoc committee, the group will go through stage 5—termination—in three weeks. The next part of this section discusses how Bonnie Sue can help the group develop to stages 3 and 4 as a situational supervisor.

APPLICATION SITUATIONS / / /

Group Development Stages **AS 11-3**

Identify the group's development stage as:

A. GDS1 B. GDS2 C. GDS3 D. GDS4 E. GDS5

_____ 11. Members have come to realize that their initial expectations are not a reality and they accept the situation.

_____ 12. The ad hoc committee has presented its recommendations to management.

_____ 13. Group members are trying to get to know one another.

_____ 14. The group set a new record level of production.

_____ 15. Members are sitting around and complaining.

Team Development and Situational Supervision

Before we discuss leading teams as a situational supervisor, complete Self-Assessment Exercise 11-2.

/// Self-Assessment Exercise 11-2 ///

Determining Your Preferred Group Leadership Style

In the 12 situations below, select the response that represents what you would actually do as the group's leader. Ignore the D and S lines; they will be used as part of Skill-Building Exercise 11-2.

1. Your group works well together; members are cohesive, with positive norms. They maintain a fairly consistent level of production that is above the organizational average, as long as you continue to provide maintenance behavior. You have a new assignment for them. To accomplish it, you would: D _____
   a. Explain what needs to be done and tell them how to do it. Oversee them while they perform the task. S _____
   b. Tell the group how pleased you are with their past performance. Explain the new assignment, but let them decide how to accomplish it. Be available if they need help. S _____
   c. Tell the group what needs to be done. Encourage them to give input on how to do the job. Oversee task performance. S _____
   d. Explain to the group what needs to be done. S _____
2. You have been promoted to a new supervisory position. The group appears to have little talent to do the job, but members do seem to care about the quality of the work they do. The last supervisor was terminated because of the department's low productivity level. To increase productivity, you would: D _____
   a. Let the group know you are aware of its low production level, but let them decide how to improve it. S _____
   b. Spend most of your time overseeing group members as they perform their jobs. Train them as needed. S _____
   c. Explain to the group that you would like to work together to improve productivity. Work together as a team. S _____
   d. Tell the group some ways productivity can be improved. With their ideas, develop methods, and make sure they are implemented. S _____
3. Your department continues to be one of the top performers in the organization. It works well as a team. In the past, you generally let members take care of the work on their own. You decide to: D _____
   a. Go around encouraging group members on a regular basis. S _____
   b. Define members' roles, and spend more time overseeing performance. S _____
   c. Continue things the way they are; let them alone. S _____
   d. Hold a meeting. Recommend ways to improve and get members' ideas as well. After agreeing on changes, oversee the group to make sure it implements the new ideas and does improve. S _____
4. You have spent much of the past year training your employees. However, they do not need as much of your time to oversee production as they used to. Several group members no longer get along as well as they did in the past. You've played referee lately. You: D _____

/// Self-Assessment Exercise 11-2 /// (*continued*)

a. Have a group meeting to discuss ways to increase performance. Let the group decide what changes to make. Be supportive. S ______
b. Continue things the way they are now. Supervise them closely and be the referee when needed. S ______
c. Let the members alone to work things out for themselves. S ______
d. Continue to supervise closely as needed, but spend more time playing maintenance roles; develop a team spirit. S ______

5. Your department has been doing such a great job that it has grown in numbers. You are surprised at how fast the new members were integrated. The team continues to come up with ways to improve performance on its own. As a result of the growth, your department will be moving to a new, larger location. You decide to: D ______
a. Design the new layout and present it to the group to see if they can improve it. S ______
b. In essence, become a group member and allow the group to design the new layout. S ______
c. Design the new layout and put a copy on the bulletin board so employees know where to report for work after the move. S ______
d. Hold a meeting to get employee ideas on the layout of the new location. After the meeting, think about it and finalize the layout. S ______

6. You are appointed to head a task group. Because of the death of a relative, you had to miss the first meeting. At the second meeting, the group seems to have developed objectives and some ground rules. Members have volunteered for assignments that have to be accomplished. You: D ______
a. Take over as a strong leader. Change some ground rules and assignments. S ______
b. Review what has been done so far, and keep things as is. However, take charge and provide clear direction from now on. S ______
c. Take over the leadership but allow the group to make the decisions. Be supportive and encourage them. S ______
d. Seeing that the group is doing so well, leave and do not attend any more meetings. S ______

7. Your group was working at, or just below, standard. However, there has been a conflict within the group. As a result, production is behind schedule. You: D ______
a. Tell the group how to resolve the conflict. Then closely supervise to make sure your plan is followed and production increases. S ______
b. Let the group work it out. S ______
c. Hold a meeting to work as a team to come up with a solution. Encourage the group to work together. S ______
d. Hold a meeting to present a way to resolve the conflict. Sell the members on its merits, include their input, and follow up. S ______

8. The organization has allowed flextime. Two of your employees have asked if they could change work hours. You are concerned because all busy work hours need adequate coverage. The department is very cohesive, with positive norms. You decide to: D ______
a. Tell them things are going well; keep things as they are now. S ______
b. Hold a department meeting to get everyone's input; then reschedule members' hours. S ______
c. Hold a department meeting to get everyone's input; then reschedule members' hours on a trial basis. Tell the group that if there is any drop in productivity, you will go back to the old schedule. S ______
d. Tell them to hold a department meeting. If the department agrees to have at least three people on the job during the busy hours, they can make changes, giving you a copy of the new schedule. S ______

9. You have arrived 10 minutes late for a department meeting. Your employees are discussing the latest assignment. This surprises you because, in the past, you had to provide clear direction and employees rarely would say anything. You: D ______
a. Take control immediately and provide your usual direction. S ______
b. Say nothing and just sit back. S ______
c. Encourage the group to continue, but also provide direction. S ______
d. Thank the group for starting without you, and encourage them to continue. Support their efforts. S ______

10. Your department is consistently very productive. However, occasionally, the members fool around and someone has an accident. There has never been a serious injury. You hear a noise and go to see what it was. From a distance you can see Sue sitting on the floor, laughing, with a ball made from company material in her hand. You: D ______
a. Say and do nothing. After all, she's OK, and the department is very productive; you don't want to make waves. S ______
b. Call the group together and ask for suggestions on how to keep accidents from recurring. Tell them you will be checking up on them to make sure the fooling around does not continue. S ______
c. Call the group together and discuss the situation. Encourage them to be more careful in the future. S ______
d. Tell the group that from now on, you will be checking up on them regularly. Bring Sue to your office and discipline her. S ______

(*continued*)

/// Self-Assessment Exercise 11-2 /// (*continued*)

11. You are at the first meeting of an ad hoc committee you are leading. Most of the members are second- and third-level managers from marketing and financial areas; you are a supervisor from production. You decide to start by: D ______
    a. Working on developing relationships. Get everyone to feel as though they know each other before you talk about business. S ______
    b. Going over the group's purpose and the authority it has. Provide clear directives. S ______
    c. Asking the group to define its purpose. Because most of the members are higher-level managers, let them provide the leadership. S ______
    d. Providing both direction and encouragement. Give directives and thank people for their cooperation. S ______
12. Your department has done a great job in the past. It is now getting a new computer, somewhat different from the old one. You have been trained to operate the computer, and you are expected to train your employees to operate it. To train them, you: D ______
    a. Give the group instructions, work with them individually, providing direction and encouragement. S ______
    b. Get the group together to decide how they want to be instructed. Be very supportive of their efforts to learn. S ______
    c. Tell them it's a simple system. Give them a copy of the manual and have them study it on their own. S ______
    d. Give the group instructions. Then go around and supervise their work closely, giving additional instructions as needed. S ______

To determine your preferred group leadership style, in the table below, circle the letter you selected in situations 1 through 12. The column headings indicate the style you selected.

	Autocratic (S-A)	Consultative (S-C)	Participative (S-P)	Laissez-faire (S-L)
1.	*a*	*c*	*b*	*d*
2.	*b*	*d*	*c*	*a*
3.	*b*	*d*	*a*	*c*
4.	*b*	*d*	*a*	*c*
5.	*c*	*a*	*d*	*b*
6.	*a*	*b*	*c*	*d*
7.	*a*	*d*	*c*	*b*
8.	*a*	*c*	*b*	*d*
9.	*a*	*c*	*d*	*b*
10.	*d*	*b*	*a*	*c*
11.	*b*	*d*	*a*	*c*
12.	*d*	*a*	*b*	*c*
Total				

Add the number of circled items per column. The total for all four columns should equal 12. The column with the highest number represents your preferred group leadership style. There is no one best style in all situations.

The more evenly distributed the numbers are among the four styles, the more flexible you are at leading groups. A total of 0 or 1 in any column may indicate a reluctance to use that style. You could have problems in situations calling for that style.

Is your preferred group leadership style the same as your preferred situational supervision style (Chapter 7) and situational communication style (Chapter 5)?

Learning Outcome 11-3

Explain the four situational supervisory styles to use with a group, based on its stage of development.

Situational supervision can be applied to the stages of group development. Chapter 7 presented the situational supervision model. In that chapter, the major focus was on supervising individual employees. Below you will find changes, with the focus on applying the model to the stages of group development. Recall the need for contingency leadership.[41] With each stage of group development, a different supervisory style is needed to help the group perform effectively at that stage and to develop to the next level.

As stated, when leaders interact with their groups, they can perform task roles, maintenance roles, or both. Here you will learn which role(s) the manager should play during the different stages of group development.

Orientation (D1 Low) = Autocratic Style The group development stage 1, orientation—low development *D1* (high commitment/low competence), uses the *autocratic supervisory style* (high task–low maintenance), S-A. When task groups first come together, leaders need to help the group clarify its objectives to provide the direction to be sure the group gets off to a good start. Because the members are committed to joining the group, leaders need to help the group develop its competence with task behavior.

Dissatisfaction (D2 Moderate) = Consultative Style The group development stage 2, dissatisfaction—moderate development *D2* (lower commitment/some competence), uses the *consultative supervisory style* (high task–high maintenance), *S-C.* Even though groups know their objectives and their roles are clear, members become dissatisfied for a variety of reasons, such as not getting along with one or more members or not being happy with the amount of influence they have in the group. When morale drops, leaders need to focus on maintenance roles to encourage members to resolve issues. At the same time, continue to play the task role necessary to help the group develop its level of competence.

Resolution (D3 High) = Participative Style The group development stage 3, resolution—high development *D3* (variable commitment/high competence), uses the *participative supervisory style* (low task–high maintenance), S-P. There is little need to provide task leadership; the members know how to do the job. When commitment varies, it is usually due to some problem in the group's dynamics, such as a conflict or a loss of interest, so focus on the maintenance behavior to get the group through the issue(s) it faces. If leaders continues to provide task directives that are not needed, the group can become dissatisfied and regress or plateau at this level.

Production (D4 Outstanding) = Laissez-faire Style The group development stage 4, production—outstanding development *D4* (high commitment/high competence), uses the *laissez-faire supervisory style* (low task–low maintenance), S-L. Groups that develop to this stage have members who play the appropriate task and maintenance roles; leaders do not need to play either role unless there is a problem.

As a leader, you should determine your group's current level of development and strive to bring it to the next stage of development. In the opening case, Bonnie Sue's committee is in stage 2—dissatisfaction. Bonnie Sue needs to play both task and maintenance roles to help the group progress to stages 3 and 4. Focusing on solving the negative norm of putting each other's ideas down works on both task and maintenance levels. Bonnie Sue also needs to provide stronger leadership in the areas of completing meeting assignments and making Kirt, Shelby, and Carlos more productive. You will learn how in the next section.

The four stages of group development, along with their appropriate situational supervisory styles, are summarized in Model 11.1.

LEADERSHIP SKILLS IN MEETINGS

With the trend toward teams, there are more meetings in the workplace.[42] Thus, you need meeting leadership skills for career success, as careers may be made or broken in the power arenas of meetings. The meeting skills presented here apply to both face-to-face and digital phone and videoconference meetings.

Let's take a few seconds for a humorist break. How do you define a committee? A committee is a group that takes minutes and waste hours; a camel is a horse put together by a committee. But it doesn't have to be. If you develop the skills in this section you can plan, run, and help lead meetings, and deal with problem members effectively. The success or failure of meetings rests primarily with the leader, but again we can all be leaders, so if the person in charge is not running the meeting effectively, you may be able to help improve the meetings.

MODEL 11.1 | Group Situational Supervision

Group Development Stage (D)	Supervisory Styles/Roles (S)
D1 Low Development *High commitment—low competence* → Members come to the group committed, but they cannot perform with competence.	**S-A Autocratic** *High task—low maintenance* Provide direction so that the group has clear objectives and members know their roles. Make the decisions for the group.
D2 Moderate Development *Low commitment—some competence* → Members have become dissatisfied with the group. They have started to develop competence but are frustrated with results.	**S-C Consultative** *High task—high maintenance* Continue to direct the group so it develops task ability. Provide maintenance to regain commitment as the group structure takes place. Include members' input in decisions.
D3 High Development *Variable commitment—high competence* → Commitment changes over time while production remains relatively constant.	**S-P Participative** *Low task—high maintenance* Provide little direction. Focus on developing an effective group structure. Have the group participate in decision making.
D4 Outstanding Development *High commitment—high competence* → Commitment remains constantly high and so does production.	**S-L Laissez-faire** *Low task—low maintenance* Members provide their own task and maintenance roles. The supervisor is a group member. Allow the group to make its own decisions.

Learning Outcome 11-4

Explain how to plan for and conduct effective meetings.

Planning Meetings

There are at least five areas in which meeting planning is needed, as discussed here.

Objectives A great mistake made by those who call meetings is that they often have no clear idea and purpose for the meeting. Leaders should state what they want to happen as a result of the meeting. Before calling a meeting, you should clearly define its purpose and objective.[43]

Participants and Assignments Before calling the meeting, the leader should decide who is qualified to attend the meeting.[44] Does the full group or department need to attend? Should some nongroup specialist be invited to provide input? Participants should know in advance what is expected of them at the meeting. If any preparation is expected (reading material, doing some research, preparing a report, and the like), they should have adequate advance notice.

Agenda The leader should identify the activities that will take place during the meeting to achieve the objective of the meeting. The agenda tells the members what is expected and how the meeting will progress. Place agenda items in order of priority. Then if the group does not have time to cover every item, the least important items carry forward. At too many meetings, a leader puts all the so-called quick items first. The group gets bogged down and either rushes through the important items or puts them off until later.

Date, Time, and Place In determining which day(s) and time(s) of the week are best for meetings, get members' input. Members tend to be more alert early in the day. Clearly specify the beginning and ending time. Be sure to select an adequate place for the meeting and plan for the physical comfort of the group. Be sure seating provides eye contact for small discussion groups, and plan enough time so that the members do not have to rush. However, to speed up meetings, some firms have stand-up meetings (yes, no chairs allowed); they tend to take about one-third less time and the quality of the decision making is about the same.[45]

EXHIBIT 11.5 | Written Meeting Plan

Time: Date, day, place, beginning and ending times.

Objectives: A statement of the purpose and/or objective of the meeting.

Participants and Assignments: List each participant's name and assignment, if any. If all members have the same assignment, make one assignment statement.

Agenda: List each item to be covered in priority order with its approximate time limit.

Leadership The leader should determine the group's level of development and plan to provide the appropriate task and/or maintenance behavior. Each agenda item may need to be handled differently. For example, some items may simply call for disseminating information, while others may require a discussion or a vote to be taken; some items may require a report from a member. Some groups rotate the role of the group moderator or leader for each meeting, with groups that are capable of doing so, to develop meeting skills.

The Written Plan After leaders have planned the above five items, they should put them in writing and make copies to be distributed to each member who will attend the meeting. Exhibit 11.5 provides the recommended contents, in sequence, of a meeting plan.

Conducting Meetings

Below, you will learn about the group's first meeting, the three parts of each meeting, and leadership, group structure and dynamics, and emotions.

The First Meeting At the first meeting, the group is in the orientation stage. The leader should use the high task role; however, the members should be given the opportunity to spend some time getting to know one another. Introductions set the stage for subsequent interactions. If members find that their social needs will not be met, dissatisfaction may occur quickly. A simple technique is to start with introductions, then move on to the group's purpose, objectives, and members' roles. For long meetings, have a break that enables members to interact informally.

Communication Skills
Refer to CS Question 8.

WORK APPLICATION 11-9

Recall a specific meeting you attended. Did the group leader plan for the meeting by stating meeting objectives, identifying participants and their assignments, making an agenda, and stating the date, time, and place of the meeting? Did the leader provide a written meeting plan to the members prior to the meeting? Explain your answers and state what you would do differently if you were the leader.

The Three Parts of Each Meeting Begin the meetings on time; waiting for late members penalizes the members who are on time and develops a norm for coming late.[46] Each meeting should cover the following:

1. *Objectives.* Begin by reviewing progress to date, the group's objectives, and the purpose or objective for the specific meeting. If minutes are recorded, they are usually approved at the beginning of the next meeting. For most meetings, it is recommended that a secretary be appointed to take minutes.
2. *Agenda.* Cover the agenda items. Try to keep to the approximate times, but be flexible. If the discussion is constructive and members need more time, give it to them; however, if the discussion is more of a distractive argument, move ahead.
3. *Summarize and review assignments.* End the meeting on time. The leader should summarize what took place during the meeting. Were the meeting's objectives achieved? Review all of the assignments given during the meeting. Get a commitment to the task that each member should perform for the next or a specific future meeting. The secretary and/or leader should record all assignments. If there is no accountability and follow-up on assignments, members may not complete them.

Leadership, Group Structure and Dynamics, and Emotions As stated in the last section, leadership needs to change with the group's level of development. The leader must be sure to provide the appropriate task and/or maintenance behavior when it is needed. The leader and members are responsible for helping the team develop an effective group structure and dynamics as it performs the task (we have already discussed how to do so in this chapter). Members may get emotional during meetings, so use your skills at dealing with emotions from Chapter 5.

Learning Outcome 11-5

Identify six problem members and explain how to handle them so they do not have a negative effect on your meetings.

Handling Problem Team Members

Certain personality types tend to emerge in team meetings that can cause the group to be less efficient than possible. Next we will discuss how to handle six problem types to make the member and the group more effective.

The Silent Member For a team to be fully effective, all group members should participate. If members are silent, the team does not get the benefit of their input.

Encourage the silent member to participate,[47] without being obvious or overbearing. The simple rotation method, in which all members take turns giving their input, helps. To build up the silent members' confidence, call on them with questions they can easily answer. When you believe they have convictions, ask them to express them.[48] Watch their nonverbal communications.

If you are a silent type, participate more often. Don't be intimidated and quiet because you are thinking others are smarter than you—they most likely are not and may have the same thoughts as you. Go to the meeting prepared with notes knowing what you want to say.[49] Know when to stand up for your views and be assertive (Chapter 6).

The Talker Talkers have something to say about everything. They like to dominate the discussion. However, if they do dominate, the other members do not get to participate and may get bored.

Slow down talkers, don't shut them up, and don't let them dominate the group. The simple rotation method is effective with talkers, as they have to wait for their turn. When not using a rotation method, gently interrupt the talker and present your own ideas or call on other members to present their ideas. Prefacing questions with statements like, "Let's give those who have not answered yet a chance" can also slow down the talker.

If you tend to be a talker, realize that as an extravert you tend to "think out loud" by speaking, whereas introverts prefer to collect their thoughts before speaking and can be overwhelmed in a group, especially a group of extraverts.[50] So slow down and give others a chance to talk and do things for themselves.

The Wanderer Wanderers distract the team from the agenda items and often like to complain and criticize.

Keep the group on track. If the wanderer socializes, cut off the conversation. Be kind, thank the member for the contribution, and then throw a question out to the group to get it back on track. If the wanderer has a complaint that is legitimate and solvable, allow the group to discuss it. Group structure and dynamic issues should be addressed and resolved. However, griping without resolving anything tends to reduce morale and commitment to task accomplishment. If the wanderer complains about unresolvable issues, make statements like, "We may be underpaid, but we have no control over our pay. Complaining will not get us a raise; let's get back to the issue at hand."

If you tend to be a wanderer, try to be aware of your behavior and stay on the subject at hand.

The Bored Member Your team may have one or more members who are not interested in the task. The bored person may be preoccupied with other issues and not pay attention or participate in the group meeting. The bored member may be a know-it-all, who feels superior and wonders why the group is spending so much time on the obvious.

Keep members motivated. Assign the bored member a task such as recording ideas on the board or recording the minutes. Call on bored members; bring them into the group. If you allow them to sit back, things may get worse and others may decide not to participate either. Negative feelings can easily be carried to other team members.

If you tend to be bored, try to find ways to help motivate yourself (Chapter 8). Work at becoming more patient and in control of behavior that can have negative effects on other members.

The Arguer Like the talker, the arguer likes to be the center of attention. Arguers enjoy arguing for the sake of arguing, rather than helping the group. They turn things into a win–lose situation, and they cannot stand losing.

Resolve conflict, but not in an argumentative way. Do not get into an argument with arguers; that is exactly what they want to happen. If an argument starts, bring others into the discussion. If it is personal, cut it off. Personal attacks only hurt the group. Keep the discussion moving on target. Try to minimize arguers' opportunities for confrontation.

If you tend to be an arguer, strive to convey your views in an assertive debate format, not as an aggressive argument (Chapter 6). Listen to others' views and be willing to change if they have better ideas.

The Social Loafer This *social loafer* problem member doesn't want to take individual responsibility and do a fair share of the work.

Following all the previously mentioned meeting guidelines helps, especially giving clear individual assignments. Don't let the group develop norms that allow social loafing, and use peer pressure to get them to do their work. Confront social loafers assertively using the conflict resolution model in Chapter 6. When necessary, threaten to go to the boss. If these methods do not work, go to the supervisor (professor or boss) and explain the situation stating the specific behavior that is lacking and that you and the group have tried to resolve the problem, but the social loafer refuses to perform to standards.

Communication Skills
Refer to CS Question 9.

Skill-Building Exercise 11-1 develops this skill.

WORK APPLICATION 11-10

Identify group problem members at a meeting you attended. Was the leader effective in handling them? What would you have done to make them more productive members? Explain in detail.

Conclusion Whenever you work in a team, do not embarrass, intimidate, or argue with any members, no matter how much they provoke you. If you do, the result will make martyrs of them and a bully of you to the team. If you have serious problem members who do not respond to the above techniques, confront them individually outside the team meeting. Get them to agree to work in a cooperative way.

In the opening case, Bonnie Sue's meetings lacked specific assignments. She needs to use more directive leadership and assign tasks to specific members to complete outside the meetings. Recall that the problem members in Bonnie Sue's group were Carlos, a talker; Shelby, a wanderer; and Kirt, an arguer. Bonnie Sue needs to use her leadership skills to slow down Carlos, keep Shelby on topic, keep Kirt from fighting with others, and resolve conflicts quickly.

APPLICATION SITUATIONS / / /

Problem Team Members AS 11-4

Identify the problem member as:

A. Silent member	C. Wanderer	E. Arguer
B. Talker	D. Bored member	F. Social loafter

_______ 16. Jamal is always first or second to give his ideas. He is always elaborating on ideas. Because Jamal is so quick to respond, others sometimes make comments to him about it.

_______ 17. Two of the group members are sitting back quietly today for the first time. The other members are doing all the discussing and volunteering for assignments.

_______ 18. As the group is discussing a problem, a member asks the group if anyone heard about the vice president and the sales clerk.

_______ 19. Kareem is usually last to give his ideas. When asked to explain his position, Kareem often changes his answers to agree with the group.

_______ 20. Aaron enjoys challenging members' ideas. He likes to have the group do things his way. When a group member does not agree with Aaron, he makes wise comments about the member's past mistakes.

PROBLEM SOLVING AND DECISION MAKING

Recall that problem solving and decision making are an important part of group structure, affecting behavior, human relations, and performance.[51] Decision making separates the successful from the also-rans and failed companies.[52] For example, News Corp. acquired MySpace for $580 million in 2005, and it was losing money, so it sold MySpace in 2011 for only $35 million and a 5 percent stake in Specific Media.[53] In this section, we discuss the relationship between problem solving and decision making, decision-making styles, and the decision-making model.

The Relationship between Problem Solving and Decision Making

In short, decisions are made to solve problems and take advantage of opportunities, and these skills are important to career success.[54] Recognizing and taking advantage of opportunities is the key to entrepreneurship success.[55] When we discuss problems, we also include opportunities, and when we discuss decision making, we are also including problem solving because they go hand-in-hand.

The ability to understand and solve problems is an important skill.[56] A **problem** *exists whenever there is a difference between what is actually happening and what the individual or group wants to be happening.* If your objective is to produce 500 units per day, but only 475 units are produced, you have a problem. Individuals typically try to reduce the discrepancy between the actual performance and the objective.[57] Thus, **problem solving** *is the process of taking corrective action in order to meet objectives.* **Decision making** *is the process of selecting an alternative course of action that will solve a problem.* Decisions must be made when you are faced with a problem or opportunity.[58] When making decisions, remember the goal of human relations is to create a win–win situation for stakeholders.

WORK APPLICATION 11-11

Give an example of a problem you face now.

In the opening case, Bonnie Sue has a problem because her team is not performing to her expectations. She needs to make some decisions about how to get the team to pull together, using the group structure and dynamics, and lead as a situational supervisor to develop the team, as discussed throughout this chapter.

Decision-Making Styles

There are various decision-making styles, including reflexive, consistent, and reflective. To determine your decision-making style, answer the questions in Self-Assessment Exercise 11-3.

/// Self-Assessment Exercise 11-3 ///

Decision-Making Styles

Select the answer (1 to 3) that best describes how you make decisions.

A. Overall I'm _____ to act.

1. quick 2. moderate 3. slow

B. I spend _____ amount of time making important decisions as/than I do making less important decisions.

1. about the same 2. a greater 3. a much greater

C. When making decisions, I _____ go with my first thought.

1. usually 2. occasionally 3. rarely

D. When making decisions, I'm _____ concerned about making errors.

1. rarely 2. occasionally 3. often

E. When making decisions, I _____ recheck my work.

1. rarely 2. occasionally 3. usually

/// Self-Assessment Exercise 11-3 /// (*continued*)

F. When making decisions, I gather ______ information.

1. little 2. some 3. lots of

G. When making decisions, I consider ______ alternative actions.

1. few 2. some 3. lots of

H. When making a decision, I usually make it ______ before the deadline.

1. long 2. somewhat 3. just

I. After making a decision, I ______ look for other alternatives, wishing I had waited.

1. rarely 2. occasionally 3. usually

J. I ______ regret having made a decision.

1. rarely 2. occasionally 3. often

To determine your style, add the numbers that represent your answers to the 10 questions. The total will be between 10 and 30. Place an X on the continuum at the point that represents your score.

Reflexive		Consistent		Reflective	
10 ------------------------	16 ------------------------		23 ------------------------		30

A score of 10 to 16 indicates a reflexive style; 17 to 23 indicates a consistent style; and 24 to 30 indicates a reflective style. You have determined your preferred personal decision-making style. Groups also have a preferred decision-making style, based on how their members make decisions. Changing the *I* to *we,* you could answer the 10 questions to refer to a group rather than to yourself.

Reflexive Style A reflexive decision maker likes to make quick decisions ("to shoot from the hip"), without taking the time to get all the information that may be needed and without considering all alternatives. This is the commonly used style of the poorly adjusted Big Five personality type.[59] On the positive side, reflexive decision makers are decisive; they do not procrastinate. On the negative side, making quick decisions can lead to waste and duplication when a decision is not the best possible alternative. If you use a reflexive style, you may want to slow down and spend more time gathering information and analyzing alternatives. Following the steps in the decision-making model, our next topic, can help you develop your skills.

Reflective Style A reflective decision maker likes to take plenty of time to make decisions, taking into account considerable information and an analysis of several alternatives. On the positive side, the reflective type does not make decisions that are rushed. On the negative side, they may procrastinate and waste valuable time and other resources and lose out on opportunities. The reflective decision maker may be viewed as wishy-washy and indecisive. If you use a reflective style, you may want to speed up your decision making. As Andrew Jackson once said, "Take time to deliberate; but when the time for action arrives, stop thinking and go on." Successful CEOs are not afraid to make decisions.[60]

Learning Outcome 11-6

List the five steps in the decision-making model.

Consistent Style A consistent decision maker makes decisions without rushing or wasting time. Consistent decision makers know when they have enough information and alternatives to make a sound decision. They have the most consistent record of good decisions. Steve Jobs was known for being a great problem solver, and especially for taking advantage of opportunities to introduce new iProducts.[61] Consistent decision makers tend to follow the decision-making steps below.

The Decision-Making Model

We all like to think that we are rational and have great intuitive judgment when making decisions. However, research reveals that people are far from rational and often act against their best interests, and that intuitive judgment is often flawed and doesn't help us make good decisions.[62] Decision making can be more rational when following a process,[63] which we call the decision-making model. Of course we have to use some intuitive judgment,[64] but using the model helps us be more rational and focus our intuitive judgment, which is called *bounded rationality*.[65] The five steps are shown in Model 11.2 and discussed here.

Communication Skills
Refer to CS Question 10.

When to Use the Decision-Making Model It is not necessary to follow all five steps in the model when making unimportant recurring decisions when the outcome of the decision is known, called certainty.[66] Risk taking is fundamental to decision making.[67] Use the model when making important nonrecurring decisions when the outcome is risky or uncertain.[68] Following the steps in the model will not guarantee success; however, following the model increases the probability of successful decision making. You most likely followed the steps in the model when selecting a college without consciously knowing it. Consciously use the model in your daily life, and you will improve your ability to make decisions. Let's examine each step here, as it is shown in Model 11.2.

Step 1: Define the Problem If you misdiagnose the problem, you will not solve it.[69] So slow down and focus only on defining the problem because when our attention is scattered, we tend to misestimate, misunderstand, and misspecify what we think we face.[70] In analyzing a problem, first distinguish the *symptoms* from the *cause* of the problem. To do so, list the observable and describable occurrences (symptoms) that indicate a problem exists. For example, Wayne, an employee with five years' tenure, has been an excellent producer on the job. However, in the last month, Wayne has been out sick and tardy more times than in the past two years. What is the problem? If you say absenteeism or tardiness, you are confusing symptoms and causes. They are symptoms of the problem. If the supervisor

MODEL 11.2 | Decision-Making Model

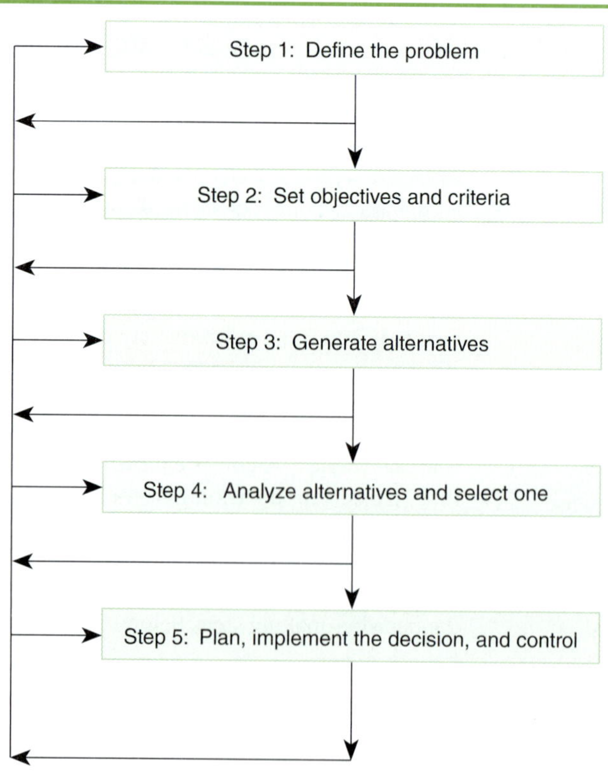

simply disciplines Wayne, he or she may decrease the tardiness and absenteeism, but the problem will not be solved. It would be wiser for the supervisor to talk to the employee and find out the reason (cause) for the problem. The real problem may be a personal problem at home or on the job.

Step 2: Set Objectives and Criteria After the problem has been defined, you set an objective (end result of the decision) to solve the problem. Refer to Chapter 8 for the setting objectives model.

Next, you identify the criteria the decision must meet to achieve the objective. It is helpful to specify *must* and *want* criteria. Must criteria have to be met, while want criteria are desirable but not necessary. For example: Objective: "To hire a store manager by June 30, 2012." The must criteria are a college degree and a minimum of five years' experience as a store manager. The want criterion is that the hiree should be a minority group member. The organization wants to hire a minority but will not hire one who does not meet the must criteria.

Continuing the example with Wayne: The objective is to improve Wayne's attendance record. The criterion is his prior good record of attendance.

Step 3: Generate Alternatives You need to generate possible methods, or alternatives, for solving the problem through decision making.[71] There are usually many ways to solve a problem; in fact, if you don't have two or more alternatives, you don't have to make a decision. When making nonroutine decisions, new, creative solutions are often needed.[72] In the next section, we discuss creativity, which is commonly used as part of this step in the decision-making model.

When gathering the information needed to generate alternatives, you can neither expect nor afford complete information. However, you must get enough information to enable you to make good decisions—the consistent decision style. It is often helpful to ask others for advice on possible solutions to your problem.[73] When generating alternatives, it is important not to evaluate them at the same time (evaluation is in step 4)—just list anything reasonable that can possibly solve the problem.

Continuing the example with Wayne: Some alternatives are giving Wayne a warning, punishing him in some way, or talking to him to determine the reason for the change in his behavior.

Step 4: Analyze Alternatives and Select One Here you must evaluate each alternative in terms of the objectives and criteria. Try to avoid distractions that can lead to poor choices.[74] Think forward and try to predict the outcome of each alternative, and try to create a win–win situation for everyone involved in the decision. One method you can use to analyze alternatives is *cost–benefit* analysis. Each alternative has its positive and its negative aspects, or its costs and benefits. Costs are more than monetary. They may include a sacrifice of time, money, and so forth. Cost–benefit analysis has become popular in the nonprofit sector, where the benefits are often difficult to determine in quantified dollars.

Another approach to improving the quality of decisions is the devil's advocate approach. The *devil's advocate technique* requires the individual to explain and defend his or her position before the group. The group critically asks the presenter questions. They try to shoot holes in the alternative solution to determine any possible problems in its implementation. After a period of time, the group reaches a refined solution.

Continuing the example with Wayne: The alternative selected is to have a talk with him to try to determine why his attendance has changed.

Step 5: Plan, Implement the Decision, and Control Step 5 has three separate parts, as the title states. After making the decision, you should develop a *plan* of action with a schedule for its implementation. Lack of planning is a common reason why decisions are not *implemented*.

Communication Skills
Refer to CS Questions 11 and 12.

Skill-Building Exercise 11-2 develops this skill.

WORK APPLICATION 11-12

Solve the problem you gave in Work Application 11-11, following the five steps in the decision-making model. Write it out clearly, labeling each step.

Decision making is a waste of time if you don't actually implement the alternative. As with all plans, *controls* should be developed while planning. Checkpoints with feedback should be established to determine if the decision is solving the problem. If not, corrective action may be needed.[75] You should not be locked into an irrational *escalation of commitment* to a decision that is not solving the problem.[76] When you make a poor decision, you should admit the mistake and change the decision by going back to previous steps in the decision-making model.

Concluding the example with Wayne: The supervisor plans what he or she will say to him during the meeting, conducts the meeting, and follows up to be sure that the problem is solved.

Model 11.2 lists the five steps in the decision-making model. Notice that the steps do not go simply from start to end. At any step, you may have to return to a previous step to make changes. For example, if you are in the fifth step and control and implementation are not solving the problem as planned, you may have to backtrack to take corrective action by generating and selecting a new alternative or by changing the objective. If the problem was not defined accurately, you may have to go back to the beginning.

CREATIVITY AND GROUP PROBLEM SOLVING AND DECISION MAKING

Creativity and innovation go together, but they are different. **Creativity** *means the ability to develop unique alternatives to solve problems.* Innovation is the organizational implementation of the creative ideas.[77] Innovation is important to organizational success,[78] and many companies are being pressured to be innovative.[79] Firms can come up with their own creative ideas, or imitate other firm innovations.[80] In this section, we'll focus on creativity that can take place during the third step of the decision-making model. Recall that when we work with others, there is a good chance that conflict will arise, so when you are in a group solving problems and making decisions, use the *conflict resolutions skills* you learned in Chapter 6.

Communication Skills
Refer to CS Question 13.

An example of creativity was introduced by Adelphi University when it wanted to expand its graduate business program. People perceived that they did not have time to further their education. The alternative Adelphi developed to solve the problem was the "classroom on wheels," which offers classes four days a week on commuter trains into and out of New York. Today, there are online degree programs. 3M is known as an innovative company. It makes thousands of products, many of which are found in other products, including the iPhone.[81]

The Creative Process

For a company to be creative, managers need to support and promote creativity.[82] They need to set creativity work goals and make creativity a job requirement.[83] For example, 3M's goal is to generate 30 percent of revenues from new products introduced in the past five years.[84] Innovative CEOs spend 50 percent more of their personal time engaging in innovation than average CEOs.[85] Steve Jobs at Apple was probably the most innovative CEO, with the ability to focus on new creative products that changed how we communicate and listen to music.[86] Some entrepreneurs innovate their way out of problems and into opportunities, like discovering new businesses and products.[87]

To improve your creativity, focus on thinking about new products, processes, and procedures that are designed to be useful, in both your personal and professional lives.[88] Follow the stages in the creative process. The four **stages in the creative process** *are (1) preparation, (2) possible solutions, (3) incubation, and (4) evaluation.* These steps are also listed in Model 11.3.

1. *Preparation.* You must become familiar with the problem. This is done during steps 1 and 2 of the decision-making model. Get others' opinions, feelings, and ideas, as

MODEL 11.3 | Stages in the Creative Process

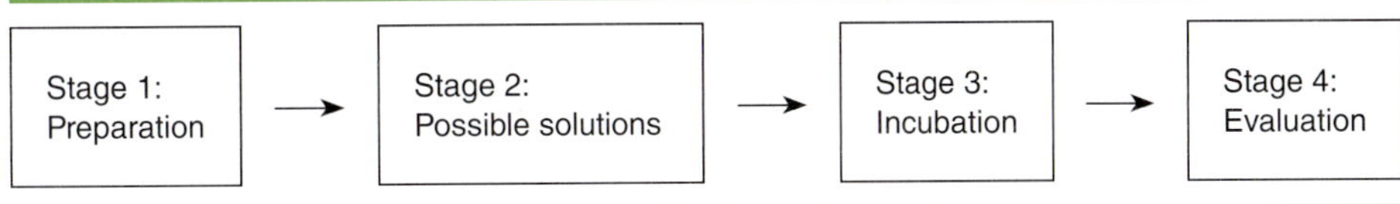

Communication Skills
Refer to CS Question 14.

WORK APPLICATION 11-13

Give an example of how you solved a problem using the stages in the creative process, or used the creative process to solve an existing problem.

well as the facts. When solving a problem, look for new angles, use imagination and invention, and don't set boundaries—think outside the box!

2. *Possible solutions.* Generate as many possible creative solutions as you can think of, without making any judgments. The brainstorming rules (discussed next) will provide details.
3. *Incubation.* After generating alternatives, take a break. It doesn't have to be long, but take time before working on the problem again. During the incubation stage, you may have an insight into the problem's solution. Have you ever worked hard on a problem and become discouraged, but when you had given up or taken a break, the solution came to you?
4. *Evaluation.* Before implementing a solution, you should evaluate the alternative to make sure the idea is practical. Evaluation through feedback often leads to more creativity.[89]

How people respond to creative ideas affects behavior. For a list of responses that kill creativity, see Exhibit 11.6. Avoid these responses and discourage others from using them as well.

Learning Outcome 11-7

Describe five techniques for generating creative alternatives.

Using Groups to Generate Creative Alternatives

In step 3 of the decision-making process, organizations today are using group input to generate creative alternatives.[90] Exhibit 11.7 lists the five techniques that are described here.

Brainstorming **Brainstorming** *is the process of suggesting many alternatives, without evaluation, to solve a problem.* When brainstorming, the group is presented with a problem or opportunity and asked to come up with creative solutions.[91] Brainstorming is commonly used for creating new products, naming products, and developing advertising slogans. Here are four interrelated brainstorming rules:

- *Quantity.* Team members should generate as many ideas as possible. More ideas increase the chances of finding an excellent solution. Generating alternatives is step 3 of the decision-making model.

EXHIBIT 11.6 | Responses That Kill Creativity

- It isn't in the budget.
- We're doing fine now, so why change?
- It costs too much.
- We don't have the time.
- That will make other products obsolete.
- We're too small/big for it.
- We've never done it before.
- Has anyone else ever tried it?
- It won't work in our company/industry.
- That's not our problem or responsibility.
- We're not ready for that.
- We tried that before and it doesn't work.
- You're years ahead of your time.
- It can't be done.
- You can't teach an old dog new tricks.
- Let's form a committee.
- It's too radical a change.
- Don't be ridiculous; let's get back to reality.

EXHIBIT 11.7 | Techniques for Generating Creative Alternatives

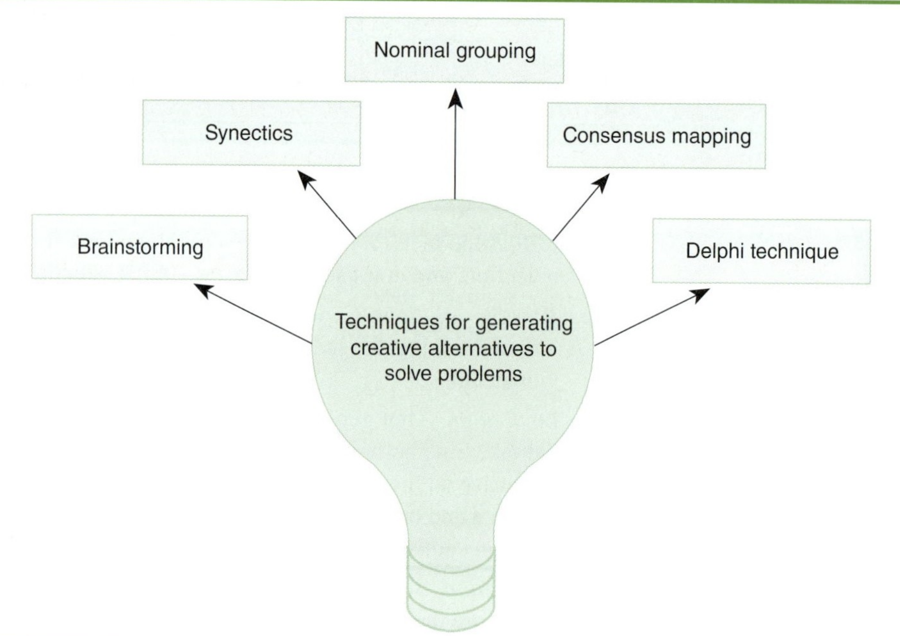

- *No criticism.* Team members should not criticize or evaluate ideas in any way during the solution-generation phase of brainstorming. Evaluation is done in step 4 of decision making—analyze alternatives and select one.
- *Freewheel.* You can't think outside the box when you are in it. You have to see things from new angles or perspectives. Team members should express any idea that comes to mind, no matter how strange, crazy, or weird—thus, the need to avoid criticism that will hinder members' creativity and to avoid responses that kill creativity (see Exhibit 11.6).
- *Extend.* Team members should try to build on the ideas of others and even take them in new directions. Remember that all ideas belong to the group, so everyone gets the credit. Extending helps build quantity and freewheeling, but watch out for criticism.
- *Brainwriting.* Brainwriting is a variation of brainstorming. To eliminate the influence of team peer pressure and other members' suggestions, participants write their ideas down. Then ideas are recorded, and members try to improve and combine ideas. It is especially relevant for use with virtual teams meeting online.

Synectics Synectics focuses on coming up with novel ideas rather than a quantity of ideas.[92] *Synectics* is the process of generating novel alternatives through role-playing and fantasizing. At first, to expand the group's thinking process, the leader does not state the exact nature of the situation. For example, when Nolan Bushnell wanted to develop a new concept in family dining, he began by discussing general leisure activities. Bushnell then moved toward leisure activities having to do with eating out. The idea that came out of this synectics process was a restaurant–electronic game complex where families could play games and purchase pizza and hamburgers. The restaurant–electronic game complex is called Pizza Time Theatre and its mascot is Chuck E. Cheese, which is also used as the restaurant's name.

Nominal Grouping It is appropriate to use nominal grouping to ensure that status difference among members doesn't influence the process and decision; some members tend to agree with the boss or informal leader and ignore low status ideas. *Nominal grouping* is the process of generating and evaluating alternatives through a structured voting method. This process usually involves six steps:

1. Each member individually generates ideas in writing (brainwriting).
2. In a round-robin fashion, members give ideas. Someone records all ideas where everyone can see them.
3. Alternatives are clarified through a guided discussion and any additional ideas are recorded.
4. Each member rates the ideas and votes; the voting eliminates alternatives.
5. An initial vote discussion takes place for clarification, not persuasion. During this time, it is recommended that members present the logic behind the reasons they gave for the various alternatives.
6. The final vote is taken to select the alternative solution presented to the leader. Management may or may not implement the decision.

Communication Skills
Refer to CS Question 15.

Consensus Mapping A *consensus* is a cooperative attempt to develop a solution acceptable to all employees, rather than a competitive battle in which a solution is forced on some members of the group. The major benefit of consensus mapping is that since the solution is the group's, members generally are more committed to implementing it. The process is to have a discussion trying to get everyone to agree on the decision to solve the problem or take advantage of the opportunity.

WORK APPLICATION 11-14

Give example situations in which it would be appropriate for a manager to use each of the five techniques for generating creative alternatives (brainstorming, synectics, nominal grouping, consensus mapping, and the Delphi technique).

Delphi Technique The Delphi technique is considered a variation of nominal grouping, without face-to-face interaction at any point, and it also includes consensus. The *Delphi technique* polls a group through a series of anonymous questionnaires. The opinions of each round of questionnaires are analyzed and resubmitted to the group in the next round of questionnaires. This process may continue for five or more rounds before a consensus emerges. The technique is used for technological forecasts, such as what the next online breakthrough will be.

APPLICATION SITUATIONS / / /

Using Groups to Generate Alternatives AS 11-5

In the five situations below, identify the most appropriate group technique to use to generate alternative solutions.

A. Brainstorming
B. Synectics
C. Nominal grouping
D. Consensus mapping
E. Delphi technique

________ 21. The supervisor wants to develop some new and different toys. She is meeting with employees and children together.

________ 22. The department is suffering from morale problems.

________ 23. The supervisor must decide on new furniture for the office.

________ 24. The supervisor wants to reduce waste in the department.

________ 25. The supervisor wants to project future trends of the business.

Skill-Building Exercise 11-3 develops this skill.

Communication Skill
Refer to CS Question 16.

ADVANTAGES AND DISADVANTAGES OF GROUP DECISION MAKING

There are advantages and disadvantages of using groups to make decisions. The challenge is to maximize the advantages while minimizing the disadvantages and the bottom line is that the group decision must have synergy. *Synergy* occurs when the group's solution to a problem or opportunity is superior to all individuals'. Unfortunately, research indicates that people often choose inferior alternatives when choosing in groups.[93] Skill Building Exercise 11-3 gives you the opportunity to see if your group can reach synergy. See Exhibit 11-8 for the advantages and disadvantages of using group decision making.

Skill-Building Exercise 11-4 develops this skill.

When to Use Groups in Decision Making Use groups when making important nonrecurring decisions when the outcome is risky or uncertain,[94] using the decision-making model. More specifically, use groups when the decision is complex, requires wide-ranging expertise, when the outcome affects a number of individuals who must share responsibility, and when there is a need to represent diverse constituencies and stakeholders.[95] The question today isn't so much about *should* we use groups to make decisions, but what level of participation should we use? Skill Building Exercise 11-4 at the end of the chapter develops this skill.

DOES TEAMWORK AND DECISION MAKING APPLY GLOBALLY?

At major global multinational corporations (MNCs), teamwork has been important for many years.[96] However, the level of teamwork does vary, and operating in an *individualistic versus a collectivist culture* does affect teamwork. In general, in collectivist cultures of Asian countries such as Japan, teamwork is considered very important and leadership and decision making are participative; the group composition is not very diversified, with shared norms and cohesiveness; and there is less conflict than within the United States and many European countries that are more individualistic. Unlike in the United States and many European countries, there are fewer status differences, as Asians don't want to stand out as being the stars—they just want to be part of the team. New technologies, especially the Internet, have made virtual teams more common and at the same time have increased the speed and quality of global communications and decisions.

The global economy requires decisions to be made that affect operations worldwide, but at the same time, country and cultural differences call for local decisions. People from different cultures don't necessarily make decisions the same way or at the same rate of speed. In countries that are not time-sensitive, such as Egypt, decisions are more reflective.

EXHIBIT 11.8 | Advantages and Disadvantages of Group Decision Making

Advantages	Disadvantages
• **Better decisions**—with synergy, including avoiding errors with the help of the devil's advocate technique • **More alternatives**—more people provide diverse idea • **Acceptance and commitment**—people tend to accept and be more committed to implement decision they help make • **Morale**—participants have more job satisfaction	• **Time**—it takes a long time to make group decisions • **Domination**—powerful individuals or a coalition may actually make the decision • **Conformity of groupthink**—members may go along with the suggested decision without questioning when they disagree with it to avoid conflict and keep social solidarity • **Responsibility and social loafing**—no one individual is accountable for the decision, so people don't take it as seriously and some don't do their fair share of the work

Communication Skills
Refer to CS Question 17.

In time-sensitive countries, such as the United States, decisions are more reflexive. Countries using participative decision making take longer than do countries that use autocratic decision making.

The level of participation in team decision making does vary by culture. In *high power-distance cultures* (for example, Mexico, Venezuela, the Philippines, and Yugoslavia), where more autocratic decisions are made, participation is not acceptable. In *low power-distance cultures* (the United States, Japan, Ireland, Australia, New Zealand, Denmark, Israel, and the Netherlands), there is greater use of participation in decision making—especially in Japan.

Let's complete Self-Assessment Exercise 11-4 to better understand how your personality affects your team behavior.

/// Self-Assessment Exercise 11-4 ///

Personality Traits and Teams and Decision Making

Read the two statements below:

I enjoy being part of a team and working with others more than working alone.

Strongly agree 7 6 5 4 3 2 1 Strongly disagree

I enjoy achieving team goals more than individual accomplishments.

Strongly agree 7 6 5 4 3 2 1 Strongly disagree

The stronger you agree with these two statements, the higher the probability that you will be a good team player. (However, not agreeing strongly does not mean that you are not a good team player.) Below is some information on how the Big Five personality dimensions and their related motive needs can affect your teamwork.

If you have a high *surgency* personality, you probably have a high need for power. Whether you are the team leader or not, you have to be careful not to dominate the group. Seek others' input, and know when to lead and when to follow. Even when you have great ideas, be sensitive to others so they don't feel that you are bullying them, and stay calm as you influence them. Be aware of your motives to make sure you benefit the team. You have the potential to make a positive contribution to the team with your influencing leadership skills. If you have a low need for power, try to be assertive so that others don't take advantage of you, and speak up when you have good ideas.

With a high need for power, you may make quick, reflexive decisions. Your preferred leadership style may tend to be autocratic or consultative. You may need to allow more participation in decision making to be more effective. Participation will also slow down your decision making.

If you are high in *agreeableness* personality traits, with a high need for affiliation, you will tend to be a good team player. However, don't let the fear of hurting relationships get in your way of influencing the team when you have good ideas. Don't be too quick to give in to others. It doesn't help the performance of the team when you have a better idea that is not implemented. You have the potential to be a valuable asset to the team as you contribute your skills of working well with others and making them feel important. If you have a low need for affiliation, be careful to be sensitive to others.

If you are high in *conscientiousness,* with a high need for achievement, you have to watch your natural tendency to be more of an individualist than a team player. It's good to have your own goals, but if the team and organization fail, so do you. Remember that there is usually more than one good way to do anything; your way is not always the best. Don't be too much of a perfectionist because you can cause problems with team members. Being conscientious, you have the potential to help the team do a good job and reach its full potential. If you have a low need for achievement, push yourself to be a valuable contributor to the group; pull your own weight.

With a high need for achievement, you may know what you want and may make quick, reflexive decisions. You may change leadership styles to help get what you want. Being conscientious, you may tend to follow the steps in the decision-making model more than the other personality types.

Being high on *adjustment,* in control of your emotions, helps the team. If you have a tendency to get emotional, make an effort to stay calm and help the team.

People low in adjustment tend to make quick, reflexive decisions and tend to push to get what they want using an autocratic style. Try not to make decisions when you are highly emotional, wait until you can think and act rationally.

If you are *open to new experiences,* you will try new things that may help the team improve. When you have ideas

(continued)

/// Self-Assessment Exercise 11-4 /// (*continued*)

that can help the team improve, share them with the team; use your influencing skills. If you are reluctant to change, strive to be more open-minded and to try new things.

People who are open to new experiences are usually more creative than those who are not. If you are reluctant to try new things, make an effort to continually look for ways to improve and be more creative.

Action Plan: Based on your personality, what specific things will you do to improve your team and decision-making skills? Should you follow the steps in the decision-making model more often?

____

____

____

____

PUTTING IT ALL TOGETHER

Communication Skills
Refer to CS Question 18.

Organizations use groups to meet performance objectives. As the people in a team interact, they develop group dynamics. The group structure is a major determinant of the group's stage of development. The more effective the group structure and dynamics, the higher the stage of development, and the higher the stage of development, the greater the level of performance of the group. The group's performance, in turn, affects its behavior and human relations. See Exhibit 11.9 for an illustration of how the factors discussed in this chapter influence teams.

As we bring this chapter to a close, you should understand the importance of the team performance model and be effective at helping the group with its structure, dynamics, and development level as you work together and during meetings. You should be able to lead the team based on its level of development using the group situational supervision model; use the decision-making model to improve your skill at solving problems and making decisions; use the creative process model to improve your creativity; and use the team situational supervision model to select the appropriate level of participation when making decisions (this last skill is developed in Skill Building Exercise 11-4).

EXHIBIT 11.9 | Team Performance Model Components

Team Performance (*f*)*	Team Structure	Team Dynamics	Team Development Stage, Leadership Style, and Decision Making
High ↔ Low	• Leadership • Composition • Problem solving and decision making • Conflict	• Objectives • Size • Norms • Cohesiveness • Status • Roles	1. Orientation; autocratic; leader makes decisions 2. Dissatisfaction; consultative; leader consults team for input on decisions 3. Resolution; participative; leader makes decisions with team 4. Production; laissez-faire; team makes decisions 5. Termination; none; none

(**f*) = is a function of.

/ / / REVIEW / / /

The chapter review is organized to help you master the 8 learning outcomes for Chapter 11. First provide your own response to each learning outcome, and then check the summary provided to see how well you understand the material. Next, identify the final statement in each section as either true or false (T/F). Correct each false statement. Answers are given at the end of the chapter.

LO 11-1 Explain the six components of team dynamics and how they affect team performance.

Team dynamics refers to the patterns of interactions that emerge as groups develop. The six components of team dynamics are: (1) *Objectives*—without clear objectives, groups will not be effective. (2) *Group size*—if the group is too large or small, it will not be effective. (3) *Group norms*—the group's shared expectations concerning members' behavior; with norms that do not support high-level performance the group will not be effective. (4) *Group cohesiveness*—the attractiveness and closeness of the group members; generally, noncohesive groups are not as effective as cohesive groups. (5) *Status within the group* —a member's rank within the group; when members are not satisfied with their status they tend to hold back group performance. (6) *Group roles*—shared expectations of how group members will fulfill the requirements of their position; when members do not understand or do not play their roles as expected, the group's performance suffers.

The best size for teams is five members. T F

LO 11-2 Describe the five stages of a team's development.

There are five stages of team development. In stage 1, *orientation* (low development level D1), members have a high commitment but low competence to perform the task. In stage 2, *dissatisfaction* (moderate development level D2), members have a lower commitment but have developed some competence. In stage 3, *resolution* (high development level D3), members' commitment varies and the competence is high. In stage 4, *production* (outstanding development level D4), members have a high commitment and high competence. In stage 5, *termination,* the group no longer exists.

Functional groups and standing committees don't usually go through a termination stage of development. T F

LO 11-3 Explain the four situational supervisory styles to use with a group, based on its stage of development.

In stage 1, *orientation* (low development level D1), the supervisor should use the autocratic style, S-A, which is high task–low maintenance. In stage 2, *dissatisfaction* (moderate development level D2), the supervisor should use the consultative style, S-C, which is high task–high maintenance. In stage 3, *resolution* (high development level D3), the supervisor should use the participative style, S-P, which is low task–high maintenance. In stage 4, *production* (outstanding development level D4), the supervisor should use the laissez-faire style, S-L, which is low task–low maintenance.

At group stage 4, the leader lets the group make its own decisions. T F

LO 11-4 Explain how to plan for and conduct effective meetings.

Areas in which meeting planning is needed include: (1) setting objectives; (2) determining who will participate, and their assignments; (3) developing an agenda; (4) setting a time and place for the meeting; and (5) determining the appropriate leadership style. In conducting the meeting, the leader should go over objectives, cover agenda items, and summarize and review assignments.

The way the manager runs the meeting should be based on the group's level of development. T F

LO 11-5 Identify six problem members and explain how to handle them so they do not have a negative effect on your meetings.

Problem group members include: (1) The silent member—bring this member into the discussion without pushing him or her; the rotation method is helpful. (2) The talker—slow down this member and gently interrupt and call on other members for their input; the rotation method is helpful. (3) The wanderer—keep him or her on the subject and gently remind the group of its objective, asking a question that will get the group back on track. (4) The bored member—keep this member interested and involved by asking for his or her input; assign tasks that will hold his or her attention. (5) The arguer—don't argue with this type of group member and keep the discussion moving; call on other members to diffuse arguments. (6) The social loafer—give him or her specific assignments, use peer pressure and conflict resolution, threaten to go to the boss, and do so if necessary.

Managers should embarrass, intimidate, or argue with members who provoke them during meetings. T F

LO 11-6 List the five steps in the decision-making model.

The steps in the decision-making model are: (1) define the problem; (2) set objectives and criteria; (3) generate alternatives; (4) analyze alternatives and select one; and (5) plan, implement the decision, and control.

The decision-making model should be used when making unimportant recurring decisions. T F

LO 11-7 Describe five techniques for generating creative alternatives.

Five techniques for generating creative alternatives include: (1) *brainstorming,* the process of suggesting as many alternatives as possible, without evaluation, to solve a problem; (2) *synectics,* the process of generating novel alternatives through role-playing and fantasizing; (3) *nominal grouping,* the process of generating and evaluating alternatives using a structured voting method; (4) *consensus mapping,* the process of developing a group consensus to solve a problem; and (5) the *Delphi technique,* which involves using a series of anonymous questionnaires to refine a solution.

The one thing these five techniques have in common is that they all involve a small group of people who get together to come up with creative ideas. T F

LO 11-8 Define the following 16 key terms.

Select one or more methods: (1) fill in the missing key terms from memory; (2) match the key terms from the end of the review with their definitions below; and/or (3) copy the key terms in order from the key terms at the beginning of the chapter.

____________________ involves working together to achieve something beyond the capabilities of individuals working alone.

The ____________________ states that a team's performance is based on its structure, dynamics, and stage of development.

____________________ refers to the patterns of interactions that emerge as groups develop.

____________________ are the group's shared expectations of its members' behavior.

____________________ is the attractiveness and closeness group members have for one another and for the group.

____________________ is the perceived ranking of one member relative to other members of the group.

____________________ are the things group members do and say that directly aid in the accomplishment of the group's objective(s).

____________________ are the things group members do and say to develop and sustain group dynamics.

A(n) ____________________ exists whenever there is a difference between what is actually happening and what the individual or group wants to be happening.

____________________ is the process of taking corrective action in order to meet objectives.

____________________ is the process of selecting an alternative course of action that will solve a problem.

____________________ is the ability to develop unique alternatives to solve problems.

The ____________________ are (1) preparation, (2) possible solutions, (3) incubation, and (4) evaluation.

____________________ is the process of suggesting many alternatives, without evaluation, to solve a problem.

____________________ are shared expectations of how group members will fulfill the requirements of their position.

____________________ are the things group members do and say to meet their own needs or objectives at the expense of the team.

/ / / KEY TERMS / / /

brainstorming 355
creativity 354
decision making 350
group cohesiveness 337
maintenance roles 339
norms 337
problem 350
problem solving 350
roles 338
self-interest roles 339
stages in the creative process 354
status 338
task roles 338
team dynamics 336
team performance model 335
teamwork 333

/ / / COMMUNICATION SKILLS / / /

The following critical thinking questions can be used for class discussion and/or as written assignments to develop communication skills. Be sure to give complete explanations for all questions.

1. Many of the TV reality shows have an element of teamwork. However, they often have members of the teams doing negative things to each other to get ahead. Do you believe that these negative examples of poor teamwork influence people's behavior in real-life groups? Can you think of any TV shows that give *positive* examples of good teamwork?
2. It has been said that the team performance model is too simplistic; group performance is much more complex. Do you agree with this statement? How can the model be used?
3. What is the difference between a rule and a norm? Do norms help or hurt groups? Is it ethical to make group members comply with group norms? Can groups stop having norms?
4. It has been said that success breeds cohesiveness, which in turn leads to more success. What does this mean? How is it supposed to work? Do you agree with the statement?
5. Select a work or sports team to which you belong/have belonged. Which team member (not the manager or coach) had the highest level of status? Identify the factors that contributed to that person's high status.
6. The younger generations have been called the "me generation" because they care only about themselves. Do you agree with this statement? How does putting oneself as number one affect group performance? Which group role is illustrated through the "me generation" statement?
7. Team development stages state that most people coming to a new group are enthusiastic, but that with time they lose some of their morale. What types of things happen in most groups to cause this decline in morale? Be sure to focus on the components of team structure and team dynamics.
8. Many people complain about meetings. Recall a meeting that you have attended. Do you have any complaints about it? State whether or not the meeting had each of the four parts of a written meeting plan (Exhibit 11.5) and whether the meeting included (1) reviewing objectives, (2) covering agenda items, and (3) summarizing and reviewing assignments. How could the meeting have been improved?
9. Identity the types of problem team members you have encountered. Did the team leader effectively handle these problem members? How could the leader have done a better job of managing these members?
10. What is the role of intuition in decision making? Should managers use more objective or subjective intuition techniques when making decisions?
11. Is following the steps in the decision-making model really all that important? Which steps of the model do you tend to follow? Which steps do you tend to not use? Will you use the model in your personal and/or professional life?
12. Should managers be ethical in their decision making? If so, how should ethics be used in decision making?
13. Are creativity and innovation really that important to all types of businesses?
14. Is it important to evaluate a creative idea before it becomes an innovation?
15. Have you used any of the five techniques for generating creative alternatives? If yes, which ones?
16. Which of the potential advantages and disadvantags of group problem solving and decision making do you think arise most frequently?
17. With virtual team members from all over the world, how does the global economy affect team performance?
18. How do your personality traits affect your teamwork and decision-making style and your interest and ability to participate in group decision making?

CASE / / / Mark Zuckerberg, Founder and CEO of Facebook

By now, it is a safe bet that most people on the planet know the name Mark Zuckerberg, yet he is a very private individual who prefers to spend much of his time with friends and family members. The interview that he gave to *Time* magazine following the announcement that he had been named *Time*'s 2010 Person of the Year is one of the few occasions that Zuckerberg allowed the media into his world. The caption went as follows:

> For connecting more than half a billion people and mapping the social relations among them (something that has never been done before); for creating a new system of exchanging

information that has become both indispensable and sometimes a little scary; and finally, for changing how we all live our lives in ways that are innovative and even optimistic, Mark Elliot Zuckerberg is *Time*'s 2010 Person of the Year.[97]

The interview revealed information about Zuckerberg's interpersonal relationship with his followers and the dynamic between them. The *Time* interviewer reveals that upon meeting Zuckerberg, the first thing that comes across is that he is very warm, with a quick smile, and he does not shy away from eye contact. His best friends are his staff. There are no offices. Zuckerberg, it is said, loves being around people. A far cry from the shy recluse that he has been portrayed as. Zuckerberg's coworkers are adamant in their declarations of affection for him. "He has great EQ," says Naomi Gleit, Facebook's product manager for growth and internationalization.

In terms of his attitude, sense of self, and values, Zuckerberg lives a very different lifestyle from what most people might think. He is not materialistic and prefers to help others with his riches. He values personal relationships over the trappings of wealth. He is someone who is truly comfortable with himself and the values he holds. Recently, Zuckerberg invited some 400 people to watch a movie. The movie was *Waiting for Superman,* a poignant documentary about America's failing public schools. The event was organized in conjunction with a group of outfits that are pushing education reform. This was Mark Zuckerberg the philanthropist, not Mark Zuckerberg the Facebook chief executive.[98] He is not motivated by material things, rather his desire is to give back and improve the lives of others. In September 2010, Zuckerberg announced that he would put up $100 million of his personal Facebook equity to help the Newark school system. Also, as part of a campaign organized by Bill Gates and Warren Buffett, Mark Zuckerberg pledged to give away at least half of his wealth over the course of his lifetime.

As a problem solver and decision maker, Zuckerberg is described as someone who can easily become impatient with followers during one-on-one meetings. "If you're not making compelling points, he kind of just tunes out," reports one of his team members. However, just as this anecdote seems to reveal something about his personality, the team member follows through with this: "He's not trying to be rude." It would appear from this anecdote that Zuckerberg is someone who puts a high premium on his time.

Facebook has been able to recruit and hire some of the best minds in the industry. According to one analyst, everyone at Facebook was a star in their previous employment. In March 2008, Zuckerberg hired Sheryl Sandberg, a veteran of Google who was the chief of staff for former Treasury Secretary Lawrence Summers. She joined Facebook as the company's chief operating officer (COO). Former Google employees soon followed. This did not stop with Google; other companies like eBay, Genentech, and Mozilla also saw an exodus of their employees to Facebook. Chris Cox, Facebook's vice president of product, was doing a master's in artificial intelligence at Stanford when Zuckerberg personally convinced him to join Facebook. "You don't get a lot of shy, retiring types at Facebook," said one writer. These are intelligent, experienced, productive, and highly sought after talents, "power nerds" to say the least. They are a highly effective team whose creativity and performance is matched only by that of its leader, Mark Zuckerberg.

Zuckerberg does not have one of those plush executive suites typical of corporate CEOs. His desk is near the middle of the office, within arm's length of his most senior employees. He is said to be a hands-on type leader. Facebook is characterized by an open corporate culture wherein little personal private space exists. Debate is the hallmark of staff meetings at Facebook and employees describe what an intense listener Zuckerberg is during these dynamic debates. It is said that he is often one of the last persons to leave the office. He leads his team by example. Most of Zuckerberg's close friends, who worked for Facebook at the start, have left. These departures, according to some analysts, could in part reflect the status that former Facebook employees have in the industry; but could also point to the difficulty some people have working for Zuckerberg.

Leadership is about having a compelling vision and being able to effectively communicate it to followers so that they become totally committed to it. In 2006, Zuckerberg turned down an offer of $1 billion from Yahoo to buy the company. For a 22-year-old to walk away from such an offer is truly remarkable and indicative of how much he believes in himself and his vision for Facebook. Facebook came out with an IPO that made Zuckerberg worth more than $20 billion, while still maintaining ownership control of the company. Unfortunately, the value of the stock dropped in value days after the IPO. By summer of 2012, Facebook is forecast to have a billion users: one of every seven people on the planet.[99]

Go to the Internet: To learn more about Mark Zuckerberg and Facebook, visit its Web site at www.facebook.com.

Support your answers to the following questions with specific information from the case and text or with information you get from the Web or another source.

1. There are four team structure components that along with team dynamics and development, affect team performance. Which of the four components does the case feature with examples?

2. How would you describe Mark Zuckerberg as a team leader?

3. Describe the team dynamics at Facebook.

4. Based on the facts of the case, at which stage would you categorize teamwork at Facebook? Base your answer on the team development stages in the text.

5. Would you describe Zuckerberg as having a reflexive, reflective, or consistent decision-making style?

Cumulative Questions

6. How do Mark Zuckerberg's values, self-concept, and ethics (Chapter 3) affect his life and leadership of Facebook?

7. According to the two-dimensional leadership style studies (Chapter 7), a leader's behavior toward followers can be classified as either initiating structure or consideration (Ohio State University Studies). The University of Michigan study classified it as job-centered or employee-centered. Which dimension(s) would you associate with Mark Zuckerberg?

Case Exercise and Role-Play

Preparation: Have students read up on the meaning of "going public" for a private company like Facebook. The question before the class is, Should Facebook go public or stay private? The chapter discusses different techniques to use in group decision making—brainstorming, synectics, nominal grouping, consensus mapping, and the Delphi technique.

In-Class Groups: Divide the class into groups of four or five students. Each group selects one of the techniques and a group leader or facilitator. Each team employs the technique it has been assigned to address the question: Should Facebook go public or stay a private company? This is the rehearsal.

Role-Play: Each team takes the stage and plays out its decision-making process using the assigned technique. Which team made the best use of its technique? The instructor or the class as a whole can vote on the outcome.

OBJECTIVE CASE /// Group Performance

Through reorganization, Christen has been assigned three additional departments that produce the same product. Aiden, Sasha, and Rashid are the supervisors of these departments. Christen would like to increase productivity, so she set up a group to analyze the present situation and recommend ways to increase productivity. The group consists of Christen, the three supervisors, an industrial engineer, and an expert on group dynamics from personnel. The group analyzed the present situation in each department as follows:

Group 1: Aiden's department produces at or above standard on a regular basis. It averages between 102 and 104 percent of standard on a monthly basis (standard is 100 percent). Members work well together; they often go to lunch together. Members' productivity levels are all about the same.

Group 2: Sasha's department produces between 95 and 105 percent on a monthly basis. However, it usually produces 100 percent. The members do not seem to interact too often. Part of the reason for the standard production level is two employees who consistently produce at 115 percent of standard. Sasha will be retiring in six months, and they both want to fill her position. There are three members who consistently produce at 80 to 90 percent of standard.

Group 3: Rashid's department achieves between 90 and 92 percent of standard on a monthly basis. Megan is a strong informal leader who oversees the productivity level. She lets members know if they produce too much or too little. John is the only member in the department who reaches production standards. The rest of the department members do not talk to John. At times they intentionally keep his level of production down. All other department members produce at about 90 percent of standard.

Answer the following questions. Then in the space between the questions, state why you selected that answer.

_______ 1. Christen, Aiden, Sasha, and Rashid make up a(n) _______ group.

a. functional *b.* task *c.* informal

_______ 2. To increase productivity, Christen set up a(n) _______ group.

a. functional *b.* ad hoc committee *c.* standing committee

_______ 3. Which group has high agreement and commitment to its own objectives (you may select more than one group)?

a. 1 *d.* 1 and 2 *g.* 1, 2, and 3
b. 2 *e.* 1 and 3
c. 3 *f.* 2 and 3

_______ 4. Which group has objectives (positive norms) in agreement with those of management (you may select more than one group)?

a. 1 *d.* 1 and 2 *g.* 1, 2, and 3
b. 2 *e.* 1 and 3
c. 3 *f.* 2 and 3

_______ 5. Which group is cohesive (you may select more than one group)?

a. 1 *d.* 1 and 2 *g.* 1, 2, and 3
b. 2 *e.* 1 and 3
c. 3 *f.* 2 and 3

_______ 6. Which group most clearly plays self-interest roles?

a. 1 *b.* 2 *c.* 3

_______ 7. Megan primarily plays a _______ role for her group.

a. task *b.* maintenance *c.* self-interest

_______ 8. Group 1 appears to be in stage _______ of group development.

a. 1 *c.* 3 *e.* 5
b. 2 *d.* 4

_______ 9. Group 2 appears to be in stage _______ of group development.

a. 1 *c.* 3 *e.* 5
b. 2 *d.* 4

_______ 10. Group 3 appears to be in stage _______ of group development.

a. 1 *c.* 3 *e.* 5
b. 2 *d.* 4

_______ 11. What would you recommend doing to increase productivity in each of the three groups?

/ / / SKILL-BUILDING EXERCISE 11-1 / / /

Team Dynamics

Note: This exercise is designed for class groups that have worked together for some time. (Five or more hours are recommended.)

Preparation (Group)

Answer the following questions as they apply to your class group.

1. Based on attendance, preparation, and class involvement, identify each group member's level of commitment to the group, including yourself. (Write each member's name on the appropriate line.)

   High commitment ____

Medium commitment ______________________________

Low commitment ______________________________

2. Our group size is:

_______ too large _______ too small _______ OK

Explain why.

3. List at least five norms your group has developed. Identify each as positive or negative.

1.

2.

3.

4.

5.

What positive norms could the group develop to help it function?

4. Based on the group's commitment, size, homogeneity, equality of participation, intragroup competition, and success, identify its cohesiveness level as:

_______ high _______ medium _______ low

How does cohesiveness affect performance? What can be done to increase cohesiveness?

5. Identify each group member's status, including your own. (Write each group member's name on the appropriate line.)

High ______________________________

Medium ______________________________

Low ______________________________

Does the group have status congruence? How can the group improve it?

6. Identify the roles members play. Write the name of each group member who plays each role on the appropriate line. You will most likely use each name several times and have more than one name on each role line, but rank them by dominance.

Task roles

Objective clarifier ______________________________

Planner ______________________________

Organizer ______________________________

Leader ______________________________

Controller ______________________________

Maintenance roles

Former ______________________________

Consensus seeker ______________________________

Harmonizer ______________________________

Gatekeeper ______________________________

Encourager ______________________________

Compromiser ______________________________

Self-interest roles (if appropriate)

Aggressor____

Blocker____

Recognition seeker____

Withdrawer____

Which roles should be played more, and which less, to increase effectiveness? Who should and should not play them?

7. Our group is in stage ________ of group development.
   1. Orientation
   2. Dissatisfaction
   3. Resolution
   4. Production

   What can be done to increase the group's level of development?

8. Identify problem people, if any, by placing their names on the appropriate line(s).

   Silent member____

   Talker____

   Wanderer____

   Bored member____

   Arguer____

   Social loafer____

   What should be done to help eliminate the problems caused by these people? Specifically, who should do what?

9. Review the answers to questions 1 through 8. In order of priority, what will the group do to improve its group structure? Specify what each group member will do to help the group's structure.

In-Class Exercise

Note: This exercise is designed for groups that have met for some time. (Five or more hours are recommended.)

Objectives: To gain a better understanding of the group structure components and how they affect group performance, and to improve group structure.

AACSB: The primary AACSB learning standard skills developed through this exercise are teamwork and leadership; in addition, communication, reflective thinking, self--management, and analytic skills are developed.

Preparation: You should have answered the preparation questions.

Experience: You will discuss your group's structure and develop plans to improve it.

Procedure 1 (10–20 minutes)

Groups get together to discuss their answers to the nine preparation questions. Be sure to fully explain and discuss your answers. Try to come up with some specific ideas on how to improve your group's process and dynamics.

Conclusion: The instructor leads a class discussion and/or makes concluding remarks.

Application (2–4 minutes): What did I learn from this experience? How will I use this knowledge in the future?

Sharing: Volunteers give their answers to the application section.

/ / / SKILL-BUILDING EXERCISE 11-2 / / /

Team Situational Supervision

In-Class Exercise (Individual and Group)

Objectives: To help you understand the stages of group development, and to use the appropriate situational supervision style.

AACSB: The primary AACSB learning standard skills developed through this exercise are teamwork and leadership; in addition, analytic skills are developed.

Preparation: You should have completed Self-Assessment Exercise 11-2.

Experience: You will discuss your selected supervisory styles for the 12 preparation situations, and you will be given feedback on your accuracy in selecting the appropriate style to meet the situation.

Procedure 1 (3–10 minutes)
The instructor reviews the group situational supervision model, Exhibit 11.1, and explains how to apply it to situation 1 in Self-Assessment Exercise 11-2. The instructor states the group's developmental stage, the supervisory style of each of the four alternative actions, and the scoring for each alternative. Follow the three steps below as you try to select the most appropriate alternative action for each of the 12 situations in Self-Assessment Exercise 11-2.

Step 1. For each situation, determine the team's level of development. Place the number 1, 2, 3, or 4 on the D ________ lines.

Step 2. Identify the supervisory style of all four alternatives *a* through *d.* Place the letters A, C, P, or L on the S ________ lines.

Step 3. Select the appropriate supervisory style for the team's level of development. Circle its letter, either *a, b, c*, or *d.*

Procedure 2
Option A (3–5 minutes): The instructor gives the class the recommended answers to situations 2 through 12, as in procedure 1, without any explanation.

Option B (10–30 minutes): Break into teams of two or three, and go over the situations chosen by the instructor. The instructor will go over the recommended answers.

Conclusion: The instructor leads a class discussion and/or makes concluding remarks.

Application (2–4 minutes): What did I learn from this experience? How will I use this knowledge in the future?

Sharing: Volunteers give their answers to the application section.

/ / / SKILL-BUILDING EXERCISE 11-3 / / /

Individual versus Group Decision Making

In-Class Exercise (Group)

Objective: To compare individual and group decision making to better understand when and when not to use a group to make decisions.

AACSB: The primary AACSB learning standard skills developed through this exercise are teamwork and leadership; in addition, communication and analytic skills are developed.

Preparation: You should have completed Application Situations 11-1 and 11-2, or the first 10 questions in the Objective Case, whichever your instructor assigned.

Experience: During class, you will work in a group that will make the same decisions, followed by an analysis of the results.

Procedure 1 (1–2 minutes)
Place your individual answers to Application Situations 11-1 and 11-2 in the "Individual Answer" column below.

Application Situation Question	Individual Answer (A-E)	Group Answer (A-E)	Recommended Answer (A-E)	Score Individual versus Group
1.				
2.				
3.				
4.				
5.				
6.				
7.				
8.				
9.				
10.				
Total score				

Procedure 2 (18–22 minutes)
Break into teams of five; make groups of four or six as necessary. As a group, come to an agreement on the answers to Application Situations 11-1 and 11-2. Place the group answers in the "Group Answer" column above. Try to use consensus rather than the voting technique.

Procedure 3 (4–6 minutes)
Scoring: The instructor will give you the recommended answers to Application Situations 11-1 and 11-2; place the answers in column 4. In column 2, place the number of individual answers you got correct (1–10) on the total score line. In column 3, place the number the group answered correctly (1–10) on the total score line. In column 5, place the number representing the gain/loss of individual versus group answers on the total score line. (For example, if you scored 8 correct and the group scored 6, you beat the group by 2—so put +2 on the total score line. If you scored 5 correct and the group scored 8, the group beat you by 3—so put –3 on the total score line. If you tied, put 0.)

Averaging: Calculate the average individual score by adding all the individual scores and dividing by the number of group members. Average.

Gain or Loss: Find the difference between the average score and the group score. If the group's score is higher than the average individual score, you have a gain of ______ points; if the group's score is lower, you have a loss of ______ points.

Determine the highest individual score ______.
Determine the number of individuals who scored higher than the group's score ______.

Integration (4–8 minutes): As a group, discuss which advantages and/or disadvantages (Exhibit 11-8) your group had while making the decisions in this exercise.

Advantages:

Disadvantages:

Improvements: Overall, were the advantages of using a group greater than the disadvantages of using a group? If your group continues to work together, how could it improve its problem-solving and decision-making abilities? Write out the answer below.

Conclusion: The instructor leads a class discussion and/or makes concluding remarks.

Application (2–4 minutes): What did I learn from this experience? How will I use this knowledge in the future?

Sharing: Volunteers give their answers to the application section.

/ / / SKILL-BUILDING EXERCISE 11-4 / / /

Using the Situational Decision-Making Model

Preparation (Individual and Group)

In this exercise, you will learn how to use the situational decision-making model. Chapter 7 discussed the situational supervision model. Chapter 5 provided a situational communication model to use when communicating. Now you will learn a similar model to use when deciding which supervisory style to use when solving problems and making decisions. Selecting the appropriate situational supervisory style includes two steps: step (1) diagnose the situation, and step (2) select the appropriate style.

Step 1: Diagnose the Situation The first step is to diagnose the situational variables, which include time, information, acceptance, and employee capability level. See Model 11.4 for a list of variables. The top half of Model 11.4 summarizes step 1.

Time You must determine if there is enough time to include the group in decision making. If there is not enough time, use the autocratic style, and ignore the other three variables—they are irrelevant if there is no time. If time permits, you consider the other three variables and selects the style without considering time. Time, however, is a relative term. In one situation, a few minutes may be considered a short time period, while in another, a month or more may be a short period of time.

MODEL 11.4 | Situational Decision Making

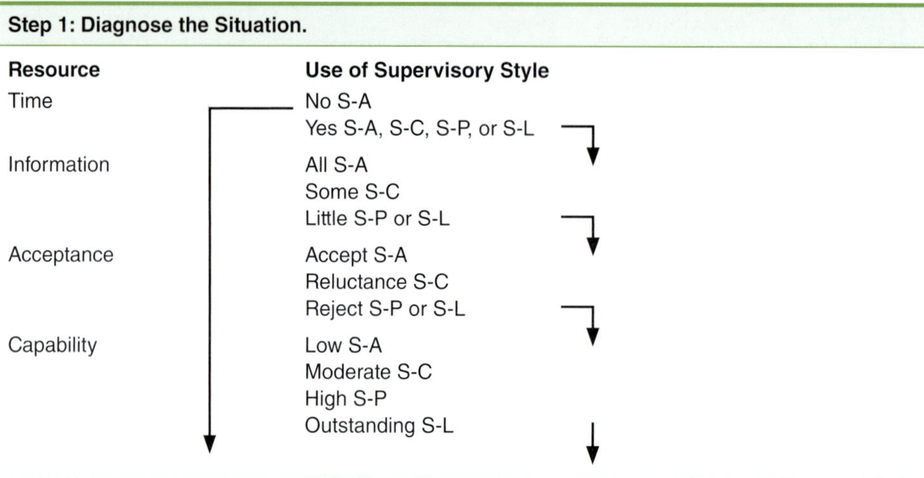

Step 2: Select the Appropriate Style for the Situation.

Autocratic (S-A)

The supervisor makes the decision alone and announces it after the fact. An explanation of the rationale for the decision may be given.

Consultative (S-C)

The supervisor consults individuals or the group for information and then makes the decision. Before implementing the decision, the supervisor explains the rationale for the decision and sells the benefits to the employees. The supervisor may invite questions and have a discussion.

Participative (S-P)

The supervisor may present a tentative decision to the group and ask for its input. The supervisor may change the decision if the input warrants a change. Or the supervisor may present the problem to the group for suggestions. Based on employee participation, the supervisor makes the decision and explains its rationale.

Laissez-Faire (S-L)

The supervisor presents the situation to the group and describes limitations to the decision. The group makes the decision. The supervisor may be a group member.

Information The more information you have to make the decision, the less need there is to use participation, and vice versa. If you have all the necessary information to make a decision, there is no need to use participation. If you have little information you need to get it through participation.

Acceptance If you make the decision alone, will the group implement it willingly? The more the team will like the decision, the less need there is to use participation, and visa versa.

Employee Capability The leader must decide if the group has the ability and willingness to be involved in problem solving and decision making. The more capable the employees, the higher the level of participation, and vice versa. Realize that a group's capability level can change from situation to situation.

Step 2: Select the Appropriate Supervisory Style for the Situation After considering the four variables, you select the appropriate style for the situation. In some situations, all variables suggest the same possible style, while other cases indicate conflicting styles. For example, you may have time to use any style and may have all the information necessary (autocratic); employees may be reluctant (consultative or participative); and the capability may be moderate (consultative). In situations where conflicting styles are indicated for different variables, you must determine which variable should be given more weight. In the above example, assume it was determined that acceptance was critical for successful implementation of the decision. Acceptance takes precedence over information. Realizing that employees have a moderate capability, the consultative style would be appropriate. See the bottom half of Model 11.4 for an explanation of how the decision is made using each of the four situational supervisory styles.

Applying the Situational Decision-Making Model

We will apply the model to the following situation:

Ben, a supervisor, can give one of his employees a merit pay raise. He has a week to make the decision. Ben knows how well each employee performed over the past year. The employees really have no option but to accept getting or not getting the pay raise, but they can complain to upper management about the selection. The employees' capability levels vary, but as a group, they have a high capability level under normal circumstances.

Step 1: Diagnose the Situation.

_______ time _______ information _______ acceptance _______ capability

Ben, the supervisor, has plenty of time to use any level of participation. He has all the information needed to make the decision (autocratic). Employees have no choice but to accept the decision (autocratic). And the group's level of capability is normally high (participative).

Step 2: Select the Appropriate Style for the Situation. There are conflicting styles to choose from (autocratic and participative):

_______ yes time _______ S-A information _______ S-A acceptance _______ S-P capability

The variable that should be given precedence is information. The employees are normally capable, but in a situation like this, they may not be capable of putting the department's goals ahead of their own. In other words, even if employees know which employee deserves the raise, they may each fight for it anyway. Such a conflict could cause future problems. Some of the possible ways to make the decision are as follows:

- *Autocratic (S-A).* The supervisor would select the person for the raise without discussing it with any employees. Ben would simply announce the decision and explain the rationale for the selection, after submitting it to the payroll department.
- *Consultative (S-C).* The supervisor would consult the employees as to who should get the raise. Ben would then decide who would get the raise. He would announce the decision and explain the rationale for it. The supervisor may invite questions and discussion.
- *Participative (S-P).* The supervisor could tentatively select an employee to get the raise, but be open to change if an employee or group convinces him that someone else should get the raise. Or Ben could explain the situation to the group and lead a discussion of who should get the raise. After considering their input, Ben would make the decision and explain the rationale for it.
- *Laissez-faire (S-L).* The supervisor would explain the situation and allow the group to decide who gets the raise. Ben may be a group member. Notice that this is the only style that allows the group to make the decision.

Selection The autocratic style is appropriate for this situation because Ben has all the information needed, acceptance is not an issue, and capability is questionable.

Below are 10 situations calling for a decision. Select the appropriate problem-solving and decision-making style. Be sure to use Exhibit 11.8, p. 358, when determining the style to use. On the time, information, acceptance, and capability lines, place S-A, S-C, S-P, or S-L, as indicated by the situation. Based on your diagnoses, select the one style you would use. Note that style on the line preceding the situation.

S-A Autocratic S-C Consultative S-P Participative S-L Laissez-faire

_______ 1. You have developed a new work procedure that will increase productivity. Your boss likes the idea and wants you to try it within a few weeks. You view your employees as fairly capable and believe that they will be receptive to the change.

_______ time _______ information _______ acceptance _______ capability

_______ 2. The industry of your product has new competition. Your organization's revenues have been dropping. You have been told to lay off 3 of your 10 employees in two weeks. You have been the supervisor for over one year. Normally, your employees are very capable.

_______ time _______ information _______ acceptance _______ capability

_______ 3. Your department has been facing a problem for several months. Many solutions have been tried, but all have failed. You have finally thought of a solution, but you are not sure of the possible consequences of the change required or of acceptance by the highly capable employees.

_______ time _______ information _______ acceptance _______ capability

_______ 4. Flextime has become popular in your organization. Some departments let each employee start and end work when he or she chooses. However, because of the cooperative effort of your employees, they must all work the same eight hours. You are not sure of the level of interest in changing the hours. Your employees are a very capable group and like to make decisions.

_______ time _______ information _______ acceptance _______ capability

_______ 5. The technology in your industry is changing so fast that the members of your organization cannot keep up. Top management hired a consultant who has made recommendations. You have two weeks to decide what to do. Your employees are normally capable, and they enjoy participating in the decision-making process.

_______ time _______ information _______ acceptance _______ capability

_______ 6. A change has been handed down from top management. How you implement it is your decision. The change takes effect in one month. It will personally affect everyone in your department. Their acceptance is critical to the success of the change. Your employees are usually not too interested in being involved in making decisions.

_______ time _______ information _______ acceptance _______ capability

_______ 7. Your boss called you on the telephone to tell you that someone has requested an order for your department's product with a very short delivery date. She asked you to call her back in 15 minutes with the decision about taking the order. Looking over the work schedule, you realize that it will be very difficult to deliver the order on time. Your employees will have to push hard to make it. They are cooperative, capable, and enjoy being involved in decision making.

_______ time _______ information _______ acceptance _______ capability

_______ 8. Top management has decided to make a change that will affect all your employees. You know the employees will be upset because it will cause them hardship. One or two may even quit. The change goes into effect in 30 days. Your employees are very capable.

_______ time _______ information _______ acceptance _______ capability

_______ 9. You believe that productivity in your department could be increased. You have thought of some ways that may work, but you are not sure of them. Your employees are very experienced; almost all of them have been in the department longer than you have.

_______ time _______ information _______ acceptance _______ capability

_______ 10. A customer has offered you a contract for your product with a quick delivery date. The offer is open for two days. Meeting the contract deadline would require employees to work nights and weekends for six weeks. You cannot require them to work overtime. Filling this profitable contract could help get you the raise you want and feel you deserve. However, if you take the contract and don't deliver on time, it will hurt your chances of getting a big raise. Your employees are very capable.

_______ time _______ information _______ acceptance _______ capability

In-Class Exercise

Objective: To develop your situational supervisory problem-solving and decision-making skills.

AACSB: The primary AACSB learning standard skills developed through this exercise are leadership and analytic skills.

Preparation: You should have completed the 10 situations from the preparation.

Experience: You will try to select the recommended problem-solving and decision-making style in the 10 preparation situations.

Procedure 1 (5–12 minutes)

The instructor reviews Model 11.4 and explains how to use it for selecting the appropriate supervisory style for situation 1 of the exercise preparation.

Procedure 2 (12–20 minutes)

Break into teams of two or three. Apply the model to situations 2 through 5 as a team. You may change your original answers. It may be helpful to tear the model out of the book so you don't have to keep flipping pages. The instructor goes over the recommended answers and scoring for situations 2 through 5. Do not continue on to situation 6 until after the instructor goes over the answers to situations 2 through 5.

In the same teams, select problem-solving and decision-making styles for situations 6 through 10. The instructor will go over the recommended answers and scoring.

Conclusion: The instructor may lead a class discussion and/or make concluding remarks.

Application (2–4 minutes): What did I learn from this experience? How will I use this knowledge in the future?

Sharing: Volunteers give their answers to the application section.

/ / ANSWERS TO TRUE/FALSE QUESTIONS / /

1. F. There is no one best size for all teams. Size is based on the team's purpose.
2. T.
3. T.
4. T.
5. F. Managers should not embarrass, intimidate, or argue with any team members.
6. F. The decision-making model should be used when making *important nonrecurring* decisions.
7. F. None of these techniques require that a small group of people get together; in fact, they can be used online. With the Delphi technique, members never get together and often don't even know who else is in the group.

CHAPTER 12

Organizational Change and Culture

LEARNING OUTCOMES

After completing this chapter, you should be able to:

LO 12-1 Describe the four types of changes.

LO 12-2 State why people resist change and how to overcome resistance.

LO 12-3 Explain how to use the Lussier change model when making changes.

LO 12-4 Explain the two dimensions of an organization's culture.

LO 12-5 Explain the seven dimensions of an organization's climate.

LO 12-6 Describe five organizational development techniques.

LO 12-7 Describe the training cycle and how training is used to increase performance.

LO 12-8 List and explain the five steps of performance appraisals and state how performance appraisals can lead to increased performance.

LO 12-9 List the steps in the coaching model.

LO 12-10 Explain the relationship between organizational culture, climate, and development.

LO 12-11 Define the following 16 key terms (in order of appearance in the chapter):

types of changes
management information systems (MIS)
automation
resistance to change
organizational culture
organizational climate
morale
organizational development (OD)
training
development
performance appraisal
standards
coaching model
survey feedback
force field analysis
team building

/ / / Ronnie Linkletter now works for the New York City Insurance Company (NYCIC). Ronnie was the manager of the claims department at Rider, a small insurance company in Danbury, Connecticut, until it was bought by NYCIC. Since the purchase of Rider, Ronnie and his peers don't know what to expect. They know there will be many changes, which they don't look forward to. They have been told by the new managers that they are a part of the NYCIC family. "Family" relates to some kind of organizational culture managers keep talking about, which has developed over many years through an ongoing organizational development program. NYCIC has been concerned about its employees' morale. Ronnie feels confused by all these new buzzwords. He wants to know how these changes will affect him. Ronnie knows that at Rider all the managers were white males, and there were very few minorities. But at NYCIC, there are women and minority managers, and more than half of NYCIC employees are minorities.

Is there a way to make changes in organizations so that people don't resist the changes? This is the major topic of Chapter 12. / / /

HOW CHANGE AFFECTS BEHAVIOR, HUMAN RELATIONS, AND PERFORMANCE

Capitalism demands that companies be innovative, flexible, and responsive to change.[1] Organizational change is an important management topic,[2] because the ability to change is crucial to success in achieving competitive advantage.[3] Human behavior and relations are the fuel that helps organizations run successfully at high levels of performance.[4] Recall in the last chapter that we discussed the importance of employee creativity, as it leads to innovation that requires change in products and processes.[5] This chapter is about how to take creative ideas and turn them into innovative changes.

Clearly, the companies that are creative and innovative are successful, like Apple. Steve Jobs has been called perhaps the most charismatic CEO in business history.[6] Jobs was incredibly innovative,[7] having been influential in changing the way we live and conduct business in several industries, more so than anyone else. He was the co-developer of the first PC; developed computer-animated feature films including *Toy Story*; developed the iPod, iTunes, and Apple Stores, clearly influencing both music and retail industries; and developed the iPhone, which has impacted wireless smartphones and telecommunications.[8]

WORK APPLICATION 12-1

Give reasons why managing-change skills are important to managers in an organization for which you work or have worked.

We can't all be another Steve Jobs, but we should realize that we need to change to be successful.[9] In this chapter, the topics of organizational culture, climate, and development are all about making changes to continually improve behavior, human relations, and performance.

MANAGING CHANGE

Change is an ongoing and never-ending process of organizational life.[10] However, changing is not easy.[11] In this section we discuss types of changes and stages in the change process. Our discussion continues in the next section, in which we examine resistance to change and change models. Before we begin, complete Self Assessment Exercise 12-1 to determine your openness to change, which relates to your Big Five personality type (Chapter 2).

/// Self-Assessment Exercise 12-1 ///

Your Openness to Change

Select the response that best describes what you would do in each situation.

1. In my daily life I:

   _____ *a.* Look for new ways of doing things.

   _____ *b.* Like things the way they are.

2. If my friends were opposed to a change:

   _____ *a.* It would not affect my changing.

   _____ *b.* I would resist the change, too.

3. In my work situation I:

   _____ *a.* Do things differently.

   _____ *b.* Do things the same way.

4. If I had the opportunity to learn to use new computer software to help me in school or at work, I would:

   _____ *a.* Take time to learn to use it on my own.

   _____ *b.* Wait until required to use it.

(*continued*)

/// Self-Assessment Exercise 12-1 /// (*continued*)

5. I like to know about a change:
   ______ *a.* Anytime. Short notice is OK with me.
   ______ *b.* Well in advance, to have time to plan for it.
6. When a work change is required, I:
   ______ *a.* Change as quickly as management wants.
   ______ *b.* Want to move slowly to implement change.
7. When leading others, I:
   ______ *a.* Use the style appropriate for their capability.
   ______ *b.* Use my distinct leadership style.

The more *a* answers you selected, the more open to change you are. The *b* answers show resistance to change. If you tend to be resistant to change, and want to have a successful career, you may want to change your attitude and behavior. You can begin by looking for different ways to do things more productively. Look at your routine for getting ready for school or work. Could you make any changes to save time?

Remember that your attitude (Chapter 3) toward change affects your openness to change. If you have a negative attitude toward change, it will affect your behavior and human relations and performance. So think positive thoughts about change.

Learning Outcome 12-1

Describe the four types of changes.

Types of Changes

There are different types of change, and types of change have various names. Organizations are composed of four interactive variables. The four variables, or **types of changes**, *are technological change, structural change, task change, and people change.* The proper metaphor for the systems effect for managing change is a balanced mobile in which a change in one variable affects the others. Because of the systems effect, you need to consider the repercussions that a change in one variable will have on the other variables, and plan accordingly.

Communication Skills
Refer to CS Question 1.

Technological Change Technological changes, such as the Internet, have increased the rate of speed at which change takes place.[12] Technology is a commonly used method of increasing productivity. For example, Wal-Mart is committed to technology. Wal-Mart's operating costs are lower, and the lower cost structure equals lower prices for customers.

Some of the major areas of technology change are the following:

Machines and Automation New machinery or equipment is introduced on an ongoing basis. The computer is a sophisticated machine that is also a part of many other machines. **Automation** *is the simplification or reduction of human effort required to do a job.* Computers and other machines have allowed some jobs, to be done by robots.

WORK APPLICATION 12-2

Describe the MIS at an organization, preferably one with which you have been associated. If you are not knowledgeable about the organization's MIS, talk with someone who is.

Process *Process* refers to how the organization transforms inputs (raw materials, parts, data, and so on) into outputs (finished goods and services, information). The change in the sequence of work in process is a technology change. With the aid of the computer, organizations have changed the way they process information. **Management information systems (MIS)** *are formal systems for collecting, processing, and disseminating the information necessary to aid managers in decision making.* The MIS attempts to centralize and integrate all or most of the organization's information such as, production, inventory, and sales information.

WORK APPLICATION 12-3

Describe an automation change in an organization, preferably one with which you have been associated.

Structural Change It is important to coordinate structure with technology. *Structure* refers to the type of organization principle and departments used, as discussed in Chapter 5.

EXHIBIT 12.1 | Types of Changes

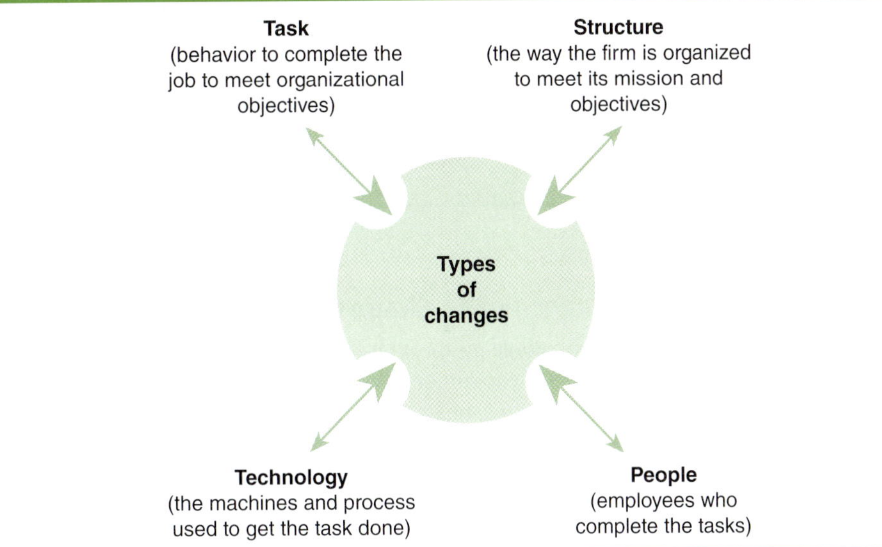

Task and People Change *Task* refers to the day-to-day things that employees do to perform their jobs. Tasks change with technology and with structural changes. As tasks change, people's skills must change. Employee retraining is an ongoing process. In some cases, organizations must hire new people with the necessary skills.

It is people that create, manage, and use technology; therefore, people are the most important resource. What people often resist are the social changes brought about by technological changes. The integration of both people and technology is known as *creating a sociotechnical system.* When changing task, structure, or technology, you should never forget the impact of change on people. Changing any of these other variables will not be effective without considering people change.

In the opening case, Rider Insurance has been bought by NYCIC. The primary change is structural. Rider is no longer a separate entity; it is part of NYCIC. NYCIC will most likely change the structure at Rider to match its present structure. With the change in structure, most likely the tasks, technology, and people will also change. See Exhibit 12.1 for a review of the types of changes.

WORK APPLICATION 12-4

Give one or more examples of a type of change you experienced in an organization. (Identify it as task change, structural change, technological change, or people change.)

APPLICATION SITUATIONS / / /

Types of Changes AS 12-1

Identify the type of change represented in each statement as:

A. Task change C. Technological change
B. Structural change D. People change

_______ 1. " Jim, from now on, you have to fill in this new form every time you deliver a package."

_______ 2. " Because of the increase in the size of our department, we will now split into two departments."

_______ 3. " Kelly is taking Chang's place now that he has retired."

_______ 4. " From now on, purchases under $300 will no longer need to be approved by the purchasing manager."

_______ 5. "Sergei, report to the training center to learn proper procedures."

EXHIBIT 12.2 | Stages in the Change Process

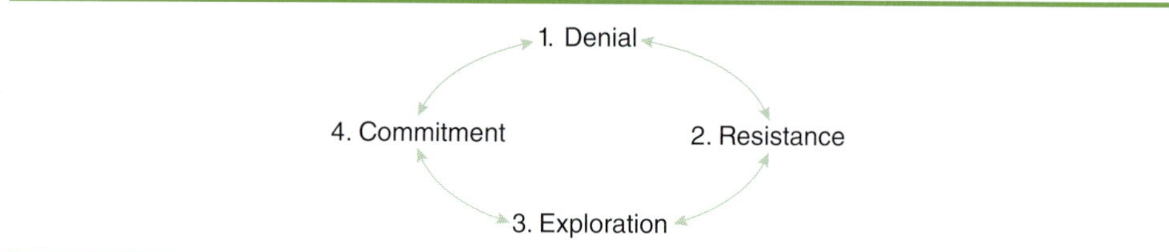

Stages in the Change Process

Most people go through four distinct stages in the change process: (1) *Denial:* When people first hear rumors through the grapevine that change is coming, they deny that it will happen at all, or to them. The "it will affect the others, but not me" reaction is common. (2) *Resistance:* Once people get over the initial shock and realize that change is going to be a reality, they resist the change. (3) *Exploration:* When the change begins to be implemented, employees explore the change. (4) *Commitment:* Through exploration, employees determine their level of commitment to making the change a success.

In the opening case, employees at both Rider and NYCIC will be going through the stages of the change process. How successfully the change process is implemented will affect the behavior, human relations, and performance of the two businesses, which are now one company.

Exhibit 12.2 illustrates the stages in the change process. Notice that the stages are in a circular formation because change is an ongoing process, not a linear one, and people can regress, as the arrows show.

RESISTANCE TO CHANGE AND HOW TO OVERCOME IT

Learning Outcome 12-2

State why people resist change and how to overcome resistance.

Communication Skills
Refer to CS Question 2.

People resist change for a variety of reasons,[13] some of which include (1) maintaining the *status quo* (people like things the way they are now, view the change as an inconvenience, or don't agree that a change is needed),[14] (2) *uncertainty* (people tend to fear the unknown and wonder how the change will affect them),[15] (3) *learning anxiety* (the prospect of learning something new itself produces anxiety), and (4) *fear* (people often fear they may lose their jobs, that they will not be successful with learning new ways, or that they may lose control over how they do their jobs), and their emotional fears can get in the way of changing.[16] Next you will learn why people resist change and how to overcome it.

Resistance to Change

Before making changes, anticipate how employees will react to or resist the change.[17] **Resistance to change** *involves the variables of intensity, source, and focus, which together explain why people are reluctant to change.* Ken Hultman identifies these three variables as the major variables of resistance to change.[18]

Intensity People often have four basic reactions to change: acceptance, tolerance, resistance, and rejection. The resistance intensity can vary from strong to weak or somewhere in between. As a manager of change, you should anticipate the intensity of resistance to change so that you can effectively plan to overcome it.[19]

Sources There are three major sources of resistance: facts, beliefs, and values. (1) *Facts:* Facts are statements that identify reality. (2) *Beliefs:* Facts can be proved; beliefs cannot. They are subjective. Our beliefs are our opinions that lead us to think and feel that a change is correct or incorrect, good or bad. (3) *Values:* Values are what people believe are worth pursuing or doing.[20] What we value is important to us.

EXHIBIT 12.3 | Resistance Matrix

Focus of Resistance (self → others → work)	Sources of Resistance (facts → beliefs → values)		
	1. Facts about self I never did it before. I failed the last time I tried. All my friends are here.	**4. Beliefs about self** I'm too busy to do it. I'll do it, but I'll mess up. I don't think I can accept the change.	**7. Values pertaining to self** I like the job I have now better. I don't want to change; I'm happy. I like working alone.
	2. Facts about others He's on probation. She has two children. Other people told me it's hard to do.	**5. Beliefs about others** She pretends to be busy to avoid extra work. He's better at it than I am; let him do it. She never understands our side.	**8. Values pertaining to others** Let someone else train her; I'm not interested. What you really think really doesn't matter to me. I don't give a . . . about him.
	3. Facts about the work environment Why should I do it? I'm not getting paid extra. I haven't been trained to do it. I make less than anyone else in the department.	**6. Beliefs about the work environment** This is a lousy place to work. The pay here is terrible. It's who you know, not what you know around here that counts.	**9. Values pertaining to the work environment** Who cares what the goals are? I just do my job. The salary is more important than the benefits. This job gives me the chance to work outside.

Source: Adapted from Ken Hultman's resistance matrix, *The Path of Least Resistance* (Austin, TX: Learning Concepts, 1979).

People analyze the facts presented from all sources and determine if they believe the change is of value to them. When the facts are clear and logical and people believe the change is of value to them, they tend to have lower resistance to the change.

Focus There are three major focuses of resistance: self, others, and the work environment. (1) *Self:* It is natural for people to want to know, "What's in it for me? What will I gain or lose?" (Self-interest.)[21] (2) *Others:* After considering what's in it for them, or when they are not affected by the change, people tend to consider how the change will affect their friends, peers (peer pressure), and colleagues. (3) *Work environment:* The work environment includes the job itself and the physical setting and climate. Employees' analysis of the facts about the current versus the changed work environment will affect their resistance to the change.

Exhibit 12.3 is an adapted version of Ken Hultman's resistance matrix, with examples of each area of resistance. For instance, in box 1, "Facts about self," note that one reason given is "I never did it before." Understanding the reasons behind a person's resistance to change will make you better able to anticipate and deal with those reasons. However, resistance may come from more than one focus and source. Use the matrix to identify the intensity, source, and focus of resistance. Once you have identified the probable resistance to change, you can work at overcoming it.

WORK APPLICATION 12-5

Describe a situation in which you were resistant to change. Identify the intensity, source, and focus. Using Exhibit 12.3, which box (by number and statement) describes your resistance?

APPLICATION SITUATIONS / / /

Identifying Resistance to Change AS 12-2

Below are five statements made by employees asked to make a change on the job. Identify the source, focus, and intensity of their resistance using Exhibit 12.3. Place the number of the box (1 to 9) that represents and best describes the major resistance.

_______ 6. The police sergeant asked Sue, the patrol officer, to take a rookie cop as her partner. Sue said, "Do I have to? I broke in the last rookie."

_______ 7. The tennis coach asked Gustavo, the star player, to have Jim as his doubles partner. Gustavo said, "Come on, Jim is a lousy player. Jamari is better; don't break us up." The coach disagreed and forced Gustavo to accept Jim.

_______ 8. The supervisor realized that Erin always uses the accommodating conflict style. The supervisor told her to stop giving in to everyone's wishes. Erin said, "But I like people, and I want them to like me, too."

_______ 9. The employee went to Sim, the supervisor, and asked him if she could change the work-order form. Sim said, "That would be a waste of time; the current form is fine."

_______ 10. Olivia, an employee, is busy at work. The supervisor tells her to stop what she is doing and begin a new project. Olivia says, "The job I'm working on now is more important."

Overcoming Resistance to Change

Below are some of the major methods for overcoming resistance to change.

- *Develop a Positive Climate for Change.* Develop and maintain good human relations. Because change and trust are so closely intertwined, the first concern should be to develop mutual trust.[22]
- *Encourage Interest in Improvement.* Continually give opportunities to develop new skills, abilities, and creativity.[23] Constantly look for better ways to do things.
- *Plan.* You need a plan to overcome resistance. Don't consider how you would react. What seems very simple and logical to you may not be to the other person. Try to see things from his or her perspective (Chapter 2). The next eight methods should be part of your plan.
- *Give Facts.* Get all the facts and plan how you will present them. Giving half-answers will only make employees more confused and angry, and hiding things and lying is a disaster. Giving the facts as far in advance as possible helps overcome the fear of the unknown.
- *Clearly State Why the Change Is Needed and How It Will Affect Employees.* People want and need to know why the change is needed and how it will affect them both positively and negatively. Be open and honest with employees. If employees understand why the change is needed, and it makes sense to them, they will be more willing to change.[24] It is important to create a sense of urgency to kill complacency and get employees to want to change.[25]
- *Create a Win–Win Situation.* Be sure to answer, "What's in it for me?" When people can see the benefits to them, and/or what they can lose, they are more willing to change.
- *Involve Employees.* Employees who participate in developing changes are more committed to them than employees who have changes assigned to them.
- *Provide Support.* Since training is very important to successful changes,[26] give as much advance notice and training as possible before the change takes place. Training helps reduce learning anxiety and helps employees realize they can be successful with the change.
- *Stay Calm.* Try not to do or say things that will make people emotional so that you don't create more resistance to change. Follow the guidelines on dealing with emotions in Chapter 5.
- *Avoid Direct Confrontation.* Trying to persuade people that their facts, beliefs, and values are wrong leads to resistance. Avoid statements that will get people emotional, like,"You're wrong; you don't know what you're talking about." Deal with conflict following the guidelines in Chapter 6.
- *Use Power and Ethical Politics.* Chapter 9 discussed how to get what you want through the use of power and politics, and it usually involves change. Use power and ethical political skills to implement changes.

EXHIBIT 12.4 | Overcoming Resistance to Change

Old			New
		Develop a positive climate for change.	
	R	Encourage interest in improvement.	
	e	Plan.	
	s	Give facts.	C
	i	Clearly state why the change is needed and how it will affect employees.	h
	s		a
	t	Create a win–win situation.	n
	a	Involve employees.	g
	n	Provide support.	e
	c	Stay calm.	
	e	Avoid direct confrontation.	
		Use power and ethical politics.	

Communication Skills
Refer to CS Question 3.

See Exhibit 12.4 for a review of the methods for overcoming resistance to change. Remember that the 11 methods for overcoming resistance to change should be a part of your plan for change. Below you will learn about planning for change.

Responding to Resistance

Below are classifications of employee resistance types, resistant statements, and responses a manager could make to the employee to help overcome resistance to change. The following are presented to acquaint you with some of the possible types of resistance you may face, along with some possible responses you could make:

- *The blocker:* "I don't want to do it that way." Manager: "What are your objections to the change? How would you prefer to do it?"
- *The roller:* "What do you want me to do?" Manager: "I want you to . . ." (Be specific and describe the change in detail; use communication skills.[27] Don't let them give up easily.)[28]
- *The staller:* "I'll do it when I can." Manager: "What is more important?"
- *The reverser:* "That's a good idea." (But she or he never does it.) Manager: "What is it that you like about the change?"
- *The sidestepper:* "Why don't you have XYZ do it?" Manager: "I asked you to do it because . . ."
- *The threatener:* "I'll do it, but the guys upstairs will not like it." Manager: "Let me worry about it. What are *your* objections?"
- *The politician:* "You owe me one; let me slide." Manager: "I do owe you one, but I need the change. I'll pay you back later."
- *The traditionalist:* "That's not the way we do things around here." Manager: "This is a unique situation; it needs to be done."
- *The assaulter:* "You're a . . . (pick a word)." Manager: "I will not tolerate that type of behavior." Or, "This is really upsetting you, isn't it?"

The above supervisory responses will be helpful in most situations, but not all. If employees persist in resisting the change, they may need to be considered problem employees and handled accordingly.

Change Models

Lewin's Change Model It is important to know how to implement change.[29] So here are two change models, providing a pro-change orientation. In the early 1950s, Kurt Lewin developed a technique, still used today, for changing people's behavior, skills, and attitudes. Lewin viewed the change process as consisting of three steps:[30]

(1) *Unfreezing:* This step usually involves reducing those forces maintaining the status quo. (2) *Moving*: This step shifts the behavior to a new level. This is the change process in

EXHIBIT 12.5 | Change Models

Lewin's Change Model	Lussier's Change Model
Step 1: Unfreezing	Step 1: Define the change.
Step 2: Moving	Step 2: Identify possible resistance to the change.
Step 3: Refreezing	Step 3: Plan the change.
	Step 4: Implement the change. Give the facts. Involve employees. Provide support.
	Step 5: Control the change (implementation, reinforcement, maintenance).

which employees learn the new desirable behavior, values, and attitudes. (3) *Refreezing:* The desirable performance becomes the permanent way of doing things. This is the new status quo. Refreezing often takes place through reinforcement and support for the new behavior.

See Exhibit 12.5 for a review of the steps.

Learning Outcome 12-3

Explain how to use the Lussier change model when making changes.

Lussier Change Model Lewin's model provides a general framework for understanding organizational change. Because the steps of change are broad, the author has developed a more specific model. The Lussier change model consists of five steps:

1. *Define the Change.* Clearly state what the change is. Is it a task, structural, technological, or people change? What are the systems effects on the other variables? Set objectives, following the guidelines in Chapter 8.
2. *Identify Possible Resistance to the Change.* Determine the intensity, source, and focus of possible resistance to the change. Use the resistance matrix in Exhibit 12.3.
3. *Plan the Change.* Plan the change implementation. Use the appropriate supervisory style for the situation. We will discuss planned change in more detail later in this chapter.
4. *Implement the Change.* Follow the 11 guidelines to overcome resistance to change in Exhibit 12.4.
5. *Control the Change.* Remember that people often resist change and may not follow your plan,[31] so you need to follow up to ensure that the change is implemented, reinforced, and maintained. Make sure the objective is met. If not, take corrective action.

WORK APPLICATION 12-6

Give a specific example of when a change model would be helpful to a specific manager.

If managers at NYCIC follow the guidelines for overcoming resistance to change and develop an effective plan using the change model, change can be implemented successfully at Rider.

ORGANIZATIONAL CULTURE

Organizational culture *consists of the shared values and assumptions of how its members will behave.*

Organizational values are important,[32] and management needs to be specific about the values and behaviors it expects from its people.[33] **Organizational culture** *consists of the shared values and assumptions of how its members will behave.* Recall the importance of creativity and innovation to success[34] (Chapter 11); to this end, many organizations develop innovative cultures,[35] including 3M.[36] In this section, we describe how people learn the organization's culture and the importance of having a strong positive culture, because it is a competitive advantage.[37]

Learning the Organization's Culture

When hiring, an important consideration is matching the person to the culture. Newcomers need to learn and be integrated into the organization's culture, and those who don't fit are often let go.[38] For example, an IBM executive was hired by Apple and was fired primarily due to his cultural incompatibility.[39] Norms are important to culture.[40] Culture is learned through observing and interacting with employees, events, and training. Here are five ways that employees learn the organization's culture.

1. *Heroes*—such as founder Tom Watson of IBM, Sam Walton of Walmart, Herb Kelleher of Southwest Airlines, Frederick Smith of FedEx, and others who made outstanding contributions to their organizations.
2. *Stories*—often about founders and others who have made extraordinary efforts, such as Sam Walton visiting every Walmart store yearly or someone driving through a blizzard to deliver a product or service. Public statements and speeches can also be considered stories.
3. *Slogans*—such as "Quality is Job 1" at Ford; McDonald's Q, S, C, V—Quality, Service, Cleanliness, and Value; The H-P Way; FedEx's People—Service—Profit philosophy.
4. *Symbols*—such as logos, plaques, pins, and jackets, or a Mary Kay pink Cadillac. Symbols are used to convey meaning.
5. *Ceremonies*—including rituals such as awards dinners for top achievers.

WORK APPLICATION 12-7

Identify the cultural heroes, stories, slogans, symbols, and ceremonies for an organization you are or have been a member of.

If you hear expressions such as, "That's not how we do things here," or "This is the way we do things here," you are learning the organization's culture.

Strong and Weak, Positive and Negative Cultures

The two dimensions of an organization's culture are strong and weak, and positive and negative.

Learning Outcome 12-4

Explain the two dimensions of an organization's culture.

Strong and Weak Cultures Organizations with clear values that are shared to the extent of similar behavior have strong cultures. Organizations that have no stated values and do not enforce behavior have weak cultures. So the more alike the values and behavior, the stronger the culture, and vice versa. Examples of strong cultures include:

IBM IBM is recognized as having a very strong culture. It has three core values. "IBMers value (1) dedication to every client's success; (2) innovation that matters, for our company and for the world; and (3) trust and personal responsibility in all relationships.[41] There is a sense of pride and of being able to distinguish yourself as an IBMer."[42]

PepsiCo, Inc. Pepsi's organizational culture stresses competition in every aspect of an employee's work life. Pepsi executives are jointly determined to surpass archrival Coca-Cola while at the same time surpassing rival executives at PepsiCo. Managers are continually pressured to increase market share; a decline can lead to a manager's dismissal.

As you can see, IBM stresses excellence; PepsiCo, competition. They have different cultures, yet they are successful organizations, which shows there is no one best organizational culture.

Positive and Negative Cultures An organizational culture is considered positive when it has norms that contribute to effective performance and productivity. A negative organizational culture is a source of resistance and turmoil that hinders effective performance.

The most effective organizational culture that leads to effective performance is strong and positive. Companies with strong positive cultures, include Apple, Johnson & Johnson, Procter & Gamble, and 3M.

Before accepting a job with an organization, you may want to learn about its culture to determine if it is the kind of organization you will enjoy working in. For example, if you are not competitive, you probably will not enjoy working for PepsiCo.

Communication Skills
Refer to CS Question 4.

In the opening case, Ronnie feels that NYCIC has a strong organizational culture, whereas Rider had a weak culture. NYCIC needs to develop the shared values and assumptions of how members should behave at Rider. Many firms experience difficulty merging cultures. The OD team-building program (discussed later in this chapter) would be an excellent way to develop the NYCIC culture at Rider.

WORK APPLICATION 12-8

Describe the organizational culture at a firm for which you work or have worked. Does or did the organization strive to have a strong positive culture? If so, how?

ORGANIZATIONAL CLIMATE

Organizational climate *is the relatively enduring quality of the internal environment of the organization as perceived by its members.* Climate is employees' perception of the atmosphere of the internal environment, which is important to organizational success.[43] Organizational climate is a broad term. Its definition will be explained throughout this section.

The major difference between culture and climate is as follows: Culture is based on shared values and assumptions of "how" things should be done (ideal environment), while climate is based on shared perceptions of the "way" things are done (intangibles of the actual internal environment). An organization can claim to have a strong culture and have a negative climate. Employees can know how things should be, while being dissatisfied with their perception of the way things actually are. For example, in some organizations managers claim that quality is very important; signs are posted telling everyone it is. But if you ask employees if quality is important, they say management only cares about how many units are actually shipped out the door.

Job satisfaction, discussed in Chapter 3, is based primarily on organizational climate. Morale is also an important part of organizational climate. **Morale** *is a state of mind based on employees' attitudes and satisfaction with the organization.* Morale can be different at various levels within the organization. Morale is commonly measured on a continuum ranging from high to low morale, based on the seven dimensions of climate listed below.

Dimensions of Climate

Learning Outcome 12-5

Explain the seven dimensions of an organization's climate.

Some of the common dimensions of climate are the following:

- *Structure.* The degree of constraint on members—the number of rules, regulations, and procedures.
- *Responsibility.* The degree of control over one's own job.
- *Rewards.* The degree of being rewarded for one's efforts and being punished appropriately.
- *Warmth.* The degree of satisfaction with human relations.
- *Support.* The degree of being helped by others and of experiencing cooperation.
- *Organizational identity and loyalty.* The degree to which employees identify with the organization and their loyalty to it.
- *Risk.* The degree to which risk-taking is encouraged.

Studies show that poor climate tends to result in lower levels of performance, but not always. Performance tends to be better when climate dimensions are logically consistent with one another. Like plants, employees require a proper climate to thrive. Working in a climate you enjoy will also affect your performance.

Communication Skills
Refer to CS Question 5.

You can develop an effective productive climate by focusing on the dimensions of climate. Often, large companies like NYCIC take over a smaller company like Rider because they are successful. In too many situations, the larger company changes the flexible entrepreneurial climate to one of bureaucracy, resulting in the small company's becoming less productive. NYCIC needs to focus on these seven dimensions of climate. The Rider employees need to shift identity and loyalty to NYCIC.

See Exhibit 12.6 for a list of the dimensions of climate.

EXHIBIT 12.6 | Dimensions of Climate

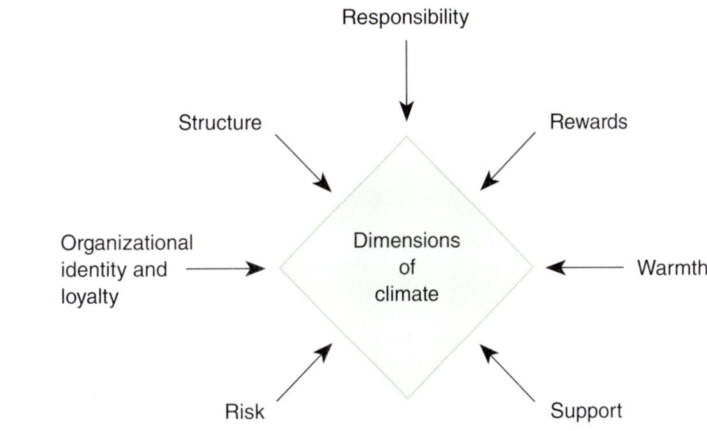

APPLICATION SITUATIONS / / /

Organizational Culture or Climate? AS 12-3

Identify each statement as being associated with:

A. Organizational culture B. Organizational climate

_______ 11. Rotary International's motto, "Service above Self."

_______ 12. "Employees were not happy with this year's raise."

_______ 13. "Please fill out this questionnaire and return it to the human resources department when you are done."

_______ 14. "The unwritten dress code is a suit and tie for work."

_______ 15. "From now on, no one but you will check the quality of your work."

WORK APPLICATION 12-9

Describe the organizational climate at a firm for which you work or have worked, based on the seven dimensions of climate. Does or did the organization measure its climate? If so, how?

WORK APPLICATION 12-10

Describe the morale at the organization.

Learning Outcome 12-6

Describe five organizational development techniques.

ORGANIZATIONAL DEVELOPMENT

So far we have discussed the importance of managing change,[44] and developing strong positive cultures and climates.[45] Now we focus on these topics as an ongoing, organizationwide process,[46] commonly referred to as organizational development (OD).[47] **Organizational development** *is the ongoing planned process of change used as a means of improving the organization's effectiveness in solving problems and achieving its objectives.*

Managing and Changing Culture and Climate through OD

The first step in organizational development is to diagnose the problem(s).[48] Indicators that problems exist, such as conflicts between diverse groups, the need for increased quality and productivity, low profits, and excessive absenteeism or turnover, lead management to call in a change agent to study the organization's problems and needs.[49] A *change agent* is the person responsible for the OD program. The change agent can use a variety of methods to diagnose problems.[50] Some methods are reviewing records, observing, interviewing individuals and work groups, holding meetings, and/or using questionnaires. After the problem has been diagnosed, OD techniques are used to solve it.

EXHIBIT 12.7 | The Training Cycle

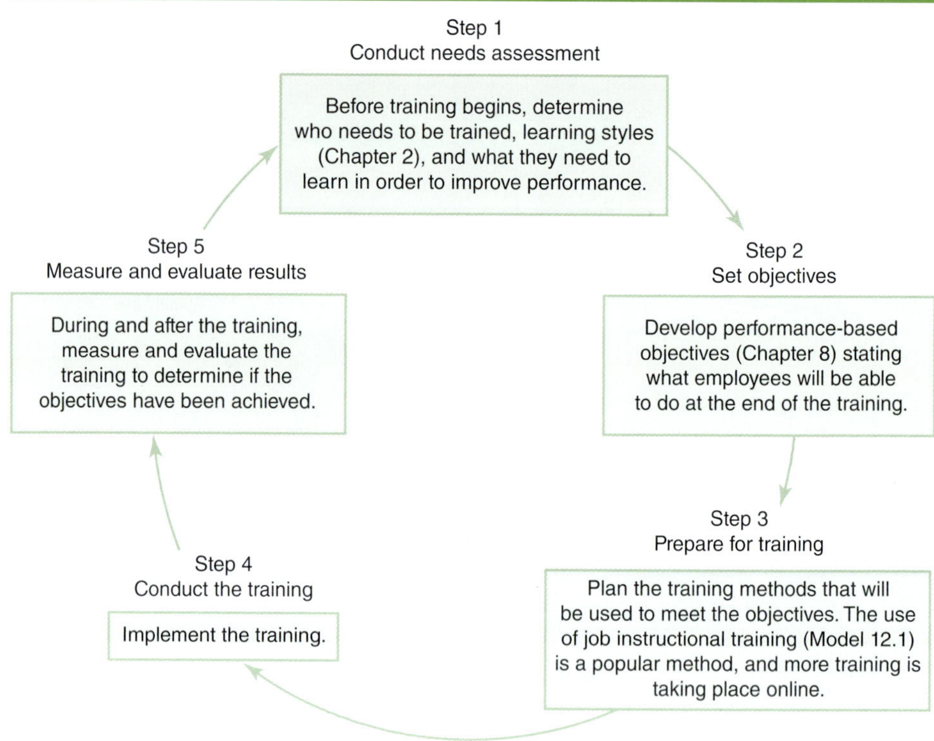

This section examines five OD techniques: training and development, performance appraisal, survey feedback, force field analysis, and team building. Training and development is presented first because the other four techniques usually include training.

Training and Development

Learning Outcome 12-7

Describe the training cycle and how training is used to increase performance.

After a position is staffed, there is usually a need to train the person to do the job,[51] and more training and development tends to lead to less turnover.[52] **Training** *is the process of developing the necessary skills to perform the present job.* **Development** *is the process of developing the ability to perform both present and future jobs.* Typically, training is used to develop technical skills of nonmanagers, while development is usually less technical and is designed for professional and managerial employees. The terms *training* and *development* are often used together; they are used interchangeably as well.

Communication Skills
Refer to CS Question 6.

WORK APPLICATION 12-11

State how you were trained to perform a specific job. Explain how the training affected your job performance. How could training at this organization be used to increase performance?

The Training Cycle Following the steps in the training cycle helps ensure that training is done in a systematic way. See Exhibit 12.7 for more details about each of the five steps in the training cycle. Model 12.1 summarizes the steps involved in conducting a job instructional training (JIT) session, which is part of steps 3 and 4 of the training cycle.

Management at NYCIC will have to determine the training needs of Rider employees, set objectives, prepare for training, conduct the training, and evaluate results so that the two units can work effectively as one organization.

MODEL 12.1 | Job Instructional Training

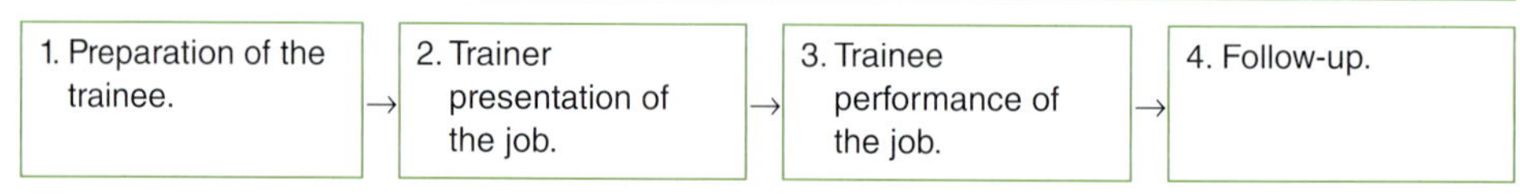

APPLICATION SITUATIONS / / /

The Training Cycle AS 12-4

Identify each of the five statements below by its step in the training cycle.

A. Step 1: Conduct needs assessment
B. Step 2: Set objectives
C. Step 3: Prepare for training
D. Step 4: Conduct the training
E. Step 5: Measure and evaluate results

_______ 16. "I will now demonstrate the proper technique."

_______ 17. "At the end of this training session, you will be able to operate the machine."

_______ 18. "In reviewing your performance, I've decided that you need more training to increase your speed."

_______ 19. "You passed the test with a perfect score; you're certified."

_______ 20. "Where did I put that JIT sheet? I need to revise it."

Performance Appraisal

After employees are hired, and during and after their training, they must be evaluated.[53] **Performance appraisal** *is the ongoing process of evaluating employee job performance.* Performance appraisal is also called *performance job evaluation, performance review, merit rating,* and *performance audit.* Regardless of the name, performance appraisal is one of the manager's most important, and most difficult, functions.[54] Conducted properly, performance appraisal can decrease absenteeism and turnover and increase morale and productivity.[55]

Communication Skills
Refer to CS Question 7.

The performance of employees is appraised according to two sets of objectives: (1) developmental and (2) evaluative. Developmental objectives are used as the basis of decisions to improve future performance. Evaluative objectives are used as the basis of administrative decisions to reward or punish past performance.

Learning Outcome 12-8

List and explain the five steps of performance appraisals and state how performance appraisals can lead to increased performance.

The performance appraisal process has five steps. These are shown in Exhibit 12.8 and steps 2 and 3 are discussed below.

Developing Standards and Measurement Methods After you determine what it takes to do the job, you should develop standards and methods for measuring performance. This is step (2) in the performance appraisal process. Poor standards are a major problem of performance appraisals.[56]

Communication Skills
Refer to CS Question 8.

The term **standards** *describes performance levels in the areas of quantity, quality, time, and cost.* Sample standards for an administrative assistant could be to type 50 words (quantity) per minute (time) with two errors or less (quality) at a maximum salary of $10 per hour (cost).

WORK APPLICATION 12-12

Describe the performance standards for a job you hold or have held. How would you improve them?

Conducting Informal Performance Appraisals—Coaching Performance appraisals should not merely be formal once-a-year, one-hour sessions. Employees need regular informal feedback on their performance.[57] The employee performing below standard may need daily or weekly coaching to reach increased productivity. Coaching is a hot topic,[58] and is growing in popularity.[59]

Learning Outcome 12-9

List the steps in the coaching model.

The coaching model is designed for use in improving ability and for dealing with motivation problems. It is important to coach low performers because they distract and drag down everyone.[60] The **coaching model** *involves these steps: step (1) refer to past feedback; step (2) describe current performance; step (3) describe desired performance; step (4) get*

EXHIBIT 12.8 | Performance Appraisal Steps

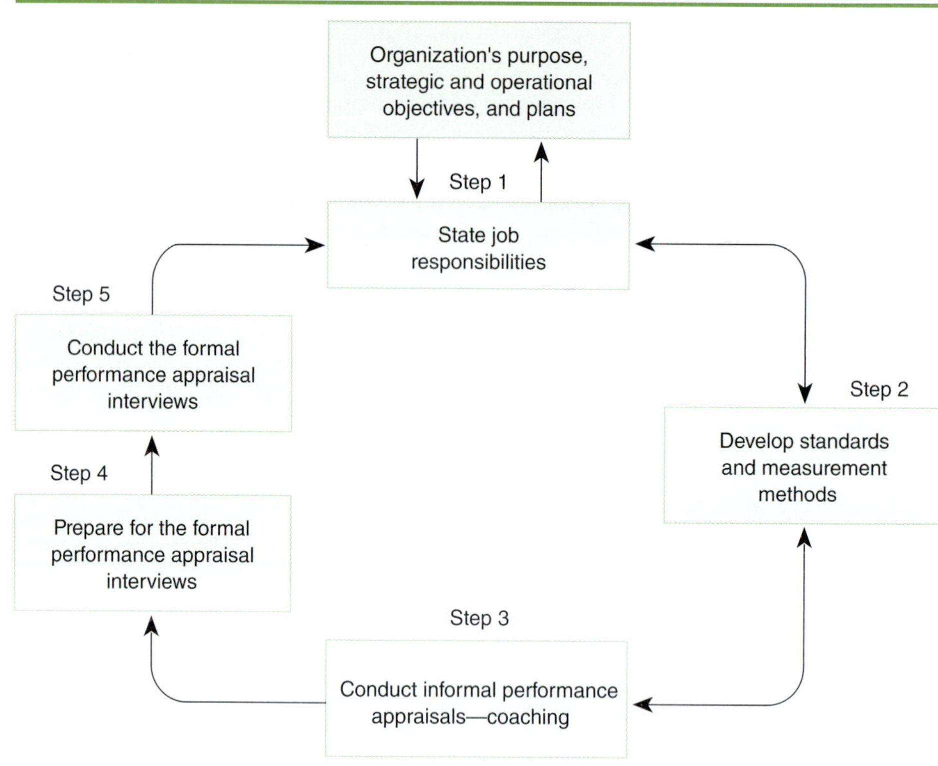

WORK APPLICATION 12-13

Identify the performance measurement method(s) used to evaluate your job performance. Describe how you would improve the method(s).

a commitment to the change; and step (5) follow up. To help you understand each step, we'll use dialogue to illustrate it. In the dialogue situation, Fran is the supervisor of vending machine repair and Dale is a relatively new vending machine repair technician. Fran is coaching Dale.

Step 1: Refer to Past Feedback This step assumes that the employee was told or trained to do something in the past and never did or no longer does it properly. If the employee has never received feedback, explain the situation.

FRAN: Hi, Dale. I called you into my office because I wanted to discuss your repair record.

DALE: What about it?

FRAN: We haven't discussed your performance since you started, but I've noticed a problem and wanted to correct it quickly.

Step 2: Describe Current Performance Using specific examples, describe in detail the current performance that needs to be changed.

FRAN: In reviewing the repair reports, I realized that you repaired vending machines at the Big Y Supermarket, the United Cooperative Bank, and the Springfield YMCA. In all three locations, you had to return to repair the same machine within a month.

DALE: That's correct. If you look at my report, you'll see that it was for different problems. I fixed them right the first time.

FRAN: I realize that. That's not the problem. The problem is that the average time before returning for any repair on a machine is three months. Did you realize that?

DALE: Now that you mention it, I did hear it in the training class.

FRAN: I want to determine why you have to return to the same machine more frequently than the average. My guess is that it's because when you go to a machine for repair, you fix only the specific problem, rather than going through the entire machine to perform routine maintenance.

DALE: My job is to fix the machines.

Step 3: Describe Desired Performance In detail, tell the employee exactly what the desired performance is. Have him or her tell you why it is important. If a skill is needed, teach it, using job instructional training (JIT). Explain why it is important for the performance to be done differently, and model the behavior.

FRAN: At the training program, did they tell you to go through the entire machine for routine maintenance?

DALE: I don't remember them saying that.

FRAN: Do you know why it is important to do maintenance rather than just to fix the machines?

DALE: I guess it's so I don't have to go back within a month and repair the same machine.

FRAN: That's right. You're more productive. From now on, I want you to go through the machines and perform maintenance rather than just fix them.

Step 4: Get a Commitment to the Change If possible, get the employee to commit to changing his or her performance. The commitment is important because if the employee is not willing to commit to the change, he or she will not make the change. It's better to know now that the employee is not going to change than to wait and find out later, when it may be too late. The employee can commit and not make the change. But at least you have done your job, and you can refer to past commitments without change when you discipline the employee.

FRAN: From now on, will you do maintenance, rather than repairs?

DALE: I didn't do it in the past because I didn't realize I was supposed to. But in the future, I will.

Step 5: Follow Up Following up is important to ensure that the employee realizes that the supervisor is serious about the change. When employees know their performance will be evaluated, they are more likely to make the change. A specific meeting is not always needed. But the employee should be told how the supervisor will follow up.

FRAN: In the future, I will continue to review the records for frequent repairs of the same machine. I don't think it will continue, but if it does, I will call you in again.

DALE: It will not be necessary.

FRAN: Great. I appreciate your cooperation, Dale. This was the only concern about your work that I had. Other than this one area, you're doing a good job. I'll see you later.

DALE: Have a good one.

Skill-Building Exercise 12-1 develops this skill.

During the discussion with the employee, preferably near the end, give positive reinforcement while correcting performance. Being positive helps motivate the employee to make the necessary change. For an example, refer to Fran's last statement above. Model 12.2 lists the five steps to increase employee performance through coaching.

MODEL 12.2 | Coaching Model

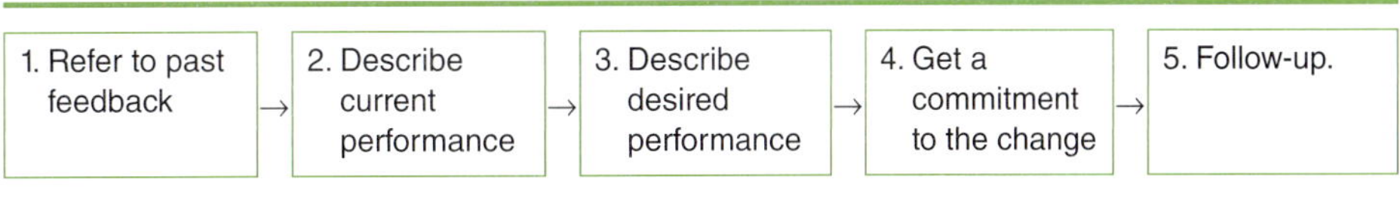

WORK APPLICATION 12-14

Describe a specific situation in which it would be appropriate to use the coaching model.

Exhibit 12.8 lists the performance appraisal steps. Notice that steps 1 to 3 are double-looped (have two-headed arrows) because the development at one step may require the manager to backtrack and make changes. For example, during an informal appraisal, the manager may realize that environmental changes require a change in the employee's job and/or performance standards. Step 5 brings the manager back to step 1.

Survey Feedback

Survey feedback *is an OD technique that uses a questionnaire to gather data that are used as the basis for change.* Different change agents will use slightly different approaches; however, a commonly used survey feedback program would include these six steps:

1. Management and the change agent do some preliminary planning to develop an appropriate survey questionnaire.
2. The questionnaire is administered to all members of the organization or unit.
3. The survey data are analyzed to uncover problem areas for improvement.
4. The change agent feeds back the results to management.
5. Managers evaluate the feedback and discuss the results with their subordinates.
6. Corrective action plans are developed and implemented.

As an example, a consultant was called by a large manufacturer to discuss training. He met with the managers of industrial engineering and manufacturing engineering. They informed the consultant of a survey that had been conducted (steps 1 to 3). The feedback results had shown engineers as being low in organizational performance (step 4). The three engineering managers had met with their engineers and discussed the reasons for the low rating and ways to change their image (step 5). They decided to have the engineers go through a human relations/communication skill-building training program to improve their ability to interact more effectively with the organizational members that they served. The consultant developed and conducted a training program that helped correct the situation (step 6).

Measuring Climate The survey feedback technique is commonly used to measure the organizational climate. Based on the results, the organization may set up training programs as described above. Some of the signs that an organization may have a climate problem include high rates of tardiness, absenteeism, and turnover. When employees have many complaints, sabotage each other's work, talk about unionization or striking, lack pride in their work, and have low morale, the organization may have a climate problem that should be corrected.

Organizational climate is measured in the same way job satisfaction is (review Chapter 3). Survey feedback is the most common approach. But the dimensions included in the questionnaire vary from organization to organization.

Force Field Analysis

Force field analysis *is a technique that diagrams the current level of performance, the hindering forces against change, and the driving forces toward change.* The process begins by appraising the current level of performance. As shown in Exhibit 12.9, the present level of performance is shown in the middle of the diagram. The hindering forces holding back performance are listed in the top part of the diagram. The driving forces keeping performance at this level are listed on the bottom of the diagram. After viewing the diagram, you develop strategies for maintaining or increasing the driving forces with simultaneous steps for decreasing hindering forces. For example, in Exhibit 12.9, the solution you select could be to have the salespeople go through a training program. You could spend more time working with the less productive salespeople. Speeding up delivery time could be worked on, while maintaining all the driving forces could lead to higher sales volume.

EXHIBIT 12.9 | Force Field Analysis

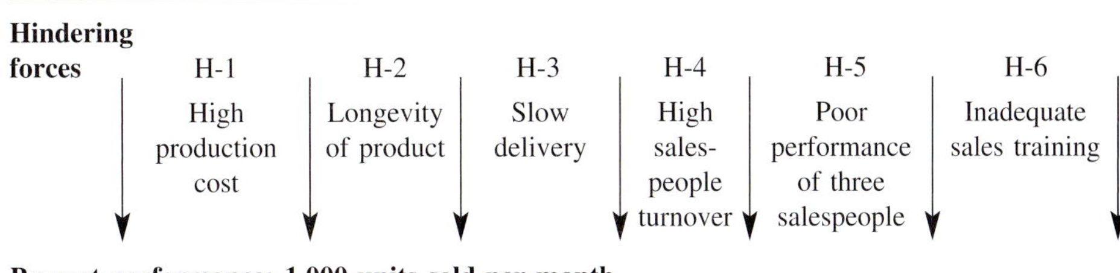

Force field analysis is particularly useful for group problem solving. After group members agree on the diagram, the solution often becomes clear to them.

Team Building

Team building is a widely used OD technique. **Team building** *is an OD technique designed to help work groups operate more effectively.* Team building is used as a means of helping new or existing groups that are in need of improving effectiveness.[61]

Team-Building Goals The goals of team-building programs will vary considerably, depending on the group needs and the change agent's skills.[62] Some of the typical goals are:

- To clarify the objectives of the team and the responsibilities of each team member.
- To identify problems preventing the team from accomplishing its objectives.
- To develop team problem-solving and decision-making, objective-setting, and planning skills.
- To determine a preferred style of teamwork and to change to that style.
- To fully utilize the resources of each individual member.
- To develop open, honest working relationships based on trust and an understanding of group members.

Team-Building Program Agenda The team-building agendas vary with team needs and the change agent's skills.[63] Typical agenda topics include the following items:

1. *Climate building.* The program begins with the change agent trying to develop a climate of trust, support, and openness. He or she discusses the program's purpose and objectives. Team members learn more about each other and share what they would like to accomplish in the session.
2. *Process and structure evaluation.* The team evaluates the strengths and weaknesses of its process. The team explores and selects ideal norms.
3. *Problem identification.* The team identifies its strengths, then its weaknesses or areas where improvement is possible. The team first lists several areas where improvement is possible. Then it prioritizes them by importance in helping the team improve performance.
4. *Problem solving.* The team takes the top priority and develops a solution. It then moves to the second priority, followed by the third, the fourth, and so on.

Skill-Building Exercise 12-3 develops this skill.

Communication Skills
Refer to CS Question 9.

WORK APPLICATION 12-15

Identify an OD technique and explain how it is used by a specific organization, preferably one with which you have been associated.

5. *Training.* Team building often includes some form of training that addresses the problem(s) facing the group.
6. *Closure.* The program ends by summarizing what has been accomplished. Follow-up responsibility is assigned. Team members commit to improving performance.

At Rider, a good starting place for OD would be team-building sessions. In teams, Rider employees could be made aware of NYCIC's OD program and how Rider will be developed. Through team-building sessions, the planned changes of NYCIC could be implemented at Rider. After a period of months, NYCIC could use survey feedback to determine how the change program at Rider is perceived. The survey could serve as the basis for understanding the need for future change at Rider. As the teams develop at Rider, they can use force field analysis to work out any problems the new changes bring and to reach higher levels of performance as part of their team-building program.

APPLICATION SITUATIONS / / /

OD Techniques AS 12-5

Below are five situations in which an OD technique would be beneficial. Identify the most appropriate technique for each.

A. Force field analysis
B. Survey feedback
C. Training and development
D. Team building
E. Performance appraisal

______ 21. "We need to teach employees statistical process control techniques."

______ 22. "We are a progressive company; we believe in developing our people. We'd like to give each employee better feedback to help them improve their performance."

______ 23. "To improve productivity, we should identify the things that are holding us back and the things that are helping us be productive, too."

______ 24. "We want an OD program that will enable us to better utilize the input of each manager."

______ 25. "Morale and motivation are low in our organization. We'd like to know why and change."

GLOBAL DIFFERENCES

As stated, the Big Five personality types are global. Therefore, individuals in all cultures are more or less open to change. However, cultural values can influence openness to change. Countries including the United States value change, whereas other cultures, including some Arab countries, place less value on change and more on tradition and religious beliefs. The United States is known for creating urgency and for setting deadlines for implementing change. However, other cultures take a slower approach and are more patient, such as many Asian and Middle Eastern countries.

Collective (i.e., Japan, Mexico) versus individual (United States and much of Western Europe) societies do affect change. Collective societies tend to want to improve the team and organizations, so individuals are often more open to change to help others even when they personally may not gain and even lose, whereas those in individual societies are more concerned about helping themselves and are more willing to resist change that hurts them personally. The Japanese generate a lot more creative ideas for improvement than do U.S. workers. The Japanese tend to focus on small incremental changes to improve processes and products, whereas Americans tends to focus on large major changes. The baseball example used is that the Japanese try to get a hit, whereas Americans go for the home run.

Some cultures are more open to power and following orders for change without questioning authority, such as France, China, and India. However, other cultures are more willing to question and resist change, such as the U.S. and Scandinavian (Denmark, Sweden, and Norway) cultures, which can cause problems for companies trying to change. Participation in change also varies by culture and country development. For example, in the United States and Japan employees are highly trained and want to participate in planning and implementing change. However, in Third World countries employees are generally neither capable nor interested in being empowered to participate in the change process.

Communication Skills
Refer to CS Question 10.

You will read more about global diversity in Chapter 13. Complete Self-Assessment Exercise 12-2 to determine how your personality affects your response to change and organizational culture.

/// Self-Assessment Exercise 12-2 ///

Personality and Organizational Change and Culture

Let's determine how your personality relates to your ability to change and the type of culture you may prefer.

On the Big Five personality traits, if you are *open to new experiences,* you are willing to change and will do well in an adaptive-type culture. If you are closed to new experiences, you will tend to do well in a bureaucratic-type culture that changes slowly.

If you score high on *conscientiousness,* with a high need for achievement, you may tend to be a conformist and will most likely feel comfortable in an organization with a strong culture.

If you have a high *agreeableness* personality, with a high need for affiliation, you tend to get along well with people and can fit into a strong culture. You would do well in a cooperative-type culture that values teamwork and empowerment.

If you have *surgency* traits, with a high need for power, you like to dominate and may not fit into a strong culture that does not reflect the values you have. You would tend to do well in a competitive-type culture that values individualism and high power.

Action plan: Would you like to work in an organization with a weak or a strong culture? What type of cultural values interest you?

____

____

____

____

As we bring this chapter to a close, you should understand why people resist change and how to overcome it using a change model, know what organizational culture is and how we learn it, and be familiar with the dimensions of climate. You should also know five organizational development techniques and be able to improve performance through training people using the job instructional training model and the coaching model.

THE RELATIONSHIP BETWEEN ORGANIZATIONAL CULTURE, CLIMATE, AND DEVELOPMENT

Learning Outcome 12-10

Explain the relationship between organizational culture, climate, and development.

Organizational culture, climate, and development are all different, yet related. Climate refers to the shared values and assumptions of the *actual internal* environment, while culture refers to the values and assumptions of the *ideal* environment. Thus, culture informs climate. Often the concept of culture encompasses that of climate. However, in recent years, the concern with culture has increased, while the importance of the concept of climate has decreased.

Organizational development is commonly used as the vehicle to change culture or climate. Organizational development programs to improve performance tend to be wider in scope than culture or climate. Culture and climate changes can be a part of an extensive OD program addressing other issues as well.

NYCIC can overcome the resistance to change at Rider through a planned organizational development program involving team building. The OD program can be based on the change model. Through team building, NYCIC can change the culture and climate at Rider to be the same as that of NYCIC.

/ / / REVIEW / / /

The chapter review is organized to help you master the 11 learning outcomes for Chapter 12. First provide your own response to each learning outcome, and then check the summary provided to see how well you understand the material. Next, identify the final statement in each section as either true or false (T/F). Correct each false statement. Answers are given at the end of the chapter.

LO 12-1 Describe the four types of changes.

The four types of changes are: (1) technology—machines and processes for creating products and services; (2) structure—organizational principles and departmentalization; (3) task—the way people perform their jobs; and (4) people—their knowledge and skill development.

Although automation is a technology change, it results in task and people changes. T F

LO 12-2 State why people resist change and how to overcome resistance.

Four major reasons people resist change are the desire to maintain the status quo, uncertainty, learning anxiety, and fear. To overcome resistance to change, one should first identify three major variables: (1) *intensity*—the strength of the intensity against change; (2) *source*—the source of resistance, whether facts, beliefs, or values; and (3) *focus*—the focus of resistance, which may be self, others, or the work environment. The 11 ways to overcome resistance to change include: (1) develop a positive climate for change; (2) encourage interest in improvement; (3) plan; (4) give facts; (5) clearly state why the change is needed and how it will affect employees; (6) create a win–win situation; (7) involve employees; (8) provide support; (9) stay calm; (10) avoid direct confrontation; and (11) use power and ethical politics.

The first reaction to rumors of change is resistance to the change. T F

LO 12-3 Explain how to use the Lussier change model when making changes.

To make a change, follow the steps in the Lussier change model: (1) define the change, (2) identify possible resistance to the change, (3) plan the change, (4) implement the change, and (5) control the change.

It is common to shorten the Lussier model to unfreezing, moving, and refreezing. T F

LO 12-4 Explain the two dimensions of an organization's culture.

The two dimensions of an organization's culture are strong and weak, and positive and negative. Organizations with strong cultures have clear values that are shared and enforced; those with weak cultures do not. Positive cultures contribute to effective performance; negative cultures hinder it.

Employees learn about the organization's culture through its heroes, stories, slogans, symbols, and ceremonies. T F

LO 12-5 Explain the seven dimensions of an organization's climate.

The seven dimensions of an organization's climate include: (1) structure—the degree of constraint on members; (2) responsibility—the degree of control over one's own job; (3) rewards—the degree of being rewarded for one's efforts and being punished appropriately; (4) warmth—the degree of satisfaction with human relations; (5) support—the degree of being helped by others and cooperation; (6) organizational identity and loyalty—the degree to which employees identify with the organization and feel loyalty toward it; and (7) risk—the degree to which risk-taking behavior is encouraged.

Morale is used to measure climate as being either high or low, based on the seven dimensions of climate. T F

LO 12-6 Describe five organizational development techniques.

Organizational development (OD) is the ongoing planned process of change to improve the organization's effectiveness in solving problems and achieving objectives. Five OD techniques are: (1) training and development, used to teach people their jobs; (2) performance appraisal, used to evaluate employee job performance; (3) survey feedback, which uses a questionnaire to gather data that are used as the basis for change; (4) force field analysis, used to diagram the current level of performance as well as the hindering and driving forces; and (5) team building, designed to help work groups operate more effectively.

Survey feedback can be part of other OD techniques, and it can also lead to the use of other techniques. T F

LO 12-7 Describe the training cycle and how training is used to increase performance.

The five steps of the training cycle are: (1) conduct a needs assessment, (2) set objectives, (3) prepare for training, (4) conduct the training, and (5) measure and evaluate training results. Employees can get more work done when they follow proper procedures.

The job instructional training (JIT) steps include: (1) preparation of the trainee, (2) trainer presentation of the job, (3) trainee performance of the job, and (4) follow-up. T F

LO 12-8 List and explain the five steps of performance appraisals and state how performance appraisals can lead to increased performance.

The five steps of performance appraisal are: (1) state job responsibilities, (2) develop standards and measurement methods, (3) conduct informal performance appraisals, (4) prepare for the formal performance appraisal interviews, and (5) conduct the formal performance appraisal interviews. Performance appraisals can provide motivation and feedback to employees on ways to do a better job.

For developmental objectives, a ranking method based on rating scales or BARS works well. T F

LO 12-9 List the steps in the coaching model.

The five steps of the coaching model are: (1) refer to past feedback, (2) describe current performance, (3) describe desired performance, (4) get a commitment to the change, and (5) follow up.

The coaching model is commonly used during the formal yearly performance review. T F

LO 12-10 Explain the relationship between organizational culture, climate, and development.

Climate refers to shared perceptions of intangible elements in the *actual internal* environment, while culture refers to the values and assumptions of the *ideal* environment. Often the concept of culture encompasses that of climate. Organizational development programs are commonly used to change culture and climate to improve performance.

As changes take place in the business environment, the organizational culture needs to change, and as culture changes, climate can deteriorate. T F

LO 12-11 Define the following 16 key terms.

Select one or more methods: (1) fill in the missing key terms from memory; (2) match the key terms from the end of the review with their definitions below; and/or (3) copy the key terms in order from the key terms list at the beginning of the chapter.

________________________ are technological change, structural change, task change, and people change.

________________________ are formal systems for collecting, processing, and disseminating the information necessary to aid managers in decision making.

________________________ is the simplification or reduction of the human effort required to do a job.

________________________ involves the variables of intensity, source, and focus and explains why people are reluctant to change.

________________________ consists of the shared values and assumptions of how its members will behave.

________________________ is the relatively enduring quality of the internal environment of the organization as perceived by its members.

________________________ is a state of mind based on attitudes and satisfaction with the organization.

________________________ is the ongoing planned process of change used as a means of improving the organization's effectiveness in solving problems and achieving its objectives.

________________________ is the process of developing the necessary skills to perform the present job.

________________________ is the process of developing the ability to perform both present and future jobs.

________________________ refers to the ongoing process of evaluating employee job performance.

________________________ is a term used to describe performance levels in the areas of quantity, quality, time, and cost.

The ________________________ involves these steps: (1) refer to past feedback, (2) describe current performance, (3) describe desired performance, (4) get a commitment to the change, and (5) follow up.

________________________ is a technique that uses a questionnaire to gather data that are used as the basis for change.

________________________ is a technique that diagrams the current level of performance, the hindering forces toward change, and the driving forces toward change.

________________________ is a technique designed to help work groups operate more effectively.

/ / / KEY TERMS / / /

automation 378
coaching model 389
development 388
force field analysis 392
management information systems (MIS) 378
morale 386
organizational climate 386
organizational culture 384
organizational development (OD) 387
performance appraisal 389
resistance to change 380
standards 389
survey feedback 392
team building 393
training 388
types of changes 378

/ / / COMMUNICATION SKILLS / / /

The following critical thinking questions can be used for class discussion and/or as written assignments to develop communication skills. Be sure to give complete explanations for all questions.

1. Which single technology change has had the largest effect on your behavior?
2. Of the four reasons people resist change, which one do you think is the most common?
3. Of the 11 methods for overcoming resistance to change, which one do you think is the best?
4. Describe your college's culture. Is it strong or weak? Are there any good slogans and/or symbols that help convey your college's culture? Give at least one new way (slogans/symbols, etc.) to promote your college's culture.
5. Using the seven dimensions of climate, describe your college's climate. Rate the morale of students as high or low, explaining your answer in detail.
6. One of the purposes of college is to train and develop students for future careers. How would you rate your overall college education?
7. A professor's job is to facilitate student learning, evaluate student performance, and assign grades. Do you believe your learning performance is evaluated effectively? How could it be improved?
8. Do your professors use consistent standards in terms of the work they require in their courses and the performance appraisal grades they give? Or do some professors require more work than others? Do some give lots of As while others give lots of lower grades? Is this diversity in work requirements and performance appraisal positive or negative? Why does it exist?
9. Which OD technique(s) can be used to improve consistency among professors in terms of work assignments and performance appraisals at your college? Which of the four reasons for resistance would be the dominant reason for faculty resistance to such a change? How would you rate the intensity, focus, and source of their resistance (see Exhibit 12.3, Resistance Matrix)?
10. Can a multinational company have one organizational culture, or does it need to have different cultures based on its business unit in each country?

CASE / / / Ursula Burns, Chair and Chief Executive Officer of Xerox

Ursula Burns joined Xerox in 1980 as a mechanical engineering summer intern. She later assumed roles in product development and planning. From 1992 through 2000, at a critical time in the company's history, Burns led several business teams including the company's color business and office network printing business. She outperformed at these mid-level managerial positions and it did not go unnoticed. In 2000, she was named Senior Vice President, Corporate Strategic Services, heading up manufacturing and supply chain operations. Alongside then-CEO Anne Mulcahy, she worked to restructure Xerox through its turnaround to emerge as a leader in color technology and document services. A key factor in the company's turnaround was its R&D of new products and technologies. At the time, Burns was responsible for leading Xerox's global research, as well as product development, marketing, and delivery. In April 2007, Burns was named president of Xerox, expanding her leadership to also include the company's IT functions, corporate strategy, human resources, corporate marketing, and global accounts. She was also elected a member of the company's board of directors. On May 20, 2010, Burns became chair of the company, leading the 140,000 people of Xerox who serve clients in more than 160 countries.

One can tell the type of corporation Burns wants Xerox to be by looking at all the recent awards the corporation has earned so far under her tenure. They underscore the company's commitments in the areas of sustainability, innovation, diversity, and ethics.

Xerox was named to the 2011 Dow Jones Sustainability Index for its commitment to sustainable innovation.

The listing identifies leaders in sustainability and gives investors a way to follow companies that embrace environmental and social values. In its third annual ranking, *Newsweek Green* rated Xerox in the top 50 for environmental performance of America's 500 largest publicly traded companies. Xerox was named to Thomson Reuters' listing of the World's 100 Most Innovative Companies. It was named one of the top companies for sales professionals in *Selling Power* magazine's annual listing of the 50 Best Companies to Sell for Now. The ranking, which appeared in the November/December issue, is based on compensation, training, and career mobility. In recognition of its commitment to inspiring employees through progressive employment practices and beneficial employee programs, Xerox Canada was named one of Canada's Top 100 Employers by Mediacorp. The Human Rights Campaign named Xerox to its 2012 Best Places to Work Corporate Quality Index, with a 100 percent rating on the survey index.

Reacting to these accolades, Burns said: "We fully appreciate that in this transparent world, who you are as a business is as important as how you perform. Frankly, at Xerox we wouldn't have it any other way." She went on to add that Xerox's approach to being respected not only as a corporate partner but also as a corporate citizen dictates its decisions and has made Xerox the brand she and everyone else at the corporation is proud to be today.

Burns's story of one of overcoming the odds. She was raised in a housing project on Manhattan's Lower East Side by a hard-working single mother who cleaned, ironed, did child care—anything to see that Burns got a good Catholic education and eventually a graduate degree in engineering from Columbia. Burns was promoted first to president of Xerox's business group operations, becoming the first woman to hold that position. She was responsible for the engineering center and five separate divisions; together her group brought in 80 percent of Xerox's profits. African Americans with Burns's background were not common at Xerox, but she never saw her race and low socioeconomic status as liabilities. "My perspective comes in part from being a New York black lady, in part from being an engineer," she said. "I know that I'm smart and have opinions that are worth being heard."

Burns has been described by many as articulate, very knowledgable, energetic, and a straight shooter when dealing with people. Burns has been credited with increasing Xerox's sales of color-capable printers and copiers, as the company brought to market 24 machines in the past two years amid competition from Hewlett-Packard and Canon. With her leadership, Xerox has gone from a company in trouble to one poised to become the leader in sales in its industry.

She is the first African American woman CEO of a firm that is included on the *Fortune* 500 list. Undoubtedly, her achievement has provided an opportunity for other people of color and women. According to Burns, she got the position through hard work and high performance.[64,65]

Go to the Internet: To learn more about Ursula Burns and Xerox, visit the company's Web site at www.xerox.com.

Support your answers to the following questions with specific information from the case, or information you get from the Web or other sources.

1. The chapter discusses four types of changes that organizations typically encounter—technological change, structural change, task change, and people change. Which of these did Burns deal with at Xerox?

2. The chapter discusses resistance to change and some of the methods managers can use to overcome resistance to change. In your opinion, has CEO Burns been a successful change agent so far?

3. Describe the type of organizational culture that Burns is trying to create at Xerox.

4. In your opinion, has Ursula Burns created a strong or weak, positive or negative culture at Xerox?

Cumulative Questions

5. Communication is a major competency for leaders (Chapter 5). Would you agree that this is a quality of Burns's, to have been as effective as she has been so far?

6. One of the characteristics of effective teams (Chapter 11) is the presence of a capable and competent team leader. Would you describe Burns as being an effective team leader?

Case Exercise and Role-Play

Preparation: Two of Burns's presidents have been in conflict with each other for a while. She has decided to assign the task to your class for resolution. Chapter 6 discusses five conflict management styles—forcing, avoiding, accommodating, compromising, and collaborating.

She wants your class to attempt to resolve this conflict using each of the conflict management styles.

In-Class Groups: The instructor forms students into small groups and assigns each group one of the conflict management styles. Group members should not know in advance which style was assigned to other groups. Each group should then develop a plan for resolving the conflict using their assigned style or approach. Each group is allowed to determined the exact nature of the conflict for their own purposes. Write out a script for dramatizing or playing out your plan.

Role-Play: Each group presents a skit of their plan to the rest of the class. The class will determine which conflict management style the group is employing in its plan. A discussion should follow in the strengths and weaknesses of each style.

OBJECTIVE CASE /// Supervisor Carl's Change

Carl was an employee at Benson's Corporation. He applied for a supervisor job at Hedges Inc. and got the job. Carl wanted to do a good job. He observed the employees at work to determine ways to improve productivity. Within a week Carl thought of a way.

On Friday afternoon he called the employees together. Carl told them that starting on Monday he wanted them to change the steps they followed when assembling the product. He demonstrated the new steps a few times and asked if everyone understood them. There were no questions. So Carl said, "Great. Start them on Monday, first thing."

On Monday Carl was in his office for about an hour doing the week's scheduling. When he came out to the shop floor, he realized that no one was following the new procedure he had shown them on Friday. Carl called the crew together and asked why no one was following the new steps.

LAMONT: We've done it this way for years and it works fine.

JENNIFER: We are all underpaid for this boring job. Why should we improve productivity? (*Several others nod.*)

LING: On Friday at the tavern we were talking about the change, and we agreed that we are not getting paid more, so why should we produce more?

Answer the following questions. Then in the space between the questions, state why you selected that answer.

_____ 1. The type of change Carl introduced was:

a. task change
b. structural change
c. technological change
d. people change

_____ 2. Using Exhibit 12.3, identify Jennifer's major resistance (box) to change.

a. 1 *b.* 2 *c.* 3 *d.* 4 *e.* 5 *f.* 6 *g.* 7 *h.* 8 *i.* 9

_____ 3. Using Exhibit 12.3, identify Ling's major resistance (box) to change.

a. 1 *b.* 2 *c.* 3 *d.* 4 *e.* 5 *f.* 6 *g.* 7 *h.* 8 *i.* 9

_____ 4. When implementing his change, Carl should have used which major step to overcome resistance to change?

a. develop a positive climate
b. encourage interest in improvement
c. plan
d. give facts
e. stay calm
f. avoid direct confrontation
g. involve employees
h. provide support

_____ 5. Lamont's response was a(n) _____ resistance statement.

a. blocker
b. roller
c. staller
d. reverser
e. sidestepper
f. threatener
g. politician
h. traditionalist
i. assaulter

_______ 6. The best OD technique for Carl to have used for this change was:

a. force field analysis
b. survey feedback
c. training
d. team building
e. performance appraisal

_______ 7. Carl followed the Lussier change model steps.

a. true
b. false

_______ 8. Lamont's statement, assuming it is representative of the group, indicates a _______ organizational culture.

a. positive
b. negative

_______ 9. Based on Jennifer's response, it appears organizational climate and morale are:

a. positive
b. neutral
c. in need of improvement

_______ 10. The conflict management style (Chapter 6) Carl should use in this situation (employees are not following the procedures) is:

a. forcing
b. avoiding
c. compromising
d. accommodating
e. collaborating

_______ 11. Assume you had Carl's job. How would you have made the change?

Note: The meeting between Carl and the employees may be role-played in class.

/ / / SKILL-BUILDING EXERCISE 12-1 / / /

Coaching

In-Class Exercise (Group)

Objective: To develop your skill at improving performance through coaching.

AACSB: The AACSB learning standard skills developed through this exercise are analytic skills, communication ability, and leadership.

Preparation: You should have read and understood the chapter.

Experience: You will coach, be coached, and observe coaching using the coaching model.

Procedure 1 (2–4 minutes)

Break into groups of three. Make one or two groups of two, if necessary. Each member selects one of the three situations below in which to be the supervisor, and a different one in which to be the employee. You will role-play coaching and being coached.

BMV 12-1

1. Employee 1 is a clerical worker. He or she uses files, as do the other 10 employees. The employees all know that they are supposed to return the files when they are finished so that others can find them when they need them. Employees should have only one file out at a time. As the supervisor walks by, he or she notices that employee 1 has five files on his or her desk, and another employee is looking for one of the files. The supervisor thinks employee 1 will complain about the heavy workload as an excuse for having more than one file out at a time.

2. Employee 2 is a server in an ice cream shop. He or she knows that the tables should be cleaned up quickly after customers leave so that the new customers do not have to sit at a dirty table. It's a busy night. The supervisor looks at employee 2's tables and finds customers at two of them with dirty dishes. Employee 2 is socializing with some friends at one of the tables. Employees are supposed to be friendly. Employee 2 will probably use this as an excuse for the dirty tables.
3. Employee 3 is an auto technician. All employees know that they are supposed to place a paper mat on the floor of each car to prevent the carpets from getting dirty. When the service supervisor got into a car employee 3 repaired, it did not have a mat, and there was grease on the carpet. Employee 3 does excellent work and will probably make reference to this fact when coached.

Procedure 2 (3–7 minutes)

Prepare for coaching to improve performance. Below, each group member writes a basic outline of what she or he will say when coaching employee 1, 2, or 3, following the steps in coaching below:

Step 1: Refer to past feedback.

Step 2: Describe current performance.

Step 3: Describe desired performance. (Don't forget to have the employee state why it is important.)

Step 4: Get a commitment to the change.

Step 5: Follow up.

Procedure 3 (5–8 minutes)

A. Role-play. The supervisor of employee 1, the clerical worker, coaches him or her (use the actual name of the group member role-playing employee 1) as planned. Talk; do not read your written plan. Employee 1, put yourself in the worker's position. You work hard; there is a lot of pressure to work fast. It's easier when you have more than one file. Refer to the workload while being coached. Both the supervisor and the employee will have to ad-lib.

The person not role-playing is the observer. He or she writes notes on the preparation steps in procedure 2 about what the supervisor did well and how he or she could improve.

B. Feedback. The observer leads a discussion on how well the supervisor coached the employee. It should be a discussion, not a lecture. Focus on what the supervisor did well and how he or she could improve. The employee should also give feedback on how he or she felt and what might have been more effective in getting him or her to change.

Do not go on to the next interview until told to do so. If you finish early, wait for the others to finish.

Procedure 4 (5–8 minutes)

Same as procedure 3, but change roles so that employee 2, the server, is coached. Employee 2 should make a comment about the importance of talking to customers to make them feel welcome. The job is not much fun if you can't talk to your friends.

Procedure 5 (5–8 minutes)

Same as procedure 3. But change roles so that employee 3, the auto technician, is coached. Employee 3 should comment on the excellent work he or she does.

Conclusion: The instructor leads a class discussion and/or makes concluding remarks.

Application (2–4 minutes): What did I learn from this experience? How will I use this knowledge in the future?

Sharing: Volunteers give their answers to the application section.

/ / / SKILL-BUILDING EXERCISE 12-2 / / /

Improving the Quality of Student Life

In-Class Exercise (Individual and Group)

Objective: To experience the quality circle approach to increasing the quality of student life at your college.

AACSB: The AACSB learning standard skills developed through this exercise are analytic skills, communication ability, teamwork, and leadership.

Experience: You will experience being part of a quality circle.

Procedure 1 (8–15 minutes)

Break into groups of five or six members. Select a spokesperson. Your group is to come up with a list of the three to five most needed improvements at your college. Rank them in order of priority, from 1—most important to 5—least important. When you are finished, or the time is up, the spokesperson will write the ranking on the board.

Procedure 2 (3–10 minutes)

Option A: The instructor determines the class's top three to five priorities for improvement.

Option B: The class achieves consensus on the top three to five priorities for improvement.

Procedure 3 (5–10 minutes)

Each group selects a new spokesperson. The group develops solutions that will improve the quality of student life for the class's three to five priority areas.

Procedure 4 (5–20 minutes)

For the first-priority item, each spokesperson states the group's recommendation for improving the quality of student life. The class votes or comes to a consensus on the best way to solve the problem. Proceed to items 2 to 5 until you finish or time is up.

Discussion:

1. Are survey feedback and quality circles (as used in this exercise) effective ways to improve the quality of student life on campus?
2. Did the class consider that quality of student life is a balance between the college, the students, and society? Are your solutions going to benefit the college and society as well as the students?

Conclusion: The instructor may lead a class discussion and/or make concluding remarks.

Application (2–4 minutes): What did I learn from this experience? How will I use this knowledge in the future?

Sharing: Volunteers give their answers to the application section.

/ / / SKILL-BUILDING EXERCISE 12-3 / / /

Team Building

Preparation (Group)

Note: This exercise is designed for permanent class groups. Below is a survey feedback questionnaire. There are no right or wrong answers. Check off the answer to each question as it applies to your class group. All questions have five choices.

Strongly Agree	Agree Somewhat	Neutral	Disagree Somewhat	Strongly Disagree
		Conflict or Fight		

1. Our group's atmosphere is friendly.

______	______	______	______	______

2. Our group has a relaxed (rather than tense) atmosphere.

______	______	______	______	______

3. Our group is very cooperative (rather than competitive).

______	______	______	______	______

4. Members feel free to say what they want.

______	______	______	______	______

5. There is much disagreement in our group.

_____ | _____ | _____ | _____ | _____

6. Our group has problem people (silent member, talker, bored member, wanderer, arguer).

_____ | _____ | _____ | _____ | _____

Apathy

7. Our group is committed to its tasks (all members actively participate).

_____ | _____ | _____ | _____ | _____

8. Our group has good attendance.

_____ | _____ | _____ | _____ | _____

9. Group members come to class prepared (all assignments are complete).

_____ | _____ | _____ | _____ | _____

10. All members do their share of the work.

_____ | _____ | _____ | _____ | _____

11. Our group should consider firing a member for not attending and/or not doing his or her share of the work.

_____ | _____ | _____ | _____ | _____

Decision Making

12. Our group's decision-making ability is good.

_____ | _____ | _____ | _____ | _____

13. All members participate in making decisions.

_____ | _____ | _____ | _____ | _____

14. One or two members influence most decisions.

_____ | _____ | _____ | _____ | _____

15. Our group follows the five steps of the decision-making model (Chapter 11).

Step 1: Define the problem.

_____ | _____ | _____ | _____ | _____

Step 2: Set objectives and criteria.

_____ | _____ | _____ | _____ | _____

Step 3: Generate alternatives.

_____ | _____ | _____ | _____ | _____

Step 4: Analyze alternatives (rather than quickly agreeing on one) and select one.

_____ | _____ | _____ | _____ | _____

Step 5: Plan, implement the decision, and control.

_____ | _____ | _____ | _____ | _____

16. Our group uses the following ideas:

a. Members sit in a close circle.

_____ | _____ | _____ | _____ | _____

b. We determine the approach to the task before starting.

_____ | _____ | _____ | _____ | _____

c. Only one member speaks at a time, and everyone discusses the same question.

_____ | _____ | _____ | _____ | _____

d. Each person presents answers with specific reasons.

_____ | _____ | _____ | _____ | _____

e. We rotate order for presenting answers.

_____ | _____ | _____ | _____ | _____

f. We listen to others rather than rehearse our own answers.

_____ | _____ | _____ | _____ | _____

g. We eliminate choices not selected by group members.

_____ | _____ | _____ | _____ | _____

h. All members defend their answers (when they believe they are correct) rather than changing to avoid discussion or conflict, or to get the task over with.

_____ | _____ | _____ | _____ | _____

i. We identify the answers remaining and reach a consensus on one (no voting).

_____ | _____ | _____ | _____ | _____

j. We come back to controversial questions.

_______	_______	_______	_______	_______

17. We make a list of other relevant questions.
18. Our group uses the ______ conflict management style.
    a. forcing *c.* avoiding *e.* collaborating
    b. accommodating *d.* compromising
18. Our group ______ resolve its conflicts in a manner that is satisfactory to all.
    a. does *b.* does not

In-Class Exercise

This exercise is designed for groups that have worked together for some time.

Objectives: To experience a team-building session and to improve your group's effectiveness.

AACSB: The AACSB learning standard skills developed through this exercise are reflective thinking and self-management, analytic skills, communication ability, teamwork, and leadership.

Experience: This exercise is discussion-oriented.

Material: Preparation for Skill-Building Exercise 12-3.

Procedure 1-a (5–30 minutes)
Climate Building
To develop a climate of trust, support, and openness, group members will learn more about each other through a discussion based on asking questions.

Rules:

1. Rotate; take turns asking questions.
2. You may refuse to answer a question as long as you did not ask it (or plan to).
3. You do not have to ask the questions in the order listed below.
4. You may ask your own questions. (Add them to the list.)

As an individual and before meeting with your group, review the questions below and place the name of one or more *group members* to whom you want to ask the question next to it. If you prefer to ask the entire group, put *group* next to the question. When everyone is ready, begin asking the questions.

1. How do you feel about this course? ______
2. How do you feel about this group? ______
3. How do you feel about me? ______
4. How do you think I feel about you? ______
5. What were your first impressions of me? ______
6. What do you like to do? ______
7. How committed to the group are you? ______
8. What do you like most about this course? ______
9. What do you plan to do after you graduate? ______
10. What do you want out of this course? ______
11. How do you react to deadlines? ______

12. Which member in the group are you the closest to? ______________________________

13. Which member in the group do you know the least? ______________________________

Other ______________________________

When the instructor tells you to do so, get together with your group members and ask each other your questions.

Procedure 1-b (2–4 minutes)
Participants determine what they would like to accomplish during the team-building session. Below are six major goals of team building; you may add to them. Rank them according to your preference.

_____ To clarify the team's objectives.

_____ To identify areas for improving group performance.

_____ To develop team skills.

_____ To determine and utilize a preferred team style.

_____ To fully utilize the resources of each group member.

_____ To develop working relationships based on trust, honesty, and understanding.

_____ Your own goals (list them).

Procedure 1-c (3–6 minutes)
Participants share their answers to procedure 1-b. The group can come to a consensus on its goal(s) if it wants to.

Procedure 2 (3–8 minutes)
Process and Structure: As a team, discuss strengths and weaknesses in group process (how the group works and communicates). Below, list norms (do's and don'ts) for the group to abide by.

Procedure 3-a (10–15 minutes)
Problem Identification: As a team, answer the survey feedback questionnaire. Place a *G* in the box to signify the team's answer. Don't rush; fully discuss the issues and how and why they affect the group.

Procedure 3-b (3–7 minutes)
Based on the above information, list 8 to 10 ways the team could improve its performance.

Procedure 3-c (3–6 minutes)
Prioritize the above list (1 = most important).

Procedure 4 (6–10 minutes)
Problem Solving: Take the top-priority item. Then do the following:

1. Define the problem.

2. Set objectives and criteria.

3. Generate alternatives.

4. Analyze alternatives and select one.

5. Develop an action plan for its implementation.

Follow the same five steps for each area of improvement until time is up. Try to cover at least three areas.

Procedure 5 (1 minute)
Training: Team building often includes training to address the problems facing the group. Because training takes place during most exercises, we will not do any now. Remember that the agendas for team building vary and usually last for one or more full days, rather than one hour.

Procedure 6-a (3 minutes)
Closure Application:

1. I intend to implement the team's solutions. Why?

2. What did I learn from this experience?

3. How can I apply this knowledge in my daily life?

4. How can I apply this knowledge as a manager?

Procedure 6-b (1–3 minutes)
Group members summarize what has been accomplished and state what they will do (commit to) to improve the group.

Sharing (4–7 minutes): A spokesperson from each team tells the class the group's top three areas for improvement. The instructor records them on the board.

/ / ANSWERS TO TRUE/FALSE QUESTIONS / /

1. T.
2. F. The first stage of the change process is denial that the change will occur.
3. F. Unfreezing, moving, and refreezing are the steps of the Lewin change model.
4. T.
5. T.
6. T.
7. T.
8. F. Ranking works well for "administrative" decisions. The critical incidents file and MBO methods work well for developmental objectives.
9. F. The coaching model is an informal performance appraisal method commonly used between formal evaluations.
10. T.

CHAPTER 13

Valuing Diversity Globally

LEARNING OUTCOMES

After completing this chapter, you should be able to:

LO 13-1 Define prejudice and discrimination and state common areas of employment discrimination in organizations.

LO 13-2 State major laws protecting minorities and women.

LO 13-3 Identify what employers can and cannot ask job applicants.

LO 13-4 List the groups that are legally protected by the EEOC.

LO 13-5 List the six areas of sexual harassment.

LO 13-6 Explain sexism in organizations and ways to overcome it.

LO 13-7 List seven areas of global diversity.

LO 13-8 List the steps in handling a complaint.

LO 13-9 Define the following 11 key terms (in order of appearance in the chapter):

prejudice	**disability**
discrimination	**sexual harassment**
minority	**sexism**
bona fide occupational qualification (BFOQ)	**multinational company (MNC)**
affirmative action (AA) programs	**expatriates**
	complaint model

/ / / A small group of white women at We-Haul in Hartford, Connecticut, were standing around the water cooler talking. These were some of the statements they made: "There is a lot of prejudice and discrimination against women around here." "There are more nonwhite faces around all the time." "We even have workers with disabilities now, and it's uncomfortable to look at them and work with them." "There are plenty of women in this company, but very few of them hold professional or managerial positions." "We women here in the offices make only a fraction of what the men in the shop are paid, and with the cutbacks, women are not getting into the higher-paying jobs." "My male supervisor recently made sexual advances, and since I shot him down, he's been giving me all the lousy jobs to do." "I've complained to management about these inequities, but nothing seems to change for us white women."

At the same time, a group of white men were also talking. Some of their statements were these: "There are more nonwhites and women around all the time." "Why can't these minorities learn to speak English like the rest of us?" "These people are always complaining about not being treated fairly, when they *are*." "We've promoted a few to management, even though they are not qualified." "They don't make good managers anyway." "The way management positions are being eliminated, it's tough enough to compete against the men, let alone these others."

Are these statements, which may have been said in many organizations, based on fact or fiction? Do these attitudes help or hurt the individuals, others, and the organization? You will learn about these and other valuing-diversity issues in this chapter. / / /

HOW DIVERSITY AFFECTS BEHAVIOR, HUMAN RELATIONS, AND PERFORMANCE

It is important to have an understanding of multicultural and diversity issues.[1] *Diversity* refers to the degree to which differences exist among members of a group or an organization. Within the workforce, the major groups include race and ethnicity, religion, gender, age, and ability. *Valuing diversity* means including all groups at all levels in an organization.

Diverse people behave differently and have different human relations in organizations.[2] However, when groups develop and oppose each other (white versus people of color, male versus female, management versus labor), behavior and human relations can suffer, leading to lower performance.[3] Recall (Chapter 11) that groups and organizations that value diversity generally outperform those that do not.

Is Diversity Really Important in America? Yes. The U.S. population continues to grow—it is around 311.6 million people currently,[4] and it is rapidly diversifying.[5] However, the white population is not growing as there is one birth for every death.[6] The population growth is coming from minorities, and more than half the growth is from Hispanics, which is now the largest minority group.[7] Today, in 10 states white children are a minority, and in 23 states minorities make up more than 40 percent of the child population.[8] One in 12 children (8 percent) born in America is the offspring of illegal immigrants, making those children U.S. citizens.[9] By around 2040, less than one-half of the total U.S. population will be white.[10] The diversification of America is clearly affecting us as individuals as well as businesses and government. It isn't surprising that CEOs of *Fortune* 500 companies have said that diversity is critically important.

Is Diversity Really Important Globally? Yes. There are 7 billion people in the world,[11] and less than 5 percent live in the United States, with over a billion people in both China (1.34 billion) and India (1.2 billion); they make up around 36 percent of the world population.[12] Clearly, American business has to compete globally to maintain and increase sales. This is why businesses are integrating global awareness into everyday action globally.[13] The world has become one large employment pool for professionals.[14] There is a good chance that during your career you will work for companies that compete with global corporations and/or do business with foreign companies. You may work for a foreign-owned corporation in the United States, and you may have the opportunity to go abroad to work. If you haven't already done so, you most likely will interact with people from other countries. You can develop your human relations skills by collaborating and learning more about people who are different from you.[15] That is what this chapter is all about.

PREJUDICE AND DISCRIMINATION

Learning Outcome 13-1

Define prejudice and discrimination and state common areas of employment discrimination in organizations.

Although progress has been made, prejudice and discrimination based on race, creed, color, and gender still exists in the United States.[16] The use of discrimination prevents equal employment opportunity.[17] Discrimination is usually based on prejudice. **Prejudice** *is the prejudgment of a person or situation based on attitudes.* As stated in Chapter 3, an attitude is a strong belief or feeling. If someone were to ask you, "Are you prejudiced?", you would probably say no. However, we all tend to prejudge people and situations. Recall that Chapter 2 discussed first impressions and the four-minute barrier. In four minutes you don't have time to get to know someone, yet you make assumptions that affect your behavior. Chapter 3 defined stereotyping as the process of generalizing the behavior of all members of a group. Your prejudice is often based on your stereotype of the group.[18] To prejudge or stereotype a person or situation in and of itself is not harmful; we all tend to do this. Although prejudice is not always negative, if you discriminate based on your prejudice, you may cause harm to yourself and other parties.[19] **Discrimination** *is behavior for or against a person or situation.*

To illustrate the difference between prejudice and discrimination, assume that Joan is a supervisor and is in the process of hiring a new employee. There are two qualified candidates: Dwane, an African American male, and Ted, a white male. Joan is white and has a more positive attitude toward whites. She stereotypes blacks as being not as productive on the job as whites. But she also believes that blacks deserve a break. Joan has a few options.

Joan can discriminate based on her prejudice and hire Ted. Selecting an employee based wholly on race or color is clearly illegal discrimination for Ted and against Dwane. In the same manner, Joan could be prejudiced for Dwane and against Ted.

Joan can be aware of her prejudices, yet try not to let them influence her decision. She can interview both candidates and select the person who is best qualified for the job. Then there would be no discrimination. This option is legal and is the generally recommended approach because it is not discrimination.

WORK APPLICATION 13-1

Discuss a situation in which you were discriminated against for some reason.

The statements in the opening case reflect negative prejudice attitudes that can lead to discrimination. Discrimination has negative consequences at the individual, team, and organizational levels.

APPLICATION SITUATIONS / / /

Prejudice or Discrimination AS 13-1

Identify each statement made by a white male as an example of:

A. Prejudice B. Discrimination

_______ 1. "Here comes Jamal [a tall black]; I'll bet he will talk about basketball."

_______ 2. "I select Dwane as my partner. Karen, you team up with Kono for this assignment."

_______ 3. "I cannot continue to work with you today, Sarah. Is it your time of the month?"

_______ 4. "I do not want to work the night shift. Can you force me to change?"

_______ 5. "The boss hired a good-looking, blonde administrative assistant. I bet she's not very bright."

Common Areas of Employment Discrimination

Historically, the five areas where discrimination in employment is most common are:

- *Recruitment.* People who hire employees fail to actively recruit people from certain groups to apply for jobs within their organization.
- *Selection.* People who select candidates from the recruited applicants fail to hire people from certain groups.
- *Compensation.* White males make more money than other groups.[20]
- *Upward mobility.* Race and gender are significant influences on advancement.[21]
- *Evaluation.* When organizations do not base evaluations on actual job performance, discrimination in compensation and upward mobility occur.[22]

WORK APPLICATION 13-2

Cite an example of employment discrimination in recruitment, selection, compensation, upward mobility, or evaluation, preferably from an organization for which you work or have worked.

Valuing-Diversity Training

To help overcome prejudice and discrimination, organizations of all types are training their employees to value (rather than simply tolerate) employee differences to help ensure high-quality relationships.[23] For example, LIMRA developed a customized diversity seminar with the following objectives: (1) to understand the current and changing demographics of the workforce, (2) to view the company's business as part of a global workforce and economy, and (3) to recognize how prejudice and discrimination can inhibit business success.

Hewlett-Packard introduced its managing-diversity program as part of the management development curriculum required of all its managers. The program stresses diversity as a competitive advantage. MetLife has a strong diversity program because it knows it affects the bottom line.

WORK APPLICATION 13-3

Have you, or has anyone you know, gone through diversity training? If yes, describe the program.

To have effective human relations with all types of people who are different from you, you need to be tolerant of people's differences, try to understand why they are different, have empathy for them and their situation, and communicate openly with them. Be aware of the human tendency to prejudge and stereotype others, and avoid discriminating based on your prejudices. Later in this chapter, we will discuss how organizations are helping their diverse workforces.

EQUAL EMPLOYMENT OPPORTUNITY FOR ALL

Valuing diversity, equal employment opportunity (EEO), and affirmative action (AA) are different. In this section, let's explain EEO and the laws it enforces, AA, and how we have gone from AA to valuing diversity.

Laws Affecting Employment Opportunity

Learning Outcome 13-2

State major laws protecting minorities and women.

You are aware that an organization cannot discriminate against a minority. Who is legally considered a minority? A minority is just about anyone who is not a white male, of European heritage, or adequately educated. The Equal Employment Opportunity Commission (EEOC) **minority** *list includes Hispanics, Asians, African Americans, Native Americans, and Alaska Natives.* Women are also protected by law from discrimination in employment, but they are not considered a legal minority because in some situations they are a majority. Disadvantaged young people, workers with disabilities, and persons over 40 and up to 70 years of age are also protected.

The EEOC has 37 offices across the nation. It offers seminars for employees who feel they aren't getting a fair shake, and it operates a toll-free telephone line (1-800-USA-EEOC) and Web site (www.eeoc.gov) around the clock to provide information on employee rights.[24] Some of the major laws and regulations affecting employment are presented in Exhibit 13.1.

EXHIBIT 13.1 | Federal Employment Laws

Law	Description
Equal Employment Opportunity	
Equal Employment Opportunity Act of 1972 (Title VII of the Civil Rights Act of 1964)	Prohibits discrimination in all areas of the employment relationship (based on race, religion, color, sex, or national origin).
Civil Rights Act of 1991	Strengthened Civil Rights Act of 1964 by providing possible compensation and punitive damages for discrimination.
Age Discrimination in Employment Act of 1967 (amended 1978, 1984)	Prohibits age discrimination against people older than 40 and restricts mandatory retirement.
Vocational Rehabilitation Act of 1973	Prohibits discrimination based on physical or mental disability.
Americans with Disabilities Act of 1990	Strengthened the Vocational Rehab Act to require employers to provide "reasonable accommodations" to allow employees with disabilities to work.
Compensation and Benefits	
Lilly Ledbetter Fair Pay Act of 2009	Amends the 1964 CRA to extend the period of time in which an employee is allowed to file a lawsuit over pay discrimination.
Equal Pay Act of 1963	Requires men and women to be paid the same for equal work.
Pregnancy Discrimination Act of 1978	Prohibits discrimination against women because of pregnancy, childbirth, or related medical conditions.
Family and Medical Leave Act of 1993	Requires employers (with 50 or more employees) to provide up to 12 weeks unpaid leave for family (childbirth, adoption, eldercare) or medical reasons.
Health and Safety	
Occupational Safety and Health Act of 1970	Establishes mandatory safety and health standards in organizations, regulated by the Occupational Safety and Health Administration (OSHA).

Communication Skills
Refer to CS Question 2.

Companies suspected of violating any of these laws may be investigated by the EEOC or become defendants in class-action or specific lawsuits. Clearly, it is important for you to be familiar with the law and your organization's EEO and AA program guidelines.

Preemployment Inquiries

Learning Outcome 13-3

Identify what employers can and cannot ask job applicants.

On the application blank and during interviews, no member of an organization can legally ask discriminatory questions. The two major rules of thumb to follow are:

1. Every question that is asked should be job related. When developing questions, you should have a purpose for using the information. Only ask legal questions you plan to use in your selection process.
2. Any general question that you ask should be asked of all candidates.

Below, we will discuss what you can (lawful information you can use to disqualify candidates) and cannot (prohibited information you cannot use to disqualify candidates) ask during a job interview. Prohibited information is information that does not relate to a bona fide occupational qualification for the job. A **bona fide occupational qualification (BFOQ)** *allows discrimination on the basis of religion, sex, or national origin where it is reasonably necessary to normal operation of a particular enterprise.* In an example of a BFOQ upheld by its supreme court, the state of Alabama required all guards in male maximum-security correctional facilities to be male. People believing that this requirement was sexual discrimination took it to court. The supreme court upheld the male sex requirement on the grounds that 20 percent of the inmates were convicted of sex offenses, and this creates an excessive threat to the security of female guards.

For a list of topics or questions that can and cannot be asked, see Exhibit 13.2.

WORK APPLICATION 13-4

Have you, or has anyone you know, been asked an illegal discriminatory question during the hiring process? If yes, identify the question(s).

APPLICATION SITUATIONS / / /

Legal Questions AS 13-2

Identify the five questions below as:

A. Legal (can be asked) B. Illegal (cannot be asked)

_______ 6. "What is your mother tongue or the major language you use?"

_______ 7. "Are you married or single?"

_______ 8. "Are you a member of the Teamsters Union?"

_______ 9. "Have you been arrested for stealing on the job?"

_______ 10. "Can you prove you are legally eligible to work?"

From Affirmative Action to Valuing Diversity

Affirmative action (AA) is a method of making up for prior discrimination in the workplace. AA requires that firms doing business with the federal government make special efforts to recruit, hire, and promote women and members of minority groups.

Affirmative action (AA) programs *are planned, special efforts to recruit, hire, and promote women and members of minority groups.* AA requires that organizations determine their racial and sexual compositions and compare these ratios with those of the available people in the population of the appropriate recruitment area. Based on these numbers, the organization plans and acts to obtain the proper percentages according to a complex calculation process.

Communication Skills
Refer to CS Question 1.

EXHIBIT 13.2 | Preemployment Inquiries

Name

Can Ask: Current legal name and whether the candidate has ever worked under a different name.

Cannot Ask: Maiden name or whether the person has changed his or her name.

Address

Can Ask: Current residence and length of residence.

Cannot Ask: If the candidate owns or rents his or her home, unless it is a BFOQ.

Age

Can Ask: If the candidate is between specific age groups, 21 to 70, to meet job specifications. If hired, can you furnish proof of age? For example, an employee must be 21 to serve alcoholic beverages.

Cannot Ask: How old are you? Cannot ask to see a birth certificate. Do not ask an older person how much longer he or she plans to work before retiring.

Sex

Can Ask: Only if sex is a BFOQ.

Cannot Ask: If it is not a BFOQ. To be sure not to violate sexual harassment laws, do not ask questions or make comments remotely considered flirtatious.

Marital and Family Status

Can Ask: If the candidate can meet the work schedule and whether the candidate has activities, responsibilities, or commitments that may hinder meeting attendance requirements. The same question(s) should be asked of both sexes.

Cannot Ask: To state marital status. Do not ask any questions regarding children or other family issues.

National Origin, Citizenship, Race, or Color

Can Ask: If the candidate is legally eligible to work in the United States, and if this can be proved if hired.

Cannot Ask: To identify national origin, citizenship, race, or color (or that of parents and other relatives).

Language

Can Ask: To list languages the candidate speaks and/or writes fluently. Candidates may be asked if they speak and/or write a specific language if it is a BFOQ.

Cannot Ask: The language spoken off the job, or how the applicant learned the language.

Convictions

Can Ask: If the candidate has been convicted of a felony and other information if the felony is job related.

Cannot Ask: If the candidate has ever been arrested (an arrest does not prove guilt). Do not ask for information regarding a conviction that is not job related.

Height and Weight

Can Ask: If the candidate meets or exceeds BFOQ height and/or weight requirements, and if it can be proved if hired.

Cannot Ask: The candidate's height or weight if it is not a BFOQ.

Religion

Can Ask: If the candidate is of a specific religion when it is a BFOQ. Candidates can be asked whether they will be able to meet the work schedules or will have anticipated absences.

Cannot Ask: Religious preference, affiliations, or denominations.

Credit Ratings or Garnishments

Can Ask: If it is a BFOQ.

Cannot Ask: If it is not a BFOQ.

Education and Work Experience

Can Ask: For information that is job related.

Cannot Ask: For information that is not job-related.

References

Can Ask: For the names of people willing to provide references or for the names of people who suggested the candidate apply for the job.

Cannot Ask: For a reference from a religious leader.

Military

Can Ask: For information on education and experience gained that relates to the job.

Cannot Ask: Dates and conditions of discharge. Do not ask about draft classification or other eligibility for military service, National Guard, or reserve units. Do not ask about experience in foreign armed services.

Organizations

Can Ask: To list membership in job-related organizations, such as union or professional or trade associations.

Cannot Ask: To identify membership in any non-job-related organization that would indicate race, religion, and so on.

Disabilities/AIDS

Can Ask: If the candidate has any disabilities that would prevent him or her from performing the specific job.

Cannot Ask: For information that is not job-related. In states where people with AIDS are protected under discrimination laws, you should not ask if the candidate has AIDS.

WORK APPLICATION 13-5

Describe the affirmative action program at an organization, preferably one for which you work or have worked.

Support for AA declined. Some of the many reasons that AA went out of favor were as follows: quotas often worked against minorities, quotas could not be met, and organizations were charged with reverse discrimination. Many believed that forced AA was not the answer to the problem of discrimination. Thus, we went from AA to valuing diversity.

Employers have legal relationships with employees.[25] Imagine the difficulty of meeting the complex, different laws in hundreds of countries at the same time, especially when the laws conflict.

THE LEGALLY PROTECTED AND SEXUAL HARASSMENT

Learning Outcome 13-4

List the groups that are legally protected by the EEOC.

The previous section presented the laws affecting minorities and other protected groups. This section discusses minorities, employees' religious beliefs, older workers, workers who are disabled, alcohol and drug abuse and testing, AIDS and AIDS testing, sexual orientation, and sexual harassment in more detail.

Minorities

EEO laws prohibit job discrimination on the basis of race, color, national origin, and religion unless discrimination stems from a BFOQ. Therefore, in the following guidelines any of these terms could replace the word *minority*.

Communication Skills
Refer to CS Question 3.

Religious Beliefs Employers are required by law to make reasonable accommodations for employees' religious beliefs, without undue hardship on the employer. "Undue hardship" is fairly clear. It involves having to pay premium wages or other costs to accommodate an employee's religious rights, defined as "all forms and aspects of religion." However, "reasonable accommodation" is ambiguous. Employers should willingly negotiate with employees and allow them to swap shifts or job dates with consenting colleagues. And employees should be allowed to take religious holidays off in place of other paid days off. Some employers allow employees to select which paid holidays they want to take. Recall (Chapter 3) that spirituality in the workplace is on the rise. But membership in religious organizations is declining.[26]

Communication Skills
Refer to CS Question 4.

Age Young and older workers have differences. Americans are aging. About one-third of the population (more than 100 million people) are age 50 or older; these people are commonly called "baby boomers."

People age 40 and older are protected from age discrimination. However, the EEOC has been criticized as being shaky in fighting age bias. Criticism may be based on the fact that hiring and promotion discrimination based on age is one of the most difficult types of discrimination for the victim to prove. People over 50 have a difficult time finding a good, full-time job. But they are often recruited for part-time jobs because they tend to have a strong work ethic.

People with Disabilities The Americans with Disabilities Act (ADA) gives equal access to employment, transportation, and buildings to millions of people in the United States with disabilities. A disability used to be commonly called a *handicap*. People with a **disability** *have significant physical, mental, or emotional limitations.* They include people with prison records, major obesity, or a history of heart disease, cancer, or mental illness that others might view as disabling. One in five Americans takes a psychiatric drug.[27] Rehabilitated alcoholics and drug abusers are also considered disabled. The law requires that employers make "reasonable accommodations" to hire people with disabilities. Individuals who are disabled can be required to meet the same productivity standards as other employees.

Communication Skills
Refer to CS Question 5.

We should focus on abilities, not disabilities, and give equal opportunity to all. ADA legislation states that reasonable accommodation "may include such areas as job restructuring, part-time or flexible work schedules, acquisition or modification of equipment or devices, the provision of readers or interpreters, and other similar actions."[28] For more information on the ADA, visit its Web site (www.ada.gov).

WORK APPLICATION 13-6

Have you ever seen any employees under the influence of alcohol or drugs at work? How did their substance use affect their ability to work?

WORK APPLICATION 13-7

How do you feel about drug testing by employers? Why do you feel this way?

Alcohol and Drug Abuse and Testing Since October 1986, when the government began to administer drug tests, drug abuse has been given much attention. According to Partnership for a Drug-Free America, 1 in 6 Americans has a substance abuse problem. Six out of 10 people say they know of someone who has gone to work under the influence of drugs or alcohol. Substance abuse has been estimated to cost American businesses over $86 billion annually in lost productivity, absenteeism, and health care costs.[29] Complete Self-Assessment Exercise 13-1 to see if you may have a potential substance abuse problem.

To help prevent drug abuse, the Federal Drug-Free Workplace Act of 1988 was enacted. Drug testing is on the increase in both the private and public sectors. Almost three-fourths (74.5 percent) of 1,200 companies surveyed said they test employees for drugs. More big companies than small ones test for substances, and more blue-collar than white-collar employees are tested.

/// Self-Assessment Exercise 13-1 ///

Your Use of Substances

For each of the following statements, select the number from 1 to 5 that best describes the frequency of your actual substance (alcohol or drug) use. Place the number on the line before each statement. You will not be asked to share this information in class.

(5) Usually (4) Frequently (3) Occasionally (2) Seldom (1) Rarely

_____ 1. I take substances in the morning.

_____ 2. I take substances to calm my nerves or to forget about worries or pressure.

_____ 3. I go to work/school under the influence of substances or take them during work/school hours.

_____ 4. I take substances when I'm alone.

_____ 5. I lie about my substance use.

_____ 6. I drive under the influence of substances.

_____ 7. I wake up and don't remember what I did under the influence of substances.

_____ 8. I do things under the influence of substances that I would not do without them.

_____ 9. I'm late for work/school because of substance use.

_____ 10. I miss work/school as a result of substance use.

_____ 11. I take substances to help me sleep.

_____ 12. I've had financial difficulties due to substances.

_____ 13. My friends take substances.

_____ 14. I plan activities around being able to use substances.

_____ 15. When I'm not under the influence of substances, I think about taking them.

_____ Total

Your score will range from 15 to 75. To determine the degree to which you have a substance problem, mark the point that represents your total score on the continuum below.

No substance abuse 15 – – – – – – – – – – 30 – – – – – – – – – – 45 – – – – – – – – – – 60 – – – – – – – – – – 75 Substance abuse

If you do have a substance abuse problem, you should seek professional help.

AIDS and AIDS Testing Human immunodeficiency virus (HIV) is the virus that causes AIDS. Acquired immune deficiency syndrome (AIDS) is the name for the condition that occurs after HIV has gradually destroyed a person's immune system, making the person prone to life-threatening infections. AIDS is not a disease affecting only homosexuals; 40 percent of all reported cases have occurred among heterosexuals. According to the World Health Organization (WHO), half of the newly infected adults are women.

WORK APPLICATION 13-8

How would you feel about working with a person who has AIDS? Why?

A person with HIV or AIDS is protected from discrimination under the ADA of 1990 and the Rehabilitation Act of 1973. In 1987, the federal government unveiled a policy barring discrimination against federal government workers who have AIDS. It also authorizes discipline for those who refuse to work with AIDS patients. For more information on AIDS, visit www.aids.gov.

Sexual Orientation A newcomer to the list of diversity groups is based on sexual orientation. *Homophobia* (an aversion to homosexuals) is the term used to refer to discrimination based on a person's sexual orientation. In most situations, companies are not responsible for determining right and wrong behavior off the job. However, all organizations are responsible for providing all workers with an environment that is safe and free of threats, intimidation, harassment, and, especially, violence. As with age, it is difficult to prove that employment discrimination is based solely on being gay, lesbian, bisexual, or transgender.

Sexual Harassment

Learning Outcome 13-5

List the six areas of sexual harassment.

Women are a legally protected group. The most common issues that prompt sex discrimination complaints, in order by numbers of cases, are discharge, terms and condition of employment, sexual harassment, wages, pregnancy, promotion, hiring, and intimidation and reprisals. Sexual harassment is one of the most sensitive areas of discrimination because it is often a matter of personal judgment. Sexual harassment charges can be made against either sex; however, the vast majority of cases are against men. Same-sex harassment is also a problem.[30]

The most frequent harassment targets are new employees, people who are on probation in their jobs, and the young and inexperienced. People who have recently experienced a personal crisis, such as separation or divorce, are frequently victims. Women in traditionally male jobs are also more subject to sexual harassment.

Behaviors considered to be sexual harassment by some are not considered harassment by others. To help people know if they have been sexually harassed, the EEOC has defined the term *sexual harassment* as follows: Unwelcome sexual advances, requests for sexual favors, and other unwanted verbal or physical conduct of a sexual nature constitute sexual harassment when (1) submission to such conduct is made either explicitly or implicitly a term or condition of an individual's employment, (2) submission to or rejection of such conduct by an individual is used as the basis for employment decisions affecting such individual, or (3) such conduct has the purpose or effect of unreasonably interfering with an individual's work performance or creating an intimidating, hostile, or offensive environment.[31] For more information, visit the EEOC Web site at www.eeoc.gov.

The federal and state courts have defined sexual harassment in six areas as grounds for lawsuits:

1. *Unwelcome sexual advances.* An employee who is repeatedly propositioned by a supervisor or coworker trying to establish an intimate relationship, on or off the job, may sue for sexual harassment even if not overtly threatened.
2. *Coercion.* An employee whose supervisor asks for a date or sexual favor with the stated or unstated understanding that a favor will be bestowed, or a reprisal made, may sue for sexual harassment.
3. *Favoritism.* Courts have ruled that an employer is liable when employees who submit to sexual favors are rewarded, while others who refuse are denied promotions or benefits. One federal court ruled that an employee who wasn't asked for sexual favors, while others were, was a victim of sexual harassment.
4. *Indirect harassment.* Employees who witness sexual harassment on the job can sue even if they are not victims. In a California state court, a nurse complained that a doctor grabbed other nurses in full view of her, causing an environment of sexual harassment.

5. *Physical conduct.* Employees don't have to be touched. Courts have ruled that unseemly gestures may constitute harassment and create a hostile work environment.
6. *Visual harassment.* Courts have ruled that graffiti written on men's bathroom walls about a female employee is sexual harassment. The pervasive display of nude or pornographic pictures also constitutes sexual harassment.

To keep it simple, DuPont tells its people, "It's harassment when something starts bothering somebody." For our purposes, **sexual harassment** *is any unwelcomed behavior of a sexual nature.*

WORK APPLICATION 13-9

Have you, or has anyone you know, been sexually harassed? If so, describe the situation(s) (use language acceptable to everyone).

WORK APPLICATION 13-10

How do you feel about the fact that certain groups are legally protected against discrimination?

Dealing with Sexual Harassment When people find themselves in a sexual harassment situation, they often feel overwhelmed, confused, unproductive, afraid, alone, and unable to find the words to confront the harasser. If the behavior is very serious, such as touching in private areas of the body, you may want to report the first offense. But if it is less obvious that sexual harassment was intentional, a warning may be given before reporting the offense. Some warning responses to the harasser, which can be revised to suit the offense, are as follows:

"I am uncomfortable when you touch me. Don't do it again or I will report you for sexual harassment."

"It is inappropriate for you to show me sexually graphic material. Don't do it again."

"I am uncomfortable with off-color jokes. Don't tell one to me again or I will report you for sexual harassment."

If the behavior is repeated, report the offense to your boss and/or some other authority in the organization. If the people in authority do not take suitable action to stop the harassment, you may take the complaint to the EEOC.

In the opening case, a woman complained about a male supervisor making sexual advances. Do you think that was sexual harassment?

APPLICATION SITUATIONS / / /

Sexual Harassment AS 13-3

Identify whether each behavior described below is:

A. Sexual harassment B. Not sexual harassment

_______ 11. Thomas tells Clair she is sexy and he'd like to take her out on a date.

_______ 12. Sue tells José he will have to go to a motel with her if he wants to get the job.

_______ 13. Marissa's legs are sticking out into the walkway. As Andrew goes by, he steps over them and says, "Nice legs."

_______ 14. For the third time, after being politely told no, Aamir says to Christina, "You have a real nice (*fill in the missing sexual words for yourself*). Why don't you and I XXXX?"

_______ 15. Josh puts his hand on Lisa's shoulder as he talks to her.

Communication Skills
Refer to CS Question 6.

Dating Coworkers Romance does change behavior and human relations at work, and it can affect performance. Some organizations have policies on dating coworkers, and some go as far as stating that employees who date may be fired. As with marriage, about half of work romances are ended. Two of the problems with dating coworkers are that once the romantic relationship ends, it can be difficult working together, and it is not unusual for one of the people to sexually harass the other to get back together.

WORK APPLICATION 13-11

What are your views on dating coworkers? Have you dated coworkers, or will you date coworkers in the future?

Political Correctness *Political correctness* is being careful not to offend or slight anyone with our behavior. Obviously, being politically incorrect hurts human relations, so we need to be careful how we behave. For example, you might think a joke about women, minorities, or any group of people is funny, but members of these groups can be offended in hearing the joke. Also, some people are very protective of political correctness, so even though the joke is not about an individual's group, he or she will still be offended and may report your behavior to management as being inappropriate. So you are better off not telling the joke, or other such behavior. Or at least ask the person if he or she wants to hear the joke before telling it.

SEXISM, RACISM, AND WORK AND FAMILY BALANCE

Learning Outcome 13-6

Explain sexism in organizations and ways to overcome it.

Sex and race are essential and pervasive sources of diversity at work, but there are inequalities.[32] **Sexism** *refers to discrimination based on sex. Racism* is discrimination based on race. Sexism and racism limit the opportunities of both women and men to choose the lifestyles and careers that best suit their abilities and interests. Men and women face discrimination when they pursue careers traditionally held by the opposite sex. Males still dominate the construction trades and women, the field of nursing, for example. Stereotyping men and women hurts not only the individuals who dare to be different but also the organization, and bias and discrimination holds both back from achieving their full potential.[33] Gender roles and racial stereotypes need to continue to change.[34]

The Negative Effect of TV, Movies, and Music Culture promotes differences in males and females, and they will always be different, but their roles can and should be equal and promote positive self-concepts.[35] Children learn these values and the media has an influence. Unfortunately, TV and movies promote sexism and depict for children a dated version of society in which females are stereotyped and very much hypersexualized.[36] Some songs and music videos also portray females as hypersexualized: "The more hours of TV a girl watches, the fewer options she believes she has in life. And the more hours a boy watches, the more sexist his views become."[37]

This section examines women in the workforce, managers, overcoming sexism and racism, changing sex roles, and work and family balance. Before reading on, determine your attitude toward women and minorities at work by completing Self-Assessment Exercise 13-2.

/// Self-Assessment Exercise 13-2 ///

Attitudes about Women and Minorities Advancing

Be honest in this self-assessment, as your assessment will not be accurate if you aren't. Also, you should not be asked to share your score with others.

Answer the 10 questions below twice: once related to women and the other related to minorities. Place the number 1, 2, 3, 4, or 5 on the line before each statement for women and at the end of the statement for minorities.

Agree				Disagree
5	4	3	2	1

Women		Minorities
_____	1. Women/Minorities lack motivation to get ahead.	1. _____
_____	2. Women/Minorities lack the education necessary to get ahead.	2. _____
_____	3. Women/Minorities working has caused rising unemployment among white men	3. _____
_____	4. Women/Minorities are not strong enough or emotionally stable enough to succeed in high-pressure jobs.	4. _____
_____	5. Women/Minorities have a lower commitment to work than white men.	5. _____
_____	6. Women/Minorities are too emotional to be effective managers.	6. _____
_____	7. Women/Minorities who are managers have difficulty in situations calling for quick and precise decisions.	7. _____

(continued)

/// Self-Assessment Exercise 13-2 /// (*continued*)

_____ 8. Women/Minorities have a higher turnover rate than white men. 8. _____

_____ 9. Women/Minorities are out of work more often than white men. 9. _____

_____ 10. Women/Minorities have less interest in advancing than white men. 10. _____

_____ Total Total _____

Women—To determine your attitude score toward women, add up the total of your 10 answers on the lines before each statement and place it on the total line and on the following continuum.

Positive attitude 10 - - - - - - - - - 20 - - - - - - - - - 30 - - - - - - - - - 40 - - - - - - - - - 50 Negative attitude

Minorities—To determine your attitude score toward minorities, add up the total of your 10 answers on the lines after each statement and place it on the total line and on the following continuum.

Positive attitude 10 - - - - - - - - - 20 - - - - - - - - - 30 - - - - - - - - - 40 - - - - - - - - - 50 Negative attitude

Each statement is a negative attitude about women and minorities at work. However, research has shown all of these statements to be false; they are considered myths. Such statements stereotype women and minorities unfairly and prevent them from getting jobs and advancing in organizations through gaining salary increases and promotions. Thus, part of managing diversity and diversity training is to help overcome these negative attitudes to provide equal opportunities for *all*.

Women in the Workforce

We now discuss *women in the workforce* as opposed to *working women*. Women who elect to work as homemakers make a great contribution to society. Unfortunately, these women are not commonly referred to as *working women* because they are not rewarded monetarily for their work. However, every female homemaker is a working woman.

How Many Women Are in the Workforce, and Why Are They Employed? Men and women are entering the workforce in equal numbers,[38] but women make up 46.3 percent of the total U.S. labor force.[39]

Women work for many different reasons, but they can generally be classified by economic necessity and self-concept needs. Women's income is critical to the support of the family. In general, women today want both a job and a family, as they are motivated to meet their needs for achievement and affiliation (Chapter 8). Actually, economic and self-concept needs are highly intertwined.

Do Men and Women Get the Same Pay? Gender differences in salary still exist, especially for female executives.[40] Women in some industries, like Wall Street, have wider pay gaps.[41] However, the pay difference is not caused simply by discrimination; women tend to work in jobs with lower pay, such as child care, education, and clerical work.[42] But discrimination is partly to blame for salary disparities, especially in management positions.[43]

Women and Minority Managers

Myths about Women Managers Two old myths about women managers are that they will leave the job to have children and that they are too emotional to be managers. Statistics show that women stay on the job. An eight-year study of male and female managers found virtually identical psychological and emotional profiles between the sexes. On all the variables that have to do with good leadership, men and women as a group show no major differences.[44] Men and women are truly equal in management ability. Another popular myth is that women are not as committed to the organization as men; research supports that they are equally committed.[45]

How Women Are Progressing in Management and the Glass Ceiling It is important to have women representatives on executive teams.[46] Today, there are more women college graduates than men, and women hold 51 percent of management and professional jobs,[47] but at each stage of advancement, men are at least twice as likely as women to be promoted.[48] Women face barriers in trying to climb the corporate ladder, one of them being operating in a male-dominated industry.[49] Women hold only about 7 percent of the senior executive jobs (chair, CEO/president, and senior VP) in big businesses.[50] The barriers to upward mobility in organizations are commonly called the *glass ceiling*, referring to the invisibility of these barriers.[51] The barriers can be insurmountable, especially for working mothers.[52]

A major problem is that inadequate career development has kept women from reaching the top rungs of the corporate ladder, and corporate America needs to do a better job coaching and mentoring women.[53] Many women are frustrated with their lack of advancement, and more women than men are starting their own businesses. One in every 11 women in the United States is an owner or co-owner of a business. Women have ownership in nearly 9 million businesses (40 percent of all businesses).[54]

Communication Skills
Refer to CS Question 7.

The United States has a federal *Glass Ceiling Commission* to help eliminate the problem, but it hasn't made much progress in recent years. In fact, there is evidence that we are falling backward on this important issue.[55] There are only 11 women CEOs of *Fortune* 500 companies (2.2 percent), down from 15 in 2010.[56]

How Minorities Are Progressing in Management and Professional Jobs Minorities are making slow progress into management and professional level jobs. However, their progress has not been rapid enough to make a significant change in the distribution of those jobs. At the same time, many successful minorities are leaving corporate America to become entrepreneurs.

Advancement Some industries have been more receptive than others to advancing women and minorities. For example, consumer products, financial services, retail, publishing, and media, and certain nonprofit and government sectors, such as health care and education, have more women and minorities in management.

Research has revealed two advancement-related traits: having a strong desire to advance and focusing on getting the job done or solving the problem. Although education and technical knowledge and skills allow entry into lower management, networks and subjective social factors allow advancement to higher levels of management, which is a disadvantage for women and minorities who can't get into the right networks to break the glass ceiling.[57] A good predictor of a woman's advancement to higher levels of management is career encouragement. As we discussed in Chapter 10, networking is critical to advancement. Having a good mentor who can give you career encouragement and get you into the right networks is also helpful.[58] Do you have the aspiration to climb the corporate ladder, and are you willing to network and get a mentor to help your advancement?

WORK APPLICATION 13-12

How do you feel about having a female boss? Why?

APPLICATION SITUATIONS / / /

Women AS 13-4

Identify each of the following statements about women as:

A. Fact B. Myth

_______ 16. "Men make better managers than women."

_______ 17. "Women work because they need the money."

_______ 18. "Male managers are more committed to their jobs than female managers."

_______ 19. "Female managers are viewed as more caring for the individual subordinate than male managers."

_______ 20. "About one out of every three managers is female."

EXHIBIT 13.3 | A Sexist (Stereotypical) Way to Tell a Businessman from a Businesswoman

Man	Woman
A businessman is aggressive.	A businesswoman is pushy.
He is careful about details.	She's picky.
He loses his temper because he's so involved in his job.	She's bitchy.
He's depressed (or hung over), so everyone tiptoes past his office.	She's moody, so it must be her time of the month.
He follows through.	She doesn't know when to quit.
He's firm.	She's stubborn.
He makes wise judgments.	She reveals her prejudices.
He is a man of the world.	She's been around.
He isn't afraid to say what he thinks.	She's opinionated.
He exercises authority.	She's tyrannical.
He's discreet.	She's secretive.
He's a stern taskmaster.	She's difficult to work for.

Overcoming Sexism and Racism

Hiring and promotion decisions should not be based on sex, though affirmative action plans may be implemented.

Sexist and Racist Language and Behavior Men and women should avoid using sexist and racist language. Sexist words such as *mailman* and *salesman* should be replaced with non-sexist terms such as *letter carrier* and *salesperson*. In written communication, the use of *he or she* is appropriate, but don't overuse it. Use neutral language and plurals—*supervisors* rather than *the supervisor,* which tends to end up needing a *he or she* as writing progresses. Avoid racist terms and jokes.

Communication Skills
Refer to CS Question 8.

Call people by name, rather than by sexist and racist terms. Working women are not girls and should not be called *girls* because this word is used to describe children, not grown women. Working men are not boys, so avoid such racist terms.

Be wary of swearing in the workplace; it is preferable not to use such language. What is really gained through swearing? You can offend someone. Are you impressed by people who swear? Are people who do not swear pressured to do so at work?

Skill-Building Exercise 13-1 develops this skill.

If anyone uses language that offends you or others, assertively state your feelings about the words used. Many times, people do not use sexist and racist language intentionally and will not use it if they are requested not to. If it continues, however, report the harassment.

Skill-Building Exercise 13-2 develops this skill.

Many working men are becoming more sensitive to sexism because they have wives and daughters entering the workforce for whom they want equal opportunities. Exhibit 13.3 illustrates negative sexist stereotyping that needs to be eliminated. Such stereotypes are a barrier to women's breaking the glass ceiling.[59]

In the opening case, there is negative sexist talk. Can these men and women change their attitudes and learn to value diversity?

How Family Sex Roles Are Changing

The traditional family in which the husband works and the wife doesn't work outside the home is no longer the pattern in the majority of American households. Two-income marriages became the norm back in 1994; today, they comprise over half of all married couples.[60] Although research shows that marriage is in everyone's best interest,[61] the number of people getting married has dropped.[62] A quarter (25 percent) of the children in America are being raised by a single parent.[63]

Communication Skills
Refer to CS Question 9.

Recall the total person approach, which holds that our personal family life affects our work life. If we can have a happier family life, we can also have a happier work life.

We will discuss some important family issues that may help improve your family life. For example, people yearn to better understand what makes a successful marriage. So, start with Self-Assessment Exercise 13-3 to check your knowledge of the facts about marriage.

/// Self-Assessment Exercise 13-3 ///

Your Marriage Knowledge

Answer each question true or false by circling its letter.

T F 1. People prefer a mate who matches them in education, class, religious background, ethnicity, and age.

T F 2. About half of marriages end in divorce.

T F 3. Living together before marriage decreases the chances of getting divorced.

T F 4. Having a baby before marriage increases the chances of getting divorced.

T F 5. Getting married young (under 18 years old vs. 25) increases the chances of getting divorced.

T F 6. Compared to people with some college, high school dropouts have a higher divorce rate.

T F 7. Most divorces happen in the seventh year—the seven-year itch.

T F 8. Couples who are very unhappy should get divorced so they will be happier in future years.

T F 9. People who go through the stress of divorce and its aftermath have health effects that may not show up until years later.

T F 10. Compared to those who are happily married, people who get divorced have more health problems and symptoms of depression.

T F 11. Compared to those who are happily married, people who get divorced smoke and drink more.

T F 12. Workaholics have a higher divorce rate than nonworkaholics.

T F 13. Arguing is helpful to a marriage.

T F 14. Couples don't need to agree and solve all their problems.

T F 15. Couples that go to church/pray together have a lower divorce rate than those that don't—the family that prays together stays together.

To determine your marriage knowledge, count the number of correct answers, using the answer key below, and place your score here:

Knowledgeable 15 14 13 12 11 10 9 8 7 6 5 4 3 2 1 Not Knowledgeable

Answers[64]

1. True. The statement that "like attracts like" is factual.
2. True. Since the mid-1960s, around half of marriages in any given year end in divorce.
3. False. Couples who live together are 50 percent more likely to get divorced. They tend to have a renter's agreement attitude that makes them less committed to sticking around through the hard times that just about all marriages go through.
4. True. People who have babies before marriage (compared to seven months or more afterward) have a 24-percent higher divorce rate.
5. True. The divorce rate is 24-percent higher for people under 18 than for those 25 or more years old.
6. True. High school dropouts have a 13 percent higher divorce rate than those with some college.
7. False. Most divorces occur in the fourth year.
8. False. Of couples that divorced, 50 percent were "happy" five years later. Of couples that were "very unhappy" but stayed together, 80 percent were "happy" five years later.
9. True. Research supports the fact that stress from divorce can show up years later.
10. True. Compared to those who get divorced, research supports the fact that people who are happily married say they are in better health, have fewer chronic health problems, and retain greater mobility in middle age.
11. True. Research supports the fact that divorced people smoke and drink more than happily married people.
12. True. According to Workaholics Anonymous, divorce is common.

(*continued*)

/// Self-Assessment Exercise 13-3 /// (*continued*)

13. True. Open-minded fair fighting often leads to resolving conflicts in any relationship. So use your conflict skills (Chapter 6) in your personal relationships.
14. True. Most successful couples never agree and solve all their problems—they outlast them through the marital endurance ethics. Have you heard the expression, "You don't want to go there" in discussions? Avoiding some less important issues helps couples stay together.
15. True. The divorce rate for church/praying couples is significantly lower, and they have better health than those who don't pray.

Marriage and Family Agreements Before entering marriage, it is very helpful to discuss and agree on career and family plans and the distribution of household and child-care responsibilities. In fact, some couples are creating family plan prenuptual agreements. These agreements are not legal documents; they are simply written lists of items relating to future family and work issues. For help preparing for marriage, most religious organizations offer courses. Two other sources include Engaged Encounter (www.engagedencounter.org) and Prep/Enrich (www.prep-enrich.com). For help making a good marriage even better, there is Worldwide Marriage Encounter, (www.wwme.org.)

Communication Skills
Refer to CS Question 10.

Although dual-career couples generally agree to split the household and child-care responsibilities evenly, most husbands often spend less time than their wives do in these areas. Some couples elect the split shift, in which one parent does household work while the other works outside the home, to avoid having to make child-care arrangements.

Fathers' Roles Are Changing In the old days, most fathers worked long hours and spent little time with their children. Today, research has clearly found that fathers are important in child care.[65] Although there are many reasons people are criminals, one contributing factor is the father's influence—or lack thereof. Fathers play an important role in criminal activity; most criminals have no real relationship with their fathers. Most males in jail don't know who their father is or have no relationship with him. In some cases, a father–child relationship virtually ends with divorce, but it doesn't have to. It's usually a choice fathers make.

Getting married and having children actually does bring about positive changes in a man's life. Today's father is spending more time with his children.[66] What some parents who work long hours are doing is coming home for dinner and/or bedtime to spend time with their children and then returning to work, usually at home, when the kids are in bed. Some others get up early to spend time with their children before going to work. More fathers routinely stay home to care for their sick children, take them to visit the doctor, and give them medicine.

Some middle-class families are finding that a second paycheck doesn't always mean living better, and some parents are opting to stay home with the kids.[67] As moms earn more, more dads are staying home to take care of the children. Like moms, some fathers work part-time or run their own businesses out of the house, and they do return to full-time work when the children get older. The "gender flip" sometimes comes as the result of a layoff. During the recession in 2008, more men were laid off than women, and without the extra income to pay for child care, more dads stay home and care for their children. But there are also more fathers who prefer to stay home with their children.

People who have made the gender flip say it does require plenty of planning and discussion, ongoing communication, and marital troubleshooting skills to make it work. Like men in traditional women's jobs, the father needs a positive self-concept to put up with the potential peer pressure to go back to work.

Mothers' Roles Are Changing In the old days, most mothers stayed home and took care of the children. Today, as discussed, mothers work outside the home. Mothers who do leave the labor force full-time tend to go back in increasing numbers as the children get older.[68]

Work at Home or in the Labor Force? People taking time off from the job to focus on home and family often sacrifice career opportunities. Thus, the decision to take a leave from work is often heart-wrenching, and although more fathers are staying home, it is more often the mother. Women tend to have two potential tracks. Those who stay on the job are on the career track, and those who leave and plan to return are on the "mommy track."[69] Unfortunately, many mothers, and fathers, who decide, for whatever reason, to stay home with the kids or to work outside the home get pressured and are made to feel guilty for the role they have chosen.

Why can't we all just let moms, and dads, make their own decisions about where they work? Let's all make an effort to stop judgmental questions and to stop making moms, and dads, feel guilty. Let's congratulate them and make them feel good about their choices and about themselves! Remember, valuing diversity is about letting people live their own lives. So let's also not pressure people to get married, to have children, or to have more or fewer children than they want.

For the stay-at-home mom, two good resources are www.athomemothers.com for motherhood lifestyle and www.familyandhome.org for tips on transitioning from work to home. For the mom in the workforce, two good resources are www.momsrefuge.com for information on juggling work and family and www.workingmom.com for strategies to simplify parenting.

Family Leave More mothers and fathers are taking maternity leave under the Family Leave Act to spend up to 12 weeks at home with their newborns. To know your legal rights, and for help getting leave, contact the Labor Department Wage and Hour Division at www.wageandhour.dol.gov and the Job Survival Hotline, operated from 9 to 5 by the National Association of Working Women, at 1-800-522-0925 or www.9to5.org.

Parenting Parenting can be stressful; many new parents experience a drop in marital satisfaction after the baby is born, and the stress can spill over onto the baby and the job.[70] If we can avoid stressful parenting, we can better manage the stress at home and work.[71] Children's basic personalities are developed during the first five years of life and affect them all their lives. Here are two simple guidelines to help develop a child's personality with a positive self-concept:

- *Engage in sensitive play.* Touch and hold children, and talk in a way they can understand. Stimulate and encourage them by making appealing suggestions for play. Refrain from unnecessary criticism; the "give more praise than criticism" rule is even more important for children than for employees. Remember that they are children—tell them they are smart and capable, help them when they need it, and praise their accomplishments.
- *Develop a warm, loving bond.* Children need to feel secure and know they are loved; sensitive play helps. Reading to children during these preschool years is a form of play that also helps academic performance in school; the more reading and less TV watching, the better the academic performance. Reading when putting children to bed and talking about their day is a great way to bond. It is much easier to bond and stay close when the child is young than to develop a relationship when they are school-age.

Work and Family Balance

Technological instant communication devices have enabled employees and their family members to communicate with each other nearly anywhere, anytime. Work tasks that can be easily completed from home are prevalent. Thus, the time designated for work and family is fuzzier, increasing the likelihood of work–family spillover. *Work–family spillover* is the effects of work and family on one another that generate similarities between the two domains. Therefore, work-related moods or attitudes are carried home, or family-related moods or attitudes are carried to work.[72]

Is the Internet and instant communications hurting the balance between work and home life? Some say yes (technoenthusiasts) it helps, but others say no (technophobes), the blur of work and family disrupts their balance.[73] Today, many pay a price in maintaining a semblance of work–family balance.[74]

People are concerned about work and family conflict and the spillover from one to the other. One role demand makes it harder to meet the other role requirement.[75] Some managers have a negative stereotype of women as having more family–work conflict than men, even though it is not always true, and this leads to glass ceiling discrimination in promotions for women.[76]

Trying to maintain a balance between work and family is stressful for many people.[77] Family relationships are important to our well-being.[78] Unfortunately, the stress can lead to nagging, which is a relationship and marriage killer.[79] Remember, when you are in conflict nagging doesn't help; use the resolving conflict model from Chapter 6 so you can successfully resolve the conflict without hurting the relationship.

Work and family balance has become so important that *Fortune, Bloomberg Businessweek,* and *Working Mother* publish lists of best places to work. Companies compete with each other to earn a place on the list and use their placements as recruiting tools.

Next, we discuss family-friendly and other policies that organizations are using to help employees satisfy their work–life needs.

MANAGING DIVERSITY

Failure to understand the importance of diversity undermines the management of diversity.[30] Managing diversity is not about tolerating differences, it is about understanding how important diversity is to the success of the organizations. Having a diverse workforce no doubt helps a company's image, and can also impact the bottom line by reducing employee turnover, boosting innovation, and attracting new business. To this end, some large corporations are adding chief diversity officers (CDOs) to the executive team. Their primary job is to create an environment where women and minorities can flourish.[81] Thus, *managing diversity* is about providing true equal employment opportunities for *all;* meeting the work–life needs of all employees. Let's face it: businesses don't just give things away. Many businesses believe in the goal of human relations, so they are giving work–family benefits because they are also benefiting.

Many organizations are offering work–life benefits packages that let the employees choose the benefits they want; these packages are also called *cafeteria benefits.* For example, one employee may select a child-care benefit, another a membership at a local gym, life insurance, or more money in a retirement account.

In addition to the many standard benefits, such as health care and retirement, here are some of the many work–life benefits being offered (the first two items describe flexible work arrangements):

- *Telecommuting,* letting employees work at home; *telecenters,* working at remote locations; and *mobile work,* working from anywhere with a laptop and cellular telephone to communicate with the office.
- *Flextime,* which allows employees to set, within limits, their starting and ending times, and sometimes to determine which days to work and which days to take off and the number of hours to work (for example, five 8-hour days or four 10-hour days). Within flextime, some organizations allow employees to take a few hours off during the day for personal reasons, such as attending a child's school activity, as long as they make up the hours.
- *Work–life,* or cafeteria, *benefits,* as discussed above.
- *Child care,* on-site or at nearby centers. This can include financial assistance and help finding child care. Some firms pay for sick child care so the employee can work. Some people are calling for a significant national child care program to cut individual costs.

- *Work–life balance classes,* to learn techniques to improve the quality of life.
- *Wellness programs,* at a company-owned facility. These programs can include payment of all or part of the cost to join a health club as well as diet and nutrition and smoking-cessation programs.
- *Tuition reimbursement,* paying all or part of educational expenses. If you want to get an advanced degree, you may want to work for a company that offers this benefit.
- *Employee assistance programs.* These programs offer professional counseling for personal, family, and/or substance abuse problems.

GLOBAL DIVERSITY

Because globalization is the number one challenge to business leaders in the 21st century, we have been discussing it in every chapter. In this section we discuss more areas of global diversity and cross-cultural relations; we begin with multinational corporations.

Multinational Companies

Advances in technology have allowed the world to become smaller through rapid communication and travel. A **multinational company (MNC)** *conducts a large part of its business outside the country of its headquarters.* Today, American corporations are growing internationally, such as Coca-Cola, which has 500 brands sold in over 200 countries,[82] and Yum! Brands' profit from its 3,700 fast-food restaurants in China surpasses those from its 19,000 U.S. restaurants.[83] Clearly, successful companies need global leaders,[84] and they need the skills to blend cultures.[85] For example, Carols Ghosn is the CEO of two companies (Renault and Nissan) on two continents.[86]

MNCs operate in virtually every major country. Complete Self-Assessment Exercise 13-4 to determine if you know in which country each MNC is headquartered.

/// Self-Assessment Exercise 13-4 ///

MNC Country of Ownership

For each item, select the country of ownership. If your answer is the United States, check the USA column. If it's another country, write in the name of that country.

Company/Brand Product	USA	Other; List Country
1. Shell gasoline	_____	____________________
2. Nestlé candy	_____	____________________
3. Unilever Dove soap	_____	____________________
4. Prudential insurance	_____	____________________
5. Barclays banking	_____	____________________
6. Anheuser-Busch ImBev beer	_____	____________________
7. Aiwa stereos	_____	____________________
8. Bayer aspirin	_____	____________________
9. Kia cars	_____	____________________
10. Cell phones	_____	____________________
11. L'Oréal facial products	_____	____________________
12. Samsung stereos/phones	_____	____________________

(*continued*)

/// Self-Assessment Exercise 13-4 /// (*continued*)

Answers:

1. The Netherlands (Royal Dutch/Shell)
2. Switzerland (Nestlé Swiss Chocolate)
3. England
4. England
5. England
6. Belgium
7. Japan
8. Japan
9. Germany
10. South Korea
11. Finland
12. France
13. South Korea

How many did you get correct? Place your score here ____.

Expatriates *are people who live and work in a country other than their native country.* Expatriates often experience culture shock, a state of confusion, and anxiety when they are first exposed to an unfamiliar culture.[87] There are changes with any move, but the changes compound tremendously when the move is to another country, especially between East and West.[88] Grasping the language and culture is difficult.[89] However, the number of expatriates is on the increase.[90]

U.S. managers using traditional American management styles often fail in an overseas business culture because managing diversity goes well beyond business etiquette. Companies need to train expatriates in language, local culture, and local business practices so they can be successful globally.[91] The trend today is to hire more local managers to run the company unit in their country.

Learning Outcome 13-7

List seven areas of global diversity.

Cross-Cultural Relations

To have successful human relations, you must be flexible and adapt to other people's ways of behaving; you are the foreigner and cannot expect others to change for you.[92] This section examines diversity in customs, attitudes toward time, work ethics, pay, laws and politics, ethics, and participative management. These seven areas of diversity are based on Hofstede's model of national cultures and the GLOBE Project, discussed in prior chapters. As you read, realize that you are being presented with stereotyped generalizations. Observations from one country or culture are not necessarily applicable to others.[93] The examples are not meant to judge "right" and "wrong" behavior. They are intended to illustrate cross-cultural differences that do affect human relations.

Diversity in Customs The Japanese and Chinese place a high priority on human relations, participative management, and teamwork. If you try to be an individual star, you will not be successful in Japan and China.[94] However, the French do not place high importance on team effort. If you are very outspoken, you will be considered impolite in Japan. If you refuse to be involved in receiving and giving gifts, you will offend Japanese people. However, don't wrap gifts in white paper because white is a sign of death. Also, don't place chopsticks straight up and down; doing so imitates an offering to the dead. Many Japanese companies start the day with exercises and company cheers. If you do not actively participate, you will be an outsider.

In Europe, management has more cultural than technical aspects and deals with value systems and religious background; it is organized more as a language than a set of techniques. While power and politics (Chapter 9) are important in the United States, they are even more important in France. It is important for a French manager to be perceived as very powerful.

Americans prefer to speak face-to-face from a greater distance than people of most other countries. If you back away or turn to the side from others, they may follow you and create a dance, and you may be considered cold and standoffish. During face-to-face communication, Latinos tend to touch each other more than Americans. Jumping when unexpectedly touched could create an embarrassing situation.

Gestures vary from country to country. For example, Americans prefer eye contact. However, the Japanese tend to look at the knot in a Japanese colleague's tie, or at the neck, to show respect. In Australia, making the "V" sign with the hand is considered an obscenity rather than a sign for victory.

Diversity in Attitudes toward Time Americans typically view time as a valuable resource that is not to be wasted, and socializing is often considered a waste of time. However, it would be considered impolite to start a business meeting with Hispanics without engaging in a certain amount of relaxed small talk. The Chinese are more long-term oriented than Americans,[95] and it takes many meetings to get to the point where they can trust you and do business.[96]

There is also a difference between respecting deadlines[97] and being on time. American and Swiss businesspeople usually expect you to be precisely on time for an appointment. However, in several countries, you could find yourself going to an appointment with a manager on time, only to be kept waiting. In some countries, if you call a meeting, most members will be late. If you get angry and yell, you could harm human relations.

Diversity in Work Ethics The work ethic, viewing work as a central life interest and a desirable goal in life, varies around the world. Generally, the Japanese have a stronger work ethic than Americans and Europeans. With a strong work ethic, and the acceptance of automation, many Japanese plants are the most productive in the world. Although there is not much difference in work ethics between Americans and Europeans, Americans work more hours than Europeans.

Americans are relatively good at getting poorly prepared workers to be productive, which is important when working with illiterate people all over the world. However, in some cultures, managers and employees have little interest in being productive. These relaxed attitudes do not do much for the bottom line of global businesses that are trying to change work ethics.

Diversity in Pay Americans, in general, are no longer the world's highest-paid employees. The Japanese and Europeans have caught up and earn as much as Americans. However, employees in Third World countries continue to be paid much less than employees in developed countries. That is a major reason so much of manufacturing is outsourced.

Pay systems also vary to meet employee values. One of the pay trends in the United States is pay for performance. However, some cultures value being paid for loyalty and following orders. Paying a salary works well in some countries, but not in others.

Diversity in Laws and Politics The legal and political environment becomes increasingly complex as multinationals do business all over the world.[98] Employee health and safety laws are generally more protective in developed countries than in Third World countries. Labor laws also vary widely from country to country. Western European nations offer good benefits, including a required four- to six-week vacation, paid holidays, and sick and family leave. Such differences change the actual labor cost per hour. It is also easier to terminate employees in some countries than in others.

In some countries, government structure and politicians are more stable than in others. A change in government can mean changes in business practices overnight. Some countries, such as Cuba, have literally taken away the plants and equipment owned by U.S. companies and sent the Americans home without any compensation.

Diversity in Ethics When conducting global business, you must rethink business ethics. In the United States and some other countries, it is illegal to take and give bribes for doing business. However, in some countries, bribing is a standard practice of doing business.[99] For example, an American businessperson complained to a local telephone company manager that the service person showed up and asked for a bribe, which was refused, so the

Communication Skills
Refer to CS Question 11.

telephone worker left without installing the phone. The businessperson was told by the telephone company manager that the matter would be investigated, for a fee (bribe). MNCs are working to develop global ethics codes.

WORK APPLICATION 13-13

Have you experienced any cultural differences in human relations with others? If so, explain.

Diversity in Participative Management In Third World nations, employees need basic skills training and may not be capable of participating in management decisions. Some cultures, like those of Japan and the United States, value participation in management whereas others do not.[100] In some cultures, employees simply want to be told what to do.[101]

Management–labor relations vary globally. In France relations are more polarized than in the United States, whereas in Japan they are more cooperative. You should realize that management and human relations become more complex as styles change from country to country.

HANDLING COMPLAINTS

Learning Outcome 13-8

List the steps in handling a complaint.

The EEOC's job is to handle complaints that are brought to it, many of which result in lawsuits. Effective management can be measured by the lack of complaints. As a manager, you should strive to meet the goal of human relations by creating a win–win situation for all employees. However, no matter how hard you try to satisfy employees' needs, complaints will arise covering a range of topics, which may include discrimination. Use the open-door policy and let employees feel as though they can come to you with a complaint. It is much better to get complaints out in the open and try to resolve them than to have employees complaining to everyone else about you.

You can use the complaint model to help you resolve employee complaints in either a union or nonunion organization. The **complaint model** *involves these steps: step (1) listen to the complaint and paraphrase it; step (2) have the complainer recommend a solution; step (3) schedule time to get all the facts and/or make a decision; and step (4) develop and implement a plan, and follow up.* Each step is discussed below.

Step 1: Listen to the Complaint and Paraphrase It Listen to the full story without interruptions, and paraphrase it to ensure accuracy. When employees come to you with a complaint, try not to take it personally; even the best supervisors have to deal with complaints. Do not become defensive and try to talk the employee out of the complaint.

Step 2: Have the Complainer Recommend a Solution Ask the complainer to recommend a solution that will resolve the complaint. Requesting a solution does not mean that you have to implement it. In some cases, the recommended solution may not solve the problem. Or the solution may not be fair to others. In such cases, the supervisor should let the employee know that the solution is not possible and explain why.

Step 3: Schedule Time to Get All the Facts and/or Make a Decision Since employee complaints often involve other people, you may find it necessary to check records or to talk to others. It is often helpful to talk to your boss or your peers, who may have had a similar complaint; they may be able to offer you some good advice on how best to resolve the complaint. Even when you have all the facts, it is usually advisable to take some time to weigh the facts before making a decision.

Generally, the more quickly a complaint is resolved, the fewer the negative side effects. Too many supervisors simply say, "I'll get back to you on this," without specifying a time period. This response is very frustrating to the employee. Some supervisors are purposely vague because they have no intention of getting back to the employee. They are hoping the employee will forget about the complaint. This tactic may get the employee to stop complaining, but it may also cause productivity and turnover problems.

Step 4: Develop and Implement a Plan, and Follow Up After getting all the necessary facts and advice from others, you should develop a plan. The plan may be developed by simply using the complainer's recommended solution. Work with the employee to find an alternative or present their own plan.

MODEL 13.1 | Complaint Model

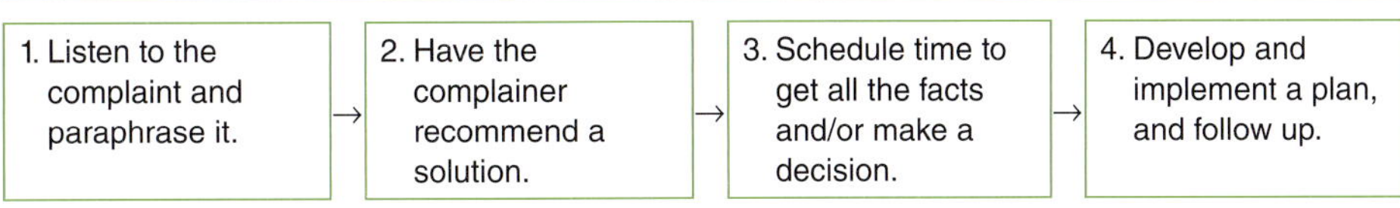

Skill-Building Exercise 13-3 develops this skill.

WORK APPLICATION 13-14

Identify a complaint you brought to a supervisor. If you have never complained, interview someone who has. State the complaint and identify the steps in the complaint model the supervisor did and/or did not follow.

In cases in which supervisors decide not to take any action to resolve the complaint, they should clearly explain why they chose not to do so. They should also state that if employees are not satisfied, they can appeal the decision to another level. The complainer should be told how to appeal the decision.

As with all plans, it is important for the supervisor to make sure that the plan is implemented through follow-up methods. It may be appropriate to set a follow-up meeting. It is also advisable to document all meetings and action.

Model 13.1 lists the four steps in the complaint model.

In the opening case, both the men and the women are complaining to each other about each other. A woman states that she did complain to management, but nothing happened. The minorities are also complaining about not being treated fairly. For things to change, management and the union have to work to resolve complaints.

Customer Complaints Handling a customer complaint is somewhat different from handling an employee complaint, especially when it involves something you and your company did wrong. The steps to follow are:

1. Admit you made a mistake.
2. Agree that it should not have happened.
3. Tell the customer what you are going to do about it, or ask what the customer recommends you do about it.
4. Take the action to make it up to the customer.
5. Take precautions to prevent the mistake in the future.

Complete Self-Assessment Exercise 13-5 to determine how your personality affects your ability to deal with diversity in the workplace.

/// Self-Assessment Exercise 13-5 ///

Personality and Diversity

If you are *open to new experiences,* you are probably interested in learning about people who are different from you.

If you have a high *agreeableness* personality, with a high need for affiliation, you tend to get along well with diverse people. You most likely do not judge peoples' behavior negatively simply because it is different. But you may need to be assertive so that you are not taken advantage of.

If you scored high in *conscientiousness,* with a high need for achievement, you may tend to be a conformist and will most likely adjust to diverse situations.

If you have a high *surgency* personality, with a high need for power, you like to dominate and may not want to accept diversity. You may need to remember, as the conscientious may too, that your ways are not always correct and are not always the best ways of doing things.

Action plan: Based on your personality, what specific things can you do to improve your ability to value and manage diversity? If you are well adjusted, you are better at dealing with a diversity of people.

____

____

____

____

____

____

As we bring this chapter to a close, you should understand some of the major laws and areas of discrimination in employment and what sexual harassment is. You should also understand the importance of valuing and managing diversity at home and globally, and how to personally avoid discrimination against anyone. Last, you should be able to handle an employee complaint using the complaint model.

/ / / REVIEW / / /

The chapter review is organized to help you master the 9 learning outcomes for Chapter 13. First provide your own response to each learning outcome, and then check the summary provided to see how well you understand the material. Next, identify the final statement in each section as either true or false (T/F). Correct each false statement. Answers are given at the end of the chapter.

LO 13-1 Define prejudice and discrimination and state common areas of employment discrimination in organizations.

Prejudice is a prejudgment of a person or situation based on attitudes. *Discrimination* is behavior for or against a person or situation. Common areas of employment discrimination include: recruitment, selection, compensation, upward mobility, and evaluation.

We all prejudge people and situations. T F

LO 13-2 State major laws protecting minorities and women.

Some of the major laws passed to protect minorities and women in the workplace include: the Equal Employment Opportunity (EEO) Act, the Civil Rights Act, the Age Discrimination in Employment Act, the Americans with Disabilities Act, the Equal Pay Act, the Pregnancy Discrimination Act, and the Family and Medical Leave Act.

The Justice Commission has the primary responsibility of ensuring equal opportunity for all. T F

LO 13-3 Identify what employers can and cannot ask job applicants.

To avoid breaking the law, employers interviewing job applicants should follow two major rules of thumb: (1) Every question that is asked should be job related, and (2) any general question that is asked should be asked of all candidates.

An organization can discriminate as long as it can prove that it is reasonably necessary to normal operation of the enterprise. T F

LO 13-4 List the groups that are legally protected by the EEOC.

Those legally protected by the EEOC include: minorities (Hispanics, Asians, African Americans, Native Americans, and Alaska Natives), women, disadvantaged young people, people with disabilities, and persons over 40.

The law states that the protected groups must be given special consideration in employment practices. T F

LO 13-5 List the six areas of sexual harassment.

The six areas of sexual harassment are: (1) unwelcome sexual advances, (2) coercion, (3) favoritism, (4) indirect harassment, (5) physical conduct, and (6) visual harassment.

Physical conduct refers to keeping your hands to yourself; touching is sexual harassment. T F

LO 13-6 Explain sexism in organizations and ways to overcome it.

Sexism is discrimination based on sex. To help overcome sexism, we should not use sexist language and behavior and we should discourage others from doing so.

Women who have been discriminated against based on gender can file a complaint with the EEOC. T F

LO 13-7 List seven areas of global diversity.

Seven areas of global diversity are: (1) diversity in customs, (2) attitudes toward time, (3) work ethics, (4) pay, (5) laws and politics, (6) ethics, and (7) participative management.

In general, American workers are the highest paid in the world. T F

LO 13-8 List the steps in handling a complaint.

The complaint model involves the following steps: step (1) listen to the complaint and paraphrase it; step (2) have the complainer recommend a solution; step (3) schedule time to get all the facts and/or make a decision; and step (4) develop and implement a plan, and follow up.

Managers don't always need to use step 3 of the complaint model. T F

LO 13-9 Define the following 11 key terms.

Select one or more methods: (1) fill in the missing key terms from memory; (2) match the key terms from the end of the review with their definitions below; and/or (3) copy the key terms in order from the key terms list at the beginning of the chapter.

________________ is the prejudgment of a person or situation based on attitudes.

________________ is behavior for or against a person or situation.

The EEOC ________________ list includes Hispanics, Asians, African Americans, Native Americans, and Alaska Natives.

A(n) ________________ allows discrimination on the basis of religion, sex, or national origin where it is reasonably necessary to normal operation of a particular enterprise.

________________ are planned, special efforts to recruit, hire, and promote women and members of minority groups.

A(n) ________________ refers to a significant physical, mental, or emotional limitation.

________________ is any unwelcomed behavior of a sexual nature.

________________ is discrimination based on sex.

A(n) ________________ conducts a large part of its business outside the country of its headquarters.

________________ are people who live and work in a country other than their native country.

The ________________ involves these steps: step (1) listen to the complaint and paraphrase it; step (2) have the complainer recommend a solution; step (3) schedule time to get all the facts and/or make a decision; and step (4) develop and implement a plan, and follow up.

/ / / KEY TERMS / / /

affirmative action (AA) programs 415
bona fide occupational qualification (BFOQ) 415
complaint model 432
disability 417
discrimination 412
expatriates 430
minority 414
multinational company (MNC) 429
prejudice 412
sexism 421
sexual harassment 420

/ / / COMMUNICATION SKILLS / / /

The following critical thinking questions can be used for class discussion and/or as written assignments to develop communication skills. Be sure to give complete explanations for all questions.

1. Clearly, women and minorities were held back from employment opportunities in the past. So shouldn't we give them special consideration today (like giving them jobs when they are qualified even though there are better qualified white males)? Should we be increasing or decreasing affirmative action programs?
2. Do we really need laws to get organizations to give equal opportunities to all? Should the current employment laws be changed? How?
3. Should religious people be given breaks and a special place to pray during their work time?
4. Some companies and jobs have a mandatory retirement age. Should the government pass a law stating a mandatory retirement age?
5. Do you feel comfortable being around people with disabilities? Should organizations make special efforts to hire individuals who are disabled? Are organizations that hire workers with disabilities just being socially responsible, or are the workers productive?
6. Do you agree that people who work together can date? How might dating lead to sexual harassment? Should organizations have policies about employee dating? If they have policies, what should the policies include?

7. Only a small percentage of *Fortune* 500 companies have female CEOs. One solution to increase the number of women CEOs would be to have co-CEOs, one male and one female. Do you think this would work? Do you have any other ideas on how to break the glass ceiling?
8. Consider the statement, "Sexist and racist jokes are just meant to be funny and no one gets hurt anyway." Do you agree?
9. The traditional family hasn't been the norm for several years. Instead, it is being overtaken by dual-income earners and single parents. Are we better off today, or should we return to the traditional family?
10. The percentage of married people has declined over the years due to divorce and people living together. Also, male and female roles have changed. Do these trends help or hurt society?
11. Consider the statement, "With the global economy, people around the world are becoming more and more alike, so why be concerned about diversity?" Do you agree? Should organizations conduct diversity training?

CASE /// McDonald's Inclusion and Diversity Programs

McDonald's is the world's leading global foodservice retailer. It is a multinational company that has served billions, with more than 33,000 locations serving nearly 68 million customers in 119 countries each day.[102] It is currently focusing growth in China where it plans to have 2,000 stores by 2013. McDonald's opened its seventh Hamburger University near Shanghai to train its new managers, and it is actually more difficult to get into Hamburger U than Harvard University (1 percent vs. a 7 percent acceptance rate).[103]

Inclusion and diversity have been part of McDonald's culture, from the crew room to the board room, for decades. Its goal is to have employees working and living to reach their full potential. Leaders hold themselves accountable for learning about, valuing, and respecting individuals on both sides of the counter. In the United States, 70 percent of its employees are women and minorities, more than 25 percent are in leadership, 45 percent of its franchise owners are women and minorities, and it has more than 5 billion diverse vendors.[104]

McDonald's takes pride in being a premier education and training institution, as it prepares restaurant managers to run multimillion-dollar businesses through their training at Hamburger University. When it comes to inclusion and diversity, it is the same story. McDonald's has developed a diversity curriculum that teaches employees how to move from awareness to action in the area of inclusion and intercultural management. McDonald's inclusion and diversity curriculum courses include:[105]

- Asian Pacific Middle East Career Development
- Black Career Development
- Hispanic Career Development
- Lesbian Gay Career Development
- Women's Career Development
- Intercultural Learning Lab

McDonald's has taken mentoring into the 21st century by introducing and offering a Web-based tool used for matching, tracking, and facilitating Adviser–Learner (mentor–mentee) relationships across an entire organization. The program incorporates the latest technology features of both informal and formal mentoring approaches, providing a virtual environment to encourage Career Engagements (one-to-one), Topical Engagements (group/peer learning/sharing), and Situational Engagements (short-term, special projects) that benefit individuals, groups, and McDonald's.[106]

McDonald's support of lesbian/gay career development has not gone unnoticed from both sides of this social issue. McDonald's scored well (85 percent in 2010 and 2011, with other corporations scoring 100 percent) in the Human Rights Campaign's (HRC) Corporate Equality Index. HRC is a national leading nonprofit organization working for lesbian, gay, bisexual, and transgender (LGBT) equal rights (www.hrc.org) that publishes the corporate survey every year.[107] This rating, however, has led to a negative publicity campaign by the nonprofit pro-family American Family Association (AFA, www.afa.net)[108] and the nonprofit anti-LGBT Americans for Truth About Homosexuality (AFTAH, www.aftah.org).[109] Both activist groups are against rewarding and subsidizing corporations that promote homosexuality; they ask businesses to be neutral on this social issue.

Go to the Internet: For more information on McDonald's Corporation and to update the information provided in this case, do a name search on the Internet and visit www.aboutmcdonalds.com.

Support your answers to the following questions with specific information from the case and text, or with other information you get from the Web or other sources.

1. Ater reading the case and visiting McDonald's' Web site, in what ways has McDonald's taken a proactive approach toward supporting and valuing diversity?

2. What structures and systems has McDonald's established to ensure that it leverages its diversity as part of the business strategy?

3. How does McDonald's propose to overcome prejudice and discrimination within the firm?

4. What actions would you recommend that McDonald's take relative to the negative publicity and statements made by the AFA and AFTAH?

Cumulative Questions

5. How do perception (Chapter 2), attitudes, values, and ethics (Chapter 3) help us understand the dynamics within this case?

6. The case indicates that the AFA and AFTAH are in conflict with McDonald's over its inclusive diversity policy (inclusion of sexual preference). What are the alternative management styles McDonald's could use to address this conflict? (Chapter 6)

7. Should McDonald's use a team approach (Chapter 11) for solving this conflict?

8. How might McDonald's organizational culture (Chapter 12) have led to the conflict described in this case?

OBJECTIVE CASE /// Lilly's Promotion

The Carlson Mining and Manufacturing Company needs a new vice president of human resources. Its headquarters are in Detroit, but the company has mining and manufacturing plants in three states and five different countries. Foreign plants account for about 70 percent of total operations.

The president, Ron Carlson, is meeting with some of the vice presidents and the board of directors to decide who will be promoted to vice president. The following are excerpts from their discussion:

RON: As you know, we are meeting today to promote someone to vice president. Ted, tell us about the candidates.

TED: We have narrowed the list of candidates to two people. You all know the two candidates. They are Rich Martin and Lilly Jefferson. Rich is 38 and has been with us for 15 years, and he has worked in human resources for 10 years. He has an MBA from a leading business school. Lilly is 44 and has been with us for 10 years. She recently finished her BS in business going to school nights at the local state college.

JIM: Lilly is an African American female with older children. She is perfect for the job, fitting into two AA classifications. We can meet our AA quotas without promoting Lilly, but it would help. Besides, there are a lot of African Americans here in Detroit; we could get some great publicity.

ED: Wait a minute. We cannot have any girls at the VP level. You know they are emotional and cannot take the pressure of the job.

RON: Their performance records are about the same, but Rich has been with us longer, and is better educated.

The discussion ended in a vote. Lilly won by a large margin. Off the record: It was because she is a qualified African American female. If she were a white male, Rich would have been promoted.

Answer the following questions. Then in the space between questions, state why you selected that answer.

_______ 1. Discrimination was used in the promotion process.

a. true *b.* false

_______ 2. The primary area discussed in this case is:

a. recruitment *c.* compensation *e.* evaluation

b. selection *d.* upward mobility

_______ 3. Affirmative action affected the decision to promote Lilly.

a. true *b.* false

_______ 4. Rich may have a case for reverse discrimination.

a. true *b.* false

_______ 5. Sexism occurred in this case.

a. true *b.* false

_______ 6. Ed's statement was:

a. factual *b.* myth

_______ 7. Ed used sexist language.

a. true *b.* false

_______ 8. With Lilly being a minority member, she will most likely encounter cross-cultural relations problems.

a. true *b.* false

_______ 9. Carlson is a multinational company.

a. true *b.* false

_______ 10. The most help Lilly got in getting to the vice president position was from:

a. AAP *c.* flexible work schedule *e.* role models and mentors

b. training *d.* child care *f.* wellness programs

11. Whom would you have voted for? Why?

12. How would you feel in Lilly's position, knowing that you are qualified for the job but that you have been selected because you are a minority? Lilly's response can be role-played.

/ / / SKILL-BUILDING EXERCISE 13-1 / / /

Sexism

In-Class Exercise (Individual and Group)

Objective: To better understand sexist language and behavior and how it affects human relations.

AACSB: The AACSB learning standard skills developed through this exercise are reflexive thinking and diversity.

Experience: You will discuss sexism.

Procedure 1 (7–15 minutes)

Option A: Students give sample words and behaviors found in the workplace that are sexist (for example, words *foreman* and behaviors [a woman being required to get the coffee]). The instructor or a class member writes the headings "words" and "behaviors" on the board and records the class members' examples. Discuss how these sexist words and behaviors affect people's behavior in organizations.

Option B: Break into teams of five or six, making the number of males and females as even as possible. As in option A, develop a list of sexist words and behaviors and discuss how they affect people's behavior in organizations.

Procedure 2 (7–15 minutes)

Option A: As a class, select a few sexist words and behaviors. Discuss how to overcome this sexism.

Option B: As a group, select a few sexist words and behaviors. Discuss how to overcome this sexism.

Conclusion: The instructor may lead a class discussion and/or make concluding remarks.

Application (2–4 minutes): What did I learn from this exercise? How will I use this knowledge in the future?

Sharing: Volunteers give their answers to the application section.

/ / / SKILL-BUILDING EXERCISE 13-2 / / /

Male and Female Small-Group Behavior

In-Class Exercise (Group)

For this exercise, some of the class members will need to bring tape recorders to class to record small-group discussions. Small tape recorders are suggested. Your instructor may assign specific people to bring them. If not, bring a tape recorder if you have one.

Objective: To see if there are any differences in male and female behavior in small groups.

AACSB: The AACSB learning standard skills developed through this exercise are analytic skills, reflexive thinking, and diversity.

Preparation: Some of the class members need to bring tape or digital recorders to class to record the small-group discussion.

Procedure 1 (15–20 minutes)

Experience: In a small group, you will make a decision that will be recorded, and then you will analyze the recording to determine if there are differences in male and female behavior.

Break into teams of five or six. Make the number of males and females as even as possible in each group. Be sure each group has a recorder. As a group, you will select a candidate for a job opening. As an individual, read the information below and think about whom you would hire in this situation. When all group members are ready, begin your discussion of whom to hire. *Be sure to record the conversation.* Discuss each candidate's qualifications fully, coming to a group consensus on whom to hire. Do not vote, unless the time is almost up. You must make a decision by the deadline stated by your instructor. Try not to finish very early, but if you do, wait for the rest of the class to finish before going on to the next procedure.

You are a member of the local school board. The board is making the decision on which candidate to hire for the open position of girls' high school tennis coach. The following is information on each candidate.

Kishana Jones: Kishana has been a history teacher at a nearby high school for 10 years. She was the tennis coach for one year. It has been five years since she coached the team. Kishana says she stopped coaching because it was too time-consuming with her young daughter, but she misses it and wants to return. Kishana's performance was rated as 3 on a scale of 1 to 5. She never played competitive tennis, but she says she plays regularly. You guess Kishana is about 35 years old.

Soren Hansen: Soren works as a supervisor on the 11 P.M. to 7 A.M. shift for a local business. He has never coached before. However, Soren was a star player in high school and college. He still plays in local tournaments, and you see his name in the paper now and then. You guess Soren is about 25 years old.

Chelsea Clark: Chelsea has been a basketball coach and a teacher of physical education classes for a nearby high school for the past five years. She has a bachelor's degree in physical education. Chelsea has never coached tennis, but she did play on the high school team. She says she plays tennis about once a week. You guess Chelsea is about 40 years old.

Lisa Williams: Lisa has been an English teacher at your school for the past two years. She has never coached, but she did take a course in college on how to coach tennis. She is popular with her students. Lisa plays tennis regularly, and you have heard she is a pretty good player. She is an African American. You guess Lisa is about 24 years old.

Hank Chung: Hank has been teaching math at your school for seven years. He was a star player in high school in Japan, and he played tennis for a successful U.S. college team. He still plays for fun regularly. He has never coached or had any type of coaching courses. He applied for the job the last time it was open four years ago but was not selected. You guess Hank is about 30 years of age.

Sally Carson: Sally has taught physical education classes at your school for the past four years. She never played competitive tennis but has a master's degree in physical education and has had courses regarding how to coach tennis. Sally taught and coached field hockey at a high school for 15 years before moving to your city. You guess she is about 48 years old.

Procedure 2 (1–2 minutes)

As an individual, answer the following questions. Circle the letter of your response.

1. Who spoke more?
   a. males *b.* females *c.* equal time
2. The one individual with the most influence in the group was:
   a. male *b.* female
3. The one individual with the least influence in the group was:
   a. male *b.* female
4. Overall, who had the most influence on the group?
   a. males *b.* females *c.* equal influence
5. Interruptions came more frequently from:
   a. males interrupting females
   b. females interrupting males
   c. equal interruption from both
6. Of the total discussion time, I spoke for about _______ minutes.

Procedure 3 (2–4 minutes)

Total the group's answers to the six questions in procedure 2. All members should write the totals next to the questions above.

Procedure 4 (20–30 minutes)

Play back the recorded discussion. As it plays, write down who talks and for how long they talk. If one person interrupts another, note it as "male interrupts female," or vice versa. When the tape finishes, add up the number of minutes each person spoke. Total the male and female times. As a team, answer the six questions in procedure 2 above. Were the answers the same before and after listening to the recorded discussion?

Conclusion: The instructor may lead a class discussion and/or make concluding remarks.

Application (2–4 minutes): What did I learn from this experience? How can I use this knowledge in the future?

Sharing: Volunteers give their answers to the application section.

Source: The idea to develop this exercise came from Susan Morse, University of Massachusetts at Amherst, in "Gender Differences in Behavior in Small Groups: A Look at the OB Class," paper presented at the 25th Annual Meeting of the Eastern Academy of Management, May 12, 1988.

/ / / SKILL-BUILDING EXERCISE 13-3 / / /

Handling Complaints

Preparation (Group)

During class you will be given the opportunity to role-play handling a complaint. Select a complaint. It may be one you brought to a supervisor, one that was brought to you, one you heard about, or one you made up. Fill in the information below for the person who will role-play bringing you a complaint to resolve.

Explain the situation and complaint.

List pertinent information about the other party that will help him or her play the role of the complainer (relationship with supervisor, knowledge, years of service, background, age, values, and so on).

Review Exhibit 13.4 (complaint model) and think about what you will say and do when you handle this complaint.

Complaint Observer Form

During the role-play, observe the handling of the complaint. Determine whether the supervisor followed the steps below, and how well. Try to have both a positive and an improvement comment for each step in the complaint model. Be specific and descriptive. For all improvement comments, have an alternative positive behavior (APB). What could have been done or said that was not?

Step 1. How well did the supervisor listen? Was the supervisor open to the complaint? Did the supervisor try to talk the employee out of the complaint? Was the supervisor defensive? Did the supervisor get the full story without interruptions? Did the supervisor paraphrase the complaint?

(positive) (improvement)

Step 2. Did the supervisor have the complainer recommend a solution? How well did the supervisor react to the solution? If the solution could not be used, did the supervisor explain why?

(positive) (improvement)

Step 3. Did the supervisor schedule time to get all the facts and/or make a decision? Was it a specific date? Was it a reasonable length of time?

(positive) (improvement)

Step 4. Did the supervisor develop and implement a plan, and schedule a follow-up? (This step may not have been appropriate at this time.)

In-Class Exercise

Objective: To experience and develop skills in resolving complaints.

AACSB: The AACSB learning standard skills developed through this exercise are analytic skills, communication ability, and leadership.

Preparation: You should have prepared to handle a complaint.

Experience: You will initiate, respond to, and observe a complaint role-play. Then you will evaluate the effectiveness of its resolution.

Procedure 1 (2–3 minutes)

Break into as many groups of three as possible. (You do not have to be with members of your permanent team.) If there are any people not in a triad, make one or two groups of two. Each member selects a number 1, 2, or 3. Number 1 will be the first to initiate a complaint role-play, then 2, followed by 3.

Procedure 2 (8–15 minutes)

A. Number 1 (the supervisor) gives his or her preparation complaint information to number 2 (the complainer) to read. Once number 2 understands, role-play the complaint (step B). Number 3 is the observer.

B. Role-play the complaint. Put yourself in this person's situation; ad-lib. Number 3, the observer, writes his or her observations on the complaint observer form.

C. Integration. When the role-play is over, the observer leads a discussion on the effectiveness of the conflict resolution. All three should discuss the effectiveness; number 3 is not a lecturer.
Do not go on until told to do so.

Procedure 3 (8–15 minutes)

Same as procedure 2, only number 2 is now the supervisor, number 3 is now the complainer, and number 1 is the observer.

Procedure 4 (8–15 minutes)

Same as procedure 2, only number 3 is now the supervisor, number 1 is now the complainer, and number 2 is the observer.

Conclusion: The instructor leads a class discussion and/or makes concluding remarks.

Application (2–4 minutes): What did I learn from this experience? How will I use this knowledge in the future?

Sharing: Volunteers give their answers to the application section.

/ / / SKILL-BUILDING EXERCISE 13-4 / / /

Periodical Articles

Preparation (Individual and Group)

Select a human relations topic that you would like to learn more about. It can be any topic covered in this book or a topic not covered, if related to human relations.

Now go to the library (usually the reference section) or online. If you are using the library, find the computer database that has business journals. Search your topic by typing it in the computer. The index should list periodical titles with the name of the author(s) and the name of the periodical in which the article appears, with its date and page number(s). You may also get an abstract of the article and a full article in the database, which you can download and/or print. Select one of the articles to read. Be sure the library has the publication in some form.

Write down the following information:

Author's name(s): ______________________________

Title of article: ______________________________

Title of the periodical: ______________________________

Date of publication and page number(s): ______________________________

Now get the periodical and read the article. Then answer the following questions. (Use additional paper if needed.)

Be sure to write neatly. You may be asked to report to the class or pass this assignment in to the instructor. Be prepared to give a three- to five-minute talk on your article.

What did the article say? (Give a summary of the most important information in the article.)

How does this information relate to me and/or my interests?

How will I use this information in the future?

When reading articles of interest to your career, always answer the three questions. Answering these questions will help you use the information rather than forget it and will develop your abilities and skills.

To continue to improve on your human relations skills after the course is over, read more articles of interest to you. When you can afford it, subscribe to a periodical of interest to you. Many employers have copies of periodicals related to their business available to employees, and they are willing to pay for employee subscriptions.

In-Class Exercise

Objectives: To become familiar with various publications. To gain some specific knowledge regarding a topic of your choice and the choices of other students in the class.

AACSB: The AACSB learning standard skills developed through this exercise are analytic skills and communication ability.

Preparation: You should have read an article of interest to you and answered the three questions in the preparation section.

Experience: Class members will share their articles.

Procedure 1 (5–50 minutes)

One at a time, students come to the front of the room and give a three- to seven-minute speech on the article they read.

Conclusion: The instructor leads a class discussion and/or makes concluding remarks.

Application (2–4 minutes): What did I learn from this experience? How will I use this knowledge in the future?

Sharing: Volunteers give their answers to the application section.

/ / ANSWERS TO TRUE/FALSE QUESTIONS / /

1. T.
2. F. The Equal Employment Opportunity Commission (EEOC), not the Justice Commission, is responsible for ensuring equal opportunity for all.
3. T. (It is called a bona fide occupational qualification [BFOQ].)
4. F. The law states that protected groups must not be *discriminated* against.
5. F. Physical conduct states that a person does not have to be touched to be sexually harassed. Touching is not harassment when it is welcomed.
6. T.
7. F. The pay of Japanese and European workers is similar to that of U.S. workers.
8. T.

APPENDIX A

Applying Human Relations Skills

LEARNING OUTCOMES

After completing this appendix, you should be able to:

LO A-1 State why human relations skills are important.

LO A-2 Identify the most important human relations concepts from the entire book.

LO A-3 Determine your strongest and weakest areas of human relations.

LO A-4 Compare your present skills assessment with the one you did in Chapter 1.

LO A-5 Explain three options in handling human relations problems.

LO A-6 Describe the four steps of changing behavior.

LO A-7 Develop your own human relations plan.

Pat O'Conner and David Fredrick, two students nearing the completion of a human relations course, were talking about the course:

PAT: This course has a lot of good practical advice that can help me develop effective human relations.

DAVID: I agree. Have you been using the information on a regular basis in your daily life?

PAT: Some of it. I'm so busy that I don't always have time to think about and actually do these things, even though I know they will help me. Have you been using it?

DAVID: Most of it. I figure that if I use these skills now rather than wait until I get a full-time job, I'll be that much ahead of the game.

PAT: Is there a way to do this?

DAVID: Yes, I've already read the appendix. It explains how to develop a human relations plan that you can put into action immediately.

PAT: Guess I'll go read it now.

DAVID: Good luck, see you in class.

Whether you are more like Pat or David, this appendix will help you develop your own human relations plan.

A REVIEW OF SOME OF THE MOST IMPORTANT HUMAN RELATIONS CONCEPTS

Learning Outcome A-1

State why human relations skills are important.

Learning Outcome A-2

Identify the most important human relations concepts from the entire book.

Let's highlight some of the most important information from each chapter in the book to tie things all together. If you cannot recall the information covered in any of the chapters, please return to the chapter for a review of the material.

Part 1. Intrapersonal Skills: Behavior, Human Relations, and Performance Begin with You Chapter 1 defined some of the important concepts used throughout the book. Can you define the following: human relations, the goal of human relations, behavior, levels of behavior, group behavior, organizational behavior, and performance? Please return to Chapter 1 and review the first few pages that state the many reasons why human relations are so important.

Can you define and discuss personality, stress, intelligence, learning styles, perception, and first impressions? If not, return to Chapter 2.

Can you define and discuss attitudes, job satisfaction, self-concept, and values? If not, return to Chapter 3.

Can you define and discuss time management and career management? If not, return to Chapter 4.

Part 2. Interpersonal Skills: The Foundation of Human Relations Can you define and discuss the importance of communications; the communication process; and how to send, receive, and respond to messages; situational communications; and how to deal with emotions and give and receive criticism? If not, return to Chapter 5.

Can you define and discuss transactional analysis, assertiveness, conflict management styles, how to resolve conflict with the collaborating conflict style, and interpersonal dynamics? If not, return to Chapter 6.

Part 3. Leadership Skills: Influencing Others Can you define and discuss trait leadership theory, behavioral leadership theories, contingency leadership theories, situational supervision, and substitutes for leadership? If not, return to Chapter 7.

Can you define and discuss content motivation theories, process motivation theories, reinforcement theory, and motivation techniques? If not, return to Chapter 8.

Can you define and discuss power, organizational politics, vertical politics, horizontal politics, and etiquette? If not, return to Chapter 9.

Can you define and discuss networking and negotiating? If not, return to Chapter 10.

Part 4. Leadership Skills: Team and Organizational Behavior, Human Relations, and Performance Can you define and discuss team dynamics, group development stages, and how to lead groups and meetings?

Can you define and discuss problem-solving and decision-making approaches and models, and creative group problem-solving and decision-making techniques? If not, return to Chapter 11.

Can you define and discuss resistance to change and how to overcome it; organizational culture and climate; and organizational development? If not, return to Chapter 12.

Can you define and discuss prejudice and discrimination, equal employment opportunity, legally protected groups, sexual harassment, sexism in organizations, global diversity and cross-cultural relations, and how to handle complaints? If not, return to Chapter 13.

Learning Outcome A-3

Determine your strongest and weakest areas of human relations.

Learning Outcome A-4

Compare your present skills assessment with the one you did in Chapter 1.

ASSESSING YOUR HUMAN RELATIONS ABILITIES AND SKILLS

For each of the 43 statements that follow, record in the blank the number from 1 to 7 that best describes your level of ability or skill. You are not expected to have all high numbers.

Low ability/skill						High ability/skill
1	2	3	4	5	6	7

_____ 1. I understand how personality and perception affect people's behavior, human relations, and performance.

_____ 2. I can describe several ways to handle stress effectively.

_____ 3. I know my preferred learning style (accommodator, diverger, converger, assimilator) and how it affects my behavior, human relations, and performance.

_____ 4. I understand how people acquire attitudes and how attitudes affect behavior, human relations, and performance.

_____ 5. I can describe self-concept and self-efficacy and how they affect behavior, human relations, and performance.

_____ 6. I can list several areas of personal values and state how values affect behavior, human relations, and performance.

_____ 7. I understand how to use a time management system.

_____ 8. I understand how to use time management techniques to get more done in less time with better results.

_____ 9. I know how to develop a career plan and manage my career successfully.

_____ 10. I can describe the communication process.

_____ 11. I can list several transmission media and when to use each.

_____ 12. I can identify and use various message response styles.

_____ 13. I understand organizational communications and networks.

_____ 14. I can list barriers to communications and how to overcome them.

_____ 15. I know my preferred communication style and how to use other communication styles to meet the needs of the situation.

_____ 16. I can describe transactional analysis.

_____ 17. I can identify the differences between aggressive, passive, and assertive behavior. I am assertive.

_____ 18. I can identify different conflict resolution styles. I understand how to resolve conflicts in a way that does not hurt relationships.

_____ 19. I can identify behavioral leadership theories.

_____ 20. I can identify contingency leadership theories.

_____ 21. I know my preferred leadership style and how to change it to meet the needs of the situation.

_____ 22. I understand the process people go through to meet their needs.

_____ 23. I know several content and process motivation theories and can use them to motivate people.

_____ 24. I can list and use motivation techniques.

_____ 25. I can identify bases and sources of power.

_____ 26. I know how to gain power in an organization.

_____ 27. I can list political techniques to increase success.

_____ 28. I have 100 people I can call on for career help.

_____ 29. I know how to open a conversation to get people to give me career assistance.

_____ 30. I know two critical things to do during a negotiation to get what I want.

_____ 31. I understand how to plan and conduct effective meetings.

_____ 32. I can identify components of group dynamics and how they affect behavior, human relations, and performance.

_____ 33. I know the stages groups go through as they develop.

_____ 34. I understand the roles and various types of groups in organizations.

_____ 35. I can help groups make better decisions through consensus.

_____ 36. I know when, and when not, to use employee participation in decision making.

_____ **37.** I understand why people resist change and know how to overcome that resistance.

_____ **38.** I can identify and use organizational development techniques.

_____ **39.** I understand how to develop a positive organizational culture and climate.

_____ **40.** I understand equal employment opportunity (EEO) and the rights of legally protected groups such as minorities, people with disabilities, alcohol and drug addicts, and people with AIDS.

_____ **41.** I can define sexism and sexual harassment in organizations.

_____ **42.** I can handle a complaint using the complaint model.

_____ **43.** I understand how to plan for improved human relations.

To use the profile form below, place an X in the box whose number corresponds to the score you gave each statement above.

Profile Form

	Your Score							Parts and Chapters in Which the Information Will Be Covered in the Book
	1	2	3	4	5	6	7	
								Part 1. Intrapersonal Skills: Behavior, Human Relations, and Performance Begin with You
1.								2. Personality, Stress, Learning, and Perception
2.								
3.								
4.								3. Attitudes, Self-Concept, Values, and Ethics
5.								
6.								
7.								4. Time and Career Management
8.								
9.								
								Part 2. Interpersonal Skills: The Foundation of Human Relations
10.								5. Communications, Emotions, and Criticism
11.								
12.								
13.								
14.								
15.								
16.								6. Dealing with Conflict
17.								
18.								
								Part 3. Leadership Skills: Influencing Others
19.								7. Leading and Trust
20.								
21.								
22.								8. Motivating Performance
23.								
24.								
25.								9. Ethical Power, Politics, and Etiquette
26.								
27.								
28.								10. Networking and Negotiating
29								
30								

(continued)

Profile Form (*continued*)

	Your Score							Parts and Chapters in Which the Information Will Be Covered in the Book
	1	2	3	4	5	6	7	
								Part 4. Leadership Skills: Team and Organizational Behavior, Human Relations, and Performance
31.								11. Team Dynamics, Creativity and Problem Solving, and Decision Making
32.								
33.								
34.								
35.								
36.								
37.								12. Organizational Change and Culture
38								
39								
40								13. Valuing Diversity Globally
41								
42								
43								Appendix A. Applying Human Relations Skills

Recall that in Chapter 1 you answered these same 43 questions. At that time you were told that you would compare your scores at the beginning and end of the course. Do so now. Turn back to your profile form in Chapter 1. Either tear it out or flip back and forth as you place your scores from Chapter 1 on the profile form here. You were asked to place an X in the boxes above. To distinguish your responses from Chapter 1, place a check or some other mark in the boxes above. If you have the same box marked for both, don't bother to check the box above. You will know it was the same response because there is only one score.

When you have finished, you will have your early and your present assessment of your human relations abilities and skills on one form. This will allow you to make an easy comparison of your scores, which represent your strong and weak areas of human relations. You will be using your profile form in the next section.

HUMAN RELATIONS PLANNING

In this section, you will learn about handling human relations problems, changing one's behavior, and developing a human relations plan.

Handling Human Relations Problems

Learning Outcome A-5

Explain three options in handling human relations problems.

In any organization, there are bound to be times when you disagree with other employees. You may be assigned to work with a person you do not like. When you encounter these human relations problems, you have to choose either to avoid resolving the problem or to confront the person to solve it. In most cases, it is advisable to solve human relations problems, rather than to ignore them. Problems usually get worse rather than better, and they do not solve themselves. When you decide to resolve a human relations problem, you have at least three alternatives:

1. *Change the other person.* Whenever there is a human relations problem, it is easy to blame the other party and expect that person to make the necessary changes in behavior to meet our expectations. In reality, few human relations problems can be blamed entirely on one party. Both parties usually contribute to the human relations problem. Blaming the other party without taking some responsibility usually results in resentment and defensive behavior. The more we force people to change to meet our expectations, the more difficult it is to maintain effective human relations.

2. *Change the situation.* If you have a problem getting along with the person or people you work with, you can try to change the situation by working with another person or people. You may tell your boss you cannot work with so-and-so because of a personality conflict and ask for a change in jobs. There are cases where this is the only solution; however, when you complain to your boss, the boss often figures that you are the problem, not the other party. Blaming the other party and trying to change the situation enables us to ignore our behavior, which may be the actual cause of the problem.
3. *Change yourself.* Throughout this book, particularly in Part I, the focus has been on personal behavior. In many situations, your own behavior is the only thing you can control. In most human relations problems, the best alternative is to examine others' behavior and try to understand why they are doing and saying the things they are, and then examine your own behavior to determine why you are behaving the way you are. In most cases, the logical choice is to change your behavior. We are not saying to simply do what other people request. In fact, you should be assertive, as discussed in Chapter 6. You are not being forced to change; you are changing your behavior because you elect to do so. When you change your behavior, the other party may also change. Remember to create a win–win situation for all stakeholders.

Changing One's Behavior

Learning Outcome A-6

Describe the four steps of changing behavior.

Improving human relations generally requires a change in one's behavior. It is hoped that over the time period of this course, you have made changes in your behavior that have improved your human relations abilities and skills. In changing behavior, it is helpful to follow a four-step approach: step (1) assess your abilities and skills; step (2) develop new skills; step (3) change your behavior; and step (4) get feedback and reward yourself.

Step 1: Assess Your Abilities and Skills You should consistently be aware of your behavior and assess it. Without becoming aware of your behavior and being committed to changing it, you cannot improve. You may know someone who has annoying behavior. The person is aware of it, yet does nothing to change. Without that commitment, this person will not change. Think about your own behavior; others may find you annoying, but do you change? What can you gain from changing? Can you make the change successfully?

You assessed your human relations abilities and skills at the beginning of the course and at the present. To continue your assessment, answer the following questions in the space provided, using your profile form.

1. Have your profile numbers (1 to 7) gotten higher compared to what they were at the beginning of the course? Why or why not?

2. Review your five objectives from Chapter 1, following your profile form. Did you meet them? Why or why not?

3. What are your strongest areas of human relations (highest numbers on your profile form)?

4. What human relations areas do you need to improve the most (lowest numbers on your profile form)?

5. What are the most important abilities and skills you have developed and/or things you have learned through this course?

Step 2. Develop New Skills The development of new skills can come in a variety of ways. In this course, you had a text to read. This information gives you the basis for new skills. In life, when there is no textbook, you can refer to libraries for periodicals and books that can give you the knowledge you need to change your behavior. You can also refer to friends and experts in the areas in which you need to improve. There may be workshops, seminars, and courses in these areas as well.

Step 3: Change Your Behavior Try to find safe, nonthreatening situations to try out your new behavior. Friends are usually willing to help; try your new behavior on them to see how it works.

Progressively change your behavior as you develop skill and confidence. For example, if you want to develop your ability to speak in front of people, volunteer and speak in class when the instructor gives you the opportunity. Take a speech class or join Toastmasters.

As with anything else in life, developing new skills takes time. Try not to be discouraged. For example, if you want to develop more positive, or less emotional, behavior, be patient; it will not happen overnight. If you catch yourself acting emotionally, be aware of it and change to more controlled behavior. With time and persistence, you will have to catch yourself less often.

Step 4: Get Feedback and Reward Yourself Being aware of people's nonverbal communication will give you feedback on your behavior, as will their intentional behavior toward you. However, others' direct feedback requested by you is often more accurate and unbiased. After trying new behavior, ask people you trust if they have noticed any difference. Get their advice on what you can do to improve. For example, if you are trying to be more positive and to give less negative feedback to others, ask them if they have

EXHIBIT A.1 | Changing Behavior Model

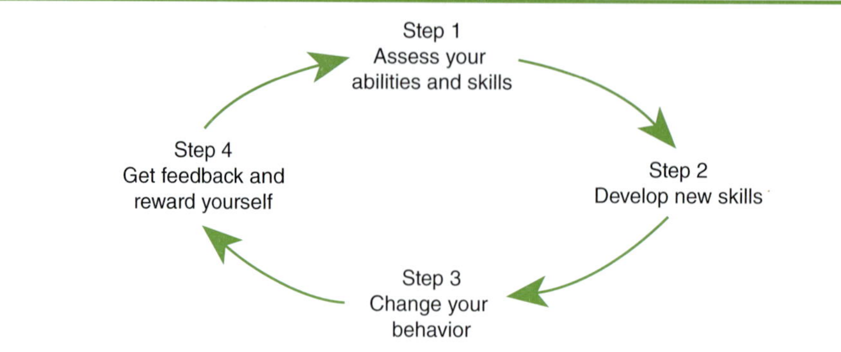

noticed any difference. Ask them to recall the last time they remember hearing you make a put-down statement. People are often willing to help you, especially when it benefits them.

You should also reward yourself for your efforts. Notice we said efforts, not total success. Build on small successes; take one step at a time. As the saying goes, "Success by the yard is hard . . . but a cinch by the inch." Your rewards do not have to be big or expensive; you can treat yourself to a snack, take a walk, or do anything you enjoy. For example, say you want to stop putting people down, and you catch yourself in the act. Stop yourself in the middle and end by complimenting the person. Focus on the success, not the failure. Reward yourself rather than be disappointed in yourself.

Exhibit A.1 illustrates these four steps.

My Human Relations Plan

Learning Outcome A-7

Develop your own human relations plan.

Follow the changing behavior model and develop a plan to change your behavior. Write in the space provided.

Step 1: Assess Your Abilities and Skills Select the one human relations area in most need of improvement. Use the information from step 1, question 4 on page 451. Write it below.

Step 2: Develop New Skills Review the material in the text that will help you develop the skill to improve your behavior. You may also talk to others for ideas, and go to the library to find articles and books on the skill. You can even look into taking a workshop or course on the subject. Below, write down some helpful notes on these skills.

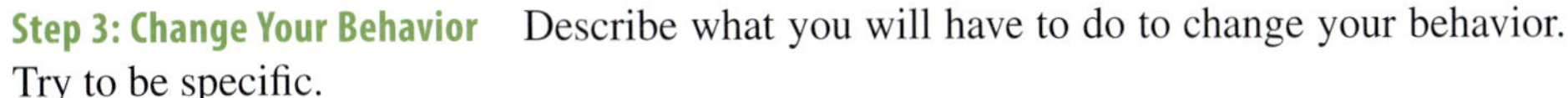

Step 3: Change Your Behavior Describe what you will have to do to change your behavior. Try to be specific.

Step 4: Get Feedback and Reward Yourself How will you get feedback on your changed behavior? How will you know if you have succeeded in changing your behavior? When will you reward yourself? How will you reward yourself?

Additional Plans If you feel you can handle working on more than one change in human relations, follow the changing behavior steps and develop another plan. However, don't try to make too many changes too quickly.

/ / / SKILL-BUILDING EXERCISE A-1 / / /

Human Relations Plan

In-Class Exercises
(Individual and Group)

Objectives: To share your human relations plan with others in order to get feedback on it.

AACSB: The primary AACSB learning standard skills developed through this exercise are reflective thinking and self-management, analytic skills, and communication abilities.

Preparation: You should have completed the human relations plan in the chapter.

Experience: This exercise is discussion-oriented.

Procedure 1 (5–15 minutes)
Break into groups of two to six persons and share your answers to the first four questions under step 1, assessing your abilities and skills. You may also look at and discuss each other's profiles, if you wish to do so. Share your human relations plans, offering each other positive feedback on your plans.

Conclusion: The instructor may lead a class discussion and/or make concluding remarks.

Application (2–4 minutes): What did I learn from this experience? How will I use this knowledge in the future?

Sharing: Volunteers give their answers to the application situation.

/ / / SKILL-BUILDING EXERCISE A-2 / / /

Course Learning

In-Class Exercise
(Individual and Group)

Objectives: To share your human relations abilities and skills developed through this course.

AACSB: The primary AACSB learning standard skills developed through this exercise are reflective thinking and self-management, analytic skills, and communication abilities.

Preparation: You should have answered the question, "What are the most important abilities and skills you developed and/or things you learned through this course?"

Experience: This exercise is discussion-oriented.

Procedure 1 (5–30 minutes)
Volunteers tell the class the most important abilities and skills developed and/or things they learned through this course.

Conclusion: The instructor may lead a class discussion and/or make concluding remarks.

A

accommodating conflict style Type of conflict management style in which the user attempts to resolve the conflict by passively giving in to the other party.

affirmative action (AA) programs Planned, special efforts to recruit, hire, and promote women and members of minority groups.

assertiveness The process of expressing throughts and feelings while asking for what one wants in an appropriate way.

attitude A strong belief or feeling toward people, things, and situations.

attribution A person's perception that the cause of behavior is either internal or external.

autocratic style (S-A) Supervisory style that involves high-directive–low-supportive (HD–LS) behavior and is appropriate when interacting with low-capability employees (C-1).

automation The simplification or reduction of human effort required to do a job.

avoiding conflict style Type of conflict management style in which the user attempts to passively ignore the conflict rather than resolve it.

B

bargaining Includes (1) developing rapport and focusing on obstacles, not on the person; (2) letting the other party make the first offer; (3) listening and asking questions to focus on meeting the other party's needs; (4) not being too quick to give in; and (5) asking for something in return.

behavior What people do and say.

behavioral leadership theories Theories that assume that there are distinctive styles that effective leaders use consistently; that is, that good leadership is rooted in behavior.

Big Five Model of Personality Model that categorizes traits into the dimensions of surgency, agreeableness, adjustment, conscientiousness, and openness to experience.

bona fide occupational qualification (BFOQ) Allows discrimination on the basis of religion, sex, or national origin where it is reasonably necessary to normal operation of a particular enterprise.

brainstorming The process of suggesting many alternatives, without evaluation, to solve a problem.

burnout The constant lack of interest and motivation to perform one's job because of stress.

business etiquette The code of behavior expected in work situations (often referred to as manners).

C

career development The process of gaining skill, experience, and education to achieve career objectives.

career path A sequence of job assignments that lead to more responsibility, with raises and promotions.

career planning The process of setting career objectives and determining how to accomplish them.

career planning model A model that includes these five steps: step (1) self-assessment; step (2) career preferences and exploration; step (3) set career objectives; step (4) develop a plan; and step (5) control.

coaching model Model that involves five steps: step (1) refer to past feedback; step (2) describe current perfromance; step (3) describe desired performance; step (4) get a commitment to the change; and step (5) follow up.

coalition A short-term network used to meet an objective.

coercive power Power that involves threats and/or punishments to influence compliance.

collaborating conflict style Type of conflict management style in which the user assertively attempts to resolve the conflict with the best solution agreeable to all parties.

communication process Consists of a sender who encodes a message and transmits it through a channel to a receiver who decodes it and may give feedback.

complaint model A model that involves four steps: step (1) listen to the complaint and paraphrase it; step (2) have the complainer recommend a solution; step (3) schedule time to get all the facts and/or make a decision; and step (4) develop and implement a plan, and follow up.

compromising conflict style Type of conflict management style in which the user attempts to resolve the conflict through assertive give-and-take concessions.

conflict Exists whenever two or more parties are in disagreement.

connection power Power based on the user's relationship with influential people.

consultative style (S-C) Supervisory style that involves high-directive–high-supportive (HD–HS) behavior and is appropriate when interacting with moderate-capability employees (C-2).

content motivation theories Theories that focus on identifying people's needs in order to understand what motivates them.

contingency leadership theories Theories that assume that the appropriate leadership style varies from situation to situation.

contingency leadership theory A theory developed by Fiedler used to determine if a person's leadership style is task- or relationship-oriented and if the situation matches the leader's style.

controlling stress plan Plan that includes step (1), identify stressors; step (2), determine their causes and consequences; and step (3), plan to eliminate or decrease the stress.

creativity The ability to develop unique alternatives to solve problems.

D

decision making The process of selecting an alternative course of action that will solve a problem.

decoding The receiver's process of translating the message into a meaningful form.

development The process of developing the ability to perform both present and future jobs.

disability Significant physical, mental, or emotional limitation.

discrimination Behavior for or against a person or situation.

distributive bargaining Negotiating over shares of a fixed pie; it creates a win–lose situation.

E

ego states Three states consisting of the parent, child, and adult.

Elton Mayo Called the "father of human relations"; he and his associates conducted research through the Hawthorne Studies from the mid-1920s to the early 1930s, known as the Hawthorne effect, that became a landmark in the human relations field. See also *Hawthorne effect*.

emotional labor Labor that requires the expression of feeling through desired behavior.

empathic listening The ability to understand and relate to another's situation and feelings.

encoding The sender's process of putting the message into a form that the receiver will understand.

equity theory A theory that is based on the comparison of perceived inputs and outputs; primarily Adams's motivation theory.

ethics The moral standards of right and wrong behavior.

expatriates People who live and work in a country other than their native country.

expectancy theory Vroom's theory that states that motivation depends on how much people want something and how likely they are to get it: Motivation = Expectancy × Valence.

expert power Power based on the user's skill and knowledge.

F

feedback The process of verifying messages.

force field analysis A technique that diagrams the current level of performance, the hindering forces against change, and the driving forces toward change.

forcing conflict style Type of conflict management style in which the user attempts to resolve the conflict by using aggressive behavior.

four-minute barrier The time people have to make a good impression (also called the four-minute sell).

G

giving praise Popularized by Blanchard and Johnson, the steps in giving praise are: step (1) tell the person exactly what was done correctly; step (2) tell the person why the behavior is important; step (3) stop for a moment of silence; and step (4) encourage repeat performance.

goal of human relations To create a win–win situation by satisfying employee needs while achieving organizational objectives.

grapevine The informal vehicle through which messages flow throughout the organization.

group behavior Things two or more people do and say as they interact.

group cohesiveness The attractiveness and closeness group members have for one another and for the group.

H

Hawthorne effect Refers to an increase in performance caused by the special attention given to employees, rather than tangible changes in the work. See also *Elton Mayo*.

horizontal communication The flow of information between colleagues and peers.

human relations (HR) Refers to interactions among people.

I

image Other people's attitudes toward an individual.

influencing process Process that begins with an objective; ethical leadership, power, politics, networking, and negotiating are used to motivate others to help reach the objective; and through trust and creating a win–win situation for all parties, the objective is met.

information power Power based on the user's information being desired by others.

initiating conflict resolution steps Three steps to follow when initiating a conflict resolution: step (1) plan to maintain ownership of the problem using the XYZ model; step (2) implement your plan persistently; and step (3) make an agreement for change.

integrative bargaining Negotiating to give everyone a good deal; it creates a win–win situation.

intelligence The level of an individual's capacity for new learning, problem solving, and decision making.

interpersonal skill The ability to work well with a diversity of people.

intrapersonal skills Skills that are within the individual and include characteristics such as personality, attitudes, self-concept, and integrity (also called self-management abilities).

J

job design The employee's system for transforming inputs into outputs.

job enrichment The process of building motivators into the job itself by making it more interesting and challenging; a means of getting job engagement.

job satisfaction A set of attitudes toward work.

job satisfaction survey A process of determining employee attitudes about the job and work environment.

job shock Occurs when the employee's expectations are not met.

job simplification The process of eliminating, combining, and/or changing the work sequence to increase performance.

L

laissez-faire style (S-L) Supervisory style that entails low-directive–low-supportive (LD–LS) behavior and is appropriate when interacting with outstanding employees (C-4).

leadership The process of influencing employees to work toward the achievement of objectives.

leadership continuum A continuum developed by Tannenbaum and Schmidt that identifies seven leadership styles based on the use of boss-centered versus employee-centered leadership.

Leadership Grid Blake and Mouton's model identifying the ideal leadership style as having a high concern for both production and people.

leadership skill The ability to influence others and work well in teams.

leadership trait theory Theory that assumes that there are distinctive physical and psychological characteristics accounting for leadership effectiveness.

legitimate power Power based on the user's position power, which is given by the organization.

levels of behavior Levels include individual, group, and organizational.

locus of control A continuum representing a person's belief as to whether external or internal forces control his or her destiny.

M

maintenance roles The things group members do and say to develop and sustain group dynamics.

management by objectives (MBO) The process in which managers and their employees jointly set objectives for the employees, periodically evaluate the performance, and reward according to the results.

management information systems (MIS) Formal systems for collecting, processing, and disseminating the information necessary to aid managers in decision making.

manifest needs theory Theory of motivation that is primarily McClelland's classification of needs as achievement, power, and affiliation.

mediating conflict resolution steps Four steps to follow when mediating a conflict resolution: step (1) have each party state his or her complaint using the XYZ model; step (2) agree on the problem(s); step (3) develop alternative solutions; and step (4) make an agreement for change, and follow up.

message The physical form of the encoded information.

minority Defined by the Equal Employment Opportunity Commission (EEOC) as Hispanics, Asians, African Americans, Native Americans, and Alaska Natives.

morale A state of mind based on employees' attitudes and satisfaction with the organization.

motivation The internal process leading to behavior to satisfy needs.

multinational company (MNC) A company that conducts a large part of its business outside the country of its headquarters.

N

needs hierarchy Maslow's theory of motivation, which is based on five needs: physiological, safety, social, esteem, and self-actualization.

negotiating A process in which two or more parties have something the other wants and attempt to come to an exchange agreement (also called bargaining).

negotiating planning Includes researching the other parties, setting objectives, anticipating questions and objections and preparing answers, and developing options and trade-offs.

negotiating process Process that has three, and possibly four, steps: (1) planning, (2) bargaining, (3) possibly a postponement, and (4) an agreement or no agreement.

networking The ongoing process of building relationships for the purpose of politicking and socializing.

networking interview process Process that includes these steps: step (1) establish rapport—praise and read the person; step (2) deliver the one-minute self-sell; step (3) ask prepared questions; step (4) get additional contacts for your network; step (5) ask your contacts how you might help them; and step (6) follow up with a thank-you note and status report.

networking process Process that includes these tasks: (1) perform a self-assessment and set objectives, (2) create a one-minute self-sell, (3) develop a network, (4) conduct networking interviews, and (5) maintain the network.

networks Clusters of people joined by a variety of links.

normative leadership theory A decision-tree model, developed by Vroom and Yetton, that enables the user to select from five leadership styles the one that is appropriate for the situation.

norms The group's shared expectations of its members' behavior.

O

objectives State what is to be accomplished within a given period of time.

one-minute self-sell An opening statement used in networking that quickly summarizes your history and career plan and asks a question.

open-door policy The practice of being available to employees.

organization A group of people working to achieve one or more objectives.

organizational behavior (OB) The collective behavior of an organization's individuals and groups.

organizational climate The relatively enduring quality of the internal environment of the organization as perceived by its members.

organizational communication The compounded interpersonal communication process across an organization.

organizational culture Consists of the shared values and assumptions of how its members will behave.

organizational development (OD) The ongoing planned process of change used as a means of improving the organization's effectiveness in solving problems and achieving its objectives.

organizational structure The way managers design their firm to achieve the organization's mission and goals.

P

paraphrasing The process of having the receiver restate the message in his or her own words.

participative style (S-P) Supervisory style that is characterized by low-directive–high-supportive (LD–HS) behavior and is appropriate when interacting with employees with high capability (C-3).

perception A person's interpretation of reality.

perceptual congruence The degree to which people see things the same way.

performance The extent to which expectations or objectives have been met.

performance appraisal The ongoing process of evaluating employee job performance.

performance formula The relationship between the three interdependent factors of ability, motivation, and resources, stated as: Performance = Ability × Motivation × Resources.

personality A relatively stable set of traits that aids in explaining and predicting individual behavior.

politics The process of gaining and using power.

power A person's ability to influence others to do something they would not otherwise do.

prejudice The prejudgment of a person or situation based on attitudes.

primacy effect The way people perceive one another during their first impressions.

priority The preference given to one activity over other activities.

priority determination questions Questions that ask (1) Do I need to be personally involved? (2) Is the task my responsibility or will it affect the performance or finances of my department? and (3) Is quick action needed?

problem Exists whenever there is a difference between what is actually happening and what the individual or group wants to be happening.

problem solving The process of taking corrective action in order to meet objectives.

process motivation theories Theories that attempt to understand how and why people are motivated.

Pygmalion effect States that supervisors' attitudes and expectations of employees and how they treat them largely determine their performance.

R

reciprocity Involves creating obligations and debts, developing alliances, and using them to accomplish objectives.

referent power Power based on the user's personal power.

reflecting statements Statements that paraphrase feelings back to the person.

reinforcement theory A theory that states that behavior can be controlled through the use of positive or negative consequences; primarily Skinner's motivation theory.

resistance to change Involves the variables of intensity, source, and focus, which together explain why people are reluctant to change.

responding to conflict resolution steps Four steps to follow when responding to a conflict resolution: step (1) listen to and paraphrase the problem using the XYZ model; step (2) agree with some aspect of the complaint; step (3) ask for, and/or give, alternative solutions; and step (4) make an agreement for change.

reward power Power based on the user's ability to influence others with something of value to them.

roles Shared expectations of how group members will fulfill the requirements of their position.

S

self-concept A person's overall attitude about himself or herself.

self-efficacy A person's belief in his or her capability to perform in a specific situation.

self-fulfilling prophecy Occurs when a person's expectations affect his or her success or failure.

self-interest roles The things group members do and say to meet their own needs or objectives at the expense of the team.

sexism Discrimination based on sex.

sexual harassment Any unwelcomed behavior of a sexual nature.

situational leadership A model, developed by Paul Hersey and Kenneth Blanchard, for selecting from four leadership styles the one that matches the employees' maturity level in a given situation.

stages in the creative process The four stages that include (1) preparation, (2) possible solutions, (3) incubation, and (4) evaluation.

standards Performance levels in the areas of quantity, quality, time, and cost.

status The perceived ranking of one member relative to other members of the group.

stereotyping The process of generalizing the behavior of all members of a group.

stress An emotional and/or physical reaction to environmental activities and events.

stressors Situations in which people feel anxiety, tension, and pressure.

survey feedback An organizational development (OD) technique that uses a questionnaire to gather data that are used as the basis for change.

systems effect When all people in the organization are affected by at least one other person, and each person affects the whole group or organization.

T

task roles The things group members do and say that directly aid in the accomplishment of its objective(s).

team building An organizational development (OD) technique designed to help work groups operate more effectively.

team dynamics Refers to the patterns of interactions that emerge as groups develop (these interactions are also called group process).

team performance model States that a team's performance is based on its structure, dynamics, and stage of development.

teamwork Involves working together to achieve something beyond the capabilities of individuals working alone.

Theory X Theory that holds that employees dislike work and must be closely supervised to get them to do their work.

Theory Y Theory that holds that employees like to work and do not need to be closely supervised to get them to do their work.

Theory Z Theory that integrates common business practices in the United States and Japan into one middle-ground framework appropriate for use in the United States.

time log A daily diary that tracks activities and enables a person to determine how time is used.

time management Techniques designed to enable people to get more done in less time with better results.

time management steps The steps include step (1) plan each week, step (2) schedule each week, and step (3) schedule each day.

to-do list The written list of activities the individual has to complete.

total person approach When an organization employs the whole person, not just his or her job skills.

training The process of developing the necessary skills to perform the present job.

transactional analysis (TA) A Method of understanding behavior in interpersonal dynamics.

trust The positive expectation that another will not take advantage of you.

two-factor theory Theory consisting of Herzberg's classification of needs as hygienes and motivators.

Type A personality The type of personality that is characterized as fast moving, hard driving, time conscious, competitive, impatient, and preoccupied with work.

types of changes Types of changes include technical change, structural change, task change, and people change.

types of transactions The three types include: complementary, crossed, and ulterior.

values The things that have worth for or are important to an individual.

value system The set of standards by which an individual lives.

vertical communication The flow of information both up and down the chain of command.

win–win situation Occurs when the organization and the employees get what they want.

XYZ model Model that describes a problem in terms of behavior, consequences, and feelings.

ENDNOTES

Chapter 1

1. Information about IBM taken from its Web sites (www.ibm.com) retrieved December 2, 2011. Olin Ready and Nancy Westwood are not actual IBM employees; the information is provided for illustrative purposes.
2. S.D. Sidle, "Personality Disorder and Dysfunctional Employee Behavior," *Academy of Management Perspectives* 25(2) (2011): 76–77.
3. H. Liao, D. Liu, and R. Loi, "Looking at Both Sides of the Social Exchange Coin: A Social Cognitive Perspective on the Joint Effects of Relationship Quality and Differentiation on Creativity," *Academy of Management Journal* 53(5) (2010): 1090–1109.
4. J.D. Hover, R.C. Giambatista, R.L. Sorenson, and W.H. Bommer, "Assessing the Effectiveness of Whole Person Learning Pedagogy in Skill Acquisition," *Academy of Management Learning & Education* 9(2) (2010): 192–203.
5. S. Lindenberg and N.J. Foss, "Managing Joint Production Motivation: The Role of Goal Framing and Governance Mechanisms," *Academy of Management Review* 36(3) (2011): 500–525.
6. K. Pajo, A. Coetzer, and N. Guenole, "Formal Development Opportunities and Withdrawal Behaviors by Employees in Small and Medium-Sized Enterprises," *Journal of Small Business Management* 48(3): 281–301.
7. K.W. Phillips, N.P. Rothbard, and T.L. Dumas, "To Disclose or Not to Disclose," Status Distance and Self-Disclosure in Diverse Environments," *Academy of Management Review* 34(4) (209): 710–732.
8. M. Korn and J. Light, "On the Lesson Plan: Feelings," The *Wall Street Journal* (May 5, 2011): B6.
9. Liao et al., "Looking at Both Sides of the Social Exchange Coin."
10. "Call for Paper—Teaching Leadership," *Academy of Management Journal* 53(4) (2010): 922.
11. Liao et al., "Looking at Both Sides of the Social Exchange Coin."
12. S.D. Sidle, "Personality Disorder and Dysfunctional Employee Behavior."
13. H. Ren, "Repairing Relationship Conflict: How Violation Types and Culture Influence the Effectiveness of Restoration Rituals," *Academy of Management Review* 34(1) (209): 105–126.
14. Hover et al., "Assessing the Effectiveness of Whole Person Learning Pedagogy in Skill Acquisition."
15. Lindenberg and Foss, "Managing Joint Production Motivation."
16. N. Karelaia, "Predictably Irrational: The Hidden Forces That Shape Our Decisions," *Academy of Management Perspectives* 23(1) (2009): 86–88.
17. M. Haynie and D.A. Sheperd, "A Measure of Adaptive Cognition for Entrepreneurship Research," *Entrepreneurship Theory and Practice* 33(3) (2009): 695–714.
18. Ren, "Repairing Relationship Conflict."
19. Sidle, "Personality Disorder and Dysfunctional Employee Behavior."
20. Phillips et al., "To Disclose or Not to Disclose."
21. S.D. Charlier, K.G. Brown, and S.L. Rynes, "Teaching Evidence-Based Management in MBA Programs: What Evidence Is There?" *Academy of Management Learning & Education* 10(2) (2011): 222–236.
22. F.W. Taylor, *Principles of Scientific Management* (New York: Harper & Brothers, 1911).
23. L. Frankel and A. Fleisher, *The Human Factor in Industry* (New York: Macmillan, 1920): 8.
24. F. Roethlisberger and W. Dickson, *Management and the Worker* (Boston: Harvard University Press, 1939): 15–86.
25. D. McGregor, *The Human Side of Enterprise* (New York: McGraw-Hill, 1960).
26. W. Ouchi, *Theory Z—How American Business Can Meet the Japanese Challenge* (Reading, MA: Addison-Wesley, 1981).
27. T. Peters and R. Waterman, *In Search of Excellence: Lessons from America's Best Run Companies* (New York: Harper & Row, 1982).
28. N.M. Pless, T. Maak, and G.K. Stahl, "Developing Responsible Global Leaders Through International Service-Learning Programs: The Ulysses Experience," *Academy of Management Learning & Education* 10(2) (2011): 237–260.
29. M.J. Chen and D. Miller, "The Relational Perspective as a Business Mindset: Managerial Implications for East and West," *Academy of Management Perspectives* 25(3) (2011): 6–18.
30. H.C. Lin and S.T. Hou, "Managerial Lessons from the East: An Interview with Acer's Stan Shih," *Academy of Management Perspectives* 24(4) (2010): 6–16.
31. Y. Mishina, B.J. Dykes, E.S. Block, and T.G. Pollock, "Why Good Firms Do Bad Things: The Effects of High Aspirations, High Expectations, and Prominence on the Incidence of Corporate Illegality," *Academy of Management Journal* 53(4) (2010): 701–722.
32. M. Kimes, "How Do I Keep My Company's Reputation Intact When Our Industry Has Been Tainted by Bad News?" *Fortune* (March 16, 2009): 30.
33. "Call for Paper—Teaching Leadership," *Academy of Management Journal* 33(4) (2010): 922; L.A. Burke and B. Rau, "The Research-Teaching Gap," *Academy of Management Learning & Education* 9(1) (2010): 132–143; P. Shrivastava, "Pedagogy of Passion for Sustainability," *Academy of Management Learning & Education* 9(3) (2010): 443–455; Charlier et al., "Teaching Evidence-Based Management in MBA Programs."
34. Quote from Johann Wolfgang van Goethe.
35. M. Port, "The Likability Factor," *Entrepreneur* (March 2010): 32.
36. J.Z. Bergman, J.W. Westerman, and J.P. Daly, "Narcissim in Management Education," *Academy of Management Learning & Education* 9(1) (2010): 119–131.
37. Lin and Hou, "Managerial Lessons from the East."
38. Port, "The Likability Factor."
39. Lin and Hou, "Managerial Lessons from the East."
40. Ren, "Repairing Relationship Conflict."
41. B. Bernstein, "I'm Very, Very, Very Sorry . . . Really?" *The Wall Street Journal* (October 19, 2010): D1–D2.
42. Ren, "Repairing Relationship Conflict."
43. Bergman et al., "Narcissism in Management Education."
44. T. Sitzmann, K. Ely, K.G. Brown, and K.N. Bauer, "Self-Assessment of Knowledge: A Cognitive Learning or Affective Measure?" *Academy of Management Learning & Education* 9(2) (2010): 169–191.
45. B. George, "A New Kind of Group Therapy," *Fortune* (November 21, 2011): 45.
46. Charlier et al., "Teaching Evidence-Based Management in MBA Programs."
47. Quote from Brian Tracy.
48. Retrieved December 3, 2011; from www.aacsb.edu.
49. R.B. Kaiser and R.B. Kaplan, "The Deeper Work of Executive Development: Outgrowing Sensitivities," *Academy of Management Learning & Education* 5(4) (2006): 463–483.
50. "Call for Paper—Teaching Leadership."
51. George, "A New Kind of Group Therapy."
52. Information taken from the W.L. Gore & Associates Web site: www.gore.com, retrieved May 2011.
53. G. Hamel, "W. L. Gore: Lessons from a Management Revolutionary," *The Wall Street Journal,* March 18, 2010; G. Hamel, "W.L.

Gore: Lessons from a Management Revolutionary," Part 2, *The Wall Street Journal*, April 2, 2010.

Chapter 2

1. Information pertaining to PepsiCo is taken from its Web site, (*www.pepsico.com*), retrieved December 5, 2011. June Peterson and Rod Wills are not employees of PepsiCo; the information is provided for illustrative purposes.
2. S.D. Sidle, "Personality Disorder and Dysfunctional Employee Behavior," *Academy of Management Perspectives* 25(2) (2011): 76–77.
3. S. Nadkarni and P. Herrmann, "CEO Personality, Strategic Flexibility, and Firm Performance: The Case of the Indian Business Process Outsourcing Industry," *Academy of Management Journal* 53(5) (2010): 1050–1073.
4. American Psychological Association (APA), *www.apa.or/helpcenter/job-stress.aspx*, retrieved December 5, 2011.
5. S.S. Culbertson, "Absenteeism: Escaping an Aversive Workplace or Responding to Resulting Illness?" *Academy of Management Perspectives* 23(1) (2009): 77–79.
6. D. Lindebaum, "Rhetoric or Remedy? A Critique on Developing Emotional Intelligence," *Academy of Management Learning & Education* 8(2) (2009): 225–237.
7. K.A. Jenh, S. Rispens, and S.M.B. Thatcher, "The Effects of Conflict Asymmetry on Work Group and Individual Outcomes," *Academy of Management Journal* 53(3) (2010): 596–616.
8. N. Karelaia, "Predictably Irrational: The Hidden Forces That Shape Our Decisions," *Academy of Management Perspectives* 23(1) (2009): 86–88.
9. R.B. Kaiser and R.B. Kaplan, "The Deeper Work of Executive Development: Outgrowing Sensitivities," *Academy of Management Learning & Education* 5(4) (2006): 463–483.
10. Nadkarni and Herrmann, "CEO Personality, Strategic Flexibility, and Firm Performance."
11. M. Brettel, A. Engelen, and L. Voll, "Letting Go to Grow—Empirical Findings on a Hearsay," *Journal of Small Business Management* 48(4): 552–579.
12. Nadkarni and Herrmann, "CEO Personality, Strategic Flexibility, and Firm Performance."
13. B. Urstadt, "The Sociopath Network," *Bloomberg Businessweek* (July 25–31, 2011). 82–83.
14. B. Schlender, "Steve and Me," *Fortune* (November 7, 2011): 115–123
15. W. Isaacson, "Steve Jobs: The Biography—His Rivalry with Bill Gates," *Fortune* (November 7, 2011): 97–112.
16. J.Z. Bergman, J.W. Westerman, and J.P. Daly, "Narcissism in Management Education," *Academy of Management Learning & Education* 9(1) (2010): 119–131.
17. Nadkarni and Herrmann, "CEO Personality, Strategic Flexibility, and Firm Performance."
18. Myers & Briggs Web site, *www.myersbriggs.org*, retrieved December 5, 2011.
19. American Psychological Association (APA), *www.apa.org/helpcenter/job-stress.aspx*, retrieved December 5, 2011.
20. Ibid.
21. M. Roizen and M. Oz, "Longevity & Wellness," *The Wall Street Journal* (April 15, 2009): D5–D6.
22. S.S. Culbertson, "Absenteeism: Escaping an Aversive Workplace or Responding to Resulting Illness?" *Academy of Management Perspectives* 23(1) (2009): 77–79.
23. APA, *www.apa.org/helpcenter/job-stress.aspx*.
24. Roizen and Oz, "Longevity & Wellness."
25. B. Reagan, "Perks with a Payoff," *The Wall Street Journal* (October 24, 2011): R3.
26. G. Cora, "Managing Work with L.O.V.E.," *Costco Connection* (February 2011): 55.
27. A. Lukits, "Feeling Groggy? Your Brain May Be Half Asleep," *The Wall Street Journal* (May 31, 2011): D4.
28. W. Amos, "Testing Positive," *Costco Connection* (April 2011): 13.
29. E. Bernstein, "Misery Poker: It's One Game Worth Losing," *The Wall Street Journal* (June 16, 2009): D1.
30. "Exercise, Quitting Smoking," *The Wall Street Journal* (January 8, 2008): A1.
31. J.C. Dencker, "Outliners: The Story of Success," *Academy of Management Perspectives* 24(3) (2010): 97–99.
32. D.B. McNatt, "Negative Reputation and Biased Student Evaluations of Teaching: Longitudinal Results from a Naturally Occurring Experiment," *Academy of Management Education & Learning* 9(2) (2010): 225–242.
33. F. Walter, M.S. Cole, and R.H. Humphrey, "Emotional Intelligence: Sine Qua Non of Leadership or Folderol?" *Academy of Management Perspectives* 25(1) (2011): 45–59.
34. D. Lindebaum, "Rhetoric or Remedy? A Critique on Developing Emotional Intelligence," *Academy of Management Learning & Education* 8(2) (2009): 225–237.
35. B. George, "A New Kind of Group Therapy," *Fortune* (November 21, 2011): 45
36. D. Holtbrugge and A.T. Mohr, "Cultural Determinants of Learning Style Preferences," *Academy of Management Learning & Education* 9(4) (2009): 622–637.
37. S. Benn and A. Martin, "Learning and Change for Sustainability Reconsidered: A Role for Boundary Objects," *Academy of Management Learning & Education* 9(3) (2010): 397–412.
38. G. Colvin, "What Really Has the 99% Up in Arms?" *Fortune* (November 7, 2011): 87.
39. Jenh et al., "The Effects of Conflict Asymmetry on Work Group and Individual Outcomes."
40. V.K. Gupta, D.B. Turban, S.A. Wasti, and A. Sikdar, "The Role of Gender Stereotypes in Perceptions of Entrepreneurs and Intentions to Become an Entrepreneur," *Entrepreneurship Theory & Practice* 33(2) (2009): 397–417.
41. J.M. Hoobler, S.J. Wayne, and G. Lemmon, "Bosses' Perceptions of Family–Work Conflict and Women's Promotability: Glass Ceiling Effects," *Academy of Management Journal* 52(3) (2009): 939–957.
42. McNatt, "Negative Reputation and Biased Student Evaluations of Teaching."
43. Ibid.
44. Jenh et al., "The Effects of Conflict Asymmetry on Work Group and Individual Outcomes."
45. K. Pajo, A. Coetzer, and N. Guenole, "Formal Development Opportunities and Withdrawal Behaviors by Employees in Small and Medium-Sized Enterprises," *Journal of Small Business Management* 48(3): 281–301.
46. E. Abrams, "The Power of the First Impression," *Wall Street Journal* (May 9–10, 200): W1.
47. Ibid.
48. Karelaia, "Predictably Irrational."
49. "You Lost Me at Hello," *Entrepreneur* (February 2009): 59.
50. H.R. Bowles and F. Flynn, "Gender and Persistence in Negotiation: A Dyadic Perspective," *Academy of Management Journal* 53(4) (2010): 769–787.
51. www.nba.com/mavericks/news/cuban_bio000329.html.
52. www.dmagazine.com/Home/D_CEO/2011/December/CEO_of_the_Year_Mark_Cuban.aspx.
53. *www.forbes.com/profile/mark-cuban/*.

Chapter 3

1. Information on the Red Cross taken from its Web site, www.redcross.org, retrieved December 9, 2011. Rayanne and Kent are not Red Cross employees; the information is provided for illustrative purposes.

2. W. Amos, "Testing Positive," *Costco Connection* (April 2011): 13.

3. P. Chattopadhyay, C. Finn, and N.M. Ashkansy, "Affective Responses to Professional Dissimilarity: A Matter of Status," *Academy of Management Journal* 53(4) (2010): 808–826.

4. S.S. Culbertson, "Do Satisfied Employees Mean Satisfied Customers?" *Academy of Management Perspectives* 23(1) (2009): 76–77.

5. T.A. Judge and J.D.K. Mueller, "Happiness as a Societal Value," *Academy of Management Perspectives* 25(1) (2011): 30–41.

6. K. Pajo, A. Coetzer, and N. Guenole, "Formal Development Opportunities and Withdrawal Behaviors by Employees in Small and Medium-Sized Enterprises," *Journal of Small Business Management* 48(3): 281–301.

7. Culbertson, "Do Satisfied Employees Mean Satisfied Customers?"

8. D. Cooper and S.M.B. Thatcher, "Identification in Organizations: The Role of Self-Concept Orientations and Identification Motives," *Academy of Management Perspectives* 23(1) (2009): 76–77.

9. J. Lehrer, "The Power Trip," *The Wall Street Journal* (August 14–15, 2010): W1–W2.

10. S.D. Sidle, "Personality Disorder and Dysfunctional Employee Behavior," *Academy of Management Perspectives* 25(2) (2011): 76–77.

11. Chattopadhyay et al., "Affective Responses to Professional Dissimilarity."

12. F.J. Flynn and S.S. Wiltermuth, "Who's with Me? False Consensus Brokerage, and Ethical Decision Making in Organizations," *Academy of Management Journal* 53(5) (2010): 1074–1089.

13. Culbertson, "Do Satisfied Employees Mean Satisfied Customers?"

14. D. McGregor, *The Human Side of Enterprise* (New York: McGraw-Hill, 1960).

15. H.C. Lin and S.T. Hou, "Managerial Lessons from the East: An Interview with Acer's Stan Shih," *Academy of Management Perspectives* 24(4) (2010): 6–16.

16. M. Brettel, A. Engelen, and L. Voll, "Letting Go to Grow—Empirical Findings on a Hearsay," *Journal of Small Business Management* 48(4): 552–579.

17. Chattopadhyay et al., "Affective Responses to Professional Dissimilarity."

18. Amos, "Testing Positive."

19. Ibid.

20. Ibid.

21. B. Farber, "Putting Ideas into Action," *Entrepreneur* (February 2009): 62.

22. Quote from Wayne Dyer.

23. J.E. Dutton, L.M. Roberts, and J. Bednar, "Pathways for Positive Identity Construction at Work: Four Types of Positive Identity and the Building of Social Resources," *Academy of Management Review* 35(2) (2010): 265–293.

24. S.S. Wang, "Is Happiness Overrated?" *The Wall Street Journal* (March 15, 2011): D1, D6.

25. Culbertson, "Do Satisfied Employees Mean Satisfied Customers?"

26. Judge and Mueller, "Happiness as a Societal Value."

27. J. Light, "Unhappy Workers Stay in Current Jobs, for Now," *The Wall Street Journal* (June 20, 2011): B7.

28. "Grateful to Be Employed, Bored Half to Death," *Bloomberg Businessweek* (June 20–26, 2011): 35–36.

29. Wang, "Is Happiness Overrated?"

30. "Grateful to Be Employed, Bored Half to Death."

31. N.M. Ashkanasy, "International Happiness: A Multilevel Perspective," *Academy of Management Perspectives* 25(1) (2011): 23–29.

32. "What Matters Most," *Fortune* (August 16, 2010): 54.

33. D.B. Montgomery and C.A. Ramus, "Calibrating MBA Job Preferences for the 21st Century," *Academy of Management Learning & Education* 10(1) (2011): 9–26.

34. What Matters Most."

35. Culbertson, "Do Satisfied Employees Mean Satisfied Customers?"

36. Judge and Mueller, "Happiness as a Societal Value."

37. Ashkanasy, "International Happiness: A Multilevel Perspective."

38. N. Bozionelos, "What Accounts for Job Satisfaction Differences across Countries?" *Academy of Management Perspectives* 24(1) (2010): 82–84.

39. Brettel et al., "Letting Go to Grow."

40. S.M. Farmer, X. Yao, and K.K. McIntyre, "The Behavioral Impact of Entrepreneur Identity Aspiration and Prior Entrepreneurial Experience," *Entrepreneurship Theory and Practice* 35(2) (2011): 245–273.

41. Dutton et al., "Pathways for Positive Identity Construction at Work."

42. B.J. Hoffman, B.H. Bynum, R.F. Piccolo, and A.W. Sutton, "Person-Organization Value Congruence: How Transformational Leaders Influence Work Group Effectiveness," *Academy of Management Journal* 54(4) (2011): 779–796.

43. J.E. McGee, M. Peterson, S.L. Mueller, and J.M. Sequeira, "Entrepreneurial Self-Efficacy: Refining the Measure," *Entrepreneurship Theory and Practice* 33(4) (2009): 965–988.

44. W.S. Weyhrauch, "Psychological Strength Training: Can It Help Employees Enhance Their Well-Being? *Academy of Management Perspectives* 24(2) (2010): 82–83.

45. Cooper and Thatcher, "Identification in Organizations."

46. J. Li and Y. Tang, "CEO Hubris and Firm Risk Taking in China: The Moderating Role of Managerial Discretion," *Academy of Management Journal* 53(1) (2010): 45–68.

47. M. Wang, H. Liao, Y. Zhan, and J. Shi, "Daily Customer Mistreatment and Employee Sabotage against Customers: Examining Emotion and Resource Perspectives," *Academy of Management Journal* 54(2) (2011): 312–334.

48. Farber, "Putting Ideas into Action."

49. Quote from Wayne Dyer.

50. M. Beck, "Silence the Voice That Says You're a Fraud," *The Wall Street Journal* (June 16, 2009): D1–D2.

51. D. Lindebaum, "Rhetoric or Remedy? A Critique on Developing Emotional Intelligence," *Academy of Management Learning & Education* 8(2) (2009): 225–237.

52. J. Lok, "Institutional Logics as Identity Projects," *Academy of Management Journal* 53(6) (2010): 1305–1335.

53. G. Cora, "Managing Work with L.O.V.E." *Costco Connection* (February 2011): 55.

54. M. Beck, "Thank You. No, Thank You," *The Wall Street Journal* (November 23, 2010): D1, D4.

55. T. Petzinger, "Talking about Tomorrow: Edward O. Wilson," *The Wall Street Journal* (January 1, 2000): R16.

56. Judi Neal, personal contact, December 10, 2011.

57. "Majority of Americans Pray, So Says Study," *AFA Journal* (February 2009): 8.

58. V. Tonoyan, R. Strohmeyer, M. Habib, and M. Perlitz, "Correction and Entrepreneurship: How Formal and Informal Institutions Shape Small Firm Behavior in Transition and Mature Market Economies," *Entrepreneurship Theory and Practice* 34(5) (2009): 803–831.

59. V.C. Edmondson, "Ethical Leadership: The Quest for Character, Civility, and Community," *Academy of Management Learning & Education* 9(2) (2010): 360–361.

60. J.R. Detert and A.C. Edmondson, "Implicit Voice: Theories: Taken-for-Granted Rules of Self-Censorship at Work," *Academy of Management Journal* 54(3) (2011): 461–488.

61. J. Lehrer, "The Power Trip," *The Wall Street Journal* (August 14–15, 2010): W1–W2.

62. R. Hurley, "Trust Me," *The Wall Street Journal* (October 24, 2011), R4.

63. "Keeping America Great," *CNBC* (aired October 16, 2009)

64. Sidle, "Personality Disorder and Dysfunctional Employee Behavior."

65. Lehrer, "The Power Trip."

66. Sidle, "Personality Disorder and Dysfunctional Employee Behavior."

67. Flynn and Wiltermuth, "Who's with Me?"
68. R. Pinheiro, "SuperFreakonomics: Global Cooling, Patriotic Prostitutes, and Why Suicide Bombers Should Buy Life Insurance," *Academy of Management Perspectives* 25(2) (2011): 86–87.
69. A. Tilcsik, "From Ritual to Reality: Demography, Ideology, and Decoupling in a Post-Communist Government Agency," *Academy of Management Journal* 53(6) (2010): 1474–1498.
70. Hurley, "Trust Me."
71. N. Karelaia, "Predictably Irrational: The Hidden Forces That Shape Our Decisions," *Academy of Management Perspectives* 23(1) (2009): 86–88.
72. Tonoyan et al., "Correction and Entrepreneurship."
73. Tilcsik, "From Ritual to Reality."
74. Tonoyan et al., "Correction and Entrepreneurship."
75. P. Schreck, "Reviewing the Business Case for Corporate Social Responsibility: New Evidence and Analysis," *Journal of Business Ethics* 103(2) (2011): 167–188.
76. Coca-Cola Web site, www.coca-cola.com, retrieved December 12, 2011.
77. Ibid.
78. Ibid.
79. Ibid.
80. Ibid.

Chapter 4

1. S. Shellenbarger, "Pressed for Time? Blame That Raise," *The Wall Street Journal* (February 22, 2011): D5.
2. J.F. Coget, "Technophobe vs. Techno-Enthusiast: Does the Internet Help or Hinder the Balance Between Work and Home Life?" *Academy of Management Perspectives* 25(1) (2009): 95–96.
3. G. Cora, "Managing Work with L.O.V.E.," *Costco Connection* (February 2011): 55.
4. G. Moran, "How to Clean Up Your Business," *Entrepreneur* (May 2011): 77–78.
5. W. Amos, "Do It Now," *Costco Connection* (June 2011): 11.
6. C. Binkley, "Cracking the Hedge-Fund Dress Code for Women," *The Wall Street Journal* (April 2009): D6.
7. M. Brzezinski, "How to Get a Raise," *Bloomberg Businessweek* (September 22, 2011): 101.
8. D. Brady, "Carol Bartz," *Bloomberg Businessweek* (August 16–29, 2010): 100.
9. B. Kowitt, "L. Hudson Tips for Climbing the Corporate Ladder," *Fortune* (March 21, 2011): 42.
10. Shellenbarger, "Pressed for Time? Blame That Raise."
11. J. Robinson, "E-mail Is Making You Stupid," *Entrepreneur* (March 2010): 61–63.
12. C. Brogan, "Watch Out for Holes," *Entrepreneur* (August 2011): 70.
13. R. Baumeister, "Concentrate," *Bloomberg Businessweek* (September 26–October 2, 2011): 81.
14. Moran, "How to Clean Up Your Business."
15. Robinson, "E-mail Is Making You Stupid."
16. Baumeister, "Concentrate."
17. Robinson, "E-mail Is Making You Stupid."
18. V. Harnish, "Five Ways to Get Your Strategy Right," *Fortune* (April 11, 2011): 42.
19. "Steve Jobs: The Biography—His Rivalry with Bill Gates," *Fortune* (November 7, 2011): 97–112.
20. L. Gallagher, "How I Managed My Time—the Covey Way," *Fortune* (March 21, 2011): 39–40.
21. W. Tsai, K.H. Su, and M.J. Chen, "Seeing Through the Eyes of a Rival: Competitor Acumen Based on Rival-Centric Perceptions," *Academy of Management Journal* 54(4) (2011): 761–778.
22. These questions are adapted from Harbridge House training materials (Boston), which was acquired by Coopers & Lybrand in 2007.
23. V. Elmer, "The Invisible Promotion," *Fortune* (February 7, 2011): 31–32.
24. S. Mohammed and S. Nadkarni, "Temporal Diversity and Team Performance: The Moderating Role of Team Temporal Leadership," *Academy of Management Journal* 54(3) (2011): 489–508.
25. B. Farber, "Putting Ideas into Action," *Entrepreneur* (February 2009): 62.
26. Robinson, "E-mail Is Making You Stupid."
27. J. Robinson, "Time Urgency," *Entrepreneur* (November 2010): 75–76.
28. Cora, "Managing Work with L.O.V.E."
29. Moran, "How to Clean Up Your Business."
30. Gallagher, "How I Managed My Time—the Covey Way."
31. Robinson, "Time Urgency."
32. F. Hesselbein, "Learning from Drucker, and the Scouts Too," *Fortune* (November 21, 2011): 41–42.
33. Amos, "Do It Now."
34. Brogan, "Watch Out for Holes."
35. M. Crouch, "Get Hired, Not Fired," *Readers Digest* (April 2011): 130–139.
36. J.Z. Bergman, J.W. Westerman, and J.P. Daly, "Narcissism in Management Education," *Academy of Management Learning & Education* 9(1) (2010): 119–131.
37. Brady, "Carol Bartz."
38. J. McGregor, "How to Make a Smart Lateral Move," *Fortune* (October 17, 2011): 55–56.
39. S.D. Sidle, "Career Track or Mommy Track: How Do Women Decide?" *Academy of Management Perspectives* 25(2) (2011): 77–79.
40. Elmer, "The Invisible Promotion."
41. Crouch, "Get Hired, Not Fired."
42. M.J. Bidwell and F. Briscoe, "Who Contracts? Determinants of the Decision to Work as an Independent Contractor Among Information Technology Workers," *Academy of Management Journal* 52(6) (2011): 1148–1168.
43. B. Farber, "Good Connections," *Entrepreneur* (January 2009): 60.
44. B. Byham, "Ace the Interview," *Fortune* (September 27, 2010): 46.
45. Crouch, "Get Hired, Not Fired."
46. V. Elmer, "How Storytelling Spurs Success," *Fortune* (December 6, 2010): 75–76.
47. McGregor, "How to Make a Smart Lateral Move."
48. R. Barnett, "I Deserve a Raise. Do I Dare Ask for One?" *Fortune* (July 5, 2010): 36.
49. Ibid.
50. Elmer, "The Invisible Promotion."
51. Brzezinski, "How to Get a Raise."
52. D.B. Montgomery and C.A. Ramus, "Calibrating MBA Job Preferences for the 21st Century," *Academy of Management Learning & Education* 10(1) (2011): 9–26.
53. P. Dappelli, "Why Companies Aren't Getting the Employees They Need," *The Wall Street Journal* (October 24, 2011): R1.
54. E. Berton, "Dress to Impress, UBS Tells Its Staff," *The Wall Street Journal* (December 15, 2010): C1.
55. Binkley, "Cracking the Hedge-Fund Dress Code for Women."
56. E. Spitzbagel, "The Tragic Decline of Business Casual," *Bloomberg Businessweek* (October 11–17, 2010): 94–95.
57. T. Wayne, "Etiquette School for Dummies," *Bloomberg Businessweek* (October 18–24, 2010): 89–91.
58. Berton, "Dress to Impress, UBS Tells Its Staff."
59. Wayne, "Etiquette School for Dummies."
60. Spitzbagel, "The Tragic Decline of Business Casual."
61. Berton, "Dress to Impress, UBS Tells Its Staff."
62. Spitzbagel, "The Tragic Decline of Business Casual."
63. Berton, "Dress to Impress, UBS Tells Its Staff."
64. Binkley, "Cracking the Hedge-Fund Dress Code for Women."
65. Spitzbagel, "The Tragic Decline of Business Casual."
66. Berton, "Dress to Impress, UBS Tells Its Staff."

67. http://en.wikipedia.org/wiki/Billboard_200.
68. http://en.wikipedia.org/wiki/Billboard_Hot_100.
69. www.reuters.com/article/2009/07/20/us-jayz-idUSTRE56J06220090720.
70. http://en.wikipedia.org/wiki/Roc-A-Fella_Records.

Chapter 5

1. Information pertaining to Ford taken from its Web site (www.ford.com), retrieved January 2, 2012. Janet Low is not an actual employee, the information is provided for illustrative purposes.
2. J.R. Detert and A.C. Edmondson, "Implicit Voice: Theories Taken-For-Granted Rules of Self-Censorship at Work," *Academy of Management Journal* 54(3) (2011): 461–488.
3. J.D. Hover, R.C. Giambatista, R.L. Sorenson, and W.H. Bommer, "Assessing the Effectiveness of Whole Person Learning Pedagogy in Skill Acquisition," *Academy of Management Learning & Education* 9(2) (2010): 192–203.
4. AACSB Web site (www.aacsb.edu), retrieved December 22, 2011.
5. K. Pajo, A. Coetzer, and N. Guenole, "Formal Development Opportunities and Withdrawal Behaviors by Employees in Small and Medium-Sized Enterprises," *Journal of Small Business Management* 48(3): 281–301.
6. A.M. Zhang, "How Does Vivid Language Shape Investor Judgments?" *Academy of Management Perspectives* 25(3) (2011): 75–76.
7. M. Krzyzewski, "Coach K on How to Connect," *The Wall Street Journal* (July 16–17, 2011): C12.
8. M. Wang, H. Liao, Y. Zhan, and J. Shi, "Daily Customer Mistreatment and Employee Sabotage against Customers: Examining Emotion and Resource Perspectives," *Academy of Management Journal* 54(2) (2011): 312–334.
9. R. Greenwood and D. Miller, "Tackling Design Anew: Getting Back to the Heart of Organizational Theory," *Academy of Management Perspectives* 25(4) (2011): 78–84.
10. F. Rojas, "Power through Institutional Work: Acquiring Academic Authority in the 1968 Third World Strike," *Academy of Management Journal* 53(6) (2010): 1263–1280.
11. J.L. Ray, L.T. Baker, and D.S. Plowman, "Organizational Mindfulness in Business Schools," *Academy of Management Learning & Education* 10(2) (2011): 188–203.
12. D. Brady, "Carol Bartz," *Bloomberg Businessweek* (August 16–29, 2010): 100.
13. M. Baer, R.T.A.J. Leenders, G.R. Oldham, and A.K. Vandera, "Win or Lose the Battle for Creativity: The Power and Perils of Intergroup Competition," *Academy of Management Journal* 53(4) (2010): 827–845.
14. Hover et al., "Assessing the Effectiveness of Whole Person Learning Pedagogy in Skill Acquisition."
15. J.A. Martin and K.M. Eisenhardt, "Rewiring: Cross-Business-Unit Collaborations in Multibusiness Organizations," *Academy of Management Journal* 53(2) (2010): 265–301.
16. Detert and Edmondson, "Implicit Voice: Theories."
17. A. Hwang and A. M. Francesco, "The Influence of Individualism—Collectivism and Power Distance on Use of Feedback Channels and Consequences for Learning," *Academy of Management Learning & Education* 9(2) (2010): 243–257.
18. AACSB Web site (www.aacsb.edu), retrieved December 26, 2011.
19. J.W. (no last name given), "CYA: The Download," *Entrepreneur* (November 2010): 26.
20. S. Cendrowski, "Bytes Beat Bricks," *Fortune* (July 4, 2011): 13.
21. M.V. Copeland, "The iPad Changes Everything," *Fortune* (March 22, 2010): 150–153.
22. "Making the Right Connections," *Forbes* (November 7, 2011): 67.
23. N. Wingfield, "Why It May be Time to Leave the Laptop Behind," *The Wall Street Journal* (October 27, 2008): R1, R3.
24. ComScore, "107 Percent," *Entrepreneur* (July 2009): 44.
25. B.J. Fogg, "Ten New Gurus You Should Know," *Fortune* (November 24, 2008): 153.
26. D. MacMillan and J. Galante, "As Mobile Shopping Takes Off, eBay Is an Early Winner," *Bloomberg Businessweek* (June 28–July 4, 2010): 27–28.
27. E. Glazer, "Problems—and Solutions," The *Wall Street Journal* (October 24, 2011): R2.
28. J. Hempel, "How Facebook Is Taking Over Our Lives," *Fortune* (March 11, 2009): 49–56.
29. A. Vance, "The Power of the Cloud," *Bloomberg Businessweek* (March 7–13, 2011): 53–59.
30. R. Cheng, "Cloud Computing: What Exactly Is It Anyway?" *The Wall Street Journal* (February 8, 2010): R2.
31. W.M. Bulkeley, "How Well Do You Know . . . The Cloud?" *The Wall Street Journal* (October 12, 2009): R1.
32. E. Taub, "Computing in the Clouds," *Costco Connection* (January 2010): 29.
33. Vance, "The Power of the Cloud."
34. R. Plant, "To Cloud, or Not to Cloud," *The Wall Street Journal* (April 25, 2011): R9.
35. Bulkeley, "How Well Do You Know . . . The Cloud?"
36. Krzyzewski, "Coach K on How to Connect."
37. Hwang and Francesco, "The Influence of Individualism."
38. B.M Galvin, P. Balkundi, and D.A. Waldman, "Spreading the Word: The Role of Surrogates in Charismatic Leadership Processes," *Academy of Management Review* 35(3) (2010): 477–494.
39. H.R. Bowles and F. Flynn, "Gender and Persistence in Negotiation: A Dyadic Perspective," *Academy of Management Journal* 53(4) (2010): 769–787.
40. N. Rothbard, "Put on a Happy Face. Seriously," *The Wall Street Journal* (October 24, 2011): R2.
41. D.R. Hekman, K. Aquino, B.P. Owens, T.R. Mitchell, P. Schilpzand, and K. Leavitt, "An Examination of Whether and How Racial and Gender Biases Influence Customer Satisfaction," *Academy of Management Journal* 53(2) (2010): 238–264.
42. D.B. Montgomery and C.A. Ramus, "Calibrating MBA Job Preferences for the 21st Century," *Academy of Management Learning & Education* 10(1) (2011): 9–26.
43. E.G. Love, D.W. Love, and G.B. Northcraft, "Is the End in Sight? Students Regulation of In-Class and Extra-Credit Effort in Response to Performance Feedback," *Academy of Management Learning & Education* 9(1) (2010): 81–97.
44. Hekman et al., "An Examination of Whether and How Racial and Gender Biases Influence Customer Satisfaction."
45. Bowles and Flynn, "Gender and Persistence in Negotiation."
46. J. Gray, *Men Are from Mars, Women Are from Venus* (New York: HarperCollins, 1992).
47. D. Tannen, *You Just Don't Understand: Women and Men in Conversation,* (New York: Ballantine Books, 1991); and *Talking From 9 to 5* (New York: William Morrow, 1995).
48. Hwang and Francesco, "The Influence of Individualism."
49. A. Pentland, "The Power of Nonverbal Communication," *The Wall Street Journal* (October 20, 2008): R2.
50. N.J. Adler, *International Dimensions of Organizational Behavior,* 7th ed. (Mason, OH: South-Western/Cengage, 2011).
51. Love et al., "Is the End in Sight?"
52. Ibid.
53. H. Meyer, "Body Talk," *Costco Connection* (May 2009): 22–23.
54. Public Radio, News Broadcast, WFCR 88.5 aired May 28, 2010.
55. C. Brogan, "The New Attention Deficit," *Entrepreneur* (December 2010): 70.
56. J. Robinson, "E-Mail Is Making You Stupid?" *Entrepreneur* (March 2010): 61–63.
57. Wang et al., "Daily Customer Mistreatment and Employee Sabotage against Customers."

58. B.A. Scott and C.M. Barnes, "A Multilevel Field Investigation of Emotional Labor, Affect, Work Withdrawal, and Gender," *Academy of Management Journal* 54(1) (2011): 116–136.
59. M. Korn and J. Light, "On the Lesson Plan: Feelings," *The Wall Street Journal* (Mary 5, 2011): B6.
60. Scott and Barnes, "A Multilevel Field Investigation of Emotional Labor, Affect, Work Withdrawal, and Gender."
61. S.C. Douglas, C. Kiewitz, M.J. Martinko, P. Harvey, Y. Kim, and J.U. Chen, "Cognitions, Emotions, and Evaluations: An Elaboration Likelihood Model for Workplace Aggression," *Academy of Management Review* 33(2) (2008): 425–451.
62. Wang et al., "Daily Customer Mistreatment and Employee Sabotage against Customers."
63. Douglas et al.,"Cognitions, Emotions, and Evaluations."
64. P. Chattopadhyay, C. Finn, and N.M. Ashkanasy, "Affective Responses to Professional Dissimilarity: A Matter of Status," *Academy of Management Journal* 53(4) (2010): 808–826.
65. W. Isaascon, "Steve Jobs: The Biography—His Rivalry with Bill Gates," *Fortune* (November 7, 2011): 97–112.
66. G. Colvin, "What Really Has the 99% Up in Arms?" *Fortune* (November 7, 2011): 87.
67. N. Rothbard, "Put on a Happy Face. Seriously," *The Wall Street Journal* (October 24, 2011): R2
68. J.Z. Bergman, J.W. Westerman, and J.P. Daly, "Narcissism in Management Education," *Academy of Management Learning & Education* 9(1) (2010): 119–131.
69. R. Kiyosaki, "Hear This," *Entrepreneur* (September 2008), p. 36.
70. S.E. Needleman, "Candidates Singing Own Praises Fall Flat," *The Wall Street Journal* (January 13, 2009), p. D4.
71. R. Wolter, "Transform Negative Reactions into Opportunities," *Entrepreneur* (March 2009), p. 104.
72. Gibson, "The Stop-Managing Guide to Management," *BusinessWeek* (June 15, 2009), p. 73
73. J. Collins, "Fall How the Mighty Fall," *BusinessWeek* (May 25, 2009), pp. 26–33.
74. A. Hemming, "Help! I've Become the Boss I Hated!" *Fortune* (June 14, 2010), p. 46.
75. R. Kiyosaki, "Don't Fear Failure," *Entrepreneur* (December 2008), p. 32.
76. L. Zalaznick, "Listen," *Fortune* (July 6, 2009), p. 49.
77. B. Farber, "Constructive Criticism," *Entrepreneur* (November 2008), p. 73.
78. T. Gutner, "Ways to Make the Most of a Negative Job Review," *The Wall Street Journal* (January 13, 2009), p. D4.
79. P.C. Bottger and J.L. Barsoux, "Do You Really Want to be a Leader?" *The Wall Street Journal* (November 30, 2009), p. R8.
80. Hemming, "Help! I've Become the Boss I Hated!"
81. K. Blanchard, D. Hutson, and E. Wills, *The One Minute Entrepreneur* (New York: Currency, 2008).

Chapter 6

1. H. Ren, "Repairing Relationship Conflict: How Violation Types and Culture Influence the Effectiveness of Restoration Rituals," *Academy of Management Review* 34(1) (209): 105–126.
2. F. Walter, M.S. Cole, and R.H. Humphrey, "Emotional Intelligence: Sine Qua Non of Leadership or Folderol?" *Academy of Management Perspectives* 25(1) (2011): 45–59.
3. K.A. Jenh, S. Rispens, and S.M.B. Thatcher, "The Effects of Conflict Asymmetry on Work Group and Individual Outcomes," *Academy of Management Journal* 53(3) (2010): 596–616.
4. K.T. Dirks, R.J. Lewicki, and A. Zaheer, "Repairing Relationships within and between Organizations: Building a Conceptual Framework," *Academy of Management Review* 34(1) (2009): 68–84.
5. P. Chattopadhyay, C. Finn, and N.M. Ashkansy, "Affective Responses to Professional Dissimilarity: A Matter of Status," *Academy of Management Journal* 53(4) (2010): 808–826.
6. H.R. Bowles and F. Flynn, "Gender and Persistence in Negotiation: A Dyadic Perspective," *Academy of Management Journal* 53(4) (2010): 769–787.
7. Dirks et al., "Repairing Relationships within and between Organizations."
8. Jenh et al., "The Effects of Conflict Asymmetry on Work Group and Individual Outcomes."
9. International Transactional Analysis Association Web site (itaaworld.org), retrieved January 2, 2012.
10. Ibid.
11. Ibid.
12. Bowles and Flynn, "Gender and Persistence in Negotiation."
13. Ibid.
14. Ibid.
15. J. O'Reilly and K. Aquino, "A Model of Third Parties' Morally Motivated Responses to Mistreatment in Organizations," *Academy of Management Review* 36(3) (2011): 526–543.
16. J.Z. Bergman, J.W. Westerman, and J.P. Daly, "Narcissism in Management Education," *Academy of Management Learning & Education* 9(1) (2010): 119–131.
17. Wang et al., "Daily Customer Mistreatment and Employee Sabotage Against Customers."
18. B.J. Tepper, S.E. Moss, and M.K. Duffy, "Predictors of Abusive Supervision: Supervisor Perceptions of Deep-Level Dissimilarity, Relationship Conflict, and Subordinate Performance," *Academy of Management Journal* 54(2) (2011): 279–294.
19. Bowles and Flynn, "Gender and Persistence in Negotiation."
20. S. Nadkarni and P. Herrmann, "CEO Personality, Strategic Flexibility, and Firm Performance: The Case of the Indian Business Process Outsourcing Industry," *Academy of Management Journal* 53(5) (2010): 1050–1073.
21. D.B. McNatt, "Negative Reputation and Biased Student Evaluations of Teaching: Longitudinal Results from a Naturally Occurring Experiment," *Academy of Management Education & Learning* 9(2) (2010): 225–242.
22. S.C. Douglas, C. Kiewitz, M.J. Martinko, P. Harvey, Y. Kim, and J.U. Chen, "Cognitions, Emotions, and Evaluations: An Elaboration Likelihood Model for Workplace Aggression," *Academy of Management Review* 33(2) (2008): 425–451.
23. S. Shellenbarger, "How to Keep Your Cool in Angry Times," *The Wall Street Journal* (September 22, 2010): D3.
24. Bergman et al., "Narcissism in Management Education."
25. Tepper et al., "Predictors of Abusive Supervision."
26. McNatt, "Negative Reputation and Biased Student Evaluations of Teaching."
27. Shellenbarger, "How to Keep Your Cool in Angry Times."
28. W. Isaascon, "Steve Jobs: The Biography—His Rivalry with Bill Gates," *Fortune* (November 7, 2011): 97–112.
29. Shellenbarger, "How to Keep Your Cool in Angry Times."
30. Douglas et al., "Cognitions, Emotions, and Evaluations."
31. Tepper et al., "Predictors of Abusive Supervision."
32. Shellenbarger, "How to Keep Your Cool in Angry Times."
33. Ren, "Repairing Relationship Conflict."
34. J.C. Santora and M. Eposito, "The Psychology of Defined-Benefit Pensions: When do They Affect Employee Behavior?" *Academy of Management Perspectives* 24(2) (2010): 85–86.
35. Chattopadhyay et al., "Affective Responses to Professional Dissimilarity."
36. F. Rojas, "Power Through Institutional Work: Acquiring Academic Authority in the 1968 Third World Strike," *Academy of Management Journal* 53(6) (2010): 1263–1280.
37. Dirks et al., "Repairing Relationships within and between Organizations."
38. Bowles and Flynn, "Gender and Persistence in Negotiation."

39. Nadkarni and Herrmann, "CEO Personality, Strategic Flexibility, and Firm Performance."
40. Jenh et al., "The Effects of Conflict Asymmetry on Work Group and Individual Outcomes."
41. Ren, "Repairing Relationship Conflict."
42. Nadkarni and Herrmann, "CEO Personality, Strategic Flexibility, and Firm Performance."
43. Chattopadhyay et al., "Affective Responses to Professional Dissimilarity."
44. Ren, "Repairing Relationship Conflict."
45. Nike Web site (www.nike.com), retrieved January 4, 2012.
46. M. Barbaro, "Slightly Testy Nike Divorce Came Down to Data vs. Feel," and "Cricket Anyone? Sneakers Makers on Fresh Turf," *The New York Times* (January 28, 2006): C1, C4.
47. Wikipedia Web site (http://en.wikipedia.org/wiki/William_Perez), retrieved January 4, 2012.
48. Nike Web site (www.nike.com), retrieved January 4, 2012.

Chapter 7

1. R.B. Kaiser and R.B. Kaplan, "The Deeper Work of Executive Development: Outgrowing Sensitivities," *Academy of Management Learning & Education* 5(4) (2006): 463–483.
2. F. Walter, M.S. Cole, and R.H. Humphrey, "Emotional Intelligence: Sine Qua Non of Leadership or Folderol?" *Academy of Management Perspectives* 25(1) (2011): 45–59.
3. "Call for Paper—Teaching Leadership," *Academy of Management Journal* 53(4) (2010): 922.
4. "Walter et al., "Emotional Intelligence."
5. Kaiser and Kaplan, "The Deeper Work of Executive Development."
6. M. Korn, "Analyze, Decide, Lead, Says Columbia's Business Dean," *The Wall Street Journal* (July 7, 2011): B6.
7. B.J. Hoffman, B.H. Bynum, R.F. Piccolo, and A.W. Sutton, "Person-Organization Value Congruence: How Transformational Leaders Influence Work Group Effectiveness," *Academy of Management Journal* 54(4) (2011): 779–796.
8. J.B. Wu, A.S. Tsui, and A.J. Kinicki, "Consequences of Differentiated Leadership in Groups," *Academy of Management Journal* 53(4) (2010): 90–106.
9. B.M Galvin, P. Balkundi, and D.A. Waldman, "Spreading the Word: The Role of Surrogates in Charismatic Leadership Processes," *Academy of Management Review* 35(3) (2010): 477–494.
10. H. Liao, D. Liu, R. Loi, "Looking at Both Sides of the Social Exchange Coin: A Social Cognitive Perspective on the Joint Effects of Relationship Quality and Differentiation on Creativity," *Academy of Management Journal* 53(5) (2010): 1090–1109.
11. X. Zhang and K.M. Bartol, "Linking Empowering Leadership and Employee Creativity: The Influence of Psychological Empowerment, Intrinsic Motivation, and Creative Process Engagement," *Academy of Management Journal* 53(1) (2010): 107–128.
12. R.M. Murphy, "The Top Companies for Leaders," *Fortune* (November 21, 2011): 165–169.
13. W. Isaacson, "Steve Jobs: The Biography—His Rivalry with Bill Gates," *Fortune* (November 7, 2011): 97–112.
14. Hoffman et al., "Person-Organization Value Congruence."
15. De Jong and Elfring, "How Does Trust Affect the Performance of Ongoing Teams?"
16. J. O'Reilly and K. Aquino, "A Model of Third Parties' Morally Motivated Responses to Mistreatment in Organizations," *Academy of Management Review* 36(3) (2011): 526–543.
17. B.J. Tepper, S.E. Moss, and M.K. Duffy, "Predictors of Abusive Supervision: Supervisor Perceptions of Deep-Level Dissimilarity, Relationship Conflict, and Subordinate Performance," *Academy of Management Journal* 54(2) (2011): 279–294.
18. M. Brettel, A. Engelen, and L. Voll, "Letting Go to Grow—Empirical Findings on a Hearsay," *Journal of Small Business Management* 48(4): 552–579.
19. R.W. Stackman and K. Devine, "Leadership and Emotional-Rational Coherence: A Start?" *Academy of Management Perspectives* 25(1) (2011): 42–44.
20. N. Gillespie and G. Dietz, "Trust Repair After an Organization-Level Failure," *Academy of Management Review* 34(1) (209): 127–145.
21. De Jong and Elfring, "How Does Trust Affect the Performance of Ongoing Teams?"
22. H.C. Lin and S.T. Hou, "Managerial Lessons from the East: An Interview with Acer's Stan Shih," *Academy of Management Perspectives* 24(4) (2010): 6–16.
23. "Call for Paper—Teaching Leadership."
24. K.E.M. De Stobbeleir, S.J. Ashford, and K. Buyens, "Self-Regulation of Creativity at Work: The Role of Feedback-Seeking Behavior in Creative Performance," *Academy of Management Journal* 54(4) (2011): 811–831.
25. "Call for Paper—Teaching Leadership."
26. E. Ghiselli, *Exploration in Management Talent* (Santa Monica, CA: Goodyear, 1971).
27. De Stobbeleir et al., "Self-Regulation of Creativity at Work."
28. T.A. Judge, R. Ilies, J.E. Bono, and M.W. Gerhardt, "Personality and Leadership: A Qualitative and Quantitative Review," *Journal of Applied Psychology* 87(4) (2002): 765–768.
29. D.A. Waldman, P.A. Balthazard, and S.J. Peterson, "Leadership and Neuroscience: Can We Revolutionize the Way That Inspirational Leaders Are Identified and Developed?" *Academy of Management Perspectives* 25(1) (2011): 60–74.
30. Staff, "What Are the Most Important Traits for Success as a Supervisor?" *The Wall Street Journal* (November 14, 1980): 33.
31. R. Likert, *New Patterns of Management* (New York: McGraw-Hill, 1961).
32. R.M. Stogdill and A.E. Coons (eds.), *Leader Behavior: The Description and Measurement* (Columbus: The Ohio State University Bureau of Business Research, 1957).
33. R. Blake and J. Mouton, *The Managerial Grid* (Houston: Gulf Publishing, 1964); R. Blake and J. Mouton, *The New Managerial Grid* (Houston: Gulf Publishing, 1978); R. Blake and J. Mouton, *The Managerial Grid III: Key to Leadership Excellence* (Houston: Gulf Publishing, 1985); R. Blake and A.A. McCanse, *Leadership Dilemmas—Grid Solutions* (Houston: Gulf Publishing, 1991).
34. Wu et al., "Consequences of Differentiated Leadership in Groups."
35. Hoffman et al., "Person-Organization Value Congruence."
36. Isaascon, "Steve Jobs: The Biography."
37. B.M Galvin, P. Balkundi, and D.A. Waldman, "Spreading the Word: The Role of Surrogates in Charismatic Leadership Processes," *Academy of Management Review* 35(3) (2010): 477–494.
38. B. Schlender, "Steve and Me," *Fortune* (November 7, 2011): 115–123.
39. Isascon, "Steve Jobs: The Biography."
40. Brettel et al., "Letting Go to Grow."
41. J.D. Davis, M.R. Allen, and H.D. Hayes, "Is Blood Thicker Than Water? A Study of Stewardship Perceptions in Family Business," *Entrepreneurship Theory and Practice* 34(6) (2010): 1093–1116.
42. A.W. Pearson and L.E. Marler, "A Leadership Perspective of Reciprocal Stewardship in Family Business," *Entrepreneurship Theory and Practice* 34(6) (2010): 1117–1124.
43. M. Farjoun, "Beyond Dualism: Stability and Change as a Duty," *Academy of Management Review* 35(2) (2010): 202–225.
44. F. Fiedler, *A Theory of Leadership Effectiveness* (New York: McGraw-Hill, 1967).

45. R. Tannenbaum and W. Schmidt, "How to Choose a Leadership Pattern," *Harvard Business Review* (May–June 1973): 166.
46. V. Vroom and P. Yetton, *Leadership and Decision Making* (Pittsburg: University of Press, 1973); V. Vroom, "Leadership and the Decision-Making Process," *Organizational Dynamics* 28 (Spring 2000): 82–94.
47. P. Hersey, K. Blanchard, and D. Johnson, *Management of Organizational Behavior: Utilizing Human Resources* 13e (Upper Saddle River, NJ: Prentice Hall, 2011).
48. Wu et al., "Consequences of Differentiated Leadership in Groups."
49. Ibid.
50. Hersey et al., "*Management of Organizational Behavior*."
51. S. Kerr and J.M. Jermier, "Substitutes for Leadership: The Meaning and Measurement," *Organizational Behavior and Performance* 22 (1978): 375–403.
52. K.S. Wilson, H.P. Sin, and D.E. Conlon, "What About the Leader in Leader-Member Exchange and Substitutability of the Leader," *Academy of Management Review* 35(3) (2010): 358–372.
53. Brettel et al., "Letting Go to Grow."
54. N.M. Pless, T. Maak, and G.K. Stahl, "Developing Responsible Global Leaders Through International Service-Learning Programs: The Ulysses Experience," *Academy of Management Learning & Education* 10(2) (2011): 237–260.
55. Y. Zhu, "Does the Relationship between Job Satisfaction and Job Performance Depend on Culture?" *Academy of Management Perspectives* 24(1) (2010): 86–87.
56. D. Holtbrugge and A.T. Mohr, "Cultural Determinants of Learning Style Preferences," *Academy of Management Learning & Education* 9(4) (2010): 622–637.
57. M.B. O'Leary, M. Mortensen, and A.W. Woolley, "Multiple Team Membership: A Theoretical Model of Its Effects on Productivity and Learning for Individuals and Teams," *Academy of Management Review* 36(3) (2011): 461–478.
58. M.R. Haas, "The Double-Edged Swords of Autonomy and External Knowledge: Analyzing Team Effectiveness in a Multinational Organization," *Academy of Management Journal* 53(5) (2010): 989–1008.
59. J.A. Martin and K.M. Eisenhardt, "Rewiring: Cross-Business-Unit Collaborations in Multibusiness Organizations," *Academy of Management Journal* 53(2) (2010): 265–301.
60. Ibid.
61. Lin and Hou, "Managerial Lessons from the East."
62. Wu et al., "Consequences of Differentiated Leadership in Groups."
63. Liao et al., "Looking at Both Sides of the Social Exchange Coin."
64. K.W. Phillips, N.P. Rothbard, and T.L. Dumas, "To Disclose or Not to Disclose: Status Distance and Self-Disclosure in Diverse Environments," *Academy of Management Review* 34(4) (2009): 710–732.
65. Galvin et al., "Spreading the Word."
66. B.A. De Jong and T. Elfring, "How Does Trust Affect the Performance of Ongoing Teams? The Mediating Role of Reflexivity, Monitoring, and Effort," *Academy of Management Journal* 53(3) (2010): 535–549.
67. K.T. Dirks, R.J. Lewicki, and A. Zaheer, "Repairing Relationships within and between Organizations: Building a Conceptual Framework," *Academy of Management Review* 34(1) (2009): 68–84.
68. R. Hurley, "Trust Me," *The Wall Street Journal* (October 24, 2011): R4.
69. C. Lechner, K. Frankenberger, and S.W. Floyd, "Task Contingencies in the Curvilnear Relationship between Intergroup Networks and Initiative Performance," *Academy of Management Journal* 53(4) (2010): 865–889.
70. Gillespie and Dietz, "Trust Repair After an Organization-Level Failure."
71. R. Hurley, "Trust Me."
72. S.S. Wong and W.F. Boh, "Leveraging the Ties of Others to Build a Reputation for Trustworthiness Among Peers," *Academy of Management Journal* 53(1) (2010): 129–148.
73. Gillespie and Dietz, "Trust Repair after an Organization-Level Failure."
74. Wong and Boh, "Leveraging the Ties of Others."
75. Hurley, "Trust Me."
76. S.S. Wang, "A Healthy Dose of Loyalty," *The Wall Street Journal* (June 21, 2011): D1–D2.
77. Phillips et al., "To Disclose or Not to Disclose."
78. J. Luft, *Of Human Interaction* (Palo Alto, CA: National Press, 1969).
79. Dirks et al., "Repairing Relationships within and between Organizations."
80. E.C. Tomlinson and R.C. Mayer, "The Role of Causal Attribution Dimensions in Trust Repair," *Academy of Management Review* 34(1) (2009): 85–104.
81. Dirks et al., "Repairing Relationships within and between Organizations."
82. Gillespie and Dietz, "Trust Repair after an Organization-Level Failure."
83. B. Bernstein, "I'm Very, Very, Very Sorry . . . Really?" *The Wall Street Journal* (October 19, 2010): D1–D2.
84. S. Shellenbarger, "How to Keep Your Cool in Angry Times," *The Wall Street Journal* (September 22, 2010): D3.
85. Starbucks Web site (www.starbucks.com), retrieved January 10, 2012.
86. The introductory paragraph updating Starbucks information was updated by Robert Lussier. The remainder of the cases and questions were written by Herbert Sherman, professor and chair of management, Long Island University.

Chapter 8

1. S. Lindenberg and N.J. Foss, "Managing Joint Production Motivation: The Role of Goal Framing and Governance Mechanisms," *Academy of Management Review* 36(3) (2011): 500–525.
2. B.L. Rich, J.A. Lepine, and E.R. Crawford, "Job Engagement: Antecedents and Effects on Job Performance," *Academy of Management Journal* 53(3) (2010): 617–635.
3. E.G. Love, D.W. Love, and G.B. Northcraft, "Is the End in Sight? Students Regulation of In-Class and Extra-Credit Effort in Response to Performance Feedback," *Academy of Management Learning & Education* 9(1) (2010): 81–97.
4. B. Anderson, "The Accidental CEO," *Fortune* (March 2, 2009): 26.
5. W. Isaascon, "Steve Jobs: The Biography—His Rivalry with Bill Gates," *Fortune* (November 7, 2011): 97–112.
6. Lindenberg and Foss, "Managing Joint Production Motivation."
7. Y. Zhu, "Does the Relationship between Job Satisfaction and Job Performance Depend on Culture?" *Academy of Management Perspectives* 24(1) (2010): 86–87.
8. N. Bozionelos, "Happiness Around the World: Is There More to It Than Money?" *Academy of Management Perspectives* 24(4) (2010): 96–97.
9. Zhu, "Does the Relationship between Job Satisfaction and Job Performance Depend on Culture?"
10. A. Maslow, "A Theory of Human Motivation," *Psychological Review* 50 (1943): 370–396; *Motivation and Personality* (New York: Harper & Row, 1954).
11. F. Herzberg, "One More Time: How Do You Motivate Employees?" *Harvard Business Review* (January–February 1968): 53–62.
12. N. Bozionelos, "What Accounts for Job Satisfaction Differences across Countries?" *Academy of Management Perspectives* 24(1) (2010): 82–84.
13. J.D. Davis, M.R. Allen, and H.D. Hayes, "Is Blood Thicker Than Water? A Study of Stewardship Perceptions in Family Business," *Entrepreneurship Theory and Practice* 34(6) (2010): 1093–1116

14. Rich et al., "Job Engagement: Antecedents and Effects on Job Performance."
15. Bozionelos, "Happiness Around the World."
16. D. McClelland, *The Achieving Society* (New York: Van Nostrand Reinhold, 1961); and D. McClelland and D.H. Burnham, "Power Is the Great Motivator," *Harvard Business Review* (March–April 1978): 103.
17. M. Brettel, A. Engelen, and L. Voll, "Letting Go to Grow—Empirical Findings on a Hearsay," *Journal of Small Business Management* 48(4): 552–579.
18. Bozionelos, "Happiness Around the World."
19. S.B. Sitkin, K.E. See, C.C. Miller, M.W. Lawless, and A.M. Carton, "The Paradox of Stretch Goals: Organizations in Pursuit of the Seemingly Impossible," *Academy of Management Review* 36(3) (2011): 544–566.
20. Lindenberg and Foss, "Managing Joint Production Motivation."
21. Zhu, "Does the Relationship between Job Satisfaction and Job Performance Depend on Culture?"
22. V. Vroom, *Work and Motivation* (New York: Wiley, 1964).
23. L.F. Edelman, C.G. Brush, T.S. Manolova, and P.G. Greene, "Start-up Motivations and Growth Intentions of Minority Nascent Entrepreneurs," *Journal of Small Business Management* 48(2) (2010): 174–196.
24. S. Adams, "Toward an Understanding of Inequity," *Journal of Abnormal and Social Psychology* 67(4) (1963): 422–436.
25. D. Loo, "Big Pharma Launches a Talent Raid in China," *Bloomberg Businessweek* (July 18–24, 2011): 21–22.
26. G. Colvin, "What Really Has the 99% Up in Arms?" *Fortune* (November 7, 2011): 87.
27. R. Pinheiro, "SuperFreakonomics: Global Cooling, Patriotic Prostitutes, and Why Suicide Bombers Should Buy Life Insurance," *Academy of Management Perspectives* 25(2) (2011): 86–87.
28. V. Harnish, "Tired of Reading the Same Old Advice?" *Fortune* (November 7, 2011): 52.
29. B.F. Skinner, *Beyond Freedom and Dignity* (New York: Alfred Knopf, 1971).
30. Author statement to clearly let the reader know that this is his interpretation of Skinner's reinforcement theory.
31. B.M Galvin, P. Balkundi, and D.A. Waldman, "Spreading the Word: The Role of Surrogates in Charismatic Leadership Processes," *Academy of Management Review* 35(3) (2010): 477–494
32. Love et al., "Is the End in Sight?"
33. Pinheiro, "SuperFreakonomics."
34. Harnish, "Tired of Reading the Same Old Advice?"
35. K. Blanchard, D. Hutson, and E. Wills, *The One-Minute Entrepreneur* (New York: Currency/Doubleday, 2008).
36. K. Blanchard and J. Johnson, *The One-Minute Manager* (New York: Wm. Morrow, 1982).
37. D. Conant, "Write a Thank-You Note," *Bloomberg Businessweek* (September 26–October 2, 2011): 104.
38. G. Hirst, D. Van Knippenberg, C.H. Chen, and C.A. Sacramento, "How Does Bureaucracy Impact Individual Creativity? A Cross-Level Investigation of Team Orientation-Creativity Relationships," *Academy of Management Journal* 54(3) (2011): 624–641.
39. E.A. Locke, "Guest Editor's Introduction: Goal-Setting Theory and Its Applications to the World of Business," *Academy of Management Executive* 18(4) (2004): 124–125.
40. L.V. Gerstner, "Fix This/Education," *Bloomberg Businessweek* (October 17–23, 2011): 98.
41. Sitkin et al., "The Paradox of Stretch Goals."
42. G. Colvin, "Wall Street Expects Corporate Miracles in 2012, and That Means Trouble," *Fortune* (January 16, 2012): 41.
43. Blanchard et al., *The One-Minute Entrepreneur*.
44. Gerstner, "Fix This/Education."
45. Blanchard et al., *The One-Minute Entrepreneur*.
46. K. Naughton, "Can Alan Mulally Take Ford's Show on the Road?" *Bloomberg Businessweek* (June 27–July 3, 2011): 21–22.
47. D. Campbell, "JPMorgan's Contrarian Bet on Bank Branches," *Bloomberg Businessweek* (June 27–July 3, 2011): 43–44.
48. C. Dawson, "Nissan Drives to Close Gap," *The Wall Street Journal* (June 27, 2011): B3.
49. Blanchard et al., *The One-Minute Entrepreneur*.
50. Ibid.
51. B.L. Rich, J.A. Lepine, and E.R. Crawford, "Job Engagement: Antecedents and Effects on Job Performance," *Academy of Management Journal* 53(3) (2010): 617–635.
52. B. Anderson, "The Accidental CEO," *Fortune* (March 2, 2009): 26.
53. G.J. Kilduff, H.A. Eefenbein, and B.M. Staw, "The Psychology of Rivalry: A Relationally Dependent Analysis of Competition," *Academy of Management Journal* 53(5) (2010): 943–969.
54. J.C. Dencker, "Outliers: The Story of Success," *Academy of Management Perspectives* 24(3) (2010): 97–99.
55. M. Kimes, "New Guru on the Block," *Fortune* (December 26, 2011): 149–152.
56. Love et al., "Is the End in Sight?"
57. Bozionelos, "What Accounts for Job Satisfaction Differences across Countries?"
58. Ibid.
59. Locke, "Guest Editor's Introduction."
60. www.underarmour.com, retrieved January 27, 2012.
61. www.inc.com/magazine/20031201/howididit.html.

Chapter 9

1. R. Greenwood and D. Miller, "Tackling Design Anew: Getting Back to the Heart of Organizational Theory," *Academy of Management Perspectives* 25(4) (2011): 78–84.
2. J.B. Wu, A.S. Tsui, and A.J. Kinicki, "Consequences of Differentiated Leadership in Groups," *Academy of Management Journal* 53(4) (2010): 90–106.
3. Y. Mishina, B.J. Dykes, E.S. Block, and T.G. Pollock, "Why Good Firms Do Bad Things: The Effects of High Aspirations, High Expectations, and Prominence on the Incidence of Corporate Illegality," *Academy of Management Journal* 53(4) (2010): 701–722.
4. Y.I. Kane and I. Sherr, "IPhone Executive Is Out at Apple," *The Wall Street Journal* (August 9, 2010): B1–B2.
5. J. Pfeffer, "Don't Dismiss Office Politics—Teach It," *The Wall Street Journal* (October 24, 2011): R6.
6. G.A. Ballinger and K.W. Rockmann, "Chutes versus Ladders: Anchoring Events and a Punctuated-Equilibrium Perspective on Social Exchange Relationships," *Academy of Management Review* 35(3) (2010): 373–391.
7. A. Dizik, "How to Charm and Do Business over Dinner," *The Wall Street Journal* (January 27, 2011): D2.
8. H.M. Haugh and A. Talwar, "How Do Corporations Embed Sustainability across the Organization?" *Academy of Management Learning & Education* 9(3) (2010): 384–396.
9. G. Colvin, "Wall Street Expects Corporate Miracles in 2012, and That Means Trouble," *Fortune* (January 16, 2012): 41.
10. B.M Galvin, P. Balkundi, and D.A. Waldman, "Spreading the Word: The Role of Surrogates in Charismatic Leadership Processes," *Academy of Management Review* 35(3) (2010): 477–494.
11. F. Rojas, "Power through Institutional Work: Acquiring Academic Authority in the 1968 Third World Strike," *Academy of Management Journal* 53(6) (2010): 1263–1280.
12. Pfeffer, "Don't Dismiss Office Politics—Teach It."
13. J. French and B. Raven, "A Comparative Analysis of Power and Preference," in J.T. Tedeschi, ed., *Perspectives on Social Power* (Hawthorne, NY: Aldine, 1974).
14. Rojas, "Power through Institutional Work.

15. J. Lehrer, "The Power Trip," *The Wall Street Journal* (August 14–15, 2010): W1–W2.
16. Rojas, "Power through Institutional Work."
17. Ballinger and Rockmann, "Chutes versus Ladders."
18. S. Shellenbarger, "Let the Boss Really See You Sweat," *The Wall Street Journal* (March 23, 2011): D1.
19. Pfeffer, "Don't Dismiss Office Politics—Teach It."
20. H. Liao, D. Liu, and R. Loi, "Looking at Both Sides of the Social Exchange Coin: A Social Cognitive Perspective on the Join Effects of Relationship Quality and Differentiation on Creativity," *Academy of Management Journal* 53(5) (2010): 1090–1109.
21. Rojas, "Power through Institutional Work."
22. Ibid.
23. Lehrer, "The Power Trip."
24. Wu et al., "Consequences of Differentiated Leadership in Groups."
25. Galvin et al., "Spreading the Word."
26. R. Pinheiro, "SuperFreakonomics: Global Cooling, Patriotic Prostitutes, and Why Suicide Bombers Should Buy Life Insurance," *Academy of Management Perspectives* 25(2) (2011): 86–87.
27. B. Schlender, "Steve and Me," *Fortune* (November 7, 2011): 115–123.
28. A.M. Zhang, "How Does Vivid Language Shape Investor Judgments?" *Academy of Management Perspectives* 25(3) (2011): 75–76.
29. Galvin et al., "Spreading the Word."
30. Ibid.
31. Zhang, "How Does Vivid Language Shape Investor Judgments?"
32. W. Isaascon, "Steve Jobs: The Biography—His Rivalry with Bill Gates," *Fortune* (November 7, 2011): 97–112.
33. Pfeffer, "Don't Dismiss Office Politics—Teach It."
34. Ibid.
35. B. Kowitt, "L. Hudson Tips for Climbing the Corporate Ladder," *Fortune* (March 21, 2011): 42
36. Kane and Sherr, "IPhone Executive Is Out at Apple."
37. Pfeffer, "Don't Dismiss Office Politics—Teach It."
38. C. Lechner, K. Frankenberger, and S.W. Floyd, "Task Contingencies in the Curvilinear Relationship between Intergroup Networks and Initiative Performance," *Academy of Management Journal* 53(4) (2010): 865–889.
39. Pfeffer, "Don't Dismiss Office Politics—Teach It."
40. Liao et al., "Looking at Both Sides of the Social Exchange Coin."
41. S.S. Wong and W.F. Boh, "Leveraging the Ties of Others to Build a Reputation for Trustworthiness among Peers," *Academy of Management Journal* 53(1) (2010): 129–148.
42. Pfeffer, "Don't Dismiss Office Politics—Teach It."
43. Liao et al., "Looking at Both Sides of the Social Exchange Coin."
44. Lechner et al., "Task Contingencies in the Curvilinear Relationship."
45. Liao et al., "Looking at Both Sides of the Social Exchange Coin."
46. Ibid.
47. T. Wayne, "Etiquette School for Dummies," *Bloomberg Businessweek* (October 18–24, 2010): 89–91.
48. Dizik, "How to Charm and Do Business over Dinner."
49. G. Moran, "How to Clean Up Your Business," *Entrepreneur* (May 2011): 77–78.
50. AACSB Web site (www.aacsb.edu). Retrieved January 21, 2012.
51. R.M. (no last name given), "Is There Proper Etiquette for Videoconferencing?" *Entrepreneur* (November 2011): 20.
52. T. Wayne, "Etiquette School for Dummies," *Bloomberg Businessweek* (October 18–24, 2010): 89–91.
53. R. McCammon, "People Are Always Misinterpreting My E-Mails. What Am I Doing Wrong?" *Entrepreneur* (January 2012): 18–19.
54. Ibid.
55. J.W. (no last name given), "CYA: The Download," *Entrepreneur* (November 2010): 26.
56. McCammon, "People Are Always Misinterpreting My E-Mails."
57. J. Robinson, "E-Mail Is Making You Stupid," *Entrepreneur* (March 2010): 61–63.
58. R.M., "Is There Proper Etiquette for Videoconferencing?" *Entrepreneur* (November 2011): 20.
59. W. Bluestein, "How to Get to the Point," *Entrepreneur* (October 2011): 46.
60. V. Tonoyan, R. Strohmeyer, M. Habib, and M. Perlitz, "Correction and Entrepreneurship: How Formal and Informal Institutions Shape Small Firm Behavior in Transition and Mature Market Economies," *Entrepreneurship Theory and Practice* 34(5) (2010): 803–831.
61. R.M., "Is There Proper Etiquette for Videoconferencing?"

Chapter 10

1. Toyota Web site, (www.toyota.com), retrieved January 28, 2012.
2. G.A. Ballinger and K.W. Rockmann, "Chutes versus Ladders: Anchoring Events and a Punctuated-Equilibrium Perspective on Social Exchange Relationships," *Academy of Management Review* 35(3) (2010): 373–391.
3. F.J. Flynn and S.S. Wiltermuth, "Who's with Me? False Consensus Brokerage, and Ethical Decision Making in Organizations," *Academy of Management Journal* 53(5) (2010): 1074–1089.
4. S. Nambisan and M. Sawhney, "Orchestration Processes in Network-Centric Innovation: Evidence from the Field," *Academy of Management Perspectives* 25(3) (2011): 40–57.
5. A. Ricadela, "How Salesforce Tames Twitter for Big Business," *Bloomberg Businessweek* (August 29–September 2, 2011): 35–36.
6. S. Nadkarni and P. Herrmann, "CEO Personality, Strategic Flexibility, and Firm Performance: The Case of the Indian Business Process Outsourcing Industry," *Academy of Management Journal* 53(5) (2010): 1050–1073.
7. T. Rutigliano and B. Brim, *Strengths Based Selling* (Gallup, 2010).
8. H.R. Bowles and F. Flynn, "Gender and Persistence in Negotiation: A Dyadic Perspective," *Academy of Management Journal* 53(4) (2010): 769–787.
9. V. Harnish, "Five Creative Money-Saving Strategies," *Fortune* (September 26, 2011): 54.
10. A. Gumbus and R. N. Lussier, "Career Development: Enhancing Your Networking Skills," *Clinical Leadership & Management Review* 17(1) (2003): 16–20.
11. Flynn and Wiltermuth, "Who's with Me?"
12. Nambisan and Sawhney, "Orchestration Processes in Network-Centric Innovation."
13. Nadkarni and Herrmann, "CEO Personality, Strategic Flexibility, and Firm Performance."
14. C. Lechner, K. Frankenberger, and S.W. Floyd, "Task Contingencies in the Curvilinear Relationship between Intergroup Networks and Initiative Performance," *Academy of Management Journal* 53(4) (2010): 865–889.
15. Gumbus and Lussier, "Career Development."
16. B. Farber, "Good Connections," *Entrepreneur* (January 2009): 60.
17. K. Blanchard, D. Hutson, and E. Wills, *The One-Minute Entrepreneur* (New York: Currency/Doubleday, 2008).
18. Nambisan and Sawhney, "Orchestration Processes in Network-Centric Innovation."
19. Nadkarni and Herrmann, "CEO Personality, Strategic Flexibility, and Firm Performance."
20. Gumbus and Lussier, "Career Development."
21. Ibid.
22. S.B. Sitkin, K.E. See, C.C. Miller, M.W. Lawless, and A.M. Carton, "The Paradox of Stretch Goals: Organizations in Pursuit of the Seemingly Impossible," *Academy of Management Review* 36(3) (2011): 544–566
23. Gumbus and Lussier, "Career Development."

24. S. Raice, "Friend—and Possible Employee," *The Wall Street Journal* (October 24, 2011): R4.
25. Farber, "Good Connections."
26. R. McCammon, "How to Enter a Room," *Entrepreneur* (August 2011): 18–19.
27. Farber, "Good Connections."
28. Ibid.
29. Ibid.
30. Ballinger and Rockmann, "Chutes versus Ladders."
31. Raice, "Friend—and Possible Employee."
32. J. Zaslow, "The Greatest Generation (of Networkers)," *The Wall Street Journal* (November 4, 2009): D1, D3.
33. Wikipedia, (www.wikipedia.org), retrieved January 30, 2012.
34. Raice, "Friend—and Possible Employee."
35. J.P. Mangalindan, "Cloud Computing for the Rest of Us," *Fortune* (March 21, 2011): 50.
36. Ricadela, "How Salesforce Tames Twitter for Big Business."
37. A. Vance, "Trouble at the Virtual Water Cooler," *Bloomberg Businessweek* (May 2–8, 2011): 30–31.
38. G.F. Fowler, "Are You Talking to Me?" *The Wall Street Journal* (April 25, 2011): R5.
39. T.L. Griffith, "Tapping Into Social-Media Smarts," *The Wall Street Journal* (April 25, 2011): R6.
40. Zaslow, "The Greatest Generation (of Networkers)."
41. R. Cheng, "So You Want to Use Your iPhone for Work? Uh-oh," *The Wall Street Journal* (April 25, 2011): R1.
42. S. Sobell, "Social Networking @ Work," *Costco Connection* (June 2011): 23–24.
43. J. Zaslow, "The Greatest Generation (of Networkers)," *The Wall Street Journal* (November 4, 2009): D1, D3.
44. Rutigliano and Brim, *Strengths Based Selling*.
45. Lechner et al., "Task Contingencies in the Curvilnear Relationship."
46. M. Crouch, "Get Hired, Not Fired," *Readers Digest* (April 2011): 130–139.
47. Farber, "Good Connections."
48. S.S. Wong and W.F. Boh, "Leveraging the Ties of Others to Build a Reputation for Trustworthiness among Peers," *Academy of Management Journal* 53(1) (2010): 129–148.
49. Lechner et al., "Task Contingencies in the Curvilinear Relationship."
50. V. Harnish, "Five Creative Money-Saving Strategies," *Fortune* (September 26, 2011): 54.
51. "Steve Jobs: The Biography—His Rivalry with Bill Gates," *Fortune* (November 7, 2011): 97–112.
52. Farber, "Good Connections."
53. Ibid.
54. Rutigliano and Brim, *Strengths Based Selling*.
55. Ibid.
56. Farber, "Good Connections."
57. Wong and Boh, "Leveraging the Ties of Others."
58. Crouch, "Get Hired, Not Fired."
59. Farber, "Good Connections."
60. Wong and Boh, "Leveraging the Ties of Others."
61. McCammon, "How to Enter a Room."
62. Bowles and Flynn, "Gender and Persistence in Negotiation."
63. Ibid.
64. Farber, "Good Connections."
65. Rutigliano and Brim, *Strengths Based Selling*.
66. Crouch, "Get Hired, Not Fired."
67. Rutigliano and Brim, *Strengths Based Selling*.
68. Wong and Boh, "Leveraging the Ties of Others."
69. Rutigliano and Brim, *Strengths Based Selling*.
70. N.J. Adler, *International Dimensions of Organizational Behavior* 7th ed. (Cincinnati: South-Western, 2011).
71. http://4020vision.com/index.php/2011/08/negotiating-women-inc-co-founder-carol-frohlinger-on-hidden-bias-in-the-workplace/.
72. www.negotiatingwomen.com/.

Chapter 11

1. P. Heugens and M.W. Lander, "Structure! Agency (and Other Quarrels): A Meta-Analysis of Institutional Theories of Organization," *Academy of Management Journal* 52(1) (2009): 61–85.
2. E.M. Spektor, M. Erez, and E. Naveh, "The Effect of Conformist and Attentive-to-Detail Members on Team Innovation: Reconciling the Innovation Paradox," *Academy of Management Journal* 54(4) (2011): 740–760.
3. Melissa Marie Sollom, St. Cloud Technical and Community College. Reviewer comment given in November 2011.
4. J.D. Hover, R.C. Giambatista, R. L. Sorenson, and W.H. Bommer, "Assessing the Effectiveness of Whole Person Learning Pedagogy in Skill Acquisition," *Academy of Management Learning & Education* 9(2) (2010): 192–203.
5. G. Hirst, D. Van Knippenberg, C.H. Chen, and C.A. Sacramento, "How Does Bureaucracy Impact Individual Creativity? A Cross-Level Investigation of Team Orientation-Creativity Relationships," *Academy of Management Journal* 54(3) (2011): 624–641.
6. K.E.M. De Stobbeleir, S.J. Ashford, and K. Buyens, "Self-Regulation of Creativity at Work: The Role of Feedback-Seeking Behavior in Creative Performance," *Academy of Management Journal* 54(4) (2011): 811–831.
7. H. Liao, D. Liu, and R. Loi, "Looking at Both Sides of the Social Exchange Coin: A Social Cognitive Perspective on the Joint Effects of Relationship Quality and Differentiation on Creativity," *Academy of Management Journal* 53(5) (2010): 1090–1109.
8. C.M. Barnes and J.R. Hollenbeck, "Sleep Deprivation and Decision-Making Teams: Burning the Midnight Oil or Playing with Fire?" *Academy of Management Review* 34(1) (2009): 56–66.
9. J.Z. Bergman, J.W. Westerman, and J.P. Daly, "Narcissism in Management Education," *Academy of Management Learning & Education* 9(1) (2010): 119–131.
10. M.L. McDonald and J.D. Westphal, "My Brother's Keeper? CEO Identification with the Corporate Elite, Social Support among CEOs, and Leader Effectiveness," *Academy of Management Journal* 54(4) (2011): 661–693.
11. Hover et al., "Assessing the Effectiveness of Whole Person Learning Pedagogy."
12. Ibid.
13. B.A. De Jong and T. Elfring, "How Does Trust Affect the Performance of Ongoing Teams? The Mediating Role of Reflexivity, Monitoring, and Effort," *Academy of Management Journal* 53(3) (2010): 535–549.
14. M.R. Haas, "The Double-Edged Swords of Autonomy and External Knowledge: Analyzing Team Effectiveness in a Multinational Organization," *Academy of Management Journal* 53(5) (2010): 989–1008.
15. M.B. O'Leary, M. Mortensen, and A.W. Woolley, "Multiple Team Membership: A Theoretical Model of Its Effects on Productivity and Learning for Individuals and Teams," *Academy of Management Review* 36(3) (2011): 461–478.
16. Haas, "The Double-Edged Swords of Autonomy and External Knowledge."
17. O'Leary et al., "Multiple Team Membership."
18. Hover et al., "Assessing the Effectiveness of Whole Person Learning Pedagogy."
19. K.A. Jehn, S. Rispens, and S.M.B. Thatcher, "The Effects of Conflict Asymmetry on Work Group and Individual Outcomes," *Academy of Management Journal* 53(3) (2010): 596–616.

20. J.B. Wu, A.S. Tsui, and A.J. Kinicki, "Consequences of Differentiated Leadership in Groups," *Academy of Management Journal* 53(4) (2010): 90–106.
21. D. Brady, "Carol Bartz," *Bloomberg Businessweek* (August 16–29, 2010): 100.
22. D.R. Hekman, K. Aquino, B.P. Owens, T.R. Mitchell, P. Schilpzand, and K. Leavitt, "An Examination of Whether and How Racial and Gender Biases Influence Customer Satisfaction," *Academy of Management Journal* 53(2) (2010): 238–264.
23. X. Zhang and K.M. Bartol, "Linking Empowering Leadership and Employee Creativity: The Influence of Psychological Empowerment, Intrinsic Motivation, and Creative Process Engagement," *Academy of Management Journal* 53(1) (2010): 107–128.
24. McDonald and Westphal, "My Brother's Keeper?"
25. G. Hirst, D. Van Knippenberg, C.H. Chen, and C.A. Sacramento, "How Does Bureaucracy Impact Individual Creativity? A Cross-Level Investigation of Team Orientation-Creativity Relationships," *Academy of Management Journal* 54(3) (2011): 624–641.
26. M.T. Dacin, K. Munir, and P. Tracy, "Formal Dining at Cambridge Colleges: Linking Ritual Performance and Institutional Maintenance," *Academy of Management Journal* 53(6) (2010): 1393–1418.
27. B.J. Tepper, S.E. Moss, and M.K. Duffy, "Predictors of Abusive Supervision: Supervisor Perceptions of Deep-Level Dissimilarity, Relationship Conflict, and Subordinate Performance," *Academy of Management Journal* 54(2) (2011): 279–294.
28. Heugens and Lander, "Structure! Agency (and Other Quarrels)."
29. E. Spitzbagel, "The Tragic Decline of Business Casual," *Bloomberg Businessweek* (October 11–17, 2010): 94–95.
30. B.J. Tepper, S.E. Moss, and M.K. Duffy, "Predictors of Abusive Supervision: Supervisor Perceptions of Deep-Level Dissimilarity, Relationship Conflict, and Subordinate Performance," *Academy of Management Perspectives* 24(3) (2010): 25–36.
31. C. Lechner, K. Frankenberger, and S.W. Floyd, "Task Contingencies in the Curvilinear Relationship between Intergroup Networks and Initiative Performance," *Academy of Management Journal* 53(4) (2010): 865–889.
32. G.N. Powell and J.H. Greenhaus, "Sex, Gender, and the Work-to-Family Interface: Exploring Negative and Positive Interdependencies," *Academy of Management Journal* 53(3) (2010): 513–534.
33. Ibid.
34. A. Bitektine, "Toward a Theory of Social Judgments of Organizations: The Case of Legitimacy, Reputation, and Status," *Academy of Management Review* 36(1) (2011): 151–179.
35. P. Chattopadhyay, C. Finn, and N.M. Ashkanasy, "Affective Responses to Professional Dissimilarity: A Matter of Status," *Academy of Management Journal* 53(4) (2010): 808–826.
36. Ibid.
37. S. Lindenberg and N.J. Foss, "Managing Joint Production Motivation: The Role of Goal Framing and Governance Mechanisms," *Academy of Management Review* 36(3) (2011): 500–525.
38. Powell and Greenhaus, "Sex, Gender, and the Work-to-Family Interface."
39. D. Holtbrugge and A.T. Mohr, "Cultural Determinants of Learning Style Preferences," *Academy of Management Learning & Education* 9(4) (2010): 622–637.
40. Ibid.
41. Wu et al., "Consequences of Differentiated Leadership in Groups."
42. Haas, "The Double-Edged Swords of Autonomy and External Knowledge."
43. B. Schlender, "Steve and Me," *Fortune* (November 7, 2011): 115–123.
44. D. Rumsfeld, "Run a Meeting," *Bloomberg Businessweek* (September 26–October 2, 2011): 84.
45. R.E. Silverman, "No More Angling for the Best Seat; More Meetings are Stand-Up Jobs," *The Wall Street Journal* (February 2, 2012): A1, A10.
46. Rumsfeld, "Run a Meeting."
47. Ibid.
48. E. Bernstein, "Speaking Up Is Hard to Do: Researchers Explain Why," *The Wall Street Journal* (February 7, 2012): D1, D4.
49. Ibid.
50. Ibid.
51. Heugens and Lander, "Structure! Agency (and Other Quarrels)."
52. J.A. Martin and K.M. Eisenhardt, "Rewiring: Cross-Business-Unit Collaborations in Multibusiness Organizations," *Academy of Management Journal* 53(2) (2010): 265–301.
53. "Bid & Ask," *Bloomberg Businessweek* (July 4–10, 2011): 46.
54. E. Glazer, "Problems—and Solutions," *The Wall Street Journal* (October 24, 2011): R2.
55. J. Kickul, L.K. Gundry, S.D. Barbosa, and L. Whitcanack, "Intuition versus Analysis? Testing Differential Models of Congnitive Style on Entrepreneurial Self-Efficacy and the New Venture Creation Process," *Entrepreneurship Theory and Practice* 33(2) (2009): 439–453.
56. P. Shrivastava, "Pedagogy of Passion for Sustainability," *Academy of Management Learning & Education* 9(3) (2010): 443–455.
57. E.G. Love, D.W. Love, and G.B. Northcraft, "Is the End in Sight? Students Regulation of In-Class and Extra-Credit Effort in Response to Performance Feedback," *Academy of Management Learning & Education* 9(1) (2010): 81–97.
58. M. Haynie and D.A. Shepherd, "A Measure of Adaptive Cognition for Entrepreneurship Research," *Entrepreneurship Theory and Practice* 33(2) (2009): 695–714.
59. J.Z. Bergman, J.W. Westerman, and J.P. Daly, "Narcissism in Management Education," *Academy of Management Learning & Education* 9(1) (2010): 119–131.
60. Brady, "Carol Bartz."
61. W. Isaascon, "Steve Jobs: The Biography—His Rivalry with Bill Gates," *Fortune* (November 7, 2011): 97–112.
62. N. Karelaia, "Predictably Irrational: The Hidden Forces That Shape Our Decisions," *Academy of Management Perspectives* 23(1) (2009): 86–88.
63. Heugens and Lander, "Structure! Agency (and Other Quarrels)."
64. D.B. McNatt, "Negative Reputation and Biased Student Evaluations of Teaching: Longitudinal Results from a Naturally Occurring Experiment," *Academy of Management Education & Learning* 9(2) (2010): 225–242.
65. A. Bitektine, "Toward a Theory of Social Judgments of Organizations: The Case of Legitmacy, Reputation, and Status."
66. M.K. Srivastava and D.R. Gnyawali, "When Do Relational Resources Matter? Leveraging Portfolio Technological Resources for Breakthrough Innovation," *Academy of Management Journal* 54(1) (2011): 797–810.
67. J. Li and Y. Tang, "CEO Hubris and Firm Risk Taking in China: The Moderating Role of Managerial Discretion," *Academy of Management Journal* 53(1) (2010): 45–68.
68. W.J. Henisz, "Leveraging the Financial Crisis to Fulfill the Promise of Progressive Management," *Academy of Management Education & Learning* 10(2) (2011): 298–321.
69. T. Keene, "EconoChat," *Bloomberg Businessweek* (July 11–17, 2011): 14.
70. J.L. Ray, L.T. Baker, and D.S. Plowman, "Organizational Mindfulness in Business Schools," *Academy of Management Learning & Education* 10(2) (2011): 188–203.
71. H.C. Lin and S.T. Hou, "Managerial Lessons from the East: An Interview with Acer's Stan Shih," *Academy of Management Perspectives* 24(4) (2010): 6–16.

72. M. Baer, R.T.A.J. Leenders, G.R. Oldham, and A.K. Vandera, "Win or Lose the Battle for Creativity: The Power and Perils of Intergroup Competition," *Academy of Management Journal* 53(4) (2010): 827–845.
73. McDonald and Westphal, "My Brother's Keeper?"
74. Ray et al., "Organizational Mindfulness in Business Schools."
75. Love et al., "Is the End in Sight?"
76. Karelaia, "Predictably Irrational."
77. F. Yuan and R.W. Woodman, "Innovative Behavior in the Workplace: The Role of Performance and Image Outcome Expectations," *Academy of Management Journal* 53(2) (2010): 323–342.
78. Srivastava and Gnyawali, "When Do Relational Resources Matter?"
79. Spektor et al., "The Effect of Conformist and Attentive-to-Detail Members on Team Innovation."
80. M. Semadeni and B.S. Anderson, "The Follower's Dilemma: Innovation and Imitation in the Professional Services Industry," *Academy of Management Journal* 53(5) (2010): 1175–1193.
81. M. Gunther, "3M's Innovation Revival," *Fortune* (September 27, 2010): 73–75.
82. Zhang and Bartol, "Linking Empowering Leadership and Employee Creativity."
83. K.E.M. De Stobbeleir, S.J. Ashford, and K. Buyens, "Self-Regulation of Creativity at Work: The Role of Feedback-Seeking Behavior in Creative Performance," *Academy of Management Journal* 54(4) (2011): 811–831.
84. Gunther, "3M's Innovation Revival."
85. "Take Time to Innovate," *Costco Connection* (February 2012): 13.
86. Isaascon, "Steve Jobs: The Biography."
87. "Take Time to Innovate."
88. Spektor et al., "The Effect of Conformist and Attentive-to-Detail Members on Team Innovation."
89. De Stobbeleir et al., "Self-Regulation of Creativity at Work."
90. Liao et al., "Looking at Both Sides of the Social Exchange Coin."
91. R.M., "What's the Secret to Better Brainstorming?"
92. Baer et al., "Win or Lose the Battle for Creativity."
93. Karelaia, "Predictably Irrational."
94. Henisz, "Leveraging the Financial Crisis to Fulfill the Promise of Progressive Management."
95. C.M. Barnes and J.R. Hollenbeck, "Sleep Deprivation and Decision-Making Teams: Burning the Midnight Oil or Playing with Fire?" *Academy of Management Review* 34(1) (2009): 56–66.
96. Haas, "The Double-Edged Swords of Autonomy and External Knowledge."
97. L. Grossman, "2010 Person of the Year Mark Zuckerberg [Cover story], *Time* 176(26) (2010): 44–75.
98. M. Helft, "Mark Zuckerberg, Philanthropist," *The New York Times* (October 11, 2010): 4.
99. www.zdnet.com/blog/btl/wsj-facebook-set-to-declare-ipo-next-week/68137; www.usatoday.com/tech/products/story/2012-01-29/pegoraro-facebook-timeline/52824342/1.

Chapter 12

1. M. Farjoun, "Beyond Dualism: Stability and Change as a Duty," *Academy of Management Review* 35(2) (2010): 202–225.
2. F. Rojas, "Power through Institutional Work: Acquiring Academic Authority in the 1968 Third World Strike," *Academy of Management Journal* 53(6) (2010): 1263–1280.
3. S. Nadkarni and P. Herrmann, "CEO Personality, Strategic Flexibility, and Firm Performance: The Case of the Indian Business Process Outsourcing Industry," *Academy of Management Journal* 53(5) (2010): 1050–1073.
4. C. Fritz, C.F. Lam, and G.M. Spreitzer, "It's the Little Things That Matter: An Examination of Knowledge Workers' Energy Management," *Academy of Management Perspectives* 25(3) (2011): 28–39.
5. X. Zhang and K.M. Bartol, "Linking Empowering Leadership and Employee Creativity: The Influence of Psychological Empowerment, Intrinsic Motivation, and Creative Process Engagement," *Academy of Management Journal* 53(1) (2010): 107–128.
6. B. Stone and P. Burrows, "The Essence of Apple," *Bloomberg BusinessWeek* (January 24–30, 2011): 6–8.
7. W. Isaascon, "Steve Jobs: The Biography—His Rivalry with Bill Gates," *Fortune* (November 7, 2011): 97–112.
8. R. Lussier, *Leadership* (Mason, OH: South-Western/Cengage, 2013).
9. S. Mohammed and S. Nadkarni, "Temporal Diversity and Team Performance: The Moderating Role of Team Temporal Leadership," *Academy of Management Journal* 54(3) (2011): 489–506.
10. A.H. Van de Ven and K. Sun, "Breakdowns in Implementing Models of Organizational Change," *Academy of Management Perspectives* 25(3) (2011): 58–74.
11. S. Nambisan and M. Sawhney, "Orchestration Processes in Network-Centric Innovation: Evidence from the Field," *Academy of Management Perspectives* 25(3) (2011): 40–57.
12. Mohammed and Nadkarni, "Temporal Diversity and Team Performance."
13. W.J. Henisz, "Leveraging the Financial Crisis to Fulfill the Promise of Progressive Management," *Academy of Management Education & Learning* 10(2) (2011): 298–321.
14. Van de Ven and Sun, "Breakdowns in Implementing Models of Organizational Change."
15. J. Lok, "Institutional Logics as Identity Projects," *Academy of Management Journal* 53(6) (2010): 1305–1335.
16. P. Shrivastava, "Pedagogy of Passion for Sustainability," *Academy of Management Learning & Education* 9(3) (2010): 443–455.
17. Fritz et al., "It's the Little Things That Matter."
18. Ken Hultman's resistance matrix, *The Path of Least Resistance* (Austin, TX: Learning Concepts, 1979).
19. Van de Ven and Sun, "Breakdowns in Implementing Models of Organizational Change."
20. Lok, "Institutional Logics as Identity Projects."
21. Ibid.
22. B.A. De Jong and T. Elfring, "How Does Trust Affect the Performance of Ongoing Teams? The Mediating Role of Reflexivity, Monitoring, and Effort," *Academy of Management Journal* 53(3) (2010): 535–549.
23. K. Blanchard, D. Hutson, and E. Wills, *The One-Minute Entrepreneur* (New York: Currency/Doubleday, 2008).
24. Van de Ven and Sun, "Breakdowns in Implementing Models of Organizational Change."
25. S. Sonenshein, "We're Changing or Are We? Untangling the Role of Progressive Regressive and Stability Narratives During Strategic Change Implementation," *Academy of Management Journal* 53(3) (2010): 477–512.
26. B. Kowitt, "Full-Time Motivation for Part-time Employees," *Fortune* (October 17, 2011): 58.
27. Blanchard et al., *The One-Minute Entrepreneur.*
28. S. Shellenbarger, "Better Ideas through Failure," *The Wall Street Journal* (September 27, 2011): D1, D4.
29. M. Farjoun, "Beyond Dualism: Stability and Change as a Duty," *Academy of Management Review* 35(2) (2010): 202–225.
30. Sonenshein, "We're Changing or Are We?"
31. Van de Ven and Sun, "Breakdowns in Implementing Models of Organizational Change."
32. D.B. Montgomery and C.A. Ramus, "Calibrating MBA Job Preferences for the 21st Century," *Academy of Management Learning & Education* 10(1) (2011): 9–26.
33. A. Rhoades, "Passionate People = A Profitable Company," *Fortune* (September 5, 2011): 22.

34. F. Yuan and R.W. Woodman, "Innovative Behavior in the Workplace: The Role of Performance and Image Outcome Expectations," *Academy of Management Journal* 53(2) (2010): 323–342.
35. N.D. Cakar and A. Erturk, "Comparing Innovation Capability of Small and Medium-Sized Enterprises: Examining the Effects of Organizational Culture and Empowerment," *Journal of Small Business Management* 48(3) (2010): 325–359.
36. M. Gunther, "3M's Innovation Revival," *Fortune* (September 27, 2010): 73–75.
37. Rhoades, "Passionate People = A Profitable Company."
38. Ibid.
39. Y.I. Kane and I. Sherr, "iPhone Executive Is out at Apple," *The Wall Street Journal* (August 9, 2010): B1–B2.
40. M.T. Dacin, K. Munir, and P. Tracy, "Formal Dining at Cambridge Colleges: Linking Ritual Performance and Institutional Maintenance," *Academy of Management Journal* 53(6) (2010): 1393–1418.
41. IBM Web site, www.ibm.com, retrieved February 22, 2012.
42. R.M. Murphy, "Secrets of the Big Blue Leader," *Fortune* (November 21, 2011): 169.
43. Yuan and Woodman, "Innovative Behavior in the Workplace."
44. Farjoun, "Beyond Dualism."
45. Yuan and Woodman, "Innovative Behavior in the Workplace."
46. Van de Ven and Sun, "Breakdowns in Implementing Models of Organizational Change."
47. Sonenshein, "We're Changing or Are We?"
48. M. Haynie and D.A. Shepherd, "A Measure of Adaptive Congition for Entrepreneurship Research," *Entrepreneurship Theory and Practice* 33(2) (2009): 695–714.
49. Lok, "Institutional Logics as Identity Projects."
50. Van de Ven and Sun, "Breakdowns in Implementing Models of Organizational Change."
51. Kowitt, "Full-time Motivation for Part-time Employees."
52. K. Pajo, A. Coetzer, and N. Guenole, "Formal Development Opportunities and Withdrawal Behaviors by Employees in Small and Medium-Sized Enterprises," *Journal of Small Business Management* 48(3): 281–301.
53. R.E. Silverman, "Yearly Reviews? Try Weekly," *The Wall Street Journal* (September 6, 2011): B6.
54. J. Pfeffer, "Low Grades for Performance Reviews," *BusinessWeek* (August 32, 2009): 68.
55. Blanchard et al., *The One-Minute Entrepreneur.*
56. Ibid.
57. Silverman, "Yearly Reviews? Try Weekly."
58. V. Elmer, "Coaching Is Hot. Is It Right for You?" *Fortune* (September 5, 2011): 19–20
59. J. Segers, D. Vloeberghs, E. Henderickx, and Il Inceoglu, "Structuring and Understanding the Coaching Industry: The Coaching Cube," *Academy of Management Learning & Education* 10(2) (2011): 204–221.
60. R. Sutton, "How a Few Bad Apples Ruin Everything," *The Wall Street Journal* (October 24, 2011): R5.
61. E.M. Spektor, M. Erez, and E. Naveh, "The Effect of Conformist and Attentive-to-Detail Members on Team Innovation: Reconciling the Innovation Paradox," *Academy of Management Journal* 54(4) (2011): 740–760.
62. Van de Ven and Sun, "Breakdowns in Implementing Models of Organizational Change."
63. Ibid.
64. S. Alleyne, A. H. Lott, J. Benton, C. M. Brown, C. Faison, K. Kanu Jr., et al., "75 Most Powerful Women in Business," *Black Enterprise* 40(7) (2010): 87–90.
65. T. A. Sykes, "The New Face of Big Business," *Essence* (Time Inc.) 40(4) (2009): 78.

Chapter 13

1. AACSB, "Learning and Assessment Standards," www.aacsb.edu, retrieved February 27, 2012.
2. S.D. Sidle, "Building a Committed Global Workforce: Does What Employees Want Depend on Culture?" *Academy of Management Perspectives* 23(1) (2009): 79–80.
3. S. Mohammed and S. Nadkarni, "Temporal Diversity and Team Performance: The Moderating Role of Team Temporal Leadership," *Academy of Management Journal* 54(3) (2011): 489–506.
4. Census, "*The Wall Street Journal* (December 22, 2011): A1.
5. National Public Radio, "News Broadcast," on WFCR (March 30, 2011).
6. C. Dougherty, "U.S. Nears Racial Milestone," *The Wall Street Journal* (June 11, 2010): A3.
7. M. Jordan, "Births Fuel Hispanic Gains," based on Census data, *The Wall Street Journal* (July 15, 2011): A3.
8. C. Dougherty, "New Faces of Childhood," based on Census data, *The Wall Street Journal* (April 6, 2011): A3.
9. M. Jordan, "Illegals Estimated to Account for 1 in 12 U.S. Births," *The Wall Street Journal* (August 12, 2010): A1–A2.
10. S. Reddy, "Latinos Fuel Growth in Decade," based on Census data, *The Wall Street Journal* (March 25, 2011): A2.
11. United Nations data, *The Wall Street Journal* (November 1, 2011): A1.
12. CIA Web site, www.cia.gov, retrieved February 27, 2012.
13. M.J. Chen and D. Miller, "West Meets East: Toward an Ambicultural Approach to Management," *Academy of Management Perspectives* 24(4) (2010): 17–24.
14. P. Tharenou and N. Caulfield, "Will I Stay or Will I Go? Explaining Repatriation by Self-Initiated Expatriates," *Academy of Management Journal* 53(5) (2010): 1009–1028.
15. N.M. Pless, T. Maak, and G.K. Stahl, "Developing Responsible Global Leaders through International Service-Learning Programs: The Ulysses Experience," *Academy of Management Learning & Education* 10(2) (2011): 237–260.
16. D.R. Hekman, K. Aquino, B.P. Owens, T.R. Mitchell, P. Schilpzand, and K. Leavitt, "An Examination of Whether and How Racial and Gender Biases Influence Customer Satisfaction," *Academy of Management Journal* 53(2) (2010): 238–264.
17. J.S. Lublin, "Coaching Urged for Women," *The Wall Street Journal* (April 4, 2011): B8.
18. H.R. Bowles and F. Flynn, "Gender and Persistence in Negotiation: A Dyadic Perspective," *Academy of Management Journal* 53(4) (2010): 769–787.
19. Ibid.
20. D. Kopecki, "Women on Wall Street Fall Behind," *Bloomberg Businessweek* (October 11–17, 2010): 46–47.
21. J.M. Hoobler, S.J. Wayne, and G. Lemmon, "Bosses' Perceptions of Family–Work Conflict and Women's Promotability: Glass Ceiling Effects," *Academy of Management Journal* 52(3) (2009): 939–957.
22. Hekman et al., "An Examination of Whether and How Racial and Gender Biases Influence Customer Satisfaction."
23. Ibid.
24. EEOC Web site, www.eeoc.gov, retrieved February 27, 2012.
25. Chen and Miller, "West Meets East."
26. C. Murray, "The New American Divide," *The Wall Street Journal* (January 21–22, 2012): C1.
27. "Psychiatric-drug," *The Wall Street Journal* (November 16, 2011): A1.
28. ADA Web site, www.ada.gov, retrieved February 29, 2012.
29. M. Corkery, "A Special Effort," *The Wall Street Journal* (November 14, 2005), R8.
30. J.L. Berdahl, "Harassment Based on Sex: Protecting Social Status in the Context of Gender Hierarchy," *Academy of Management Review 32*(2) (2007): 641–658.

31. EEOC Web site, www.eeoc.gov, retrieved February 29, 2012.
32. Bowles and Flynn, "Gender and Persistence in Negotiation."
33. Hoobler et al., "Bosses' Perceptions of Family–Work Conflict and Women's Promotability."
34. Bowles and Flynn, "Gender and Persistence in Negotiation."
35. D. Cooper and S.M.B. Thatcher, "Identification in Organizations: The Role of Self-Concept Orientations and Identification Motives," *Academy of Management Perspectives* 23(1) (2009): 76–77.
36. G. Davis, "The High Cost of the Gender Gap," *The Wall Street Journal* (November 21, 2011): R14–R15.
37. Ibid.
38. R. Blumenstein, "A Blueprint for Change," *The Wall Street Journal* (April 11, 2011): R1.
39. U.S. Census data, www.census.gov, retrieved March 2, 2012.
40. R. Ren, "Executive Compensation: Is There a Gender Gap?" *Academy of Management Perspectives* 24(4) (2010): 93–95.
41. Kopecki, "Women on Wall Street Fall Behind."
42. Ren, "Executive Compensation."
43. M.C. Sonfield and R.N. Lussier, "Family Business Ownership and Management: A Gender Comparison," *Journal of Small Business Strategy* 15(2) (2005): 59–75.
44. Bowles and Flynn, "Gender and Persistence in Negotiation."
45. L.L. Brennan, "Working around the Family: Is There a Gender Divide?" *Academy of Management Perspectives* 21(2) (2007): 81–82.
46. D. Lee, "The High Cost of the Gender Gap," *The Wall Street Journal* (November 21, 2011): R14–R15.
47. G.N. Powell and J.H. Greenhaus, "Sex, Gender, and the Work-to-Family Interface: Exploring Negative and Positive Interdependencies," *Academy of Management Journal* 53(3) (2010): 513–534.
48. R. Blumenstein, "A Blueprint for Change," *The Wall Street Journal* (April 11, 2011): R1.
49. Ren, "Executive Compensation."
50. Hoobler et al., "Bosses' Perceptions of Family–Work Conflict and Women's Promotability."
51. Bowles and Flynn, "Gender and Persistence in Negotiation."
52. Lublin, "Coaching Urged for Women."
53. Ibid.
54. P.S. Davis, E. Babakus, P. D. Englis, and T. Pett, "The Influence of CEO Gender on Market Orientation and Performance in Service Small and Medium-Sized Businesses," *Journal of Small Business Management* 48(4) 2010): 475–496.
55. Blumenstein, "A Blueprint for Change."
56. Ibid.
57. Lee, "The High Cost of the Gender Gap."
58. Lublin, "Coaching Urged for Women."
59. Bowles and Flynn, "Gender and Persistence in Negotiation."
60. Brennan, "Working around the Family."
61. R.G. Davis, "Until Death Do Us Part," *AFA Journal* (December 2011): 16–17.
62. Murray, "The New American Divide."
63. "A quarter of" *Wall Street Journal* (April 28,2011): A1.
64. Question and answer for 1: S. Begley, "Evolution Psychology May Not Help Explain Our Behavior After All," *The Wall Street Journal*, (April 29, 2005): B1.

Questions and answers for 2, 3, 7, 8, 12–15: The study was conducted by the Universities of Wisconsin and Minnesota and reported by Jeffrey Zaslow, "Divorce Makes a Comeback," *The Wall Street Journal* (January 14, 2003): D1, D10.

Questions and answers for 4, 5, 6: S. Shellenbarger, "No Comfort in Numbers: Divorce Rate Varies Widely from Group to Group," *The Wall Street Journal* (April 22, 2004): D1.

Questions and answers for 9, 10, 11: S. Shellenbarger, "Another Argument for Marriage: How Divorce Can Put Your Health at Risk," *The Wall Street Journal* (June 16, 2005): D1.

Questions and answer references more current supporting 2, 4, 5, 15: "The National Marriage Project," *AFA Journal* (February 2007): 12–13. S. Shellenbarger, "In Search of Wedded Bliss: What Research Can Tell Us," *The Wall Street Journal* (March 20, 2008): D1.
65. Davis, "Until Death Do Us Part."
66. Ibid.
67. J. Novack and S. Fitch, "When Work Doesn't Pay," *Forbes* (October 5, 2009): 88–93.
68. Ibid.
69. S.D. Sidle, "Career Track or Mommy Track: How Do Women Decide?" *Academy of Management Perspectives* 25(2) (2011): 77–79.
70. R. Ilies, K.S. Wilson, and D.T. Wagner, "The Spillover of Daily Job Satisfaction onto Employees' Family Lives: The Facilitating Role of Work–Family Integration," *Academy of Management Journal* 52(1) (2009): 87–102.
71. J.C. Santora, "Dual Family Earners: Do Role Overload and Stress Treat Them as Equals?" *Academy of Management Perspectives* 24(4) (2010): 92–93.
72. Ilies et al., "The Spillover of Daily Job Satisfaction Onto Employees' Family Lives."
73. J.F. Coget, "Technophobe vs. Techno-enthusiast: Does the Internet Help or Hinder the Balance between Work and Home Life? *Academy of Management Perspectives* 25(1) (2009): 95–96.
74. Santora, "Dual Family Earners."
75. Powell and Greenhaus, "Sex, Gender, and the Work-to-Family Interface."
76. Hoobler et al., "Bosses' Perceptions of Family–Work Conflict and Women's Promotability."
77. Santora, "Dual Family Earners."
78. E. Bernstein, "She Talks a Lot, He Listens a Little," *The Wall Street Journal* (November 16, 2010): D1.
79. E. Bernstein, "Meet the Marriage Killer," *The Wall Street Journal* (January 25, 2012): D1–D2.
80. P. Chattopadhyay, C. Finn, and N.M. Ashkanasy, "Affective Responses to Professional Dissimilarity: A Matter of Status," *Academy of Management Journal* 53(4) (2010): 808–826.
81. L. Kwoh, "Firms Hail New Chiefs (of Diversity)," *The Wall Street Journal* (January 5, 2012): B10.
82. Coca-Cola Web site, (www.cocacola.com), retrieved March 9, 2012.
83. I. Boudway, "Yum! Brands Earnings," *Bloomberg Businessweek* (July 11–17, 2011): 16.
84. Pless et al., "Developing Responsible Global Leaders through International Service-Learning Programs."
85. H.C. Lin and S.T. Hou, "Managerial Lessons from the East: An Interview with Acer's Stan Shih," *Academy of Management Perspectives* 24(4) (2010): 6–16.
86. D. Brady, "Carlos Ghosn," *Bloomberg Businessweek* (December 12–18, 2011): 112.
87. G. Chen, B.L. Kirman, K. Kim, C.I.C. Farh, and S. Tangirala, "When Does Cross-Cultural Motivation Enhance Expatriate Effectiveness? A Multilevel Investigation of the Moderating Roles of Subsidiary Support and Cultural Distance," *Academy of Management Journal* 53(5) (2010): 1110–1130.
88. M.J. Chen and D. Miller, "The Relational Perspective as a Business Mindset: Managerial Implications for East and West," *Academy of Management Perspectives* 25(3) (2011): 6–18.
89. J. Nair, "Meeting Cross-Cultural Challenges," *Fortune* (May 4, 2009): 58.
90. Tharenou and Caulfield, "Will I Stay or Will I Go?"
91. Nair, "Meeting Cross-Cultural Challenges."
92. C. Rose, "Charlie Rose Talks to John Mack," *Bloomberg Businessweek* (January 31–February 6, 2011): 16.
93. Y. Zhu, "Does the Relationship between Job Satisfaction and Job Performance Depend on Culture?" *Academy of Management Perspectives* 24(1) (2010): 86–87.
94. Sidle, "Building a Committed Global Workforce."

95. Chen and Miller, "The Relational Perspective as a Business Mindset."
96. Rose, "Charlie Rose Talks to John Mack."
97. D. Holtbrugge and A.T. Mohr, "Cultural Determinants of Learning Style Preferences," *Academy of Management Learning & Education* 9(4) (2010): 622–637.
98. Nair, "Meeting Cross-Cultural Challenges."
99. V. Tonoyan, R. Strohmeyer, M. Habib, and M. Perlitz, "Correction and Entrepreneurship: How Formal and Informal Institutions Shape Small Firm Behavior in Transition and Mature Market Economies," *Entrepreneurship Theory and Practice* 34(5) (2010): 803–831.
100. A. Hwang and A. M. Francesco, "The Influence of Individualism—Collectivism and Power Distance on Use of Feedback Channels and Consequences for Learning," *Academy of Management Learning & Education* 9(2) (2010): 243–257.
101. N.D. Cakar and A. Erturk, "Comparing Innovation Capability of Small and Medium-Sized Enterprises: Examining the Effects of Organizational Culture and Empowerment," *Journal of Small Business Management* 48(3) (2010): 325–359.
102. McDonald's Web site, www.aboutmcdonalds.com, retrieved March 12, 2012.
103. M. Wei, "East Meets West at Hamburger University," *Bloomberg Businessweek* (January 31–February 6, 2011): 22–23.
104. McDonald's Web site, www.aboutmcdonalds.com.
105. Ibid.
106. Ibid.
107. Human Rights Campaign Web site, www.hrc.org, retrieved March 12, 2012.
108. American Family Association Web site, www.afa.net, retrieved March 12, 2012.
109. Americans for Truth About Homosexuality Web site, www.aftah.org, retrieved March 12, 2012.

INDEX